The Rise and Fall of the Soviet Union

Martin McCauley

PEARSON
Longman

Harlow, England • London • New York • Boston • San Francisco • Toronto • Sydney • Singapore • Hong Kong
Tokyo • Seoul • Taipei • New Delhi • Cape Town • Madrid • Mexico City • Amsterdam • Munich • Paris • Milan

Pearson Education Limited
Edinburgh Gate
Harlow
Essex CM20 2JE
England

and Associated Companies throughout the world

Visit us on the World Wide Web at:
www.pearsoned.co.uk

First published 2008

ISBN 978-0-582-78465-9

British Library Cataloguing-in-Publication Data
A catalogue record for this book is available from the British Library

10 9 8 7 6 5 4 3 2
12 11 10 09 08

Typeset in 10/14pt Sabon by 35
Printed and bound in Malaysia, (PJB CTP)

The publisher's policy is to use paper manufactured from sustainable forests.

For Emma Balmer

Contents

List of Tables

List of Figures

List of Text Boxes

List of Maps

List of Illustrations

Preface

In the early 1970s when *The Soviet Union since 1917* was being written, the country was at its apogee. It was a superpower and some commentators even expected it to outstrip the United States. However, less than 20 years later, it disappeared from the map. This astonishing turnaround is reminiscent of the great empires of the pre-Christian era. To take one example, the Hittite empire which held sway in Asia Minor and Syria. It appears earthquakes may have played a major role in its demise. In the case of the Soviet Union, the natural disasters were all political. Poor leadership led to its collapse; an unintended cause of policies which were geared to achieving other goals. No one yet is clear about the reasons for the outbreak of the First World War. Likewise, the reasons for the collapse of the Soviet Union are little understood. Scholarship is only at the beginning of the journey of discovery.

The Soviet Union was a remarkable phenomenon. It was the first Marxist state, and only survived because it was huge and had abundant natural resources. The Marxist experiment, based on eliminating the profit motive for private gain and the market economy, could not have prospered in a small country. The need to import raw materials and other goods would have forced it to trade internationally and thereby to observe the laws of the market economy. Marxism could only survive in countries such as China, India and the United States. China was a Marxist state and, at times, it looked as if India might make that journey as well. The best way to understand Marxist philosophy is to think of it as a search for a black cat in a dark room. However there is no black cat there. Marxism-Leninism, its Russian variant, was thus a search for a non-existent black cat in a dark room. Leninists went further; they claimed to have caught the black cat! Given the tension between objective reality and the guiding philosophy, leaders were obliged to use coercion to force through their revolution. Marx expected a successful socialist revolution to occur when capitalism had matured and could develop no further. Instead, the first Marxist state was an underdeveloped state, in the industrial sense of the term. To survive, the Bolsheviks had to industrialise from above.

Another complication was that the Soviet Union was a multinational empire. As the inefficiency of the system became more and more apparent, from the 1960s onwards, non-Russians became convinced that they could run affairs more effectively. This promoted nationalism.

The profit motive for private gain and the market cannot be suppressed. The planned economy rendered them illegal but they re-emerged in a new guise. Enterprises could produce goods privately from defective spare parts. These were bartered or sold on. The militia, KGB, Party and government officials wanted their cut. Organised crime developed as pickings became richer. Corruption was endemic to the Soviet system but began to expand under Nikita Khrushchev (1953–64) and bloomed under Leonid Brezhnev (1964–82). Belief in the black cat was strongest during the initial phase of the revolution. Then it surged again the 1930s. Khrushchev was convinced he had caught the black cat but he did more to undermine the faith than any other leader. He proclaimed that citizens would be living under communism, an era of plenty, in 1980. This led to widespread ridicule as reality proved otherwise. The new Soviet man and woman had to emerge in order to build socialism and then communism. They were to be selfless and dedicated to the common good. It turned out that most wanted an easy life. A highly educated Russian professor once said to me: 'I don't want to be a member of the masses. I want to be me.' Individualism only became legitimate under Mikhail Gorbachev. The greatest tribute one can pay the Soviet communism is that it miraculously survived over 70 years. Even more impressive, the Red Army defeated the German Wehrmacht over the years 1941–45. In 1941, the Wehrmacht was the most powerful army in the world. In 1945, the Red Army had become the most powerful army in the world. By then, middle ranking officers were superior to their German opposite numbers. How does one explain all this?

The end of the black cat myth spurred a search for an alternative. The country went back to its roots and nationalism grew. The inefficiency of the economy promoted the black market and bribe taking and giving. A joke sums this up nicely: 'Is it true that the Soviet Union has atomic bombs?' 'No, because if it had they would be on sale in the Odesa market.' If one had the right connections and the money, one could obtain anything.

Another way of looking at it would be to say that the Russian people, despite being subjected to a utopian ideology, fought back and eventually overturned that ideology. This book is a tale of the Russian and other Soviet peoples overthrowing their masters and their world view. Reality reasserted itself. In other words, communism foundered because it could not meet the political, economic and social expectations of society. It promised the earth but did not deliver. Communism, under Gorbachev, was seen as morally indefensible by many. This applied especially to Gorbachev and Aleksandr Yakovlev, the driving force behind glasnost.

The latter hoped for a Reformation which would usher in a moral and just society based on private property. Gorbachev was not willing to go that far.

Jokes often illuminate one's understanding and add to the pleasure of studying other cultures; they are in italics throughout the text. Russians are well known for their acerbic humour. For some reason many of the best Russian jokes are either Jewish or Armenian. The following is a classic example. *A Jewish family emigrates from the Soviet Union to New York. Moshe, the ten year old son, is very bright and keen to learn about the Catholic faith. A priest is holding a class and Moshe slips into the back row. 'Kids, I have a special question today. Whoever answers it correctly will receive five dollars. The question is: who was the most influential person who ever lived?' 'Napoleon', answers one boy. 'Very good, but not quite right', says the priest. 'Julius Caesar', replies another. 'No, not exactly.' 'George Washington', suggests another. 'No, no.' Moshe stands up and says: 'Jesus Christ.' 'Absolutely right', says the priest, 'here is your five dollars. But you are a Jewish boy so why did you not say Moses?' Moshe replies: 'I'll tell you, Father. It's quite simple. Moses is Moses but business is business.'*

I owe much to a host of friends and colleagues who have, over the years, helped me in my quest to understand Russia. Some of my experiences in the Soviet Union are related in this book. Others will forever remain private. I am particularly grateful to Albert Axell and Peter Duncan for reading and commenting on part of the text. I am deeply indebted to John Keep and Katya Kocourek for reading and commenting on the whole manuscript. They pointed out some egregious errors and made some valuable suggestions. They are in no way responsible for the shortcomings of the book. Katya was also an indefatigable research assistant and an inspiration. She contributed to the text of various chapters. Alexander Nekrassov was a brilliant guide to the intricacies of Soviet life and politics.

Thanks are also due to Bruce Adams (2005), Edward Lucas, Allen Mechen, Andrew Rozeik, Ksenia Skvortsova and Radek Sikorski for their jokes, ditties and illustrations. David McCron provided some valuable diagrams.

A special word of thanks is due to Rabbi Abraham Hochwald (1997) for the Jewish jokes. The Rabbi has a particular interest in Jewish humour and has worked in the Israeli Ministry of Social Affairs, in the agency for Jewish education in southern France and has served as a Rabbi in Bavaria, Lower Saxony and the Rhineland.

The major Russian source for the period after 1945 is Pikhoya (1998). The sections on crime and corruption under Khrushchev, Brezhnev and Gorbachev are based on information in the open Soviet press, especially *Moskovskaya Pravda*, *Liternaturnaya Gazeta*, *Izvestiya* and *Komsomolskaya Pravda*. Fedor Razzakov, *Bandity vremen sotsializma (Khronika rossiiskoi prestupnosti 1917–1991)* (www.chelny.ru) was also useful.

Chapters end with a list of questions which broadly encompass the factual and thematic content of the chapter. Their purpose is two-fold: i) to stimulate and guide discussion about particular aspects of the subject in the classroom, seminar or tutorial; and ii) to assist students revising for examinations. They can also be adapted into essay-style questions for those wishing to conduct more in-depth research.

Chinese names and places are in Pinyin rather than Wade Giles orthography. Hence Peking (Wade Giles) is Beijing (Pinyin); Mao Tse-tung (Wade Giles) becomes Mao Zedong and so on.

All dollars are US dollars and a billion is a thousand million.

Martin McCauley
May 2006

Acknowledgements

Edward Lucas for 'Oh my Stalin'

The Jamestown Foundation and Nikolai Getman (1917–2004) for the gulag paintings; Getman spent eight years (1946–54) in the Kolyma camps in northern Siberia

Publisher's Acknowledgements

We are grateful to the following for permission to reproduce copyright material:

Table 6.1 and Figure 10.1 from The Political Economy of Stalinism: Evidence from the Soviet Secret Archives, Cambridge University Press, Gregory, P. 2004; Figure 8.1 from Stalin & Stalinism, Longman, McCauley, M. 2003; Figure 11.1 from Against Their Will: The History and Geography of Forced Migrations in the USSR, Central University Press, Pavel, P. 2004; Table 11.1 from The Road to Terror: Stalin and the Self-Destruction of the Bolsheviks, Yale University Press, Getty, J.A. & Oleg, V.M. 1999; Figure 20.2 and Figure 21.3 from The Rise and Fall of the Soviet Economy An Economic History of the USSR from 1945, Longman, Hanson, P. 2003; Table 20.2, Table 21.1 and Table 21.2 from Sovetsky Soyuz: Istoriya Vlasti 1945–1991, Pikhoya, R.G. 1998; Figure 23.1 from Bandits, Gangsters and the Mafia, Longman, McCauley, M. 2001; Table 23.1 and Table 23.2 from Russia: An Abnormal Country in European Journal of Comparative

Economics, Università Carlo Cattaneo, Rosefield, S., 2005. Illustration 19.1 is a 1959 Herblock Cartoon, copyright by The Herb Block Foundation.

Maps

Map 1.1, Political-Administrative Map of the USSR until 1991 from The Soviet Union 1917–1991, Longman, McCauley, M. 1993; Map 3.1, The Civil War from The Soviet Union 1917–1991, Longman, McCauley, M. 1993; Map 4.1, Central Asia from Bandits, Gangsters and the Mafia, Longman, McCauley, M. 1993; Map 4.2, The Caucasus Region from Bandits, Gangsters and the Mafia, Longman, McCauley, M. 1993; Map 10.1, The Expansion of Soviet Industry under Stalin from The Soviet Union 1917–1991, Longman, McCauley, M. 1993; Map 14.1, Invasion of the Soviet Union 1941–2 from A War to be Won, Belknap Press, Murray, W. & Millet, A.R. 2001; Map 14.2, The Eastern Front November 1942– June 1943 from A War to be Won, Belknap Press, Murray, W. & Millet, A.R. 2001; Map 15.1, Soviet Territorial Gains in Europe 1939–49 from The Soviet Union 1917–1991, Longman, McCauley, M. 1993; Map 19.1, The Soviet Union and the Middle East from The Soviet Union 1917–1991, Longman, McCauley, M. 1993; Map 19.2, War and Advance of Communism in Indo-China from The Soviet Union 1917–1991, Longman, McCauley, M. 1993.

In some instances we have been unable to trace the owners of copyright material, and we would appreciate any information that would enable us to do so.

Notes

The Party and the government

The USSR was sometimes described as a Party-government state. The main features of the relationship between the Party and the government are shown below. The approximate equivalence of Party and governmental bodies is given at each territorial level.

Party	Government
Politburo (Presidium between 1952–66), Communist Party of the Soviet Union (CPSU)	Presidium of the USSR Council of Ministers
Central Committee (CC)	USSR Council of Ministers
CPSU Congress	Presidium of the USSR Supreme Soviet
Republican (e.g. Ukrainian) Party Secretariat	Republican Council of Ministers
Republican CC	Presidium of Republican Supreme Soviet
Republican Party Congress	Republican Supreme Soviet
Regional (krai, oblast) Party Committee	City, krai or oblast soviet
Regional Party Conference	No equivalent
District (raion, etc.) Party bodies	Raion-village soviet
District Party Conference	No equivalent
Primary Party organisations (enterprises, collective farm, etc.)	No equivalent
Rank and file Party members	Voters

Note on Russian names

Russian names consist of a first name, patronymic (father's name) and a surname. Hence Mikhail Sergeevich Gorbachev or Mikhail, the son of Sergei Gorbachev. A sister would have been called Anna Sergeevna (the daughter of Sergei) Gorbacheva. Gorbachev's wife was Raisa Maksimovna, Raisa, the daughter of Maksim, née Titorenko. (Titorenko is a Ukrainian name, hence does not end in the feminine a.) Another Russian name is Rimashevsky (masculine) and Rimashevskaya (feminine). The latter denotes both the daughter and the wife.

Many Russian names end in ov and ev. This is the genitive plural. Gorbachev, (pronounced Garba-choff) has an ev ending because it follows ch. The stress is at the end, on the ev. He would have been addressed formally as Mikhail Sergeevich, as the title gospodin (mister or lord) had been dropped in 1917. It is now again in use in Russia. He could also be addressed as Tovarishch (Comrade) Gorbachev.

Most Russian names have a diminutive. Sasha for Aleksandr, Volodya for Vladimir, Kolya for Nikolai, Seryozha for Sergei, Misha for Mikhail, Nadya for Nadezhda, Tanya for Tatyana, Raya for Raisa, and so on. Children, animals and close friends are addressed with the diminutive. There is also Ivan Ivanovich Ivanov: Ivan (John), the son of Ivan Johnson. Donald MacDonald, Donald, the son of Donald, would be Donald Donaldovich Donaldov in Russian.

Ukrainian names sometimes end in a: e.g. Kuchma, but this is both masculine and feminine. As above, Titorenko is masculine and feminine. Some names end in o; e.g. Chernenko. This would be Chernenkov in Russian. There are also names ending in enko, chenko, lenko, denoting the diminutive: e.g. Kirilenko, little Kiril or Cyril; Mikhailichenko, little Mikhail or little Michael. A common Armenian surname ending is yan: e.g. Mikoyan (the stress is always at the end). Common Georgian surname endings are vili, adze, elli: e.g. Dzhugashvili (or Djugashvili); Shevardnadze; Tsereteli; Chekhidze. Muslim surnames adopt the Russian ending ov or ev: e.g. Aliev, Kunaev, Rakhmonov, Nazarbaev.

Note on orthography

In this book the Russian endings ii, yi have been rendered y: e.g. Malinovsky, Podgorny. The phonetic y has been omitted: e.g. Efimov, not Yefimov. The exception is Yeltsin as this is now the accepted English spelling. The soft sign in Russian has been omitted throughout.

The present-day names of the republics are given in the text. Hence Moldova, not Moldavia, Kyrgyzstan, not Kirgiziya.

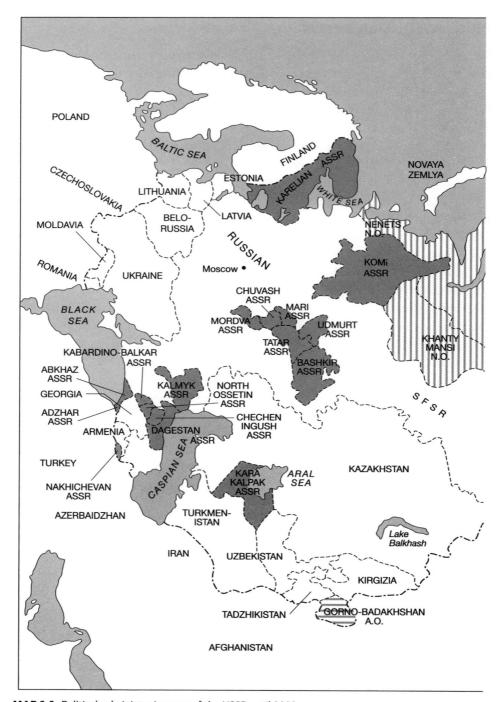

MAP 1.1 Political-administrative map of the USSR until 1991

MAP xxix

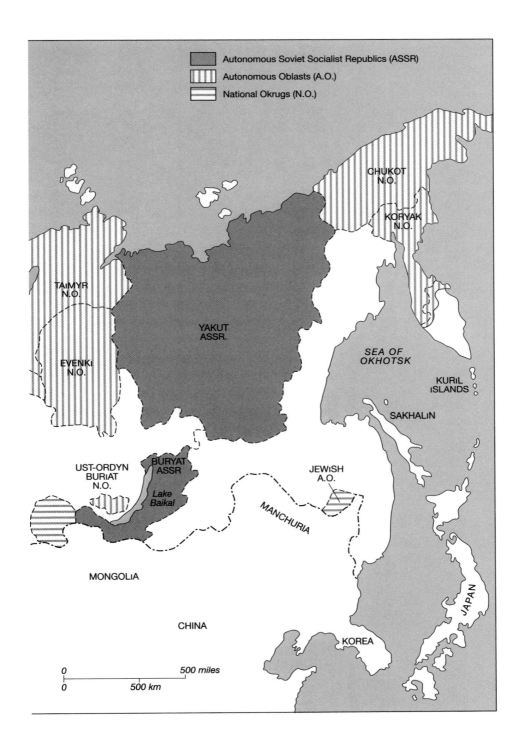

Autonomous Soviet Socialist Republics (ASSR)
Autonomous Oblasts (A.O.)
National Okrugs (N.O.)

CHUKOT
N.O.

KORYAK
N.O.

TAIMYR
N.O.

YAKUT
ASSR.

SEA OF
OKHOTSK

EVENKI
N.O.

KURIL
ISLANDS

SAKHALIN

UST-ORDYN
BURIAT
N.O.

BURYAT
ASSR

JEWISH
A.O.

Lake
Baikal

MANCHURIA

MONGOLIA

JAPAN

CHINA

KOREA

0   500 miles
0   500 km

CHAPTER 1

Ave Atque Vale

*Jesus Christ joins an Aeroflot flight from Irkutsk to Vladivostok in Siberia.
He approaches a passenger. 'I can grant you any wish you like.' 'Oh, I should
like all communists to disappear from the face of the earth.' 'Yes, that can be
arranged.' He moves on to another passenger. 'And do you have a special
wish?' 'Yes, I want all fascists to be done away with.' 'All right, I can arrange
that.' He then comes to another passenger, a Jew. 'Is it really true that you are
going to do what those two gentlemen requested?' 'Of course. After all, I am
the son of God.' 'Well, in that case, I should just like a cup of coffee.'*

*The moral of this story is that divine intervention is needed to get a cup of
coffee on an Aeroflot flight. The planned economy is so inefficient it cannot
even deliver such a simple request.*

This book begins with the event which sealed the fate of the Soviet Union (also
known as the Union of Soviet Socialist Republics or USSR), the attempted coup of
August 1991. The reason for this is to highlight the dramatic conflict which posed
those who wanted to move towards a more democratic country against those who
wished to retain an authoritarian regime. The inability of the USSR to manage
political and social change sealed its fate. The gulf between the ruling class, called
the nomenklatura, and the population was too wide. The ruling Communist
Party of the Soviet Union (CPSU) was hopelessly split by August 1991. Many of
Mikhail Gorbachev's supporters advised him to leave the Party and set up a Social
Democratic Party which would manage the transition to a more democratic society. He declined to do so and thereby sacrificed much support from radicals and
democrats. He was a see-saw leader – always trying to find the golden mean
between extremes. The timing of the attempted coup coincided with the proposed

signing of a treaty establishing a Union of Sovereign States to succeed the Soviet Union. It was to be a real federation rather than the sham federation which had been the USSR. Economic power was to flow to the republics with only defence, security and foreign affairs being left to the President in Moscow. How strong he would be would depend on how much tax flowed from the republics to Moscow. Vladimir Kryuchkov, head of the Committee of State Security (KGB), was the mastermind behind the attempted coup. The account which follows sees events mainly through his eyes. His memoirs map out the path (Kryuchkov 1996). Differing versions of the coup are provided by Mikhail Gorbachev (1996) and Vladimir Medvedev (1994), Gorbachev's chief of personal security at Foros. Another major source is R. G. Pikhoya (1998) who, although not present at Foros, interviewed many who were. He spent many years reconstructing the events of the attempted coup.

Until the attempted coup it appeared that President Boris Yeltsin of Russia – the largest republic of the Soviet Union – was in favour of a Union of Sovereign States. The dramatic events of 18 August changed all that. He seized the opportunity to press the claims of Russia ahead of all the other republics. He could now consider another option. Break away from the Soviet Union and restore Russian independence. In other words, Russia would be the successor state to the Soviet Union. Russia or the Russian Soviet Federated Socialist Republic (RSFSR) had been subsumed in the Soviet Union and only acquired its own Communist Party, Academy of Sciences, etc. in 1990. The CPSU had administered Russia. Russia did have its own government but this was secondary to the government of the Soviet Union. Moscow was the capital of the Russian Federation and the Soviet Union. The Kremlin was the seat of power of both Russia and the USSR. This chapter can be read in conjunction with Chapter 21 on the Gorbachev era. Beginning at the end of the story in August 1991 encourages the reader to look backwards not only at the events leading up to the attempted coup but also the long term reasons and factors (or historical antecedents) that contributed to the demise of the USSR.

17 August 1991

General Vladimir Kryuchkov, chair of the KGB, leaves his office at the Lubyanka, not far from the Kremlin, steps into his sleek, official car and orders his driver to take him to the ABC complex, on the outskirts of Moscow. The complex is the KGB's idea of paradise. It is a sanatorium with all mod cons: a swimming pool, a cinema, saunas, a gymnasium and masseuses. It is where senior KGB officers relax after a demanding shift protecting the Soviet Union against its enemies, both inside and outside the country. It is surrounded by guards and high walls to ensure that no prying Russian catches a glimpse of the luxurious lifestyle within. Part of the secret of the power of the CPSU is to enshroud its decision-making process in mystery. Its leaders, of which Kryuchkov is one, arrive at decisions in ways unfathomable to the average citizen. The leaders claim special knowledge of the laws of history, revealed to them by Karl Marx and his chief Russian disciple, Vladimir Lenin. The gap between the leaders and the led is as wide as the Volga.

But all is not well. The disciples cannot agree among themselves on how to maintain their power. Some of them know enough theology to remember the parable about the house divided. A house divided against itself will not stand. The problem is the leader, Mikhail Gorbachev. He is manifesting symptoms of madness. What does one do when the leader is deranged and capable of bringing the whole house down around his ears?

Kryuchkov has a picnic table brought out in the balmy evening weather and covered in Russian delicacies with generous libations of vodka and spirits. He has selected his guests with care. Together they are to attempt something momentous: the removal of the leader. Prime Minister Valentin Pavlov is there looking anxious. Further along sits Oleg Shenin, a member of the Politburo (see Glossary); Oleg Baklanov, deputy head of the Security Council and the most important representative of the military–industrial complex in the Soviet leadership; Valery Boldin, Gorbachev's Chief of Staff; and General Dmitry Yazov, Minister of Defence. The deputy head of the KGB and two deputy defence ministers are also there. The Minister of Internal Affairs, Boris Pugo, has not been invited.

Pavlov cannot contain himself and complains that the situation is catastrophic. The country is in total chaos and facing famine. The harvest is not being brought in and there is a shortage of fuel. Nobody will obey an order. The only hope for the country is a state of emergency. The others murmur their agreement.

Kryuchkov informs them that he briefs Gorbachev on a regular basis. However, the General Secretary (Gensek) does not grasp what he is being told. He interrupts Kryuchkov, changes the subject and is generally distracted. The ascetic KGB chief had implored Gorbachev on numerous occasions to declare a state of emergency and restore order before it is too late.

The seeds of a coup against the leader had been germinating in Kryuchkov's mind ever since November 1990. Only a coup supported by the KGB could succeed in the Soviet Union. He is the obvious comrade to mastermind such an operation. Does he not spend his time in the world of espionage? Conspiracy is second nature to him.

Time is of the essence. On 20 August Gorbachev is planning the grand ceremony of the signing of the Union Treaty which will end the Soviet Union and usher in the Union of Sovereign States. This will be a real federation, not the sham federation which the Soviet Union has been. Even worse, the new federation might turn out to be a confederation, a loose association of states with a weak centre. Another problem is that Soviet republics such as Estonia, Latvia and Lithuania want to leave the Soviet Union and become independent. They do not want to be part of any successor state. Clearly, drastic action is needed to keep the country welded together.

Fortunately for the plotters Gorbachev and his family had decamped on 4 August to Foros, the palatial three storey summer residence which 4,000 military construction workers, over the years 1986–88, had built for Gorbachev in Crimea, on the shores of the Black Sea. Advisers were staying nearby and could be consulted on a regular basis. Gorbachev and his close associates had always considered a coup a possibility. Hence the leader's decision to abandon Moscow to the plotters must rank as one of the most astonishing misjudgements of recent times. One does not have to be Sherlock Holmes to work out that the more advisable course of action would have been to sign the Union Treaty and then disappear to the luxuries of the south.

The last coup in the Soviet Union had been the bloodless removal of Nikita Khrushchev as Prime Minister and Party leader, in October 1964. The leader had alienated almost every elite in the country. His son apprised him that a plot was being hatched but the leader, in his supreme insouciance, just ignored the information. History was to repeat itself with Gorbachev.

This time around things are not so simple. In 1964, when the KGB gave an order it was obeyed. Nowadays most people have lost their fear of the security services. Kryuchkov has to scare the population. There is going to be an armed uprising against the leadership. They are going to seize strategic points in Moscow: the Kremlin, the railway stations, the Ostankino TV complex, two hotels, and so on. The motherland is in grave danger. There is no time to lose. His co-conspirators think to themselves: 'Who are they?' Since the Minister of Defence is one of the conspirators, who will lead the revolt? Marshal Sergei Akhromeev, Chief of the General Staff, and one of the top brains in the military? But he is on holiday in the south. In other words, the KGB has unearthed a conspiracy in the military right under the nose of the Minister of Defence? Nobody considers General Yazov very bright but could he be so dim as not to notice a plot to take over the country?

18 August 1991

A beautiful, sunny Sunday. At 8 a.m. Yazov calls a meeting in the Ministry of Defence. General Kalinin, commander of the Moscow military region, is ordered to get the 2nd guards motor rifle division and the 4th guards tank division ready to enter Moscow. General Pavel Grachev is to do the same with the 106th Tula airborne division. At 11 a.m. Kryuchkov orders Vice-Admiral Zhardetsky, head of the KGB third main directorate, and General Vorotnikov, head of the department for the defence of constitutional order, to prepare and send KGB groups to Estonia, Latvia and Lithuania. Kryuchkov's deputy, Lebedev, is instructed to shadow and, if necessary, arrest a number of persons. There are 70 names on the list, ranging from the leaders of the Russian government to those in retirement, such as Eduard Shevardnadze. Yeltsin's dacha, at Arkhangelskoe, 30 km from Moscow, is to be put under surveillance.

The plotters need to reassure Gorbachev that everything is normal. Kryuchkov phones the leader four times and Gorbachev also talks to Gennady Yanaev, his Vice-President, Oleg Shenin, Valentin Pavlov and the deputy Prime Minister, Vladimir Shcherbakov.

At about 4 p.m. Georgy Shakhnazarov phones and asks about details of the trip back to Moscow the following day. He also asks about Gorbachev's health and the leader says everything is fine except his bad back. Gorbachev has finished his speech for the signing of the treaty and wants to spend the rest of the day with his wife Raisa, daughter Irina, son-in-law Anatoly and granddaughter, Oksana.

At 4.50 p.m. Foros security informs the leader that there are visitors to see him. This is odd as Gorbachev has not invited anyone. He picks up one of the many phones on his desk to find out more. It is dead as well all the others. The leader's worst suspicions are coming true. Gorbachev paces the room and tries to think of what to do.

How do the plotters gain access? General Yury Plekhanov, head of the KGB's ninth directorate, responsible for the security of the leadership, is with them. He simply orders the Foros security staff (all KGB operatives) to let them in. He is accompanied by KGB General Generalov, Oleg Shenin, Oleg Baklanov, General Valentin Varennikov, commander-in-chief of ground forces, and Valery Boldin. Gorbachev quickly realises that the Party, military and KGB have betrayed him.

Gorbachev keeps them waiting for some time. Then he allows them to enter his study. Boldin informs the General Secretary they have come to discuss a series of issues about the state of the country.

'Whom do you represent? Whom are you speaking for?', he asks.

Baklanov, Varennikov and Boldin begin talking about the need to adopt plans drawn up on his orders to cope with the critical situation. They inform the Gensek that it is necessary to introduce a state of emergency; the Supreme Soviet and government are opposed to the signing of the Union Treaty as it has not been agreed with them. Gorbachev thinks for a while and then asks if the state of emergency will also apply to the Russian government. The reply is positive. The Gensek then comments that it would be better to achieve these goals by 'democratic methods'. He shakes hands with each as they leave. 'Damn you all, go ahead!' (Medvedev 1994).

Gorbachev's chief of personal security, Vladimir Medvedev, then reports that all communications have been cut. He fears a Khrushchev-like coup. Medvedev states that Boldin has brought documents for Gorbachev to sign. The latter declines to sign them. When Boldin leaves Gorbachev, he appears disappointed but calm, as if he had expected this outcome all along (Medvedev 1994).

Gorbachev's account is different. To the question, whom do you represent, the reply is:

'The committee; the committee established in connection with the state of emergency'.
'Who appointed this committee? I did not and neither did the Supreme Soviet.'

They explain to him in a condescending manner that Gennady Yanaev has assumed the presidency and that a state of emergency has been declared. Gorbachev wants to know the members of the State Committee for the State of Emergency which has assumed power. Baklanov provides the names:

- Vladimir Kryuchkov, head of the KGB;
- Dmitry Yazov, Minister of Defence;
- Boris Pugo, Minister of Internal Affairs;
- Oleg Baklanov, deputy head of the Security Council;
- Valentin Pavlov, Prime Minister;
- Gennady Yanaev, deputy President;
- Aleksandr Tizyakov, chair of the Association of State Enterprises;
- Valery Starodubtsev, head of the Peasants' Union.

Baklanov adds the name of Anatoly Lukyanov and says that the Russian President, Boris Yeltsin, will be arrested on his return from Almaty, Kazakhstan. If Gorbachev does not sign the document imposing a state of emergency, he is to hand over his powers to Yanaev. 'Relax', says Baklanov, 'We'll carry out the "dirty work" and then you can return' (Gorbachev 1996). Two hundred and fifty thousand pairs of handcuffs had been ordered from a factory in Pskov.

The leader tries to take it all in. He regards Kryuchkov as an educated comrade. Hence he can see further than the four walls of the Lubyanka. Yazov, well he had been brought back from command in the Russian Far East. He had been chosen specifically because he was a nonentity, someone incapable of masterminding a military coup. Yazov, afterwards, thought of himself as a dolt, which he was. Boldin is a terrible disappointment. He had linked up with Gorbachev in 1978 when the latter had arrived in Moscow to join the Party elite. Boldin had risen to be Gorbachev's trusted Chief of Staff, the comrade who handled every piece of paper on the leader's desk. Yanaev had been handpicked by Gorbachev as someone utterly incapable of pushing him aside. His aides did his work for him while he devoted his energies to his two great passions: women and drink. He was capable of humour at times. When asked by a parliamentary deputy, during his confirmation hearing, whether he enjoyed good health, he replied: 'My wife has no complaints'. The defection of Lukyanov, a friend and confidante since university days, is a body blow to Gorbachev.

Why did Gorbachev not arrest the plotters? Presumably, he concluded that since the main plotters were in Moscow nothing would be served by arresting their messenger boys in Foros. Medvedev saw the matter quite differently. His key concern was to decide whether the President was in danger of arrest or being physically harmed. He concluded that there was no risk of either happening. The handshakes at the end of the discussion with Gorbachev confirmed this. Medvedev stated that had the order been given to arrest the plotters they would have been arrested. The guard remained fully armed and loyal to the President. Medvedev had a TU-134 plane and a helicopter at his disposal. The plotters could have been taken to Moscow without any trouble.

The coup continued because the plotters hoped Gorbachev would come round to their point of view. Had Gorbachev acted decisively it might have been nipped in the bud. He remained passive, thus allowing the initiative to pass to the plotters.

The plotters had worked out three plans:

- Plan A envisaged Gorbachev conceding defeat when confronted with opposition from the Party, defence industries, military and militia. This was the most desirable and, on the face of it, legal. When the state of emergency was in place, the Supreme Soviet could meet and replace Gorbachev as President. This would make it a constitutional change.

- Plan B, more realistic, envisaged Gorbachev playing for time. He would remain silent on the state of emergency. He had successfully used this tactic after the Tbilisi events of April 1989 but less successfully after the Vilnius events of January 1991. On these occasions the authorities used violence against demonstrators. He could then claim that he did not know or was informed about it. A group of communications specialists accompanied the plotters to Foros to cut off Gorbachev. He could then claim he had been isolated and thereby avoid responsibility. Yanaev could then become acting President. Gorbachev's future would depend on how the state of emergency developed. He could come back to Moscow, negotiate with the plotters and regain his position. If the plotters turned out to be very powerful, he would lose his position. In this case, he could claim to have opposed them from the very beginning.

- Plan C was the least desirable. Gorbachev would come out strongly against the coup; call on his personal guard to arrest or kill the plotters; appeal to the people of the Soviet Union to come to his aid. He would also ask for foreign help. If this occurred, there was a group in the power ministries who would use force to smash any attempt to restore Gorbachev as President. Persistent rumours were disseminated that Gorbachev was mentally confused and could not perform his duties effectively. This was part of Plan C. A group of Moscow psychiatrists were on standby to prepare a medical bulletin about the mental illness of the President. He could then be replaced, constitutionally, by Yanaev. This scenario did not envisage Gorbachev surviving. He would simply be too dangerous to the plotters. Since he was mentally ill, he could die quite suddenly (Pikhoya 1998).

When they get back to Moscow the plotters report the bad news to Kryuchkov. This now means Plan B, without Gorbachev, will have to be adopted. Kryuchkov immediately convenes a meeting of all the conspirators. Boris Pugo, Minister of the Interior and a former KGB chief in Latvia, is also there. There is another complication. Lukyanov states that, as chair of the Supreme Soviet, he cannot join the Extraordinary Committee. This would allow Lukyanov to claim afterwards that he had not been privy to the deliberations of the plotters. The weak link is Yanaev. He will not sign the document setting up the Committee and he does not want to be President. He is told it will only be a temporary appointment. When Gorbachev has recovered, he will return to Moscow and resume his duties. Yanaev, after long consideration, signs the document assuming the duties of President (Remnick 1993).

Then Aleksandr Bessmertnykh, the comrade who had succeeded Eduard Shevardnadze as Gorbachev's Foreign Minister, arrives. Kryuchkov explains that the country is in mortal danger and that a Committee has been set up to save it. He wants Bessmertnykh to join the Committee. However he senses danger. He enquires if the President had set up the Committee. Kryuchkov explains that the President is not well. Bessmertnykh would like to see a medical report. He eventually declines, explaining that joining the Committee would make life very difficult for him as Foreign Minister (Pikhoya 1998). For the next three days he refuses to leave his apartment, claiming that he is ill.

19 August 1991

Gennady Yanaev becomes President but is in no fit state to understand his duties. He has spent most of the night drinking with Pavlov. Yazov repairs to the Ministry of Defence and spins the story of an imminent military attack on Soviet power. He hopes the officers do not think he is also drunk. All military units are put on red alert and soldiers ordered back from leave. The Tamanskaya guards motor rifle division and the Kantemirovskaya tank division are ordered into Moscow. The Tula airborne division is also deployed. The Extraordinary Committee also has at its disposal the elite Alpha unit and the Beta group, skilled in diversionary tactics. The Ministry of Internal Affairs (MVD) provides OMON special forces and the Dzierzynski special motor rifle division. General Varennikov flies from

Foros to Kyiv to inform the Ukrainian leadership that it is to obey the Extraordinary Committee. Otherwise a state of emergency will be introduced. It appears that everything is running smoothly. When the Kantemirovskaya enter Moscow they are greeted by insults.

Something is wrong with Pavlov. A Kremlin doctor is dispatched to his dacha at 7 a.m. He reports later that the Prime Minister was not only drunk but hysterical.

The country and the world hear about the coup at 6 a.m. Funeral music by Chopin creates an atmosphere of crisis. The announcers look shocked and bewildered. A state of emergency has been introduced. The motherland is in mortal danger and Gorbachev's reforms – perestroika, glasnost and democratisation – have led the country into a cul-de-sac. Soviet institutions are being undermined by the unprincipled actions of a minority which are bent on seizing dictatorial power. A tidal wave of sex and violence threatens to drown the motherland. Millions of citizens are demanding action to repel the octopus of crime and shameless immorality. The names of the members of the Extraordinary Committee are then read out. There is no mention of socialism, communism or the Party.

The newsreaders announce that, according to Anatoly Lukyanov, the Union Treaty is unconstitutional and ignores the wishes of the millions who had voted on 17 March 1991 to retain the Soviet Union. As President Gorbachev is seriously ill, his duties have been assumed by Gennady Yanaev.

Boris Yeltsin, an early riser, is having breakfast at his dacha in Arkhangelskoe, just outside Moscow, when the news of the coup breaks. Ruslan Khasbulatov, later speaker of the Russian parliament, and other top Russian politicians are in dachas nearby. They rapidly converge on Yeltsin. Anatoly Sobchak, mayor of Leningrad, now St Petersburg, receives a telephone call in his hotel room and immediately orders his driver to take him to Yeltsin's dacha. Tanks and armoured personnel carriers are moving in the opposite direction. Yeltsin, Sobchak, Aleksandr Yakovlev – the father of glasnost – and dozens of other reform politicians are on KGB arrest lists. However the mighty security service contents itself with arresting some small fry, leaving the big fish to swim away.

President Yeltsin of Russia contacts Presidents of other republics throughout the Soviet Union but the response is muted. Everyone is playing it cool. They want to know who will win before taking sides. Yeltsin decides to take a tremendous gamble. He and his entourage set off for the White House – the parliament and the seat of government in the Russian Federation. He may not make it; he may die in the attempt. The goal is to call parliament into session; condemn the coup as unconstitutional; call for the release of Gorbachev and involve the whole world in the struggle. Sobchak follows in his car and then sets off for Sheremetevo airport to return to Leningrad. At the airport, three Russian KGB men approach him. He thinks it is all over. 'Comrade Sobchak we are from the Russian KGB and have orders to ensure that you board your flight to Leningrad', they inform him.

Boris Yeltsin makes the White House at about 10 a.m. The dashing, debonair Aleksandr Rutskoi (born 1947), Russian vice-President and an Afghan war hero, and Ruslan Khasbulatov, the smooth-talking Chechen, begin broadcasting appeals from the White House. Andrei Kozyrev, Russian Foreign Minister, is dispatched to Paris to solicit foreign support and to set up a government in exile if the worst comes to the worst. Oleg Lobov, deputy Prime Minister, and a long time confidant of the President, takes a group with him secretly to Sverdlovsk, where they will be secure.

When Yeltsin arrives at the White House, he desperately needs some military support. He phones General Pavel Grachev, who is commander of Soviet airborne troops. Grachev promises to defend the Russian Federation. This is the same Grachev who had participated in the preparations for the coup. Eventually Grachev decides to remain neutral. Another piece of good fortune for Yeltsin is that General Karpukhin, the Alpha commander, when ordered to place Yeltsin's dacha under surveillance and later to arrest him and take him to Zavidovo, a hunting lodge outside Moscow, simply ignores the order. The reason for this appears to have been the fact that he was given the order orally and not in written form. If something went wrong, Karpukhin would be blamed. He decided not to take the risk.

When Anatoly Sobchak arrives in Leningrad he is told that General Viktor Samsonov, commander of the Leningrad oblast region, has gone over to the rebels. He has declared on TV that the Committee has taken over from Gorbachev and that a state of emergency is in place. Sobchak goes immediately to see him. As mayor of Leningrad, he has the city behind him, but will the General listen? Samsonov does, and changes sides.

Yeltsin immediately invites diplomats and foreign journalists to the White House. Ivan Silaev, Russian Prime Minister, reads out the appeal 'To the citizens of Russia'. Yeltsin asks those present to inform the world about the position of the Russian government. At 12.10 p.m. Yeltsin signs Decree No. 59. It claims that the statement by the Extraordinary Committee is unconstitutional and that they are attempting a coup d'état. They are state criminals. All decisions of the Committee are illegal and are not to be implemented on the territory of the Russian Federation. Legal authority in the Russian Federation rests with the President, the Supreme Soviet and Prime Minister. Officials implementing decisions of the Committee in Russia will be prosecuted.

Then, by accident or design, the President pulls off a masterstroke. He creats an image which flashes round the world and symbolises the three day resistance. Boris, in his bulletproof vest and surrounded by aides protecting him from snipers' bullets, emerges from the White House and climbs on top of a T-72 tank of the Tamanskaya guards division. 'Citizens of Russia', he booms, 'the legally elected President of the country has been deposed . . . What we have is a right-wing, reactionary, anti-constitutional, coup d'état . . . We declare all the decrees and decisions of the Committee to be illegal . . . We call on the citizens of Russia to reject the plotters and to demand a return to normal constitutional development'. He is followed by General Konstantin Kobets, chair of the State Committee on Defence. He would organise the military resistance to the coup.

General Kobets distributes the few weapons there are in the White House. A propaganda war breaks out. Opponents of the coup plaster Yeltsin's appeal on the walls of the Metro. Yeltsin appeals on the radio for the soldiers to change sides and not to spill the blood of the people. He calls for reinforcements at the White House and by the end of the day there are about 25,000 there, the vast majority civilians. They are poorly armed but three military men instruct them how to build makeshift barricades.

Astonishingly, the junta has not cut the Soviet Union off from the outside world. Telephones, telexes and faxes function normally. The BBC, CNN, CBS and Radio Liberty are working flat out on the story of the decade. Russian reporters can file their stories and radio stations transmit the latest news to the provinces. *Izvestiya*, the government newspaper, puts the Committee's appeal on page one and Yeltsin's counter-appeal on page two.

At 10.50 a.m. the CC apparatus sends a telegram to all first secretaries of republics, krais and oblasts instructing them to organise support for the Extraordinary Committee. An extraordinary session of the Soviet Supreme Soviet will take place on 26 August. The republics hope that the measures will only apply to Russia. In the Kremlin hospital the finishing touches are put to the report on Gorbachev's serious illness.

The Committee waits until evening before calling a press conference which will be televised worldwide. They need someone with the charisma and popular appeal of Yeltsin. The star performer chosen is the new President, Gennady Yanaev. He looks very nervous, his fingers drumming the table. He resembles a cat on a hot tin roof. The star performer should have been Kryuchkov, with his glasses, high forehead and total conviction that he is right. However, the show has to be presented as a legal, constitutional transfer of power. Kryuchkov would have given the impression it was a KGB coup. Yazov's presence would have signalled a military coup. Yanaev looks like a clown in search of a script. He is clearly not completely sober. His answers become less and less credible. The journalists begin to laugh at him. Immediately after the press conference, Soviet television shows a montage of foreign and domestic reaction to the attempted coup. Yeltsin is shown on his tank condemning the Committee. Anatoly Sobchak, from Leningrad, does the same. He states that the Committee's writ does not extend to the city or Leningrad oblast. The Committee begins to fall apart. Boldin is admitted to hospital during the morning and Pavlov during the day. During the evening, Baklanov prepares to jump ship. General Valentin Varennikov, commander of ground forces, writes an angry letter to the Committee. It appears to him that the security services have not carried out a single order. He demands action be taken to 'liquidate' Yeltsin.

The other clown, Valentin Pavlov, the Prime Minister, has found a script. He convenes the government at about 6 p.m. He spins them the story of the imminent military coup and the need to support the Committee in order to save the Motherland. Almost every minister supports him. Afterwards Pavlov phones Yazov with the good news. Yazov realises that Pavlov is drunk again when he proposes a simple solution to resolve the crisis: 'Arrest them all.' Pavlov then checks into the Kremlin hospital.

20 August 1991

The White House is a hive of nervous activity. The risk of an imminent attack focuses minds. All available arms are distributed and well-wishers have brought in food and drink. Then at 8 a.m. General Pavel Grachev orders General Aleksandr Lebed to withdraw his airborne battalion from the White House. Their machines, decorated with Russian flags, begin withdrawing at 11 a.m.

The Committee, annoyed by the press coverage, resolves to stop publication of all newspapers which criticise it. Only officially sanctioned state stations and channels will be permitted to broadcast. It turns out that, except for Estonia, Latvia, Moldova and Kazakhstan, republican Party leaders support the Committee or prefer to remain neutral. A meeting of the top 20 or so military takes place in the General Staff building. A plan to storm the White House is worked out. It involves joint action by units from the Ministry of Defence, MVD and the KGB. Airborne troops, commanded by Lebed, and the KGB Dzierzynski division are to blockade the White House, scatter the civilians and permit OMON forces, backed up by tanks, to break through the barricades. Alpha and Beta group are to rush through and force their way into the White House. Alpha is to arrest Yeltsin and Beta is to eliminate all opposition inside the building, using special measures. Helicopters are to provide air support. Operation Thunder is timed for 3 a.m. on 21 August.

Yeltsin calls a huge demonstration for midday and about 200,000 respond. The national flags of Russia, Ukraine, Lithuania and Georgia flutter in the breeze. This time Yeltsin appears on the White House balcony and roars out his defiance. He is followed by a huge cast, ranging from politicians to a comedian who imitates Gorbachev to a tee, grammatical slips and all. Evgeny Evtushenko weighs in with an apposite poem.

The situation inside the White House changes. Weapons appear and professional military and reserve officers assume responsibility for its defence. A flood of information comes into the White House about military intentions. General Pavel

Grachev, commander of the airborne units, and later to become Yeltsin's Minister of Defence, has orders from General Valentin Varennikov to attack. Grachev ignores the order. General Evgeny Shaposhnikov orders his men to shoot down any military helicopters en route to the White House. Communications between units, subordinate to the Committee, are listened in to by the White House defenders.

The Russian leadership takes the political initiative. At 10 a.m. a delegation consisting of Rutskoi, Khasbulatov and Silaev hand Lukyanov a note demanding a meeting with President Gorbachev within 24 hours; a medical examination of the President, to include specialists from the World Health Organisation; the lifting of the state of emergency; the return of the troops to their barracks; and the dissolution of the Extraordinary Committee. Lukyanov tries to distance himself from the Committee, claiming that more time is needed to study the situation.

In Foros, the luxury counts for nothing, Raisa is a bag of nerves. Mikhail paces the rooms and corridors and hatches a plan with son-in-law Anatoly. They have a transistor radio which picks up the BBC and Voice of America so they have some idea of what is happening in the outside world. Anatoly sets up a video camera and Gorbachev records a message of desperation and defiance. Four recordings of the message are made. The film is cut into parts, to be smuggled out by various people.

The elite KGB Alpha group, consisting only of officers, refuses to storm the White House without written orders. They demand these from their commander, General Karpukhin, but he says all orders were oral. They are being asked to shed Russian blood. If the White House is stormed foreign journalists may also be killed. There are many famous Russians inside, including Mstislav Rostropovich, the world renowned cellist. Who will answer for their deaths?

The plan gets under way. General Kalinin, military commander of Moscow, orders a curfew from 11 p.m. This is to get rid of the crowds around the White House. Firing near the Belorussian railway station and the Ukraina hotel, opposite the White House, plays on everyone's nerves. Information reaches the White House that the assault will begin at 2 or 3 a.m. Yeltsin is offered protection in the US embassy close by the White House. At midnight, he and mayor Popov, deputy mayor Luzhkov and a few others move to the spacious White House bunker in the basement. Luzhkov orders building materials to form a barrier. Yeltsin talks to the world on his private telephone. Grachev knows if his airborne troops launch an attack, all the others will follow. He decides not to attack. An armoured personnel carrier, on patrol, gets stuck in a barricade. It is pelted with stones and other materials. The troops open fire and shoot three demonstrators dead. The White House reads this as the beginning of the attack. Yazov is responsible for the first bloodletting. He changes tack and orders his troops to halt.

The military is split down the middle. Generals Aleksandr Lebed, Boris Gromov and Pavel Grachev are not going to spill rivers of Russian blood. Gromov and Grachev keep Yeltsin informed about the latest thinking of the plotters. Yazov concludes that there are not enough troops to take the White House. He does not have the guts to order up more. The resolve of the KGB also wavers. Kryuchkov will slaughter Russians but his key subordinates will not. Anyway, Yeltsin and his colleagues will not be conveniently waiting on the fifth floor to be taken. They are already in a bunker protected by a 50 cm thick steel door. It will probably not come to that. Generals Grachev and Shaposhnikov agree that if an assault is launched, they will order the bombing of the Kremlin.

Kryuchkov sits in the Lubyanka and contemplates the pile of telegrams on his desk. They are all reporting support for the Committee throughout the country. He sets off for the short journey to the Kremlin to bring the glad tidings to the Committee, which is to convene at 8 p.m. 'President' Yanaev is again in an agitated state. He says that he has heard rumours that the White House is to be stormed. The thing to do is to go on television and scotch the rumours. There is silence. Then Yanaev asks if there is really anyone who wants to storm the White House. Again there is silence. It is broken by the spymaster reporting nationwide support for the Committee. Yanaev contradicts him by reporting that all his telegrams report the opposite.

21 August 1991

3 a.m. Gennady Burbulis, one of Yeltsin's aides is called to the telephone in the White House. Kryuchkov is on the line. 'Everything is normal. You can now go to sleep.' The coup has collapsed. At 6 a.m. the generals meet in the Ministry of Defence. Yazov asks his senior commanders what should now be done. The majority advise that the troops be returned to barracks as soon as possible. Yazov should leave the Committee but he refuses (Remnick 1993).

Since early morning, militia units from MVD schools have begun arriving in Moscow. They are loyal to the Russian President. The Supreme Soviet convenes at 10 a.m. Deputies, arriving from all parts of the country, are welcomed jubilantly by the crowds. The Russian Supreme Soviet deals the death blow to the Committee. It approves all Yeltsin's decrees and confers on him legislative power. He can now promulgate decrees in his own name. The retreat begins at Red Square at 11 a.m. when the first tanks wheel round and by 1 p.m. the roads are chock-a-block with tanks and armoured personnel carriers. The soldiers are delighted that it is all over.

Kryuchkov phones Yeltsin and suggests they fly together to see Gorbachev. The Russian President senses a trap. He decides to stay in Moscow and send his Vice-President, Aleksandr Rutskoi, his Prime Minister, Ivan Silaev and the Minister of Justice, N. Fedorov, Evgeny Primakov and Vadim Bakatin. Then there are Colonel Aleksandr Sterligov, an aide to Rutskoi, and 36 officers of the MVD and the Russian presidential security service. It is possible that the Russian delegation, on landing at Foros, might be arrested by KGB units guarding Gorbachev and loyal to the Committee. They take a TU-134. Kryuchkov, Yazov, Baklanov, Tizyakov and Vladimir Ivashko, deputy Gensek, fly in a separate plane. Anatoly Lukyanov, to give the impression that he is not associated with the plotters, commandeers his own plane. Yanaev, dead drunk as usual, stays in the Kremlin. No one bothers to enquire about Pavlov (Pikhoya 1998).

The Ukrainian leadership waits another two days, until 23 August, when it is clear that the Committee is defunct, to announce the independence of the republic. A referendum on independence will be held on 1 December. Georgian leader Zviad Gamsakhurdia changes course. He had recognised the new regime but now claims independence for Georgia. Azerbaijani leader Mutalibov, in a telegram, praises Yeltsin to the skies for saving the country. Embarrassingly for him, he had told journalists that the removal of Gorbachev was the natural consequence of policies which had led to chaos. The Supreme Soviets of Estonia, Latvia and Lithuania, on 21–22 August, seize the opportunity to declare independence and to restore their pre-1940 constitutions.

President Nazarbaev announces his resignation from the Politburo, the CC, his leadership of the Communist Party of Kazakhstan, as a CPSU member and his intention of setting up a Kazakh party. The leadership of the Russian Communist Party, which had insulted Gorbachev at every turn and hated Yeltsin, declares that they had never had any contact with the Committee.

The Committee leaders arrive at about 4 p.m. Gorbachev refuses to speak to the plotters or Lukyanov (Gorbachev 1996). The Russian delegation arrives at about 8 p.m. Gorbachev is already a free man as he is in 'control of the situation'. He has been telephoning for four hours and the Kremlin guard has changed sides. He has talked to President George Bush and several republican leaders, including Yeltsin, Nazarbaev and Dementev, the Belarusian leader. When Raisa sees Rutskoi approaching with his sub-machine gun, she becomes alarmed. 'Have you come to arrest us?', she asks. 'No', replies Rutskoi, 'to free you' (Pikhoya 1998). The Russian delegation thinks Gorbachev looks remarkably well. Not so Raisa. She can hardly walk, having suffered a nervous collapse and partial paralysis. Gorbachev immediately invites the Russian delegation to spend the night at Foros.

About midnight, the plane with the Russian delegation and the Gorbachev family takes off. Kryuchkov is with them. He is there to ensure that the KGB does not shoot down the plane. He is profoundly depressed and cannot control his hand and facial movements. The other plotters are in another plane.

22 August 1991

Gorbachev's plane arrives at Vnukovo at about 2 a.m. The Gensek is held back until it is clear that there will be no hostile reception. He walks down the gangway, followed by Raisa and the family. He knows he has returned to a different country but it is more different than he thinks. On the apron, the leader heads for the TV camera. Before he can utter anything, Evgeny Primakov, intervenes. 'The President is too tired to say anything', he explains. This symbolically underlines the fact that the leader is no longer number one. Primakov represents Russia and Russia is now dominant. The Soviet Union and its leader will be forced to play a secondary role from now on.

Gorbachev should have headed for the White House, the centre and symbol of the resistance. Had he done so, he would have received a muted or perhaps a warm welcome. Instead he convenes, at midday in the Kremlin, a meeting of his loyal supporters, the Chief of Staff General Moiseev, the Procurator General, the chair of the Supreme Court and the Foreign Minister. Moiseev is named Minister of Defence and the deputy KGB chair, Kryuchkov's successor. Moiseev's appointment raises eyebrows as he had been actively involved in planning the takeover. Aleksandr Bessmertnykh retains his position as Foreign Minister even though the plotters wanted him as their Foreign Minister.

Then Gorbachev goes to the White House to meet Russian and foreign journalists. He makes another catastrophic mistake. He reconfirms his commitment to socialism and argues that the Party can be renewed and the work of perestroika completed. This turns his listeners against him. Had not the Party played a key role in the coup? To the average person, the Party was dead but Gorbachev was insisting that he could give it the kiss of life. Overwhelmed with questions he cannot answer, Gorbachev breaks off the press conference. 'You will never know the complete truth', he tells the journalists (Pikhoya 1998).

23 August 1991

'I have come from Foros to a different country and I, likewise, am a different person', Gorbachev bitterly comments (Gorbachev 1996). It is payback time for Boris Yeltsin. Gorbachev has dissipated any sympathy he had garnered and has no grasp of the new political realities. He is forced to rescind the appointments he had made. He, the President of the Soviet Union, is then invited to the White House by the President of Russia, to meet the Russian Supreme Soviet. Yeltsin humiliates and denigrates Gorbachev at every turn. He stands above him and points his finger down at him. He forces the President to read out the minutes of the meeting of the government on 19 August. Every minister, with two exceptions, had supported the coup. 'You appointed that government', says the President of Russia gloatingly. 'And now on a lighter note, shall we sign the decree banning the Russian Communist Party?' Gorbachev can only splutter that this is news to him. 'I haven't read the decree', he says plaintively. The Party has lost power in Russia. Yeltsin also signs a decree seizing the assets of the Communist Party of the Soviet Union on Russian territory.

While Gorbachev is speaking, a huge crowd besieges the CC building, on Old Square. Those inside begin destroying documents; some seek to take documents with them as they leave the building. They have to face an angry populace. The more senior officials are evacuated by the special underground which links the building to the Kremlin.

24 August 1991

Gorbachev resigns as Secretary General of the CPSU and its Central Committee (see Glossary) is dissolved. The Communist Party, which had so triumphantly seized power on 7 November 1917, has expired. The Bolshevik era is over.

The Party is not the only one to die. Marshal Sergei Akhromeev, arguably the top brain in the military, hangs himself in his office. He attempted suicide twice but the rope broke the first time. He left several notes. One explains that he will try again with all his might. One is addressed to Gorbachev and explains why he cut short his vacation in order to join the coup. Another is to his family, in which he writes that he cannot live while the motherland is dying. Another is to pay an outstanding mess bill; rubles included. When they come for Boris Pugo, they are shocked by what they see. His wife lies dying from a bullet wound while he is dead from a bullet in his head. His wife's aged father, in the final stages of dementia, is wandering around the small flat as if nothing has happened. Pugo leaves a note for his children and grandchildren. 'Forgive me, it was all a mistake.' Others jump out of windows to their deaths.

Gorbachev convenes the fifth and final USSR Congress of People's Deputies on 2 September 1991 in the Kremlin. The three Baltic States, Moldova and Georgia have declared independence so only the remaining ten Soviet republics are represented. They agree to dissolve the Congress and draft a new Union Treaty to establish a Union of Sovereign States. Gorbachev envisages a federation in which the centre will have responsibility for defence and foreign policy. Yeltsin disagrees and announces that the President of the new Union will play a ceremonial role 'just like the Queen of England'. Gorbachev was always the master of the bribe. He promises the deputies that after the dissolution of the parliament they will still be paid their salaries and retain all their privileges, such as free air travel. They vote for dissolution.

Gorbachev works indefatigably to make the new Union a reality. However, there is someone else in Moscow who is working against the new Union, Boris Yeltsin. On 8 December 1991, in Belovezh forest, outside Minsk, the Presidents of Russia, Ukraine and Belarus dissolve the Union of Soviet Socialist Republics and set up the Commonwealth of Independent States (CIS). Yeltsin phones President

George Bush with the news and leaves it to Stanislau Shushkevich, the Belarusian leader, to inform Gorbachev. Gorbachev has every right to feel insulted. Yeltsin has duped him. One Russian puts it quite graphically: 'Yeltsin had Gorbachev by the balls' ever since he returned from Foros. Rustic but right. The CIS will not have a President. On Christmas Day, 25 December 1991, Gorbachev goes on television to announce his resignation as President of the USSR. The Russian flag now flies over the Kremlin. The Soviet Union, just like its creator, the CPSU, is no more. *Ave Atque Vale* or Hail and Farewell.

Why was there a coup and why did it fail?

- A conservative group, headed by Kryuchkov, wished to retain the old Soviet Union. They wanted the existing political class to stay in power. This meant rejecting the process of democratisation which had gathered momentum. If Gorbachev did not agree to their plans, he would be eliminated. A seriously ill leader could, after all, die suddenly. Medical specialists were to prepare a bulletin on his deteriorating health and subsequent death.

- Gorbachev conspired with Kryuchkov to restore some order in the country. The coup leaders would do Gorbachev's 'dirty work for him'. This implied arresting Yeltsin and the leading reformers and putting an end to the rise of Russia within the Soviet Union. Then Gorbachev would recover from his 'illness' and resume his duties as Soviet President. He would then be a more conservative leader, stressing law and order, and warning of the dangers of the break-up of the country.

- Kryuchkov misunderstood Gorbachev and believed he had the go-ahead for a coup. This is the cock-up theory of Soviet politics. Gorbachev was a master political infighter and very skilled at sending out different signals to various groups. This explanation concludes that he was too clever by half and totally confused Kryuchkov. Anyway, he should have stayed in Moscow until the new treaty was signed and then gone on holiday.

- Understanding the attempted coup is still a problem. Why did Gorbachev shake hands with the plotters as they left Foros on 18 August? They had wanted him to sign a document introducing a state of emergency. He refused. Vladimir Medvedev, the head of his personal guard, maintains that he could have arrested the plotters and restored communications, had he been given the order. He also claims that Gorbachev's personal safety was never in danger. Why did Gorbachev not demand that communications be restored immediately? Anyway, he did have access to an outside phone in the servants' quarters. Apparently he did not have the plotters arrested because he hoped they would see reason. This is an astonishing conclusion by a President whose power is being usurped. One would expect him to have arrested them and given orders to crush the coup. His passivity nurtured in them the hope he would come round to their way of thinking. Why did the plotters travel again to Foros on 21 August? They knew they had lost so what was there to gain by talking again to Gorbachev? When they arrived they were arrested with ease and communications restored immediately. Gorbachev then began telephoning everyone. When the Russian delegation arrived, four hours later, to liberate Gorbachev, they found him a free man and acting like a leader. Very curious. Also why did he say to journalists: 'You'll never know the whole story'? Another problem is understanding why Kryuchkov, the most loyal of comrades, turned on his master.

- Had the coup been launched in 1988 or 1989 it would, almost certainly, have succeeded. This means that Gorbachev's reforms had transformed the political culture by 1991. The intelligentsia – the educated classes – and many ordinary workers and others were no longer in awe of the Party and the KGB. Glasnost had emboldened many and they were unwilling to go back to the old days.

- Even though opposition to the Gensek was widespread, no one had the temerity to organise his removal. Party discipline held even though the situation was getting out of hand. The inbred conviction that the Gensek should be obeyed held.

- There was no big idea to win over middle and lower level officers in the military and KGB. No attempt was made to win over the intelligentsia. Kryuchkov took the usual KGB attitude to the educated: crack the whip and they would fall in line. They are only babblers anyway. There was no charismatic figure to counter Yeltsin's popularity. A blueprint to regenerate the Soviet economy was absent.

- The economic consequences of the coup had not been considered. Probably the United States would announce an embargo on food and other exports and call on other countries to follow suit. Soviet hard currency debt, mainly in US dollars, was climbing rapidly by 1991. It could be forced to default and become a pariah in the international financial markets.

- No attempt was made to rally the population behind a crusade to defend socialism and communism. The appeal was to save the motherland from the octopus of sex, crime and violence which was threatening the health of society. Hence the powerful weapon of patriotism or nationalism was not used. Contrast this with Yeltsin's potent use of Russian patriotism.

- It is astonishing that the plan was so inept, given that Kryuchkov had been shaping it since November 1990. Only one of the eight members of the Committee, Oleg Baklanov, travelled to Foros. He was not even an important member of the Soviet establishment. Just why Kryuchkov thought that the leader could be intimidated by second level personnel, only he knows. The plan was very simple. Ask Gorbachev to sanction a state of emergency and then the Committee would run the country. According to the Gensek, he swore at them, called them 'penises' and spent over two hours arguing with them. This was round one.

■ The comrade chosen to succeed Gorbachev as President was Gennady Yanaev. A sorry apology for a top politician, he had been chosen by Gorbachev to be his Vice-President because he was much more concerned about women and drink. At the first press conference he made a disastrous impression, drumming on the table with his fingers and clearly the worse for wear. He looked and sounded like a clown without a script. During the three days of the coup, he lived in the Kremlin, went without sleep, and smoked and drank interminably.

■ Valentin Pavlov, the Prime Minister, was intellectually superior to Yanaev but of weak character. It was his responsibility to get the government behind the coup and he did so. He just told the ministers that if they failed to support it they would be out of a job and would lose their privileges. He should have appeared on television to explain how he was going to turn the economy round.

■ Many middle and lower level KGB officers were not convinced that spilling Russian blood was justified. The KGB had been willing to spill Azerbaijani blood in Baku, Georgian blood in Tbilisi, Lithuanian blood in Vilnius and Latvian blood in Riga but many operatives baulked at spilling Russian blood to take the White House. They perceived that it would be an infamous act and they would not be easily forgiven for it. Hence many of them played both sides and provided Yeltsin's men with vital intelligence. Another reason why they did not want to turn the clock back in the Soviet Union was that they were going into private business. Many ex-KGB officers now ran private businesses and there were many opportunities for serving officers. The smart ones linked up with Party and government officials to enrich themselves. The more daring entered into alliances with organised crime, which mushroomed in the Gorbachev era. The elite Alpha group was not willing to follow oral orders and demanded written orders in order to protect itself if things went badly.

■ Changes had also taken place in the military. Yeltsin, after becoming President of Russia in June 1991, devoted a lot of time to cultivating the military. His argument was that the military units on Russian soil were Russian and not Soviet. He told them he wanted to make Russia great again and that the rest of the Soviet Union was holding Russia back. There was a perception that Russia produced about three-quarters of Soviet national income but only about half of this remained in Russia. The other republics were exploiting Russia. Many top generals played both sides.

- Yazov was a third rate general. He had been plucked out of the Russian Far East and made Minister of Defence because he was so ordinary. He saw himself as a dolt and could not work out why he had become involved in such an incompetent coup. Marshal Sergei Akhromeev, probably the top brain in the military, was a member of Yazov's group. Had he taken over command things would have been different since he thought it worth dying to save the Soviet Union.

- Had Yeltsin and his aides been arrested on the first day of the coup, it would probably have succeeded. KGB officers watched him leave his dacha but did not arrest him because they had not been given a written order to do so.

- Yeltsin was a brilliant populist and knew how to arouse passions. He was astute enough to demand the return of Gorbachev. He avoided the impression of going for power himself. The legal, constitutional norms had to be observed.

- Yeltsin appealed to Russian patriotism. The coup was anti-Russian as the Committee wanted to force Russia back into the old Soviet Union. This message struck a responsive chord among the intelligentsia. They knew that their lives would be blighted if the Committee secured power. Many workers were indifferent. Things had been going from bad to worse in the late Gorbachev era. Why should they suddenly improve if the leader came back? Yeltsin's answer was that we Russians can do it, if we are permitted to. Let us regenerate Russia together.

- Oleg Shenin, with the wisdom of hindsight, offered the following to *Trud-7* newspaper readers on 19 August 2004.

> 'A basic mistake by the Committee was that it did not dissociate itself from Gorbachev clearly enough. It should have demonstrated that perestroika, good in itself, was going disastrously wrong because of Gorbachev's actions. They were certain to lead to the collapse of the Soviet Union. The Committee should have concentrated attention on the need to save the Soviet Union – something which the vast majority of Soviet citizens agreed with. The message should have been: "Gorbachev's return to Moscow means the end of the Soviet Union".'

By August 1991 the majority of the Soviet people 'had already rejected Gorbachev. They were ready to accept anyone, even the devil, and they got Yeltsin'. It was an error to bring in so many troops but, once they were there, they 'should have been used. I assumed automatically that once the Committee had issued its declaration, swift action would follow'. The arrest of Yeltsin 'had been agreed in advance. He should have been detained in Kazakhstan, where he was the day before. We should also have isolated Popov, Luzhkov and others. I do not understand why it was not done. It was stupid'. Asked why he had not given orders to the special services on behalf of the Party, he replied:

> 'I could not. If I could have, I would have. We created Party committees in the KGB, the Ministry of Defence and Ministry of the Interior which were subordinate to the organisational department of the Party's Central Committee; in fact to me. However article 6 of the constitution [conferring on the Party a monopoly of power] was no longer valid and heads of economic and law-enforcement structures doubted Party decisions.'

The fact that Alpha did not storm the White House 'suggests that the Party was not obeyed at all', commented the *Trud-7* journalist.

> 'I had nothing to do with it. The Committee did not take the necessary decisions. The special task forces or the army did not refuse to carry out the order [to storm the White House] because there was simply no order. Had the Alpha group received an order, it would have complied. But they were afraid to give it. It was discussed in Kryuchkov's office with the generals present. Baklanov and I insisted on storming the White House. The others were against it. It was dangerous and blood would be spilt. But Baklanov and I believed that shedding a little blood now would lead to a normal country later. This was preferable to a lot of blood later when the country collapsed. The others did not support us. I am absolutely convinced this was a mistake. All the more so because I was aware of Alpha's abilities. There would not have been any blood. They would have arrested the yellers and then everything would have calmed down.'

Questions

1 What was the main reasoning behind the coup and who was the driving force behind it?

2 'The coup was more about revenge than a desperate bid by the old elite to hold on to power.' Discuss.

3 'Too many ideologies were competing for power within the Soviet Union between 1989 and 1991. In this respect a coup was inevitable.' Discuss.

4 Distinguish between 'reform radicals' and 'reform conservatives' and explain why there are significant distinctions for the period 1989–91.

5 Is there anything Gorbachev could have done differently that would have kept the Soviet Union together?

6 The coup leaders afterwards maintained that Gorbachev had been a willing participant in the coup against himself. He had favoured a crackdown but could not be associated with it directly because of his international reputation. Afterwards he could return to Moscow and wash his hands, like Pontius Pilate, of responsibility for the coercion. Comment on the precise nature of Gorbachev's role in the August 1991 coup.

Further reading

David Remnick, *Lenin's Tomb: The Last Days of the Soviet Empire* (1993); Mikhail Gorbachev, *Memoirs* (1996); *The August Coup: The Truth and Lessons* (1991).

CHAPTER 2

1917: days of hope and days of despair

There were two revolutions in 1917: the February and October revolutions, according to the Julian calendar and the March and November revolutions, according to the Gregorian. (The Bolsheviks moved to the Gregorian calendar on 1 February 1918 which became 14 February 1918. The Russian Orthodox Church still retains the Julian calendar. The reason is that it does not accept the authority of the Roman Catholic Pope Gregory.) The first revolution removed the Tsar and the second brought the Red Tsar to power. It was not supposed to be like that. These two revolutions were intended to make Russia the most democratic country in the world. Social justice would be achieved and everyone would live in plenty. It turned out quite differently. Why?

Russia was once described as an autocracy tempered by assassination. Tsar Alexander II, the liberator of the serfs, was killed in 1881; Prime Minister Petr Stolypin was gunned down in 1911; an assortment of ministers and governors were terminated. The midwife of reform in Russia was violence. The lost Crimean War (1854–56) provided the impetus for the reforms of Alexander II. Russia had to become more like its European competitors or it would become a colony of one of them. The 1905–07 revolution revealed the desperate situation of most peasants. Russia's most successful period was the years 1909–13. War, in 1914, was a disaster for Russia. However, had it held out to 1918 it would have been one of the victor powers of the entente. When the February revolution broke out, there was no reason to assume that the situation on the eastern front was any worse than on the western front. Germany succumbed to revolution in 1918 as did Austria-Hungary and the Ottoman Empire. Russia was the only 'victor' power to fall to revolution. Revolution meant a social revolution. In February 1917, the social revolution was achieved with limited violence but, in October 1917, the social revolution was extremely violent.

The peasant problem

The peasant problem dominated Russian politics. In 1900, over half the peasants could not survive on agriculture alone. A major reason was the rapid increase of the population. It grew by almost 50 per cent between 1885 and 1913. Almost 5 million peasants migrated to Siberia and Central Asia in the two decades before 1917. Others made for the cities. Peasants concentrated on producing grain. In 1914, about 90 per cent of arable land was sown to grain, mainly wheat and rye.

Peasants were emancipated in 1861. Black slaves in the United States were emancipated after those of Russia. However, of the total US population of 31.2 million, only 4 million were slaves. In other words, just over 12 per cent of the population were emancipated. However, in Russia, emancipation 'freed' 82 per cent of the population. Most of these peasants were no better off after 1861 than before.

Peasants lived in communes (*obshchina* or *mir* in Russian) or villages. In central Russia they had up to 80 households. In drier regions, it could be up to 1,000. The commune acted as the agent of the government. It collected taxes, selected young men for military service and imposed order. It practised collective responsibility (*krugovaya poruka*). This involved combining to prevent crime and apprehending criminals, the maintenance of roads and bridges and solving social conflicts. If one household did not pay its taxes or provide a son for the army, the others had to make up the deficit. Collective responsibility had a profound impact on the peasants' attitude to land. It was God's and was not the property of any person. There were periodic redistributions to cope with the fact that some households had expanded and others contracted. Since not all land was good, fertile land, the solution adopted was to provide households with some good, some average and some poor land. This meant that the strips could be quite some distance apart. The male heads of households formed a village assembly (*skhod*) to run affairs. An elder or *starosta* was elected to chair meetings, ensure decisions were implemented and liaise with the state authorities.

Women were kept in their place in a male-dominated environment. 'The more one beats the *baba* (old woman), the tastier the soup will be', says it all. However, the interests of younger males were often neglected. The average Russian peasant was not a farmer in the western sense. The Russian peasant had a deeply ingrained suspicion of the rich and the poor. Being poor meant that one's taxes had to be paid by others. Being rich meant that one's behaviour was suspect, perhaps criminal. 'Wealth is a sin before God and poverty a sin before one's fellow man', went a folk saying. Villagers helped one another out in sickness and need. The downside was that peasants kept a close eye on each other since one peasant's behaviour could harm others.

Violence was the constant companion of rural life in Russia. Life was based on a lack of personal responsibility. All important decisions were taken by others. Introducing the profit motive into such a way of life was a challenge. After 1906, Prime Minister Stolypin promoted the consolidation of the household's various strips into a single farm outside the village. Overall it proved a failure. The peasant did not want capitalist farming. Capitalism was high risk but the vast majority of peasants wanted a low risk life.

The commune was a barrier to raising the efficiency of agriculture. It was patriarchal but it was also consensual and collectivist. One could say it was social-ist by nature. Peasant socialism was articulated by the Socialist Revolutionary Party, the SRs. As it spoke for the peasants, it was the largest party in Russia. The problem was that the SRs favoured a market but rejected capitalism.

The peasant's loyalty was to the village and the region. He did not think of himself as a member of a wider Russian nation. He accepted the Tsar, calling him 'little father', and blamed all his ills on the nobles and bureaucrats. When a prob-lem arises in western society, a search begins for its political, economic and social roots. In Russia, one looks around for someone to blame. The natural order was ordained by God and the peasant opposed strongly any attempt to change tradi-tion. The world was full of spirits, good and bad. Witches, spells, the evil eye and magic were everyday phenomena. A man's reputation was important. He was deeply offended if laughed at.

Peasants lived in an *izba*. It was dirty, full of smoke, windows without glass were stuffed with hay or rags to keep out the wind and rain, it was dark, dank and packed with humans. Hens lived under the rough-hewn table. A large oven provided heat and permitted rudimentary cooking and washing. There was no chimney for the smoke to escape. An important factor in commune life was geo-graphical isolation. It was often quite a distance to the next village. Villages were routinely cut off in winter. There was no electric light, radio or television, of course. Distance to the market was one factor holding back the commercialisation of agriculture. Another was the lack of urban centres. In large stretches of Russia there were no cities, only small and larger villages. However the younger members of the commune sought seasonal work in the towns. They normally returned to help with the harvest.

The nobility

At the opposite end of the social scale were the nobles. They mistrusted one another and most wanted the Tsar to remain an autocrat. This was preferable to the constitutional monarchies of Western Europe. Many of them lived in grand houses, even palaces. They were educated after a fashion and the young delighted in tasting the pleasures of the 'civilised' world. They were not a ruling class, rather a governing class. The landed nobility saw themselves as the ruling class in the countryside. However by the end of the nineteenth century the urban and court nobility was more influential. There was a table of ranks; 14 in all. Bureaucrats or officials who rose to a certain state rank automatically became members of the service nobility. This also applied to the military.

The Tsar was forced to grant a constitution in 1905. Nobles dominated the upper house, the State Council, and many were members of the lower house, the Duma, due to property qualifications. A group of landed nobles emerged as a powerful interest group. They made land and political reform very difficult. They perceived this to be in their interests and those of the Tsar but, in reality, they deepened the crisis of the regime. They were digging their own graves.

The bureaucracy

If the nobility went to the grave, another tsarist institution, the bureaucracy, skilfully survived the two revolutions of 1917 and was reborn as the nerves and sinews of the new Bolshevik state. This underlined a basic truth about Russian bureaucracy. It does not serve the people; it serves the leader and his retinue. There was, and is, no tradition of public service. The bureaucracy expanded rapidly in the nineteenth century and numbered almost 400,000 by 1917. Its rapid growth meant that education and achievement became more important than noble birth. The service nobility over time outnumbered the hereditary nobility. The bureaucracy would have preferred the emergence of rules and regulations encased in law. This would have promoted the rule of law. The Tsar preferred to rule in an arbitrary fashion. His attitude was patrimonial; Russia belonged to him. In this environment, the person who had the ear of the sovereign was in a powerful position.

The Russian Orthodox Church

The Russian Orthodox Church was a significant pillar of the autocracy. The Tsar was head of church and state. Over time, the church lost power and influence among the ruling elites. It existed on state subsidies, with the humble parish priest often as poor as a church mouse. Spirituality did not reside among the elites but among the peasants. The church was much more influential in the villages. The intelligentsia or educated class regarded the church as a reactionary pillar of tsardom. The Reformation and the European Enlightenment of the eighteenth century passed it by but there was a flowering of theology at the beginning of the twentieth century.

The Orthodox Church was unlike the Roman Catholic Church with its emphasis on morality and learning. Russian church services are dominated by ritual. There is no preaching in the Catholic or Protestant tradition. Moral guidance is not given. There is no catechism which lays down the beliefs of the faithful or guides behaviour. The Orthodox mass is a spiritual experience; the senses not the intellect dominate. The upper classes were struck by the spirituality of the peasant. Out of this came the idea that the peasants' faith was the source of Russia's unique character. This belief fused with national pride, creating the myth that the nation was founded on the special goodness of the people. This special virtue would one day save mankind.

Capitalism in Russia

There were natural capitalists in Russia, men who were capable of turning one ruble into two, but most of them were not ethnic Russians. Germans, Jews and Muslims were ahead in the money-making stakes. Trade was the source of most wealth but foreign capital began flowing into Russia towards the end of the nineteenth century. Russia was rich in minerals and fuel and the markets of the world beckoned. The Russian nobility had the same disdain for money making as its English and French counterparts. Russia's great writers, Dostoevsky among them, poured contempt on the money-grubbing bourgeoisie. A few nobles grasped the opportunities offered in the late nineteenth century and developed commercial agriculture. Enterprising peasants, the Bolsheviks were later to call them kulaks, prospered and rural stratification grew. Textiles and sugar refining were two of the traditional Russian industries. Engineering developed, especially iron and steel. The main customer was the state. The domestic Russian market was small so the state began to play the role of the largely absent bourgeoisie. It began a vast programme of public works, such as building the Trans-Siberian Railway. In fact it was state capitalism and the budget was overspent. This was deficit financing before John Maynard Keynes made it popular. The tsarist state promoted industrialisation successfully decades before Stalin.

Russian philosophy

In the western sense of the term, there was no Russian philosophy. The problem of the acquisition of scientific knowledge, central to European philosophy since Descartes, was absent. So too were the mathematical and logical preoccupations of modern analytical philosophy. Philosophy as an academic discipline, with its own jargon and rules of debate, never put down roots in Russia. There have been many Russian philosophers but they have overwhelmingly been writers, poets, revolutionaries and journalists. Abstract speculation had to serve a higher cause: the destiny of Russia and the burning question of social justice. The thinker could not be detached from everyday life. He had a moral responsibility to the people. The populist activist Petr Lavrov underlined the searing responsibility of the philosopher: 'Mankind has paid a heavy price so that a few thinkers can sit in their studies and discuss its progress'. Many philosophers in the West were churchmen, but not in Russia.

Rational enquiry or scientific method never became part of Russian intellectual life. The reason for this is that the Renaissance, Reformation and Enlightenment (so called because it lit up the mind) never took hold in Russia. European philosophy, from Descartes to Kant, was predominantly a critique of reason. This is the title of Kant's famous work: *Kritik der reinen Vernunft*. Its goal was to sharpen and refine methods of rational enquiry. This would allow any new idea or proposition to be tested by criteria which all accepted. Secular thought developed apace. The gulf between philosophy and theology widened. Secular thought entered Russia in the form of socialism, democracy and nationalism. Since there was no tradition of secular thought, these new ideas were grafted on to prevailing moral, religious thought. A part of this was messianism or the hope or faith in a coming Messiah who would solve all problems. Russians stressed the moral dimension of socialism, democracy and nationalism. They lacked the analytical tools to examine rigorously these doctrines. German philosophers proved enormously popular, from Kant, Fichte, Schelling and Feuerbach to Hegel (they all began as theologians), Marx and Nietzsche. Theoretical debates were conducted according to accepted rules. Since Russia lacked this tradition, enthusiasts read the texts literally, not as components of a debate. German philosophy moved on and left the Russians behind. This is especially true of the reception of Marxism in Russia. Marx never maintained that he had arrived at the final analysis of scientific socialism. His thought was always evolving. The Russians, because they lacked such a philosophical tradition, were literalists. They concentrated on certain passages and passionately defended them against all comers. The essence of good philosophy is intellectual scepticism. The Russians did not accept scepticism, they were looking for certainty. They found what they were looking for in Marx, simplified and codified him and made him fit Russian tradition.

The advent of Marx

'Who becomes a communist in the West?' 'Someone who has given up hope of becoming a capitalist.'

The first language into which *Das Kapital*, the magnum opus of Karl Marx (1818–83), was translated was Russian, in 1872. An English edition was published much later.

Why should Marx's work have aroused such interest in Russia, an underdeveloped country, and so little interest in Britain, the most advanced capitalist country of the day? Marx's analysis of the formation of capital led him to the conclusion that capitalism would fail because it was based on the exploitation of labour. Workers, meaning industrial workers, would rebel and sweep the owners of the means of production, distribution and exchange aside. This would herald the dictatorship of the proletariat or wage earners. Socialist society would have dawned. One might have expected this doom-laden analysis of the market economy to have sent shock waves through the capitalist establishment. Not a bit of it. The barons of industry leafed through a few pages and concluded that it was nothing but gobbledegook. No worker could understand it. After all it was based on the philosophy of Karl Wilhelm Friedrich Hegel (1770–1831), a German whose writings were almost impenetrable even to Germans. The Russian censors came to the same conclusion.

The main reason why Marx's writings struck such a responsive chord in Russia was that young, educated Russians were appalled by his analysis of European capitalism and the emergence of bourgeois society. Such a misfortune must not befall Russia. They wanted to retain the virtues of a pre-industrial society. They were known as populists and were later to articulate their programme through the SR party. Hence the SRs were not Marxists. They wanted to fashion a peasant-based socialism.

Marx's analysis of the creation of capital struck a responsive chord among Russians. If I own a house worth £500,000 I can borrow, say, £200,000 on it in order to buy another house. I have created £200,000 of capital. I can then mortgage the new house and raise, say, £100,000. I can buy another house with this money. The old adage is true: money makes money. The more capital I have the more I can create and the richer I become. All I need to raise the original £200,000 is to prove I have legal title to my house. Marx found the creation of capital extremely immoral. It produced a profoundly inegalitarian society. He believed that one's wealth should be earned by doing socially useful work. Marx identified private ownership of property as the source of inequality. Under socialism there would be no private property. It would all be socially owned. Hence one would not get a bank loan on the house one lived in. Young radical Russians considered banking immoral. One should not obtain income from bank deposits and investments. One should work for one's living. Populists, therefore, were opposed to the buying and selling of land. There should be no land market. Marxists agreed with them. Hence the approach to economics among most Russians was moral.

By the 1890s, it became clear that capitalism had put down roots in Russia. The problem was how to reduce the exploitation of the Russian peasant turned worker. The most brilliant expositor of Marxist thought in Russia was Georgy Plekhanov (1856–1918). Gifted with a mellifluous prose style, he seduced a whole generation. The coming revolution in Russia would be bourgeois when the capitalists and middle classes would rule. The task of Marxists was then to forge the conditions which would permit the working class to move forward to the next stage, the socialist revolution.

Marxism, to Russians, had a seductive moral dimension. Capitalism was a necessary evil but it laid the foundations for a socialist society; a classless, just society. Peace and harmony would reign when society became so productive it could meet the needs of every member. Many young Russians, wrestling with the problems of how to promote a more just society, were bowled over by Marx's writings. Not only did he offer a bright future; it was inevitable.

Plekhanov was no revolutionary. He was content for economic forces to develop to the point when a socialist revolution became inevitable. The organiser of revolution, the master of insurrection, was Vladimir Ilich Ulyanov (1870–1924). He is better known as Lenin. He was born in Simbirsk into a family which had enjoyed upward mobility. His father, an inspector of schools, had joined the service nobility. Vladimir or Volodya was a brilliant student but was liable to fly off the handle at times. Various reasons have been advanced to explain his behaviour, including the fact that he fell on his head as a child. Some specialists believe he died of syphilis. It takes about 20 years for this disease to kill and produces certain personality traits. He adored his elder brother, Aleksandr. It was a terrible shock to him when Aleksandr was executed for attempted regicide in 1887. He would have been spared had he asked for clemency. However the senior Ulyanov wanted to die a martyr. Volodya was thrown out of Kazan University for participating in a student protest. He completed his law degree at St Petersburg University by correspondence. He became a leading light in the capital's Marxist circles. He met his future wife Nadezhda Krupskaya there. Soon he was known as the 'old man' because of his baldness, wispy beard and serious demeanour. Lenin had two faces. One he showed to opponents. It was aggressive, arrogant, abusive and violently personal. The other was to his inner circle. Here he was charming, modest and at times humorous. Promoting revolution obsessed him. The working class was incapable of understanding what was in its own best interests; revolution. This insight had to be brought to them from outside, by social democrats who came from the intelligentsia. Workers were only capable of advancing to 'trade-union consciousness'. Hence Lenin was indispensable. This arrogance was typical of the rising star. The other side of the coin was his utter moral certainty that he was right.

Lenin spelled out his vision of a professional, revolutionary party in *What Is to Be Done?*, published in 1902. He sketched out a 'party of a new type', one full of dedicated revolutionaries. Lenin split the Russian Social Democratic Labour Party (RSDRP) at its second Congress in Brussels in 1903. The decisive question was who could be a party member. Lenin's vision collided with that of Iuly Martov. The latter favoured a mass party along the lines of the German Social Democratic Party (SPD), at that time the leading Marxist party in the world. Lenin won and his faction, in the majority, became known as Bolsheviks. Martov's faction, in the minority, became Mensheviks. This was an historic split. After 1918 the political left divided into those who favoured Lenin's line and those who wanted a more democratic approach. The former set up Communist parties and the latter Social Democratic parties.

Crisis and war

The Revolution of 1905–07

In 1903, Father Georgy Gapon, encouraged by the Okrana (secret police) established the Assembly of Russian Workers. Within a year it had over 9,000 members. When four members of the Assembly of Russian Workers were dismissed from the Putilov Metallurgical Works, Gapon called for industrial action. In late December over 110,000 workers in St Petersburg were on strike. Gapon appealed directly to the Tsar to resolve the dispute. He drafted a petition calling for an eight hour working day, higher wages and better working conditions, the vote for all citizens and an end to the Russo-Japanese war. Over 150,000 signed the petition and on 9 January (22 January according to the Gregorian calendar) 1905, Gapon led a large procession of workers to the Winter Palace to present the petition to the Tsar. When they reached the Palace police and Cossacks opened fire and killed over a thousand, leaving many more wounded. It became known as Bloody Sunday and signalled the start of the revolution of 1905–07.

At times during 1905 the regime almost collapsed. The government lost control of certain towns as workers went on strike in massive numbers. Peasants rebelled. There were mutinies in the army and navy. The most famous was on the battleship *Potemkin*, in the Black Sea. A nationwide strike in October 1905 paralysed the country. Workers set up their own councils, or soviets. St Petersburg set up a soviet to represent everyone. It was briefly led by Lev Bronstein, known as Trotsky (1879–1940). He was a brilliant orator and writer and became the idol of the left. Small concessions failed to stem the tide. It was the conclusion of the war with Japan in the summer (which Russia lost) which turned the tide. Troops could now be brought back to suppress peasant and worker discontent. In October, the Tsar signed the October Manifesto which granted a limited constitutional regime. Rights of assembly and speech were guaranteed. A bicameral parliament, the Duma and the State Council, were to be set up. Political parties and trade unions became legal. The liberals now sided with the Tsar, fearing anarchy. Troops put down an uprising of Moscow workers in December 1905. The St Petersburg soviet was disbanded and Trotsky arrested. Separatist movements were crushed and order restored with great brutality. The revolution dragged on until 1907 but the monarchy was now safe – for a season.

The final crisis

The period also produced a gifted politician on the right, Petr Stolypin. He was Prime Minister from 1906 to 1911 when he was assassinated attending the opera with the Tsar in Kyiv (Kiev in Russian) by a person linked to the police. He was no democrat or respecter of due legal process. He saved the monarchy by deploying brutal methods. His work was in vain because he was followed by inconsequential politicians. Part of the problem was the interference of the Tsarina Alexandra. She was virulently opposed to representative government and political parties. Her only son, Aleksei, was a haemophiliac. This disease, often accompanied by excruciating pain, is transmitted through the female line. However, the monk Grigory Rasputin, probably through hypnosis, was able to help. He enjoyed a wild reputation and this deepened the alienation felt by the educated towards the monarchy. The Tsar was weak, the Tsarina strong willed (pig-headed would be a better description) and Rasputin was regarded as dissolute. (Rasputin in Russian means a dissolute.) Paradoxically, the years before 1914 were very successful economically. However, this compounded the crisis. The expanding industrial economy created a demand for more and more workers. The urban industrial class felt more and more alienated from the rest of society.

Was Russia capable of overcoming the crisis? Historians are divided into two main groups. Those who are politically right of centre saw Russia as capable of riding the storm and successfully industrialising. The huge mineral and fuel wealth of the country was waiting to be exploited. The market economy was developing apace and this would lead to businessmen gaining more and more political influence. The left of centre historians have no faith in the market economy. Bad government would exacerbate the situation and revolution would become inevitable. The tsarist regime was quite incapable of acting in its own interests.

The First World War

The line-up was impressive: Russia, France and Britain against Germany, Austria-Hungary and Turkey. A host of other players entered the fray. Russia stood to gain hugely. It was to get the Straits (which linked the Black and Aegean Seas), among other things, and this would resolve once and for all the perennial problem of egress from the Black Sea to the Mediterranean for its warships. However, to Lenin, the working class should not fight for the Tsar but against him. The imperialist war could be turned into a civil war. This would bring down tsardom.

Russia was ill equipped industrially to fight a modern war. Its military reforms were only partially completed and anyway their battle plans had been acquired by the Austrians. They thought they could make up for technical deficiencies by sheer numbers of men. On balance, the Russians lost the war against the Germans but won against the Austrians and Turks.

The February revolution

No one anticipated the collapse of communism in Eastern Europe in 1989 and in the Soviet Union in 1991. Neither did anyone foresee the fall of the Romanov dynasty in February 1917. It came as a bolt from the blue. Even that sea-green optimist, Vladimir Lenin, was gloomily reminiscing in January 1917 that his generation would not 'live to see the decisive battles of the coming revolution'.

The Tsar's residence was in St Petersburg or rather Petrograd. The name had been changed on 18 August 1914 because it sounded too German. In reality, the name is from the Dutch. It was also the seat of government and the Duma. However, he was not in his capital but at Mogilev, to the west. He was at general staff headquarters as he believed it his duty to lead his army but he had no military training. Various schemes were hatched to remove the Tsar while retaining the monarchy. The gulf between him and educated society widened. There was no dialogue between the ruler and the conservative and liberal politicians, the Progressive Bloc, which wanted a government of national confidence.

The event which changed the history of the world occurred, appropriately, on International Women's Day, 23 February 1917. Women, angry and hungry, decided to strike and marched to other factories, calling on workers to join them. By the next day half the industrial workers of Petrograd were on strike. Women, queueing in vain for bread, joined them. The mounted Cossacks refused orders to disperse the strikers. The Duma called for a government responsible to it. However, the conservatives and liberals did not want revolution. They were afraid that anarchy could tear the country apart.

The left was, as usual, split. The Socialist Revolutionaries, SRs, spoke for the peasants who made up the vast majority of the army. They broke down into three groups: the right wanted victory and strong government; a centre, led by Viktor Chernov, which wanted peace; and a militant left which gradually gravitated towards the Bolsheviks. The Social Democrats, SDs, could not agree. Some Mensheviks and Bolsheviks supported the war (defensism), some opposed the war (internationalists) and others call for Russia's defeat (defeatism).

On 25 February over 300,000 workers marched and were joined by students and office and shop employees. It was wildly exciting to demonstrate against the Tsar. The next day some police officers attempted to disperse the crowds but were killed. The Tsar acted. He ordered the Duma to disperse and it obeyed him. Soldiers began shooting at the crowds. The fate of the revolution was on a knife-edge. Demonstrators were not intimidated by gunfire but became angrier. Suddenly the turning point was reached. An elite guards regiment mutinied and joined the crowds. The tide had turned. Had the soldiers been willing to defend the monarchy there would have been no revolution. By the evening of 27 February, 66,000 soldiers had gone over to the insurgents. Duma members formed a Provisional Government. They met in the Tauride Palace. In another wing of the palace, deputies, elected by workers, came together to set up the Petrograd soviet of workers' deputies. They were carrying on where they had left off in 1905.

On 2 March, Tsar Nicholas II abdicated and handed nominal power to his brother, Grand Duke Michael. He was sharp enough to decline. Nicholas then abdicated in favour of his haemophiliac son, Aleksei. When told that if the Tsarevich became Tsar he would never see him again, Nicholas accepted that he would have no successor. This ended the 300 year old Romanov dynasty.

The revolution ushered in multiple sources of power. Dual power refers to the coexistence of the Provisional Government and the Petrograd soviet. Conservatives and liberals set up the Provisional Government (it was to act until a Constituent Assembly was elected). Most military officers and government officials supported it. Workers, peasants and the lower orders elected their own government, the soviet.

Numerically the soviet represented the overwhelming majority of citizens. The period between March and October 1917, when the Bolsheviks seized power, can be regarded as a failed experiment. That is, from the point of view of liberal or bourgeois values: a market economy, the development of civil society, the rule of law and representative institutions – first and foremost a parliament. The latter would mediate social conflicts and elect a government and agree a constitution. This agenda envisages gradual change. However Russian soldiers, workers and peasants wanted social change speeded up.

Conservatives and liberals were handed power after the revolution. The left did not want it. From a Marxist perspective, the February revolution was a bourgeois revolution in which the capitalists and their supporters would rule. The task of Marxist parties was to put pressure on the government to grant concessions to workers.

The Petrograd soviet was dominated by moderate SRs and Mensheviks. Military officers wanted their authority restored but the rank and file did not favour giving up their revolutionary gains. On 1 March, the soviet passed the famous 'Order No. 1' which stated that soldiers were only to obey orders which did not 'contradict the orders and decrees' of the Petrograd soviet of workers' and soldiers' deputies. Hence power was shared by the Provisional Government and the soviet. In reality, the soviet wielded more power than the government. This was a recipe for weak, indecisive government at a time when Russia needed strong, incisive leadership. The uneasy relationship between the Petrograd soviet and the Provisional Governments represented dual power which lasted until October 1917. It was one of the unintended consequences of the February revolution.

Relations between the two institutions always swung between cooperation and rivalry. Trotsky, dismissively, referred to dual power as dual powerlessness. He was right. Neither institution, in effect, ruled.

Factory owners granted many concessions: an eight hour day; higher wages; recognition of workers' councils. Inflation soon wiped out wage increases and owners balked at compensating for inflation. Bolshevik agitators said the only solution was for the workers to take over the factories. Peasants wanted land and the peasants in uniform wanted peace. They were keen to return to the village to claim more land. They deserted en masse.

The revolution brought the Bolshevik leaders back from internal and external exile. Vyacheslav Molotov and Aleksandr Shlyapnikov, in Petrograd, headed the Bureau of the Bolshevik Central Committee. They also edited *Pravda*, the Party's newspaper. The line they took was outright opposition to the Provisional Government. When Iosif Stalin and Lev Kamenev arrived back in Petrograd from Siberian exile they expected to be acknowledged as leaders of the Central Committee. They proposed a conciliatory attitude towards the government. When the Bureau of the Central Committee was newly elected on 12 March Stalin was excluded. He created such a fuss that he was elected to the Presidium of the Bureau on 15 March. He and Kamenev joined the editorial board of *Pravda*. Molotov was kicked off the Bureau. It ceased to demand the removal of the Provisional Government. However, Stalin and Kamenev favoured the Petrograd soviet over the Provisional Government. They articulated a policy aimed at splitting the Mensheviks and attracting its left wing to the Bolshevik cause. The goal appeared to be the fashioning of a broadly based left-wing party which would gradually become the dominant party in Russia.

Everything changed on 4 April when Vladimir Lenin arrived at the Finland station, in Petrograd, from exile in Switzerland. The German Kaiser and his government thought that Lenin, dedicated to the defeat of Russia, would help the German cause by opposing the war inside Russia. He was granted passage through Germany in a sealed train. Lenin and the Bolsheviks had been receiving subventions from the Germans. Lenin was furious at the Bolsheviks' lack of opposition. His firebrand approach, articulated in the April Theses or proposals, shocked the Party. It also shocked Stalin and Kamenev to the core. From being the leaders of the Bureau they were now relegated to the substitutes' bench. Trotsky, soon to abandon his own group and join the Bolsheviks, commented that the Party was as unprepared for Lenin as it had been for the February revolution. How did Stalin react to Lenin's rebukes? He simply changed sides and became a firm supporter of Lenin. Stalin recognised that Lenin was a winner.

Lenin's analysis was a recipe for action. Russia was in transition from the first stage of revolution to the second stage, which 'would place power in the hands of the proletariat and poor strata of the peasantry'. He acknowledged that Bolsheviks were often a tiny minority in the soviets of workers' deputies throughout the land. The SR-Menshevik majority was dismissed as 'petty bourgeois opportunist elements'. However, the soviet of workers' deputies was the 'only possible form of revolutionary government'. Therefore the goal was not a parliamentary republic (the Constituent Assembly would solve nothing) but a 'republic of soviets of workers', agricultural labourers' and peasants' deputies throughout the country'. Thus war was declared on the government and the moderate leadership of the soviet. Victory would come when the soviet was led by Bolsheviks. Lenin's theses are a development of Marxism. He formulated two new concepts: the shortening of the period between the bourgeois and proletarian revolutions and a soviet republic would implement the dictatorship of the proletariat. According to Lenin, the latter 'presupposes the application of mercilessly brutal, swift and decisive violence to strangle the opposition of exploiters, landowners and their hangers-on'.

The first head-on confrontation between the government and the soviet occurred at the end of March. The soviet formulated its attitude to the war as 'revolutionary defensism'. This involved fighting to defend the revolution but simultaneously struggling for a 'democratic peace'. The Foreign Minister, the Constitutional Democrat or Kadet, Pavel Milyukov, wanted victory and compensation which included control of Constantinople (now Istanbul) and the Straits. Articulating the old tsarist goals was like a red rag to a bull. Thousands jammed the streets of Petrograd demanding the dismissal of the 'capitalist ministers', first and foremost Milyukov. The moderate soviet leadership strove to prevent the parties and groups which had supported the revolution splitting along class or interest group lines. It did not want to join the 'bourgeois ministers' in a coalition government. When the Minister of War, the Octobrist or conservative Aleksandr Guchkov resigned, the soviet became nervous. Was the right planning a military coup? This forced the hand of the soviet leadership and they voted to join a coalition government on 1 May. Two days later Pavel Milyukov resigned. Another two days and the first coalition government took office. The soviet leadership had now fallen into the trap it had been trying to avoid: assuming responsibility for rapidly deteriorating conditions in Russia.

The new Minister of War was the SR Alexander Kerensky. He was a brilliant lawyer and orator. He regaled the troops with the wonders of the post-war world and encouraged them to fight the Germans. A new offensive, called the Kerensky offensive, was launched with predictably disastrous results. The distribution network became less and less efficient. This meant shortages and higher prices. Factories closed because of lack of inputs. Worker resentment and militancy grew. The harvest was good but the grain was not reaching the cities. Soviets were set up throughout Russia and they took over local government.

All contentious economic decisions were avoided. The Constituent Assembly would resolve them. The alliance of the middle classes and moderate socialists gradually broke down amid mutual recrimination. This widened the gulf between the right and the left. The right blamed the workers for national decline and the left blamed the 'capitalist ministers' and captains of industry. The centre began to disappear. The slogan 'all power to the soviets' appeared for the first time at the end of May in the Petrograd soviet.

The first All-Russian Congress of Peasants' Soviets, in May, banned the buying and selling of land. It was to be transferred to land committees for equitable redistribution. The Minister of Agriculture, the SR leader Viktor Chernov, began drafting proposals to implement this. Landowning interests in the government opposed land committees and a ban on buying and selling of land. Chernov, frustrated, resigned on 20 July. Peasants did not wait for the Constituent Assembly to resolve the land question. They set up committees of people's power which sanctioned the taking over of uncultivated land. The Assembly would be expected to legalise the redistribution. They took over noble estates and the manor houses. They were used to running their own affairs, through their assemblies. Now they seized the opportunity to expand their writ, ignoring the weak central government.

The first All-Russian Congress of Soviets convened in June. The moderate socialists were in the majority. However, Bolshevik influence was growing among workers and soldiers. Irakly Tsereteli, the silver tongued Menshevik, proudly stated that there was no political party in Russia ready to take power from the government. Lenin cut him short: 'Yes, there is'. Bolshevik delegates loved his audacity but everyone else laughed. To the moderate socialists the enemy was on the right, not the left. Congress banned all street demonstrations. When the Bolsheviks called for a mass protest against the capitalist ministers, it decided to hold its own demonstration. To its dismay, it discovered that most slogans proclaimed Bolshevik policies: 'all power to the soviets' and 'down with the ten capitalist ministers'.

The July days

On 2 July the government began to disintegrate as Kadet ministers resigned. They would not accept regional self-rule for Finland and Ukraine. Armed soldiers took to the streets, workers joined them, sailors from the naval base at Kronstadt arrived and the whole throng moved to Bolshevik headquarters. Power was being offered to Lenin. He prevaricated and finally came out against such a démarche. Frustrated, the crowd moved on to the Tauride Palace. Chernov was brave enough to address the angry demonstrators. 'You bastard, take power when it is offered you', shouted a voice from the crowd. The government was preparing to arrest one of Lenin's associates who was bringing money from Germany. The newspapers got hold of the story and blew the operation. They then declared Lenin an agent of the Kaiser. The mood changed completely. Many soldiers changed sides. Lenin and

Grigory Zinoviev were advised to go into hiding but many other Bolshevik leaders, among them Lev Trotsky, ended up in jail. Iosif Stalin evaded arrest and became the link between the Bolsheviks in Petrograd and Lenin, in Finland.

With Lenin in Finland and the Bolsheviks in retreat, the government had an opportunity to reassert its authority. The problem was that there was no government until 24 July. Three vital weeks were squandered. The new Prime Minister was Alexander Kerensky, as full of eloquence as he was empty of self-doubt. He chose General Lavr Kornilov as the new commander-in-chief. A fellow general was unflattering: 'He has the heart of a lion but the brain of a sheep'. The government's programme alienated the right-wing Kadets and a rag-tag army of oppositionists coalesced to fight socialism. At a state conference on 14 August, in Moscow, Kornilov was given a tumultuous reception when he called for a no-holds-barred struggle against anarchy. This was code for the soviets. He discussed with Kerensky the possibility of the military taking over Petrograd and closing down the soviet. As a lawyer he was clever with words. He gave Kornilov, who had no practice in reading the minds of politicians, the impression he was on his side. Then he changed his mind and declared Kornilov a rebel. The workers of Petrograd received arms to defend the revolution and railway workers stopped Kornilov and his men reaching the capital.

The Kornilov rebellion was a turning point. Workers were now armed and could effect an insurrection. On 31 August, Bolsheviks achieved a majority in the Petrograd soviet (workers' and soldiers' sections voting together) for the first time. The government fell and a new coalition government was formed. Its power only existed on paper. Only two scenarios were credible. Either the moderate socialists fashioned a coalition of all socialist parties or the Bolsheviks would take over. The right was discredited after the Kornilov affair and the conservative and liberal parties were hopelessly divided. This meant that the Menshevik and right SR policy of promoting a bourgeois revolution was no longer feasible. Now there was a stark choice: dictatorship from the right or the left.

The Bolsheviks were riding the crest of a wave. In late September, they secured a majority in elections to the Moscow soviet. Around the country the story was the same. The Bolsheviks were giving expression to the anger and frustration of almost all segments of society. In Petrograd, Trotsky became the chair of the soviet. Lenin, still in Finland, advocated an armed uprising but was met with scepticism. Lenin slipped back into Petrograd and passionately argued his case to the Central Committee on 10 October. Armed insurrection was put on the agenda. Moderate Bolsheviks were upset. Lev Kamenev and Grigory Zinoviev penned a rejection of Lenin's dangerous radicalism. It was published and told the whole world that the Bolsheviks were planning an armed insurrection. This confirmed what Kerensky suspected and plans were drawn up to deploy troops to counter the Bolshevik attack. The Petrograd soviet set up a military revolutionary committee, chaired by Trotsky. The soldiers of the Petrograd garrison agreed to implement its orders. Kerensky tried to arrest the members of the military revolutionary committee and to close down Bolshevik newspapers. On 24 October, Lenin, in disguise, made his way to the Smolny Institute, the Bolshevik headquarters. Troops took over key points in the city, meeting little resistance. Government ministers, ensconced in the Winter Palace, were called upon to resign. The cruiser *Aurora* fired a salvo. It was the signal for soldiers and Red Guards to storm the palace and arrest the ministers. Kerensky evaded them, dressed as a female nurse.

Early the next morning, 25 October, the 2nd All-Russian Congress of Soviets convened and declared soviet power. It was a bit of a damp squib because the Bolsheviks had taken power, in the name of the soviets, the evening before. Moderate socialists marched out in protest, leaving the Bolsheviks to do as they pleased. Why did Lenin pre-empt the Congress? Was he afraid that Congress would declare soviet power in the name of all socialist parties? Seizure of power beforehand permitted the Bolsheviks to present it to Congress as a fait accompli. The Bolshevik majority in Congress would then vote to legitimise the Bolshevik seizure of power. Soviet power meant Bolshevik power. However by rejecting a multi-party socialist government, Lenin was heading deliberately in the direction of dictatorship and civil war.

Why was there a February revolution?

■ Successful revolutions usually start in capital cities. Petrograd had a large concentration of soldiers and war industry workers. They all had grievances which had been festering since the 1900s. Given the right circumstances these could explode into violence.

■ The military changed sides. Had the soldiers followed orders and dispersed the demonstrations, in rivers of blood if necessary, the revolution would not have occurred.

■ Why did soldiers mutiny? They were peasants in uniform and land grievances were uppermost in their minds. They distrusted their officers. Defeats at the front had demoralised many. They were radicalised by the crowds. Without the influence of the demonstrators they would, almost certainly, not have refused to follow orders.

■ There were shortages of bread and basic foodstuffs in Petrograd. They were available in other parts of Russia but the dislocation of war led to a breakdown of communications.

■ The Tsar was not in Petrograd but in Mogilev. Had he been in his capital it is possible that a personal appeal by him might have influenced the demonstrators.

- The gulf between the Tsar and educated society was never as wide as in February 1917. Almost no one came to his defence. This underlines the fact that Russia was not a cohesive society. Its various elements, peasants, workers, middle classes and nobility, inhabited different social worlds.

- The Progressive Bloc in the Duma (formed in the summer of 1915 when Pavel Milyukov brought together the three leading parties of the Duma, the Kadets, Octobrists and the Progressives, to form a political coalition to put pressure on the Tsar to appoint liberal ministers) was loyal but the Tsar would not heed their appeal for a government of national confidence. Liberals and conservatives wanted a Tsar as a centre of authority.

- The revolution was spontaneous, therefore popular and democratic. No political party played a key role in ending tsardom. It was leaderless and this caused problems afterwards. No recognised figure personified the revolution; quite unlike October.

- The demonstrations developed a momentum of their own. A mood of rebellion swept through the city. Even the middle classes and some nobles joined in. They wanted a more modern Russia.

Why was there an October revolution?

- Lenin is the key figure. Without him there would have been no Bolshevik insurrection in October. He cajoled the Central Committee into going for power.

- The Petrograd soviet had a Bolshevik majority. The Bolshevik and left SRs set up the military revolutionary committee and this became the general staff of the revolution. The Kornilov revolt had led to the arming of workers by Kerensky in Petrograd. They never handed their weapons back. A Bolshevik armed insurrection thus became possible.

- The third coalition government of 25 September was very weak. It lost the capacity to influence events in the capital and the country. It forfeited legitimacy. Kerensky gave orders to move troops to counter the upcoming Bolshevik insurrection. They were ignored as the Petrograd garrison had agreed to take orders only from the military revolutionary committee.

- The coalitions between the moderate socialists in the soviet and the upper and middle classes had failed. The concept of moderates from all classes combining to administer the country was revealed as a chimera. The failure of the alliance between the upper and middle classes and moderate socialists polarised political opinion.

- Landowners would not give up any of their land so no agreement could be reached with the moderate SR leader, Viktor Chernov. This increased direct action by peasants.

- Industry was shutting down due to a lack of inputs and labour disputes.

- Inflation inevitably rose as the government printed money to meet its obligations. This exacerbated an already tense situation and radical solutions, offered by the Bolsheviks, became more attractive.

- The Constituent Assembly might have saved the day for the moderate socialists. Had it been convened during the summer of 1917, the SRs, Mensheviks and other moderate socialists would have been in a majority. It would then have offered its support to a government of the middle classes. However, the upper and middle classes would not give up land and this would have led to a confrontation with the Assembly. Had the Assembly met, the Bolsheviks could not have seized power in the name of the soviets. The party which eventually dominated it, the SRs, had already split into right and left SRs and the right SRs into various factions. By October 1917, the SRs and other moderate socialists were a spent force. They had gambled on the middle classes taking power and lost. The way was open for dictatorship: on the left or the right.

- The mistaken military policy of the government. The Kerensky offensive in June was political suicide and played into the hands of the Bolsheviks. It was carried out in response to Allied appeals to attack the Germans in the east when the Allies were launching an offensive in the west. The government felt honour-bound to respond but it should have declined.

- The Bolsheviks were brilliant at propaganda. They came up with short, snappy slogans which caught the public imagination: peace and bread, all power to the soviets and down with the ten capitalist ministers. They very skilfully gave expression to the frustration, anger and impotence felt by the majority of the population.

- The weakness and incompetence of the government was legendary. They appeared to be their own worst enemies. In July, it took three weeks after branding Lenin a German agent to form a new coalition. Momentum was lost.

- The general mood was that the threat of a coup would come from the right. No one took seriously the possibility of a left-wing party staging a successful insurrection.

- Lenin judged that a revolutionary situation (the ruling classes are incapable of ruling and the rest of the population will not tolerate their miserable lot) existed in Russia in September 1917. He had misjudged the situation in the past but this time he was right.

Why were the Provisional Governments so weak?

- They were provisional or interim governments. They regarded themselves as caretaker governments. Such administrations always avoid contentious issues and prevaricate.

- All the key questions would be resolved by the Constituent Assembly. This seriously undermined the resolve of successive Provisional Governments.

- The first government reflected the fact that the February revolution was regarded by socialists as handing power to the bourgeoisie. It consisted of representatives of the upper and middle classes. The odd man out was Kerensky, who was nominally an SR but in reality belonged to the middle classes.

- Real power rested with the soviet not the government. Order No. 1 made it impossible to reimpose discipline in the army. Dual power was a recipe for weak government. Hence there was always a conflict between the popular legitimacy of the soviets and the power of the government. The latter, as a consequence, suffered from diminished legitimacy.

- The soviet did not wish to assume responsibility for running the country. That was the task of the bourgeoisie.

- The soviet was obliged to join a coalition government in May. It quickly became evident that the upper and middle classes and the moderate socialists could not agree on much.

- Had Germany not facilitated Lenin's passage through Germany, the government almost certainly would have survived until the Constituent Assembly took over. There would have been no Bolshevik takeover. Lenin's refusal to support the government in any way made life very difficult for it. His relentless attacks sapped the will of the soviet to be a coalition partner.

- The government wished to show that it was democratic. This meant avoiding the use of coercion. It had to be different from the tsarist government. Its refusal to use force meant that its writ did not extend far.

Why was there no bourgeois revolution in 1917?

- Moderate socialists regarded a bourgeois revolution in February 1917 as legitimate. Capitalism was only in its initial phase in Russia and the middle class was the only group capable of developing it.

- This presented the main liberal party, the Kadets, with a dilemma. It was to take power during a war and a revolution. The economy was in tatters and industrialists were finding it more difficult to manage their enterprises.

- Pavel Milyukov, the Kadet leader, was a lawyer. His main worry in February 1917 was the collapse of the Russian state. His declared objective was to retain the monarchy. The problem was that it was hopelessly discredited.

- Milyukov pulled out of government in April 1917 and never considered re-entering a Provisional Government. There were Kadets in later governments but they served as individuals.

- Milyukov regarded Kerensky as ineffectual and sympathised with General Kornilov when he attempted a coup against Kerensky's government. Milyukov was against a military dictatorship but wanted a strong leader to head off the anarchy and chaos which was threatening to engulf Russia.

- Hence the Kadets had hoped that a monarchist general would restore order and then prepare the way for a liberal, democratic Russia.

- Milyukov did not believe that a constitutional monarchy could be restored in the short term. What was needed was a military dictatorship (this meant in essence handing power to what became known as the Whites). The problem was that they were monarchists opposed to the Duma and representative government. It is worth noting that the Kadets and Lenin agreed on the options facing Russia: a dictatorship from either the left or the right.

- The anti-Bolshevik left (right SRs and Mensheviks) was committed to a democratic solution to Russia's woes. However, a disintegrating country, rising inflation, empty state coffers and increasing unrest, especially in the countryside, led to many democrats thinking the unthinkable: a strong state to impose order.

- The last desperate attempt by the democrats to save themselves was the convening of the Democratic Assembly on 14 September 1917, and its election of a pre-parliament. The deliberations in the Assembly quickly revealed that every party had broken up into various factions. The pre-parliament was to have a majority of property owners; in other words, representatives of the middle classes. Those from the soviets were to be in the minority. The Democratic Assembly elected 250 members from among its members and 250 others were added ex officio from the middle classes and business. The pre-parliament was to support the government. This was necessary, as one delegate ruefully admitted, because the government enjoyed no support at all in the country.

- The irony of the situation was not lost on the non-Bolshevik left. Moderate socialists were trying to entice the bourgeoisie into political activity at a time when the socialists enjoyed mass support in the country and the bourgeoisie none. The bourgeoisie was fragmented many ways and, anyway, did not wish to participate in government.

■ A Provisional Council of the Republic was to be set up in early October. The discussions on its composition highlighted the weaknesses of the democrats. The left insisted on peace and a solution to the agrarian question; the Kadets would not countenance this. Decisive policies to save Russia were needed. All the delegates produced was hot air.

Questions

1 Explore the Bolshevik justification for revolution in 1917.

2 Why was the Kornilov revolt significant?

3 'Lenin adapted Marxism to suit Russia's internal needs.' Discuss.

4 Outline the distinguishing policies and ideology of the SRs, Mensheviks and Bolsheviks between February and October 1917.

5 'The Bolshevik revolution was a result of the mistakes and miscalculations of the Provisional Government.' Discuss.

6 'Lenin was an ideologue rather than a tactician.' Discuss.

7 What were the main grievances of workers, peasants and soldiers in 1917? What was common to all of them?

8 'Revolutions are made by individuals not by masses.' Discuss.

9 'The October Revolution was not an isolated event, but part of a much larger wave of change in Russia during 1917.' Discuss.

10 Compare Lenin's views on revolution, and how they changed, in *What is to be Done?* (1902) and *The State and Revolution* (1917).

Further reading

On the competing historiographies of the Bolshevik Revolution see Edward Acton, *Rethinking the Russian Revolution* (1990). Acton distinguishes between three 'traditional' interpretations of the revolution in October 1917 (1. Soviet view; 2. liberal; 3. libertarian) and 'Revisionism', which underlines the role played by those other than the main political actors, for instance, the masses; Harold Shukman, *Lenin and the Russian Revolution* (1977); Sheila Fitzpatrick, *The Russian Revolution* (1994); Robert Service, *The Russian Revolution, 1900–1927* (1999); Moshe Lewin, *The Soviet Century* (2005).

CHAPTER 3

Soviet power, terror and civil war

An historiographical overview

Lenin's decision to go it alone meant that the Bolsheviks were in a minority in Russia from the outset. Marxist ideology was a guiding light but it was uncertain where it would shine next. There was no Marxist road to socialism mapped out for them. Marx had assumed that the dictatorship of the proletariat would dawn when industrial capitalism had reached its apogee. Workers would then take over the running of the state and eventually do away with it. None of this applied to Russia. Lenin, in launching the Bolshevik bid for power, hoped that it would provoke a chain reaction of socialist revolutions throughout the advanced capitalist world. Without this, the revolution in Russia would go under. Later he changed his mind. Revolution flickered in Germany until 1923 but then it became evident that Soviet Russia was on its own. As there was no blueprint they would have to arrive at solutions by trial and error. Civil war was inevitable. If the Bolsheviks did not fashion a military force to defeat their enemies, power would slip away. Does this mean that the communist dictatorship was inevitable?

There are three main views:

1   It was inevitable. Russia is a vast empire and in order to keep it together strong central rule is necessary. Democracy was putting up tender shoots before 1914 but there was no tradition of representative rule. Civil society – autonomous social and professional organisations independent of the government – hardly existed. Russia was an illiterate, peasant country topped by a thin layer of the educated. Industrial capitalism had only put down roots in the 1880s and was thus a tender plant. The intelligentsia was incapable of ruling. The bureaucracy ensured the functioning of the state and its loyalty was to the leader and his circle. Economic and cultural backwardness meant

that catching up with Western Europe would take decades. Those who share this view would regard Bolshevism as a continuation of tsarist rule. A ruler, surrounded by a personality cult, a bureaucracy beholden to him, political police to ensure that opposition was restricted, control of the means of communication so as to project a single ideology and a claim that the gods of history were on his side are the basic constructs. The red Tsar ruled in Moscow. The Holy Scriptures were the writings of Marx and the leader; first Lenin, then Stalin. They understood the laws of history and would lead the people to paradise. The fact that the Soviet Union attempted to build socialism in international isolation meant that it became military socialism. It was not possible to industrialise rapidly without exploiting the people. They had to be inspired, and, if that failed, coerced into sacrificing themselves for the good of socialism. The autocratic system may fail from time to time: as in 1917 and 1991. However, the mean for Russia is dictatorship. Russia will always regress to the mean. This view can be called the continuity approach. Russia remains Russia irrespective of who is in power.

2   Another approach is to see the Bolsheviks as the victims of circumstance. Lenin took power against the will of the majority, banking on international revolution. He had no choice but to use coercion to stay in power. The Bolsheviks demonstrated fierce self-belief and willpower to succeed. They were relying on the placebo principle. They provoked a civil war by refusing to share power. Lenin thought the soviets would do his bidding. He was wrong. The industrial working class regarded October as their victory. They would now take over the factories and run them in their own interests. Lenin had other ideas. He wanted to run the enterprises in the interests of the state. The peasants took the land and the Bolsheviks acknowledged this. However, the Red Army, the Bolshevik Party, the political police (Cheka) and the urban dwellers had to be fed. Surpluses had to be extracted from the peasants using coercion. Foreign armies intervened in an attempt to overthrow the Red regime. Lenin thought that war communism would lead to full communism. Again he was wrong. It is amazing that he and the Bolsheviks survived. Out of this morass a new system was forged. It can be called military socialism. After Lenin died in 1924 the master builder turned out to be Stalin. He took military socialism to its zenith. This approach would emphasise that the Bolsheviks had no fixed idea of how to rule. It was just a matter of circumstance. They discovered, almost by accident, that military socialism was viable.

3   Another view would be to start with Marx. The most powerful formative force was ideology, first as conceptualised by Lenin and then Stalin. The most powerful belief was that the Bolsheviks were right and everyone else wrong. Numbers did not matter. The whole country could be against them

but this signified nothing. Lenin once conceded that the Russian working class had ceased to be a working class. The Bolsheviks claimed to be democrats. However, democracy was the rule of the working class and poor peasantry. Lenin and his cohorts had the right, no the duty, to interpret what was in the best interests of the working class. Hence everything they did was democratic. Fired with secular religious zeal, Bolsheviks were willing to sacrifice themselves for socialism. In a poor, backward country, they craved leadership. Given that the level of literacy was low, the ideology had to be expressed in very simple terms. Slogans were the best way to do this. They were fundamentalist Marxists because they were unsophisticated. Certainty was what the cadres were looking for. They took the peasant route to argument – shout or use force. The cadres worked by simple rules: if someone wore a tie, he was a bourgeois. As such he was a class enemy and a counter-revolutionary. He was unfit for the new society which was being built so he could be exterminated. All enemies of soviet power were counter-revolutionaries. The best medicine for them was death. It was a Manichean world: everything was either black or white. In a religious country such as Russia, it was viewed as a struggle between good and evil, between God and the devil. God was a Bolshevik God. The Bolsheviks had total moral certainty. Everything they did to defend the revolution was moral. If they did not eliminate opposition, they were behaving immorally. Ruthlessness and an absence of mercy were needed to build the new Jerusalem. Decisions were often taken on the run without much time to consider the alternatives. This approach accepts that the Bolsheviks never did anything by accident. They tied every decision to their understanding of ideology. The majority of the population were peasants and did not share their ideology. How did the Bolsheviks solve the peasant problem? Predictably they used force. They came to regard the ideology as providing quick solutions.

Building Soviet power

As was usual for meetings in Russia, the 2nd All-Russian Congress of Soviets started late in the evening of 25 October 1917 and ran on through the night. The Bolsheviks and their allies, the left SRs, were in the majority. The right SRs and some Mensheviks declared that they were leaving in protest at the use of force the day before. Trotsky, in the chair, then made his famous remark. They were miserable, bankrupt wretches and they were destined for the 'rubbish bin of history'. Trotsky was often an erring prophet but on this occasion he was right. The Winter Palace fell and Congress voted in soviet power. More Mensheviks left. Lenin then proposed his decree on peace. There should be an immediate armistice. There were no dissenting voices. Then Lenin introduced the decree on land. He simply took over SR land policy and handed the land – state, church and landlord land – over to the peasants. The peasants themselves could work out an equitable redistribution. In reality, it did not solve the problem of land hunger. The average peasant household acquired between 0.1 and 1 hectare. Hence Lenin was handing over the countryside to the peasants. Was this not un-Marxist? No, because it was only tactical. Lenin sought peace in the countryside while the Bolsheviks set about consolidating their position in the towns.

On 9 February 1918 land was socialised and private ownership abolished. The land now belonged to the whole nation. Local soviets were to promote state and collective farms at the expense of the peasant holding. In 1919, 4.6 per cent of land was in state farms and only 1.7 per cent in kolkhozes or collective farms. Socialist farming was more rational because the farms were larger. However, the peasant preferred his smallholding.

A new government was formed. It was called the Soviet (Council) of People's Commissars (Sovnarkom). Its chair was Lenin. The Bolsheviks wanted to avoid the use of minister and council of ministers. They were too bourgeois. The ever resourceful Trotsky came up with the new name. 'I like that', said Lenin, 'it smells of revolution'. All commissars were Bolsheviks. Stalin, as a Georgian, became Commissar for Nationalities. Trotsky became Commissar for Foreign Affairs. Lenin had toyed with the idea of making him Commissar of Internal Affairs. He desisted. Having a Jew as the new policeman of Russia would not go down well with ethnic Russians, many of whom were anti-Semites. It might look like a Jewish conspiracy to take over Russia. Aleksei Rykov took over Internal Affairs.

There was fierce fighting in Moscow and some resistance around Petrograd but workers and Red Guards carried the day. Thirteen right-wing Bolsheviks resigned from the Central Committee and Sovnarkom. They forced Lenin to accept a coalition, socialist government. However, he would only accept left SRs as commissars. The first socialist coalition government took office but the left SRs did not occupy any of the strategic commissariats. The coalition lasted four months, until March 1918. The Treaty of Brest-Litovsk was too much for the left SRs and they left the government.

A raft of legislation was promulgated. Ranks were abolished and everyone was now a citizen. Bureaucratic salaries, indeed all salaries, were capped. Banks were nationalised. Large houses ceased to be property of the owners. They were divided up among needy families, meaning those with the right connections. Privilege came in with the revolution. Church and state were separated and all religions were put on an equal footing. The courts were abolished and people's courts and revolutionary tribunals took their place. Lay persons sat with professional judges to ensure revolutionary justice. Men and women became equal before the law and all ethnic groups were to be treated as equal. Soldiers' committees ran military units. It was all wildly exciting.

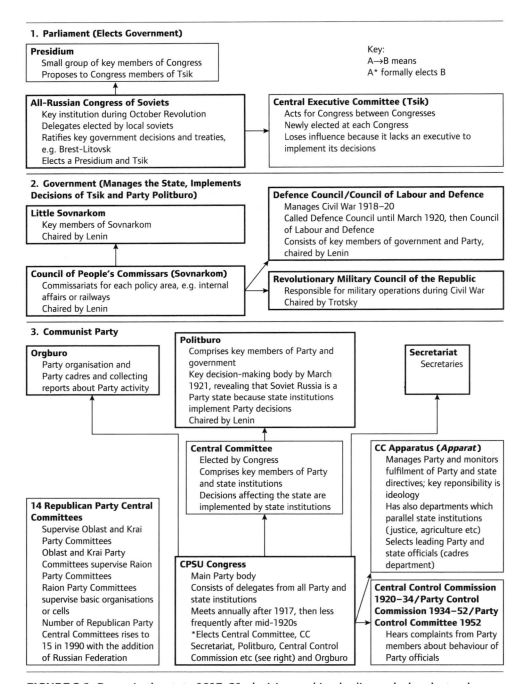

1. Parliament (Elects Government)

Presidium
Small group of key members of Congress
Proposes to Congress members of Tsik

Key:
A→B means
A* formally elects B

All-Russian Congress of Soviets
Key institution during October Revolution
Delegates elected by local soviets
Ratifies key government decisions and treaties,
e.g. Brest-Litovsk
Elects a Presidium and Tsik

Central Executive Committee (Tsik)
Acts for Congress between Congresses
Newly elected at each Congress
Loses influence because it lacks an executive to
implement its decisions

**2. Government (Manages the State, Implements
Decisions of Tsik and Party Politburo)**

Little Sovnarkom
Key members of Sovnarkom
Chaired by Lenin

Defence Council/Council of Labour and Defence
Manages Civil War 1918–20
Called Defence Council until March 1920, then Council
of Labour and Defence
Consists of key members of government and Party,
chaired by Lenin

Council of People's Commissars (Sovnarkom)
Commissariats for each policy area, e.g. internal
affairs or railways
Chaired by Lenin

Revolutionary Military Council of the Republic
Responsible for military operations during Civil War
Chaired by Trotsky

3. Communist Party

Orgburo
Party organisation and
Party cadres and collecting
reports about Party activity

Politburo
Comprises key members of Party and
government
Key decision-making body by March
1921, revealing that Soviet Russia is a
Party state because state institutions
implement Party decisions
Chaired by Lenin

Secretariat
Secretaries

Central Committee
Elected by Congress
Comprises key members of Party
and state institutions
Decisions affecting the state are
implemented by state institutions

CC Apparatus (*Apparat*)
Manages Party and monitors
fulfilment of Party and state
directives; key reponsibility is
ideology
Has also departments which
parallel state institutions
(justice, agriculture etc)
Selects leading Party and
state officials (cadres
department)

**14 Republican Party Central
Committees**
Supervise Oblast and Krai
Party Committees
Oblast and Krai Party
Committees supervise Raion
Party Committees
Raion Party Committees
supervise basic organisations
or cells
Number of Republican Party
Central Committees rises to
15 in 1990 with the addition
of Russian Federation

CPSU Congress
Main Party body
Consists of delegates from all Party and
state institutions
Meets annually after 1917, then less
frequently after mid-1920s
*Elects Central Committee, CC
Secretariat, Politburo, Central Control
Commission etc (see right) and Orgburo

**Central Control Commission
1920–34/Party Control
Commission 1934–52/Party
Control Committee 1952**
Hears complaints from Party
members about behaviour of
Party officials

FIGURE 3.1 Power in the state 1917–21: decision-making bodies and who elects whom
*Formally elects: delegates presented with single list drawn up by leadership; CC plenum could also
elect or demote Politburo members
Council of Labour and Defence (STO) lasted until 1930s
Little Sovnarkom later became Presidium of Sovnarkom
Sovnarkom renamed Council of Ministers, April 1946
Revolutionary Military Council of Republic; dominated by Trotsky, loses influence after Civil War
Secretariat (see Glossary)

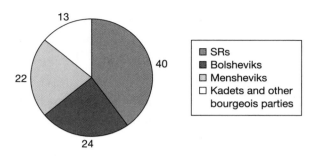

FIGURE 3.2 Parties in the Constituent Assembly (%)

Elections to the Constituent Assembly took place in mid-November. As expected, the SRs were the largest party, with about 40 per cent of the vote. The Bolsheviks came second with 24 per cent. However, the Reds won in the major cities, such as Petrograd and Moscow, and in military units. What would Lenin do? Recognise the Assembly as an alternative centre of power? Stalin was put in charge of convening the Assembly. This was a clear signal about what was going to happen. The Assembly met on 5 January 1918 and Lenin demanded it recognise Soviet power. Chernov, in the chair, ignored this and proceeded to debate the issues of land and peace, even foreign policy. The deputies passed laws. Early the next morning, Chernov was informed that the guards were tired and they should vacate the building. When they returned to the Tauride Palace they found the doors locked. Lenin had signed a decree disbanding the Assembly. There were a few protests.

The nature of the new state was not high on the Bolshevik agenda. Their primary task was to retain power until the socialist revolution broke out abroad. Lenin expected Berlin to become the socialist capital of the world. The German comrades would then help the Russians to build socialism. The commune state could fill in meanwhile. It would give expression to the dictatorship of the proletariat which would effect the transition to socialism. The state would be democratic, expressing the will of the majority of workers and poor peasants. Coercion and terror would be used to eliminate opposition.

Economic policy in this period goes through various phases:

■ **State capitalism:** October 1917–July 1918. Factories would be run in the national interest. Managers would have targets set by the state. Factory committees and workers' control were to maximise production. The beginnings of central planning emerge. 'Bourgeois specialists', the former management were to be inveigled into running their old enterprises. Lenin tried in vain to restrict workers' control to mere supervision of management. The radical left, called Left Communists, pushed for nationalisation and worker management. Wildcat nationalisation became an epidemic. On 1 December 1917, the Supreme Council of the National Economy (Sovnarkhoz) was set up to run a mixed economy of state and private sectors. Lenin's appeal to bourgeois management failed.

■ **War communism:** July 1918–March 1921. A wild, disastrous experiment during the Civil War. Lenin and the Bolshevik leaders thought they could advance to communism without going through the preparatory stages. Factories were nationalised, even those employing one or two workers; private trade banned; workers disciplined; and peasants forced to hand over their surpluses. A goal was to abolish money. Wholesale nationalisation was carried out in the summer and autumn of 1918. In other words, before the Civil War really got going. Workers, because they lived in towns, suffered more than peasants. There were over 3.6 million workers in manufacturing, metallurgy and mining in 1917 but only 1.2 million by the end of 1920. There were another 3.5 million workers employed at home and in urban and rural workshops in 1917. Probably only a third were still there by late 1920. The workers who had formed the backbone of Bolshevik support in Petrograd, about 400,000 in October 1917, dwindled to about a third of this number in 1920. The population of Moscow dropped by half. Prices were fixed, bread and the basic essentials were rationed. Only workers and those perceived to be serving the Soviet state got ration cards. Money gradually lost its value. The natural response was to resort to barter and the black market. About 60 per cent of city bread passed through illegal channels in 1918–19. The Bolsheviks declared the private trader, labelled a speculator, the arch enemy. The failure to feed the cities inevitably affected labour discipline. During the first half of 1920, there were strikes in 77 per cent of large and medium-sized enterprises, mostly over the lack of food.

The working day, in those enterprises still operating, lengthened to 10 or 11 hours. In January 1919, the mobilisation of workers made the labour situation so tight that those left behind were not permitted to change their jobs. In May 1920, the penalties for absenteeism became draconian. Places such as Kazan and Kaluga declared themselves autonomous. One group prospered however: the bagmen. They carried life-sustaining produce on their backs into the towns and traded it at incredible prices to desperate customers. The middle class pawned everything, sometimes even their daughters. In October 1918, compulsory labour was decreed for all able bodied citizens between the ages of 16 and 50. In late 1919, with the end of the Civil War in sight, Trotsky proposed a novel solution to the labour crisis. Workers would be treated as soldiers. They would not be permitted to leave their place of employment without permission. Labour armies could be formed and sent wherever the economic situation was critical. Lenin was also keen on the idea and it became law. It was, not surprisingly, hugely unpopular. Black markets were closed down and traders conscripted into labour armies. Strict military discipline was to prevail. Predictably, the militarisation of labour failed. Lenin, ever keen to increase labour productivity, became enamoured of the ideas of the American time and motion pioneer, F. W. Taylor. They flopped in Soviet Russia but were to be resurrected by Stalin in 1936. An enthusiastic American visitor told the folks back home that he had seen the future and 'it works'. He must have been observing the Soviet Union at night, wearing dark glasses.

It is not surprising that this moneyless, marketless and private propertyless experiment failed. What is amazing is that the Lenin team attempted to implement it during a period of great political conflict. One is tempted to say that war communism was brutal Marxism in practice. The Soviet argument that war communism was forced on the Lenin team by the exigencies of war is false. The most extreme nationalisation decree was promulgated in November 1920 when the Civil War had been won. War communism has been called the greatest economic failure in history.

■ **New Economic Policy (NEP)**: March 1921–October 1928. Soviet Russia faced economic collapse in March 1921 and Lenin ordered a retreat. The market returned; money acquired value; trade became legal again; taxes were expressed in monetary terms not in kind; cooperatives and small businesses thrived; foreign capital and expertise were sought. No wonder the average Bolshevik was bewildered. Was this not going back to capitalism? Central planning concentrated on the 'commanding heights' of the economy. They were in state hands.

The Cheka

The first Extraordinary Commission (Cheka) was formed to guard the Revolution's headquarters in Petrograd. However, Felix (the name means happy in Latin) Dzierzynski, on 20 December 1917, persuaded Lenin to expand the Cheka into the Extraordinary Committee to Combat Counter-Revolution and Sabotage. The guidelines were scribbled on the back of an envelope. A fuller decree was to be elaborated later. It never was. Leonid Krasin, an engineer who had worked for Siemens in Germany, and later People's Commissar for Foreign Trade, had a low opinion of Dzierzynski:

'Lenin has become quite insane. If anyone has influence over him, it is comrade Felix Dzierzynski, an even greater fanatic. He is, in essence, a cunning piece of work who scares Lenin with counter-revolution and the idea that this will sweep us all away. And Lenin, I am finally convinced, is very much a coward, shaking in his boots. And Dzierzynski plays on that.'

Krasin is not quite fair to Lenin. Thousands of criminals had been released to fight at the front by the tsarist authorities. They killed their officers and roamed the cities of Petrograd and Moscow looking for 'exploiters' to liquidate. The Kerensky government had freed more criminals. Many of them were to be recruited by the Cheka and the Red Army. The Cheka had the right to terminate anyone it judged a counter-revolutionary. By June 1918 every soviet was setting up its own Cheka.

Over time the Cheka expanded its operations. It became responsible for counter-espionage, the military, the railways, it intercepted personal mail and telegrams and it also sent spies abroad. Within two years the organisation numbered 20,000 men and women. There was plenty of small arms, machine guns and ammunition left over from the First World War. A particular enemy was the typhus louse. Lenin once remarked that either the typhus louse would kill the revolution or the revolution would kill the typhus louse. It had a special liking for woollen greatcoats – the standard issue. Dzierzynski seized a consignment of leather jackets, forwarded by the western allies for Russian air force pilots. Now his agents were safe from the predatory louse. Lenin was in no doubt about the type of comrade needed for Cheka work. One honest man to nine bastards was the norm.

The left SR Commissar for Justice opposed the use of terror to defend the revolution. Under him the Cheka, more or less, was kept on a leash. Left Communists, such as Bukharin, wanted revolutionary war but Lenin's priority was to extract Russia from a war it could not win. An armistice was signed on 15 December 1917 and this recognised Soviet Russia in international law. The Germans agreed to recognise an independent Poland, Estonia, Latvia and Lithuania, at that time occupied by Germany. The left would not contemplate a peace treaty with Germany and its allies; Trotsky sat on the fence and wanted neither peace nor war; but Lenin wanted peace at any price. The Bolsheviks signed the Treaty of Brest-Litovsk on 3 March 1918. The agreement gave Germany dominance in the Baltic States and Ukraine, and Turkey had a free hand in Transcaucasia. Soviet Russia lost the western part of the Russian Empire. The capital had moved from Petrograd to Moscow.

The Bolsheviks desperately needed grain to feed their supporters and the cities and set up committees of the poor (*kombedy*). This set poor peasants against richer peasants but little grain flowed to the state. Workers' detachments were sent from the towns. They collected grain because they had rifles. On 6 July 1918, Yakov Blyumkin, a left SR, assassinated the German ambassador, Count Wilhelm von Mirbach, in an attempt to rekindle the war against Germany. Left SRs took over the main post and telegraph office in Moscow. One of those captured was 'Iron Felix', who succumbed to an hysterical fit, bared his chest and invited them to shoot him. The rebellion only lasted a day. There were several other revolts along the Volga. Cheka ruthlessness carried the day. SRs were then purged from the Cheka. So depressed was Dzierzynski by his inability to protect Lenin from attack that he resigned. He shaved his hair, forged Polish papers in the name of Felix Domanski, and dropped in on his wife and son in Switzerland. Lake Lugano soothed his troubled spirit and he returned to Moscow to resume his Cheka duties.

Officially Red Terror dates from 1 September 1918 following the shooting of Moisei Uritsky, the head of the Petrograd Cheka on 30 August. Ironically he was one of the few who opposed the use of terror. Lenin, on the other hand, proposed hanging 100 'kulaks, rich men and blood suckers' for all to see. The Tsar, his family and servants were murdered in Ekaterinburg, in the Urals, on 16 July 1918. They were shot by local Bolsheviks who feared they might be rescued by the advancing White forces. Lenin talked of victory or death.

After addressing a meeting, on 30 August, Lenin was shot twice by Fanny Kaplan, an SR (some sources argue that another SR did the shooting). The Cheka exacted a terrible revenge in the old capital. Over 1,000 were shot and 6,000 arrested. The Red Terror had begun in earnest. Most of those who died were prominent pre-revolutionary figures. Lenin survived but one of the two bullets was left in his body. In January 1919, Moscow ordered 'mass terror against wealthy Cossacks'. They were to be 'extirpated completely'. Local Reds executed thousands before a halt was called. Red Terror was countered by White Terror. Workers and anyone associated with the Bolsheviks were mown down. It was exterminate or be exterminated. Kornilov was one of the most bloodthirsty. Captured Red commanders were immediately shot. Red Terror may have claimed over 100,000 lives; White Terror probably more. Jews were a special target of the Whites.

Ethnic Russians were a minority in the Cheka and its successor organisations until the mid-1930s. Poles, Jews, Latvians, Georgians and other Caucasians dominated. Felix was a Pole whose family, originally Jewish, had converted to Catholicism. He hated Russians or rather upper and middle class Russians. They were held personally responsible for his and other prisoners' sufferings in tsarist jails. He had spent 11 years in tsarist prisons, penal servitude or exile. He had intended to train for the Catholic priesthood but, at the age of 19, suffered a crisis which destroyed his Christian faith. He transferred it to Marxism. He preached the new secular religion with evangelical zeal. He never missed an opportunity in jail to tell other prisoners that Marx was the saviour of the working class. The legacy of his years in prison was an unnatural pallor. Very pale pupils gave his eyes an X-ray intensity. It appeared he was staring through one to the wall behind. Prison was used to hone many skills. Dzierzynski chaired unofficial prisoners' courts to discover if someone was an informer, double agent or simply a plant. He developed a great understanding of human psychology. These skills were then codified and used by the Cheka and its successor organisations. He regarded the Cheka as the sword and shield of the revolution. The Cheka developed a formidable esprit de corps. The model Chekist was a man with a 'warm heart, a cool head and clean hands'. Felix scorned creature comforts. He worked tirelessly in his unheated Lubyanka office wrapped in a greatcoat, sipping mint tea and eating bread. There was a softer side to him. His relationship with a sister was close and he had several wives and offspring. Lenin trusted him but did not afford him much respect. Trotsky denigrated the Cheka chief as a deformed fanatic. Stalin saw that he could be useful and cultivated him.

Dzierzynski liked to surround himself with other Poles. One was Jozef Unszlicht (Iosif Unshlikht), a survivor of the Warsaw underground, who disliked Russians as much as his superior. He became commander of 300,000 paramilitaries, used as special units against peasants, Cossacks and any other perceived enemy. Latvians were even more prominent in the Cheka and Red Army. The Latvian riflemen, formed in April 1918 and disbanded in November 1920, were a formidable force. They saved the Bolsheviks in the summer of 1918 when the SRs revolted. When Latvia gained its independence in 1919 communist agitators were not welcome and over 200,000 Latvian leftists settled in Soviet Russia. In 1919, about three in four of the Cheka central management were Latvian.

Among prominent Latvians in the Cheka were Jekabs Peterss (Yakov Peters) and Martins Lacis (Martin Latsis). Peterss took part in the Sidney Street siege in London, in 1911, but was acquitted of murder. He harboured a lifelong animosity towards Winston Churchill, the minister responsible for the police. Lacis was quite a man of letters. His poetry was published before the revolution and he wrote comic verse and plays. He made his name in the People's Commissariat of Internal Affairs (NKVD). In May 1918, he uncovered a monarchist plot and was promoted to the Cheka. In Kyiv, he and Peterss devised clever traps for the unsuspecting middle class. They opened a Brazilian consulate and offered visas for large sums of money. Once they had paid, the unsuspecting were arrested by the Cheka. Latsis spelled out Cheka philosophy:

> 'When interrogating, do not seek material evidence or proof of the words or deeds of the accused against Soviet power. The first question to be asked is: what class does he belong to, what education, upbringing, origin or profession does he have? These questions must decide the fate of the accused. This is the being and essence of Red terror . . . It does not judge the enemy, it strikes him . . . it shows no mercy . . . we, like the children of Israel, have to build the kingdom of the future under constant fear of enemy attack.'

Jews flocked to the Bolshevik cause. They were promised liberation and the chance to become as equal as any other citizen. The *shtetl*, the Jewish township in western Russia and Ukraine, was a natural breeding ground. They had suffered pogrom after pogrom. Karl Marx was a Jew. Lenin was partly Jewish and there were many Jews in the Bolshevik leadership: Trotsky, Zinoviev, Kamenev and Sverdlov, to name only the most prominent. Many of them saw their chance to take revenge on middle and upper class Russians. They had excluded Jews and now the Jews would exclude them.

Zinoviev, a Jew, on a trip to Ukraine, remarked that there were too many Jews in the communist leadership. Lazar Kaganovich, a Jew, and head of the Party in Ukraine, in the mid-1920s, reduced the quota of Jews at Kharkiv university from 40 per cent to 11 per cent. Ukrainians replaced them. In 1922, Jews made up 15 per cent of communists (and 3 per cent of the population), second only to ethnic Russians with 65 per cent.

Victims had their property and possessions confiscated. The Tsarina's jewellery filled ten suitcases. It brought in millions of dollars when sold abroad. Nothing was wasted. The victims' clothing was stored for further distribution. Lenin received a suit, a pair of boots, a belt and braces worn by someone who had no further use for them. Underwear was given to the Red Army. Gold teeth were extracted and implanted in someone else's mouth. Such ghoulish work took its toll. A poet among the Chekists wrote: 'There is no greater joy, nor sweeter music than the crunch of broken lives and bones . . . up against the wall! Shoot!'

The Civil War, accompanied by famine and epidemic diseases, cost over 10 million lives, most of them non-combatants. The Red Army and Cheka lost about 2 million men during the revolution and Civil War; the Whites lost half a million; 300,000 Ukrainian and Belarusian Jews perished in pogroms; and 5 million died of starvation in the Volga region in 1921. Two million Russians emigrated to Europe and Asia. This was a demographic disaster. The males in the military and Cheka were predominantly in their twenties; their victims were the educated portion of society. Those who emigrated were among the country's cultural and scientific elite. A by-product of the mayhem was an army of hundreds of thousands of homeless children. The Cheka set up colonies for them. They would provide the recruits for the Stalin revolution.

Stalin and Dzierzynski were dispatched to Perm, which had just surrendered. They were so ruthless that they had to be relieved of their duties in February 1919. The two appeared again in tandem in Georgia after the Red Army had occupied the country, in February 1921. Stalin wanted to subsume Georgia in a Transcaucasian soviet federation. The Georgians wanted to remain a republic. They were annoyed that Abkhazia had been detached and appended to the Russian Federation as an autonomous republic. The Georgian communists complained to Lenin. This infuriated Stalin and Sergo Ordzhonikidze. The latter slapped one of the Georgians in the face for calling him 'Stalin's mule'. Lenin asked Stalin and Dzierzynski to investigate and resolve the problem. They absolved Ordzhonikidze of blame. Dzierzynski was now a member of Stalin's inner circle.

Felix thought that no ordinary mortal could serve more than two years in the Cheka. Nervous breakdowns, hysteria, heart attacks and constant headaches appeared to be part and parcel of the job. He was no exception. He and senior members of the Cheka took annual breaks on the glorious Abkhaz coast. Sergo Ordzhonikidze wrote to Nestor Lakoba, Stalin's associate, in September 1922:

Dear comrade Lakoba,

Comrades Dzierzynski, Yagoda and others are coming to stay with you for two months. They must be put in the best villa . . . on the sea front. You must be in every way a very hospitable host, in the Abkhaz manner . . . Yours, Sergo.

Another comrade whose health failed from time to time was Trotsky. His wife recalled that after an important meeting, her husband would come home bathed in perspiration. This was the effect that Stalin had on him. He was given to fainting fits and was also a hypochondriac. Lenin instructed Dzierzynski, in May 1921, to look after Trotsky's health. The commissar was dispatched to Abkhazia. This was an astute move as the lines of communication with the Kremlin would go through Stalin.

Box 3.1 *The secret police*

Cheka	December 1917
GPU (State Political Administration) (part of NKVD)	February 1922
OGPU (Unified State Political Administration)	July 1923
GUGB (State Administration of State Security) (part of NKVD)	July 1934
NKGB (People's Commissariat of State Security)	February 1941
GUGB (part of People's Commissariat of Internal Affairs (NKVD)	July 1941
NKGB	April 1943
MGB (Ministry of State Security)	March 1946
MGB and MVD (Ministry of Internal Affairs) merged	March 1953
KGB (Committee of State Security)	March 1954– December 1991

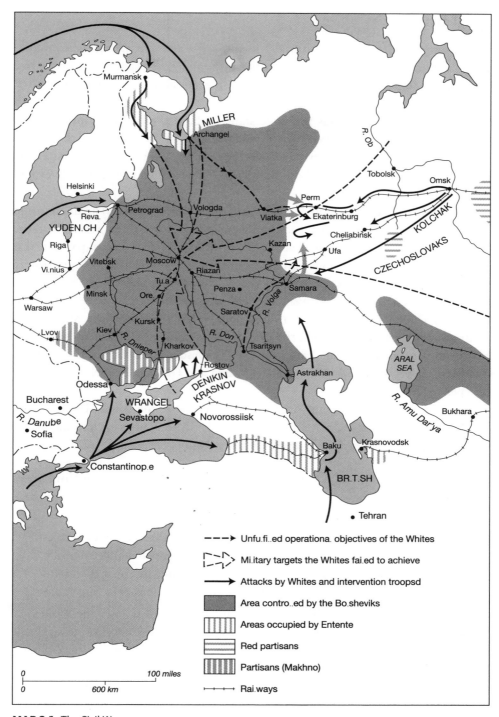

MAP 3.1 The Civil War

Civil war

Civil wars are normally more brutal, violent, cruel and corrupting than international conflicts. Murderers, sadists, masochists and psychopaths are given free rein. The Judeo-Christian adage: an eye for an eye and a tooth for a tooth often becomes two eyes for an eye and all teeth for a tooth. Bloodletting can become an addiction. Man reverts to his primitive state. Perhaps the best description of the Russian Civil War is to revert to Darwin: survival of the fittest. In this world the moral imperative is to survive. The means are irrelevant; the end goal everything. The Reds were convinced they would be exterminated if they lost. They had to win.

Many disparate groups made up the opponents of the Reds. The main group were the dispossessed upper and middle classes. Then there were the SRs, Mensheviks and all left of centre activists who wanted a democratic, pan-socialist Russia. Anarchists and various nationalist groups in Ukraine saw the opportunity to secure autonomy. Peasants wanted the Bolsheviks off their backs and to run their own lives. Then there were the Germans who wanted to extend their influence. There were also the eighteen nations which constituted the Allied intervention, including Great Britain, the United States and Serbia. They were concentrated in the north. In the Far East the Japanese were eying territory, from Vladivostok westwards. In Azerbaijan, Armenia and Georgia local elites strove for independence from Moscow.

The Civil War was fought over three main fronts: the south (Don, Kuban, north Caucasus and Ukraine); the east (Volga, Urals and Siberia); and the northwest (Baltic and Poland). There were also three distinct periods:

- **From the Bolshevik takeover to the end of the First World War, in November 1918.** The protagonists were forming. The Allies intervened, so did the Japanese and the Germans. Romania occupied Bessarabia (present-day Moldova).

- **From November 1918 to November 1919.** This was the period of greatest success for the Whites, General Nikolai Yudenich threatened Petrograd in the north; General Anton Denikin, in the south, made his most successful advances. Admiral Aleksandr Kolchak, in the east, was also having success.

- **November 1919 to March 1921.** By the end of November 1919 the Whites were on the run and never recovered. This period is one of Red success. The Poles intervened and reached Kyiv but were driven back. The British, French and other interventionists departed in late 1920. The Japanese were eventually forced to leave by the United States. The Treaty of Riga ended the Soviet–Polish war in March 1921. The Reds penetrated Georgia and removed the Menshevik government. Red rule was proclaimed in Armenia and Azerbaijan.

Allied forces landed in Murmansk on 6 March 1918, at the invitation of Lenin and the local soviet. The soviet leader was afraid that the Germans might seize the port and other strategic targets. Few of the soldiers wanted to remain after November 1918 but the Allies were committed to helping the Whites with men, matériel and advice.

The major concern for the Bolsheviks in 1918 was the south. The Don Cossacks were totally opposed to Red rule and formed the backbone of the Volunteer Army. The Whites were second best and might have been wiped out had the Germans not come to their rescue. General Petr Krasnov, the ataman of the Don Cossacks, backed German ambitions and declared an independent republic. In Ukraine, the Reds were driven out in early 1918 and the Rada (council) declared Ukrainian independence. A Soviet government held power in Kharkiv (Kharkov in Russian), a mainly Russian-speaking mining area. After the Treaty of Brest-Litovsk, the Germans removed the Rada and installed General Pavlo Skoropadsky as Hetman (from the German Hauptmann, meaning captain). Skoropadsky played the same role as Krasnov. His government was full of Kadets.

Fortunes changed for the Whites in the summer of 1918. They cleared the region between the Black and Caspian Seas of Reds. The Whites were severely weakened by the refusal of Generals Denikin and Krasnov to cooperate. Krasnov attempted to take Tsaritsyn (later Stalingrad, now Volgograd). Had he succeeded, the Whites in the east and south could have linked up. When General Baron Petr Wrangel forced the Reds out of Crimea he instituted a reign of terror. The goals of most Whites in Siberia were different. They wanted the Constituent Assembly reconvened and a democratic Russia.

Many Czechs and Slovaks had surrendered to the Russian army because they refused to fight for the Austrian Kaiser. There formed a group of about 40,000. Lenin wanted rid of them and they were put on trains to Vladivostok from whence they would be shipped to Europe. Near Chelyabinsk, in the Urals, they encountered some Hungarian prisoners of war. A fight ensued and the outcome was that the Czechs and Slovaks took over the city. The local soviet had tried to arrest them. They then moved along the Trans-Siberian line overthrowing soviets on the way. When they got to Omsk, in western Siberia, local anti-Bolshevik groups linked up with them and a new anti-Bolshevik administration was formed. The Czechs fanned out to take control of Simbirsk (later Ulyanovsk) Kazan, the capital of modern-day Tatarstan and Ufa, the capital of present-day Bashkortostan. Right SRs took over. They were repressive and were dependent on the Czechs and Slovaks to retain power. The Czechoslovak Legion was never strong enough to threaten Bolshevik power but they kept the Civil War going in the east.

The end of the First World War brought a welcome respite for the Bolsheviks. The Germans withdrew from Ukraine and southern Russia. The Turks left

Transcaucasia. They had ruled in Baku, Azerbaijan. The British quickly moved into Baku, a centre of the oil industry. The French appeared in Crimea. In January 1919, the Red Army took Riga, the capital of Latvia, Vilnius, now the capital of Lithuania, Kharkiv, their Ukrainian capital and Kyiv. The Allies requested that German forces in Latvia and Lithuania stay to pre-empt a Bolshevik takeover. In the east there was disarray among the White elements. An All-Russian Directorate was set up in September in Ufa dominated by right SRs. It was overthrown by military officers in November. They installed Admiral Aleksandr Kolchak as Supreme Ruler of All Russia. In March 1919 his forces took Ufa but the Reds counter-attacked under the very able Mikhail Frunze and retook the city. Hopes of linking up with White forces in the south were finally at an end.

In January 1919, the Volunteer Army launched an offensive which was crowned with great success. General Denikin's troops took Tsaritsyn, Kharkiv and Kyiv. In May, General Yudenich began moving from his base in Estonia towards Petrograd. Denikin's forces reached as far as Orel, about 300 km south of Moscow. The Reds faced extermination. They rallied and drove Denikin out of Orel and into headlong retreat. A great Red counter-offensive carried them through Ukraine to Rostov-on-Don. In Siberia they retook Omsk. Yudenich had to retreat to Estonia. The British pulled out in September 1919 and left Kolchak to his own devices. Wrangel became commander of all White forces. His troops retreated to Crimea where they were evacuated by the French in November 1920. Kolchak was caught and executed. The Czechoslovak Legion struck a deal with the Reds and left Russia. When the Reds retook territory they executed huge numbers of so-called collaborators.

By February 1921 they were in Tbilisi, Georgia, and the whole of the Caucasus was theirs. In the same year the Reds conquered Central Asia. There was some unfinished business in Poland. War between Warsaw and Moscow had been under way since 1918. Lenin was very optimistic about the prospects of revolution in Poland and pushed for a Red Army invasion. Dzierzynski worked on his victory speech in Warsaw. He fancied himself as the new Polish Minister of Education. The defeat of the Red Army, called by the Poles the 'miracle on the Vistula', in August 1920, was a bitter blow. Lenin had expected Polish workers to welcome the Red Army but they met them with pitchforks. Polish workers had no desire to be put back under the Russian boot. Stalin took his revenge when he massacred Polish officers, in captivity at Katyn, in 1940. The defeat of the Red Army was very significant for the prospects of revolution in the rest of Europe. Had the Red Army penetrated Germany it is possible that the communists might have taken power. Red power might have swept through Europe.

The Civil War cost millions of lives. At least a million died in combat or fell victim to Red or White terror. Another 3 million died of hunger, disease and the cold.

The Comintern

The leading Marxist party in the world, the SPD, supported Germany's war aims. The vast majority of socialists backed their own countries during the war. This appalled Lenin. He was determined to set up an organisation to replace the Second International founded in 1889. In March 1918, the Bolsheviks changed the name of their party. The Russian Social Democratic Labour Party (Bolsheviks) became the Russian Communist Party (Bolsheviks). It was cutting its links with social democracy. Lenin encouraged radicals to leave their socialist parties and set up communist parties. This happened in Finland and Latvia, in August 1918. Austria, Germany, Poland and Hungary followed several months later.

The leaders of the German Communist Party (KPD), Karl Liebknecht and Rosa Luxemburg, opposed Lenin's desire for a separate Communist International. They feared that it would be dominated by Russia. Communists launched a bid for power in Berlin in January 1919. It failed and Liebknecht and Luxemburg were killed by members of a right-wing *Freikorps* unit. Luxemburg, a Polish-born Jewess, was sharply opposed to the Bolsheviks' dictatorial ways and Russian nationalism.

'The ultra-centralism advocated by Lenin is permeated in its very essence by the sterile spirit of a night watchman rather than by a positive and creative spirit. He concentrates mainly on *controlling* the party, not on *fertilising* it, on *narrowing* it down, not *developing* it, on *regimenting* and not on *unifying* it.' (1918)

On 2 March 1919, the Communist International met for its 1st Congress in the Kremlin. A major problem had been contacting Lenin's sympathisers abroad. One tactic employed was to sew invitations into the clothing of 24 prisoners of war who were then sent home with instructions to contact the desired person. They were very pleased to take the money but forgot everything once over the Russian frontier. The Congress was so short of delegates that one Rutgers represented The Netherlands, the USA and even Japan. After all, he had spent two months in Japan. The KPD delegate, Hugo Eberlein, had been instructed to oppose the founding of the Comintern. However, the deaths of Liebknecht and Luxemburg weakened his resolve and he did not vote against. Grigory Zinoviev chaired the new body. The language of the Congress was German because it was expected that Berlin would become the socialist capital of the world. German remained the language until Lenin's death.

The 2nd Congress convened in Petrograd on 19 July 1920 but repaired to Moscow and remained in session until 7 August 1920. This Congress was much more representative of left-wing opinion and delegates from 41 countries attended.

The Congress adopted the famous 21 conditions of admission. Although signed by Grigory Zinoviev, head of the Comintern, they had been penned by Lenin. Communist parties were to be set up in each country and modelled on the Russian party. Implacable opposition was declared to social democracy everywhere. A party's first loyalty was to the Soviet state not their home country.

In Germany the communists could only claim the allegiance of a minority of the working class. When the KPD launched an armed uprising in March 1921, with the blessing of the Comintern, their weakness became all too apparent and the uprising was easily suppressed. The French Communist Part (PCF) was founded in December 1920 and again many socialists did not join. The same happened in Italy. The upshot was that the rift between the Communist Party (PCI) and the socialists so weakened the left that it was in no position to effectively resist the rise of fascism.

The Party bans factionalism

This occurred at the 10th Party Congress, in March 1921. Lenin had requested that every delegate declare his or her adherence to one of the platforms at the Congress. The Congress was certain to be fractious as Lenin had decided to introduce the New Economy Policy (NEP). This was, in reality, a retreat from Bolshevism. During the Congress, the rebellion of the Kronstadt (an island fortress in the Gulf of Finland) sailors reached its climax. The Congress was suspended while Trotsky and some 300 deputies repaired to Petrograd to suppress the uprising. The sailors, among the most ardent supporters of the October Revolution, were demanding soviet democracy. Fortunately for the Bolsheviks, the ice around the island fortress permitted an assault by 50,000 Red Army soldiers. The uprising was suppressed in rivers of blood. The Red Army was commanded by (later Marshal) Mikhail Tukhachevsky. For the first time, the Bolsheviks had spilled Red blood.

The Congress reconvened in sombre mood. Some of the deputies had perished at Kronstadt. The stage was set for the outlawing of dissent, labelled factionalism. The Workers' Opposition (WO), dominated by trade unionists, lost its battle against the central direction of the economy. The Democratic Centralists, who wanted more democracy, lost out. They were banned. A resolution was passed entitled 'On the syndicalist and anarchist deviation in our Party'. It outlawed the views of the WO and declared that the propagation of such ideas was incompatible with Party membership. Another resolution, 'On the Unity of the Party', banned factionalism. Party members could discuss issues but the formation of groups with platforms of their own was forbidden. Once a Party decision was taken, complete obedience was demanded. Those who infringed this rule could be expelled from the Party. A CC member could be expelled by a two-thirds vote of members. This was so controversial at the time that it was only made public knowledge three years later. Lenin conceived of it as an emergency measure to force through the New Economic Policy. He understood that the Party might fall into 'error' in the future.

The ban on factionalism revealed that the Party was riven with dissent. The NEP had to be forced down their throats. Another group, the Mensheviks, was bound to see NEP as a vindication of its position. A retreat to state capitalism meant that the Bolsheviks could not build socialism in Soviet Russia. Lenin solved the problem by having about 2,000 Mensheviks, including the entire CC, arrested just before the introduction of NEP. Many of them were later released and the leading Mensheviks went into foreign exile. After the Congress, Lenin asked Stalin to ensure that his victorious faction achieved dominance in the central Party apparatus. The way to do this, thought Lenin, was to make Stalin Party General Secretary (Gensek). Stalin, of course, would only appoint comrades who would do his bidding. Gradually his personnel network expanded.

Twelve steps towards dictatorship

Soviet Russia, by a process of trial and error, became a militarised state. It had a commander-in-chief, Lenin, and a general staff to develop policy. Officers – Party officials – were to implement orders. One can trace 12 steps towards dictatorship. It should be underlined that Lenin and the Bolshevik leadership did not mechanically plan a dictatorship, beginning in October 1917. It was more a matter of events shaping them rather than the reverse.

1 The dissolution of all non-Bolshevik parties.
2 The establishment of a one party government.
3 The sidelining of the soviets.
4 The nationalisation of industry.
5 The nationalisation of land.
6 The transformation of trade unions into instruments of Bolshevik rule.
7 The sidelining of factory committees.
8 The emergence of the Bolshevik Party as the sole legitimate party.
9 The outlawing of factions within the Bolshevik Party.
10 The emergence of a dominant faction within the Bolshevik Party.
11 The transformation of the Red Army, an instrument to save Soviet Russia, into an instrument to keep the Bolsheviks in power.

12 The transformation of the political police (Cheka), an instrument to defend
the revolution, into an instrument to protect the power of the Bolshevik
leadership.

Why did the Reds win the Civil War?

- They had to. They feared extermination if they lost.

- The need to win produced some brilliant military commanders. One example
was Mikhail Frunze.

- The Bolsheviks had a unified command structure. Trotsky was in charge and
only Lenin could overrule him.

- Trotsky was a gifted military coordinator; he learnt strategy quickly on the
hoof; he understood the need to milk the military experience of former
ex-tsarist officers (military specialists).

- The Reds discovered that ruthlessness paid dividends. Trotsky was always
ordering the shootings of Whites or 'class enemies'.

- The First World War had trained millions of peasants to fight. They wanted to
be rid of landlords and to keep the land they had seized.

- The Reds' territory was concentrated in the north-west and centre of Russia.
They controlled the most densely inhabited part and the core of Russian
industry. They never lost Petrograd or Moscow. Soviet-held Russia numbered
about 60 million people but White territory never accounted for more than
10 million.

- Red lines of communication and supply were shorter than those of
the Whites.

- The Reds were able to appropriate the war matériel of the tsarist army.

- The Reds had a big idea. They were brilliant at slogans: all power to the
soviets; land to the peasants; away with the landlords and capitalists; workers
and poor peasants are the new ruling class.

- The peasants did not want the Reds or the Whites. The most powerful
argument the Reds had was: back us and you keep the land; back the Whites
and the landlords will return. On balance the peasants supported the Reds.
Most of the 5 million Red Army soldiers were peasants.

- Lenin promised self-determination to the nationalities. This was seductive.
If the Whites returned they would lose their autonomy. This was of great
significance in a multinational empire.

- The military experience shaped the Party. It was gradually organised along
military lines and proved effective. Party officials were conduits for Politburo

decisions; they were responsible for implementation using whatever methods they thought appropriate; they were only accountable to a higher level official. Enthusiasm and self-sacrifice were all that the Party offered in 1918 but over time it became clear the Reds would win. Becoming a Party cadre became attractive as a career.

■ The Reds were willing to pay an awesome price for victory: a devastated country; a sullen peasantry; empty factories; millions brutalised by war and hordes of orphans reverting to an uncivilised state.

Why did the Whites lose the Civil War?

■ On paper they should have won because their armies included so many experienced officers and men. They failed to drive home this advantage. The Reds were given time to develop military expertise.

■ No central command structure.

■ Too many fronts. Their men and matériel were spread over a vast territory.

■ They never managed to link up the eastern and southern fronts. This would have allowed joint offensives.

■ White commanders fought among themselves. Krasnov would not join Denikin in an assault on Tsaritsyn.

■ The Reds called them the lackeys of the imperialists because they accepted foreign matériel and advice. The Reds were defending Russia but the Whites were handing it over to foreigners.

■ No big idea. The nearest they came to one was Great Russia. However this meant a return to the tsarist past in the eyes of most Russians.

■ No policy to win over the nationalities. The Whites retained Great Russian nationalism. This was read as Great Russian imperialism by non-Russians.

■ No land policy to counter the Bolshevik slogan of land to the peasants. The landowners who supported the Whites would not allow a land reform.

■ The Whites did not come up with a concept for a new Russian state to challenge the Bolshevik slogan of a Soviet state. The Whites wanted to reimpose the pre-February 1917 Russia.

■ The Whites fatally underestimated the Reds in the beginning.

■ In White-controlled areas there were frequent peasant uprisings. They had to be put down.

■ White commanders were not as ruthless as Red commanders.

■ Red military expertise increased over time. This cannot be said of the Whites.

Questions

1 What were the immediate problems facing the Bolsheviks after their assumption of power between 1917 and 1921?

2 Did the Bolshevik Revolution come to an end in 1921 with the conclusion of the Civil War?

3 Why was there so much violence in Russia during 1917 and 1918?

4 Were the Bolsheviks really trying to eradicate class distinctions in Russia between 1918 and 1921?

5 Did Lenin make ideological concessions in order to maintain power between 1918 and 1921?

6 'The period 1917–21 was one of transition in which the rudiments of the Soviet state order were established.' Discuss.

7 What new methods of Bolshevik rule were institutionalised during the period 1918–21 and were they necessarily brutal or merely pragmatic reactions to a desperate situation?

8 'Democratic centralism replaced Lenin's dominance of the Bolshevik Party between 1918 and 1921.' Discuss.

9 Discuss the role of Trotsky in securing Bolshevik victory in the Civil War.

10 'Bolshevism was a new form of autocracy.' Discuss.

Further reading

Alec Nove, *An Economic History of the USSR 1917–1991* (1992); T. H. Rigby, *Lenin's Government: Sovnarkom, 1917–1922* (1979); Evan Mawdsley, *The Russian Civil War* (2000); Rex Wade (ed.), *Revolutionary Russia: New Approaches* (2004).

CHAPTER 4

Muslims and others and revolution

Russia's first contact with Muslims in the modern era was in the sixteenth century when they captured Kazan, the Tatar capital, on the Volga. It is the capital of modern-day Tatarstan. After the conquest, the Tatar nobility was offered the opportunity of joining the Russian nobility. Many of them did and in this way were russified and converted to Orthodoxy. It was only in the 1880s that the Russians attempted to russify Muslims and convert them to Orthodoxy. They failed.

In sweeping across Siberia to the Pacific Ocean, Russia acquired more Muslim subjects. Buddhists and animists were also caught up in the imperial net. Catherine the Great (1762–96) was a highly successful imperialist. She swept down to the Crimea and then across the Caucasian mountains. Armenia came in seeking protection from the Ottoman Turks and Georgia did the same. Crimea was taken from the weak Ottoman empire and Azerbaijan from an equally weak Persian empire. The Azerbaijani people were thus partitioned between the Russian and Persian empires. The Crimean Tatars and Azerbaijanis were overwhelmingly Muslim. The Armenians were Armenian Orthodox and the Georgians Georgian Orthodox. Armenia and Georgia have their own alphabets and have retained their distinctive version of Orthodoxy until the present day. The last great Muslim frontier was Central Asia. By the end of the nineteenth century Russian power was ensconced throughout the region. The Russian appetite for Muslim lands was insatiable. They occupied northern Persia in the early eighteenth century but were forced to leave.

Among the Bolshevik leadership, Lenin was the most sensitive to nationality issues. The first Muslim in the Party Politburo, N. A. Mukhitidinov, only appeared at the 20th Party Congress in February 1956. Jews were wary of Russian nationalism but were also keen to prevent the growth of national feeling among the over 100 nationalities in the former Russian empire. They favoured a strong, central Soviet

MAP 4.1 Central Asia

state. Stalin, the assimilated Georgian, and Dzierzynski, the assimilated Pole, agreed. However, tactical concessions had to be made to convince non-Russians that Soviet power was not tsarist power in a red mantle. Stalin became Commissar for Nationalities in the first Soviet government. On 3 November 1917, he and Lenin published the Declaration of the Rights of the Peoples of Russia. It proclaimed an end to national and ethnic privileges. The various nations had the right to secede. The goal was a voluntary and honourable union. In other words, a unitary state. This did not go down very well. Lenin changed tack and declared that a future Russian and Ukrainian government should be founded on the principle of federalism. Later, in the Declaration of the Toiling and Exploited Peoples, he developed the concept of a 'free union of nations as a federation of Soviet republics'. In January 1918, he proclaimed the Russian Socialist Federated Soviet Republic (RSFSR).

The 'Russian' in the new state's name was not *Russkaya* but *Rossiiskaya*. The significance of this was that *Russkaya* signified ethnic identity, the latter was geographic. It signalled that the country was peopled by many nationalities. Lenin was indicating to non-Russians that Russians, though in the majority, would not be accorded a privileged role in the new state. All the nations of the former Russian empire would be welcome in the RSFSR. The response was decidedly lukewarm. Finland had gained independence in December 1917. Poland was promised independence after Germany was defeated. Estonia, Latvia and Lithuania were scrapping to escape Petrograd's control.

Transcaucasia

In Azerbaijan, Muslim organisations proliferated and saw the February and October revolutions as affording them freedom of choice. However, the capital Baku was dominated by Russians and Armenians. This was due to the oil industry. In March 1918, Muslims tried to take over Baku city soviet but were defeated by the Russians and Armenians. The Baku commune, which ruled Baku from April to July 1918, tried in vain to promote Soviet power in Transcaucasia. Nationalist Azerbaijanis sided with the Ottoman Turkish army when it marched on Baku. Once there, Azerbaijanis took their revenge on Armenians, slaughtering about 30,000. The nationalists had declared Azerbaijan independent in May 1918 but they were always in a precarious situation. There was a Bolshevik tradition in

MAP 4.2 The Caucasus region

Baku (Stalin was one who cut his teeth there). The nationalists had to rely on the Ottoman Turkish and afterwards the British army to stay in power. When Britain left, the door was open for the Red Army to take Baku, almost unopposed, in May 1920.

Armenians were quintessentially merchants and could turn almost any deal into a good one for themselves. They were a diaspora, spread out from the Ottoman empire to Russia and India. Between 1915 and 1922 the Turks killed upwards of 2 million Armenians in Anatolia. They were perceived as a threat to the Ottoman empire and, after its collapse, to the Republic of Turkey. Those who found refuge in Russian Armenia survived. Armenians congregated around Erevan, their capital. Independence was declared in May 1918 but the Red Army re-established Soviet power in the republic in December 1920.

After February 1917, in Georgia, the Mensheviks dominated the soviets and found themselves running the 'bourgeois revolution'. The Mensheviks fashioned a viable socialist government and began economic and social reforms. However they could not defend themselves militarily and relied on Britain for security. Britain left. A faction within the Bolshevik leadership, led by Stalin and Sergo Ordzhonikidze, another Georgian, and supported by Felix Dzierzynski, the Pole, pushed for a military invasion to support an 'uprising'. In February 1921, the Red Army marched in and the Mensheviks fled. They attempted to regain power in 1924 but were ruthlessly dealt with. Red imperialism had proved victorious.

Central Asia

Central Asia or Turkestan (the land of the Turks) was of considerable geopolitical significance for centuries. It can be divided into eastern and western Turkestan. Part of eastern Turkestan now forms part of the Chinese autonomous province of Xinjiang. Here live Uigurs, Kazakhs and other Muslim Turkic peoples who have been divided by history from their kinsmen and women in Central Asia. Western Turkestan stretches to the Caspian Sea.

Today, Kazakhstan, Kyrgyzstan, Uzbekistan, Turkmenistan and Tajikistan comprise Central Asia, which occupies an area of over 1.5 million square miles. This is about half the territory of the United States. The states vary greatly in size. They range from Kazakhstan, the largest, with over a million square miles, to the smallest, Tajikistan, which is just over 55,000 square miles. As far as population is concerned, Uzbekistan is the largest and Turkmenistan the smallest.

About 60 per cent of the region is desert. Hence water is the key natural resource. The region is dominated by two great rivers, the Amu-Darya and the Syr-Darya. The region was always a battleground between the nomad on his horse and the sedentary population. The nomad's domain was Kazakhstan with its vast steppes. Two factors unify the peoples of Central Asia: language and religion. All (except the Tajiks) speak a Turkic language. They were not distinct languages before 1917, rather dialects of Turkish. The Soviet authorities, in order to prevent the emergence of a unified Turkestan, deliberately fragmented the region. They set up new states and new languages. For instance, Kazakh and Kyrgyz were very similar but their division gradually led to two distinct languages emerging. Islam is the dominant religion. First brought to Turkmenistan in the eighth century by Arab invaders, it was not until the fourteenth century that it was adopted throughout the region. Sunni Muslims dominate.

The Russians come

The nomadic Kazakhs could only offer sporadic resistance to the Russian tide and by the middle of the nineteenth century the Russians had penetrated to the Syr-Darya. The Russian revolution of 1905–07 was a watershed for Turkestan. The Russian naval defeat at the hands of the Japanese ended the aura of Russian invincibility. Russians in Central Asia became quite radical during the revolution but excluded Muslims from their deliberations. They therefore began to organise. Among their demands were equality with Russians and the establishment of a Muslim religious organisation in Tashkent. This was ignored but they did elect some Muslim deputies to the Russian Duma or parliament.

Turkestan exploded in 1916. In June 1916 the tsarist authorities issued an order mobilising Muslims exempted from military service to do agricultural service in the rear. This brought all the Muslim grievances to a head. The Kazakhs and Kyrgyz wanted restitution of their confiscated lands (settled by Russians); others thought that a great opportunity now existed to bring down the Russian Empire. The first armed conflict was in July when Muslims attacked Russians and sabotaged railway installations in Samarkand and elsewhere. Pillage and rape spread. A holy war (jihad) was declared against the infidel. The Russian army put down the rising after a week but the Kazakhs and Kyrgyz carried on their struggle until the February 1917 revolution. The total Kazakh population, in 1916, was just over 5 million. Almost a million perished between 1916 and 1922 and another 400,000 fled to China, Mongolia, Afghanistan, Turkey and Iran.

Russians and Muslims welcomed the February 1917 revolution with considerable enthusiasm. The Provisional Government decreed an end to national, ethnic and religious discrimination. All citizens were recognised as equal. But inequality between nations persisted. Soviets or councils sprouted like mushrooms after a shower of rain in Soviet Russia and began to run affairs. A soviet of workers' and soldiers' deputies, which mirrored the one in St Petersburg, was established in Tashkent, the most important Russian city in Turkestan. However, it was entirely composed of Russian deputies. It saw itself as the new power in the land and totally ignored Muslim aspirations.

The communists come

Lenin thought he had the answer to the national problem. He perceived that 'Great Russian chauvinism' (bellicose nationalism) was so strong that a unitary state would not work. This chauvinism was amply illustrated by the behaviour of the Tashkent soviet which arrogated to itself the right to decide the future of Muslims – without bothering to consult them. Lenin proposed the self-determination of nations within the Russian Empire. He admitted that Soviet Russia could not live without its non-Russian territories. The grain and industrial resources of Ukraine, for instance, were vital to Russia's well-being. Lenin's answer was audacious. Russians had to fight for the right of self-determination of all nations in Russia. This would convince non-Russians that Russians were no longer imperialist. After the victory of the proletariat (working class), the oppressed nations would no longer need to exercise their right to secede. The victory of socialism would lead to nationality being transcended. Workers would all want to be part of one big happy socialist family.

Some readers may assume that Lenin had taken laudanum before he fashioned the above theory but he was stone-cold sober. Protests by other Bolsheviks, especially Jews, that Lenin, far from weakening nationalism, was in fact promoting it, were brushed aside. As time would show, Lenin's nationality policy was to prove one of the greatest political misjudgements of the twentieth century.

Without realising it, Lenin was a Russian nationalist. All those who joined a socialist state would be assimilated and it would become a 'centralised, monolingual state'. Assimilation was Lenin's answer to all national problems, including the most difficult one, the Jewish question. The principal goals of socialism would be the economic, political and ethnic fusion of all nations.

Kazakhs (still called Kyrgyz by the Russians) were delighted that they were to be recognised as a nationality. However, there had been a long legacy of conflict over land, with Russians colonists settling in fertile areas. The Kazakhs demanded the return of their ancestral land before they were recognised as a nationality. The Bolsheviks had to fashion a policy which appealed to two disparate groups, the Russian colonists, who regarded themselves as the masters, and the nomadic natives, still smarting from the 1916 rising. A Kazakh Revolutionary Committee was set up in June 1919 and was parachuted in to establish Soviet power. The result was violent conflict. Despite this a Kazakh Autonomous Republic was established in October 1920, leaving the Kazakhs and Russians to find a way of living together. The Kazakhs did gain one concession: there was to be no more Russians colonisation. An anti-Bolshevik Kazakh national government, the Alash-Orda, was set up but it soon collapsed.

In the rest of Turkestan an original solution was adopted by Moscow. There were two irreconcilable revolutions: a proletarian revolution among Russian workers and soldiers, based in Tashkent, and a nationalist Muslim revolution, led by the educated bourgeoisie, which established an autonomous power base in Kokand. The Turkmen set up a government in the Transcaspian region. The Bolsheviks had little success in promoting revolution outside Tashkent. The Bolshevik Party of Turkestan, composed of Russians, found it impossible to promote national self-determination. Such a policy would have swept the communists off the political map.

In May 1920, Muslims proposed to Lenin that an Autonomous Republic of Turkestan be set up and become part of the RSFSR. He watered down their demands but eventually they gained more autonomy than expected. The main reason for this was the distance between Moscow and Tashkent. However, this was only a tactical move by Lenin as he was waiting for the apposite moment to divide up Turkestan.

How then did Moscow attempt to reshape Turkestan? The chosen instrument was the People's Commissariat of Nationalities (*Narkomnats*). It had sections for each nationality. All local demands had to be channelled through it. In 1921, official representatives of the Republic of Turkestan were installed and were to advise Moscow of local problems via *Narkomnats*. They were also to relay Moscow's wishes to the locals. Soon every significant initiative had to go to Moscow to be resolved. Then federal committees for each policy area were set up. The locals resented Moscow's interference but the fact that it occurred through *Narkomnats*, which represented national interests, sugared the pill. On reflection, the Bolsheviks turned out to be sophisticated imperialists. Appearance and reality diverged widely.

A federal or a unitary state?

The first Soviet constitution came into force in January 1924. Lenin and Stalin disagreed strongly on the nature of the new Soviet state. Stalin wanted only one republic, the Russian Federation. All other ethnic regions, such as Ukraine, Belarus and Central Asia, would become autonomous republics within the Russian Federation. Azerbaijan, Armenia and Georgia should be grouped together in a Transcaucasian autonomous republic in order to contain nationalism in each republic. Stalin's reasoning was that local elites would form in the various republics and make it difficult for Moscow to impose its priorities. Lenin, on the other hand, insisted that the non-Russian republics (Ukraine, Belarus, Uzbekistan and Turkmenistan) should have the same legal status as the Russian Federation within the new state. (Tajikistan acquired the same status in 1929 and Kazakhstan and Kyrgyzstan in 1936.) However, he agreed with Stalin that Armenia, Azerbaijan and Georgia should be grouped together in a Transcaucasian Federation.

The conflict between Lenin and Stalin had momentous consequences for nationalities in the new Soviet state. (This conflict is based on documents dictated by Lenin on 30 and 31 December 1922. Their authenticity has now been questioned.) In Lenin's eyes, the only way to overcome the distrust engendered by centuries of tsarist imperialism was to grant them the right to run their own economies. Only defence and foreign affairs would be the prerogative of Moscow. Lenin thought that local communist elites would run their territories better than bureaucrats in Moscow. To this end, a policy of promoting non-Russian elites, called *korenizatsiya*, was introduced. This was to overcome the great deficit of native cadres, especially in Central Asia. Hence Lenin envisioned a genuinely federal state.

Stalin, supported by Dzierzynski and Ordzhonikidze, disagreed. They wanted power concentrated in Moscow. They favoured a traditional Great Russian model for the new Soviet state. To Lenin this was Great Russian chauvinism. The row came to a head over Georgia. The Georgians objected strongly to Stalin's proposal that they enter the Soviet Union as part of a Transcaucasian Federal Republic. They favoured being a republic – on a par with the Russian Federation. Lenin agreed that Georgia would be a republic but only as part of the Transcaucasian Federal Republic.

On paper, Lenin won but, in reality, he lost. The new Soviet constitution ushered in a federal state. However, the comrade who succeeded Lenin did not favour a federal but a unitary state. Lenin lost because he fell ill at a critical moment. On 9 March 1923, on the point of imposing his will on Stalin during what was called the Georgian affair, he suffered a massive stroke. This ended his political career. Lenin had wanted his draft constitution and the thinking behind it published. On 5 March, Lenin had asked Trotsky to 'take upon yourself the defence of the Georgian case in the Party Central Committee'. On 6 March 1923, in a letter to Kamenev, Trotsky wrote that 'Stalin's resolution on the national question is worthless and a sharp turn is needed'. This was Lenin's position. However, later in the letter Trotsky did a U-turn.

> 'I am against liquidating Stalin and expelling Ordzhonikidze: but I agree with Lenin in principle: nationalities policy should be radically changed; persecution of the Georgians must cease; administrative methods of pressuring the Party must cease . . . the intrigues must stop. We need honest collaboration.'

Trotsky had let Stalin off the hook. Why did Trotsky fold like a pack of cards when offered this opportunity to defeat Stalin? The main reason may have been his state of health. In June 1922, five specialists gave their diagnosis. Trotsky was suffering from a 'chronic functional colitis [inflammation of the lining of the colon], a slight hypertrophy of the heart and a tendency to fainting fits, due to anaemia'. He needed a special diet and was to avoid physical and intellectual exertion (Lewin 2005).

Hence, at a crucial juncture in the evolution of Soviet Russia, beginning in March 1923, the leadership was deprived of its two main actors: Lenin and Trotsky. Had the latter prevailed, the Soviet Union would have become a different state. The hyper-centralisation, promoted by Stalin and his supporters, would have been avoided.

Islam and communism

Almost all the communists in Central Asia were Russian. The party had no recruitment problem. Indeed it was the other way round. Every Russian bureaucrat and colonist wanted to join. This led Muslims to set up their own Communist Party. Sultan Galiev, the most charismatic Muslim communist, in March 1918, set up the Russian Party of Muslim Communists (Bolsheviks), independent of the Russian Communist Party. Lenin wanted more Muslim members in the Communist Party of Turkestan. Locals rushed to join and were soon in the majority. They then demanded that it be reconstituted as an independent Turkestani Communist Party. Things were getting out of hand. To make matters worse, the Basmachi, freedom fighters supported by the local population, attacked Russians and all symbols of Soviet power. They severely undermined Soviet power in Turkestan. The bases of the Basmachis were in northern Afghanistan. After the conclusion of a treaty with the emir of Afghanistan, in 1921, Moscow was able to move into Afghanistan to attack Basmachi bases.

Moscow's response was swift and brutal. It declared that the Communist Party of Turkestan was a regional organisation of the Russian Communist Party. Wholesale purges followed. The party was rebuilt, based on class criteria, and sensitive to the population balance. Workers were Russian and Muslims were peasants. This meant that almost all leading positions were occupied by Russians, with Muslims only occupying minor positions. Over 150 Russian communists were seconded from Moscow to assist the process.

Muslim traditions, ways of life, social attitudes and laws were far removed from the Russian legal system. The Bolsheviks, in December 1917, abolished the existing legal system and replaced it with people's courts. In October 1924, the RSFSR criminal code was extended to Turkestan. Various Islamic practices were outlawed. Muslim law was now administered underground. The imposition of Soviet law led to a marked improvement in the status of women. In public life, their rights were the same as men's. Abducting a fiancée and the payment of a bride price became criminal offences. Divorce was by mutual consent and replaced a husband's repudiation of his wife. Polygamy was strictly forbidden and men had to pay alimony. The vendetta, a part of life in the Caucasus and Central Asia, was declared illegal.

The communists set themselves the task of ending traditional Muslim education which took place in *mektebs* and consisted of reciting the Quran. The *madrasas* trained a small number of students. The great majority of the population remained illiterate. The Bolsheviks were not going to transform attitudes in Central Asia overnight. How did they set about it? They organised the 'indignant masses' who attempted to stamp out vestiges of tradition which had been outlawed. If they found a woman on the street with a veil, she was forcibly unveiled. They monitored weddings and were particularly keen to stop the coming together of old men and young girls – marriages which had been arranged by the girls' parents. The 'indignant masses' roamed Turkestan enforcing modernisation whether the locals wanted it or not. Another ploy by the Bolsheviks was to develop women's sections in the Communist Party. Females were the most difficult to reach and the women's sections soon appeared in every workplace and social organisation. The Komsomol, the Communist Party's youth organisation, engaged in many recruitment drives. They were very successful but failed miserably when it came to enrolling girls – a major success indicator. Less than 5 per cent of Komsomol members in Central Asia were female.

In 1925, the Bolsheviks set up socialist republics, autonomous republics and autonomous oblasts to promote political and cultural diversity. The Kazakhs and Kyrgyz were separated. Since there was no accepted Kyrgyz language, a dialect of Kazakh was chosen and declared to be the national language. The Uzbeks and Tajiks were divided. In many ways this was reasonable as Tajiks spoke Farsi (Persian). During the 1920s the Bolsheviks called on all colonial peoples to rise up in revolt against their imperial masters. The anti-colonial revolution was taken seriously by Russian historians. They presented Russia's expansion over four centuries as one of unmitigated disaster for the natives. Wherever Ivan went, rape, pillage, desecration, murder, mayhem and destruction were bound to follow. Russia apologised for its previous sins of empire.

Questions

1 Was Bolshevik nationality policy born of pragmatic thinking, ideological concerns, or did it represent a real commitment to regulate centre–periphery relations?

2 'The USSR never managed to complete the transition from an empire to a true multinational federation.' Discuss.

3 'Lenin was a devout internationalist, Stalin a Russian nationalist.' Discuss.

4 'Soviet-style federalism was essentially a phoney federalism.' Discuss.

5 How did Lenin and Stalin's attitudes differ on the nationality question?

6   What was the Treaty of Brest-Litovsk and why was it important for future Bolshevik nationality policy?

7   'Inter-dependency was the key to regulating centre–periphery relations in the USSR.' Discuss.

8   'The Bolsheviks ruled the USSR by a policy of ethnic divide and rule.' Discuss.

9   'Lenin justified the Bolshevik revolution on promises he was later unable to keep.' Discuss in relation to the nationality question.

10   How did Lenin attempt to solve the nationality question after 1918?

Further reading

Dominic Lieven, *Empire: The Russian Empire and its Rivals* (2000); Jeremy Smith, *The Bolsheviks and the National Question, 1917–1921* (1996).

CHAPTER 5

Women and revolution

The position of women changed radically with the adoption of Byzantine or Orthodox Christianity. It is traditionally male-dominated and as early as the twelfth century women were segregated in churches. During the period of the Tatar yoke (1240–1480) the position of women deteriorated further. Tsar Peter the Great (1689–1725) modernised and militarised society. He removed the word 'motherhood' and decreed that Russia was now a 'fatherland'. The Batyushka (little father) Tsar would no longer marry Matyushka (little mother) Rus during the coronation ceremony. Women ruled Russia at various times, some with distinction, such as Catherine the Great. The concept of equality found expression in the work of Dostoevsky and Turgenev. Both featured female heroines and revolutionaries, however both conceived of the equality of males, not the equality of the sexes. Women headed the household in the village commune when the men went to work in the towns. They took their place in the village assembly. About a third of the population of St Petersburg at the turn of the century were female servants. In Moscow it was 25 per cent. By 1914, women made up about 40 per cent of the factory labour force.

The intellectual roots of Bolshevik feminism

Feminism insists on the equality of the sexes; women have no designated roles to play, irrespective of nature or social or intellectual convention; often an intellectual pursuit.

Women's liberation is the transformation of women's role in society; involves a revolution in existing social and cultural values on the part of men and women; has to be formalised in institutional terms (e.g. women's suffrage).

The Russian revolutionary movement had a long tradition of welcoming women into its ranks. The Russian female radical emerged from the middle ranks of society and the nobility, with large numbers also from the working class. Twenty per cent of them were teachers. Less than 10 per cent were of peasant background; and one-third came from the working class. Over 50 per cent were ethnic Russians, with a strong minority of Jewish women. Almost half (48 per cent) of all women who joined the revolutionary movement had a good secondary education and most joined the revolutionary movement during their late teens or early twenties (Clements 1997). Women joined political movements such as nihilism and populism. Of those charged with political crimes between 1873 and 1879, around 15 per cent were female. There were about 700 women revolutionaries listed in the 1870s. A woman, Sofia Perovskaya, led the group which assassinated Tsar Alexander II in 1881. She became the first woman to be hanged for a political crime. Women began their careers as revolutionary purists, whose beliefs were conditioned and largely determined by what they perceived as the socio-economic injustices of the modern age. Many were attracted to Marxism and peasant socialism (later the SR party) during the 1890s, at a time of major social change when thousands of women all over Europe were drawn into professional work.

Later their commitment to the revolutionary 'cause' (*delo*) was strengthened by political ferment, such as that witnessed during the first Russian revolution of 1905–07. (Women in Finland, then part of the Russian Empire, had obtained the vote in 1904.) The constitution wrung out of Tsar Nicholas II in October 1905 granted limited male suffrage but women were not mentioned. However, following the revolution, female universities opened and the St Petersburg Women's Technical Institute produced 50 engineers between 1906 and 1916. In 1910, there were over 1,500 women doctors in Russia, more than any another western state. Women constituted 10 per cent of the membership of both of the leading revolutionary movements, with 8,000 female SRs in 1907 and 10,000 female social democrats. In *Bolshevik Women* (1997), Barbara Clements speculates that as many as 2,000 female members of the Social Democratic Party later became *Bolshevichki*, that is, followers of Lenin. However some started as Mensheviks, such as Alexandra Kollontai, later switching to the Bolsheviks.

The most renowned Russian female revolutionaries were Nadezhda Krupskaya (1869–1939) and Alexandra Kollontai (1872–1952). Krupskaya (later to be Lenin's wife), the de facto founder of a Russian revolutionary feminism, published *The Woman Worker* (*Rabotnitsa*) in 1900. It was the first Russian Marxist study of Russian female factory workers. The Bolsheviks added equal rights to their party programme after 1903. However they rejected feminism. Women would be emancipated as part of the working class and not through their own political activity. Kollontai was a legend in her own lifetime and is perhaps the most famous Marxist woman in Russian history. She was the most prolific author on the women's question in the Russian Social Democratic Labour Party. She founded the Proletarian Women's Movement in 1905. She opposed feminism (it was considered bourgeois) and campaigned in factories for women to join the workers' struggle. Kollontai had to flee Russia in 1908.

Marxism appealed to Alexandra Kollontai, Evgeniya Bosh, Konkordiya Samoilova and Elena Stasova because it offered a critique of patriarchal society. August Bebel's *Women Under Socialism* (1879), which advocated the complete emancipation of woman from male tutelage, was a sensation. It became the Marxist bible for feminists. He advocated female suffrage, the right of women to enter professions, to divorce and to own property. He touched a sore point when he argued that it was not only capitalism which oppressed women. Men were just as guilty. Whereas other writers had advocated more rights for middle class women, Bebel was the first to do the same for working class women. Female revolutionaries believed that women's inequality was rooted in the institution of private property; women were economic slaves of men, the predominant money earner. The liberation of the female therefore began with a reassessment of domestic social roles (childrearing; sexual relations) and particularly the institution of the family, a point later echoed by Lev Trotsky.

Leading theorists and champions of the equality of the sexes, Kollontai and Inessa Armand (1879–1920), claimed that women's liberation was only possible under socialism. Armand has gone down in history as Lenin's great love. She insisted on the socialisation, and ultimate transformation, of domestic labour, particularly childcare, and the family unit in ensuring female self-determination. The theories of these revolutionaries had one major weak point. They did not consider gender roles as important in the emancipation of woman. The plight of the modern woman was therefore reduced to a simple equation of exploitation by individuals and classes in a morally bankrupt capitalist world. However Armand and Kollontai distinguished themselves from 'bourgeois feminists' in their belief that working women were responsible for freeing themselves from 'economic and social oppression', something that would later justify the creation of special women's organisations after the Bolshevik Revolution.

The period between 1900 and 1917 witnessed the consolidation of their revolutionary characteristics. These included fiery personas, superb oratorical skills, an uncompromising 'hardness' (*tverdost*) as regards revolution, and an absolute commitment to revolutionary virtues, such as devotion to the working class and the cause of socialist equality. Some began their careers as Bolshevik women by joining the editorial board of the Party newspaper, *Iskra* (*The Spark*). The underground work performed by these revolutionaries was largely of a grass-roots, organisational, technical and secretarial nature. However, they performed similar tasks to their male colleagues such as the distribution of illegal revolutionary literature and participation in the same secret discussion groups.

There were thousands of female radicals in Russia between 1910 and 1914. But only a minority of these actually became revolutionaries. Armand and Lenin's sister, Anna Elizarova, had planned to launch a newspaper, *Rabotnitsa* (*Woman Worker*), on International Women's Day in 1914. However, most of the editorial board were arrested and exiled. An underground press brought out the publication and it appeared illegally until war broke out in 1914. It recommenced publication in 1917. Female political parties competed for influence. Both Mensheviks and Bolsheviks intensified their efforts to win over women workers. Women, as elsewhere in Europe, joined the war. One was a pilot, others made up female battalions, suffering fearful losses.

The February Revolution began on International Women's Day when militant women demonstrated for peace and bread. They marched to the Putilov armaments factory and called on the men to join them. When they found a bakery, they ransacked it and called on the queuing women to join them. They sought out the jails and freed male prisoners. They looted the food shops they judged to be charging excessive prices. The demands of the women strikers were simple: food and protection for them and their children. They did not demand suffrage or equality with men. Soon they were linking up with male strikers. Now the demand was for an eight hour day, freedom of assembly and a republic. Women strikers dominated International Women's Day. The next day male strikers took over. The exclusively male Provisional Government granted women the vote. They were also accorded equal rights and pay. Women could now serve on juries and be lawyers.

On the eve of the dramatic events of 1917, several leading female revolutionaries had developed their own distinct populist visions of revolution. Revolution was justified on the basis of a unified workers' movement dedicated to channelling the spontaneous energies of the masses towards liberation. They conceived of 'duty' in egalitarian terms. Their first concern was the plight of the masses and the greater collective good rather than developing their own political careers. They believed that grass-roots organisational work was as important as any other type of revolutionary work, and the political party, rather than the individual leader, was the main transmitter of the revolutionary message. They were deeply mistrustful of 'politics', a world dominated by men. Their brand of Marxism was impassioned and different to the majority of male Bolsheviks. As 1917 drew nearer, their understanding of equality became firmly rooted in the assumption that the liberation of the proletariat was synonymous with female emancipation. Socialism was a basic prerequisite for the successful completion of these processes. Leading female Bolshevik revolutionaries spent much of the First World War abroad, in exile. Bosh and Kollontai returned from Scandinavia in March; Armand and Krupskaya from Switzerland in April 1917. Some, like Samoilova, had been hiding in Moscow and Siberia. When Lenin returned to Petrograd in April 1917 he recognised the importance of women workers. The Bolsheviks were more successful than other political parties because of the firebrand Alexandra Kollontai and her team. The Bolsheviks set up a Bureau of Women Workers and it sent groups of women into the factories. Women were active in trade unions. They also played an important role in demonstrations and strikes.

Women in revolution

By 1917, female revolutionaries had proved their mettle. Those who had actively participated in the underground movement before 1917 now assumed key positions in soviets, party organisations and the Military Revolutionary Committee prior to the main revolution in October 1917. The Bolshevik Party was more welcoming of women than any other political organisation in Russia at the time. Before and during 1917 education rather than class background (this changed during the 1920s) was the main prerequisite for admission to Party ranks. The period between February and October constituted the high point of political activity for women revolutionaries. During this time women continued to work as they had done before 1917, primarily as 'political agitators' preparing the groundwork for the Party's seizure of power. Women contributed clerical and journalistic work, made speeches, ran committees, helped plan the coup, trained with pro-Bolshevik militia units and the Red Guards and wrote and distributed pamphlets and leaflets. Women confirmed their reputations as political agitators *par excellence* during this period. They were in many respects the grass-roots, public face of revolution. The charismatic Alexandra Kollontai showed off her skills as an orator, addressing soldiers and sailors on the theme of the Bolshevik cause in 1917. Other revolutionaries were also established public speakers such as Evgeniya Bosh (known as the 'flaming evangel' of the Bolshevik Revolution), who later led an infantry regiment. Rozaliya Zemlyachka (née Salkind) became the organisational secretary of the Moscow city committee, which at that time was the basic unit of the Bolshevik Party; Vavara Yakovleva became secretary of the Moscow regional Party committee.

Women were more likely to become members of Bolshevik committees and serve as Party officials than be elected to a city's soviet executive committee. There were few *Bolshevicki* in the top ranks of the Party leadership but Elena Stasova was elected a temporary member of the Politburo between July and September 1919 and Alexandra Kollontai was elected to the Party Central Committee in August 1917. Women occupied positions in the lower levels of the Party hierarchy, with a few exceptions such as Bosh, Kollontai, Stasova and Zemlyachka. Kollontai's appointment as Commissar for Social Welfare made her the first women ever to hold a cabinet position in a European government. She drafted the first legislation on maternity insurance in January 1918. Kollontai advised on the rewriting of the marriage law and went on to draft labour regulations on the health of female workers and quickly became the leading Party spokesperson on women. Others worked in local Party organisations, wrote newspaper articles and pamphlets, spoke at neighbourhood committees and continued in the same type of missionary work as before the revolution. Bosh pursued a career as a political agitator and ruthless military leader. She participated in the attempt to bring Ukraine under Bolshevik rule in 1918, rapidly becoming one of the most feared Bolsheviks. In January 1918, Bosh took up the position of Commissar of Internal Affairs in the Bolshevik People's Secretariat in Kharkiv. Most prominent Bolshevik women, such as Kollontai and Bosh, were enthusiastic supporters of Lenin and his views about the liberation of women. Lenin believed that female liberation began in the home, with the transformation of the domestic role of 'slave-owner' between husband and wife. He also believed that women should be encouraged to work in the public sector. Real equality of the sexes could only be achieved by raising the political consciousness of both men and women about the work of the Party.

The year 1917 strengthened feminism, as Barbara Clements (1997) explains:

'The revolution actually intensified the Party's long-standing practice of engaging women in all its activities, because it sustained the crisis atmosphere that had nurtured egalitarianism throughout the underground years, and it strengthened the commitment most Bolsheviks professed to women's equality. The revolutionary year 1917 was so filled with general ideas of freedom that in fact it quickly became a special point of official pride with the Bolsheviks that they had so many working in their organization.'

Women conceived of their revolutionary roles largely in revivalist terms, inspiring and initiating female members of the proletariat in the idea of revolution. In 1917, they revived the newspaper *Rabotnitsa* (closed down in 1914), which later became the leading voice of political agitation amongst female members of the proletariat. The newspaper, which was circulated to thousands of Party members and beyond, became the foundation stone of Bolshevik feminism. It made the liberation of women a high priority of the revolution and proclaimed women's rights to polit-ical and legal equality, protective labour regulations, improved wages, and female representation on factory committees and union boards.

The female Bolshevik as political agitator

The regime recognised women were important given that they constituted 43 per cent of the industrial labour force in 1917, up from 26 per cent in 1914 (Clements 1997). In theory, women revolutionaries remained loyal to their original pre-mise that the successful achievement of socialism was conditional upon women's liberation. However, they faced the complex task of combining utopian aspirations unleashed by the revolutionary ferment of 1917 with the political demands and ideological requirements of the new regime. The 'women's question' had to fit into the current concerns of the Party. Women revolutionaries believed that legislation was not enough to ensure 'liberation'. That depended on several factors, including the restructuring of family life and the transformation of social patterns and relations. It had to become part of the official Party programme and women's political consciousness had to be raised; so too their appreciation of the nature of the process of 'liberation'. In order to fulfil the Bolshevik feminist criterion of self-liberation, the process should begin from 'below' (grass-roots level) but be directed from above. A special institution would have to be created to coordinate this process.

The Women's Department of the Central Committee apparatus (or Department for Work Among Women), the *Zhenotdel*, was established by Armand, Kollontai, Samoilova, Nikolaeva and Krupskaya, with Armand appointed head of the organisation in the autumn of 1919. (Kollontai took over leadership of the *Zhenotdel* following the death of Armand in 1920. Kollontai distinguished herself in her demands for the increased representation of women on trade union committees.) The *Rabotnitsa*, re-established in 1917, became the voice of the department and of Bolshevik feminism in general. However, Krupskaya later became the editor of the department's official newspaper, *Kommunistka*, which appeared in 1920. The *Zhenotdel* provided an opportunity for the lobbying of women's issues in the Bolshevik Party. It was accountable directly to the Party Central Committee and was in regular contact with the Orgburo (see Glossary) and the CC apparatus (see Glossary). This meant that it was not able to criticise the Party in any way, but it could exert pressure on the government in adopting policies directly affecting women, such as the legislation legalising abortion in 1918.

Zhenotdel was as much about feminism as it was about politics: it was to a) favourably transform women's attitudes towards the revolution and Soviet power; b) create loyal citizens of Soviet women by outlining the nature of their new social obligations, thereby extending the influence of the Party to working class and peasant women; c) enlighten women about politics in the new state; d) socially mobilise women by drawing them into the new state via work in trades unions, cooperative organisations and the soviets; and e) ensure the liberation of all women through the development of social networks and support organisations such as nurseries, public dining rooms, and so on. Indeed, female revolutionaries were convinced that the Party could not achieve legitimacy without the support of women. However, women could not be useful for the construction of socialism until the realities of their daily lives were transformed. As far as the Party was concerned, it created a crucial point of contact between female Bolsheviks and politically inactive women. In Bolshevik terms, politically conscious women meant liberated women. The problem was that women were not joining the Party in sufficiently large numbers. The Party conceived of the *Zhenotdel* primarily as a propaganda department through which women could be encouraged to participate in the Civil War and support the Red Army. In their work after 1917, therefore, female revolutionaries faced the challenging task of balancing emancipation with the immediate requirements of the Party.

Reaching, teaching, mobilising and politicising female workers and peasants was not an easy task. Deeply entrenched views about gender persisted, not to mention institutions such as the peasant commune, bastions of traditional family virtues. The starting point was to address the unequal treatment of female workers in the workplace and in education. This work began with the organisation of various congresses and delegations, such as the 1st All-Russian Congress of Working Class and Peasant Women, which established committees for working females. Next was the creation of delegate meetings, women's clubs and discussion groups, through which women became acquainted with the nature of Marxist feminism and Soviet politics. The delegates' meetings provided a means by which women could be elected to local soviets. However, not all delegates joined the Party. Delegate meetings reached large numbers of women in the 1920s. In 1922, there were 95,000 delegates, rising to 620,000 in 1927 and to 2.2 million in 1932. Nevertheless, the 620,000 delegates in 1927 only comprised 0.9 per cent of the total female population.

Female participation in regional soviets increased from 18 per cent in urban areas and 10 per cent in rural areas in 1926 to 32 per cent and 27 per cent in 1934 (Clements 1994). During the 1920s about 20 per cent of city soviet deputies were women but only 10 per cent of members of soviet executive committees were female. Ten per cent of the members of trade union factory committees, but less than 7 per cent of the highest ranking members of trade union governing boards, were women. The net effect of this was that female membership of the Party increased from 9.9 per cent in 1924 to 11.9 per cent in 1926, but this fell well below targets. Nevertheless, these changes did not eradicate deeply embedded attitudes, both on the popular and Party level, about the political immaturity or 'backwardness' of women. Through this delegation work a new generation of communist women were recruited and trained for various professions, including teaching, medicine, engineering and administration. During the 1920s Party Congresses endorsed and supported the work of the *Zhenotdel*, although its status remained uncertain throughout the 1920s. Even the women leaders of the organisation were obliged to soften their feminist rhetoric so as not to alienate male members of the Party. Feminism was potentially a counter-ideology to Marxism.

Despite these initial advances, female revolutionaries of the 'older generation', those who had played an active part in the pre-1917 underground movement and the revolution of 1917, gradually became disillusioned with the new regime. Russia's surrender to Germany in the Treaty of Brest-Litovsk (March 1918), followed by the increasing centralisation of power of the Party, and movement away from 'democratic centralism', alienated those such as Kollontai, who had championed egalitarianism, Party democratisation and the independence of local Party organisations. She resigned her position as Commissar for Social Welfare in 1918, and became an outspoken member of the Left Opposition led by Bukharin, and, later, Workers' Opposition in 1921. Inessa Armand and Varvara Yakovleva also became affiliated with the Left Opposition at this time. By 1921 male Bolsheviks held practically all leading positions in the Party; they formed alliances with other men, not women.

Initially two main issues dominated Party thinking as far as women were concerned: sexual morality and the marriage law (promulgated in 1926). The family code of 1918 abolished the concept of illegitimacy. Women could inherit property; obtain their own internal passports and petition for divorce; and the new marriage law better underlined a woman's right to child support and the importance of entering marriage freely and leaving it without restriction. Women could also retain their maiden name after marriage. Equality of the sexes existed on paper but not in reality. The Russian male expected women to wait on him. Drunkenness was a constant problem in the home. Husbands could just abandon their wives and children. One communist activist complained that some men had 20 wives. They simply refused to be responsible for their own children's upbringing. Not surprisingly, divorce was common. In 1927, four out of every five marriages ended that way. The most common complaint reported by *Zhenotdel* was that factory management regarded female workers as part of their harem.

The emergence of the new Bolshevik woman: 1921–29

The Civil War period (1918–21) was significant for three reasons: i) it unleashed a belief in revolutionary possibilities and heralded new calls for women to liberate themselves; ii) it revolutionised the concept of womanhood and 'equality' in the minds of female revolutionaries; and iii) it witnessed the coming of age of a new generation of female revolutionaries who had joined the Bolshevik Party after October 1917; their activities slowly overshadowed the work of the older generation of *Bolshevichki*. The 1917–18 period in which women and men had undertaken similar revolutionary work was now over. In 1922, the Party had 30,547 female members of whom 29,172 had joined since the February revolution. The latter figure constituted the 'new generation' of female revolutionaries who had developed their understanding of 'equality' against the background of the Civil War. Thirty-seven per cent of the 1917–21 group came from the working class. They were utterly subservient to the **Party and** its ideological missives.

Unlike the older generation, who developed their own feminist Marxism, they had no distinct revolutionary ideas of their own. The Party was their family and the roots of their identity. They were devoted to the idea of 'revolution' for it was this, rather than any other underground work, that enabled them to become politically active. These revolutionaries believed in their right, which equalled that of men, to defend the revolution, even if this meant combat. In the autumn of 1920, 66,000 women were serving in the Red Army, or 2 per cent of the total (Clements 1997). Twenty-five per cent of these were female recruits from the new generation. Most of the young women sent to the front by the Party, after receiving basic training in first aid and Marxism, worked as clerks and nurses. Others acted as spies (behind White lines), couriers and, most significantly, as 'political officers'. The latter worked as agitators, lecturing troops in Soviet politics, helping soldiers overcome demoralisation and maintaining the commitment of those on the front line to the Bolshevik cause. Many women fought in partisan units and in uprisings against the White forces.

The position of the 'political worker' was revolutionary; it challenged existing norms and perceptions of the role of the female Bolshevik. However, female political workers constituted a small minority, 10–15 per cent, of the Red Army. Some women were as young as 17 when they became commanders of platoons. Only a few women achieved high rank in the Red Army, such as Valentina Suzdaltseva, the 22 year old head of agitation, the political department of the army; and Larisa Reisner, was secretary of the Volga fleet Party organisation and headed an intelligence department. Nevertheless, female Bolshevik veterans Evgeniya Bosh and Rozaliya Zemlyachka remained the best known female military commanders. Zemlyachka requested a military assignment in December 1918 and became chief political officer of the Eighth Army operating in Ukraine; later she became chief political officer of the Thirteenth Army. In 1922, Zemlyachka received the Order of the Red Banner for her work in the Civil War, the highest military decoration in the USSR. Bosh played an equally crucial role commanding troops in Ukraine. Some female recruits served on Party control, and purge, commissions during the war. In many respects women 'energised' the Red Army. In total, 13 per cent of the old Bolshevik generation and 8 per cent of the Civil War generation died between 1917 and 1921 from various diseases, including cholera, typhus and influenza (Clements 1997). Inessa Armand, Lenin's lover, died in the autumn of 1920, followed by Samoilova eight months later, both of cholera. During the Civil War women suffered more than men. *Zhenotdel* organised women's units, including cavalry units, sharpshooters, sabotage groups, reconnaissance personnel and all the other skills needed in wartime. The casualty rate was high.

The 'new woman' who emerged from the Civil War was shaped by the militarisation of the collective identity of the Bolshevik Party. The virtues of this new female 'Redness' were determination, toughness, brutality, reliability, discipline, fierceness and utter devotion to the regime: 'during the Civil War, *tverdost* [hardness] was joined to conceptions of hierarchy and discipline that had been far less highly valued before 1917'. The new *Bolshevichki* learned not just hardness, although that was still highly prized, but also obedience to their superiors and submission to the will of the 'great stern family' (of the Party). In 1920, the new Soviet woman was described on the pages of *Kommunistka*: she was independent, socially active and independent in her personal life.

Contradictions in the Bolshevik message about 'emancipation' came to the fore during the Civil War. The war merely confirmed the masculine nature of Bolshevik political culture and the role of women in a supporting role to men, who took the key decisions. Between 1917 and 1921 the percentage of female Bolsheviks who held Party positions declined. During the Civil War, 43 per cent of

5.1 Alexandra Kollontai
Source: Satirikon, Paris, 1931.

the older generation and 39 per cent of the younger worked in full-time Party jobs; these figures fell in the New Economic Policy years to 32 per cent and 25 per cent respectively (Clements 1997). By 1922 most of the former prominent female Bolsheviks had disappeared from the public scene: in February 1922 Kollontai was removed as head of *Zhenotdel*. She later became a diplomat. She was packed off to the Soviet embassy in Oslo (thus becoming the world's first female ambassador) and later made ambassador to Sweden. Only Zemlyachka and Bosh remained, and with them elements of the old Bolshevik feminist identity. The Civil War exposed two quite distinct mind-sets about revolution: one was a newly revitalised belief in a socialist utopia strengthened by victory in the Civil War (harboured by the young generation); the other was a distrust of the autocratic, militarised political culture resulting from the war experience (older generation).

With the end of the Civil War, cities swelled with people, especially women. Many made for Moscow and Petrograd after losing their husbands and homes. The number of female and child prostitutes in these cities soared in 1920 and 1921. The Party declared work among women a 'top priority' in 1924. The Bolsheviks introduced the most far-reaching changes in the status of women in modern times. The extent of the social revolution was clear by the mid-1920s: education had been opened up to the lower classes; women had entered govern-ment posts; divorce and abortion were legalised in 1918 and 1920 respectively; and state-sponsored social mobility created new employment opportunities. The measures resulted in revolutionary changes: peasants and textile workers become factory directors and members of the Soviet government.

Barriers against change in the countryside had been weakened by the revolu-tion. Of the 620,000 women who served as delegates to *Zhenotdel* conferences in 1927, 384,400 (62 per cent) were peasants (Clements 1997). Dramatic changes in literacy rates also point to social improvement: in the 1897 census 13 per cent of women were recorded as literate; in 1920 this rose to 25 per cent. In 1918, 67 per cent of young female factory workers were literate and, in 1926, 42.7 per cent of all Russian women were able to read (Kelly and Shepherd 1998). Female unem-ployment disappeared with the massive expansion of the labour force ushered in by the first Five Year Plan, beginning in October 1928.

Party propagandists pointed to the presence of women in government as evidence of full emancipation. However, after October 1917 women were only marginally involved in high politics. This was underlined by the fact that women were not involved in patron–client networks at the apex of Bolshevik power. In any case, from the mid-1920s onwards, entry into government positions was deter-mined by class background. Managerial roles became the preserve of men, leaving women with clerical work. The highest positions achieved by women were during the the first Five Year Plan (1928–32), when the demand for skilled labour was at its highest. In general, members of the older generation of revolutionaries worked in the middle and upper ranks of governmental institutions like Narkompros (education), whilst the younger generation (those less well educated) worked in low ranking Party jobs. The most intensive political work performed by women was undoubtedly during the period of the Civil War when 35 per cent of the older generation and 20 per cent of the younger generation worked in government departments (Clements 1997).

The women's movement was torn apart by the political struggles of the 1920s. Klavdiya Nikolaeva was removed from her position as head of *Zhenotdel* in 1925 because of her support for Zinoviev; and Vavara Yakovleva lost her job as deputy Commissar of Education in 1929 because of her backing of Bukharin. Others such as Bosh criticised the Party leadership and supported Evgeny Preobrazhensky in 1923; and Krupskaya sided with Zinoviev and Kamenev. In 1924, Bosh committed suicide. She was not the first Bolshevik to suffer from depression; Armand had as well. The Party had not evolved in the way female Bolsheviks had hoped or envisaged. Most of the older generation favoured increased Party democracy and opposed the NEP. Conversely, those who campaigned in favour of the Stalin group in the mid-1920s rose in *Zhenotdel*. Zemlyachka, for instance, proved a staunch supporter of Stalin and his confrontational style of politics. In 1927, she was appointed to the Party Central Control Commission in the Urals; she was the only woman to serve on the Council of People's Commissars (Sovnarkom) under Stalin.

Women were mobilised for the first Five Year Plan. In 1929, liberation became synonymous with plan fulfilment. The pace of women's 'liberation' was dictated from above and had little to do with female demands from below. By the end of the 1920s, women were yearning for security, which they found in the traditional, patriarchal institution of the family. In many respects this contradicted the ideas of those such as Kollontai and Armand. In the early 1920s, the Party's outlook was influenced by Marxist feminism and it pursued a liberal agenda, but by the late 1920s this had changed with the consolidation of a new sexual code that prescribed premarital chastity and monogamy. A tension between the perception of female utility and their status as women existed in official Bolshevik ideology. It was never resolved.

The economic mobilisation of the 'New Women': the 1930s

By the beginning of the 1930s the older generation of Bolshevik revolutionaries had disappeared. The libertine image of the 1920s was to be reversed by 1937 with the proclamation in *Pravda*, and later by Stalin himself, of the existence of a 'new Soviet woman'. In the first Five Year Plan women were to make a distinct contribution to the construction of socialism. By 1929, liberation was synonymous with plan fulfilment. There were clear political reasons for complete emancipation. The 1920s witnessed the 'active' liberated women, whilst the 1930s were portrayed by the Party as a decade which provided a 'solution' to the women's question. In 1930, when *Zhenotdel* was closed down, the Party proclaimed the 'official' liberation of women, and thereby removed 'the striving for equality' from the Party agenda. The arguments of the 1920s relating to domestic labour, motherhood, marriage and sexuality were eclipsed by official rhetoric. International Women's Day provided an opportunity for the public dissemination of sweeping assertions about the equality of the sexes. Following the closure of *Zhenotdel*, a *zhensektor* (women's sector) was set up under the department of agitation of Party committees at republic, krai, oblast, town and district (raion) levels. The work of these bodies concentrated on political tasks amongst women rather than women's issues. The aim of the women's sector was to encourage women to join collective farms. This would, or so the Party claimed, result in the liberation of peasant women. The sector was abolished in 1934, but by then the aim of drawing women into social production, and eradicating social backwardness, had been overcome, according to official propaganda. Women, therefore, were very much a part of Stalin's grand modernising project of the 1930s. They were considered a vital economic resource and an integral part of the new society. They were, according to Stalin, the 'pride of the Soviet people'. In 1928, there were 3 million female workers; this was to rise to 13 million in 1940. Women also came in useful in legitimising Stalin's cult of personality from the mid-1930s onwards.

The need to restructure the domestic milieu was no longer mentioned. In the 1930s and 1940s equality was supposedly granted and guaranteed through the economic policies of industrialisation and collectivisation. Women were now part of a 'great army of labour' in industry, agriculture and, later, the Great Fatherland War. This liberation was accompanied by the strengthening of the family (of which the woman was the leading representative), which became the cornerstone of the regime. However, women's equality had to be justified in order to legitimately bring them into the economy and place a new series of demands on their shoulders. Newspapers such as *Izvestiya* declared that the October Revolution of 1917 had itself guaranteed emancipation and equality of the sexes.

According to Stalin, equality was brought to rural areas through the collectivisation of agriculture: 'Without collective farms – inequality. With collective farms – equal rights' and 'only kolkhoz life can obliterate inequality and put women on their feet' (*Izvestiya*, 17 March 1933). Women were destined to play a special role in 'annihilating inequality' in the countryside. This new proposition provided a range of employment opportunities for women. These would also challenge existing gender perceptions. In performing a new set of tasks (such as farm management, tractor driving), women assumed a new patriotic duty first to the state, then to her extended family, and only then to her personal life. It was assumed that women were likely to advance in the workplace if their political consciousness was raised; and this was best achieved by political education in the factory or on the farm. The most politically aware – expressed through the fulfilment and over-fulfilment of tasks – would be promoted.

Although collectivisation bludgeoned the countryside, it did yield certain benefits for women. Patriarchy was weakened in the cities as a result of the Five Year Plans. Between 1932 and 1937, women made up 82 per cent of all workers entering the paid labour force for the first time. During the 1930s, women were urged to attend schools and job-training programmes in the countryside, thus becoming a more educated and skilled workforce. By the end of 1930s, literacy among peasant females under the age of 50 had risen to 80 per cent; and 57 per cent of farm operatives were women. The number of female tractor drivers went up from several thousand in 1930 to 57,500 in 1938 (Clements 1994).

In 1936, a quarter of all female trade unionists were classified as norm-breaking (Stakhanovite) women. Heroic feats of production were favoured over all others when singling out peasant women (Stakhanovite heroines) for praise, medals, awards and adulation in the press. Nineteen thirty-six was declared Stakhanovite Year. Stakhanovism shaped the new evolving image of women as economic warriors committed to the realisation of the tasks set by the Stalinist regime, regardless of self-sacrifice. In overfilling norms and increasing productivity they were performing their duty and loyalty to the state, confirming the trend that in 1930s duties took precedence over rights. Paradoxically, by performing duties one was acquiring new rights. Women were also obliged to inspire their husbands to overproduce and do great deeds for the Soviet state. A woman's political consciousness was measured by self-sacrifice (public sphere) and devotion to her husband (domestic sphere). However, old rural attitudes towards women remained unchanged. Collectivisation did not propel women into leadership posts. Men occupied 97 per cent of the managerial jobs in Soviet agriculture throughout the 1930s. The number of female deputies in rural soviets was as low as 4 per cent in some districts. In 1932, about 16 per cent of Party members were female. The proportion of female delegates to Party Congresses by 1939 never reached 10 per cent. Only seven women were elected to the Party Central Committee: none to the Politburo (Clements 1994).

During the 1930s, about one-sixth of Party administrative posts (the apparat) were filled by females. These were normally minor positions. Similarly, in the economic sphere, the Five Year Plans did not eradicate inequality because the emphasis on the development of heavy industry favoured jobs performed by men, at the expense of social services and consumer goods; female labour was concentrated in low-paid industry. However, women did benefit from the technical revolution and in 1939 one-third of all engineers were women. Most teachers and doctors were female.

The legislation relating to social policy which was passed in the 1930s confirmed the increased demands on women in both the home and the workplace in the form of a 'double-shift' lifestyle. The 1936 marriage law and the outlawing of abortion in the same year underlined the importance of the growth and stability of the nuclear family and with it the cult of motherhood. The marriage law made divorce more difficult; increased child-support payments and penalties for non-payment; the abortion law could bring a social reprimand and fine of 300 rubles. The processes institutionalised in this legislation served to reinforce traditional patriarchalism, albeit in a modern guise. In the economic sphere, the Soviet leadership cleverly paid lip service to the Marxist principle that housework should be abolished, whilst reasserting the traditional role of women by officially endorsing feminine domesticity. Nevertheless, new work by Mary Buckley (in Edmondson 2001) suggests that the image of the new Soviet woman shaped by the radical changes of the 1930s was a 'liberation of sorts':

'Women could break out of the confines of traditional expectations of their gender. They could assume new roles on tractors and combine harvesters, often amid opposition from men and women alike. They could become what they had never hitherto been. Moreover, they could even legitimately compete with men in socialist competitions and win. They could demonstrate that they were "better" in a culture where women were seen by men as "inferior". They could realize socialist ideology on equality by showing that they were equal to any task performed by the male . . . they could do this at a time when leaders were reinstating family values and attempting to instil stability in family life. One unintended consequence of female Stakhanovism was a challenge to the interpersonal status quo of gender relations.'

Contrary to propaganda, women were not passive workers, utterly subservient to the state. They asserted their rights in the economy through trade unions and harboured their own distinct professional ambitions. Many stakhanovites demanded recognition for their work and many did not fulfil their role as a 'Soviet mother' and remained single and childless throughout the 1930s. The 1930s provided a new framework through which women could realise their potential and demonstrate their abilities. The fact that some women worked better and more effectively than men was suggested at the All-Union Congresses of Collective Farm Shock Workers (Stakhanovites) which convened throughout the 1930s. However, this was not in line with official ideology which prescribed that men and women were equal. Women had as much interest in maintaining the new system as did men; after all many increased their social status through plan fulfilment (Edmondson 2001).

The emergence of the New Soviet Woman was announced during 1937–38. The main attributes of this image can be summarised as follows:

- New Woman combined the best attributes of both images relating to her gender, the rational (practical, determined, hard-working, self-confident, innovative, ambitious) and the romantic (motherhood, femininity, beauty, intuition, diffidence, emotion, submissiveness).

- New Woman triumphed over technology; she mastered modern machinery.

- New Woman was a force to be reckoned with; she was assertive, independent and had a mind of her own.

- New Woman was a great, active force in industry, agriculture and in the home; she was a high achiever in the workplace and in the family; she performed a multiple of tasks as citizen, worker, housekeeper, wife and mother and, most important, as a duty-bound, loyal servant of the Soviet state.

- New Woman was driven by duty, hard work, self-sacrifice and love of the motherland; any personal ambition was directed to the wellbeing of the new society as a whole and the greater collective good; she gained satisfaction from serving others.

- Overall, New Woman was a symbol of progress, status and achievement; she served the purposes of ideology and the elite; she provided economic and social services to society by working hard, cultivating obedient members of society in her family; she represented the modern nuclear family as the cornerstone of the new regime.

Women were affected by the purges of the 1930s. This was on the basis of guilt by association – many were the wives of disgraced Bolsheviks arrested in 1937. They were usually sent to labour colonies. The Civil War generation benefited most from the changes; they were promoted to the vacancies created by the purges. The Bolshevik veteran, Rozaliya Zemlyachka, for instance, was promoted on several occasions and showered with awards in the late 1930s. In May 1939, she became chair of the Commission of Soviet Control. Many leading women collaborated in the process of denouncing colleagues to the police.

'Superwoman' and the Great Fatherland War

Over 800,000 women served in the armed forces during the war. Nineteen forty-three was a record year for new female recruits entering the military. The female contribution to the war effort was divided between the military and industrial spheres. The division of labour according to gender disappeared between 1941 and 1945, and largely represented a continuation of demands upon women, except on a grander and more dramatic scale. In 1940, for instance, women constituted 38 per cent of the non-agricultural labour force; by 1943 that figure had climbed to 57 per cent. Over 12 million men left farm work and this meant that in 1944 there were four female to every male farm worker. In June 1941 women and girls were mobilised for wartime work. By December 1942 women's battalions existed and by 1943 the majority of political officers in the air corps were women. Women served in all-female units within the larger command structure of the Red Army. Several thousand women went into direct combat and served in the infantry as snipers. Over 26,000 women joined the partisans. More than 100,000 women received military decorations (91 as Heroes of the Soviet Union) for their service to the Red Army during the war (Clements 1994). Some women excelled as sharpshooters.

Women played a central role in the wartime mobilisation of national patriotism. They became inextricably linked with the iconography of war. After 1941 the New Soviet Woman became Mother Russia. The primary concern of the female was the protection of her loved ones by defending the state. These maternal instincts made women effective fighters. Soviet women were committed to both production and defence. These images were cleverly combined with the masculine fatherly symbol of Stalin and captured in the rousing slogan: 'For the Motherland. For Stalin!' This emotionally charged propaganda was intended to raise the morale and fighting spirit of the troops at the front. The nature of the 'enemy' became clearer by elucidating the rationale for war – the defence of land and female kin. This served a dual purpose for the regime: it promoted patriotism at home and at the front and brought women into warfare either through combat or industrial work vacated by men. The regime insisted that women were leading patriots, equal to men at the front.

The wartime patriotic duty of a woman, which largely reaffirmed her primary role as mother rather than worker, was extended further at the end and immediately after the war. Over 28 million Soviet citizens died during the Great Fatherland War and therefore it was the duty of women (who outnumbered men by almost 26 million in 1946) to replenish the population and overcome wartime losses. The 1944 family law attempted to promote large families by awarding military-style decorations for motherhood. Women with five children earned a second-class Motherhood Medal; those with six won a first-class Motherhood Medal; Motherhood of Glory went to mothers of seven, eight and nine children. Ten children brought the title Heroine Mother and a certificate of the USSR Supreme Soviet Presidium. The 1944 legislation encouraged even unmarried women to reproduce. Single parents could choose to rear children with the help of the state. The traditional virtues of motherhood were asserted with this legislation: women's happiness was supposedly rooted in having children rather than directing farms or factories. By the end of 1945 the 'New Woman' was primarily maternal and domestic, thereby overshadowing the short-lived wartime status of 'Superwomen'.

Questions

1 Why were so many women attracted to Bolshevism? Identify and define the main tenets of Bolshevik feminism.

2 Why did Lenin's penchant for a centralised Party and state lead to the exclusion of women from leading positions?

3 Distinguish between the ideological stances of the 'new' and 'older' generation of female revolutionaries following the October 1917 Revolution.

4 'Advances in women's politics were determined by the political priorities of the Party leadership at any one time.' Discuss.

5 'The Civil War militarised the image of the female revolutionary indefinitely.' Discuss.

6 What was the most important revolutionary task performed by female revolutionaries in the period between February and October 1917? Why was this the high point of female revolutionary activity?

7 Compare and contrast the feminist ideas of Inessa Armand and Alexandra Kollontai. Were their ideas misguided? How did they contribute to the work of the *Zhenotdel*?

8 Discuss the proposition that revolution, collectivisation and industrialisation guaranteed women's rights and that through these changes, women achieved what they wanted.

9 'The 1920s were libertine whilst the 1930s were draconian as regards the question of female liberation.' Discuss.

10 'The Great Fatherland War presented "Soviet woman" with the challenge of balancing motherhood and worker with that of warrior.' Discuss.

Further reading

Marilyn French, *From Eve to Dawn: A History of Women*, Vol. III (2003); Richard Stites, *The Women's Liberation Movement in Russia: Feminism, Nihilism and Bolshevism, 1860–1930* (1991); Barbara Evans Clements, *Daughters of Revolution: A History of Women in the USSR* (1994); *Bolshevik Women* (1997); Catriona Kelly and David Shepherd (eds), *Constructing Russian Culture in the Age of Revolution: 1881–1940* (1998); Linda Edmondson (ed.), *Gender in Russian History and Culture* (2001); Sheila Fitzpatrick and Yuri Slezkine (eds), *In the Shadow of Revolution: Life Stories of Russian Women from 1917 to the Second World War* (2000).

CHAPTER 6

The New Economic Policy

Five decisive issues

Paul Gregory suggests that there were five key issues during the 1920s:

1   What economic system should be chosen? The continuation of a mixed economy, the NEP economy, or forced collectivisation, the elimination of the kulaks and super-industrialisation? The right favoured a mixed economy; the left rapid collectivisation and industrialisation.

2   Would the Party have one common policy – a general line – or would it tolerate a variety of views? Would the Party permit factions or was every comrade to unite under one policy banner? Politburo members were permitted to have their own views. However, Party discipline required everyone to fall behind a decision once it had been taken. Bukharin, Rykov and Tomsky, a trade union leader, disagreed with the Great Breakthrough of 1929 but loyally defended it. Rykov, as Prime Minister, began to implement it even though he disagreed with it. However, Stalin wanted a Politburo of like minds. He had to manufacture deviations from the general line in published articles or speeches in order to remove critics from the leadership. Bukharin was astonished to hear that he was being expelled, in July 1929, for making 'masked attacks' against the Party line in his speeches and articles. Rykov, in June 1930, was framed. He was accused of organising an opposition group.

3   Would the state have its own power base separate from that of the Party or would state institutions be subservient to the Party? In essence, a Party-state. Lenin devoted little attention to this question. But it was of acute concern to Stalin as his main opponents controlled the reins of government. Rykov, the Prime Minister, survived the first round of expulsions from the Politburo.

However he was removed in December 1930. Stalin could now appoint his own Prime Minister. Politburo decrees were now either promulgated as Central Committee decrees or as government directives. Important Politburo decrees were joint Party–government decrees. A government decree could be rejected by Stalin. Most decrees were top secret and not published.

4   How much democracy should be allowed to the rank and file of the Party? Should they be able to influence the central Party apparatus? The leadership had to ensure that workers did not take matters into their own hands. The Soviet Union was a workers' state but the Party had to ensure that this was not taken literally.

5   Was there to be a collective leadership or a single dictator? Stalin deployed great political skill in the 1920s. He needed to win the support of some 40 regional and national leaders in the Central Committee to expel the Left Opposition, in 1926, and the Right Deviationists, in 1929 and 1930. He needed the support of delegates at the 15th Party Congress, in December 1927, to push through the Great Breakthrough. A tactic he deployed to gain the support of regional Party bosses was to award them investment projects. In this way he outflanked the Right Deviationists.

The General Secretary (Gensek)

Stalin had accumulated an impressive range of offices before he became Gensek: People's Commissar for Nationalities (1917–23); of State Control (from 1919); and of the Workers' and Peasants' Inspectorate (Rabkrin) (1920–22); member of the Military-Revolutionary Council of the Republic (Revvoensovet) (1918–20); the Party Secretariat (from 1918); Orgburo (from 1919) and the new Politburo (from 1919). Yakov Sverdlov would have been the natural candidate for Gensek but he was dead. No one else was as well qualified as Stalin. This made some of his Politburo colleagues a little queasy but they identified Trotsky as a greater danger to their ambitions than Stalin. This was again a piece of good fortune for the Gensek. He had a file on everyone. He was the best informed comrade in the Kremlin by simply eavesdropping on every conversation on the Kremlin telephone system, the *Vertushka*. Dzierzynski was a useful ally in the collection of intelligence. Stalin was particularly keen to identify Trotsky's supporters among Party officials and run-of-the-mill communists.

Stalin's tactic was quietly to build up a Party apparatus which paralleled that of government commissariats. Krupskaya complained to Lenin, in 1921, that Stalin had built up a large agitation and propaganda (agitprop) department which looked like a 'full-blown new commissariat'. It duplicated the political education department, which she headed, of the Commissariat for Enlightenment

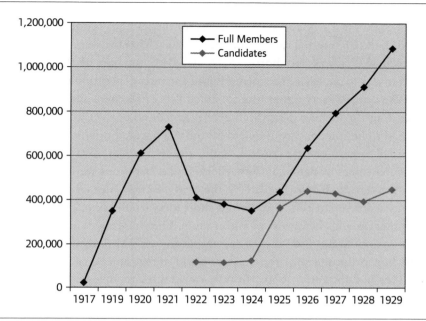

FIGURE 6.1 Party membership, 1917–29

Source: Based on data in Richard Overy, *The Dictators: Hitler's Germany and Stalin's Russia* (2004).

(Narkompros). Lenin asked Stalin not to bother himself with agitprop. Stalin fudged the issue by challenging the numbers but also claimed that he had been forced to assume responsibility for this department. He refused to give it up (Lewin 2005).

Stalin struck up a tactical alliance with Zinoviev and Kamenev. They would meet before Politburo meetings, either in Zinoviev's flat or Stalin's Central Committee office, to discuss the agenda. They would agree on policy and the roles to be played by each member of this troika. They proved so effective that they out-manoeuvred Trotsky and the Left Opposition in 1923–24. In 1924–25, the troika became the group of seven with the addition of Nikolai Bukharin, Aleksei Rykov, Mikhail Tomsky and Valerian Kuibyshev. They had one principal aim: prevent the rise of Trotsky.

In theory, the Politburo took decisions and the Orgburo allocated resources. Gradually decisions of the Orgburo acquired the weight of decisions of the Politburo; and decisions of the Secretariat became decisions of the Orgburo. The only way a decision of the Secretariat could be nullified was by a motion passed at a CC plenum. Stalin was the only person who was a member of the Politburo, Orgburo and Secretariat.

The minutes of the Orgburo and the Secretariat reveal a stunning number of items on the agenda of each meeting. They attempted to micromanage a huge country from Moscow. They go into the minutest detail. There are telegrams, signed by Stalin, to Party and state agencies, for instance, to supply nails to a building site or build an internal railway in a steelworks. There were many about barbed wire which was always in short supply. Another function of the Orgburo and Secretariat was to supervise the formation of the next generation of specialists and cadres. The central Party apparatus compiled lists of teachers and students and set up colleges and academies. Since Stalin believed that no one was irreplaceable, there always had to be someone available to fill the slot vacated by some unfortunate.

In order to gain greater control, Stalin set up a private secretariat, called the general department or personal chancellery. Its deliberations were kept secret from the CC Secretariat. It was headed by the very discreet Aleksandr Poskrebyshev. Stalin was a short man and he preferred short men around him. Poskrebyshev was so small that only his head was visible at table. The chancellery had a secret line of communication. Stalin used this to communicate with Molotov. The latter would forward him proposals and the master would agree, amend or veto them. If he agreed, they had the force of law. In this way Stalin circumvented Sovnarkom and other institutions.

Other loyal allies were the Armenian Anastas Mikoyan, who had a flair for commerce; Lazar Kaganovich, who became Stalin's deputy during the 1930s and retained his position by being sycophantic and brutal; Sergo Ordzhonikidze, a fellow Georgian, but who was to find Stalin too demanding; Kliment Voroshilov, who could keep an eye on the military; and Georgy Malenkov, who was to prove himself a skilful manager. And there was Felix Dzierzynski. All these comrades recognised Stalin as someone who was upwardly mobile. They hitched themselves to his chariot.

Trotsky's problem was that he disagreed fundamentally with Lenin on certain issues. One of these concerned the role of trade unions. After NEP was introduced, Lenin was keen to give the trade unions more autonomy in order to develop the economy. However, Trotsky favoured continuing with paramilitary methods to discipline the labour force. The issue was to come to a head at the 11th Party Congress, in 1922. Weakened by illness, Lenin asked Stalin to spearhead the campaign against Trotsky. He did this with considerable relish. Every comrade could see that Trotsky opposed Lenin and that Stalin represented Lenin.

Trotsky was unable to benefit from Lenin's denigration, in the first addendum (dated 4 January 1923) to his testament or will, of Stalin's talents. (One Russian scholar thinks the testament was a forgery (Kuromiya 2005).) In the addendum Lenin had suggested that 'comrades think of a way of removing Stalin from that post [Gensek]'. The need for Party unity was paramount and an outward show of solidarity was imperative. Trotsky had a lot to complain about. In October 1923 he had penned a letter to the CC complaining about the practice of nominating rather than electing persons to important Party posts. Then, in October, the Platform of the Forty Six, castigated current practice. 'Free discussion within the Party has practically disappeared . . . the secretarial hierarchy . . . decides the composition of conferences and congresses.' The latter had become the executive assemblies of the new hierarchy. Needless to say, the CC declared that Trotsky and his allies were profoundly wrong in their analysis.

With Lenin's death imminent, Trotsky was packed off to Abkhazia for two months. The Kremlin commandant, in Stalin's pocket, wrote to Nestor Lakoba, on 6 January 1924:

'I consider the best place for him is . . . where you used to accommodate comrades Dzierzynski and Zinoviev. Comrade Trotsky has been prescribed complete rest by the doctors and although our people will provide Trotsky's guards, I never the less ask you, dear comrade Lakoba, with your sharp eye and care, to take comrade Trotsky under your wing . . . I am sure you understand me completely. Obviously there are to be *no* meetings or formal parades.'

On 18 January 1924, three days before Lenin died, Dzierzynski made it even plainer to Lakoba that Trotsky was to be isolated:

'Comrade Lakoba! Dear comrade! Because of the state of Trotsky's health, the doctors are sending him to Sukhumi [to the south of Abkhazia and even further from Moscow] . . . Because of his state of health, comrade Trotsky will not generally be able to leave his dacha and therefore your main task is to prevent any outsiders or unknown persons entering.'

After Lenin's death, Stalin dictated a telegram to Trotsky:

'To Yagoda; to be given immediately to Trotsky. I regret that it is technically impossible for you to arrive in time for the funeral. There are no reasons to expect complications. Under these circumstances we see no need to interrupt your treatment. Naturally we leave a final decision to you.'

Trotsky acknowledged that he was in no fit state to make public speeches. The thought occurs to one that since Stalin and Dzierzynski supervised Trotsky's medical treatment, they had an interest in ensuring that this troublesome comrade did not recover quickly. He was out of Moscow at a vital time. He presumed that he would get the call at the 13th Party Congress, in May 1924. But supreme office does not just fall like manna from heaven; it has to be grasped. Stalin understood this. Trotsky had the ammunition to damage Stalin at the Congress – Lenin's testament. However, when it was read to CC members, Trotsky remained silent. A majority of CC members voted for Stalin to retain his post of Gensek. At the Congress everyone voted for Stalin to retain his post. At the CC plenum after the Congress the same happened. Then Stalin offered to give up his position in the Politburo, Orgburo and Secretariat and be sent to Turkhansk, Yakutsk or overseas. Again Stalin received unanimous support to retain his positions. Presumably the reason why Trotsky was reluctant to challenge Stalin was fear of being accused of splitting the leadership so soon after Lenin's death. Unity was the norm. This was another occasion on which Stalin's luck held. Tactically Stalin wanted Trotsky inside the Politburo and not outside. If expelled from the Party he could become a loose cannon. Even after losing his last great state office, People's Commissar of the Army and Navy, in January 1925, Stalin voted to keep him on the Politburo.

The scissors' crisis

Nineteen twenty-one was a hungry year but 1922 was better. In 1924, agricultural output was back to 1913 levels. However, peasants were consuming more. Peasants only marketed 60 per cent of what they produced in 1913. Industry did not fare as well. Global output in 1924 was only 45 per cent of the level of 1913. One of the reasons for this was that agriculture was providing fewer inputs to industry. The state had to export grain and agricultural products in order to import vitally needed machinery. Hence the key question concerned the terms of trade between the town and the countryside. Foreign trade was a state monopoly but most domestic trade was in private hands. Merchants and traders – the nepmen – held back industrial goods to ensure higher prices. Industrial prices therefore rose but the good harvest of 1922 saw agricultural prices drop. Trotsky graphically labelled this the scissors' crisis. Industrial goods were twice as expensive as in 1913 but agricultural goods only half as valuable. In simple terms, this could mean that a peasant had to supply four bags of grain to buy an industrial product which had only cost him one bag in 1913.

The price of industrial goods was high not because output was low but because of an imperfect market. In late 1923, the government had to act. Bukharin, the most enthusiastic promoter of NEP, demanded lower industrial prices. This would stimulate demand and eliminate high-cost producers. The retail prices of basic necessities such as salt, paraffin and sugar were not to exceed certain limits, decreed the government. The harvest of 1923 was good and the state began exporting grain again. As a result, grain prices rose and the scissors' crisis faded away. The economy jogged along for the next three years while the Party barons fought for supremacy.

Socialism in one country

Trotsky, ever the orthodox Marxist, averred that a socialist economy in Soviet Russia would only be possible after the victory of the proletarian revolution in some advanced capitalist countries. Stalin called this Menshevism. He, unlike Trotsky, had faith in the Russian working class. He claimed that Lenin had been the first to come up with the idea of socialism in one country. This was completely untrue. Stalin's group came up with a clever idea. Socialism could be built in Soviet Russia but the final victory of socialism required the support of the world proletariat. The chief ideologue was Bukharin, now on the right. He was proud of his command of dialectical materialism. He could mesmerise Stalin and other comrades with his scintillating Marxist analyses. Stalin hired a private tutor to teach him dialectics. He could not make head or tail of it so he gave up. Intellectually Bukharin was Stalin's superior but politically Stalin was his superior.

The move to socialism in one country formally ended the period of banking on revolution outside. Trotsky's argument that revolution should be promoted abroad was now rejected. Stalin espoused the idea that Soviet Russia should become autarchic. In other words, produce almost everything itself and become independent of world trade. Trotsky, almost naturally, adopted the opposite approach. He argued that the country should become part of the world economy and in so doing acquire technology and know-how from advanced capitalist countries. Europe needed grain and Russia needed European technology. Why should communist Russia develop advanced technology which could be purchased abroad? Again Trotsky's logic was impeccable.

The United Opposition

The gulf between the left (Trotsky, Evgeny Preobrazhensky), which wanted more rapid industrial growth paid for by the peasants, and the right (Stalin and Bukharin), which was content to allow the peasants to become more prosperous, was unbridgeable. The left thought the state was degenerating and becoming excessively bureaucratic (meaning fewer and fewer officials were taking decisions and more and more were implementing them). In April 1925, Bukharin called on the peasants to enrich themselves. This was too much for Zinoviev, who began making strongly pro-worker speeches and claimed that NEP would not lead to socialism in one country. Zinoviev thought he was impregnable in his Leningrad Party base. At the 14th Party Congress, in December 1925, the left could only muster 65 votes with 559 against. After the Congress, Vyacheslav Molotov, Mikhail Kalinin and Kliment Voroshilov travelled to Leningrad and convinced Party workers to change sides. Sergei Kirov became Party leader there.

Given the popularity of left policies among the proletariat (favouring workers over peasants), how was it possible that the left only mustered 65 votes at the Congress? The answer rests with Stalin's personnel policy. His dominance of the Orgburo permitted him to place his nominees in Party post after Party post. They, in turn, were elected as delegates to the Congress. The Congress then elected a new Central Committee. Each successive Party Congress saw an increasing Stalinist majority. He had become the chief Party patron. Stalin, more than any other Bolshevik, was the master of patronage politics.

Zinoviev was still head of the Comintern and tried to use it in domestic infighting. In July 1926, Zinoviev and Kamenev joined Trotsky and they were labelled the United Opposition. They seemed strange bedfellows. Quite clearly, it was a tactical move forced on them because of the rising power of Stalin. They presented their opposition in the Declaration of the Thirteen. It was a vigorous attack against the pro-peasant views of the majority. This was factionalism. Zinoviev was immediately dropped from the Politburo. He also ceased to head the Comintern. Sergo Ordzhonikidze became a candidate member of the Politburo. In October 1926, Trotsky ceased to be a member of the Politburo and Kamenev was dropped as a candidate member. The United Opposition had had some of their teeth extracted. They were excluded from publishing in the official media and had to revert to clandestine methods. The OGPU, the new name of the Cheka, traced the publications and destroyed the printing presses and broke up their meetings. Bukharin called on them to bow their heads before the Party and say: 'Forgive us for we have sinned against the spirit and the letter and the very essence of Leninism'.

But they were not yet finished. In spring 1927, Trotsky drafted a no-holds-barred attack on the Stalin team. Eighty-three oppositionists signed it. They wanted a more revolutionary foreign policy, rapid industrial growth and a thoroughgoing democratisation of the Party and soviets. They were arguing that the Politburo was taking the revolution in the wrong direction. Heady stuff.

International affairs came to the aid of the United Opposition. Britain broke off diplomatic relations with the Soviet Union in May and Chiang Kai-shek massacred Chinese communists in April. Trotsky berated the Politburo's ham-fisted handling of international affairs. He even declared that his loyalty was to the socialist fatherland and not to Stalin. Their mutual loathing was clear for all to see. Stalin waited until October to apply the coup de grâce. A joint CC and Central Control Commission plenum had a huge anti-left majority. Trotsky, Zinoviev and Kamenev were voted off the CC. In November, Trotsky and Zinoviev were expelled from the Party. In December 1927, at the 15th Party Congress, another 75 leftists, including Kamenev, were removed from the Party.

The economy compounded the problems facing the Stalin leadership. The 1927 harvest was down on the previous year. However, the state offered low prices and there were few industrial goods to buy. The peasants withheld grain and sold higher value products such as meat and dairy produce. As such they were acting in a rational economic manner. To make matters worse, industrial production declined in 1927. This meant that imports of foreign goods had to be curtailed. The government could have adopted the 1925 policy of raising grain prices to bring more grain on to the market, but refused. The only other option was coercion. Grain would be requisitioned to fund industrial expansion.

Kamenev and Zinoviev could not bear life outside the Party and humbly begged for readmission. They acknowledged that their views were anti-Leninist. Stalin readmitted them in June 1928. Trotsky was made of sterner stuff. He and 30 supporters, including Preobrazhensky, were sent into internal exile. Trotsky found himself in Alma Ata (now Almaty), on the Chinese frontier. His wife, secretaries and archive accompanied him. He was permitted to communicate with his supporters inside the country. This was an astute move. It made it simpler for the Chekists to identify Trotskyites.

The 15th Party Congress adopted a Five Year Plan (1928–32) of economic development. The 'socialist offensive' was under way. Capitalist elements in the towns and countryside were to be liquidated. This sounded like a victory for the left. Even Bukharin and Rykov, on the right, supported the more rapid expansion of industry. Stalin still played the role of the moderate. He warned that the kulak had to be countered by using economic means and socialist legality.

Not enough grain and food products were reaching the cities at the end of 1927. Members of the Politburo set off for Ukraine, the Volga and the north Caucasus – the traditional food surplus regions. Stalin made for the Urals and Siberia. Ostensibly he was there to investigate why agricultural products were not coming on to the market. In reality, he reverted to the tactics of war communism using article 107 of the USSR Penal Code. This envisaged three years in prison for 'speculation', meaning high prices. Villagers were brought together and asked who was hoarding grain. Those who informed would receive some of the grain themselves. The grain was then seized and this tactic, dubbed the 'Urals-Siberian method', was deployed throughout the country. In February 1928, Stalin returned in triumph to Moscow with wagonloads of seized grain. *Pravda* celebrated his success, Bukharin was outraged. The FYP had proposed voluntary collectivisation. The 15th Congress had actually envisaged that in 1933 three-quarters of the peasant population would still be living in private households.

Stalin unilaterally substituted his own plan. Collectivisation was to remove not only the kulak but also the individual peasant producer as a supplier of grain and food products to the state. In early 1928, Molotov added a significant remark. Referring to the reluctance of the kulak to sell to the state, he argued that the kulaks should be dealt such a blow that the 'middle peasants would jump to attention'. In 1927, middle peasants made up 62.7 per cent of the peasantry. There were only about a million kulak households or 3.9 per cent of all peasants.

TABLE 6.1 Output, state procurement and prices of grain

	1926–27	1927–28	1928–29
Grain production (million tonnes)	74.6	72.8	72.5
Grain Procurement (million tonnes)	11.6	11.1	9.4
Wheat price in private market (rubles per tonne)	86.1	89.2	112.0
State procurement price (rubles per tonne)	64.8	62.2	61.1

Source: Paul Gregory, *The Political Economy of Stalinism* (2004).

Hence state procurement prices for grain declined from 1926–27 onwards while private market prices rose. The procurement crisis was restricted to state procurements. It was provoked not by a kulak conspiracy, but by state pricing policy. State grain prices, by 1928–29, were below average production costs. So the peasants began switching to industrial crops, such as flax, and feeding more grain to their animals. This was because the profit from producing technical crops and meat and milk products was much higher than for grain. Some peasants actually burnt their grain rather than sell it to the state.

Was Stalin an economic illiterate who thought that peasants would sell grain to the state at half price? No. He had a good grasp of the working of the agricultural market. The Preobrazhensky model of primitive capital accumulation required the state to acquire grain at low prices. It could then sell the grain at much higher retail prices and export the rest. If the grain was sold to private traders the state lost its profit. Stalin's correspondence with Molotov, who became chair of Sovnarkom or Prime Minister in December 1930 when Stalin turned down the job himself, clearly underlines the link between procuring grain at low prices and the use of force. Stalin was quite aware that the peasant would not sell at half price to the state.

All this sounded the death knell of NEP. Bukharin could protest in vain but Stalin now had a Politburo majority in favour of coercive collectivisation and rapid industrialisation. In November 1929, Bukharin was voted off the Politburo. At the 16th Party Congress, in July 1930, Mikhail Tomsky was not re-elected to the Politburo. In December 1930, Aleksei Rykov lost his Politburo seat and Sergo Ordzhonikidze moved into the Politburo. Hence in 1930 the right was destroyed and Stalin could adopt the policies of the left. By great tactical skill, he had flitted into and out of alliances. Bukharin, in his naivety, had believed that he was the main beneficiary of the rout of the United Opposition. Stalin was not yet the master of all he surveyed. He had to wait until 1937 before he acquired the power of life and death over everyone, including his Politburo colleagues. Payback time for all the real and imagined insults of the previous two decades was just beginning.

Box 6.1   *Opposition*

Left Opposition (1923–24)   Trotsky and his supporters against Stalin, Zinoviev, Kamenev and Bukharin; they opposed socialism in one country; they favoured international revolution; they criticised the decline of intra-Party democracy.

Right Opposition (also known as Right Deviation) (1928–29)   opposed rapid industrialisation and forced collectivisation and favoured the continuation of NEP; the retention of the class alliance between workers and peasants; Bukharin, Rykov and Tomsky leading members.

United Opposition   formed in mid-1926; Trotsky, Zinoviev, Kamenev against Stalin and Bukharin; opposed their pro-peasant policies; favoured faster rates of industrial growth; defeated in 1927.

Democratic Centralists (1919–21)   opposed increasing centralisation; militarisation; and bureaucratisation.

Workers' Opposition (1919–21)   opposed central management of economy; one-man management; favoured collective management at enterprise level.

The Party apparatus

Stalin had a clear vision of the type of apparatus he wanted to fashion. Party cadres were to be cogs in a machine which was to build a strong state. Then it was to launch industrialisation. Trotsky and others often railed about the bureaucratisation of the Party and government. By this, they meant that the leading cadres took the decisions and their subordinates implemented them. This flew in the face of Party democracy. Bureaucratisation had also afflicted Soviet bodies at the local and national level. The Party Control Commission was inundated with complaints from Party organisations about the behaviour of Party bosses. The Party's information service summarised these complaints for the use of its top cadres. There were many strikes and the reaction of Party members who had participated in them was described. Often the bulletins sided with the strikers and criticised the incompetence of Party and government bosses.

The Party was a pyramid. At the top, the Politburo, Orgburo and Secretariat; their executive was the central Party apparatus; in the middle the republican, krai and oblast committees, each with its own apparatus; and at the bottom all the raion committees and their apparatuses. There were two other, much larger, pyramids: the soviets and Sovnarkom, the government. The Party apparatus was to monitor the activities of these two pyramids. By 1929, the Supreme Soviet of each republic was subordinate to the USSR Supreme Soviet. Local soviets were, of course, subordinate to their own republican Supreme Soviet. They were also subordinate to the local agencies of Sovnarkom. The Party CC apparatus, to carry out its functions of supervision, established parallel bodies. Hence there were two parallel apparatuses: the governmental and the Party. The task was made easier by the fact that the Prime Minister and other important government commissars were members of the Politburo. At the base, each workplace had a Party cell. These were integrated into a Party organisation embracing the enterprise or commissariat. Furthermore, most key positions in government administration were held by Party members. A major problem facing the Party apparatus was how to monitor a growing governmental administration.

Many Party apparatchiks, in the 1920s, had been though the fires of the Civil War and had given their all to the Party. A significant proportion became disillusioned during the 1920s. The increasingly hierarchical structures rendered their work routine. They quickly became bored. 'Working in the apparatus depresses me', was a complaint which tells one a lot about the new apparatus coming into being. Christian Rakovsky, exiled to Astrakhan as a supporter of Trotsky, provided a perceptive analysis of what was happening. He saw the Party as an aggregate of hundreds of thousands of individuals. What united them was not an ideology but a fear for their own safety. Rakovsky knew that the Party could not be regenerated. He saw the second FYP (1933–37) as promoting the 'total separation of the Party bureaucracy from the working class'. It would become a 'ruling stratum supported by the state apparatus' (Lewin 2005).

What about rank and file Party members? Many of them joined the league of the disillusioned. Between 1922 and 1935 around 1.5 million left the Party. The usual way of doing this was failing to pay dues or when one moved jobs or addresses omitting to register with the local Party branch. This was done without fear of reprisals. However, these ex-members, now labelled enemies of the people, were one of the targets of the purges of 1937–38.

Was NEP in crisis in the late 1920s?

■ From the point of view of a market economy, NEP was not in crisis. The reason for the difficulties of the time was the refusal of the state to pay market prices for grain. The peasant acted as a rational economic actor and declined to sell in the hope prices would rise.

■ From a Marxist point of view NEP was in crisis. The number of kulaks was declining because a farm with, say, three horses, was divided into three farms, one retained by the father and the other two taken over by sons. This was a reaction to the heavy taxes imposed on kulaks. Some poor peasants were joining up with other poor peasants to produce a viable farm holding. This had led to the number of middle peasants increasing. From a Marxist point of view this was very confusing. Marxists expected the number of kulaks to rise, the number of middle peasants to decline and the number of poor peasants to increase. This was because the kulaks would gradually squeeze out the middle peasants and acquire their land. Middle peasants would gradually become poor peasants. Gradually, the countryside should be dominated by kulaks surrounded by an army of poor peasants. This was not happening. The danger, from a Marxist point of view, was that capitalism would become stronger in the countryside and delay the move to socialism.

- In a country which was still dominated by peasants, the above scenario was depressing. Stalin's response was to engineer a crisis in grain procurements and then to advocate collectivisation as the only solution to the grain problem.

How did Stalin become top dog?

- Stalin was never seen as a future national leader. Hence he was not regarded as a threat to the ambitious.
- This made him appear modest and moderate.
- He understood the importance of personnel policy better than anyone else.
- This permitted him to place his nominees in positions of power. However, in the early years he could not openly advocate loyalty to himself. He could only hint that a person would progress if he supported him.
- He was a brilliant personnel manager. He could select the right person for the right task.
- He was a member of the CC Secretariat. This permitted him to influence the composition of Party committees, the CC and Party Congresses.
- He was a member of the Orgburo which allocated resources under the direction of the Politburo.
- He was a member of the Politburo.
- He was a member of Sovnarkom.
- As Commissar for Nationalities he was responsible for all non-Russians.
- He was head of the Workers' and Peasants' Inspectorate (Rabkrin).
- He was a member of the Revolutionary Military Council (Revvoensovet).
- He was a member of the Council of Labour and Defence (STO).
- He was the best informed person in the leadership through his personal chancellery, phone tapping of Kremlin lines and Cheka informants.
- Yakov Sverdlov died in March 1919 thus removing the natural candidate for Gensek in 1922.
- His alliance with Dzierzynski meant that the Cheka could be used to Stalin's advantage.

- The ban on factionalism in the Party offered great opportunities to someone who could muster a Politburo majority. ·

- Lenin's death intervened before he could be removed as Gensek.

- He portrayed himself as Lenin's chief disciple after his death even though he had clashed with the 'old man' on several issues.

- Tactically, he was the most skilful of the Bolshevik leadership after Lenin's death.

- In *The Foundations of Leninism*, in 1924, he presented a clear, simple analysis of Lenin's thought. Party members appreciated this. Hence this contributed to his growing reputation as the chief interpreter of Lenin's legacy. He added a little of his own. He declared that socialism could be built in one country, something which Lenin had never said.

- He brilliantly exploited the fact that Russia was a religious country. Marxism-Leninism became the new scriptures which were literally true. He was a fundamentalist. This meant that no revisionist interpretation of Lenin's writings was to be permitted except by Stalin personally. The Party was the church. Party leaders were the bishops. Workers would carry portraits of the leaders in the form of icons. Bukharin once called on the left to admit that they had sinned against the spirit and the letter and the very essence of Leninism. Extraordinary language for an atheist Marxist to use. However, it was very fitting in the Russian context.

- After Lenin's death, Lenin's body was embalmed against the wishes of his widow. Everyone could visit his holy shrine, the Lenin mausoleum in Red Square, Moscow. Stalin, after all, had trained as an Orthodox priest.

- The Trotsky threat was deliberately exaggerated and this permitted the troika of Stalin, Zinoviev and Kamenev to gain an advantage.

- This troika met before Politburo meetings to coordinate policy; later, seven met. The leader was always Stalin although Bukharin thought he was the leader of this latter group.

- The kulak threat was deliberately exaggerated to promote collectivisation.

- Stalin was naturally on the left but could not reveal this while Trotsky was a threat.

- When Trotsky was sidelined he moved to the left.

- His support of NEP was tactical. He was just waiting for the opportune moment to launch a socialist industrial economy.

- His policy of socialism in one country caught the public mood. It increased Russian self-confidence.

Three Marxist models

There were three main Marxist models of development during the 1920s.

■ The Bukharin model
A mixed economy with agricultural growth fuelling industrial expansion. The commanding heights of the economy (heavy engineering, defence-related production, hydrocarbons (oil and gas), electricity generation and distribution, water supply, railways, the post and telephony) would remain in the state's hands. The state monopoly of foreign trade would continue. The state would stimulate agricultural output through market signals. It would tax the better off. The state would buy grain at market prices. It would export grain to earn hard currency to import machinery and industrial equipment. Other commodities, such as minerals and timber, could also be exported. No coercion would be used to stimulate growth or extract a surplus from the peasants. The Bukharin model expected small agricultural holdings to be consolidated so as to achieve economies of scale. The peasant would gradually become a farmer – someone whose economic activity was regulated by market prices. Cooperation among producers would increase and follow the pre-1914 pattern. As Russia industrialised so the share of the agrarian sector in gross domestic product would diminish. Russia would resemble a developed capitalist country with agriculture gradually becoming less important. (New Zealand is an exception to this trend.) Russia's agrarian problem would resolve itself over time. The motor for change would be the market. The Bukharin model can be labelled soft Marxism.

■ The Trotsky model
Trotsky was always an advocate of rapid industrial growth. He found the slow pace of industrialisation during the 1920s very frustrating. The economist, Evgeny Preobrazhensky, developed the concept of primitive capital accumulation in a socialist state. Marx had written about primitive capitalist accumulation under capitalism. Since 80 per cent of citizens were peasants, Preobrazhensky concluded that the capital for socialist expansion would have to come from the agrarian sector. The state would pay low prices for grain and then export as much as possible. The more hard currency that was accumulated the faster industrial development could proceed. There was one major flaw in Preobrazhensky's analysis which he never addressed. Why should a peasant sell grain to the state at low prices? Since the peasant was a rational economic actor he would prefer to sell grain to the private sector at higher prices. If prices in the private sector were low he would store his grain until prices rose. If he accumulated lots of rubles and found that industrial consumer goods were in short supply he would produce less the following

year. Again this was rational behaviour. Preobrazhensky's approach rejected the fundamentals of the market.

Trotsky feared that the Bukharin model could lead to the richer peasants dictating the growth of the industrial economy. As they became richer they would move back to capitalism rather than forward to socialism. Trotsky's supporters were urban workers and Party and government officials around the country. They wanted rapid industrialisation. This would lead to a rise in their living standards. Who would decide industrial growth rates and where would the necessary capital come from? The Party bureaucracy was increasingly falling under the dominance of Stalin. Hence it could not be a Party body. Trotsky favoured a committee of experts – economists, mathematicians, engineers – who would come up with an optimal plan. An optimal plan is one in which the resources of the state are deployed to maximum effect. Gosplan could perform this function. The operational plan – implementing the optimal plan – would be the responsibility of Sovnarkom, the government. Again professionals should dominate – not Party bureaucrats. Naturally Trotsky would be the leader of the country and would have the final say about growth rates. A way would have to be found to extract grain surpluses from peasants at low prices. Trotsky was never given the opportunity of finding a solution to this conundrum. One thing was certain. He would not use the market to stimulate sales.

■ The Stalin model
Stalin wanted rapid industrialisation as much as any other comrade. He had a solution to the problem which Preobrazhensky had skirted around. How were surpluses to be extracted at low prices? As the peasant was a rational economic actor he would not sell to the state at low prices. The solution was simple. Use coercion. Who would fashion the optimal plan? Stalin and his team. It would be the task of Sovnarkom to implement their programme. The rate of capital formation would be directly related to the amount of grain which could be marketed abroad. The state would have to ensure a rising tide of exports to permit the import of more and more machinery and equipment. Dependency on grain exports would be greatest during the initial stages of industrialisation. This dependency would gradually weaken as new machine-building enterprises came on stream in the Soviet Union. Hence the first, say, five years would be the most critical. Since no country had ever attempted to do what the Stalin team had in mind, there were no blueprints. They would have to base their goals on guesswork. This would impose an enormous strain on the planners, Party and government officials and managers responsible for turning dreams into reality.

This model involved constant tension and conflict. In the 1920s F. A. Hayek, a brilliant Austrian economist, assessed the chances of a planned economy succeeding. In the absence of the market, a leader would have to be brutal in order to force through his operational plan. Without using force, the principal at the centre would find that his agents implemented operational plans which maximised their benefits. Local interests would always take precedence over central, state interests. The brutal leader and his team would have to find ways to punish the recalcitrant. In a country the size of the Soviet Union, this would be a mammoth undertaking. If his brutal methods were not successful, he would be forced to become even more brutal. However, there were limits to his brutality. Too much could result in a drop in production. He would have to find the optimal level of brutality. Since no one knew what the optimal level of brutality was, the leader would have to experiment. He would need to deploy enormous political skill to keep control and achieve high growth rates. The brutal leader would, by definition, be a risk taker, even a high risk taker. The Stalin model can be classified as brutal Marxism.

Was the victory of the brutal model inevitable? The Bukharin model, which involved taking advantage of the market economy, would not have resulted in brutality against the peasantry and others. Eliminating the market meant that some mechanism had to be developed to replace market signals. Stalin conceived of the Soviet Union as one giant factory with himself as managing director. His orders had to be implemented. He did not need to work out a detailed operational plan; that was the responsibility of his team. The latter produced mountains of paper and orders. They were responsible for checking that managers met production targets. There was no such thing as a fixed production target; it was always changing. Managers were encouraged to exceed their production targets. They automatically requested more inputs. However, if they obtained more inputs another enterprise obtained less. Stalin's team had the task of managing this high-tension and conflict-ridden system. The amazing thing is that it did not simply collapse.

Had Trotsky defeated Stalin would he have become a brutal dictator? He might have simply phased out the market economy over a period of time rather than abruptly ending it as Stalin did. However, Trotsky was a comrade in a hurry. He would have needed to become a brutal dictator in order to achieve high industrial growth rates. He might have found another method of extracting grain from peasants at low prices. But it is difficult to resist the conclusion that he would have been brutal towards the peasants. His ruthlessness during the Civil War revealed that he was capable of brutality. He would have been presented with the same problems of principal and agent as Stalin. How does one implement one's targets? Human nature almost always chooses the easy option. Rapid industrialisation required huge sacrifices by everyone. How could one achieve success without a certain level of brutality in a non-market environment? Trotsky would, most likely, also have been a brutal dictator. Although it is difficult to imagine his being as brutal as Stalin.

Questions

1   Did NEP contradict Bolshevik ideology – if so why?

2   How viable was NEP?

3   What were the most obvious consequences of NEP for industry, trade and social structure?

4   'Had NEP been retained there would have been no need to collectivise and industrialise in the late 1920s and early 1930s.' Discuss.

5   'Economic crises forced the Bolsheviks to alter their understanding of ideology.' Discuss.

6   Distinguish between and summarise the different types of opposition groups (including the Bolshevik factions) in the 1920s.

7   'The secret to Stalin's success was that he was able to play varying factions within the Bolshevik Party off against one another.' Discuss.

8   'Economic Stalinism as devised in the late 1920s was a far more brutal package than anything that had happened since 1917.' Discuss.

9   Were there any alternatives to Stalin's 'socialism' in the 1920s, and if so what were they?

Further reading

Alec Nove, *An Economic History of the USSR 1917–1991* (1992); Sheila Fitzpatrick, *The Russian Revolution* (1994); Sheila Fitzpatrick, Alexander Rabinovich and Richard Stites (eds), *Russia in the Era of NEP: Explanations in Soviet Society and Culture* (1991).

CHAPTER 7

Diplomats and spies

'An ambassador is an honest man sent to lie abroad for the good of his country.'

Henry Wotton, 1604

The Bolsheviks thought they would have no need for diplomacy or diplomats when they took power. Trotsky, the first People's Commissar for Foreign Affairs, saw himself as the conductor of the world revolution. His task was to prevaricate at Brest-Litovsk until the German comrades took power in Berlin. The German diplomats would then be swept into the rubbish bin of history. In order to undermine the whole concept of diplomacy, the young Soviet state published the secret treaties of the defunct tsarist state. This underlined the predatory, imperialist nature of tsarism. From the communist point of view, acquiring more territory was a thing of the past. Come the revolution, all frontiers would be swept away. One huge, happy socialist family would inhabit the earth. The Bolsheviks also thought they would have no need for a militia or standing army. All that changed in the spring of 1918. The commune state had to give way to a revolutionary state. Diplomats, spies, a militia, a secret police and standing army were all needed.

What were the goals of the new Soviet diplomacy, a despised art until events forced a rethink? They were quite simple: guarantee the security of the state by preventing the coming into being of hostile anti-Russian alliances; and the promotion of revolution abroad. Hence Soviet diplomacy always had two prongs: one based on Realpolitik or the interests of the state and the other promoting revolution. Of course, the two enjoyed a symbiotic relationship. The more countries moved to socialism, the more secure Soviet Russia would become.

The Russian state was weak so its foreign policy was that of a weak state. Lenin came up with the notion of peaceful cohabitation or coexistence with capitalist states. That was on the level of inter-state relations. All the time the Comintern, the Cheka and local Communist parties were gnawing away at the capitalist body politic. Lenin did not see this as a contradiction. It was an example of the dialectic in action.

As diplomatic recognition for the young Soviet state was unlikely, the Bolsheviks concentrated on what they believed capitalists could not resist: making money through trade. Great Britain, then perceived by Moscow as the most important country in Europe, was a special target. Trade negotiations began in June 1920 and resulted in the Anglo-Soviet trade treaty, in March 1921. De facto, this afforded Soviet Russia diplomatic recognition. The talks almost foundered when it was discovered that Kamenev was handing out money to left-wing British newspapers.

This marked the beginning of a more moderate phase in Soviet foreign policy. The failure of the German communist uprising, in March 1921, was another factor. The Comintern also reflected this more pragmatic approach. Even Trotsky pulled in his horns. He told the 3rd Comintern Congress, in June 1921, that in 1919 he had expected revolution in months; now it would take years. Lenin denounced preparations for an armed uprising. Communists were too weak to take on the might of the bourgeois state at present. At the end of 1921, the Comintern called for a united workers' front. Communists were to collaborate with other socialists and trade unions in the common pursuit of a better life for workers. This volte-face was as radical as NEP in domestic policy.

The main stumbling block in normalising relations with capitalist powers was the pre-revolutionary debts of the Russian state. They were the largest in the world at that time. Soviet Russia was bankrupt into the bargain. No agreement could be reached with Britain or France. Indeed it was only under Gorbachev that these debts were repaid, after a fashion. Soviet representatives met envoys from the major European powers, in Genoa, in April 1922, to discuss debts. Lenin would have liked to attend but was advised that if he did so he would probably return to Moscow in a coffin. During the negotiations, the Soviet and German delegations secretly repaired to Rapallo and signed a treaty there on 16 April 1922. The two outsiders had come together to outflank the victor powers. Soviet grain paid for German machinery. The Reichswehr, the German military, could collaborate with the Red Army in producing new weapons and aircraft. The Versailles treaty had restricted Germany to a peacetime army of 100,000 but the agreement with Soviet Russia permitted the training of many more. This agreement, which benefited Moscow more than Berlin, only came to an end with the accession to power of Adolf Hitler in 1933.

The failure of yet another German communist bid for power, in October 1923, caused hardly a ripple in German–Soviet relations. The uprising had been encouraged by the Comintern. The defeat of revolution made communists everywhere even more dependent on the Russian Communist Party.

The parlous nature of Anglo-Soviet relations was evident just before the general election of 1924. A letter, purportedly written by Zinoviev, head of the Comintern, was published in the British press. It called on British communists to form cells in the army as a first step towards a British Red Army. The letter was a forgery but it had its desired effect. Labour lost the election. Germany joined the League of Nations. Moscow proposed a military alliance but Berlin declined. It had decided it could achieve more by looking westwards. Soviet diplomacy was more successful elsewhere. Soviet Russia concluded a treaty of friendship and mutual non-aggression with Turkey (December 1925), Afghanistan, Lithuania, Latvia, Estonia and Persia by the autumn of 1927. Poland refused to sign such a treaty.

The country which held out the greatest hopes for revolution was China. The Guomindang (also known as the Nationalist Party), a political party founded in 1911 by Sun Yatsen, concluded a pact of mutual recognition in May 1924. The USSR was the only European power which was not trying to expand its extra-territorial rights there. It already held the largest concession, about 1,000 sq km, of any foreign power in China. Moscow recognised Chinese sovereignty in Mongolia and it had a long border with the Soviet Union. Moscow instructed Chinese communists to work within the Guomindang. The tactic was to subvert from within and plant communist moles in the organisation. Chiang Kai-shek, the Guomindang Chief of Staff, had trained in Japan and went on a three month mission to Moscow, in 1923. This instilled in him an aversion to communism. However, he was astute enough to conceal this from the Russians. They thought he belonged to the left wing of the Guomindang. The Russians provided advisers and matériel to help the Guomindang in its bid to take over China. When Sun Yatsen died, in March 1925, Chiang sided with those who believed the communists were Trojan horses within the movement. China policy was decided by Stalin but he misjudged Chiang. He thought of him as a lemon which could be squeezed until it was dry and then discarded.

On 6 April 1927, the Beijing authorities raided Russian premises and seized documents which revealed that Moscow's policy was to overthrow the existing government and replace it with their client. Other documents made clear the close links between Moscow and the Communist Party of China (CPC). This outraged Chinese public opinion. Unless the Guomindang acted and dissociated itself from the communists, it could be seen as colluding with Moscow to transform China into a Russian satellite. On 12 April 1927, Chiang gave orders to cleanse the Nationalist Party of communists. He acted first in Shanghai, the headquarters of the CPC. Thousands of communists were killed but the leadership remained almost intact. This spelled disaster for Comintern policy in China but Trotsky was not able to capitalise on Stalin's folly. On the contrary, the Chinese communists had to confess that they had been at fault. A Chinese communist, on a visit to

Moscow in 1928, had the impression that the Comintern was no longer the 'general headquarters of the world revolution' but had become 'Stalin's plaything for bullying communists of various nations'.

After the Shanghai debacle, Stalin ordered the CPC to establish its own army and to occupy territory. The long term aim was to take China by military force. About 20,000 communists led by Zhou Enlai, later to become Mao's number 3 in the People's Republic, left Chiang's forces but many moles remained. They were to play a major role in subverting Chiang's strategy in the war against Japan and in 1947–49. A large secret military aid system was set up in Russia and Russian military agents were sent to major Chinese cities. Comintern agents, often German and Dutch, were to guide policy. Mao now came out with his famous dictum: 'Power comes out of a gun'.

The Whites invaded Outer Mongolia in 1920. However, with the help of the Red Army the locals defeated them and also drove out the Chinese in 1921. The Mongolian People's Republic was officially proclaimed on 24 November 1924. This was the only country to go communist between 1917 and 1945. It was a small return for all the sacrifices of revolutionaries, inspired and marshalled by Moscow. The main reason for the lack of success of the world communist movement was the political and economic weakness of the Soviet Union.

Spies

The Cheka learnt a lot from the tsarist Okhrana. The latter was particularly good at penetrating anti-state organisations and introducing *agents provocateurs*. The Bolsheviks had been at the receiving end. Roman Malinovsky, a comrade whom Lenin trusted, turned out to be an Okhrana agent. He was shot in the Kremlin on the first anniversary of the October Revolution. In the beginning, the Cheka concentrated on domestic matters as an organ for the 'revolutionary settling of accounts with counter-revolutionaries'. The first agent sent abroad was Aleksei Filippov. He had been a newspaper proprietor and was recruited by Dzierzynski at the end of 1917 to go to Finland to gather intelligence on bankers, industrialists and nationalists. Lenin decided that the Finnish communists stood a better chance of taking power if Finland were an independent state. A delegation of Finnish ministers visited Petrograd and were invited to ask for independence. A declaration of secession was signed on 6 December 1917. Finland seceding from the former Russian empire verified Lenin's statement that non-ethnic Russian territories could secede. Of course, Lenin expected a communist Finland to apply for readmission to Russia. Finnish communists launched a coup at the end of January 1918, aided by the Russian military and naval garrison in Helsinki, and took the capital and much of southern Finland. However, the former tsarist general, Karl Mannerheim, rallied nationalist forces. Filippov's main task was to shadow

Mannerheim and find out about his links with the Germans. In April 1918, the Germans intervened and the communists were shattered. Filippov had to return to Soviet Russia post-haste.

In July 1918, Lenin warned of a vast, well planned conspiracy of capitalist powers, first and foremost Britain and France, preparing to choke the life out of the new state. The conspiracy only existed in Lenin's imagination but it set a trend. The Bolsheviks were acutely insecure in a hostile capitalist world. As Marxists they did not believe that anything that happened could be an accident. It had to be part of something else.

The Red Army and the Cheka had to fight for their lives during the Civil War. They were fortunate that the White forces were not coordinated and directed from one centre. During the Civil War the Cheka claimed to have unmasked a series of conspiracies. The first was the 'envoys' plot'. Its moving spirit was Robert Bruce Lockhart, a junior British diplomat. The plot involved diplomats from various embassies and some colourful adventurers.

One of these was Sidney Reilly. He was born Sigmund Rosenblum in Odesa, the illegitimate son of a Jewish doctor. He studied chemistry in Vienna before going to Brazil. He became attached to British intelligence and changed his name to Reilly in 1899. He reported to London on Baku oil, Persian affairs and Russian naval facilities in Port Arthur, Manchuria. In 1905, he was instrumental, disguised as a French Catholic priest on the Riviera, in gaining oil concessions for Britain in Persia, in the face of fierce French competition. Or so the story goes. As manager of a German shipbuilding agency in St Petersburg, he gained access to German naval plans and relayed them to London before 1914. He made many sorties behind German lines during the war. On one occasion he attended a meeting of the German General Staff in the presence of Kaiser Wilhelm II. At least this is what he claimed. The mixture of fact and fantasy led to his dismissal from the British Secret Intelligence Service. He arrived in Moscow on 7 May 1918 and made sure he was noticed. He marched up to the gates of the Kremlin, declared that he was an emissary of Prime Minister David Lloyd George and demanded to see Lenin. The guards ignored him (Andrew and Mitrokhin 1999).

The most sophisticated part of the envoys' plot was contributed by the Cheka. In August 1918, a Cheka *agent provocateur* managed to convince Bruce Lockhart, the French consul-general and Reilly that a commander of a Latvian regiment in the Kremlin was ready to lead an anti-Bolshevik uprising. Reilly gave him 1.2 million rubles. Reilly came up with some startling ideas. One was to capture Lenin and Trotsky, remove their trousers and parade them, in their briefs, through the streets of Moscow! As the whole world laughed, the Bolshevik revolution would collapse. On 30 August, Moisei Uritsky, the Cheka chief of Petrograd, was shot dead and Vladimir Lenin was shot. The Cheka had no more time for the envoys' plot and declared on 2 September that they had liquidated it. The Cheka claimed that the envoys were the 'organisers' of the attack on Lenin and the 'real murderers' of Uritsky. Red Terror descended on the land. The Cheka executed hundreds in Petrograd and arrested thousands more. Among the victims was Aleksei Filippov, the Cheka's first foreign agent.

The Cheka sent an increasing number of agents behind enemy lines during the Civil War. The number increased so rapidly that a special illegal operations department had to be set up. 'Illegal' operations now became an integral part of foreign intelligence. On the third anniversary of the founding of the Cheka, on 20 December 1920, a new foreign department (INO) was established to run all operations beyond the borders of the Soviet state. Initially almost all agents abroad were illegals. However, as diplomatic and trade missions were set up, legal agents could be placed there. The head agent was called the *rezident* or resident. Only the ambassador knew his identity but, of course, the ambassador could be the *rezident*. Illegals did not report to the *rezident* but to the INO in Moscow.

The Cheka, in late 1919, boasted that it had wiped out '412 underground anti-Soviet organisations'. Lenin and Dzierzynski were convinced that every western agency was an integral part of the worldwide capitalist conspiracy against Soviet Russia. They were particularly suspicious of the American Relief Association (ARA) which they had been forced, in August 1921, to allow into the country to relieve the terrible famine. They thought that food was being used as an instrument of subversion. Starving Chekists were not to be fed by the Americans lest they succumb to 'imperialist temptations'. The Cheka thought that 200 of the 300 aid workers were agents who could become 'first class instructors for a counter-revolutionary coup'. ARA's large food reserves in Vienna were, in reality, a support base for a White seizure of power. Soviet intelligence remained convinced that the whole operation was an espionage exercise. A quarter of a century later all Russian employees had to sign a declaration that they had been American spies.

The first significant head of INO was Mikhail Trilisser, a Russian Jew. His main pre-revolutionary occupation had been tracing police spies among Bolshevik émigrés. Lenin was keenly interested in foreign intelligence. He regarded Arthur Ransome, who later became a successful British novelist, as an important source. Ransome may not have been a Soviet agent but his Russian wife certainly was. The defeated Whites settled in France, Germany and other countries. Penetrating their organisations became an important task for INO. Lenin thought there were up to 2 million White émigrés and everyone was plotting the downfall of the communist regime. In truth there were White anti-Bolshevik groups in Paris, Berlin and Warsaw (Andrew and Mitrokhin 1999).

Another perceived threat was from the remnants of the Ukrainian nationalist forces which had escaped abroad. A General Tutyunnik was identified as promoting a network of nationalist underground cells. The task was to lure Tutyunnik back to Ukraine and arrest him. The ploy was to set up fictitious anti-Bolshevik underground groups which would welcome Tutyunnik and other White generals as leaders of an uprising. He returned in June 1923, assured by one of his close associates that everyone was waiting for him. The associate was, in reality, a double agent. Those waiting for him were the Ukrainian GPU. Letters were written in his name to prominent Ukrainian nationalists abroad stating that the struggle was hopeless and that he had changed sides. He was executed six years later.

The OGPU identified Boris Savinkov as a particularly dangerous White Guard plotter. He had served as a deputy minister of the Provisional Government and was known to Winston Churchill, who wrote effusively about him. Later Savinkov formed a Russian army which fought with the Poles against the Red Army. This made him a Bolshevik *bête noir*.

According to recent research, the first Czechoslovak President, T. G. Masaryk, was apparently involved in a plot to assassinate Lenin between 1917 and 1921. In March 1918, following a meeting with Boris Savinkov in Moscow, Masaryk supposedly instructed the secretary of the Czechoslovak National Council in Russia, the legionary Jiří Klecanda, to pay Savinkov 200,000 rubles to coordinate and carry out the deed. During cross-examination at his trial in Moscow in August 1924, Savinkov confirmed these details.

Savinkov established an anti-Bolshevik organisation in Warsaw which sent agents into Soviet Russia. The Chekists had a mole in the Warsaw organisation. A show trial was arranged for 44 captured members. Savinkov then repaired to Paris. An agent, posing as an anti-Bolshevik, visited Savinkov and invited his aide to come to Moscow to link up with an underground organisation. When the aide got to Moscow, he was arrested by the Chekists and changed allegiance. He returned and spun a convincing tale. Savinkov and some of his supporters crossed the Soviet border and fell into the arms of the Chekists. At his trial he was sentenced to 15 years in prison. He failed to realise that his cell-mate was a Chekist officer. He patiently debriefed him over a period of eight months. When the Chekists decided that there was nothing more to learn, Savinkov was pushed out of a window to his death. Other sources maintain it was suicide.

In 1921, the OGPU invented the Monarchist Association of Central Russia (MOR) to entice royalists back to the country. A Chekist officer, a Soviet foreign trade representative, pretended to be a secret MOR member and won the confidence of a Grand Duke and a White general. The operation was also intended to net Sidney Reilly. He was increasingly confusing reality with fantasy. On one occasion, apparently, he was convinced he was Jesus Christ. In September 1925, he fell for the same ploy as Savinkov. He believed he was to meet MOR members. Once across the border, he was arrested. He wrote a letter to Dzierzynski promising to tell all he knew about British and American intelligence and the Russian émigré community. In November 1925, he was taken for a walk in the woods. He was dispatched with a bullet in the back. The MOR deception was finally exposed in 1927, to the huge embarrassment of British, French and other intelligence services. They had been completely taken in by it. The Russians were becoming masters of deception.

Security in British embassies was almost non-existent at this time. The first major coup for INO was penetrating the British embassy in Rome, in 1924. An Italian employee was recruited to pass on secret documents and even a diplomatic cipher. The technique was quite simple. The Italian was made an offer he could not refuse: bags of money. He also provided copies of Foreign Office analyses of world events which were forwarded regularly to ambassadors. For a decade or so he supplied about 150 pages of classified material a week. Moscow's reading of this goldmine of information was that Britain was probably planning an attack on the Soviet Union. The Rome *rezident* was instructed to acquire 'details of the English plan' (Andrew and Mitrokhin 1999).

If 1924 was a golden year, 1927 was a disaster. Sooner or later western intelligence services were bound to strike it lucky. Early Russian cipher systems were not sophisticated. A large number of inexperienced agents were being sent from Moscow and the Comintern was turning out a stream of enthusiastic comrades for work in the West. One of these was Richard Sorge, a German in Tokyo, who became one of the century's most successful spies.

In March 1927, the Poles uncovered a large OGPU spy ring, probably by breaking ciphers. Soviet spies were detected in Turkey, Switzerland, China and France. In May, the Austrian government trapped some of their Foreign Office officials passing documents to the *rezident*. The greatest blow of all came when the British Home Secretary announced the discovery of complex spy networks which had been operating in Britain. Britain broke off diplomatic relations with the Soviet Union. The Home Secretary had a field day reading out extracts from decoded telegrams. It was a Pyrrhic victory. The Home Secretary, in publicising a great British counter-espionage success, was revealing to Moscow that its codes had been broken. It then introduced a cipher system which western cryptanalysts could not break until after the Second World War.

The break in relations with London was serious as Britain was perceived to be the most dangerous enemy of the Soviet Union. Japan also turned out to be a serious threat. In 1925, INO had succeeded in intercepting the secret communications of the Japanese military mission and consulate-general in the north-east Chinese city of Harbin. Incredibly, the Japanese communicated with Tokyo by using the Chinese postal service. The Russians recruited agents to intercept, open and photocopy these letters. Then they forwarded the documents to Tokyo in new envelopes with Japanese seals. One of the most alarming documents was acquired in July 1927. In it, Gi-ishi Tanaka, the Japanese Prime Minister and Foreign Minister, advocated the conquest of Manchuria and Mongolia and the eventual occupation of China. He expected Japan sooner or later to have to 'cross swords with Russia'. A second copy of the document was obtained by the Soviet embassy in Japanese-occupied Seoul. It was extracted from the Japanese chief of police's safe. So alarmed was Moscow that INO leaked the document to the US press. The impression was given that the material had come from US intelligence.

The diplomatic break with Britain and the Japanese memorandum convinced Stalin that war was imminent.

> 'It is not a question of some indefinite and immaterial "danger" of a new
> war. It is a matter of a real and material threat of a new war in general,
> and war against the Soviet Union in particular.'

Agents were instructed to search for a similar British memorandum outlining plans for war against the Soviet Union. Their failure to detect one did not alter Stalin's belief that Britain was planning war. In reality, there was no war plan being drawn up in London.

When the Chekist officers arrived at Trotsky's flat, in January 1928, to take him into exile, they found him still in his pyjamas. Stalin had decided Almaty, on the Chinese frontier, was a suitable place. He had originally thought of dispatching him to Japan. Trotsky refused to open the door so the officers broke it down. He was astonished to discover that the officer in charge was a former bodyguard from Civil War days. The officer was overcome with emotion. 'Shoot me! Shoot me!', he wailed. Lev Davidovich comforted him and told him it was his duty to carry out orders, even if they were contemptible. Trotsky would not cooperate. The officers then took off his pyjamas, put on his clothes and carried him to a car to take him to the station. He was put on the Trans-Siberian express.

Trotsky spent most of his time in Almaty writing and receiving telegrams and letters. These ran into thousands. Trotsky was convinced, probably correctly, that many more did not reach him. The Chekists prepared a summary of intercepted correspondence monthly for Vyacheslav Menzhinsky, who had taken over from Dzierzynski, and Stalin. The correspondence contained copious references to Stalin and his entourage. They were called 'degenerates'. Once can imagine Stalin's reaction. The Chekists found Trotskyite prisoners insolent and they enjoyed wrecking their jail from time to time. Stalin concluded that Trotsky was too dangerous within the borders of the Soviet Union. In February 1929, he, his entourage and archive, were deported to Turkey. The Chekists gave him $1,500 to ease his resettlement. This demoralised many of Trotsky's followers. The Chekists were able to turn some of them and they became informers. It declared with pride that it had defeated the Trotskyite menace by the second half of 1929. Stalin was not convinced.

Stalin soon regretted his decision to expel Trotsky from the Soviet Union. It was an astonishing move. An event occurred in the summer of 1929 which confirmed Stalin's worst fears. Yakov Blyumkin, the murderer of the German ambassador in July 1918 and a brilliant Orientalist, paid a secret visit to Trotsky. This would have been of little significance had not Blyumkin been the OGPU's chief illegal resident in the Middle East. He agreed to take a message to Karl Radek, one of Trotsky's former colleagues.

The idea was to link up with like-minded comrades throughout the Soviet Union. INO had a mole in Trotsky's entourage so Moscow knew immediately of the visit. The INO head, Trilisser, baited a trap for Blyumkin. He instructed a sensational blonde to seduce Blyumkin and debrief him in bed. This technique was later dubbed the 'honey trap'. The OGPU and its successors deployed it with exquisite skill on many occasions. She lured him back to Moscow and the Chekists pounced. Blyumkin was interrogated and shot (Andrew and Mitrokhin 1999). The sensational blonde married the Berlin (and later New York) *rezident*. This was about as high as a woman could go in the male-dominated OGPU.

Questions

1 Which factors (internal/external/institutional/ideological) proved decisive in influencing the goals of the new Soviet diplomacy after the Bolshevik Revolution?

2 Outline the key phases of Soviet foreign policy between 1917 and 1921.

3 Why was the Comintern so important for the development of Soviet diplomacy?

4 How did the Bolsheviks attempt to normalise relations with other European countries?

5 'The Bolshevik Party produced great spies but very poor diplomats. This was inevitable given the nature of Party ideology.' Discuss.

6 Which countries were the Bolsheviks eager to maintain good diplomatic relations with and why?

7 What do you regard as the main turning point in the development of Soviet diplomacy between 1917 and 1929? Explain your answer.

8 Why were Germany and China initially so important to Bolshevik diplomacy?

9 'The USSR was not an expansionist state because it was fundamentally weak.' Discuss.

10 What role did the Cheka play in shaping Soviet diplomacy and its perception of foreign powers in the 1920s?

Further reading

Christopher Andrew and Vasili Mitrokhin, *The Mitrokhin Archive: The KGB in Europe and the West* (1999); Christopher Andrew and Oleg Gordievsky, *KGB: The Inside Story of its Foreign Operations from Lenin to Gorbachev* (1990); W. G. Krivitsky, *In Stalin's Secret Service* (2004); G. Edward White, *Alger Hiss's Looking-Glass Wars: The Covert Life of a Soviet Spy* (2004); Victor Cherkashin with Gregory Feifer, *Spy Handler: Memoir of a KGB Officer* (2005).

CHAPTER 8

Society and culture

Winners and losers

Marx divided society into classes. Under capitalism the two main classes were the capitalist class and the working class. The former were the oppressors and the latter the oppressed. Come the socialist revolution, the roles would be reversed. Class was related to the means of production. If one owned a factory and employed labour one was a capitalist. The same applied to a shop. The working class or proletariat sold its labour. Everyone who worked for a wage was a member of the working class. Or were they? What about a doctor who worked for the state? Marx never defined exactly what he meant by class. This caused the Bolsheviks huge problems when they came to divide the new Soviet society into classes. The vast majority of the population were peasants, office workers and employees. One group of peasants could be classified as workers: the landless labourers. Hence the winners in the new society were the industrial workers and landless peasants. However this left the majority of the population unclassified.

Defining class was of crucial importance to the Bolsheviks. They needed to be clear about who their friends were and who their enemies were. During the transition period, called the dictatorship of the proletariat, their enemies could not be recognised as full citizens. The first task was to decide who were the allies of the capitalist class, the bourgeoisie, and who were the allies of the working class. By the early 1920s there were few capitalists left in Russia. Most of the aristocracy had fled or were dead. Who now made up the bourgeoisie? The Bolsheviks, many of them uneducated workers, identified the intelligentsia as the bourgeoisie. They stood out as being educated and hence better off. Other groups were added to the bourgeoisie. Often they had nothing in common with capitalism. They were lumped together and referred to as 'former' people. They included ex-industrialists, nobles, pre-1917 bureaucrats, officers of the Imperial and White armies and priests. Nepmen, who were the traders and manufacturers of the NEP period, formed the new Soviet bourgeoisie. The new ruling class was the proletariat. The vanguard of that class was the Bolshevik Party. But many of the leaders were not of working class origin. The problem was solved by declaring that they were 'proletarians by conviction'. The peasants were either poor peasants, middle peasants or rich peasants. The last, the kulaks, were exploiters since they employed labour.

There were various social groups which formed a swamp between the proletariat and the poor peasantry. There were the white collar workers, or employees, the middle peasants (who were self-sufficient and did not employ regular labour) and artisans. These groups appeared natural allies of the Bolsheviks but the Party was wary of them in the 1920s. The main reason was that it was afraid they would dilute the class-consciousness of the proletariat. The 1918 Russian Federation constitution conferred full citizenship and the right to vote only on workers and poor peasants. Virtually all Soviet institutions during the 1920s practised class discrimination. They deliberately excluded the sons and daughters of non-proletarians from secondary and further education. Needless to say, many classified as 'class aliens' managed by bribery, subterfuge or fraud to penetrate the bureaucracy, Party and higher education. Vigilant communists 'unmasked' them and they were then periodically purged. The courts handed out class justice. A worker received a more lenient sentence than a kulak. It was possible to appeal against one's social classification. Documents, real or forged, were produced to back up one's claim. Hence discrimination promoted corruption and dissimulation.

The 1926 Soviet census (the population was put at 147 million) divided society into two categories: wage earners, the proletariat; and proprietors or those who employed anyone in the town or the countryside. All peasants (except poor peasants) fell into the latter category. A sharp distinction was made between those who employed labour and those who employed only family members. Naturally the losers sought to disguise themselves so that they appeared among the winners. A priest could dress as an employee and become a bookkeeper. The wife of a former official could work as a sales assistant. Everyone spied on everyone else and hoped to benefit from 'unmasking' a 'class alien'. It was just like village life. Trust was a commodity in short supply in Soviet society.

Unmasking aliens reached a fever pitch at the end of the 1920s. The liquidation of the kulaks as a class had been decreed. This meant the confiscation of their property and deportation to the inhospitable east and north. All those regarded as kulak hangers-on were also sent packing. The nepmen were suppressed as urban trade was nationalised. A cultural revolution began which resulted in many 'bourgeois specialists' losing their posts in commissariats, research institutes and enterprises. All 'outsiders' risked losing their jobs, being evicted from their homes

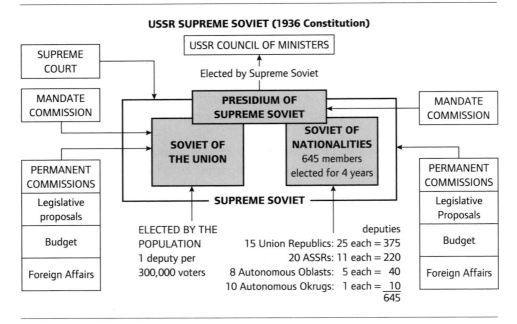

FIGURE 8.1 USSR Supreme Soviet (1936 constitution)
Source: *Stalin and Stalinism*, Pearson Education (McCauley, M. 2003).

and being denied ration cards. Their children were thrown out of universities, the Komsomol and the Young Pioneers (for 10–14 year olds). Hence rural school-teachers who were the sons of priests were sacked. Priests who had gone into industry were unmasked, shamed and rendered unemployed. Even after the elimination of the kulaks as a class, their influence would live on, asserted Stalin. He had in mind their bourgeois mentality, their values and their world view.

Gradually economic rationality reasserted itself. The contribution of the outsiders was recognised and by 1936 all the laws discriminating against non-proletarians were repealed. The 1936 constitution conferred the vote on everyone. On paper everyone was equal. However some were more equal than others. The working class was still the ruling class. The other class was the collective farm (kolkhoz) peasantry. The educated were classified as the intelligentsia and described as a stratum. Internal passports, with one's class recorded, were introduced in 1932. They were issued by the OGPU, the Cheka's successor. Peasants were excluded. They could only move if granted permission by their farms. This was a reversion to the practice of the pre-1917 communes. Hence the 1920s was a period when the majority of the population pretended to be someone else and to move into the coveted category of worker. The Party had a rule that seven years of service qualified one for promotion to the working class. The 'Lenin enrolment' brought many more workers into the Party. Stalin supervised this surge in recruitment and one can presume that many of the new comrades looked to him as their leader. Being a worker and a Party member meant that one had joined the new society's elite.

However, in the mid-1920s it was still possible to be a worker and a Party member and be unemployed. The Red Army slimmed down from 4.1 million to 1.6 million in 1921 and many of the demobilised made for the towns. They were given preferential treatment but the economy was not expanding fast enough to accommodate all of them. There were also peasants streaming in from the miserable conditions in the countryside. Workers' living standards did rise in the 1920s but were still below those of 1913. Women, who had filled the shoes of the men in industry until 1921, were displaced by the returning males. They were normally less skilled and hence earned less. Some industries, such as textiles and tobacco, had a predominantly female labour force. This meant that wages were low.

Traditional forms of association, carried over from the peasant past, flourished in industry, mining, lumber work and construction. Groups of 5–50 workers formed *arteli* to sell their labour. They were normally from the same village or locality. They elected leaders who negotiated terms of employment. They also distributed earnings according to agreed rules. One was to pay the person with the longest beard the highest wages! The older men passed on their skills to the younger. In December 1924, the *arteli* were accorded the right to enter into contracts, hire labour and raise capital. However, their members were excluded from trade unions. The Party was wary of them since they were based on a locality or village and not on class. Paradoxically, the Party did not favour the collectivity and egalitarianism of the *artel*. Aleksei Gastev, an enthusiastic follower of American practice, argued in favour of piece rates. This rewarded those who worked harder with higher wages. The days of the *artel* were numbered. The need to raise labour productivity took precedence during the first Five Year Plan (1928–32). Some *arteli* survived, now called *brigady* (brigades) but they were shorn of their elected leaders. Nevertheless, resourceful workers found new ways of resisting the relentless drive to raise productivity. The Party recruited workers to become leaders and to push aside those whom the workers looked up to. Given the mixed state and private economy of the 1920s, it is not surprising that a class-conscious working class did not emerge.

Peasant resourcefulness

Marx once disparagingly referred to peasants as akin to potatoes in a sack. Even if one put them all together, they remained separate. The Russian revolution had been urban; peasants had made their own and were hard to control as the Bolsheviks were just an island in a sea of peasants. It was much easier to weld workers together. The village commune actually enjoyed greater independence from the state than before the revolution. This was not by design. The communists were weakly represented in rural areas and the village assembly (*skhod*) was more influential than the village soviet. The latter tended to meet, take decisions and then disperse, whereas the assembly, dominated by the richer peasants, had greater influence over day to day affairs. This had to change. Communist efforts to entice peasants into collective farms and cooperatives met with little success. Normally only the losers in the countryside were attracted to this type of farming.

There were about 20 million peasant households in the Soviet Union in the 1920s and upwards of 400,000 communes. Middle and poor peasants accounted for over 95 per cent of the peasantry and they produced about 75 per cent of the marketed grain. The kulaks, making up perhaps 4 per cent, marketed 25 per cent of the grain. Over 40 per cent of rural children did not go to school. More children would have gone to school had it not been for the fact that there was one teacher to every 700 rural dwellers. Doctors were even in shorter supply. There was one for every 17,000 rural dwellers. Just over half of the adults could be classified as literate. The vast majority of illiterates were poor peasants.

Given the above, it is not surprising that the Party was thinly spread in the countryside. Less than 0.3 per cent of rural dwellers were Party members. The chair of the village soviet was usually a communist. He was often a former Red Army man of peasant origin. On average, however, there was not even one communist per village commune in 1929. In that year, about 15 per cent of Party members were classified as peasants. Factory workers made up 42 per cent but 43 per cent were officials and white collar professionals.

Culture

The overwhelming majority of the artistic and cultural intelligentsia welcomed the downfall of tsarism. Most teachers did as well. Exactly the reverse was true about the October revolution. In 1928, there was not a single communist among the academicians of the Academy of Sciences. They regarded the terms Bolshevik and scholar as an oxymoron, a contradiction in terms. Other educated groups were not as hostile. When the Bolsheviks called on intellectuals to attend a meeting to express solidarity with Soviet power, one did turn up: Vladimir Mayakovsky, the poet. Even Maxim Gorky, the darling of the left, turned his nose up at the Bolsheviks. Lenin had spent quite some time courting him in places like Capri before 1917.

The Russian intelligentsia occupied a proud place in European culture. Artists such as the painter Marc Chagall, the pianist Vladimir Horowitz and the composer Igor Stravinsky were not only famous in Europe but throughout the world. Paradoxically, the conservative political culture of Russia had produced some of the world's most radical, experimental artistic talent. Lenin had no desire to take on the intelligentsia after the revolution. He had to secure his political base first. Naum Gabo, the sculptor, has recounted that Lenin visited his studio. After wandering around, Lenin remarked that he could not understand what was going on but, as an artist, Gabo had the right to be creative. Most Bolshevik leaders were educated. Trotsky was above average. Lenin was a cultural conservative but so nervous he feared listening to Beethoven's 'Appassionata'. It deflected his thoughts from revolution!

Eventually the winners were those who wanted to fashion a new revolutionary culture. If the working class was the ruling class then culture should be working class culture. When Stalin became influential he favoured a new Russian intelligentsia, one which would help in the building of the new socialist society. He began to turn this vision into reality from 1929 onwards. Until then many of the old intelligentsia clung on to the hope that scholarship, creativity and respect for the artist and writer would prevail.

The Russian intelligentsia can be divided into various groups. There were those who turned their back immediately on Russia and made for the West. Among these were Ivan Bunin and Vladimir Nabokov, both of whom were to win the Nobel Prize for Literature. Others, like Chagall who was a commissar in Vitebsk for a while, flirted with the new regime but quickly concluded that they could not coexist. They also left. Others went into internal migration, ceased to participate in politics and hoped that the Bolshevik wind would blow over. These included the poet Nikolai Gumilev (shot by the Cheka in 1921) and his wife Anna Akhmatova. Lenin conceded that the communists could not compete intellectually with their critics and deported 160 of them in 1922.

Some members of the intelligentsia left but returned because they could not abandon Russia. These included the composer Sergei Prokofiev, the poetess Maria Tsvetaeva, and the writers Ilya Ehrenburg and Maxim Gorky. The last saw himself as the conscience of the revolution. He was a one comrade loyal opposition but he engaged in some good works. He found employment as a translator for many needy writers. Ill, Lenin encouraged him to go abroad in 1921. He fell for Stalin's flattery in 1931 and returned. He was not allowed to go abroad again and died in 1936. Dark rumours circulated that his death had not been entirely natural.

The Commissar for Enlightenment, 1917–29, was Anatoly Lunacharsky (1875–1933). A Bolshevik from the beginning but nevertheless a civilised man, he had wide cultural interests. He supported Constructivist and Suprematist artists. He and his brother-in-law, Aleksandr Bogdanov (1878–1928), developed the idea that Marxism was a secular religion. Gorky was also taken by this concept. They were disparagingly dubbed God-builders and ridiculed by Lenin in his only major attempt at philosophy, *Materialism and Empiriocriticism* (1908).

Socially conscious writers had been part and parcel of Russian culture. However, at the turn of the century movements evolved which centred on individual human development. The revolution opened up vistas for writers and artists who had yet to make their name. They identified with the workers' and peasants' state and wished to become leading lights in the new proletarian firmament. A group formed, called Proletkult. Some held that the new culture could be built on bourgeois foundations, others that the old culture had to be rejected and replaced by a collectivist worker culture. There should be workers' universities, workers' encyclopaedias and a completely new workers' theatre.

The Party accommodated a wide range of literary and artistic views until 1928. A group called the All-Russian Association of Proletarian Writers (VAPP), formed in 1920, tried to gain a monopoly. In May 1924, a conference decreed that no single group or school or movement should speak for the Party. Bukharin was a leading light in the literary world and a restraining influence. Trotsky regarded the vast majority of artists and writers as fellow travellers. The two leading lights of Bolshevik culture during the 1920s were the poet Sergei Esenin (1895–1925) and Vladimir Mayakovsky (1893–1930). Esenin, of peasant origin, visited the United States but could not cope with urban culture. He wrote that he was glad he was a Bolshevik. Although at heart a pessimist, he was immensely popular. In a fit of depression, he hanged himself and composed a poem in his own blood while dying. Mayakovsky hated Esenin and produced bombastic poetry glorifying the revolution. His poem 'Vladimir Ilich Lenin' came after the leader's death. Lenin regarded most of his work as pretentious nonsense. Depressed by criticism, he shot himself.

The Bolsheviks quickly grasped the potential of the cinema. They used trains as rolling cinemas to impress the peasants. Film makers revelled in the new freedom after February 1917. They quickly discovered that there was a huge market for pornographic films. The Bolsheviks were puritanical and frowned on the depiction of the naked, human body. Some great film directors emerged, headed by Sergei Eisenstein. He became famous for his *Battleship Potemkin* (1925) and *Ten Days that Shook the World* (1927).

Cultural revolution

Lenin understood this term to mean raising the cultural level of the proletariat and peasantry and teaching them good manners and civilised behaviour. From 1928, it meant the militant left attacking fellow travellers and bourgeois specialists. Art and culture were now to serve the Party. It promoted similar campaigns against bureaucrats and bourgeois specialists in industry and education. The way was being prepared for new elites to take over. Students of working class origin now flooded into universities and other centres of higher education. There were only about 40,000 of them in 1928 but five times this number now stormed the gates of academia. In 1930, compulsory primary education was introduced. Workers were upgraded to engineers and managers and the incumbents pushed aside. Previously engineers had received a wide, general education. Now they were given crash courses in narrow specialisms.

There were several schools of Marxist philosophy in the 1920s. That changed at the end of the decade as the evolving philosophy of Marxism-Leninism was accorded dominance. In April 1928, the Academy of Science was forced to admit communists for the first time. In 1930, the Academy was reorganised and admitted postgraduates. They, of course, were communists. The Academy was to function as the main centre of research throughout the country. Academies of Science were set up in the various republics. Entry to the academies was much sought after as they became centres of privilege.

The cultural wars ended in 1932. The Party had won. Literature and art were now to serve the building of the new society. They were to educate the public in the spirit of the new socialist era. They were to depict heroic self-sacrifice and boundless dedication to the new world. Pessimism was banned. Russian Association of Proletarian Writers (RAPP) and other proletarian writers' associations were dissolved in April 1932. All artists and writers were drafted into trade unions. Stalin favoured the emergence of one leader in each discipline. Subdivisions of a discipline were also to be headed by one comrade. This made it easier to check on the implementation of directives. An unkind critic remarked that Stalin was attempting to produce myriads of little Stalins in every field of endeavour.

Why was there so much non-political intellectual diversity during the 1920s?

- The two leading lights of the period 1917–24, Lenin and Trotsky, were educated men. They were intolerant in politics but tolerant of diversity in other spheres.

- Art, literature, science and technology enjoyed considerable freedom to evolve. There was censorship, of course, but there was only one viewpoint which was inadmissible: rejection of the revolution.

- Lunacharsky was commissar until 1929. He was eclectic in his views.

- During the years 1917–28 politics took pride of place. The intellectual world was less important.

- Artistic, cultural and scientific norms were set by the dominant Party group. No political group dominated to the extent that it could set these norms.

- Lenin and Trotsky prevented any single group or movement achieving dominance and acting in the name of the Party.

- Pluralism in intellectual affairs was desirable since it was impossible to decide which group or association represented the best way forward.

- Competing groups and movements looked for patrons among the Party leadership such as Bukharin, Trotsky and Stalin.

- Had one faction won before 1928, its preferred cultural line would have been imposed.

- Science and technology were left unmolested before 1928 because the economy only needed a certain number of scientists and engineers. The first FYP required a huge increase. This meant that standards had to drop. Left to themselves the institutions would not have accepted a dilution of standards.

- The first FYP required a new type of specialist, one who was willing to attempt to do the impossible.

Questions

1 Why was the Bolshevik Revolution an urban affair given that a majority of the population lived in the countryside in November 1917?

2 Initially how did the Bolsheviks interpret 'class' and how and why did their conception change over time? Did they define class according to orthodox Marxism, or was it determined by circumstances inside Russia?

3 How did the role of the cultural intelligentsia change during the 1920s?

4 'The idea of a classless society is nonsense. Even the Bolsheviks practised class discrimination when they prescribed that everybody should become working class.' Discuss.

5 How did peasants attempt to cope with daily Bolshevik life in the 1920s?

6 Why was the Bolshevik Party so poorly represented in the countryside?

7 'The Bolshevik experiment constituted not one but several cultural revolutions.' Discuss.

8 'The cultural sphere provided the best medium for the dissemination of Bolshevik ideology.' Discuss.

9 'The true nature of Bolshevik ideology was exposed in culture rather than in acts of terror and repression.' Discuss.

10 'The Bolsheviks could not have remained in power had they not managed to capture public imagination through cultural means.' Discuss.

Further reading

Sheila Fitzpatrick, *The Cultural Front: Power and Culture in Revolutionary Russia* (1992).

CHAPTER 9

Collectivisation: turning private peasants into state peasants

'Comrade Stalin, should power be based on loyalty or fear?' 'Fear', replied Stalin, 'because loyalty can change.'

'My grandfather grew up in a village where he worked the land with his brother and their children. His neighbour, Petya, was a layabout who slept on the porch of his ramshackle hut and spent the evenings drinking and beating his miserable wife. He would watch with disdain as we sweated in the hot sun building a new barn or bringing home a new cow. When times were hard, Petya would turn up at our door begging. In 1929, Petya appeared at my grandfather's door accompanied by a handful of thugs, sporting a military uniform and cap bearing a red star, and declared: "In the name of Soviet power, I order you to hand over all your property and land to the collective". This is why my grandfather hated communism and Soviet power all his life.'

Source: Paul Gregory, *The Political Economy of Stalinism*, 2004

Stalin and his team felt exhilarated after their forays into the grain surplus areas in early 1928. They came back to Moscow with the booty they had been looking for: grain. Coercion could extract surpluses from peasants. It was only one step from this to the belief that peasants could be herded into collective farms and made to produce surpluses for the state.

The Japanese Prime Minister, in 1927, had given notice of his country's inevitable clash with the Soviet Union. Japan was a resource-poor country and needed to secure raw materials to build up its power. As a country with ambitions to expand its territory it needed to ensure that the Soviet Union and China were not in a position to block it. In 1927, the Red Army could not have coped with the

Japanese army. Then there was the point that every Bolshevik activist wanted rapid industrialisation and the expansion of the industrial working class. If Stalin and his supporters dallied, Trotsky and the Left Opposition might make a comeback.

Was collectivisation inevitable? Was a war against the private peasantry always on the Marxist agenda? There are two main schools of thought. Until the 1970s the received wisdom in the West and the Soviet Union was that coercive collectivisation was inevitable. The Soviet state wished to industrialise rapidly and build up the defences of the country. It needed to secure a food base before it began massive industrialisation. The Red Army had to be fed.

Stalin and the leadership decided that their only option was to confiscate grain surpluses. Private peasants would be corralled into collective farms and effectively become state labourers. They would produce all the grain and food that was needed by the state. Marxists do not accept that the market is efficient. Small peasant plots are also inefficient. Consolidating many smallholdings into large collective farms would permit the use of machinery. This was a rational economic policy. Communists believed that the larger the unit of production the more efficient it should be. The industrialisation of agriculture would end rural backwardness. The peasant labourers would be paid according to what they produced. Payment would come after the harvest was in. If the harvest was poor they could end up with little or nothing. This was a good deal for the state since it paid low prices to the farms. The state would have the produce and could sell it at a handsome profit in the towns and could export the surplus. The capital for industrialisation would mainly come from the work of rural labourers. Once Stalin and the leadership had decided on rapid industrialisation the above scenario was the only possible one. Since living standards in the countryside would be miserably low, the more ambitious peasants would move into the towns and building sites and provide the necessary labour for industrialisation. The level of coercion to be used would depend on the peasant labourer. If he proved recalcitrant, he would be forced to work. It permitted the government to control the peasants to an extent never before achieved.

In the 1970s some historians in the West began to challenge the thesis that collectivisation was necessary in order to industrialise more rapidly. It was patently clear in the 1970s that agriculture was the Achilles' heel of the Soviet economy. The Soviet Union began importing grain from North America in 1963 and imports accelerated under Brezhnev. Why was a potentially rich agricultural country unable to feed itself? The answer was that the decision to collectivise had been a colossal blunder. It was argued that the state should have continued with the market to acquire food for the cities, Red Army and export. Russian agricultural cooperatives in 1914 had been the most developed in the world. Hence there was a tradition which could have been built on. Peasants were rational economic actors and would have reacted to market signals set by the government. Taxation could have been used to regulate the incomes of the kulaks. The war on the countryside meant that a huge coercive apparatus had to come into being.

Had NEP continued the Soviet economy would have expanded but at a slower tempo. A more prosperous agricultural sector would have provided taxes and exports to fuel industrialisation. The agony of the 1930s could have been avoided. It could be countered that the Great Depression, which began with the Wall Street crash of October 1929, would have cut demand for and prices of Soviet grain. This is true but the prices of machinery would also have dropped as manufacturers desperately sought markets for their products. The Soviet Union imported large quantities of machinery during the first Five Year Plan (1928–32). Henry Ford, for instance, built the tractor plant at Volgograd. Had NEP continued there would have been more grain to export and higher levels of machinery imports. The logic of this argument is that forced collectivisation was a political and not an economic decision. The state was willing to pay an economic price to achieve control over agricultural production. Many Russian historians adopted this view in the 1990s.

This analysis is convincing if the long term perspective is adopted. Soviet agriculture was high cost and inefficient. By 1991, about one-third of the harvest was being lost between field and table. The private plots, which covered about 3 per cent of the arable land, produced about 33 per cent of the global agricultural output. The government paid huge subsidies because it was afraid to raise food prices from the late 1960s onwards. It feared popular revolt. Hence agriculture was a huge loss-making sector until 1991. Foreign currency, mainly acquired through sales of gold, had to be spent on importing food. This meant that other sectors, such as health, were starved of foreign equipment.

One can only concur with this argument if the long term view is taken. However, the scenario changes if the short term view is adopted. If it is accepted that war against Nazi Germany was inevitable then the Soviet Union had to be prepared to fight it. Stalin and the leadership accepted that war against capitalist powers was inevitable. Without the rapid industrialisation of the 1930s – geared first and foremost towards defence – would the Red Army have defeated Hitler? The answer is almost certainly no. The continuation of NEP could have resulted in the demise of the Soviet Union. It can be argued that a wiser leadership would not have entered into a pact with Hitler and then failed to heed all the warnings that he was preparing to attack in June 1941. Perhaps, but Stalin had read Hitler's *Mein Kampf* and was aware that a war between national socialism and communism was inevitable. He hoped to launch an attack when he was ready: perhaps in 1943.

Stalin was also aware that Japan would eventually attack. Fortunately for the Soviet Union the Japanese waited until 1939 before attacking the Red Army in Mongolia. However, the Soviet leadership did not know how much time it had to prepare its defences in 1928. Had Japan decided to strike against the Soviet Union after occupying Manchuria in 1931, it might have conquered Siberia. Luckily for

Moscow, Tokyo decided to consolidate its position in China before considering a war against the Red Army. Stalin had to contemplate the nightmare scenario that Germany and Japan might coordinate their attacks. It is unlikely that the Soviet Union could have won this two-front war.

One of the great ironies of history is that the brutal collectivisation of the private peasant, one can argue, saved the Soviet state. Without it, the military industries could not have expanded as rapidly as they did. The sacrifices of the peasants also saved western civilisation. Had Hitler won, Europe would have returned to the Dark Ages.

An intriguing question remains: was Stalin's policy of coercive collectivisation Marxist? Would the continuation of NEP have been un-Marxist? Or the other way round? Marx expected capitalism to develop to its full potential and then collapse. Hence the continuation of NEP with its reliance on capitalist markets was a Marxist policy. Russian agriculture had not developed to the point where, according to Marx, it was on the point of collapse. A Marxist scenario in the countryside would have been agriculture dominated by a few large farms and everyone else a rural labourer. The vast majority would have been exploited (because they were not paid according to the productivity of their labour) by a minority of exploiters. This situation had not been reached in Soviet Russia. Given the fact that prosperous farmers were dividing up their farms among their sons the likelihood of it happening was slim. This latter development was very perplexing for a Marxist. The number of poor peasants (those who had to work most of the time for another in order to feed their family) was declining as they banded together to become middle peasants – peasants capable of producing enough to sustain their families. This made the rural sector, from the Marxist point of view, well nigh incomprehensible. Marx expected peasant farming to give way to commercial farming and then disappear. Hence NEP was Marxist.

Was Stalin's forced collectivisation un-Marxist? Marx did not envisage a Marxist party taking power in an underdeveloped country. Moving to socialist agriculture via forced collectivisation was something he had not contemplated. Marx did not shy away from violence. He expected bloodletting during the dictatorship of the proletariat when the bourgeoisie fought to retain their wealth and power. Force was acceptable but it would be used against rich farmers by their labourers. In using coercion Stalin creatively developed Marxism. Hence his policy amounted to unorthodox Marxism, whereas the continuation of NEP would have been orthodox Marxism.

Collectivisation step by step

Collectivisation went through various phases. It began with the forced requisitioning of grain in 1928. After Stalin's defeat of Bukharin, in 1928, he launched a policy of forcing the kulaks, the most efficient farmers, off the land in 1929–30. Kulaks were regarded as a rural cancer and could not be allowed to join collective farms so as to turn them into centres of anti-communist resistance. This led to the policy of dekulakisation, the elimination of the kulaks as a class. The more prosperous they were the more likely they were to be shot. Vyacheslav Molotov, at a secret meeting of the Stalin leadership in February 1930, put forward the idea of drowning or shooting all kulaks. If this were not possible, he suggested camps in Siberia. Only then did his mind turn to the nature of the work they could be forced to do: felling timber (Baberowski 2003). It is worth noting that this was not the first time that the Bolsheviks had considered wiping out successful farmers. It was advocated as a solution to the peasant problem at a closed session of the 10th Party Congress in 1921.

A total of 1.8 million were deported as kulaks and another 31,000 shot during the years 1928–32. Children were dealt with very harshly and the mortality rate was high. Why were children treated so badly? The most convincing explanation is that the Bolsheviks believed in the inheritance of acquired characteristics. In other words, the children of kulaks inherited the traits of their fathers. The evil had to be torn up by the roots. The violence against the kulaks was a warning to the middle peasants. If they refused to join collectives they were simply called kulaks and dealt with accordingly.

Throughout 1928 Stalin made it clear that a momentous change was coming. He warned Party members that the alliance with the peasantry meant an alliance with the kulaks. That was against the spirit of Leninism. Many communists found this perplexing as Stalin had defended the alliance with the peasantry against the United Opposition a short time before. Stalin went further. He revelled in the prospect of class war in the villages. The prospect horrified Bukharin. He espoused the orthodox Marxist view that the alliance with the peasantry should continue. To him, Stalin's unorthodox Marxism was 'ignorant nonsense'.

The battle for supremacy in the Politburo between Stalin and his allies and Bukharin and his supporters raged during 1928. During the summer, Stalin and his supporters tried to make the seizure of grain surpluses normal government policy. Bukharin hit back with 'Notes of an Economist', a scathing attack on those who were destroying the alliance with the peasantry. It was published in *Pravda* in September. He echoed Trotsky's complaints about the bureaucratisation and centralisation of Party and state organs. Stalin riposted through his control of personnel policy. The Moscow Party chief, a supporter of Bukharin, was ousted. Lazar Kaganovich, Stalin's man, moved into the trade union hierarchy as a counter to Tomsky. Stalin talked about a Right Deviation which was attempting to slow economic growth.

The conflict came to a head in February 1929. Bukharin, Rykov and Tomsky presented their case and accused Stalin of engaging in the 'military-feudal exploitation' of the peasantry and destroying Party democracy. Industrialisation should proceed at a slower tempo and the market be retained. They were convinced they had a majority in the Politburo but they miscalculated. They were outvoted. Bukharin was sacked as editor of *Pravda* and head of the Comintern. Tomsky was ousted from the leadership of the trade unions. Both left the Politburo. Rykov was removed as head of the Russian government. Inevitably there was a purge of their followers in other institutions. Stalin and his coterie had scored a crushing victory.

Stalin could now espouse policies which collectively can be called Stalinism. He had been a moderate and centrist in 1926 but by 1929 he was further to the left than the left. He and his supporters had created the grain crisis by refusing to raise state prices. The crisis then forced extraordinary measures. He was a risk taker and revelled in crises. In September 1929, he declared that there should only be one state purchaser of grain. Prices could be kept down by having one monopoly buyer.

Stalin never liked the quiet life. He always wanted tension, conflict and intrigue. He was convinced that force and punishment had to be used to achieve objectives. His orders are full of expressions such as 'begin punitive measures', 'turn them over to the courts' and 'fight vile wreckers'. In August 1929, he instructed Molotov to 'expose and hand over to the courts' and dismiss all officials caught trying to meet their procurement targets by obtaining grain from outside their region. Collectivisation achieved Stalin's main economic target: guaranteed supplies at low prices. Between 1929 and 1938, state grain procurement increased steadily despite no rise in output.

Dealing with the kulaks

Bread rationing had to be introduced in 1928. Tea and sugar followed and then, in autumn 1929, meat. This indicated that the peasant was not producing as much marketable food as previously. The 1928 grain harvest was 5 million tonnes below that of 1926, a record year. The state did import some grain in June 1928 but Stalin rejected this use of foreign currency in 1929. More grain had to be squeezed out of the peasants. Stalin's Urals-Siberian method was applied to the whole country in the summer and autumn of 1929. Anastas Mikoyan, an Armenian who had been a close aide of Stalin since the Civil War, spearheaded the foray into the countryside. Over 100,000 Party members were mobilised for rural duties. Grain flowed to the cities as peasants were cajoled and forced to hand over surpluses. Anything the activists could lay their hands on was a surplus. It was no use saying it was seed grain needed for the spring sowing.

Collectivisation accelerated after the defeat of the Bukharinites. At the 15th Party Congress, in December 1927, a resolution stated that the task of the Party in the countryside was to gather small peasant farms into large collectives. This would take 10–15 years. It was an immense task as only 1.2 per cent of the sown area was inside collective farms. A further 1.5 per cent was to be found in state farms. The first FYP envisaged 26 million hectares in state and collective farms, accounting for 15 per cent of global agricultural output. All perfectly feasible. But that changed at the end of 1929. Stalin announced that all agriculture was to be collectivised. However, he excluded Central Asia, Transcaucasia and some northern regions. The kulaks were to be eliminated as a class. The tame ones were to be resettled locally. The obstreperous ones were to be deported to inhospitable areas in Siberia, the Far North and Kazakhstan.

On the tenth anniversary of the October Revolution, Stalin triumphantly declared that the middle peasants were rushing headlong into the collectives. Like many of Stalin's statements this was pure myth. Molotov waxed eloquent about the 'cunning and dangerous enemy' in our midst, the kulak. In early 1930, the whole countryside was to be socialised. Since there were about 400,000 villages, over a quarter of a million communists descended on the countryside to introduce the new order. The simple method was to merge several villages and call them a kolkhoz. They were given splendid names such as 'Lenin's Testament' and 'Forward to the Victory of Communism'.

Stalin needed a comrade as ruthless as himself as Commissar for Agriculture. In 1929, he chose Yakov Yakovlev (né Epshtein), deputy head of Rabkrin, for the job. Anastas Mikoyan, Commissar for Trade, became head of grain procurements. Politburo members were made responsible for grain collections in specific regions. They had to deliver. Until April 1931, executions, in theory, could only be ordered by the Party Central Committee. It was then extended to the OGPU and the republican courts. In March 1930, the Politburo began permitting certain officials to order the death penalty.

Peasant opposition

The peasants hit back. In 1930, there were 13,754 mass peasant demonstrations; over half opposed to collectivisation. In 1930 alone, the Chekists executed more than 20,000 peasants. These statistics are from secret police reports. The flavour of these reports is always negative: the countryside is hostile to Soviet power. Was this entirely accurate or were the gatherers of statistics telling Stalin and his team what they wanted to hear? The message was clear: the peasant class was the enemy of Bolshevism. Stalin regarded his victory over the peasants as one of his greatest triumphs.

Kulaks were outlaws and lamented their fate. In December 1929, Stalin excluded them from collective farms. This meant deportation, execution or flight. Stalin was brutally frank.

'It is ridiculous and foolish to talk at length about dekulakisation . . .
When the head is off, one does not grieve for the hair. There is another
question no less ridiculous: whether kulaks should be allowed to join
collective farms? Of course not, for they are the sworn enemies of the
collective farm movement.'

Genrikh Yagoda, head of the NKVD, informed Stalin in early 1932 that
since 1929 540,000 kulaks had been deported to the Urals, 375,000 to Siberia,
over 190,000 to Kazakhstan and over 130,000 to the Far North. Another
secret police report reveals that on 1 January 1933 there were 334,000 in the gulag
and 1,142,000 in special settlements. Almost all of these were kulak victims of
collectivisation.

The message that the countryside could explode was brought back to Moscow
by shattered communists. If the mayhem continued, the spring sowing would not
take place. Stalin decided to act and announced a tactical withdrawal. He placed
all the blame on local Party officials in a speech, on 2 March, entitled 'Dizziness
from Success'. They had become inebriated with the wine of success. Coercion was
unacceptable. Collectivisation was to be voluntary. Desperate Party officials tried
to ensure that peasants did not get hold of that day's *Pravda*. Of course Stalin was
engaging in massive hypocrisy. He had put pressure on Party officials to up the
tempo and to use as much violence as was necessary. He became a hero to the
peasants. Stalin was a hypocrite but he was also a clever tactician. He wanted to
ensure that the spring sowing took place. Collectivisation could recommence at
harvest time. However, he kept one promise he made. Each household was to
retain a vegetable garden, an orchard and some livestock. The size ranged from
0.1 hectare in fertile areas to 1 hectare in inhospitable regions.

Before Stalin's 'Dizziness from Success' speech, about 15 of the 20 million
peasant households had been collectivised. Three months later less than 5 million
households were in collectives. Of these the great majority were poor peasants.
Those who bolted were almost exclusively middle peasants. A message for the
future was provided on 30 July 1930. The village gathering (*skhod*) was abolished.
The soviet was the only institution between the peasant and the state. It did not
matter if the new chair could not distinguish a cow from a bull. This led to a joke
about a kolkhoz chair who was asked how many teats a cow had. He replied:
'I'm not certain but I can tell you how many a woman has'. Technical expertise
was not the main criterion. Loyalty to comrade Stalin was.

Despite the mayhem, the 1930 harvest was excellent, about the same as the
record harvest of 1926. Nevertheless, the output of meat and dairy products
declined by about a quarter. This was due to large scale slaughtering of livestock
during the previous winter. The evidence appeared to support collectivisation;
at least from the standpoint of state needs. Although collectivised peasants only

accounted for a quarter of the peasantry, they delivered 40 per cent of state procurements. The government was able to export about 3 million tonnes of grain in 1930 and 4.8 million tonnes in 1931. This declined to 1.8 million tonnes in 1932 and 1.7 million tonnes in 1933. There was rationing in the cities and some peasants starved. The net result was that the state imported 1.5 billion rubles' worth of equipment for heavy industry between 1928 and 1933.

Forced collectivisation resumed in the autumn of 1930. Again they slaughtered, feasted and broke farm implements. Mikhail Sholokhov, the prize-winning chronicler of collectivisation, described the mood.

> 'Slaughter, you won't get meat in the kolkhoz, crept the insidious rumours. And they slaughtered. They ate until they could eat no more. Young and old suffered from indigestion. At dinner time tables groaned under boiled and roasted meat. Everyone had a greasy mouth, everyone hiccoughed as if at a wake. Everyone blinked like an owl, as if inebriated from eating.'

Between 1928 and 1933 they slaughtered 26.6 million head of cattle or 46.6 per cent of the total Soviet herd; 15.3 million horses or 47 per cent of the total and 63.4 million sheep or 65.1 per cent of the total. For the peasants, collectivisation was Armageddon or the end of the world. They had no thought for the morrow. They were inviting famine.

Famine in Ukraine

'What do you feed those chickens on?'
'What business is that of yours?'
'I want to lose some weight too.'

Ukraine was one of the bread baskets of the Soviet Union. Its grain steppes rival those of the Mid West plains in the US. By the middle of 1932, about 70 per cent of peasant households were in collective farms. In 1930, state procurements hoovered up about a third of the Ukrainian harvest. In 1931, the state wanted 42 per cent. In 1932, a poor harvest year, it was to be one-half. Party officials advised Moscow that it was taking too much grain but to no avail. Molotov made clear there would be no concessions. Activists were sent from the cities to procure the grain. They took all the grain they could find and left the peasants to starve. The cities and the Red Army took precedence.

Despite the sequestration of grain, state procurement targets were not met. Ukrainian Party officials, suspected of being soft on the peasants, were dismissed. Stalin regarded tales of famine in Ukraine and elsewhere as anti-Soviet propaganda.

The Soviet press made no mention of famine. The *Daily Worker*, the organ of the Communist Party of Great Britain, declared that tales of famine were false. However, the *Daily Worker* correspondent was aware of the real situation and informed western correspondents. Some, like Malcolm Muggeridge, reported the famine while others, such as Walter Duranty, a Pulitzer Prize-winning correspondent of the *New York Times*, kept silent. He sympathised with the Soviet regime and did not want to risk losing his accreditation.

The famine reached its apogee in the early months of 1933. By May, the situation began to improve. At least 5 million died agonising deaths from lack of sustenance. Whole families disappeared, corpses lined the roads and cannibalism reappeared. Railway passengers could see for themselves what was happening in the Ukrainian countryside. They kept the news to themselves or passed it on to close confidantes. Contradicting comrade Stalin meant instant arrest as a counter-revolutionary.

The human tragedy was observed by the schoolgirl Nina Lugovskaya (1918–93). Nina's diary begins in October 1932. Her father, an economist, was a Socialist Revolutionary and had been exiled to Siberia during the reign of Nicholas II. In 1929 he was exiled to the Far North for three years. His wife lost her job as well but found work as a school administrator. Her wages were not sufficient to feed her three daughters. Food was rationed in Moscow in the early 1930s and priority was given to Stakhanovite workers, then ordinary workers and, if any was left over (usually not), to office staff. Nina did not discuss her thoughts with her family. She was appalled by the treatment of Ukrainian famine refugees and the summary executions after the murder of Sergei Kirov, the Leningrad Party leader, on 1 December 1934.

The last diary entry is on 2 January 1937. Two days later the NKVD confiscated the diary. She was found guilty of 'planning a terrorist act against Stalin' and sentenced to five years' hard labour in Kolyma, followed by seven years of exile in Siberia. Her mother and two sisters received the same sentence. Her father was arrested in 1935 and accused of being the 'leader of a counter-revolutionary terrorist and insurrectional SR organisation in Moscow oblast', which in 1936 had been planning terrorist acts against Party leaders and the Soviet government. In July 1937, he was sentenced to ten years' hard labour in Kazakhstan. Hence the whole family ended up in the gulag. Her mother died in exile in Magadan oblast but was rehabilitated in 1961. Her father returned to Moscow in 1947 and died in the late 1950s. He was rehabilitated posthumously in 1959.

Nina married an artist, a former political prisoner, in Magadan in the late 1940s. They worked together as stage designers and eventually settled in Vladimir, in central Russia. Nina petitioned Nikita Khrushchev for rehabilitation. She stated that the confessions she had made had been forced out of her under duress. She had been threatened with everything, including execution and driven to such despair that it 'didn't matter what I signed, I just wanted it all to be over'. She was rehabilitated in 1963. Her friends remembered her as a reticent and kindly person. No one was aware of what she had suffered.

> 'Strange things are going on in Russia. Hunger, cannibalism . . . People from the provinces say there isn't time to remove the corpses from the streets, that provincial towns are full of starving, ragged peasants. Everywhere there's terrible thieving and banditry. And Ukraine? . . . It's a dead, silent steppe . . . Refugees are doggedly and ceaselessly converging on the big cities. Often they are driven out again, entire long trainloads – back to certain death. But the struggle to survive has taken over; people are dying in railway stations, in trains and still they get to Moscow.'
>
> (31 August 1933) (Lugovskaya 2003)

The OGPU also reported strange things:

> 'Citizen Gerasimenko ate the corpse of her dead sister. Under interrogation Gerasimenko declared that for a month she had lived on rubbish, not even having vegetables . . . Citizen Doroshenko, after the death of his father and mother was left with infant sisters and brothers, ate the flesh of his brothers and sisters when they died of hunger . . . In Sergienko's apartment was found the corpse of a little girl with the legs cut off, and boiled meat.'
>
> (March 1933)

Stalin was afraid the foreign press might get wind of these horrors:

> To Molotov, Kaganovich
>
> 'Do you know who let the American correspondents in Moscow go to the Kuban? They've produced some filth about the situation in the Kuban . . . This must be stopped and these gentlemen must be banned from travelling throughout the USSR. There are enough spies as it is.'
>
> (February 1933)

Some western historians have argued that the famine was deliberate. It was in response to Ukrainian nationalism, which Stalin found particularly exasperating. He did not permit food to be delivered to the starving areas. However, not only Ukrainian families but German, Jewish, Russian and others died of hunger. There was famine in the north Caucasus and the Volga region. The nomadic Kazakhs were forced into kolkhozes and died in large numbers. The total of all Soviet victims was between 6 and 7 million. Millions of the survivors became chronically ill or handicapped. Many of them moved into towns, spreading epidemics. Crime soared. Legislation was draconian. Petty theft could bring the death sentence or 10 years in the gulag. A starving peasant, attempting to steal five sheaves of wheat, could be shot.

Another explanation would be that the famine was mainly the result of the confusion engendered by forced collectivisation. The other aspect which contributed to the catastrophe was the utter inflexibility of the Stalin leadership. Stalin talked about the 'great turn' in policy. There was simply no going back.

Down on the farm

The majority of peasants regarded the new kolkhozes (set up on existing farmland) and state farms (set up on previously uncultivated land) as a renewal of serfdom. New elites formed. The collective farm chair or the manager of the state farm (sovkhoz) became the new boss. He (rarely she) was appointed by the local Party organisation and he gathered around himself new white and blue collar elites. They were the accountants, brigade leaders and other administrators. Then there were the tractor drivers, machine operators and blacksmiths. These groups did not work in the fields. That was left to those at the bottom of the ladder. It was normal for the white and blue collar elites to be predominantly male. Since many of the leading positions entailed a better lifestyle, competition for these positions was sharp. This permitted the local Party officials and chairs to expect favours for the most attractive positions. Since there were shortages, those farms within reach of a city had the opportunity of earning extra 'on the side'. In other words, they could work the black market.

Kolkhoz markets

In 1932, Stalin was obliged to make kolkhoz markets legal. The surplus produced on private plots could be sold here. If farms produced more than their plan targets they could sell it in these markets. There was little profit in selling grain as all flour mills belonged to the state. The best lines were meat, eggs, fruit and vegetables. An enterprising farm manager could link up with Party and police officials and steer produce to the private market. They could declare that state procurement targets for the lucrative products had been met and delivered to the state. If they were pilfered en route to the state storehouse, it was not the farm's fault. It was common practice when picking potatoes to pick only those near the surface. In the evening those lower down could be dug up for private consumption.

Most peasants became passive and forgot what initiative was. They waited until given an order and then did as little as possible. This alarmed Stalin. In June

1932, he ordered a flood of manufactured consumer goods be sent to the grain, sugar and cotton producing areas. He told Molotov, in 1933, that coercion had worked and there was no need to continue with it in the countryside. In September 1934, Stalin decreed that the state procurement prices for wheat and rye be increased. He was forced to accept a basic law of economics: workers need an incentive to work.

In 1935, the kolkhoz model charter was adopted. It made private plots legal. The peasant could keep a cow but not a horse. The leadership was embarrassed by the popularity of kolkhoz markets. In 1940, kolkhoz markets accounted for 19 per cent of the retail trade turnover in food products. Prices were, of course, higher there. Azeris quickly established themselves as the best market traders. So rife was economic crime that an amnesty was declared in the same year. Freedom of religion was included in the 1936 constitution and for a time in the mid-1930s things improved for former kulaks. Every citizen was now granted the franchise. Priests and their families were the only group still excluded from joining kolkhozes. Farms provided a rudimentary social security and health system. Schools catered for the farm children. However, living standards were so low that the enterprising left. Girls were as keen to better themselves as boys. Burgeoning industry had an insatiable appetite for labour. After military service, few found farm work attractive. A natural order soon established itself. Those over 35, the lazy and the drunkards stayed; the ambitious left. Needless to say, those in positions to enrich themselves also remained.

Things changed in 1937. Then Stalin ordered the deportation and execution of thousands of former kulaks and criminals. Priests again became a target for state repression. In 1939, Stalin imposed a minimum number of labour days on the farm. Penalties for labour indiscipline became more severe. The private plot was reduced in size.

The balance sheet

Paul Gregory (2004) concludes that the Preobrazensky model of primitive capital accumulation was infeasible when enunciated in the mid-1920s. Stalin added force and made it feasible. It was a policy conceived and executed at the highest level. Gregory finds that the grain procurement crises did not prove that private agriculture failed. Agriculture grew rapidly under NEP and only slowed down as the result of increasing state intervention. Peasants produced more, ate more and fed more to their livestock during NEP than ever before. The Bolsheviks believed that NEP delivered too much to the peasants and too little to the cities. Force was decreed to reverse this scenario.

The Bolsheviks held to four fundamental values:

1   state ownership;

2   a planned economy;

3   primitive capital accumulation;

4   the leading role of the Party.

The 'Right Deviation' wanted the continuation of a mixed economy. This would have forced the Bolsheviks to concede at least one of their core values. According to Marx's model of reproduction, an underdeveloped country must create capital as fast as possible. Any policy which cuts consumption increases savings. Primitive accumulation appeared to work as investment in the economy doubled between 1928 and 1937. Was this the result of squeezing peasant incomes or were workers' incomes also squeezed? Abram Bergson, a leading American economist, concluded that workers fared as badly as peasants during the 1930s.

To justify Stalin's gamble, one would need to show that agriculture produced a surplus: the flow of goods from the countryside to the towns exceeded the flow of industrial goods to the countryside. Unfortunately for Stalin, those economists who have studied this problem conclude that there was virtually no surplus. Why was this? One reason was the lack of motivation of the rural labour force. Another was the massive slaughtering of livestock. Traditionally horses and oxen provided the traction power in the countryside. In 1933, livestock numbers were only 40 per cent of those of 1928. The deficit had to be made up by producing more tractors and farm machinery for the farms. Hence the living standards of farm and industrial workers were cut to increase the rate of investment. The economic premise on which coercive collectivisation had been based turned out to be false: extract a large surplus from the peasants in order to accelerate the rate of industrial investment. A side effect of Stalin's economic misjudgement was that the agrarian sector did not produce enough food for the population. The 1930s were years of hunger for the vast majority of people. In fact, Soviet agriculture never managed to feed the population well.

Jokes about kolkhoz life reflect the deep indifference to the works of the founding fathers, especially Lenin.

At a kolkhoz ceremonial meeting, prizes are being awarded. 'For excellent work in the fields, comrade Ivanova is warded a sack of grain.' (Applause) 'For excellent work in the dairy, comrade Petrova is awarded a sack of potatoes.' (Applause)

'For excellently performing public services, comrade Sidorova is awarded Lenin's Collected Works.' (Laughter, applause, shouts from the hall: 'Just the thing for that bloody old bitch.')

Questions

1 Who were the kulaks and what was the dekulakisation campaign?

2 What were the main controversies surrounding the dekulakisation campaign?

3 'The "kulak" was merely an ideological category which served the Bolsheviks nicely in enabling them to commit further atrocities.' Discuss.

4 Which phase of the collectivisation campaign was the harshest?

5 'Collectivisation signified the misguided attempt to solve economic problems by ideological means.' Discuss.

6 'Collectivisation was a necessary evil.' Discuss from an economic point of view.

7 How did Stalin justify collectivisation?

8 'Collectivisation was a good idea on paper but wrongly executed.' Discuss.

9 Was there an alternative to the strategy of forced collectivisation and rapid industrialisation adopted in 1928–29?

10 'The Bolsheviks were modernisers and engineers of social change.' Discuss.

Further reading

Sheila Fitzpatrick, *Stalin's Peasants: Resistance and Survival in the Russian Village After Collectivization* (1994); R. W. Davies and Stephen G. Wheatcroft, *The Years of Hunger: Soviet Agriculture, 1931–1933* (2003); Paul Gregory, *The Political Economy of Stalinism* (2004).

CHAPTER 10

Industrialisation

'Human will is the essential factor in achieving the economic plan.'

Stalin (This is the placebo principle)

'Our task is not to study the economy but to change it . . . we prefer to stand for higher tempi rather than sit [in prison] for lower ones.'

Strumilin

'There are no fortresses which Bolsheviks cannot storm.'

Stalin

The four Bolshevik core values are:

- state ownership;
- a planned economy;
- primitive capital accumulation;
- the leading role of the Party.

These were in place by 1929. Inevitably, a Stalin-like figure was needed to drive this system forward. Workers were promised a glorious tomorrow but wanted a fair wage. In 1929 and 1930, they felt that fair wages were not being paid and economic growth suffered. In came food rationing. Stalin wanted to reward those who put in more effort and cut the rations of the rest. It proved unmanageable. It led to greater fraud and corruption as ration cards became currency. Along came Stakhanov and his miraculously high labour productivity. Workers would be paid for higher productivity. This did not work as it drove up wages as well. Draconian labour laws had to be introduced. Clearly most workers felt they were not being paid a fair wage.

Stalin was a strong leader in 1929 but he still had to consult his team. He could not run the economy on his own. Gosplan was responsible for drafting plans. However it had no executive power. An operational plan was needed, one which would implement the national plan. The main plan was the Five Year Plan. However, it was more for show than anything else. Eugene Zaleski (1980) showed that FYPs were not turned into operational plans and the record of fulfilment was poor. They were 'visions of growth' to inspire the population. There were none during the war (1941–45) but they were resurrected afterwards because they were useful propaganda tools.

To Stalin, planning meant that he and his team set targets which Gosplan and the government implemented. The talented economists in Gosplan were ruthlessly weeded out and replaced by new comrades who would not tell Stalin that he was attempting the impossible. He found that the Supreme Council of the National Economy, responsible for the whole industrialisation portfolio, was too unwieldy. It was split up into various commissariats in 1932. Sergo Ordzhonikidze switched to become Commissar for Heavy Industry, the key ministry. Lazar Kaganovich became Commissar for Transport. This was also a very important ministry as it had to solve the logistics of the industrialisation drive. Vyacheslav Molotov became Prime Minister in December 1930. Stalin and Molotov took a general view of the economy but Ordzhonikidze became a strong advocate of the interests of heavy industry This dismayed Stalin. Other ministers also lobbied for their own commissariats. This led to fierce debates in the Politburo with Stalin playing the role of conciliator.

Commissariats were divided into glavki or departments. For instance, the Commissariat of Heavy Industry was subdivided into glavki representing the various sectors of heavy industry. Subordinate to each glavk were the enterprises of its sector. Stalin soon found that planning was a complicated process. Scientific planning turned out to be a myth. Gosplan and the CC apparatus did not have sufficient staff to plan from the top down. It was impossible for the centre to lay down each enterprise's plan.

By 1941, there were over 20 million products. The main task of the centre became the calculation of material balances. In other words, the inputs needed to produce the outputs. Stalin's main influence was to dictate the amount of investment and investment priorities. These were expressed in rubles. Naturally, heavy industry took priority. The government's task was then to implement Stalin's priorities. It was up to the commissariats and their glavki to work out how to do this. Needless to say, every ministry, glavk and enterprise lobbied for more resources, claiming that they could not meet targets with what they were to get. Enterprises wanted easy plans. What eventually emerged was quite different from that envisaged by Stalin and his team. Enterprises turned out to be most influential in the allocation of resources. Annual plans were constructed after the event and based on performance. It was bottom up planning. The simple task was to produce a little more than the year before.

As labour turnover was high, factories had to find ways to retain valuable workers. Since there was a perpetual shortage of inputs, they needed to pay over the odds if they were to make up the difference. If factory A produced a valuable product it could barter or sell this to factory B for a product it needed. All this horizontal activity was, of course, illegal. An army of fixers came into being. They roamed the country to find the vitally needed inputs. They did deals and expected favours in return. In order to finance this illegal activity, each enterprise needed a slush fund. This was built up by obtaining more inputs from the state than they needed to meet the plan. The problem was that state suppliers did not provide all plan deliveries. Stalin compounded the problem by intervening incessantly in the economy. The plan was forever changing. The imperative was to meet the plan. He permitted enterprises to break the law in order to achieve this. Even this did not always achieve the results he required. Intense lobbying led to him reducing some plans on occasions. He accepted they were simply unrealistic. Sometimes he would provide more inputs to achieve the targets.

Breaking the law became a way of life for enterprises. It led to a massive increase in fraud and crime. The shadow economy – all economic activity outside the official, planned economy – mushroomed. Concerns were permitted to sell up to 5 per cent of their plan targets in special shops. Defective goods and spare parts could be sold on. A remarkable number of 'defective' goods were produced. In reality, the great majority had only been labelled defective. The easier the plan was to fulfil the more could be produced for the shadow economy. Another common practice was to 'lose' goods in transit. They were then simply written off. State officials, the militia and the Chekists all had to be compensated to turn a blind eye to this illegal activity. Cars were a highly prized commodity. Some cars for export were sold instead to the Chekists and private dealers at knock-down prices. Shop assistants in state stores placed anything in great demand under the counter. Many state goods were siphoned off into the shadow economy. Officials concerned with distribution could divert goods into the unofficial economy.

What did Stalin do to combat the illegal activity which was undermining his grand vision? He deployed the only policy he knew: force. There were four heads of Gosplan and three Commissars for Heavy Industry during the 1930s but little changed. Planners, 'bourgeois specialists', scientists, philosophers, ministers, managers, workers and peasants were slaughtered. The pressure told on Ordzhonikidze. He took his own life in February 1937. Stalin saw this as a betrayal. Clearly Sergo had not been up to the job. Stalin had to be ruthless. He needed mini-Stalins everywhere. They made life miserable for their subordinates and their superiors made

«АПОКАЛИПСИСЪ»

Рис. А. Шараю.

И безумецъ пришелъ, и навьялъ.

10.1 Stalin as slave driver
Source: Satirikon, Paris, 1931.

life miserable for them. However, Stalin was capable of taking his foot off the pedal. In 1933 and 1937 he reduced investment and growth targets.

'Cadres decide everything' was a favourite saying. 'For us, objective difficulties do not exist. The only problem is cadres. If things are not progressing, or if they go wrong, the cause is not to be sought in any objective conditions: it is the fault of the cadres' (Lewin 2005). Hence Stalin held that rules and regulations were fine but what really mattered was the comrade in charge.

Under Stalin the Politburo devoted more time to personnel matters than to anything else. This was in line with his maxim: 'Every functionary must be closely studied, from every angle and in the most minute detail'. It was irrelevant if the comrade in charge broke every law there was; what was important was that he met his plan targets. Hence human robots were of no use to Stalin. He needed comrades who could get the job done, irrespective of the cost. If something went wrong, the only thing to do was to identify a culprit and punish him. This applied even if no one was at fault. A case in point happened during the war when Stalin sent a telegram to Roosevelt. The latter did not answer. Stalin assumed that the telegram had not been sent. So Molotov had to find the guilty party. He chose the head of the cipher department. He was expelled from the Party and disappeared without trace.

Decision making

Strange as it may seem, Stalin and the Politburo only took three types of economic decision during the 1930s:

1 the investment budget;
2 the allocation of foreign exchange (for instance, Stalin forbade the import of Rolls Royces);
3 grain procurements.

All other decisions were taken by subordinates. Some of these only took a small proportion of necessary decisions. For instance, Gosplan took no more than 10,000 of the millions of resource allocation decisions made annually. The overwhelming majority of these decisions were taken by lower level personnel. These acted as opportunists and followed sectional interests. There was constant war between Stalin and his subordinates. The latter provided distorted information which placed them in the best possible light. Stalin was always complaining that he was surrounded by liars and rascals. He was. Subordinates were showered with orders which they could not fulfil. They had to ensure that someone else took the blame when they failed. Since there was a lot of failure there was a lot of blame to apportion. A ritual ensued. If blamed for something, it was important not to contest the allegation. The best course of action was to admit one's guilt and beg for mercy. It was akin to the religious concepts of sin and repentance. Stalin became very angry if a victim refused to acknowledge his guilt. Every now and then some sacrificial victims were shot. It was irrelevant if they were innocent. Plan failure demanded human sacrifice. Stalin had no trust in his subordinates, even his close aides, and the subordinates, in turn, did not trust their subordinates.

The above became known as the command administrative system. Even though it had been cobbled together in great haste and by trial and error, it proved remarkably durable and lasted until 1988.

The battle for investment

Regional Party bosses were delighted by the Great Breakthrough of 1929. It promised an investment bonanza. The Urals wanted more engineering (e.g. Uralmash or Urals Machinery Enterprise); the Far East wanted gold and silver mines; Uzbekistan wanted irrigation projects; the central Black Earth region wanted metallurgical and tractor plants. Stalin encouraged the view that the sky was the limit. Reality proved otherwise. Regions had to fight one another for investment. Annual plans went through numerous variants before Stalin and his team took the final decision. For instance, in 1935, the investment plan oscillated between 18 billion and 27.1 billion rubles. The latter figure won. In 1936, the fluctuation was even greater: from 17 billion to 35 billion. Ordzhonikidze could out-shout anyone. Needless to say, he inflated his investment demands. When rebuffed he launched into tirade after tirade. Since he was responsible for the most important ministry, heavy industry, he could argue that rejecting his proposals amounted to undermining the nation's defence potential. Stalin needed nerves of steel to face down such challenges.

Rationing

Workers needed consumer goods to motivate them but more consumer goods signified fewer investment goods. Stalin came up with the idea of rationing. He personally drafted the legislation which was promulgated in December 1930. Stalin was attempting to limit consumption without lowering labour productivity. Priority sector workers should receive more while everyone else got less. A slogan in the early 1930s summed up the thinking: 'He who does not work to industrialise the country shall not eat'. It was hoped that those in non-priority sectors, such as agriculture, could be forced to produce as much as before. They would face severe punishments, even the gulag, if they did not. Workers in important industrial areas, such as Moscow and Leningrad, were to receive more. Stakhanovite workers were entitled to more within their factories. The military and the Chekists were granted generous rations. Best of all were the elites in Moscow. Those at the top received a 'Moscow ration'. The gulag was not forgotten. Prisoners were to receive 20 per cent less while their norms remained the same. Ration cards were only distributed to non-agricultural workers and employees. All others had to fend for themselves. Rationing was in place during the crucial period, December 1930 to late 1934.

Rationing was abandoned for various reasons. Bureaucrats could not cope with its complexity. Once shock workers finished their meal, hungry workers took their place. The administrative system was only able to feed the elite groups, numbering fewer than 5,000. Rationing provoked a vast increase in speculation and crime. Ration cards became currency and were sold to the highest bidder. Rationed goods were diverted into the private sector. The state lost this revenue. Petty and large scale theft became a minor industry. In 1935, over 100,000 persons were sentenced for speculation. This was only the tip of the iceberg. Those with resources could bribe their way out of trouble. Even the death sentence did not halt the expansion of the shadow economy. It turned out that priority workers did not consider their rations to be a fair wage. The low prices of rationed goods, in comparison to the private market, resulted in a considerable loss of revenue. In order to get peasants to produce technical crops (for instance, flax and cotton), they had to be given ration cards and provided with industrial consumer goods. Rationing was abandoned in early 1935. Much higher prices now prevailed. However, private, illegal, trade had taken root. Theft from one's workplace became a way of life. Theft, speculation and crime were now daily companions.

A worker is asked about pay in his factory. 'Not bad but the take-home pay is better.'

'Will there be theft under communism?' 'No, everything will have been stolen under socialism.'

Class divisions are clearly visible from these entries in the diary of the schoolgirl Nina Lugovskaya (2003):

'All Moscow stores are divided into four categories:

- the commercial stores . . . the counters are thronged with ladies wearing makeup, fine clothes and perfume; the Soviet aristocracy composed mostly of Jewish women and the wives of communists and state officials . . . there are no workers inside. For nearly two years now the state has engaged in this sort of speculation, ruthlessly destroying private nepmen while creating state nepmen.
- modest shops full of goodies. There is often a sign: Limited Distributor. Not everyone can buy food here.
- Torgsin [trade with foreigners] shops. Here you find everything. [foreigners pay in hard currency; Soviet citizens in gold and silver].
- state cooperatives, kiosks. These are the most numerous . . . Most of the time there is no one in them except on those days when workers and office staff receive their coupons for food rations. There are huge queues and you hear people squabbling and swearing.'

(21 August 1933)

'Life in Moscow . . . was disagreeable to an alien to me. And the people
– elegant city people, neatly dressed, with white, well-cared-for hands
and faces – were equally disagreeable . . . I looked at the women in their
bright, extremely low-cut dresses, at their heavily made up faces and
dyed hair, and I thought of those other women who worked for days on
end for a crust of bread, dirty, ragged, with rough but such sweet faces.'

(30 July 1934)

Stakhanovism

The end of rationing in early 1935 signalled that the Politburo could no longer
hope to distribute consumer goods to priority workers while depriving others.
It then turned to Stakhanovism as a way of raising labour productivity. Stalin's
famous dictum 'Cadres decide everything' was coined in May 1935. He went on to
assert that mastery of new technology could 'lead to miracles'.

On 30 August 1935, Aleksei Stakhanov, a miner, produced 102 tonnes of
coal in 5 hours and 45 minutes. His norm had been 7 tonnes. This phenomenal
achievement had been staged by the mine supervisor and the Party representative.
All the technology worked. It appears it was not inspired by the Politburo but
was an initiative from below. Of course, it was immediately seized upon and the
Stakhanovite movement spread like wildfire. Within a few weeks it took hold in
the car, engineering, textile and footwear industries. Had the Politburo discovered
a magic formula for rapidly raising labour productivity? There were hidden dangers. Stakhanovism was based on piece rates. If workers produced more and were
paid more, investment would fall. The average daily wage of industrial workers,
between August and December 1935, rose by 16 per cent. It also fomented resentment. Research has revealed that the movement only had an ephemeral impact.
Labour productivity did not perceptibly increase during and after the Stakhanovite
movement. The OGPU files reveal that many managers opposed Stakhanovism.
They regarded it as disruptive. It provoked worker sabotage. So serious was the
situation that anti-Stakhanovite behaviour was classified as terrorism in December
1935. Accidents, damage to machinery and poor quality work were now treated
as crimes.

The application of compulsion to the whole labour force became policy in
December 1938. The worker's contract with the enterprise was extended to five
years. The new labour book (each worker had one) had to list all his misdemeanours, including the reason, if necessary, why he was sacked. Workers were to
be punished for arriving 20 minutes late and laziness, sloppy workmanship and
drunkenness became criminal offences. The working week was extended from six
to seven days and workers could not change jobs at will. In 1940, over 3.3 million
workers were accused of violations of labour discipline. Of these 1.8 million were

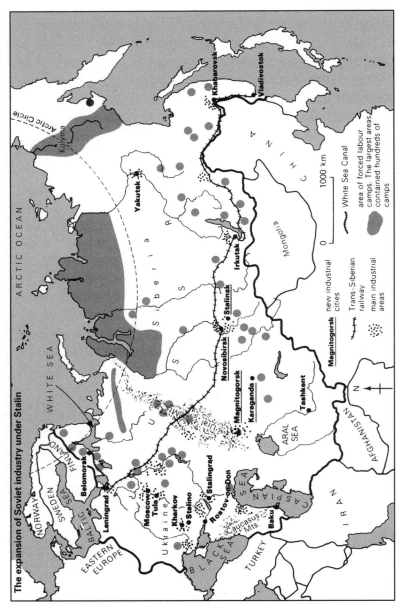

MAP 10.1 The expansion of Soviet industry under Stalin

sentenced to six months' corrective labour at the workplace and 322,000 (another source gives 500,000) went to prison for two to four months. If the judges were lenient they too were sentenced. This labour legislation remained in force until the mid-1950s.

Control figures

Control figures are output targets, such as steel, coal or freight train journeys, to be produced in some future quarter or year. There were hundreds of thousands of control figures to decide but the Party leadership could only decide a few of them because its staff was very small. In January 1930, the CC apparatus only employed 375 persons. The Politburo only had ten members and a very small staff, so could only keep track of a few commodities. Stalin's team was overworked and drowning in paper, petitions and inspections. Each member of the elite had to become a specialist in some economic area.

Success meant rapid promotion. Andrei Zhdanov (agriculture) was elected a full member of the Politburo in February 1935. Nikolai Ezhov became Commissar of the Interior in 1936 and a full member of the Politburo in October 1937. He was then charged with implementing the Great Terror. Politburo members roamed the country, inspecting factories and collective farms. Among themselves they prattled endlessly about steel, iron, grain, freight trains and the like. Some Politburo meetings were exclusively devoted to one industrial subject such as the best way to produce cars. The Politburo discussed a wide range of issues from the strategic to the banal. They even spent time on the price of bread and Metro tickets in Moscow. However, most of their time was consumed by personnel and economic subjects. Finding the right comrade for the right economic task was very important.

The Politburo only set about 20 important output targets in the second FYP (1933–37). This was the norm for the whole Stalin period as the directives for 1955, laid down in 1951, only involved about 20 indicators. Stalin provided little guidance on why he had arrived at a specific output target.

If FYP plans provided little guidance why did they survive? They were 'visions of growth' and very useful as propaganda. In fact, no FYP was ever fulfilled and this did not concern the leadership. They were debated in the Politburo, at Party Congresses and endlessly in the press. They were for public consumption. I asked a Party member, in the late 1960s, what he thought of *Pravda*'s trumpeting of the success of economic plans. 'I look in the shops', was his telling reply. The fact that economic plans were debated in public signalled that they were not important. The Soviet state was extraordinarily secretive about its modus operandi. An indication of this was that operational plans, on the other hand, were discussed behind closed doors. They were to remain secret from the public.

10.2 Millions of watts for the Motherland!; For 38 million tonnes of oil and gas in 1941!
Source: *Russia in Global Affairs*, Vol. 4, No. 2, 2006.

The conclusion is that the command administrative system was not directed by FYPs. It was run by quarterly and annual plans. Operational plans were the results of negotiations between producers and their superiors. They often did not exist halfway through the year. They were cobbled together later on the basis of actual results. Producers had to suffer endless interventions by state and Party officials. Hence the operational plan could literally change daily.

Haggling

Stalin had four economic priorities:

1 the priority of defence;
2 heavy over light industry;
3 investment over consumption;
4 quantity over quality.

These were not clearly articulated in policy documents. However, those involved in resource allocation had an almost instinctive grasp of them and acted accordingly.

Production was carried out by enterprises which were controlled not by central authorities but by intermediate industrial and regional agencies which were held responsible for the results of the enterprises subordinate to them. The principle of one man management (*edinonachalie*) applied. The minister was responsible for the ministry plan, the glavk director for the glavk plan and the enterprise manager for the enterprise plan. The plan was law. It was a breach of Party discipline to criticise the plan. Plans were always drafted on the basis of inadequate information. This permitted astute managers to haggle for easy plans which suited their own sectional interests.

The planner's task was to make life difficult for managers and prevent them producing for the shadow economy. Ministries withheld information in order to delay the drafting of the plan. The archives confirm that enterprises cheated. However, ministers and high ranking Party officials colluded with enterprises. One case which reached Stalin's desk in 1933 concerned the decline in the quality of textiles. In order to fulfil the plan in metres, an enterprise managed to stretch the cloth. Someone buying a man's shirt found that, after washing, it had shrunk to the size of a child's. Double counting was common practice. Combine harvesters were delivered to farms with essential parts missing. The producer could claim that they had been stolen en route and it was therefore not responsible. (In the 1970s, some enterprises did not even bother to assemble farm machinery. Everything arrived in kit form.)

The military economy

Rapid rearmament was decided in 1928 but due to the opposition of Aleksei Rykov, head of Sovnarkom, little progress was made. The Manchurian crisis in 1931 changed matters. The economy was now placed on a permanent war footing. Targets were raised rapidly and this caused considerable disruption of the economy. The civilian economy took a backseat. Much matériel was produced which was already obsolete ten years later. The defence budget grew from 1.2 to 6.4 milliard rubles between 1928 and 1932, according to Stone (2000). This is five times higher than the published Soviet figures. This is a salutary warning to readers not to take Soviet statistics at face value. In and after 1936 defence spending accelerated. It became an increasing burden as manpower and material resources were mobilised. In 1936 alone, defence spending increased by 60 per cent. In that year weapons procurement was three times that of 1933. However, in 1937 the military economy only produced two-thirds of the planned target. Stalin's decapitation of the military is one reason for the failure.

Reese (2000) concludes that the military leadership failed to soften the opposition of their peasant recruits to forced collectivisation. Efforts to increase the number of officers of humble origin produced disappointing results. They were incompetent and 'criminal activity among officers manifested itself at an astonishingly high rate', notably the embezzlement of their men's pay. The army shifted to greater professionalism in the late 1930s.

The Politburo's dilemma

During the 1930s, the Politburo took between 2,300 and 3,500 economic decisions annually. In the early 1930s there were about 50 items on a Politburo agenda but by the mid-1930s this rose to between 100 and 1,000 items. The central Party apparatus only counted about 400 persons and the Central Statistical Administration, 900, in the early 1930s. Clearly there was not enough technical staff to do the job Stalin had in mind.

The dictator, or Stalin, is represented by the government and the Party leadership. These two had a symbiotic relationship because the top ministers were members of or hoped to become members of the Politburo. Theoretically, the government was supposed to run the economy, guided by the 'general line' of the Party. In reality the two were fused as the Party was deeply involved in economic management.

The state and the Party had their own control commissions (police force) headed by a senior Politburo member. The Party control commission began as the Workers' and Peasants' Inspectorate (Rabkrin) and then became the Party Control Commission. It was greatly feared. The state agency, the Committee for State Control, also had wide ranging investigative functions. It normally worked with the Procuracy and the Ministry of Justice. Crimes and misdemeanours by higher ranking Party officials came under the jurisdiction of the Politburo. It could even impose a death sentence.

Stalin discovered, much to his chagrin, that Politburo members, when appointed to oversee economic portfolios, immediately became defenders of sectional interests. There were very few generalists, those looking at the economy as a whole. Stalin and Molotov were the two main generalists. Anastas Mikoyan, Commissar for Supply and Trade, even tried to establish grain reserves in his own ministry. Politburo members protected their own ministries from criticism. Stalin's solution was to strengthen Gosplan and other central agencies. The government used Gosplan to evaluate the flood of requests it received from ministries. Gosplan was not held responsible for economic failure until the purges of 1937–38.

The shadow economy

The shadow economy covers everything outside the plan. It includes the private, semi-legal and black economies and organised crime. It was divided into various sectors:

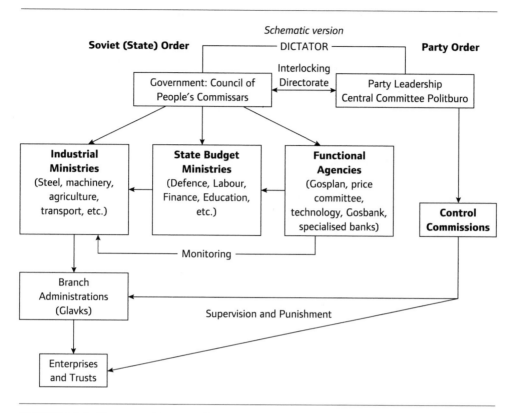

FIGURE 10.1 The central Soviet administration
Source: Paul Gregory, *The Political Economy of Stalinism* (2004).

- kolkhoz markets and the *tsekhy* (workshops) whose output could be sold privately;
- embezzlement of state produce, speculation and bribes. State produce could be stolen or bought for state prices and then sold at higher prices. Products could be declared defective and sold;
- the black market or underground economy. This included hard currency, gold and anything else for which there was a pent-up demand; organised crime.

The easier the plan, the more there was for the shadow economy. Vehicles were a much desired commodity. This led to a burgeoning of illegal, horizontal trans-actions. Vehicles could be written off as lost or so badly damaged they were scrap. The Chekists were well placed when it came to acquiring cars at knock-down prices. Vehicles for export could be redirected into private hands. Slick traders acted as the go-betweens. The allocation of vehicles was decided by the Politburo. One would presume that this left no leeway for the private market. The opposite was true. If resourceful entrepreneurs could trade in vehicles, which were tightly regulated, one can assume that private trade in other sectors, less closely regulated, was vast. Money was only part of the equation. One could amass a million rubles and be able to buy very little. Hence obtaining another desired commodity in return was part of the deal.

Theft was an ever present problem. Chubin, an official of the State Control Commission, took a pragmatic attitude to the stealing of grain, in Kursk:

> Chubin: Our inspectors, who are honest people (laughter in hall),
> together with the grain procurement agency official decided to check on
> warehouses, at night. They approached one: it was unlocked. They took a
> sack of grain away with them. They entered another warehouse and took
> another sack of grain. They took a sack from a third one and nobody even
> noticed.
> Voice from hall: And are they honest people? (Laughter in the hall)
> Chubin: Yes, they are because grain is stored in such a way that every
> honest man can help himself to it. (Laughter in hall)
>
> Source: Paul Gregory, *The Political Economy of Stalinism* (2004).

Party bosses were in a position to demand favours from enterprises. Soon it became a mutual greasing of palms. In this way, Party apparatchiki could acquire the wherewithal of the good life. The lure of materialism led many apparatchiki into corruption.

Labour

In 1928, the non-agricultural labour force consisted of 9.8 million workers and 3.9 million employees (neither a worker nor a peasant). Of these, industry employed 3.6 million workers and 500,000 employees (engineers, technicians). In 1940, there were 21 million workers and 12 million employees. Together they accounted for over half the national labour force. Of these, 11 million workers were employed in industry as were 2 million employees. In 1913, women made up a quarter of industrial workers (predominantly in textiles) but in 1940, 43 per cent of industrial workers were female. It should be pointed out, however, that few women were to be found in leading positions. The values of the villages were transferred to the towns. This ensured that the patriarchal culture of the country-side found a new lease of life at the workplace. What also emerges from the above is that the structure of the working class had changed beyond all recognition. Industry was flooded with raw recruits who had to learn on the job.

Employees included a group of key importance for the development of the economy: specialists. Mainly engineers, they had completed higher technical or specialist secondary education. There were 521,000 in 1928 (233,000 of whom had university qualifications) but on 1 January 1941 their numbers had swollen to 2.4 million or one in four employees. In order to arrive at a figure for the intelligentsia, one needs to add scientists, artists and writers. Altogether there were 2.5 million. On 1 January 1941, for every 1,000 workers, there were 110 engineers and technicians. However two-thirds were *praktiki*, those learning on the job. The average industrial worker, in 1939, had had four years of primary education. Hence anyone with elementary literacy skills was at an advantage. Many became office workers, accountants and so on. They were, not surprisingly, better paid than workers. In 1940, on average, a worker earned 31 rubles a month and an employee 54 rubles.

The rapid increase in the number of employees underlines the increasing stratification of Soviet society. With low living standards and education, even a small advance was important. The most important group, the specialists with advanced education, were in pole position.

The bosses

The top bosses were called *nachalniki*. They were heads of Party and state institutions at Union, republican, krai and oblast levels. In 1939, there were 68,000 in urban and 5,000 in rural areas; a grand total of 73,000 (Lewin 2005). Below them were the *rukovoditeli*. In 1939, there were 445,000 managers of firms, construction sites and in administrative agencies and their departments. Another 757,000 held posts at lower levels. In the countryside there were 280,000 chairmen and deputy chairmen of kolkhozes. This produces a grand total of 1.5 million *rukovoditeli*.

The emergence of the *nachalniki* and *rukovoditeli* is a highly significant phenomenon. They, as members of the technical intelligentsia, enjoyed high status which permitted them to articulate and defend their interests. They became pressure groups which often got their way.

The ever expanding government administration

An insight into the reasons behind the rapid expansion of the administration, and the bosses, is provided by two reports (Lewin 2005).

The first is a speech, in early 1929, by Valerian Kuibyshev, chair of the State Inspectorate, to his department heads. It was composed of members of the Party's Central Control Commission and the Workers' and Peasants Inspectorate. His conclusion was alarming. Soviet administration was almost a carbon copy of the tsarist administration. He listed the main defects. There were now so many abuses and scandals that action was necessary. Changing personnel would not solve the problem. One lot of swindlers would be sacked but they would be replaced by a new set of swindlers. Everyone was aware of the inter-agency disputes which raged. No department was willing to accept the solutions advanced by another department, especially if it involved the slightest inconvenience. The higher government agencies, which had the task of coordinating the activities of lower bodies, were themselves racked by quarrels. Their decisions were often the result of fortuitous majorities. Supra-ministerial bodies, such as the Council of Labour and Defence, or the economic councils, at regional level, were insufficiently powerful. The aggrieved party could appeal to Sovnarkom and often won.

The second is an editorial in *Izvestiya* in July 1941. A 'huge expansion of superfluous departments and agencies can be observed in our state administration, innumerable superstructures where employees do nothing but write, conduct enquiries and answer correspondence. All too often, this paper trail leads to nothing'. Details were given of the expansion of supply agencies. For instance, in Gorky (now Nizhny Novgorod), there were already 60. Every commissariat had several supply agencies; each agency employed large numbers of employees, and running expenses continued to mount. The agencies duplicated one another as they performed virtually the same tasks. The administrative budget had doubled in 1940. This phenomenon was not confined to Gorky but was to be observed throughout the country.

Why was the government administration expanding so rapidly? One reason is that the local bosses were Stalin's agents. In post, they became patrons and gathered around themselves a swarm of clients. The patron needed to find posts for his clients. As he extended them this favour, he expected favours from them. It was logical for every commissariat to set up its own supply agencies. They could do deals with other agencies to the mutual benefit of the bosses. Every commissariat and agency sought to develop its own empire and fend off incursions by others.

Another reason was the extreme centralisation of power. Stalin and his team insisted on taking all key decisions. This meant that subordinates were afraid to take decisions and referred them upwards. Everything was written down. Large numbers of officials were needed at the centre to sift through the requests. There were so many orders emanating from the centre that commissariats could not keep up. Stalin discovered that thousands of directives and decrees had not been properly filed. His suspicious mind turned this sloppiness into a threat to his regime. In reality, the reason for the failures he unearthed were due to the bottlenecks the system suffered from. Even the most efficient capitalist economy suffers from bottlenecks. They are simply the result of objective circumstances. However, Stalin did not recognise that these existed. Some comrade had to be the source of the problem. The Stalinist system has been diagnosed as suffering from systemic paranoia. Refusal to recognise that bottlenecks are bound to occur led to blaming individuals or groups for the crises. They, of course, were the class enemy. The more bottlenecks there were, the greater the perceived threat to the regime.

The Politburo served as an appeal court until 1991. If ministries could not arrive at a decision, the matter was sent to the Politburo. This reached an absurd climax under Leonid Brezhnev when the subject of ladies' underwear appeared on the agenda. The lingerie was so dreadful it had to be seen to be believed. It was a real passion killer. Perhaps this was a deliberate ploy by the planners. The male's sexual energy could then be channelled into material production.

The new socialist city

The new society was to be predominantly urban. Over 23 million peasants moved from the countryside to the towns between 1928 and 1939. Two million of these headed for Moscow. In 1939, one in three citizens was living in an urban area. Soviet Russia had inherited 640 towns and had added another 450 by 1939. The fastest increase was registered in medium sized towns (50,000–100,000 inhabitants). This revealed the influence of industrialisation. Rural mores and traditions moved with the migrants. Most new towns were just large villages dependent on industry instead of agriculture. The population of Moscow and Leningrad doubled in the decade to 1939; Gorky tripled. New towns sprang up almost overnight. Manitogorsk (Magnetic City) was a striking example.

The 1930s revealed a population in flux with huge flows of migrants. Millions of peasants, after sampling urban life in one city, abandoned it, went elsewhere or returned to their villages. Housing conditions were often appalling. The existing housing stock could not cope with the influx and many new workers had to live in barracks. Others lived in holes in the ground. The lucky ones obtained a corner of a room, or four or five families could share a communal kitchen. The less said about sanitary conditions the better. Family life was shattered as everyone battled against hunger and disease. The huge flows of people in and out of cities imposed an enormous strain on human relationships. Women had to work during the day and then begin work again at home in the evening. This led to higher death rates and lower birth rates.

Homo Sovieticus

Stalin was a firm believer in the inheritance of acquired characteristics. This was backed up by social psychology based on the theories of Ivan Pavlov (1849–1936). Broad roads, public buildings, high-rise blocks of flats, amenities and parks were envisaged. Life was to be communal, just like the village. There were communal kitchens, toilets and services. Electricity, gas and water were not metered. Rents were to be low. Such grandiose thinking was hugely expensive. Reality, including military reality, forced a rethink. The largest building in town was the Party head-quarters, followed by the town soviet. They were situated on the main square, always called Stalin (then Lenin) Square. There was also the ubiquitous statute of Stalin, later Lenin. The nomenklatura lived in the finished apartments; workers in huts and tents. They moved into apartments when they became available. They were seldom finished. It was up to the occupant to complete them. Since one could not buy building materials these had to be stolen or bought on the black market. In Magnitogorsk, a newly built industrial town in the Urals, the elite lived in neat cottages well away from the hoi polloi. There was even a special village, set in a birch grove, called Amerikanka, for the American specialists. When they left, the bosses moved in. They came to work in chauffeur-driven cars. Workers depended on public transport.

Moscow was transformed as it was remodelled as a capital city. Huge squares appeared capable of hosting large demonstrations. Grandiose parks made life more pleasant. The Cathedral of Christ the Saviour dominated the Moscow sky-line. This irritated Stalin. It was pulled down and a palace of soviets, the tallest building in the world, was to replace it. However the engineers found that the cathedral had been built on marshy land. They could not solve the technical prob-lems involved in constructing such a huge edifice. Later, a large outdoor swimming pool occupied the space. During the 1990s, the swimming pool was demolished and the cathedral rebuilt. One of the great successes was the building of the Moscow Metro, a splendid underground system. Nikita Khrushchev, Party boss in Moscow, supervised the work. Human lives were sacrificed to complete the project on time. It was conceived of as a foretaste of the communist future. It was a fairy-tale world for the average passenger. The Metro was built deep underground to serve also as a bomb shelter.

The state administration and the Party apparatus

There were 10 People's Commissariats in 1924, 18 in 1936 and 41 in 1940. State committees, such as Gosplan and grain procurement, enjoying the status of com-missariats, multiplied. Their staffs did as well. If a new commissariat or state com-mittee was created a new Party department in the Central Committee apparatus followed suit. Hence the two apparatuses expanded in parallel. By 1939, the ap-paratus had departments for every branch of government and state activity. There were about 45 departments at the centre. This was paralleled at the republican level by a similar apparatus. Each krai, oblast and raion Party organisation had its own apparatus. They kept on remorselessly expanding.

What was life like at the bottom of the pile? The head of the cadres' depart-ment of the CC apparatus reported, after an inspection visit to Vladivostok, that he found something akin to a 'railway station in total chaos'. Between January

1933 and January 1934 Party membership had also halved in the Far East krai. Some had been expelled, some downgraded to sympathisers and others had simply vanished.

Communists were living in scandalous conditions: in dugouts, toilets, five persons lived in one 6 square metre room, and so on. The food situation was just as bad. Even worse, the krai committee was doing nothing to remedy the situation. All it did was move cadres from one area to another. This sorry state of affairs was probably common throughout the country. Resources were quite inadequate for the tasks to be undertaken (Lewin 2005).

How powerful was Stalin?

The chapters on collectivisation and industrialisation suggest that Stalin was not necessarily the master of all situations; he was reacting, more often than not, to events. The new planned economy was close to breakdown on more than one occasion. The totalitarian model argues that Stalin was aiming for total control. These two chapters reveal that he never achieved it. During the revolutionary transformation of the economy Stalin could only hold the reins, inspire, guide and cajole everyone forward. Passivity was his greatest enemy. There was an inchoate opposition but it never coalesced into anything resembling a real threat to Stalin's leadership. A one party dictatorship could be enforced in public but this did not eliminate opposition in private. Seeing Stalin as dependent on his agents (members of his team) is one way of grasping his position. The agents, in turn, became patrons and they, in turn, gathered sub-agents around themselves. Everyone acted in his own interests. Stalin had to ensure that they collectively did not derail his dream of fashioning an economically powerful state.

Questions

1   When did rapid industrialisation begin and how successful was it?

2   What was Gosplan and why was it so important?

3   Were the first Five Year Plans successful in laying the foundations of an industrially developed economy?

4   'The concept of the plan served ideological purposes and nothing more.' Discuss.

5   'Industrialisation produced the first examples of the new Soviet man and woman.' Discuss.

6   'Industrialisation resulted in the institutionalisation of a distinct command administrative system without which the Soviet Union was ungovernable.' Discuss.

7   'The shadow economy owes its origins to industrialisation.' Discuss.

8 'Industrialisation laid the seeds of Stalinism as a distinct ideology.' Discuss.

9 What did Stalin's doctrine of 'Socialism in one Country' mean in practice?

10 'Stalin's industrialisation spawned the emergence of a new technocratic elite class.' Discuss.

Further reading

William G. Rosenberg and Lewis H. Siegelbaum (eds), *Social Dimensions of Soviet Industrialization* (1993); Sheila Fitzpatrick, *Everyday Stalinism: Ordinary Life in Extraordinary Times: Soviet Russia in the 1930s* (1999); Paul Gregory, *The Political Economy of Stalinism: Evidence from the Soviet Secret Archives* (2004); Moshe Lewin, *The Soviet Century* (2005).

CHAPTER 11

Terror and the gulag

Gulag: literally the main administration of labour camps run by the OGPU and NKVD. This term covers camps, special settlements; those sentenced to hard labour, exile and deportation.

> 'Whoever attempts to destroy the unity of the socialist state . . . that man is an enemy, a sworn enemy of the state and the peoples of the USSR. And we shall destroy each and every such enemy, even if he was an Old Bolshevik [member of the Pary before October 1917]; we will destroy all his kin, his family. We will mercilessly destroy anyone who, by his deeds or his thoughts – yes, his thoughts – threatens the unity of the socialist state.'
>
> Stalin, 1937

One day, Stalin misplaced his pipe and, after a long and thorough search, decides someone had stolen it. He summons a guard to find it. After some time he accidentally came upon his pipe and notified the guard to drop the matter.

'We can't', the latter explained, 'we have arrested ten suspects.'

'Release them', ordered Stalin.

'We can't', the guard explained, 'They have all confessed.'

Show trials, so called because most, if not all, the evidence was fabricated, meant that they became a piece of political theatre. It was to demonstrate to the public that there were enemies of the revolution everywhere and everyone had to be vigilant. The accused were obliged to confess their 'crimes' and admit their guilt. They were also expected to repent of their 'sins'. The show trials can be regarded as morality plays.

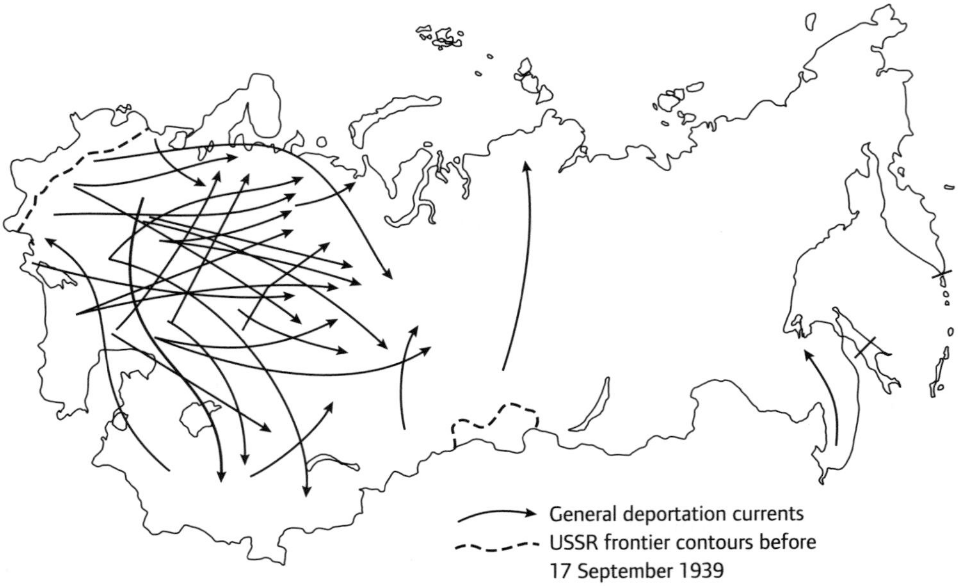

General deportation currents

USSR frontier contours before
17 September 1939

FIGURE 11.1 Kulak exile, 1930–31

Source: Pavel Polian, *Against their Will: The History and Geography of Forced Migrations in the USSR* (2004).

The Shakhty trial, in May 1928, the Union Bureau of Mensheviks, the Union for the Liberation of Ukraine, the Industrial Party and the Trade trials, in 1929–30, are only a few which squashed the old intelligentsia and bourgeois specialists. The evidence at all these trials was fabricated. One of those sentenced wrote to the USSR Procuracy in May 1967.

'No such body as the Union Bureau of Mensheviks existed in reality.
Those convicted in this case did not all know each another and not
all of them had been members of the Menshevik party . . . The first
"organisational" session of the "Union Bureau" took place a few days
before the trial began . . . At this "meeting" the accused became
acquainted with one another and agreed what conduct they would
adopt in court.'

The trials had four goals.

1   Stalin wanted to weaken the threat from the 'Right Deviationists';
2   remove former Menshevik or non-party specialists;

3   get rid of moderates in planning and industry;

4   he also needed scapegoats for the dire economic conditions of the early years of planning.

The prosecution's case always rested on the confessions of the accused. These had been beaten out of them. In the Shakhty trial, 53 engineers were accused of sabotage and five were sentenced to death. In June 1930, 48 officials of the People's Commissariat of Trade were accused of sabotage. They were all shot.

The Chekists were inundated with deported peasants and had to expand the number of camps and special settlements rapidly. Gradually, by a process of trial and error, they arrived at a system for the exploitation of this labour force. The Politburo decree of 30 January 1930 'On measures to liquidate kulak farms in the areas of total collectivisation' set targets. About a million persons were to be deported in 1930. Local Chekist agencies set up troikas (one representative each from the OGPU, the local Party and Procuracy) to try those arrested. They were divided into two groups: those who were sent to camps and those to settlements. In 1930, the Chekists arrested 330,000 persons and executed 20,000. Housing was totally inadequate and conditions so harsh that many children and old people died. Males were separated from their families and dispatched to do forced labour.

The OGPU documents state that in 1930–31, 1.8 million were exiled but on 1 January 1932, only 1.3 million special settlers were registered. This reveals that many of the able-bodied had escaped, leaving the camps full of old people, the handicapped and children. Settlers were subjected to extreme cruelty and hunger.

The decision to build a canal between the White and Baltic Seas, in May 1930, was a defining moment in the history of the gulag. It was the OGPU's first large project. The canal was to employ 120,000 prisoners and to be completed in two years. The average prisoner died after two to three months. The canal was completed ahead of schedule, in 1933. Stalin was pleased. However, it proved of limited value. It was too shallow to take ships which could cope with the Arctic winter and was only ice free half the year.

The Chekists had gained valuable experience in the management of large projects, something they would put to good use in the coming years. They identified prisoners who could be promoted to management positions. One of the most notable was N. A. Frenkel. He won plaudits from the OGPU and then moved on to other projects. He was head of construction on the Baikal–Amur railway (BAM; it was resurrected under Brezhnev) and later became an NKVD general. He is well known because of his role in Alexander Solzhenitsyn's *Gulag Archipelago*.

The gulag was centralised in late 1932 to become a vast network of camps servicing huge economic projects. Besides the White–Baltic Sea canal there was the Moscow–Volga canal, the Kolyma, Ukhta, Pechora mines (in the Arctic) and the supplying of Leningrad and Moscow with firewood.

The government then turned its attention to gold mining. Gold could be sold abroad and the proceeds used to purchase machinery and equipment. The site chosen was the traditional area along the Kolyma river. In November 1931, the Politburo set up a special trust, directly subordinate to the Party CC. Genrikh Yagoda, head of the OGPU, was to supervise the extraction. A target of 2 tonnes was set for 1931, rising to 25 tonnes in 1933. These targets remained on paper. Only 791 kg was produced in 1937. Over 11,000 prisoners panned for gold.

The Shakhty and Industrial Party trials provided the Chekists with much needed engineering expertise. These prisoners were placed in special design laboratories and even farmed out to individual enterprises. The state attitude to bourgeois specialists changed in the summer of 1931. Many 'wreckers' were released and returned to work in industry and transport. The White–Baltic Sea canal was always short of engineers. The Chekists increased the supply by arresting whole design bureaux and transforming them into the OGPU design bureaux. The Chekists was very pleased with the work of the design bureaux (*sharashki*). They became a feature of Soviet life. Solzhenitsyn's *First Circle* is about life in a *sharashka*.

The exploitation of camp labour led to appalling conditions. A commission which inspected the Solovetsky camp in 1930 reported some chilling details (Khlevniuk 2004). Mass violence and murder were commonplace. Some guards were prosecuted. The report stated:

11.1 The day's task: women prisoners are divided into groups of five

Source: 'First Group of Five Move Out', *The Gulag Collection*, Nikolai Getman, (The Jamestown Foundation, 2001).

'There are various ways of terrorising and torturing prisoners. Besides beating them with poles . . . in summer prisoners stand at attention, naked, so that the mosquitoes can feast on them; others squat on narrow benches and are not allowed to move or make a sound all day long . . . At night, they leave those prisoners who do not fulfil their norms in the forest, where their extremities become frostbitten . . . Unbearable conditions at work led to mass cases of self-inflicted injuries; for example, prisoners hacked off their fingers and toes . . . Everyone, from team managers to guards beat up the prisoners . . . There were special cells, one metre high, with sharp twigs stuck in the floor, walls and ceiling. The prisoners locked there could not stand it and died.'

The murder of Kirov and its aftermath

The situation changed dramatically after the murder of Sergei Kirov, the Leningrad Party leader, on 1 December 1934, by one Leonid Nikolaev. Stalin grasped the opportunity to draft the extraordinary law which was approved by the Politburo on 3 December 1934. Opposition activity was now labelled terrorism. The accused was to be indicted one day before the trial, there was to be no lawyer for the defence, no appeal and the death sentences was to be carried out immediately after the verdict. Stalin, without any evidence, implicated Zinoviev, Kamenev and their supporters in the murder. Former oppositionists were convicted in closed trials.

A Politburo resolution of July 1935 affected a large proportion of the rural population. Collective farmers (kolkhozniki), but not kulaks, serving sentences of five years or less were to have their sentences quashed. Those convicted of counter-revolutionary crimes or to more than five years were not included. Between April 1935 and March 1936, almost 557,000 collective farmers had their convictions rescinded. Another 200,000 had been pardoned in Ukraine in 1934. Rural officials, convicted of economic crimes, were also pardoned.

Counter-revolutionary crime

A conversation in the gulag. 'How many years did they give you?' 'Twenty. How about you?' 'Also twenty. What are you in for?' 'Nothing.' 'Liar. For nothing they give you ten.'

The definition of counter-revolutionary crime changed over time. The article in the criminal code on counter-revolutionary crimes was amended in 1926. Previously it had involved a clearly proven 'intention followed by action' before prosecution followed. The GPU became very skilful in avoiding supervision by

11.2 Waiting to be executed: these prisoners listen to their death sentence
Source: 'Waiting to be Shot', *The Gulag Collection*, Nikolai Getman, (The Jamestown Foundation, 2001).

prosecutors who were required to monitor the legality of their actions. Investigators no longer had to prove 'intention followed by action'. It could be used by Stalin to attain any desired objective. Old Bolsheviks could be accused of mentally opposing the Party line. This, in itself, was now a counter-revolutionary act. This approach may have been borrowed from medieval Christianity with its concept of heresy. A thought could be a sin and could be heresy.

The GPU could label anyone a heretic. It gradually escaped control by law and the legal authorities and became quite arbitrary. Stalin could use it against anyone. He had a lot of scores to settle. The malicious, vindictive side of his nature was now given free rein. He played with the oppositionists: allowing them back into the fold if they repented of their sins. They caved in to Stalin but this did not save them. The gene of heresy was in their bodies.

Juvenile crime

Juvenile crime was an ever present headache. Kliment Voroshilov, in a letter to Stalin, stated that there were over 3,000 registered 'juvenile hooligans' in Moscow. Of these about 800 were 'gangsters'. About 100 hooligans and homeless children were arrested every day. Voroshilov complained that the authorities had nowhere to send them because no one would accept them. He proposed a solution. 'I do not understand why we cannot just shoot these scoundrels. Do we have to wait until they grow up to be even greater thugs?' The criminal code did not permit the shooting of anyone under the age of 18. In April 1935, the Politburo allowed the shooting of children who were 12 or older. In late 1935, the police took into custody about 160,000 homeless children, of whom 62,000 were sent to correction centres and 10,000 were arrested. The rest were sent home to their parents or orphanages.

The Great Terror

The Great Terror is the term applied to the mass repressions of the period between July–August 1937 and November 1938. The archives reveal that they were a series of centrally planned punitive actions. Mass executions reached a level never hitherto experienced during the Stalin era. The terror devastated the country and worsened the condition of prisoners in the gulag.

The Great Terror is often called the *Ezhovshchina* (Ezhov times), named after Nikolai Ezhov, the head of the NKVD. He was called the 'bloody dwarf' since he was only just over one and a half metres tall (4 ft 10 in) and had an ugly face and body. Stalin (about 5 ft 8 in tall) liked to surround himself with comrades shorter than himself. For instance, he chose the diminutive Ivanov as his English interpreter. In reality, Ezhov was only Stalin's executioner. Stalin set the tasks and Ezhov was to use his ingenuity to accomplish them.

Ezhov became an entrepreneur specialising in fabrication, cruelty and violence. Stalin picked him for a special mission in late 1934. He was to head the team implicating Kamenev and Zinoviev in the murder of Kirov. As a reward for excellent work, Stalin made him a CC secretary and head of the Party Control Commission. Then he was delegated to the NKVD to deal with Trotskyites and Zinovievites. This peaked in the August 1936 show trial of Kamenev, Zinoviev and other former oppositionists. This trial signalled an intensification of repression against anyone who had directly or indirectly supported the opposition. In September 1936, Stalin made Ezhov People's Commissar for Internal Affairs. He made his decision known in a letter from Sochi, where he was on vacation, to the Politburo.

> 'We [Stalin always used the first person plural] consider it absolutely essential to appoint comrade Ezhov as People's Commissar for Internal Affairs. Yagoda was obviously not up to the task of exposing the Trotskyist-Zinovievite bloc. The OGPU is four years late in [accomplishing] this task.'

Yagoda was made People's Commissar for Communications. He was aware that he was living on borrowed time. Some called him the Mephistopheles from

Terror and terrorism

Deployed upwards
- By an individual or group
- Against persons seen, rightly or wrongly, as members or supporters of an oppressive ruling establishment or political ideology

Terrorism is the use of violence deliberately designed to maim, kill or terrify

Deployed downwards
- By the state (counter-terror or state terrorism or repression or oppression)
- To eliminate physically those whose opinions are held to be subversive or perceived to pose a potential ideological threat to the legitimating idea of the state

Counter-terror = state's response to terrorism from below
State terrorism = state violence against perceived opponents
Repression = state violence to eliminate all political opposition that threatens the power base of the leader
Oppression = state violence against distinct groups of the population in order to maintain the collective good, but in reality to eliminate groups which challenge the ideological claims of the state

- Terror is a defining characteristic of modern dictatorships
- Terror serves specific political and socio-economic purposes
- The unleashing of terror (either as repression or oppression) on particular groups in society reveals how the regime seeks to legitimate itself
- The depiction of the 'perpetual enemy' (counter-revolutionaries in a Marxist society; Jews in Nazi Germany) is crucial to understanding the justification of particular methods of repression or oppression

FIGURE 11.2 Terror and terrorism

the (Jewish) Pale. He knew his position was a sinecure and spent his time making paper aeroplanes. He commented when arrested: 'I have long been expecting you'. He was one of the accused at the third show trial and was executed in March 1938.

Ezhov was more successful at fabricating evidence and beating confessions out of the accused than Yagoda. Another show trial began in Moscow in January 1937. Seventeen defendants, including such Bolshevik luminaries as Karl Radek, the leading communist wit, and Georgy Sokolnikov were lumped together in an 'anti-Soviet Trotskyist centre'. They were either shot or sentenced to long prison terms. Preparations for the show trial against the 'Right Deviation' got under way. The main targets were Nikolai Bukharin, Aleksei Rykov and Mikhail Tomsky. Tomsky evaded the bullet in the neck by committing suicide in August 1936. The plenum judged them guilty of setting up a terrorist organisation. In March 1938, the third great show trial began. They were all shot.

The court concluded that there were right-wing terrorist organisations throughout the country. In May 1937, a Politburo resolution exiled former oppositionists and expelled Party members and their families from Moscow, Leningrad and Kyiv. Other cities were later added to this list. Suspicion then fell on the military. Arrests of military leaders began in 1936 and peaked in the June 1937 trial of the 'anti-Soviet Trotskyist military organisation'. Among those executed was Marshal Mikhail Tukhachevsky, deputy People's Commissar for Defence. It was claimed that he had links with Nazi generals and was conspiring against Stalin. A dossier 'framing' Tukhachevsky was put together by anti-Soviet elements in Paris and the German *Abwehr* (counter-intelligence) and allowed to fall into the hands of President Eduard Beneš of Czechoslovakia. He passed it on

11.3 Debin River Camp

Source: 'Upper Debin Camp', *The Gulag Collection*, Nikolai Getman, (The Jamestown Foundation, 2001).

to Stalin. Tukhachevsky, a military genius, fascinated Stalin. Initially he rejected his views on mechanised warfare and then adopted them. Had he still been alive in 1941, the Soviet Union would not have suffered its initial, catastrophic defeats.

A fifth column

After dealing with political opposition, Stalin turned his attention, in July 1937, to unreliable social and national groups. Repression of the broad population now began. Stalin targeted not only those whom he judged guilty or under suspicion but those who, because of their thinking, could potentially join the opposition. In other words, he was setting out to eliminate those whom be believed formed or could form a fifth column. All kulaks and criminals who had returned to their villages were to be registered.

TABLE 11.1 Order No. 00447 (two zeros in front of an NKVD directive revealed that it had been issued on the personal orders of Stalin) (extract)

	First Category	Second Category	Total
Azerbaijan	1,500	3,750	5,250
Armenia	500	1,000	1,500
Belarus	2,000	10,000	12,000
Georgia	2,000	3,000	5,000
Kyrgyzstan	250	500	750
Tajikistan	500	1,300	1,800
Turkmenistan	500	1,500	2,000
Uzbekistan	750	4,000	4,750
Bashkortostan	500	1,500	2,000
Dagestan	500	2,500	3,000
Azov–Black Sea krai	5,000	8,000	13,000
West Siberia krai	5,000	12,000	17,000
Leningrad oblast	4,000	10,000	14,000
Moscow oblast	5,000	30,000	35,000
Sverdlovsk (Ekaterinburg) ob.	4,000	6,000	10,000
Chelyabinsk oblast	1,500	4,500	6,000

Source: J. Arch Getty and Oleg V. Naumov, *The Road to Terror: Stalin and the Self-Destruction of the Bolsheviks* (1999).

In July 1937, the NKVD was ordered to arrest all foreigners, naturalised foreigners and those with relatives abroad employed in water stations and researching in microbiology. It believed that the German General Staff and the Gestapo (*Geheime Staatspolizeiamt*) were stepping up espionage and subversion. All German nationals who had worked, or were working, in military enterprises and in strategic economic positions were to be arrested. This was then extended to other sectors of the economy. Other national groups were then targeted. In August 1937, Polish 'subversive groups' were to be liquidated. This was followed by the repression of Romanians, Estonians, Latvians, Finns, Greeks, Afghans, Iranians, Chinese, Bulgarians and Macedonians. In late 1937, Koreans living near the border with Korea, totalling 172,000, were deported to Kazakhstan and Uzbekistan.

This order, issued in July 1937, opened the floodgates of repression. It was to deal with 'former kulaks, criminal and other anti-Soviet elements'. They were divided into two categories. All those in the first category were to be shot. Those in the second category were to be sentenced to 8–10 years imprisonment. Altogether 268,950 persons were to be arrested, of whom 72,950 were to be shot. Each region had its quota. Local leaders could request an increase in their quota. Many did. The families of the victims were either sent to camps or exiled.

In January 1939, Stalin confirmed, in a telegram, that the use of 'physical methods [torture]' was still justified. In another document, in 1938, he also gave his consent to the execution of 138 high ranking military officers. During 1937–39, Stalin and Molotov personally signed 400 lists of those to be executed. These totalled 44,000 names.

The elevation of the NKVD

In 1937, Stalin increased the salaries and perks of leading NKVD officers. Now the top comrades qualified for their own dachas and huge bonuses. Even more significantly, Stalin bestowed on them the ultimate accolade: they became the 'armed detachment of our Party'. This meant, in reality, that they had become Stalin's own Praetorian Guard. As such they were now beyond the control of the law or the legal institutions. They were also above the Party and government.

What was morale like inside the NKVD? A 1935 report listed over 11,000 offences and crimes committed by officers. The high incidence of crimes, over 5,600, alarmed the writer of the report. Many of these had been committed by the top echelons. It turned out that almost two-thirds of the leading cadres at regional and city level had been disciplined. Sloppy work, debauchery, drunkenness and disobeying orders were commonplace. Theft and embezzlement were also prevalent.

Even in the more elite GUGB, one of the predecessors of the KGB, things were no better. Over the period October 1936–January 1938, almost 4,000 officers were arrested, dismissed or transferred to the reserves. In addition, another 1,400 were punished for being members of counter-revolutionary groups or being in contact with Trotskyites and so on. Another 600 were dismissed for being morally corrupt and a further 500 were discovered to have served with the Whites. Early deaths and suicides swept away another thousand (Lewin 2005).

Beria

The conclusion of the Great Terror, by a Politburo decree in November 1938, marked the end of Nikolai Ezhov. He was arrested in April 1939 and shot in February 1940. There was irony in the fact that he was condemned for being head of a counter-revolutionary organisation.

Beria receives a telephone call from Stalin inviting him to his Kremlin office.

'Good day, Lavrenty Pavlovich, how are you?'

'Comrade Stalin, I am well.'

'Good. We have some very good news for you. We have decided to appoint you People's Commissar of Internal Affairs. Ezhov is no longer up to the job. There are war clouds on the horizon so you will have to fulfil very demanding tasks. How you achieve them is up to you. You have a free hand to act as you like. However, we shall not tolerate failure.'

Beria was exhilarated. He was aware that every time Stalin said 'we' he meant 'I'. He, and he alone, would decide his, Beria's, fate. Yagoda had worked for a season and had then been discarded and shot. Ezhov was certain to be shot. He knew too many secrets. Beria was confident that he was cleverer than the two of them combined. He had to ensure that Stalin did not treat him as he had Yagoda and Ezhov.

Lavrenty Beria was close to Stalin and a fellow Georgian. He faced a huge challenge. The NKVD was in disarray as many of its officers had been arrested and sentenced. Molotov and Kaganovich were pretty good administrators but Beria was in a class of his own. He was absolutely brilliant. What does that mean? Administration is like Legoland™. The brilliant administrator is able to break down a task into small parts. He can see how they all fit together. As such, he can give each group clear orders about what he wants them to achieve. Each group is a piece of Lego. When a bottleneck occurs, he can immediately arrive at a solution so that the whole project keeps moving. Part of the skill is to select the right personnel for the right job. They all need to fit together like Lego. Beria had the mind of a top scientist but he also had the mind of a top criminal. An irresistible combination. He could put the fear of Marx into any comrade. He was the 'merchant of death', a past master in cruelty, especially psychological torture, and as deadly as a viper. An added advantage was that he wore his Marxism lightly. He had a pragmatist's mind. In his flat cap, pince-nez and open-necked shirt, he looked like a refugee from the intelligentsia. He knew he could read the boss like a book. Beria had prodigious energy. He also had a gargantuan sexual appetite. His men would pick up damsels he fancied and deliver them to his bedchamber. Some of them even enjoyed the experience and recalled him decades later as a gentle lover. He had a charming, sensitive wife who could see through Stalin at ten paces. She regarded him as a hood and a malevolent influence and wanted Lavrenty Pavlovich to concentrate on a technical career.

Beria's first major task was to eliminate the presumed fifth column in the territories acquired as a result of the Hitler–Stalin (or Ribbentrop–Molotov) non-aggression pact of August 1939. The Soviet Union later took over the Baltic States of Estonia, Latvia and Lithuania, western Ukraine and western Belarus (previously in Poland) and northern Bukovina and Bessarabia (from Romania). There were four large scale deportations from these territories to the east, involving 370,000 persons or about 3 per cent of the population. Others were simply shot. There was collusion between the NKVD and the Gestapo. In March 1940, the Politburo decided to execute 4,443 Polish officers at Katyn, in Belarus, and 16,000 at other sites. Another 5,000 members of the Polish civilian elite were also murdered. They were regarded as inveterate enemies of Soviet power. Their families were deported to the east.

NKVD tasks

On the eve of war, in June 1941, the NKVD was an enormous economic conglomerate. It was charged with constructing, as rapidly as possible, a host of military and strategic projects. Hundreds of thousands of convicts were moved around the country in a vain attempt to fulfil the targets.

In 1940, Beria's proposal of moving another 50,000 prisoners to the Kolyma gold mines was approved. In order to expand rapidly the output of nickel from Norilsk Nickel and Northern Nickel, in the polar north, these and other metal producing enterprises were transferred to the NKVD. Hence Beria became responsible for a large number of strategically important enterprises. In March 1941, the NKVD was charged with building airports for the People's Commissariat for Defence. Over 400,000 prisoners were needed for this vitally important strategic undertaking.

The huge workload of the NKVD led to its reorganisation. In February 1941, the NKVD was split into the NKVD and the People's Commissariat for State Security (NKGB). Beria stayed as head of the NKVD and his deputy, V. N. Merkulov, became head of state security. The gulag became one of the administrations of the NKVD.

'What is Rabinovich doing in exile?' 'Scientific work. He married a Chukcha [nationality in Arctic] and is breeding frost-resistant Jews.'

Beria and football

Football was wildly popular in the Soviet Union and one of the reasons was that a football ground was the only place a person could vent his frustration and opposition. Beria was a passionate football fan. He became the patron of Dinamo Moscow, the NKVD team. He wanted Dinamo to win everything. Nikolai Starostin and his three brothers did not want to play for Dinamo and built up Spartak Moscow as one of the most successful teams of the 1930s. They enjoyed taking the NKVD down a peg. Nikolai had played against Beria in Georgia. 'He was a crude, dirty, left half.' In 1939, in the semi-final of the Soviet Cup, Spartak beat Dinamo. Beria was so furious he ordered the game replayed. Again Spartak won and Beria kicked every chair in sight. Spartak went on to win the double that year. Beria had had the patron of Spartak arrested and shot. But he could not touch a top footballer. His chance came in March 1942, when the country was at war. Starostin and his three brothers were arrested and sent to the gulag for ten years. Among the accusations against Nikolai was that he played football in a 'bourgeois way'! Stalin's son Vasily also wanted to build up a team to challenge Dinamo. In 1952 he tried to get Starostin released to play for his team. Beria was obdurate. However, Vasily smuggled Starostin into his apartment in Moscow. He was rearrested and sent back to the gulag. When Beria was executed the Starostin brothers were released and Nikolai returned to Spartak and achieved spectacular success as president.

The gulag

There were 528 gulag camps scattered over the country. A state control inspector found there was a propensity to set up new agencies in Moscow or other desirable cities where the officials 'could have a good time without concerning themselves at all about the camps'. Another aspect of the gulag which has not yet been explored in the published literature was production for the black market. Those who gained most were the gulag camp administrations and the central gulag administration. To cite only one example: wooden chess sets, skilfully carved by prisoners, were sold at low prices. However it was almost impossible to buy one. The black market price was about three times the state price.

   In the early 1930s, about one in six of the adult Soviet population was subject to repression or persecution. Stalin and his team viewed these socially alien elements, ex-Party members and the others, as a nascent fifth column. The drive to eliminate this potential fifth column led, inexorably, to the Great Terror.

11.4 Prisoners sometimes built settlements for native people: these are Chuchki but not prisoners
Source: 'A Northern Settlement', *The Gulag Collection*, Nikolai Getman, (The Jamestown Foundation, 2001).

According to the estimates of the USSR Ministry of Justice in 1958, the normal courts convicted 7.1 million persons in 1937–40 and a further 3.1 million in 1941. When the OGPU extra-legal courts are added, the number of convicted persons in 1937–40 rises to 8.6 million. The courts sentenced about 20 million persons between 1930 and 1940. Another 3 million were exiled or deported. According to the 1939 census there were 37.5 million Soviet families and 4 million single adults (total population was 162 million). This reveals that the majority of Soviet families were touched by the tragedy of repression.

Why did the purges end? One suggestion is that Stalin was satisfied that Party and state cadres had been rejuvenated. A new cohort was in place ready for new battles. Party and state agencies had been devastated. For instance, in 1937–38, there was a turnover of 75 per cent among senior and middle level cadres (managers and technicians) in the Commissariat of Railways. Kaganovich had masterminded this mayhem. At the 18th Party Congress, in March 1939, Stalin proudly announced that between April 1934 and March 1939 over half a million cadres had been recruited to revivify Party and state administration, especially at the highest levels. In early 1939, the number of nomenklatura posts filled by the Central Committee apparatus was 33,000. Just under a half of these had been appointed in 1937–38. Many had not yet graduated before their elevation. The rulers of the post-Stalin Soviet Union (except Gorbachev) came from this cohort.

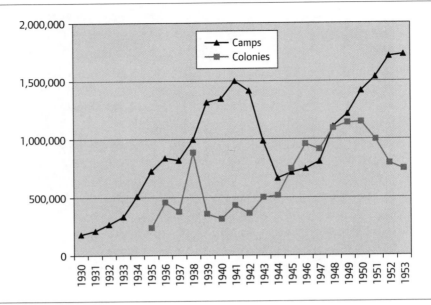

FIGURE 11.3 Number of prisoners in the gulag (camps and colonies), 1930–53
Source: Based on Richard Overy, *The Dictators: Hitler's Germany and Stalin's Russia* (2004).

The impact of the war

The war brought even greater hardships. Rations were cut and about 2 million died of starvation. Numbers were made up by enemy POWs (2 million in 1945 but only 19,000 in 1953, many Germans having been repatriated to the GDR) and waves of new prisoners. The gulag reached its zenith during the last years of Stalin, when special camps were set up. This is the period when the *vory v zakone*, literally thieves in law, expanded. They were professional criminals and were sworn enemies of the Soviet system. They fought for dominance in the camps and the victors emerged after Stalin's demise to spread over the country. The political prisoners became even more alienated. Stalin did not realise how uneconomic and potentially explosive the gulag had become.

The rehabilitation committee

Aleksandr Yakovlev, the father of Gorbachev's glasnost, devoted much effort to chronicling the crimes of the Stalin era (Litvin and Keep 2005). As chair of the rehabilitation committee, he looked into millions of cases. He estimated, on incomplete data, that 5.95 million persons were arrested for political offences between 1921 and 1953. Of these, 4.06 million were sentenced by regular courts and extra-judicial tribunals (e.g. troikas). Over 3.5 million were victimised as a result of their ethnic identity between 1936 and 1961. In the RSFSR, for example, 11 nations were deported in their entirety and another 48 suffered this penalty in part. Yakovlev estimates that, during the Soviet era, the number of persons who lost their lives for political reasons (executed or died in the camps or prisons) was between 20 and 25 million. This figure includes the victims of famines: 5.5 million during and immediately after the Civil War and 5 million in the 1930s. The number of persons convicted in the RSFSR, between 1923 and 1953, was over 41 million. If one adds those in other republics, the figure is astronomical.

An overview

The campaigns of mass repression may be summarised as follows (Litvin and Keep 2005):

Stage 1: Dekulakisation was an attempt to wipe out the rural elite; it was a gigantic settling of accounts; there was much improvisation and loss of life. Its prime motivation was political, the eradication of the kulak menace, and not economic. Officials east of the Urals were always appealing for more labour. Hence there was a coincidence of interests between the Stalin leadership and local officials.

Stage 2: In 1932 some of those arrested were released; a man-made famine ensued causing greater loss of life than Stage 1.

Stage 3: Simultaneously and especially after 1934 the NKVD was ordered to carry out sweeps of 'former people' and other marginals from the towns who were regarded as anti-Soviet: those with irregular political backgrounds; infringers of internal passport regulations (obligatory from November 1932); beggars and petty criminals. The archives show a steady rise in repression. Stalin and his team were very skilled at sending out contradictory signals simultaneously. This tactic was to confuse the opposition. The murder of Kirov changed the climate among the leaders. Stalin's complicity in Kirov's murder remains unproved. Stalin was a nervous, insecure leader. These traits infected his team. They all came to believe that there were plots or potential plots everywhere. As Marxists they thought in class terms. All those who did not support the general line of the Party were class enemies.

Stage 4: The NKVD now applied the techniques it had mastered in Stage 3. There was action on two levels: i) at the top against political opponents (ex-oppositionists in the Party, military leaders) culminating in the show trials; ii) about a dozen secret mass operations against various groups such as those living in borderlands and social marginals. This was partly based on previously compiled lists (from applications for internal passports, residence permits, job applications or information from informers); quotas of those to be arrested were sent down to the local police.

The show trials were designed to increase the vigilance of the population, especially Party members. They were judicial farces, like modern-day morality plays, and public reaction was carefully noted. Stalin, by a decree in August 1937, made use of resentment over shortages by promoting public events at which locals could vent their anger at former bosses under arrest. These paralleled the show trials in Moscow. This deflected blame away from the Stalin team, the real culprits for the shortages.

Stage 5: This stage began during Stage 4, and was concerned with ethnic cleansing. The targeted groups included Poles from western Ukraine and western Belarus, annexed in 1939–40; most were deported but some were shot (Katyn massacre); later the Volga Germans and other Germans, in 1941, and many, mostly Muslim, nationalities in the north Caucasus, in 1943–44. They were accused of collaborating with the invading Germans; trials were dispensed with.

Stage 6: This involved two groups of prisoners of war: i) repatriated Red Army soldiers (1.8 million) or civilian forced labourers (over 3.5 million); these were regarded as collaborators; ii) enemy POW and enemy nationals rounded up in east Germany or Austria after 1945; politically unreliable elements in the Eastern European people's democracies; those who engaged in partisan or political activities against the reimposition of Soviet hegemony in Ukraine and the Baltic States. Partisan activity (especially in western Ukraine and Lithuania) continued until 1953. The total number in the gulag was about 5.3 million, about half in camps and half in exile. Roughly 90 per cent of the exiles were non-Russians.

Interpretations

Scholars can be divided into four groups:

1   the intentionalists;

2   the revisionists;

3   the post-modernists or culturalists;

4   the new political historians.

Intentionalists

The leading intentionalist is Robert Conquest, the doyen of terror studies. His *Great Terror: A Reassessment* (1990; first published 1968) is the benchmark study. The intentionalists regard the terror as functional, an integral part of the regime's objective of eliminating class enemies and forming the new socialist man and woman. They regard Bolshevik ideology as all-important: the ruling Party exercised a monopoly of force, which was its chief tool in forging the new socialist society. Policies were drafted at the centre by the leader and his team within the Politburo, which as an institution had been rendered powerless, and passed down to local leaders (mini-Stalins) to implement. Adherents of this school concede that

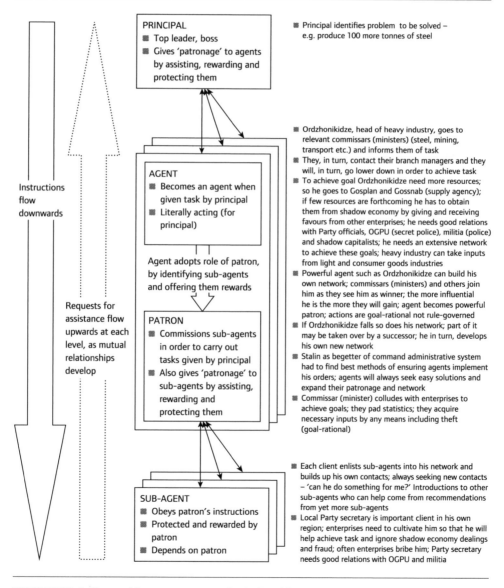

FIGURE 11.4 Networking structures and relationships

local officials were sometimes able to use their initiative, for instance, in regard to the quotas handed down of those to be repressed (purged). Hence, the totalitarian model needs refinement in certain particulars, but basically holds good since popular input into the process was not significant. Some students of Soviet governance (Richard Löwenthal, Moshe Lewin) discern a struggle between two 'logical systems': personal rule by the dictator versus a bureaucracy that sought greater security and regularity in managing a modern state, especially one intent on fashioning a socialist economy and society.

Nicolas Werth, a French scholar, has made a thought-provoking contribution to the debate (2002). Werth agrees with the revisionists that the state bureaucracy was in a chaotic state, given the impossible demands made on it and the constant changes in Party policy. Successive campaigns created an atmosphere of panic and crisis. Under these circumstances, the principal, Stalin, could not effectively control his local subordinates, his agents. The principal was constantly trying to limit their autonomy by periodic purges. There was always the fear that a fifth column could emerge to challenge his authority. In response to the revisionist argument (see below) that it is naive to attribute the terror to one individual, one principal, Stalin, Werth sees the entire leadership as suffering from 'institutionalised paranoia'. The Great Terror was a great 'social cleansing' which created a subservient technocratic elite. But as the number of agents grew, the principal's problems increased and Stalin could not always get his way since officials kept to their own self-serving routines. Even so, the Soviet system of government by fear was extended to the satellite countries of Eastern Europe, most of which experienced leadership purges, concentration camps, etc.

Werth also focuses on the violence of the regime. He finds four 'repressive logics' which operated together to make Stalin's regime so violent. They were

1   Stalin and his team's paranoia;
2   its desire to centralise all key decision making;
3   the criminalisation of all activities outside the official, planned economy;
4   the rise of Great Russian chauvinism.

Another important factor was the simultaneous combination of legal and extra-legal methods. Policy was often not made explicit, and so officials, and still more the populace generally, had to guess what was wanted of them. State violence was applied rather indiscriminately and with various degrees of intensity against constantly shifting targets.

The most encompassing and impressive study of the gulag is that by Anne Applebaum (2003). The first part of her study is devoted to the administrative system and its economic rationale. As regards the reasons for the terror, she is firmly in the intentionalist camp. Most of her book is devoted to the experiences of the inmates. It is a classic case study of the problems inherent in the principal–agent relationship. Rules specified a minimum of welfare but were disregarded in practice; survival often depended on arbitrary acts by guards and even criminals, who treated prisoners as subhuman. Food was used as an instrument of control. Hierarchies developed among the prisoners. A dominant group were the *vory v zakone*. They were professional criminals and the gulag system permitted them to recruit and to pass on their skills. Thieving had to be skilful and booty had to be shared with one's fellow thieves. No foreigner was permitted to join. It was an exclusive Russian phenomenon. A member could only murder another with the permission of the group. Anyone who betrayed the group was executed. A member could leave the fraternity but he was to remain silent about his past.

Most western scholarship on the terror supports the intentionalists. Russian scholars have published many key documents and have explored central and local archives; these new sources highlight the callous cruelty of the system.

The revisionists

If Robert Conquest is the doyen of the intentionalist school, the founding father of the revisionist school is J. Arch Getty. His *Origins of the Great Purges* (1985) was the bible of the revisionists. He attempted to escape the straitjacket of the totalitarian school which saw the principal as all-powerful and his agents obeying him out of fear. Getty's approach was to see Stalin as just another decision maker, whose will was mediated through cadres with a limited de facto ability to interpret it as they chose. There was pressure from below as well as from above. Hence, whereas the totalitarians were concerned, first and foremost, with central decision making, Getty looked away from leadership politics and allotted a central role to the agents. In 1999, he and the Russian scholar, Oleg Naumov, published a striking volume of documents with extensive commentary. He toned down his arguments about input from below but the drift it is still there. Getty sees struggles between the central and regional bodies as power struggles rather than just as contests between senior and junior officials. It is clear from the documents that locals were competing with one another in harshness and cruelty.

Some NKVD cadres were from orphanages, had no experience of family life, and regarded Stalin as a father figure. A few of them tried to limit the centre's lust for violence but the majority were willing helpers. They enthusiastically helped to shape and implement policies. For example, they drew up the lists which were used to implement Order No. 00447 of 30 July 1937 (see Table 11.1). They could take life and death decisions in the regions. They could not overfulfil the plan on their own initiative. They had to petition Moscow. Ezhov then passed on the request to Stalin. He usually scribbled 'I agree' in the margin. It was rather like Stalin letting the dogs of violence off the leash. But he remained the master and reined them in from time to time.

The revisionists saw themselves as essentially social historians, concerned primarily with the fate of the working class, and to a lesser extent the emergence of the new elites. They sought to write history 'from below'. Their leading exponent, Sheila Fitzpatrick, is little concerned with leadership policies and never seeks to examine Stalin's agenda or the infighting at the top. She reveals that the new elites were essentially peasant in origin and brought into their administrative work something of the old Russian patriarchal and collectivist mentality. For example, networking was a way of life. Promotion always depended on whom one knew. Patron–client relations were important, even in the intelligence services. The nuclear physicists were the exception to this rule. Another aspect which fascinates Fitzpatrick is the cultural revolution which accompanied industrialisation and collectivisation. New cohorts of writers, poets, dramatists, film producers and musicians emerged.

Post-modernists or culturalists

What is post-modernism (PM)? This highly influential trend originated in France where philosophers, almost all Marxist, became disillusioned after the failure of the revolutionary New Left in 1968. There was a great variety of views among them, but most assert the fragmentary and plural character of reality. They question the power of reason to depict or explain historical processes, and consider it a waste of time to try to ascertain the causes or consequences of events; what matters are not the 'facts of history', deemed unknowable, but relationships. They are sceptical towards the claims of grand social theories or narratives, whether Marxist, liberal or Christian. There are no universal truths. They were used in the past to legitimate the power of those who know and deny power to those who do not know, and so should be criticised ('deconstructed').

Hence, with regard to the Stalin era, the PM thinkers stand at the opposite pole to the intentionalists. In their universe the difference between right and wrong, good and evil, is blurred.

Cultural historians, sometimes termed 'culturalists' or 'culturologists', belong to a related school of thought which has been influenced by the intellectual nihilism of the PM philosophers. They do not concern themselves with how people take decisions but seek to elucidate their inner thoughts. They ask, for example, how ordinary men and women 'constructed' a new identity for themselves under the pressure of the Stalinist state. Was their new 'self' modern, socialist, Russian nationalist, or what? They have examined the diaries a few citizens kept, or the autobiographies they had to compile when asked to prove their loyalty, along with police documents, to seek clues as to their inner state of mind. Critics of this school allege that they are looking for something for which there is not sufficient evidence. They warn that it is misleading to apply criteria to a totalitarian state that have been developed in examining how people interact in a free society. In sum, they are barking up the wrong tree: what we should really be trying to get at is the responsibility of various actors, high and low, for their behaviour. A culturalist might respond that that will only become clear when we have built up a full picture of the whole society: i.e. the doings of every subject and actor. Susanne Schattenberg puts the case for the culturalists succinctly (2002):

> 'If we proceed from the assumption, not that an omnipotent state
> maltreated a powerless population of victims, but that each individual was
> also subject and actor, then it is relevant to ask what the criteria were
> according to which each person acted and thought, and how these criteria
> were influenced and changed. The subjective view of the historical actors
> would then become the key to [understanding] the objective history of
> violence and [solving] the problem of why such deeds could happen.
> The new cultural history can help to explain . . . how an idea can be
> transformed into violent acts. It establishes the nexus between the state's
> plans and aims on one hand and the behaviour of various segments of the
> population on the other, by focusing on the point that each "system" is
> conditioned by the other, and studies this interaction. In this way, culture
> is the transmission belt, so to speak, whereby the Politburo, appealing to
> pre-existing patterns and traditions, manages to influence [the actors']
> view of reality, their norms, values, and motives for doing what they did.'

The new political historians

New work on Stalin and Stalinism published in 2004–06 by historians Richard Overy, Robert Service, E. A. Rees and Geoffrey Hosking has attempted to forge a middle ground between old totalitarian (or 'intentionalist') models and the revisionists. This new political history has largely built on and developed some 'intentionalist' ideas such as T. H. Rigby's earlier characterisation of Stalinism in the 1930s as a 'mono-organisational system', that is the centralised coordination of all social activities, which in practice was made workable by the initiative of Party officials 'below'. However, the new literature has moved further away from the top-heavy political system envisaged by Robert C. Tucker in which orders originating from the leader, Stalin, were handed down to subordinates and perfectly subservient lower level Party officials in an attempt to realise a socially engineered 'revolution from above'. Society is important, but it is the way in which it played, or was manufactured to play, its part in legitimating Stalinist political culture in the 1930s that is at issue. The concepts of legitimacy and authority in understanding the ways in which power was rationalised and perceived by both individuals and groups have become important once again to students of Russian history. Hence, the refocus on the concept of dictatorship, for the one-party systems developed in Germany and the Soviet Union during the inter-war period can only be understood by breaking down the antecedents, means and methods of political rulership. 'Dictatorship' does not necessarily infer the straightforward rule by one man or one political party. It is the product of the combination of a variety of social, cultural, economic, ideological and institutional factors. Themes dominating new work include: the ideological foundations of the one party state, the precise mechanics of Soviet power in the 1930s, the legitimation of state power, the nature of personal dictatorship, and the intellectual antecedents of ideology. The result is not necessarily a new characterisation of Stalinism, but a clearer understanding of the quirks of Soviet rulership and its corresponding ideology.

In *The Dictators: Hitler's Germany and Stalin's Russia* (2004), Richard Overy's concern is with the practical substance of dictatorship and its distinct forms, hence state-sponsored repression or terror and the 'cult of personality' are broadly identified as the clearest markers of such systems. Political legitimation is taken as a core feature of political practice and therefore these two aspects are discussed in relation to the role played by the gradual moulding and application of a distinct type of revolutionary ideology as the ultimate source of personal and state legitimacy. On a superficial level, Stalin legitimated his political position on Lenin's legacy of 'revolution'. Overy discusses the two-fold purpose of the cult as a political tool by which the leader is able to a) consolidate his political position and b) harness social or public consent for the new moral universe represented by the revolutionary ideology of the state. The cult of personality thus enforces the image of the leader as a leviathan figure, solely representative of a general will. But the legitimacy of the image of leader and the system he represents would not be complete without public affirmation of his political status through rallies and other en masse gatherings and ideological rituals such as Party meetings.

A closer study of 'terror' reveals much about how the dictatorships functioned in practice. The original 'intentionalist' contention, that Stalin instituted and directed various kinds of purges during the 1930s, is affirmed in the 'new history'. What is new is the analysis concerning the conditions of state-sponsored terrorism and its specific political function and rationale. Overy argues that the escalation of the terror between 1936 and 1938 can indeed be explained by factors 'from below'. It is far more instructive, however, to consider that Stalin created a distinct framework within which social forces (ordinary Soviet citizens and party officials) could express their resentment and self-interest in the process of endorsing the guilt of, for instance, unpopular figures. (Overy cites the example of Stalin instructing local officials to hold show trials in the provinces in 1937.) However, society was not necessarily bludgeoned into submission in a climate of fear of reprisal in the way described by the 'intentionalists' or 'totalitarian thinkers'. Stalin did not demand social subservience; he sought to harness spontaneity, discontent and existing social attitudes in underpinning the 'total' terror process of class enemy victimisation, and there was an abundance of human capital for this task. 'Show trials' of various kinds, furthermore, provided evidence of the existence of a threat, thus consolidating the impression that 'enemies of the people' actually existed. Stalin also built on existing social mores, particularly prejudices, which in some cases pre-dated 1917, on top of the culture and language of revolution associated with the 1920s. In these ways terror was deemed legitimate. Stalin was a political mastermind who, as Robert Service writes in *Stalin: A Biography* (2004), created a chaotic atmosphere that suited his purposes. In many respects the terror process was self-propelling, but it was in fact a tightly coordinated operation directed and instituted from above. The inspiration for the escalation of terror in 1937 and its end, albeit in consultation with Politburo colleagues, in 1938 was Stalin. Overy adopts a functionalist approach to Stalin's terror, specifically the Great Purge (1936–38), and argues that it had a distinct, albeit perverse logic. The purge was a formal way of ensuring Party subservience to Stalin, institutionalising Party self-discipline and eliminating political incompetence. It was a crude mechanism by which to achieve elite turnover in order to maintain ideological standards. More crucially for Stalin's own populist cult of personality, the terror was used as a mechanism to show that the leader was not the repressor of Party-state and society but an overbearing guardian of the revolutionary principle of state power by ridding the system of malign elements. In this role, he becomes the source of state legitimacy. This was a revolutionary regime that legitimised itself through the elimination of counter-revolutionary actions. As Overy explains, the 'creation of the idea of the perpetual enemy' was indispensable for Stalin. The purges were not simply a product of Stalin's despotic paranoia, but were in fact a response to the presumed existence of political enemies in the top echelons of power, a point jointly confirmed by Robert Service.

'Sociological utopia', as characterised by Overy, is the ideological foundation stone upon which Stalin justified his actions and political goals. It encapsulates the rationale of social engineering and the ideal of a classless, unified and 'organic' community. The modernising project was based on the assumption that through the creation of the right type of socio-economic conditions, scientific progress and the evolution of a Soviet new man and woman was ensured. It is this that distinguishes Stalin's Soviet Union from Hitler's Germany. Overy uses a metaphor to explain the point: 'the new community constituted a "body" that was in need of therapy and healing . . . the Soviet object was to identify and ameliorate the "social illness" through the positive pursuit of prophylactic remedies, not to gouge out those elements through violent medical intervention'. Stalin's vision of dictatorship can best be distinguished in his concern for social cleansing and social regeneration, something quite distinct from Hitler's exclusivist 'biological utopi-anism' predicated on principles of race.

In *Stalin: A Biography*, Robert Service goes further than Richard Overy in arguing that Stalin relied on a complex combination of existing Party structures and the Bolshevik mind-set in legitimating terror: indirect incriminations, inten-tionally fabricated evidence produced by state security agencies and disagreements with orders at Politburo level all propelled the process further. More often than not the Central Committee was 'shocked' into submission. The 'terror' was a major operation that required input from several spheres, including the police, people and Party officials. Stalin was not therefore an isolated figure who operated in a political vacuum; even he was obliged to consult with associates on those to be arrested (such as, most notably, Ezhov, the head of the NKVD prior to Beria). The collaboration and consent of other Party officials, that is, the context of 'terror', was key to both diffusing exclusive responsibility and endorsing the process. The Communist Party was marginalised during the 1930s but some important factions remained and horizontal rivalry continued. Stalin played institutions off each other.

The essence of Stalin's personal despotism can best be understood in the pre-meditated exploitation of the systemic defects (such as 'misinformation') for his own purposes.

Service readdresses the state–society dichotomy deconstructed by the revision-ists and concludes that terror was most definitely directed from above, although initiative from below seeking Stalin's endorsement (for instance, for more arrests of local Party officials) was not discouraged, indeed quite the opposite. The flow of information between centre and periphery was much more fluid than assumed by revisionists: Stalin remained deeply involved in the terror process via his personal envoys who oversaw events on the ground. Service captures the essence of the new political history in the following extract from *Stalin* (2004):

> '[T]his was not a totalitarian dictatorship, as conventionally defined,
> because Stalin lacked the capacity, even at the height of his power, to
> secure automatic universal compliance with his wishes. He could purge
> personnel without difficulty. But when it came to ridding the Soviet order
> of many informal practices he disliked, he was much less successful.'

The second pillar of Service's argument concerns two different structural con-straints placed on Stalin's rule: the first relates to the persistence of informal prac-tices (the patronage network) without which the Soviet system was unworkable, and which were not, despite Stalin's original aim, eradicated by the Great Purge; the second relates to Stalin as the inheritor of a Soviet order created and consolid-ated by Lenin between October 1917 and March 1919, and whose fundamental characteristics remained unchanged in the 74 years of the Soviet experiment. This order (characterised by Service as 'one-party dictatorship; centralised party; one-ideology state; legal nihilism') imposed a framework within which Stalin was obliged to develop his policies and which at times even forced compromise or change of viewpoint in processes of reform and reaction. Service's third main argument concerns the determinants of Stalin's despotism. Stalin was a very cunning leader who supplemented his rule by a tightly regulated 'cult of impersonality' (an empty cult), which kept close associates guessing, but was powerful enough to manipulate public opinion. The cult of leadership during the 1930s left people in doubt about who was primarily responsible for 'terror', and social discontent was widespread in both town and country and cannot be underestimated. Society was not traumatised into permanent compliance. It is this fact that leads Service to conclude that Stalin's despotism was not fuelled by clinical paranoia, but by a very real sense of insecurity. The revisionists fail to distinguish between different types of causes in explaining the terror of the 1930s. Distinction must be made, argues Service, between instigative and facilitating causes in determining the nature of Stalin's reaction to an existing situation (major social discontent) and the course of action adopted as a result. Stalinism should not be viewed as having existed as a distinct ideological bubble independent of the other periods of Soviet history; as Service notes, its study reveals various unifying themes of Soviet historical experience that should not be ignored.

Overy's discussion of the 'moral universe of dictatorships' is a key theme of E. A. Rees's exploration of the Machiavellian character and intellectual substance of Stalin's dictatorship in *Political Thought from Machiavelli to Stalin: Revolutionary Machiavellism* (2004). The parallels between Niccolò Machiavelli's (1459–1517) thinking about politics and Stalin's are striking, particularly with regard to the self-perception of the ruler and his political duties and obligations in the consolidation of the state. (Stalin possessed a copy of Machiavelli's *The Prince*.) Stalin may not have created, but merely tinkered with the system over which he ruled, but he did adapt a revolutionary culture of the pragmatic pursuit of a utopian goal in which the ends justified the means. As Rees explains:

> '[Stalin's] policy of promoting cadres coincided with Machiavelli's advice not to hold youth back. The "revolution from above" and the terror of 1936–38 coincided with Machiavelli's prescription that states constantly need to renew themselves, by returning to the original founding principles, to guard against corruption and to restore virtù. Revolution was a great consumer of human energy, which needed to be replenished. Machiavelli's advice to tyrants was that, to preserve their rule, they should keep everything in constant ferment . . . In accordance with Machiavelli's view, the state-builder creates the basis for morality; therefore his own actions are above moral censure.'

The ultimate goal of politics becomes intertwined with the role of the leader as the protector and guarantor of the wellbeing and survival of the state and its legitimising principle, for this simultaneously enables him to maintain and preserve power. In this perverse rationalisation of the political obligation of the leader to the state, morality is separated from politics, justifying the application of violence (or terror) in politics. The absolute conviction of the 'righteousness of the [utopian] cause' is the basic characteristic of the moral universe of dictatorship. Other methods of Stalinist rule analogous to Machiavelli's political philosophy include the elimination of all forms of political opposition; the cultivation of a distinct populist cult of personality in which the leader is transformed into heroic defender of the state and draws inspiration from the support of the masses for the state idea; the advantages arising from 'inventing conspiracies'; the ability to adapt ideology to suit circumstance. The aim of Rees, following on from Overy, is to explore the broader European context from which Stalinist and Nazi ideologies evolved, and to suggest that they shared many intellectual roots with other political phenomena of the time.

Geoffrey Hosking, *Rulers and Victims: The Russians and the Soviet Union* (2006), adopts a novel approach to explain the nature of ideological continuity and change in the Soviet Union. According to Hosking, the tumultuous 1930s represented a clash of two messianic visions, Russian (split into an ethnic and imperial, statist conception of Russian identity and Russia's role in the world) and socialist, later Soviet (a supra-national, Marxist-inspired vision that envisaged the 'emancipation of humanity through an international proletarian movement' and the creation of a perfect society of comrades). The first was retrospective by nature, whilst the latter was forward looking and utopian. The collectivisation of agriculture during the early 1930s represented the clearest exposition of this clash, which witnessed the dismantling of the peasant commune and the de-legitimisation of Russian Orthodox Christianity, the clearest markers of 'Old Russian' identity. However, the mid-1930s (after Stalin signalled the creation of a new social memory to complement the ensuing ideological change and strengthen the legitimacy of the regime in the face of the spectre of Nazi Germany) witnessed the evolution of a new Soviet revolutionary messianism, a mass Russian-Soviet patriotism, that drew more heavily on the imperial statist tradition of Russia's past, rather than more populist conceptions of 'Russianness'. More often than not 'New Russia' was in many respects a reflection, albeit a superficial one, of 'Old Russia', and symbols of Russian national identity and traditions of collectivism were used to reinforce Bolshevik revolutionary culture. As Hosking explains:

> '[T]he Soviet Union was in a real sense Russian. Bolshevism revived
> elements of the inherited system of Russian myths and symbols dating
> right back to the sixteenth century: the idea that Russia has a special

mission in the world, to practise and disseminate Truth and Justice (*Pravda*) based on egalitarianism and the frugal way of life of ordinary toiling people. This was *krugovaya poruka* [collective responsibility] in modern dress . . . By virtue of this special mission, so the assumption went, Russians were entitled to exercise patronage or protection over the less well developed or "capitalist" world; this was a form of service to them, what one might call "Russia's burden." Such an outlook was fully compatible with Soviet Communism, and it constituted the practical, working ideology of many Russians employed by the Soviet state . . . the Soviet Union represented Russia's crisis of messianism. It was the state form in which the Russian sense of being a chosen people worked itself out in reality.'

The nature of the Soviet messianic vision changed in 1945 following the Great Fatherland War, as Hosking notes, 'it became backward looking, fixated on the great victory achieved in the past. In its attitude to the future it crystallised around the ambition to become a great world power', and efforts were concentrated on transforming the USSR into a 'militarist society'. However, whether backward or forward looking this 'messianic' mission was deeply flawed because it failed to represent properly the core ethnic tradition of Russian nationhood (the devotion to Orthodox Christianity) represented by the peasantry. The Soviet experience represented the development and dominance of thinking about the state and 'neo-Russian empire' at the expense of ethnic Russia.

Questions

1 Were the roots of the terror Marxist or a reflection of the despotic paranoia of Stalin and his team? How was it possible for Stalin and his team to deploy terror on such a scale and survive?

2 Draw up a balance sheet of the advantages and disadvantages of using coercion so massively.

3 Are the terms 'one party state' and 'mono-organisational society' adequate in describing political reality in the Soviet Union in the 1930s?

4 What do you understand by the term Stalinism? How can it best be defined?

5 Does the term 'cult of personality' remain an adequate term to describe the Soviet Union in the 1930s given the 'new political history'?

6 What have revisionist interpretations contributed to the understanding of the way the political system functioned under Stalin? What if anything have the culturalists added to the debate about the revolution from 'above' and 'below'?

7 Which groups were most affected by Stalin's purges and which groups or individuals contributed most to the terror process?

8 Why did the initial purges of 1934–35 lead to the Great Purge of 1936–38? Was there a certain political rationale for the terror process?

9 Discuss the Great Purge as part of everyday life in the Soviet Union and as a consequence of social engineering

10 How important were visions of utopia for the 'moral universe' (Richard Overy) of dictatorship? Discuss in relation to the ways in which Stalin attempted to legitimate his power and maintain his power base during the 1930s.

Further reading

E. A. Rees, *Political Thought from Machiavelli to Stalin: Revolutionary Machiavellism* (2004); Evan Mawdsley, *The Stalin Years: The Soviet Union 1929–1953* (2003); Harold Shukman (ed.), *Redefining Stalinism* (2003); Robert C. Tucker (ed.), *Stalinism: Essays in Historical Interpretation* (1999); David L. Hoffmann (ed.), *Stalinism: The Essential Readings* (2003).

CHAPTER 12

State and society

'In our country – a country in which the socialist order has triumphed completely, where there is no unemployment, where every citizen of the Soviet Union has every opportunity to work and live honourably, any criminal act by its very nature can be nothing other than a manifestation of class struggle.'

Genrikh Yagoda, 1935

The Party renewed

The Party was always being purged (repressed) in order to remove the heretics and doubters. In 1921, about a quarter of Party members were expelled. Sixty per cent of Party members in 1933 no longer held a Party card in 1939. Of the 139 members and candidate members of the CC elected at the 17th Congress, in 1934, 78 per cent were arrested and shot, mainly in 1937–38. Of the 1,966 delegates to the Congress, 60 per cent were arrested as counter-revolutionaries. Only six of the ten Politburo members in 1934 survived until 1939. Besides Stalin, of Lenin's first Sovnarkom only one comrade was then still alive, Lev Trotsky. His head was pierced by an ice pick in Mexico in 1940.

On the face of it, the above statistics testify to widespread opposition to the Party line. True, there were dissenters but not enough to justify the wholesale purges of the 1930s. No official objected to one party rule. There were merely reservations about the pace and wholesale use of violence. A case in point was Beso Lominadze, Party boss in Transcaucasia. In 1930, appalled by the costs of collectivisation, he began contacting like-minded officials. He told one that the whole Party leadership had to go. 'What about the General Secretary?'

'When there is a spring cleaning, every stick of furniture has to go, including the largest piece.' Stalin soon heard of this. Lominadze was expelled from the CC and sent to Magnitogorsk as Party boss. In January 1935, Stalin summoned him to Moscow. His chauffeur reported: 'We were on Urals high road . . . Suddenly I heard a bang like a shot. I stopped, turned to Lominadze, and said in annoyance: "A tyre's burst". He replied: "No, it's not a burst tyre, I've put a bullet in my chest".' There is another way of looking at it. Stalin, as principal, regarded all Party members as his agents. The purges reveal that the agents were difficult to discipline.

The 14th Congress, in 1925, was a turning point. Stalin and his team had a majority at the Congress and used it to end intra-party democracy. He and his supporters always claimed to be defending the Party's interests. Stalin openly admitted that he ignored democracy in the interests of the Party. This Congress also legitimised denunciations of a Party member by another Party member for deviations from the general line. One Russian historian claims that this Congress saw the birth of the nomenklatura. He continues:

> 'The 16th Congress, in 1930, and the 17th, in 1934, were no longer arenas where like-minded souls exchanged views, where a collective effort was made to decide matters with respect for minority and majority opinion. Instead they became something akin to conclaves of Hitlerite storm troopers ready to carry out the Führer's orders even if they knew they were criminal.'

The most clearly articulated opposition to the emerging Stalin dictatorship was drafted by Martemyan Ryutin and his confrères, in 1932. The Ryutin 'platform' (it ran to about 1,000 pages) saw Stalin and his team destroying Bolshevism. It discerned a growing disillusionment with socialism among the population, especially the peasantry. A softer line had to be taken in order to rebuild confidence in socialism. Ryutin and 17 of his supporters were arrested and expelled from the Party (Ryutin was later shot). They were accused of trying to set up a 'bourgeois, kulak organisation to re-establish capitalism . . . by underground activity under the fraudulent banner of Marxism-Leninism'. Stalin wanted the death penalty for Ryutin but Sergei Kirov and other moderates stayed his hand. A gnawing fear gripped Stalin. How many other Ryutin groups were there? He demanded more vigilance to 'unmask' the enemy within.

Any Party comrade who opposed the general line was now guilty of trying to restore capitalism. Did Stalin believe this? He was fed report after report by the secret police which pointed to the existence of opposition groups. They had orders to produce evidence so they fabricated it. Stalin and his team believed that they were surrounded by an ocean of class and potential class enemies.

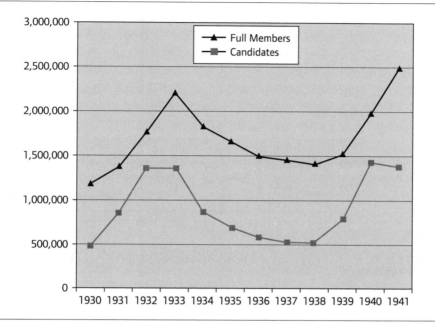

FIGURE 12.1 Party membership, 1930–41

Source: Based on data in Richard Overy, *The Dictators: Hitler's Germany and Stalin's Russia* (2004).

The Politburo

Figure 12.2 shows the number of meetings and the total number of hours spent by Stalin consulting members of the Politburo in his Kremlin office between 1931 and 1939. The information is taken from the visitors' book which recorded all those summoned to Stalin's presence and how much time they spent with him. One is struck by Stalin's tremendous workload. The busiest year is 1937. Of course, he sometimes saw more than one Politburo member at a time.

The Politburo met 83 times in 1930, 87 times in 1931 but only 33 times in 1933 and 9 times in 1936. There were 2,857 items on the agenda in 1930, 3,878 in 1931, 3.245 in 1933 and 3,367 in 1936. This meant that, in 1936, that the average Politburo meeting dealt with over 370 issues. In other words, the vast majority of questions had been decided beforehand and only needed formal approval. Another conclusion is that Stalin increasingly consulted his team and took decisions outside Politburo meetings.

Voroshilov was responsible for defence; Zhdanov succeeded Kirov as Party leader in Leningrad and also supervised culture; Kaganovich was an all-purpose administrator and a master at reading Stalin's moods. He once said there were six Stalins (Stalin was a new person after the suicide of his wife in 1932); Molotov

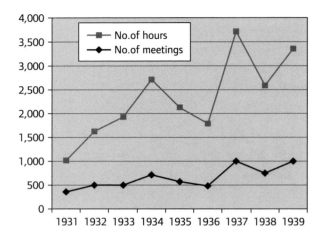

FIGURE 12.2 Number of meetings and hours devoted by Stalin to consulting Politburo members, 1931–39

Source: Calculated from data in Oleg V. Khlevniuk, *The History of the Gulag* (1996).

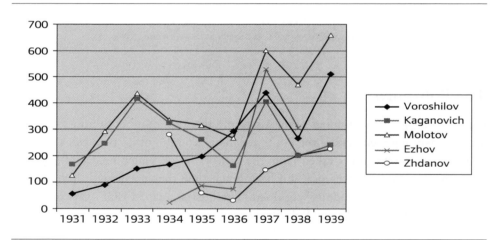

FIGURE 12.3 Number of hours devoted by Stalin to consulting key members of his team, 1931–39

Source: Calculated from data in Oleg V. Khlevniuk, *The History of the Gulag* (1996).

was Stalin's right-hand comrade – he argued with Stalin but always gave way; he was a major adviser on foreign policy; Ezhov was the secret police chief.

The relative importance of policy areas can be gauged from the frequency of meetings. During the 1930s the most important members of the team to Stalin were Voroshilov, Kaganovich and Molotov. Ezhov was a star in 1937; he was the second most consulted person then. This underlines the role of the purges. The

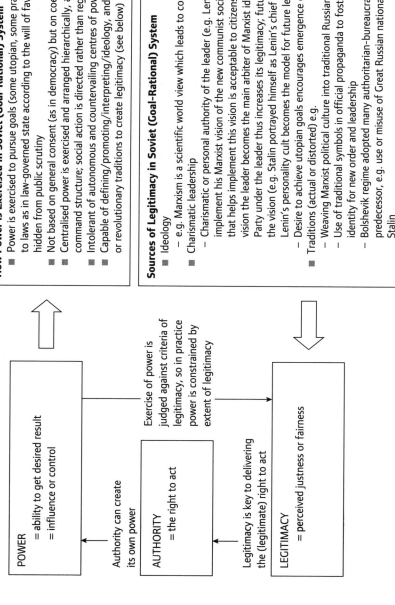

How Power is Exercised in Soviet (Goal-Rational) System

- Power is exercised to pursue goals (some utopian, some practical), not according to laws as in law-governed state according to the will of favourably placed individuals hidden from public scrutiny
- Not based on general consent (as in democracy) but on coercion/force and control
- Centralised power is exercised and arranged hierarchically, analogous to military command structure; social action is directed rather than regulated
- Intolerant of autonomous and countervailing centres of power (e.g. civil society)
- Capable of defining/promoting/interpreting/ideology, and using/abusing ideological or revolutionary traditions to create legitimacy (see below)

Sources of Legitimacy in Soviet (Goal-Rational) System

- Ideology
  - e.g. Marxism is a scientific world view which leads to communism
- Charismatic leadership
  - Charismatic or personal authority of the leader (e.g. Lenin) persuades many to implement his Marxist vision of the new communist society. Any action or policy that helps implement this vision is acceptable to citizens. By remaining true to this vision the leader becomes the main arbiter of Marxist ideology; the Communist Party under the leader thus increases its legitimacy; future leaders continue the vision (e.g. Stalin portrayed himself as Lenin's chief disciple) and Lenin's personality cult becomes the model for future leaders
  - Desire to achieve utopian goals encourages emergence of a strong leader
- Traditions (actual or distorted) e.g.
  - Weaving Marxist political culture into traditional Russian culture
  - Use of traditional symbols in official propaganda to foster political culture and identity for new order and leadership
  - Bolshevik regime adopted many authoritarian-bureaucratic features of its imperial predecessor, e.g. use or misuse of Great Russian nationalism or chauvinism under Stalin

POWER
= ability to get desired result
= influence or control

Authority can create its own power

Exercise of power is judged against criteria of legitimacy, so in practice power is constrained by extent of legitimacy

AUTHORITY
= the right to act

Legitimacy is key to delivering the (legitimate) right to act

LEGITIMACY
= perceived justness or fairness

FIGURE 12.4 Power, authority and legitimacy

three most active years for Stalin were 1933, 1937 and 1939. The importance of defence grew inexorably during the 1930s. Stalin consulted most with Voroshilov and Molotov in 1939.

The above reveals that Stalin, in effect, had emasculated the Politburo by 1937. He did this by dispersing and diluting the power of his team. In February 1937, Kaganovich, previously number two, lost this position. He was replaced by Andrei Andreev (1895–1971). Ezhov, although not a Politburo member, ran key departments and supervised the police for the Party. He only became a candidate member in October 1937. Zhdanov was dispatched to Leningrad but was to spend ten days a month in Moscow. Stalin increased the number of CC secretaries from three to five. The post of his deputy was abolished. Stalin's rise to absolute power can be traced in Kaganovich's letters to him. In 1935–36, they are sycophantic and replete with obsequious phrases. Previously Kaganovich had been more of a colleague; now he was a servant.

The full Politburo rarely met. It broke down into groups of seven, five, three and two. Often meetings took place around the dinner table at Stalin's dacha. Mikoyan states that a G5 (Stalin, Molotov, Malenkov, Beria and himself) existed in the Politburo until 1941. It decided operational matters and foreign affairs. Other issues were decided by a G3 or G2. The G5 became the G6 after war broke out when Voroshilov joined. He was dropped in 1944. In 1945 Zhdanov joined and later Voznesensky.

The new society

Paul Kammerer, a German Marxist biologist, was a comrade with a mission. He was upset by the dominance of Gregor Mendel's school of genetics. Mendel (1822–84) had published his work in 1866 but it was ignored by the scientific community until 1900. Kemmerer was a follower of Jean Baptiste Lamarck (1744–1829), the French biologist. The latter had popularised the concept of the inheritance of acquired characteristics. Marx found this attractive as it appeared to confirm that the social environment was the key factor in human behaviour. Transform the environment and the new man and woman would emerge. Children of these parents would be free of the stains of the previous generation. Mendel overturned this and argued that the environment was secondary to the genes one inherited.

Kammerer experimented on the midwife toad and 'proved' that Lamarck was correct. When his experiments were repeated, it was discovered that he had cheated. He committed suicide. However, the Soviet Union of the 1930s was looking around for Marxist heroes of science. A film glorifying his work was made in Moscow. Kammerer's work did not turn Stalin into a Lamarckist; he was already a convinced believer in the inheritance of acquired characteristics. He was an avid plant experimenter at his numerous dachas on the Black Sea coast.

Given his commitment to Lamarckism, Stalin set out to create the perfect environment to engender the new Soviet man and woman. He and his team proclaimed the victory of socialism in the Soviet Union in 1934. Hence any deviation from socialist norms of behaviour after that would be due to the survival of bourgeois values. They would then have to be extirpated to ensure they did not contaminate the new society which was forming. Were the kulaks and their offspring irredeemably bourgeois or could they be redeemed and become loyal Soviet citizens? What about the 'social marginals': the petty criminals, prostitutes and so on? Could socially useful labour redeem them?

Socialist realism

The cultural revolution (1928–31) was a period when left proletarian writers and artists were let loose on 'fellow travellers' and 'bourgeois intellectuals'. According to Richard Stites (1992), they assaulted 'science fiction, detective stories, fairy tales, folk music, jazz and escapist films'. These were produced by decadent intellectuals for degenerate businessmen. They wanted the foxtrot and the saxophone banned as well as Tchaikovsky's operas. These radicals attacked corruption in the Party as well. This ended in 1932. All literary organisations gave way to the Union of Soviet Writers (USW), in 1934. One could not publish if one was not a member. Two of the country's greatest poets, Osip Mandelstam and Anna Akhmatova did not join. Glavlit set the norms and awarded the prizes and threw the brickbats. The censors, directed by the OGPU, went through everything with a fine-tooth comb. Cows and pigs could not be called commissar, Pravda, proletarian, deputy, cannibal or Yid. Some readers might make a connection! Folk tales, in which heroes had to decide whether to take the road on the left or the right, were rewritten. They now had to choose between a side road and a main road. Stalin, a great reader, was often the editor and censor of novels, plays, poems and film scripts.

At the founding congress of the USW, some delegates drafted an appeal to foreign writers. The OGPU confiscated it but never discovered the authors.

'We Russian writers are like prostitutes in a brothel, with just one difference, they sell their bodies while we sell our souls; just as they have no way out of the brothel, except death by starvation, neither do we . . . In your countries you set up committees to save victims of fascism, you convene anti-war congresses . . . But why do we not see you acting to save victims of our Soviet fascism, run by Stalin? . . . Personally we fear that in a year or two Stalin will not be satisfied with the title of world-class philosopher but will demand, like Nebuchadnezzar, to be called at the very least the "sacred bull".'

What was socialist realism?

'Artists are the engineers of human souls.'

Stalin, October 1932

'It is optimistic because it is the literature of the rising class of the proletariat, the only progressive and advanced class . . . it is the only permissible style of writing . . . the task is to remould and re-educate working people in the spirit of socialism.'

Zhdanov, 1934

'Music which is incomprehensible to the people is not needed by the people.'

Zhdanov, 1948

In	Out
Optimism; joie de vivre; comradely devotion, biting satire of deviant behaviour; acceptable formulas; puritanical; depict the future now; heroic sculpture and painting; simple inspiring message; happy ending; a bright, glorious future is inevitable; simple plots – hero overcomes impossible odds to ensure fulfilment of plan	Self-pity; introspection; pessimism, sex; pornography (it could entail a five year prison sentence from 1935); free-wheeling comedy; lampooning or criticism of those in authority; experiment; wallowing in the past; avant-garde theatre and art; complex plots and characters who are unsuccessful
Nikolai Ostrovsky's *How the Steel was Tempered* (1934); Mikhail Sholokhov's *And Quiet Flows the Don* (1928–40); Sergei and Georgy Vasilev's film *Chapaev* (a Civil War hero who actually dies but is avenged by Red forces) (1934); Aleksei Tolstoy's *Peter the* Great (1929–40); after 1934 the Russian classics (now the Soviet classics) in literature and music (many great writers were reclassified as revolutionary democrats including Pushkin, despite his having an official position at the Russian Court);	Dmitry Shostakovich's opera *Lady Macbeth of Mtsensk* (or *Katerina Izmailova*); the classics until 1934; Vsevolod Meyerhold and his avant-garde theatrical productions; all forms of abstract art and sculpture; Sergei Eisenstein's film *Bezhin Meadow* (1935), but never completed because of censors' objections. It was based on the story of Pavel Morozov, murdered by his relatives for denouncing his father as a kulak. (This was later revealed to be a myth.)

Konstantin Stanislavsky and the
Moscow Art Theatre: now the officially
approved style of theatre; the films
Peter I (1937–38), *Minin and*
Pozharsky (1939); and *Suvorov* (1941)
glorified the Russian past as the
country armed for war.

Maxim Gorky (1868–1936) was the doyen of socialist realism. He returned in 1928 to Moscow from Italian exile. Feted as the greatest Soviet writer, he still returned to Italy every year until 1934. It did not concern him that Italy was a fascist country. His sixtieth birthday was celebrated with great pomp and stage-managed praise. One of his fellow writers noted in his diary:

'Gorky's jubilee was arranged by the Soviet government in the same way as all other state festivals. Today the government says: "Kiss Gorky" and everyone kisses him. Tomorrow they'll say: "Spit on Gorky" and they'll all spit on him. Unless there is a change of policy Gorky will soon become a nullity.'

Gorky was vain but not vain enough to fail to realise that it was all a charade. He complained to a woman writer: 'They're paying me honours everywhere. I'm an honoured baker, an honoured pioneer. If I visited an insane asylum today, they'd make me an honoured madman'.

Yet he turned out the prose the regime wanted. In 1932, commenting on the Solovetsky camps, part of the gulag, he effused about the 'unprecedented, fantastically successful experiment of re-educating socially dangerous people in conditions of free, socially useful work'. He carried on a vigorous correspondence with Stalin and Yagoda, the secret police chief, who was close enough to be almost family. The latter defined his role to Gorky: 'Like a dog on a chain, I lie by the gates of the republic and chew through the throat of anyone who raises a hand against the peace of the Soviet Union'. Even in Italy, Gorky's letters to Stalin were full of extravagant praise. He referred to the OGPU as the 'tireless and valiant guardian of the working class and the Party'. He told Stalin he was a 'good person', a 'resolute Bolshevik' whose courage made him irreplaceable. Hence Gorky lived in two worlds. He enjoyed his role as the muse of socialist realism and its fairy-tale world. On the other hand, he knew the real world was often brutal and unfair. He could vent his spleen on members of Stalin's team. He dismissed Voroshilov, Kaganovich and Molotov as 'camp-following rubbish'. He was typical of many writers and artists. They had to make compromises in order to survive.

Women

As Stephen Kotkin has shown in his fine study of Magnitogorsk (1995), the wives of the ruling elite did not work but were expected to supply emotional and other support to their husbands. These wives could revert to bourgeois values with lace curtains and new furniture. They were encouraged to teach their social inferiors hygiene and to organise drama and study groups. The gulf between the labouring and non-labouring Soviet woman grew wider by the day. One of the reasons why bourgeois values could reappear was that socialism had finally triumphed in the Soviet Union. Hence borrowing from the past was no longer subversive. Better off women were not permitted to form groups or societies for the promotion of a female agenda. It was a male-dominated world. It is interesting to note that at a time when Stalin was extolling the virtues of marital life, he himself was living the life of a promiscuous widower. After his wife, Natasha, committed suicide in November 1932, he declined to marry. He preferred short term liaisons.

The schoolgirl Nina Lugovskaya (2003) was dismayed by the second-class status of women:

> 'Women are so one-sided and narrowly developed . . . To be sure, this is largely the result of our awful legacy from the older generation . . . We must strive for equality with men. Are we women striving now? No, we're sitting in our same dirty pit dug over dozens of centuries and screaming phrases which men have "thought up" for us: *Long live equal rights! Make way for women!* Not one of us has taken the trouble to realise that these are empty phrases: they soothe the feminine pride of some, while others (the majority) are simply unaware of their humiliating position.'
>
> (28 October 1936)

Education

Progressive schooling where pupils were not disciplined but encouraged to reveal their creativity was abandoned in 1931. Back came more traditional norms. Anton Makarenko became the acknowledged authority. His goal was a 'stern collective' not freewheeling individualism. Each subject had a set book. In 1935, the traditional grading system, 1–5 (5 was the highest grade), reappeared. So did school uniforms. When I first saw the girls' black dresses and white pinnies, in 1957, I thought they looked like pre-1914 ladies' maids.

Mikhail Pokrovsky dominated history writing until his death in 1932. He regarded almost everything the Tsars did as bad. Even Minin and Pozharsky who had led a popular revolt against the Poles in Moscow in 1612, were dismissed as counter-revolutionaries. Stalin stepped in and called Pokrovsky's book anti-Leninist. He wanted to forge a new Soviet patriotism and identity and needed Russian heroes. Soviet history now began with the founding of Kievan Rus. A new history of the Soviet Union appeared in 1935 and remained the set text for the next 20 years. It lauded the successes of the Tsars in their battle to extend the borders of the Russian state. The Bolsheviks had inherited that state and would not permit anyone to destroy its 'indivisible unity'. Hitherto national histories had praised local resistance to tsarist expansion. Now tsarist rule was seen as a modernising force.

The Stalin cult

Stalin grew in self-conceit after 1929. He began to see himself as having a special historical role. The Stalin cult began in earnest on his official fiftieth birthday, in December 1929. Seven of the eight pages of *Pravda* were devoted to him. Never the less, he was always insecure. He was careful not to profile himself as the chief decision maker. He always presented himself as part of a collective leadership. In 1934, he was addressed as Dear Leader; there were now emotive overtones to his leadership. Many women found him physically very attractive and adored him. Children were taught to regard him as a kindly father figure. He cultivated a modest image. An old peasant woman wrote to the Dear Leader that she had a spare cow and would he like her. He replied: 'Thank you very much, but I spend all my time in town in the service of the Soviet people and I don't have a farm; just keep your cow and carry on'. Stalin knew how to cultivate the common touch. However, one observer warned: 'He catches everything on the radio station of his brain, which operates on all wave lengths . . . Be on your guard if he is being charming. He has an enormous range of anaesthetics at his disposal'.

One of the goals of the cult was to give citizens a focus in a period of enormous social upheaval. With Stalin at the helm, the Soviet ship of state was in wise hands. Another way of restoring some normalcy to life was the plethora of festivals, carnivals and celebrations. There was one almost every month. Red Army Day was on 23 February; International Women's Day was 8 March. Then there was May Day and, of course, 7 November, the anniversary of the Bolshevik revolution. Only 7 November was a public holiday. The persecution of religion had relented by the mid-1930s. This permitted the reappearance of the New Year's Tree in 1935 (banned in 1928) and Father Frost (a Russian version of Father Christmas). It was again possible to buy the ingredients to make the traditional Easter cake. 'Life has become better, life has become more joyful', intoned Stalin.

Great stress was laid on physical fitness. There were endless parades of gymnasts, athletes and other sportsmen and women. There were competitions galore and the winners received generous prizes. The Soviet Union tried to achieve world records in everything. For instance, a Soviet pilot flew higher than anyone else. All the record holders were careful to attribute their feats to the wise leadership of comrade Stalin. He was their inspiration.

There were those who harboured quite opposite sentiments. One of these was Nina Lugovskaya (2003).

> 'Then they refused to stamp Papa's passport. I didn't know what to do.
> I was filled with rage, helpless rage. I began to cry. I ran around the room
> swearing. I decided I had to kill the bastards. Ridiculous as that sounds,
> but it's no joke. For several days I dreamed for hours while lying in bed
> about how I'd kill him [Stalin]. His promises, his dictatorship, the vile
> Georgian who has crippled Russia. How can it be? Great Russia and the
> Great Russian people have fallen into the hands of the scoundrel. Is it
> possible? That Russia, which for so many centuries fought for freedom
> and which finally attained it, that Russia has suddenly enslaved itself.
> I must kill him as soon as possible. I must avenge myself and my
> father.'
>
> (24 March 1933)

She was also puzzled by her inability to get her sisters to comprehend the sham of Soviet reality:

> 'How can I refute their [my sisters'] mechanical arguments: "If you're not
> for the Bolsheviks, you're against Soviet rule; this is all temporary, things
> will get better?" Were those five million deaths in Ukraine temporary? . . .
> How can I with such strong weapons as the facts and the truth, not prove
> to my sisters the lie of the Bolshevik system? I must be extremely inept.'
>
> (11 December 1934)

Becoming a new Soviet man and woman

What was it like to live through the social revolution of the 1930s? It was easier for the minority who were workers by origin. Most people did not fall into this category. If they were to make a career they had to overcome their social origin and become a new man and a new woman. Stepan Podlubny (born 1914) was one such. He confided his thoughts to a diary between 1931 and 1939. It provides many insights into the agony of consciously becoming a different person. He is often appalled by those around him. They are not as serious as he is. The son of a kulak, he and his mother obtained forged papers showing them to be of worker origin and moved to Moscow in 1931. He lived in perpetual fear of being unmasked. He obtained work as an apprentice printer and eventually became a medical student.

'A thought that I can never seem to shake off . . . is the question of my psychology. Can it really be that I will be different from the others? The question makes my hair stand on end, and I start shivering. Right now, I am a person in the middle, not belonging to one side or the other.'

(13 September 1932)

'My daily secretiveness, the secret of my inside – these don't allow me to become a person of independent character. I can't come out openly or sharply, with any free thoughts. Instead I have to say what everyone [else] says.'

(8 December 1932)

He overcame his fears in 1935.

'The thought that I've become a citizen of the common Soviet family like everyone else obliges me to respond with love to those who have done this. I am no longer with the enemy, whom I fear all the time, every moment, wherever I am . . . I am just like everyone else.'

(2 March 1935)

His social origin was uncovered but he continued to study. His mother was arrested in December 1937 and accused of Trotskyism. In order to help her, he abandoned the medical institute.

'Of course, there are many rumours about the arrest of various people . . . But to number Mama, a half-literate woman, among the Trotskyites would never have occurred to me.'

(18 December 1937)

Now his life lacked purpose and suicide became a possibility. However, he recovered his sense of self and became an open critic of the regime. Stalin was Russia's Nero. He visited his father who had resettled in Yaroslavl, to the east of Moscow. He shared a room with other workers, a pig and colonies of bugs and lice. He was amazed to find that this was commonplace. Yet everyone told him they were doing well. Progress was a sham. Instead backwardness and barbarism were everywhere. However, he still believed that the path to communism was pre-ordained by history. Hence he did not challenge the legitimacy of the regime.

On the other hand, Nina Lugovskaya is exasperated by the new world:

'Yesterday stands out because of Stalin's wife's funeral. There were loads of curious people and I didn't like the sight of their happy, animated faces as they jostled ahead in the queue for a look inside the coffin. Little boys were rushing about outside and shouting; "Hurrah!" I walked back and forth, listening in to the conversation of passers-by, and the few words I caught expressed surprise and malicious irony. I didn't feel sorry for that woman. Stalin's wife, after all, couldn't be the tiniest bit good, especially since she was a Bolshevik. And why did they have to announce it in the newspapers? It only set people against her even more. As if she were someone special!'

(12 November 1932)

'And now they've taken Ira's father away, destroyed their happiness and peace, their way of life, all their habits, everything that was dear to their hearts. We lived well, too, until Papa's arrest, but then from out of the blue came deprivation and disturbances. And now they, who always had butter and coffee for breakfast, they too will lose everything if Ira's father is exiled to some godforsaken little town in the North . . . Oh, Bolsheviks! What have you sunk to, what are you doing? Yesterday we had a class on Lenin and the new society we are building. It was so painful to hear those outrageous lies from a teacher I worship . . . And to whom is she lying? To children who don't believe her, who smile to themselves and say: "Liar! Liar!" '

(21 January 1933)

'Around eleven they announced that comrade Kirov, a member of the Politburo, had been killed in Leningrad . . . I felt a little ashamed that nothing inside me shuddered at this report. On the contrary, I felt glad: that means there's still a struggle going on, there are still organisations and real people. Not everyone is gobbling the slops of socialism.'

(2 December 1934)

Questions

1 'Stalin was a social moderniser.' Discuss.

2 'The idea of the New Soviet citizen traces its roots to the 1930s.' Discuss.

3 'The Party was sacrificed in the 1930s for the sake of Stalin's social revolution.' Discuss.

4 Was Stalin's rule uncontested during the 1930s?

5 Was Stalin's Soviet Union really a 'one party state' in the 1930s?

6 Why did the Politburo meet so irregularly after 1936?

7   What does Stalin's commitment to Lamarckism reveal about his conception of ideology and the role it played in shaping society?

8   As far as policy is concerned, what was the top priority during the 1930s and why?

9   How did the Stalinist regime harness culture in its sociological transformation of Soviet society?

10   'Reform in education was the greatest achievement of Stalin's social revolution era.' Discuss.

Further reading

Sheila Fitzpatrick, *Everyday Stalinism: Ordinary Life in Extraordinary Times: Soviet Russia in the 1930s* (1999); Stephen Kotkin, *Magnetic Mountain: Stalinism as Civilization* (1995); Lewis Siegelbaum and Andrei Sokolov, *Stalinism as a Way of Life: A Narrative in Documents* (2000).

CHAPTER 13

Pursuing peace and preparing for war

'We are living not only in a state, but in a system of states, and the existence of the Soviet Republic side by side with imperialist states is in the long run unthinkable. But until that end comes, a series of the most terrible conflicts between the Soviet Republic and bourgeois states is inevitable.'

Stalin

Stalin also took it for granted that external enemies would conspire with internal enemies. 'Only blind braggarts or disguised enemies of the people would dispute this elementary logic.' Hence for Stalin it was an article of faith that war was inevitable. The task of Soviet diplomats and agents was to discover the war plans of bourgeois states. Naturally, 'enemies of the people', first and foremost Trotskyites, would be conspiring with the enemies of the Soviet Union. For instance, since German fascism was the mortal enemy of Soviet socialism, and Trotskyism was also a mortal enemy, it was logical that they would team up against the Soviet Union. Stalin devoted an enormous amount of effort, during the 1930s, to eliminating Trotsky and his supporters.

Another important aspect was recruiting agents to penetrate the corridors of powers of the bourgeois states. Moscow was spectacularly successful in Britain. The magnificent five, Guy Burgess, Donald Maclean, Anthony Blunt, John Cairncross and Kim Philby, provided volumes of intelligence for their masters in Moscow. They had been recruited by a brilliant Austrian Jew, Arnold Deutsch, possible the most talented illegal to work for Moscow. However, Stalin did not trust them until the war had got under way. He suspected that they were *agents provocateurs*. He was notoriously suspicious of intelligence since he was well aware of how it could be massaged to support a particular viewpoint. He did not want analysis, just facts. He turned out to be a very poor analyst.

Hunting down 'enemies of the people' took precedence over intelligence gathering during the 1930s. The main task of the NKVD in France was the infiltration and neutering of the Trotskyite movement. The top comrade was Lev Sedov, Trotsky's son. A Soviet agent, Mark 'Étienne' Zborowski, became his indispensable assistant. In 1936, Moscow was told that Sedov was selling part of his archive to the Paris branch of the International Institute of Social History in Amsterdam to raise money. It ordered Zborowski, a service engineer at a Paris telephone exchange, to cause a fault in the institute's telephone line. This would allow Zborowski time to locate the archive when repairing the fault. The burglary went off without a hitch. Sedov assured the Paris police that Zborowski was above suspicion. The archive, in reality, was of little significance compared to Trotsky's main archive which ended up at the Hoover Institution.

In 1937, the order went out to abduct and bring to the Soviet Union General Miller, the head of a White Guard organisation, and Lev Sedov. Miller was abducted in broad daylight in Paris, drugged, placed in a trunk and put on a Soviet boat at Le Havre. He was interrogated and shot in Moscow. Sedov escaped a trip to Moscow by falling ill and dying in hospital. One cannot be sure if he died of natural causes. With Sedov out of the way, Zborowski took over as editor of the *Bulletin of the Opposition* and as Trotsky's most trusted supporter in France. Aleksandr Orlov, head of a hit squad during the Spanish Civil War, had defected to the United States. He warned Trotsky that there was an NKVD agent in Paris and described Zborowski. Trotsky thought it was disinformation. The next target was Rudolf Klement, secretary of Trotsky's Fourth International. He was abducted and his headless corpse surfaced in the river Seine.

The NKVD in Mexico was always dreaming up ways to liquidate Trotsky. On one occasion, in May 1940, they machine gunned his villa outside Mexico City but Trotsky, his wife and son escaped by diving under their beds. The Mexican police picked 73 bullets out of the plaster. The hitmen took with them the American guard, who had colluded with them by opening the gate, and shot him. He could have blown their cover. It was decided that one person should worm himself into Trotsky's confidence and then kill him. The comrade chosen was Rámon Mercader. He put an icepick through the back of Trotsky's head on 20 August 1940. Stalin breathed a sigh of relief. Mercader went to jail but never uttered a word about the assassination. His mother, who had convinced him to become the hitman, was feted in the Kremlin by Beria and Stalin. She was awarded the Order of Lenin. Later, she bitterly regretted what she had done.

Kremlin thinking

The diplomacy of the Soviet Union during the 1930s was that of a weak state. The country needed time to build up its defences. Soviet military doctrine was offensive. The next war was going to be fought on someone else's territory. The furious development of the war economy in the second half of the 1930s created a feeling of security.

Marxists found fascism's appeal very hard to understand. Italy, Germany, Austria, Spain, Romania and other European countries embraced it to varying degrees. It fused nationalism, racism, anti-communism and anti-capitalism into a potent mix. Marxist analysts eventually regarded it as the wolf-like face of finance capital. As such it was bound to collapse under its own contradictions. How could a movement which championed workers and small business against big business, but at the same time embraced big business, survive? Stalin had read Adolf Hitler's *Mein Kampf* (My Struggle) and was well aware that Hitler regarded the obliteration of communism as a necessary step towards world domination. German national socialism was expansionist and *Lebensraum* (living space) would be carved out of other states. Slavs, along with Jews and gypsies, were *Untermenschen* (subhumans). To the Nazis, they were a superior form of cattle.

Stalin had considerable respect for the German Chancellor. He admired his ruthlessness. He was a mesmeric public speaker but Stalin hypnotised people in private. Stalin thought he had Hitler's measure but he consistently misread him. Communists and Nazis had collaborated against the ruling social democrats (SPD), especially in Berlin, before 1933. Social democrats were ridiculed as social fascists. The Great Depression, which began in 1929, devastated capitalist economies. World production halved in the decade to 1939; world trade shrank by two-thirds. Communists, from Beijing to Berlin and Bogotá, fervently believed that capitalism would be dead within five years. However, Roosevelt's New Deal, based on public works, saved the US economy.

After 1918, the only friend the Soviet Union had in Europe was Germany. Both were outcasts. Lenin always saw Germany as the key country for revolution making in Europe. But Berlin began moving closer to Britain and France in the second half of the 1920s. Maxim Litvinov, a sophisticated, polyglot Jew, with an English Jewish wife, took over as Commissar of Foreign Affairs in July 1930. He was to remain the acceptable face of communism for almost a decade. His approach was to present the Soviet Union as a partner. He favoured closer relations with Britain and France. He had to face formidable obstacles. Britain cut off trade relations and anti-imperialist propaganda in British and French colonies in India, Indo-China and elsewhere raised the hackles of London and Paris. Revolution was not on his mind; that was left to the Comintern.

In 1931 Japan invaded Manchuria and set up the puppet state of Manchukuo. The League of Nations did not react. This posed a potentially lethal threat to Russia. Would Tokyo attack the Soviet Union or would it attempt to conquer China first? Litvinov then proposed a treaty of non-aggression and trade with all contiguous states. In 1931, treaties were signed with Afghanistan and Turkey. Treaties with Finland, Estonia, Latvia, Poland and France followed in 1932.

Romania and Japan refused to sign. The Soviets discovered that they could gain influence by supporting the peace movement. Litvinov eloquently argued the case for disarmament and peace.

Collective security

The Comintern and the German communists (KPD) were delighted when Hitler became Reich Chancellor in January 1933. In May 1933, they exulted that the fascist dictatorship, which was destroying democracy, was speeding up the proletarian revolution in Germany. The Soviet Union renewed its treaty of alliance in May 1933. In November 1933, Litvinov travelled to Washington and achieved his goal, the diplomatic recognition of the Soviet Union. The Politburo declared that the basis of its foreign policy was collective security. The USSR joined the League of Nations in late 1934 and in May 1935 treaties were signed with France and Czechoslovakia. However, the treaty with Czechoslovakia only obliged the Soviet Union to come to Czechoslovakia's assistance if France acted first. A problem was that Czechoslovakia did not have a common frontier with the Soviet Union. Poland and Romania did but they would not agree to a treaty.

The Comintern realised in 1935 that it had catastrophically misjudged fascism. It now favoured a popular front with socialists and bourgeois parties. The Spanish Civil War (1936–39) offered Italy and Germany the opportunity to hone their military skills. The Soviet Union provided the Republican government with aid but its primary objective was to ensure that the Trotskyite POUM did not win. Communists linked up with republican forces to crush an insurrection by anarchists, always strong in Spain, and Trotskyites in Barcelona in May 1937. Moscow preferred a victory by Franco's Falangists to a Trotskyite Spain.

Britain and France were in no position militarily to adopt aggressive policies towards Italy and Germany. When Italy invaded Ethiopia in October 1935, the Soviet Union imposed economic sanctions but London and Paris did nothing. Emperor Haile Selasse appealed to the League of Nations, whose charter called for sanctions against aggressors, but was ignored. A diplomat wryly observed when he heard the popping of champagne bottles: 'Listen to the artillery of the League of Nations'. Germany signed an agreement with Italy (Hitler was a great admirer of Mussolini), in October 1936, and with Japan the following month. Here, in effect, was an anti-Comintern pact.

A Chinese saviour

Despite all the gloom something happened which may have saved the Soviet Union from oblivion. Stalin desperately wanted to see Japan embroiled in a general war in China. Japanese forces were concentrated in the north and only had small garrisons elsewhere. One of these centres was Shanghai. A communist mole, Zhang Zhi-zhong, was commander of the Shanghai-Nanjing garrison. His troops shot dead two Japanese military in August 1937. A Chinese prisoner, under sentence of death, was dressed in a Chinese uniform and then shot dead. The aim was to give the impression that he had been killed by the Japanese. Chiang Kai-shek wanted to resolve the problem. Zhang escalated the conflict by bombing the Japanese flagship and troops and naval planes on the ground. Zhang then issued a press release falsely claiming that the Japanese had attacked Shanghai. Chiang had to agree to an all-out offensive. The Japanese rapidly brought in reinforcements. The result was disastrous. The Chinese may have lost about 400,000 and the Japanese 40,000.

Stalin signed a non-aggression pact with Chiang and began to supply China with weapons on an unprecedented scale. Over 1,000 planes, as well as tanks and artillery, were sent. A Soviet air force group came as well. During the next two years over 2,000 Russian pilots flew combat missions. They even bombed Japanese-occupied Taiwan. There were about 300 military advisers, headed by the future Marshal Vasily Chuikov, who spoke Chinese. Moscow poured in matériel over the next four years (Chang and Halliday 2005). Stalin was very pleased. With the Japanese embroiled in the south of China there was less likelihood that they would attack the Soviet Union in the near future. Zhang may have been more important to Moscow than their brilliant spy in Tokyo, Richard Sorge.

Stalin wanted the Reds to fight the Japanese but Mao had other ideas. He agreed with Chiang that the Reds were not to be used in battle, only as auxiliary troops. Mao's plan was for the communists to occupy territory behind Japanese lines. Stalin wanted Chiang to defeat the Japanese but Mao wanted the Japanese to defeat the nationalist army. The Reds only fought the Japanese in one important battle during the years 1931–45, but it was fought against Mao's wishes.

Germany

Germany annexed Austria in March 1938. Moscow did not condemn the move. Then Hitler demanded the Sudetenland, a German-populated area in Czechoslovakia. The Soviet Union declared it would defend the country if France did the same. In September 1938, the British and French Prime Ministers met Hitler and Mussolini in Munich and ceded the Sudetenland. They had not consulted the Soviets or the Americans or the Czechs. Neville Chamberlain came home waving the agreement which he claimed he had brought 'peace for our time'. Winston Churchill growled that it made war more likely. In March 1939, the Germans occupied Prague and declared Slovakia an independent state. Britain's reaction to the occupation of the Czech lands was to promise Poland, Romania and Greece support if attacked. This decision was rash as the only way of helping Poland, for example, was to march through Germany. London intended it merely as a way of warning Germany off.

'If you live among wolves, you must howl like wolves.'

Stalin

On 3 May 1939, Litvinov was replaced as Foreign Minister by Molotov. Collective security had failed. The Soviet Union negotiated with Britain and France and simultaneously with Germany. The world was shocked when, on 23 August 1939, in Moscow, Ribbentrop, the German Foreign Minister, concluded a non-aggression pact with Stalin and Molotov; a second treaty of friendship was signed on 28 September which divided Poland and parts of Eastern Europe into spheres of influence, one Soviet, one German; a comprehensive treaty was signed on 11 February 1940, exchanging Soviet raw materials and food for German machinery and military equipment; a supplementary treaty was signed on 10 January 1941, confirming the economic relationship for another year. Stalin confided to an aide that he had always admired Hitler: 'I should like to drink his health', he went on.

On 1 September 1939, Germany attacked Poland and two days later Britain and France declared war on Germany. Stalin waited until 17 September before claiming his part of Poland. The two armies did engage in some joint operations against the hopelessly outnumbered Poles. The Germans were struck by how nervous Red Army officers were and the poor quality of their equipment. Stalin seemed to fear that the Wehrmacht would continue its offensive into the heartland of the Soviet Union. In October 1939, the people's assembly of western Ukraine voted to join the Soviet Union.

The Baltic states of Estonia, Latvia and Lithuania fell within the Soviet sphere of influence. They were obliged to permit the stationing of Soviet troops on their territory. Finland, also in this zone, refused to make any concessions and the Red Army invaded in November 1939. Things did not go well as the Finns were much more skilful at winter war than Ukrainian peasants, for example. The Soviet bulldozer forced the Finns to sign a disadvantageous peace treaty in March 1940. The Soviets took Hangö, Viipuri (Vyborg) and Finnish Karelia. However, Finland remained independent. The Red Army's performance was poor (in mitigation, the best equipment was not deployed). There was a desperate shortage of officers as over 22,000 had been arrested during the terror.

The Nazi–Soviet pact was a body blow to foreign communists. The British (CPGB) and French (PCF) parties still supported the war against Hitler until the Soviets disciplined them. The CPGB then declared that Britain was fighting an imperialist war. The PCF was immediately banned. By late September 1939, only two communist parties, the CPGB and the Swedish, were legal in Europe.

Yet there was one communist leader who was excited by the Nazi–Soviet pact: Mao Zedong. He harboured hopes that Stalin would do a deal with Tokyo and partition China. He would become the master of the Soviet zone in China. He regarded the division of France into a German-occupied zone and the rest administered by the puppet Vichy regime as a good omen. Stalin began talks with Japan immediately after signing the Nazi–Soviet pact. To improve relations, Mao's agent supplied the Japanese with intelligence about Chiang's forces. A deal was struck by the Maoists and the Japanese in central China. The Reds were to be unmolested in return for not sabotaging railway or other communications.

The 'phoney war' – so called because there was no real fighting – ended in the spring of 1940. Germany invaded Denmark and Norway in April and moved against Belgium, the Netherlands and Luxembourg, in May. Then the advance continued into France, which fell in June. Remarkably, Britain was able to evacuate over 300,000 troops from Dunkirk. The German commander, General (later Field Marshal) von Rundstedt (1875–1953), on his own initiative, had halted the advance outside the town. Bombers were then deployed but bombs which fell on sand did not explode.

In June 1940, the Red Army occupied Lithuania and the following month the parliament voted to join the USSR. The same happened in Latvia and Estonia. In August, the USSR Supreme Soviet officially welcomed the Estonian, Latvian and Lithuanian Soviet Socialist republics into the USSR. Bessarabia and northern Bukovina were taken from Romania and added to the Moldovan Soviet Socialist Republic. Hitler transferred Transylvania from Romania to Hungary in August 1940. After the fascist Iron Guard took over in September, German troops entered Romania. It bordered on the Soviet Union. Moscow did not want the Balkans to fall under Germany sway but Berlin saw it as a strategic goal. Molotov travelled to Berlin in November 1940 to attempt to iron out differences. The Soviets would not budge on the Balkans. Molotov proposed that the Soviet Union join the Tripartite Pact – the alliance of Germany, Italy and Japan – but Hitler was not interested. While they were negotiating, a British air raid forced them to repair to a bunker. Molotov enquired of Ribbentrop: 'What will England do?' 'England is finished', snorted the German Foreign Minister. 'If that is so, what are we doing in this bunker and whose bombs are falling?'

In July 1940, Hitler decided to attack the Soviet Union in the spring of 1941. He needed allies and Slovakia, Hungary, Romania and Bulgaria came on side. Finland also joined. Turkey skilfully avoided committing itself. A tripartite alliance with Italy and Japan was also agreed. Operation Barbarossa, the attack on the USSR, was approved on 5 December 1940. Italy stumbled in its attempt to take over Greece and needed German assistance. In March 1941, there was a coup d'état in Yugoslavia and the pro-German regent was overthrown. The new government concluded a treaty of friendship and non-aggression with Moscow in April. Hitler was furious and ordered the invasion of Yugoslavia. Italy came in as well and also moved into Albania. By May, German troops had taken over Yugoslavia and Greece and had entered Bulgaria. This held up the attack on the Soviet Union. It was now planned for Sunday 22 June 1941.

Japan

Stalin's nightmare was a two front war: against Germany in the west and Japan in the east. Japan was a resource-poor country and hence needed fuel and raw materials. It invaded Manchuria in 1931 and the rest of China in 1937. The main Pacific power was the United States. Since Tokyo's aim was to dominate the Pacific it had to take on the Americans sooner or later. The Japanese tested Soviet resistance at Lake Khasan in mid-1938. About 15,000 Red Army soldiers were involved. The result was inconclusive. In May 1939, the Japanese penetrated Mongolia at Khalkin Gol, near the Soviet border. The conflict dragged on until August when General (later Marshal) Georgy Zhukov (1896–1974) launched an offensive. He used tanks for the first time in Soviet mechanised warfare. He had over 112,000 troops under his command. Again the results were unclear but the Red Army believed it had come off better. A truce was agreed in September 1939. Fortunately, the Japanese never attempted to move westwards again. Ironically, Zhukov deployed tactics elaborated by the executed Marshal Mikhail Tukhachevsky. Examples of these were: armour must strike out independently; operations must be conducted in depth; good intelligence must always be ensured; and deception and pre-emption must be afforded high priority. These were to form the core of Zhukov's method of warfare.

Interpretations

There are two main interpretations of Stalin's diplomacy in the run-up to the war (Litvin and Keep 2005):

- the classical;
- the realist.

Classical

This view sees Stalin as hedging his bets. His policy was short term, pragmatic, flexible and ambivalent: options were kept open as long as possible before a final decision was taken. This was based on a hard-headed calculation of the balance of forces and state interests. The collective security policy, associated with Maksim Litvinov was only finally abandoned in mid-August 1939, a mere two weeks before the signature of the Ribbentrop–Molotov pact. The key reason why the Soviet Union prevaricated so long was its perceived military weakness in relation to Germany and Japan, the most likely aggressor states. The Red Army needed several years to match German and Japanese military might. In the meanwhile, the Soviets could not afford to be seen to be aggressive by either Berlin or Tokyo. The search for allies in the West was given priority. However the Soviets were aware of Anglo-French appeasement of Germany which was partly based on their perceived military weakness.

Moscow harboured the suspicion that Paris and London would like to turn German military might against it. This would allow France and Britain to remain neutral and give them more time to build up their defences. Stalin had another option. If Germany became embroiled in a war with France and Britain it would not be in a position to attack the Soviet Union. Such a war was likely to be long drawn out. When the bourgeois powers had exhausted themselves, the Red Army could intervene, 'liberate' these countries and introduce socialism there. The socialist revolution might engulf the whole of Western Europe. This option also held out the prospect of territorial 'adjustments' at the expense of the smaller Eastern European states.

Geoffrey Roberts (1995) is the most eloquent representative of this view; Jonathan Haslam (1984 and 1992) provides a finely balanced account.

Realist

These authors begin with Stalin's Marxist world outlook and his penchant for Byzantine intrigue. Some see his deep antagonism to Anglo-French bourgeois power, strengthened by the Allied intervention in the Russian Civil War, and his desire for a temporary understanding with Nazi Germany as the driving forces behind his diplomacy. He perceived Germany's social base to be weak and this increased its revolutionary potential. The Red Army would be ready to come to the assistance of progressive forces when the moment was ripe. Hence the Soviet military build-up in the 1930s had twin motives: defending the country but also gearing for military intervention abroad. Leading authors who present this view are Robert Tucker (1991), Richard Raack (1995) and Joachim Hoffmann (1999).

It is an over-simplification to divide authors into these two camps as some incorporate elements of both approaches in their writing. All major contributions are assessed in Gabriel Gorodetsky's (1999) book, the major study of the topic. He is highly critical of Stalin, Hitler, Britain and France for the errors committed. His tome covers, in exhaustive detail, the period between the pact and the German invasion.

Realists seize on remarks in Georgi Dimitrov's diary (2003). He was head of the Comintern from 1935 to 1943. He reports that, on 7 September 1939, Stalin commented:

'We see nothing wrong in their having a good, hard fight and weakening each other . . . We can manoeuvre, pit one side against the other and set them fighting one another as fiercely as possible. The non-aggression pact is to a certain degree helping Germany. Next time, we'll urge on the other side.'

Caroline Kennedy-Pipe (1998) identifies two competing groups in Moscow: those who favoured collective security and the others who were for a rapprochement with Germany (Molotov, Kaganovich, Zhdanov and Vyshinsky). She falls into the classical group as she views the Soviet Union in the 1930s as a country under siege. It badly needed allies but Stalin was over-suspicious of the western powers. The Baltic States served as buffer zones. On the Munich crisis, the view is that the Soviet Union had no intention of coming to Prague's aid. Decisive French action might have changed things but Moscow thought this unlikely. Litvinov's dismissal as Foreign Minister was due partly to the fact that he was Jewish, but also to his support for the Anglo-French proposals. The critical decision to choose an agreement with Germany was taken on 11 August 1939, three days before Voroshilov met the Allied mission. He made demands which he expected to be rejected.

The Soviet Union overfulfilled its commitments under the economic terms of the pact while Germany fell further and further behind in its deliveries of finished goods. By 22 June, the Soviets had delivered 2.2 million tonnes of grain, 1 million tonnes of oil and 100,000 tonnes of cotton. These deliveries, especially of oil, proved essential for the Wehrmacht's conduct of the coming invasion. Stalin rejected all information which warned of an imminent German attack. These sources ranged from Winston Churchill to Chiang Kai-shek. The latter gave the date of the invasion as 21 June 1941. Richard Sorge, a brilliant German communist spy, had penetrated the German Embassy in Tokyo and provided Stalin with the exact date of the attack. Stalin's response was to call him a 'lying shit who has set himself up with some small factories and brothels in Japan'. An NKVD report from Berlin was dismissed with the comment: 'You can tell your "source" from the German air force to go and fuck his whore of a mother!' Beria wrote to Stalin on 21 June:

'I again insist on recalling and punishing our ambassador to Berlin, Dekanozov, who keeps bombarding me with "reports" on Hitler's alleged preparations to attack the USSR. He has reported that this attack will start tomorrow . . . But I and my people, Iosif Vissarionovich, have firmly embedded in our memory your wise conclusion: Hitler is not going to attack us in 1941.'

The Soviet military reported Germany massing 4 million troops on the Soviet border. Why did Stalin ignore these warnings? Gorodetsky adduces a range of reasons:

- Soviet intelligence was not viewed very highly by Stalin.
- He expected Hitler to attack the Soviet Union after he had defeated Britain. This would avoid the nightmare of a two front war.
- He expected moderates in the Wehrmacht to stay the hand of the more aggressive.
- He expected Berlin to present an ultimatum with limited demands which could be accommodated.
- June 1941 was too late to launch an full-blooded attack on the Soviet Union.
- He was very suspicious of British motives, especially after Rudolf Hess's flight to Britain – understood by Stalin as an attempt to negotiate a separate peace.
- London harboured intentions of encouraging the Wehrmacht to move eastwards. This last reason may have been the decisive one.

What of the view that Stalin was planning a preventive strike but was beaten to it by Hitler? After all, Soviet military doctrine was offensive. The next war would be fought on someone else's territory. The argument in favour was articulated in the 1990s by Viktor Suvorov (Viktor Rezun), a former military intelligence (GRU) officer. Hitler had, of course, justified his attack by arguing that it was necessary to neuter a Soviet attack. Stalin's speech to military academy graduates of 5 May 1941 is viewed as crucial. He urged them to take the offensive. Semen Timoshenko (1895–1970), Commissar for Defence, and Georgy Zhukov, Chief of Staff since January 1939, took the speech seriously and began preparing the army for war and a preventive strike in Poland. Stalin was annoyed and told them that his purpose had been only to boost morale and not to think of the Wehrmacht as invincible. The Red Army was in no condition to attack Germany so Stalin was playing for time. He had not told the military chiefs that he was involved in diplomatic manoeuvrings. He only consulted Molotov and Voroshilov. Probably only Molotov knew the details. Pons (2002) gives short shrift to the view that Stalin was planning a pre-emptive strike in June 1941. Gorodetsky (1999) takes the same view. Barros and Gregor (1995) provide details of the disinformation campaign waged by the intelligence services of both sides. Their conclusion is that Stalin vastly overestimated his ability to guide events and the extreme secrecy of the

Soviet system was eventually self-defeating. Hitler was much craftier than Stalin gave him credit for.

The Comintern had its wings clipped, to please Berlin, and Stalin would have closed it down had the invasion not intervened. After its formal abolition in 1943, it continued to function in secret as institutes 99, 100 and 205. It remained in the Comintern building. The Chinese, for example, complained that it was still issuing them orders. It is clear that Stalin envisaged it playing an important role in countries liberated from German rule in Eastern Europe.

The Stalin–Hitler pact gave rise to some splendid satire.

To the tune of *Clementine*

Oh my Stalin

In Old Moscow, in the Kremlin
In the spring of '39
Sat a Russian and a Prussian
Working out the Party Line.

(Chorus)
Oh my Stalin, Oh my Stalin,
Oh my Stalin party line
First he changed it, then rearranged it
Oh my Stalin Party Line.

Leon Trotsky was a Nazi
We all knew it for a fact
Pravda said it, We all read it
'fore the Hitler–Stalin pact.

Once, a Nazi, would be shot see
That was then the Party line
Now a Nazi's, hotsy-totsy
Volga boatmen sail the Rhine/
I can bend this spine of mine.

Now the Führer and our leader
Stand within the Party line
All the Russians, love the Prussians
Trotsky's laying British mines.

Party comrade, Party comrade,
What a sorry fate is thine!
Comrade Stalin does not love you
'Cause you left the Party Line.

Oh my Stalin, Oh my Stalin,
Oh my Stalin Party Line;
Oh, I never will forsake you
for I love this life of mine.

To the tune of Auld Lang Syne

And should old Bolshies be forgot,
and never brought to mind,
you'll find them in Siberia,
with a ball and chain behind.
A ball and chain behind, my dear,
a ball and chain behind.
Joe Stalin shot the bloody lot
for the sake of the Party Line.

Questions

1 'Stalin's foreign policy prior to the Great Fatherland War was based on misinformation, self-delusion and naivety.' Discuss.

2 How did the Soviets perceive the Germans? Did they understand the reasoning behind a racial utopia?

3 Did the Soviets neglect the cultivation of diplomatic relations with their neighbours?

4 Why did the USSR sign the Molotov–Ribbentrop pact? Was it such a surprising move given that the two dictatorships shared many commonalities?

5 According to Soviet thinking, what were the distinctions between 'Fascism' and 'Marxism' and why were they antithetical?

6 Why did Stalin discount all warnings of a German attack?

7 Why was the Soviet Union so badly prepared for war in 1941? Does the fault lie with Stalin alone or with some structural defect?

8 'Stalin's great political skills were only truly revealed by the catastrophic impact of total war.' Discuss.

9 What accounts for Stalin's misreading of Hitler's intensions towards the Soviet Union?

10 Outline the core features of the 'classical' and 'realist' interpretations of Stalin's pre-war diplomacy.

Further reading

Viktor Suvarov, *Icebreaker. Who Started the Second World War?* (1990); David Glantz criticises Suvarov in *Journal of Military Studies*, vol. 55 (April 1991), pp. 263–4; David Glantz, *Stumbling Collosus: The Red Army on the Eve of War* (1998); Alter Litvin and John Keep, *Stalinism* (2005); Gregor Suny, *The Soviet Experiment: Russia, the USSR, and the Successor States* (1998); Donald Rayfield, *Stalin and his Hangmen: An Authoritative Portrait of a Tyrant and Those Who Served Him* (2004); Christopher Andrew and Vasili Mitrokhin, *The Mitrokhin Archive: The KGB in Europe and the West* (1999); Alexander Dallin and F. I. Firsov, *Dimitrov and Stalin, 1934–1943: Letters from the Soviet Archives* (2000); Zhores A. Medvedev and Roy A. Medvedev, *The Unknown Stalin*, translated by Ellen Dahrendorf (2003); Ivo Banac (ed.), *The Diary of Georgi Dimitrov, 1933–1949* (2003); David E. Murphy, *What Stalin Knew: The Enigma of Barbarossa* (2005).

CHAPTER 14

Total war

'All wars start with a misunderstanding.'

Saturday 21 June 1941: just before midnight

> 'Gefreiter Hans Krebs, 74th Infantry Division, reporting, Genosse. I have
> come to inform you that our unit has been ordered to attack tomorrow
> morning at 4 a.m. As a communist, I feel it my duty to report this to you.'

> Zhukov: 'Comrade Stalin, we have a German soldier who claims that his
> unit is going to attack in the morning.'

> 'Another bloody *agent provocateur*. Interrogate him; when you have
> finished; shoot him!'

The same evening, in the Kremlin

Stalin had ordered Marshal Semen Timoshenko, Commissar of Defence, and
Marshal Georgy Zhukov, Chief of the General Staff, to come to his office. When
they arrived they found others there, including Beria, Malenkov and Molotov.

'Comrades, we are here to discuss the present situation.' He looked at the
military men. 'What now?' There was silence. Eventually Timoshenko said: 'We
must place all troops on the western frontier on full battle alert.' Stalin thought a
moment and replied:

> 'No, it would be premature to issue such an order now. It may still be
> possible to resolve the situation by peaceful means. We should issue a
> short order stating that we might attack if provoked by German action.
> The border units must not permit themselves to be provoked into doing

anything which might cause difficulties . . . They are not to yield to any provocation. I think Hitler is trying to provoke us. Surely he has not decided to go to war.'

The troops were to move closer to the border and stay on high alert during the night. Zhukov and Timoshenko left at 10.20 p.m. Stalin conferred with the others until 11 p.m. He then headed for his dacha at Kuntsevo, just outside Moscow. Zhukov phoned him at 0.30 a.m. on 22 June. He reported what Krebs had said. The *vozhd* (boss) did not react. The Wehrmacht attacked at 3.30 a.m. Krebs was still being interrogated. The invasion saved his life.

Zhukov phoned Stalin again. 'Comrade Stalin, Germany has attacked.' Silence. 'Comrade Stalin, have you understood what I said?' Again, silence. Zhukov repeated his question again. 'Yes, comrade Zhukov, I understand. Bring Timoshenko to my Kremlin office immediately.' When they arrived they found Molotov, Beria and Lev Mekhlis (1896–1953) already there.

Stalin was still not sure if elements in the German High Command had ordered the attack without the knowledge of Hitler. He waited until 7.15 a.m., almost four hours after the invasion, before giving an order to Soviet troops to 'go on to the offensive'. What was needed was an order to go on to the defensive. Going on to the offensive actually increased Soviet casualties. Anyway, this order was futile. Many of the units on the frontier had already been destroyed.

Some of the German troops brought their pets with them. One crossed the frontier with an owl on his fist. The owl was the sacred bird of the goddess Athena. He had stolen it from the Acropolis, in Athens, a few weeks earlier.

Operation Barbarossa launched Army Group North against the Baltic States and Leningrad; Army Group Centre against Belarus and Moscow; and Army

---

Box 14.1 *The players*

Allied forces	Axis forces	Neutrals
Great Britain, United States, Soviet Union, China, Canada, France, Belgium, Netherlands, Luxembourg, Yugoslavia, Greece, Norway, Denmark, Estonia, Latvia, Lithuania, Poland, Czech Lands, Australia, New Zealand, India, South Africa, British and French colonies	Germany (including Austria), Japan, Finland, Italy, Slovakia, Romania, Hungary; Spain and Bulgaria provided troops but did not declare war on USSR	Portugal, Switzerland, Sweden, Turkey, Ireland

Group South against Ukraine and Kyiv. The Romanians and the German Eleventh Army were to come in as reinforcements and the Finns were to be ready to join the German thrust against Leningrad, beginning on 11 July. Hungarian, Slovak, Italian and Spanish troops were to join the invasion after 24 June.

Stalin was in shock. He could not bring himself to tell the Soviet people that war had begun. Molotov stood in for him at midday. He managed to keep his stutter under control. Stalin would not set up a general headquarters or assume the role of commander-in-chief. He claimed he needed more time to think.

Stavka, responsible for all land, sea and air operations, was set up on 23 June. Timoshenko was named chair and Stalin was listed as one of the members. This was odd, to say the least. The reason was that Stalin was still not ready to assume overall responsibility. On 26 June, Stalin panicked. He ordered Beria to contact Berlin about ending the war. He was willing to hand over the Baltic States, Ukraine, Bessarabia and Finnish territory he had recently acquired. If that were not enough, what more did Hitler want? Beria wanted the Bulgarian ambassador in Moscow to transmit the message to the Führer.

The desperate plea may never have reached Berlin. Had it done so, Hitler would have tossed it aside. He felt certain of victory. After a meeting in the Commissariat of Defence, on 29 June, Stalin was despondent: 'Lenin left us a great inheritance, and we, his heirs, have fucked it all up'. Stalin ordered more counter-attacks, senselessly sacrificing his troops. He went off to his dacha but did not show up the next day. He refused to answer the telephone.

Late in the afternoon of 30 June, Vyacheslav Molotov, Lavrenty Beria, Georgy Malenkov, Anastas Mikoyan and Nikolai Voznesensky gathered in Molotov's office. Molotov was regarded as the depressed master's number two. Beria proposed a State Committee of Defence (GKO) with Stalin as chair. Molotov was sceptical as Stalin was in a state of near collapse. Voznesensky, who was to play a key economic role during the war, misread this remark and proposed Molotov as leader. However, the latter was slavishly submissive to Stalin and refused to entertain the idea. The group of six had it then within their power to end the tyrannical reign of Stalin. But they could not conceive of a Soviet Union without the *vozhd* (Pleshakov 2005).

When they arrived Stalin fully expected them to remove him from power. He was sitting in an armchair. 'He looked up and asked: "Why have you come?" There was a strange look on his face. The question was also strange since he should have summoned them. Molotov mumbled: "We need you so as to concentrate all power in your hands". Stalin looked surprised and merely muttered: "Fine".'

This provided him with a new lease of life. On 3 July he addressed the nation on the radio. 'Comrades! Citizens! Brothers and sisters! Soldiers and sailors!', he began. He appealed to everyone, not in the name of the Party, but in the name of

TABLE 14.1 Soviet and German production of aircraft, tanks and artillery, 1941–45

Year	Country	Aircraft	Tanks	Artillery
1941	SU	15,735	6,590	67,800
	Germany	11,776	5,200	7,000
1942	SU	25,436	24,700	127,000
	Germany	15,409	9,300	12,000
1943	SU	34,845	24,089	130,000
	Germany	28,807	19,800	27,000
1944	SU	40,246	28,963	122,400
	Germany	39,807	27,300	41,000
1945	SU	20,102	15,419	62,000
	Germany	7,540	–	–

Source: Based on I. C. B. Dear (ed.), *The Oxford Companion to the Second World War* (1995).

patriotism. 'Forward to victory!', he concluded. This war was not between the Soviet and German armies but one between the whole Soviet people and Germany. Millions volunteered to fight the fascists.

A Front consisted of a number of armies and each had a Political Commissar, who was a member of the Politburo, added to it. This led to conflicts between the military and the commissars. Stalin resolved these conflicts. In this way he remained in overall control. Below the Fronts, armies were the largest formations. On 22 June 1941 there were 30 armies but their number grew rapidly. An army's size varied according to the theatre of war. There were 'shock' armies, used to launch attacks to break through the enemy's lines.

At the outbreak of war there were 5.37 million soldiers and 5 million more were added by 1 July. The Red Army had more tanks and aircraft than the Germans. There were 1,861 T-34 and KV tanks which were superior to anything the Wehrmacht had (German intelligence failed to detect this). Even the older T-26s were superior to the German T-1 and T-IIs. The new T-III and T-IVs were no match for the T-34 or KVs. The first Soviet rocket, the BM-14, or Katyusha, could propel shells up to 2 km. The Germans never developed anything comparable. Stalin had not realised its potential but after war began it was put into production. On paper, the Red Army should have been able to repel the German attack given its superiority in numbers of men and matériel. The breakdown of communications led to catastrophe. German saboteurs had cut communication cables which were obligingly carried by telegraph poles.

In 1942, the Soviet Union produced 8.5 million tonnes of steel compared to Germany's 35 million tonnes. Despite this it easily outproduced Germany in war

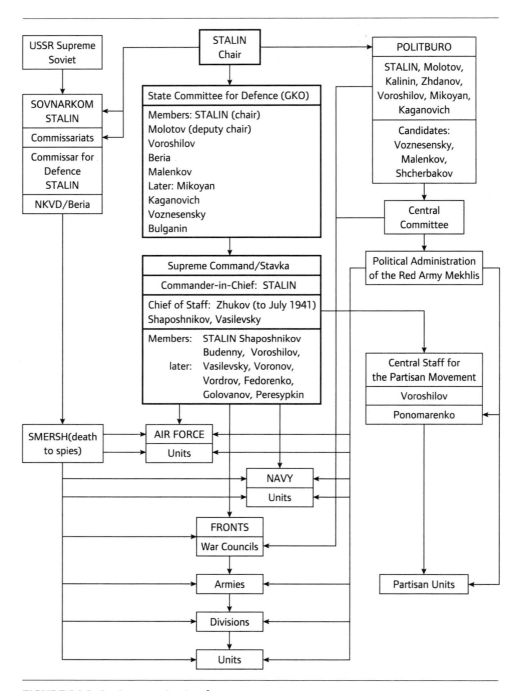

FIGURE 14.1 Soviet organisation for war

Source: Based on I. C. B. Dear (ed.), *The Oxford Companion to the Second World War* (1995).

matériel. Why was this? In the 1920s the Soviets had adopted an American mobil-isation model which gave priority to dual purpose technology in arms production and supplies. They built, with US help, huge state of the art tractor and motor plants while the tractors and motors were so designed that their key parts could be used in the production of tanks and aircraft. The Germans, on the other hand, chose to create specialised military production facilities which were very labour intensive. In the 1930s, the Soviets did not give priority to military production or building up a huge army (about 800,000 men in 1939). Gosplan focused on developing metallurgy, the fuel and energy complex and basic sectors which could be mobilised in case of war (Shlykov 2006).

A decision-making body without an executive arm, the implementation of GKO's orders was the responsibility of the Party, government and soviet bodies. Hence the Party CC, Sovnarkom and its people's commissariats were of crucial importance. GKO and Stavka collaborated closely. GKO members reported on their sector of the economy or problem area to the GKO chair. Generals, people's commissars and other key officials appeared when necessary. There was no formal agenda. It functioned like a war cabinet. GKO members called together experts to find a technical solution to a problem. When resolved, Gosplan, the people's commissariats and other agencies were instructed to implement it. Stalin was a good chair because of his incredible memory and his ability to ask questions which penetrated to the core of a problem. He was also temperamental. He normally tried to check recommendations with other specialists. He could be persuaded but his decision was final.

German goals

In March 1941, Hitler outlined his approach to the coming conflict to his generals. 'Communism is an enormous danger to our future . . . This is a *Vernichtungskrieg*, a war of extermination . . . War against Russia: extermination of Bolshevik com-missars and the communist intelligentsia.' Red Army commissars were to be shot on capture. This approach completely ignored the deep resentment against Stalin's policies which seethed below the surface. Hitler classified all Soviet citizens as Russian and failed to distinguish between Russians, Ukrainians, Georgians and so on. Hence he did not capitalise on the animosity against Russians in the Soviet Union. The Germans forced Soviet citizens to back Stalin. Hitler wanted a massive blow along the border to shatter the Red Army. The Soviets had to be defeated by winter 1941. Equipping a huge invasion force meant that weapons and vehicles had to be assembled from all over Europe. What happened when they broke down? The vehicles were built only to travel on good roads, not the roadless Russian ter-rain. Astonishingly, as of 22 June, the Germans had not yet agreed on the cam-paign's next objectives. They assumed that the decisive battles would be near the frontier. If the Red Army did survive, the Wehrmacht's logistical (provision of equipment, food, etc.) system was in no position to keep the army supplied as it penetrated deep into Russia.

The German Luftwaffe achieved total aerial dominance very quickly. During the first eight and a half hours of combat the Soviets lost 1,200 combat aircraft.

MAP 14.1 Invasion of the Soviet Union, 1941–42

Source: Reprinted by permission of the publisher from A WAR TO BE WON: FIGHTING THE SECOND WORLD WAR by Williamson Murray and Allan R. Millett pp. 116, 274, Cambridge, Mass.: The Belknap Press of Harvard University Press, Copyright © 2000 by the President and Fellows of Harvard College.

By 26 June, they had lost over 3,800. Stavka put out a communiqué on 22 June stating that attacks by German forces were being repulsed and losses inflicted. This was pure fiction. The Red Army, ordered to attack, was mown down. The Wehrmacht made rapid progress towards Leningrad. The Finns attacked but remained within the 1939 frontiers. The greatest Soviet disasters occurred in the centre where General Pavlov lost control. Stalin ordered Pavlov shot. Many soldiers fought on when completely outnumbered. By 25 June, the Germans had bagged over 324,000 POWs and as many again were dead. By early August, the Germans had advanced deep into Russia; they were almost at Leningrad and Ukraine west of Dnepr appeared to be within their grasp. However, once again, they had no clear objective.

German military planning had assumed that after the battles at the frontiers, Moscow would not be able to call up many reserves. This was soon proved completely false. By the end of June, the Soviets had called up 5.3 million reservists. Whereas they had deployed 97 divisions during the summer of 1941, they added another 194 new divisions by the winter. Another unwelcome surprise was the effectiveness of the Soviet T-34 and KV tanks in combat. A further blow was the unsuitability of many vehicles: about 25 per cent had to be written off with little hope of replacement. This meant that German units were not being provided with the ammunition they needed. Luftwaffe units were seriously short of fuel and ammunition by early July.

The Wehrmacht made little progress in August. By 1 September, the Germans had suffered 410,000 casualties (dead and wounded) out of the 3.78 million soldiers at the beginning of the invasion. There were not enough reserves to replace them. About half of the panzers were out of commission. This testifies to the tenaciousness of Soviet resistance.

In late September, German troops reached the outskirts of Leningrad. Hitler ordered them to lay siege and to starve the population to death and destroy every building. To avoid accusations of defeatism, the city authorities had not stockpiled food or fuel. Neither had the old and children been evacuated. The city was soon encircled with only a temporary corridor over frozen Lake Ladoga to ferry in supplies. Over a million Leningraders would die during the siege.

Army Group South was making good progress in its attempt to take Kyiv. Over 665,000 Soviet POWs were taken. Hitler then gave the order to take Moscow. This caught Stavka by surprise. It had not expected a major offensive so late in the year. German troops had no winter clothing and over half of the panzers were out of operation. Zhukov had stabilised the situation in Leningrad and was then called back to defend Moscow in mid-October. He was a brilliant, brutal, domineering commander. He did not accept failure. On one occasion he took a knife and sliced off the tips of the fingers of an officer who was indicating on a map why he had failed.

On 4 December, the temperature fell to −32°C. German soldiers suffered frostbite and many of the wounded died. The commanders were afraid to retreat. Army Group Centre was in trouble. Army Group North was sitting in the snow outside Leningrad. Army Group South abandoned Rostov-on-Don. The commander was sacked by Hitler but his successor reissued the order to retreat (Murray and Millett 2001).

Then came the Japanese attack on Pearl Harbor, in Hawaii, on 7 December 1941. Four days later Hitler declared war on the United States. Some historians see this decision as sealing the fate of the Third Reich. It was based on misconceptions: Hitler regarded the United States as a nation of mongrels; he agreed with the navy that the U boats could defeat the US Navy. He and his generals celebrated. Then he said: 'By the way, where is Pearl Harbor?' No one knew. Amazingly, no strategic assessment was made of the role the United States − the richest country in the world − could play in a global war. It was a stroke of good fortune for the Soviet Union and the other Allies.

The battle for Moscow

On 5 December, in appalling weather, Zhukov counter-attacked outside Moscow. He thought he could decimate the exhausted Army Group Centre by the spring. However, Stalin had other ambitions. He withdrew divisions from Moscow and spread them out along the whole front from the Black Sea to Leningrad. He was going for the knock-out blow. Despite this, Army Group Centre almost buckled. It retreated in disarray. Some soldiers threw away their weapons, put a rope around a calf and set off westwards. Others pulled sledges loaded with potatoes. Hitler sacked all his commanders. He assumed overall command himself. By early March 1942, the Germans had stabilised the front. The Red Army was not capable of encircling the Germans. The decisive factor had been Hitler's willpower. He had prevented a retreat degenerating into a rout.

The Red Army paid a terrible price for survival. In March 1942, there were 3.6 million Soviet POWs. Among them was Stalin's son, Yakov. Later, Hitler offered to exchange him for Marshal Paulus but Stalin refused. Yakov deliberately provoked his own death in a German concentration camp, in 1943. Only 100,000 POWs were capable of working in industry. The rest were dead or dying. Germany had no policy other than neglect for the POWs. The commissar order, to shoot all commissars and communists, was carried out. A German soldier told me that his unit, disgusted at having to shoot prisoners, resolved not to take any more prisoners. Waffen SS units did not take prisoners. Military and SS units cooperated in murdering Jews. At Babi Yar, outside Kyiv, an SS-Sonderkommando unit executed almost 34,000 Jews and Soviet citizens in two days. Their criminality was self-defeating. It only boosted resistance. Stalin gave the go-ahead for penal battalions in the summer of 1942. Recruits from the gulag struck fear into the Germans. They fought ferociously. They could only move forward. If they tried to retreat the NKVD put a bullet in their backs.

Operation Blau

Hitler judged that the Red Army had to be defeated in 1942 before the western powers could mobilise their military and economic resources. But the battering the Wehrmacht had taken in the autumn of 1941 limited this option. By April, Hitler was ready to launch Operation Blau (Blue), to take Stalingrad and the Caucasian oil fields.

Oil was a problem which continued to plague the Germans. However Army Group South was 25 per cent below strength. Romanian, Hungarian and Italian divisions had to be brought in to protect the rear. The Italians had to be sandwiched between the two Balkan armies to prevent them fighting one another. The Germans thought the Red Army was now exhausted. But it was recovering quickly. The Soviets lost Crimea and 175,000 men on 19 May. Timoshenko counter-attacked at Kharkiv but seriously underestimated German strength. The Red Army suffered almost 280,000 dead or wounded and lost 1,200 tanks. Stalin changed tactics. Now the Soviets avoided head-on confrontations and ceded territory for time. That changed on 28 July when Stalin issued his order: Not a Step Back. Any soldier who deserted his post would now be shot.

On 3 September, Luftwaffe bombers devastated Stalingrad. Losses mounted, though, and by 10 October half of the Luftwaffe aircraft were non-operational. The Germans failed to destroy the Soviet petroleum industry because it was not a top priority. Cutting off fuel to the Red Army would have dealt a crippling blow to Soviet mechanised power. Taking Stalingrad was accorded a higher priority.

The battle for Stalingrad was ferocious and continued during September, October and November. Zhukov launched an offensive against Army Group Centre at Rzhev, in November. It had two objectives: defeat the Germans and prevent troops being sent to help at Stalingrad. It was an unmitigated disaster. The Red Army lost over 100,000 dead and 235,000 wounded. It was Zhukov's greatest defeat.

On 19 November, the Red Army counter-attacked and smashed through the Romanian army. The German Sixth Army, under Field Marshal Paulus (1880–1957), was being encircled. It should have retreated but Marshal Göring assured Hitler that the Luftwaffe could supply the city. In reality, the Luftwaffe had no chance of doing this. The losses sustained by its transport and bomber fleets did irreparable harm. Hitler ordered the Sixth Army to fight to the death. Paulus, 22 generals and 91,000 men, surrendered on 2 February. Only 6,000

MAP 14.2 The eastern front, November 1942–June 1943

Source: Reprinted by permission of the publisher from A WAR TO BE WON: FIGHTING THE SECOND WORLD WAR by
Williamson Murray and Allan R. Millett pp. 116, 274, Cambridge, Mass.: The Belknap Press of Harvard University Press,
Copyright © 2000 by the President and Fellows of Harvard College.

eventually returned to Germany. It was the greatest military victory the Red Army had yet achieved. It was a turning point. The last offensive operational success the Wehrmacht could claim came in February 1943 (Murray and Millett 2001).

Kursk

The battle for the Kursk salient, in July 1943, was to be another turning point. It was the world's largest tank battle until the Gulf War. Zhukov correctly pinpointed the site of the battle and massive defensive preparations began. Soviet skill at *maskirovka* (deception) was so great that the Germans did not realise what was going on. This was the pattern for the rest of the war: Red Army preparations for every major offensive were hidden from German eyes. More worrying for the Wehrmacht was the fact that a new generation of young Red Army commanders was emerging. They were equal or superior to anything the Wehrmacht had.

The Allies landed in Sicily on 8 July and this caused Hitler to call a halt at Kursk. He had to switch to defending the Mediterranean. However most of Germany's mobile forces in the east had been destroyed at Kursk. The time of reckoning was at hand.

By the summer of 1943, Soviet forces enjoyed a significant numerical superiority. Whereas the Red Army had 5.76 million men, the Wehrmacht could only muster 3.1 million. The advantage was even greater in tanks, artillery and aircraft. Soviet intelligence gathering, deception and the execution of operations were superior. American Lend-Lease deliveries of food, raw materials and machine tools had an impact. In addition, by the end of the war, the Americans had delivered 11,900 locomotives and railway wagons; 409,000 lorries, many of them four-wheel drive; and 47,000 jeeps. These proved invaluable in keeping the Soviet offensives moving.

Kharkiv was liberated on 21–22 August 1943. Things were going well in the south but an attack on Army Group North failed miserably. Attacks on Army Group Centre were also unsuccessful. Red Army successes in the south led Hitler to order Army Group South to retreat but it was too late. In October, Kyiv was retaken. The Soviets were now concentrating their efforts in the south and leaving Army Group Centre for a later date. The balance of forces was swinging more and more in the Soviets' favour. At the end of 1943, the Germans had 2.5 million men and an extra 700,000 allied troops. The Red Army had 6.4 million troops. The Soviets had four aircraft for every Luftwaffe machine. In men and matériel, Moscow now had a three to one advantage. The 900 day siege of Leningrad finally ended on 27 January 1944.

On 30 March 1944, Hitler recalled Field Marshal von Manstein (1887–1973), his most successful Army Group South commander, to Berlin. He sacked him. He told von Manstein that the days of grand offensives were over. What he needed now were commanders who would fight to the death. Now the Field Marshal displayed his grasp of military and political reality. He took his considerable redundancy payment, added his family savings and bought a large estate in East Prussia in October 1944. At this point, the Red Army was preparing an offensive which would sweep the Germans out of East Prussia.

The summer 1944 offensives

Five great offensives were planned. The first blow was against Finland, on 10 June 1944. The Soviets had a two to one advantage in men and matériel. The Finns sued for peace in August and Stalin did not press home his advantage. Finland retained its independence.

Operation Bagration was launched on 22 June 1944, the third anniversary of the German attack, against Army Group Centre. Within four days, the latter had lost operational control over its forces. Minsk was liberated on 3 July. Vilnius was taken on 13 July. In the south Marshal Konev's forces smashed their way through to Lviv. On 20 July, a bomb went off in Hitler's headquarters in East Prussia. It did not kill him. Now several commanders were purged. Army Group North's new commander demanded to know how many commanders of his division had been shot or were being shot for cowardice. Senseless self-sacrifice was now demanded. On 30 July, the Red Army was within 10 km of Warsaw. On 31 July, Soviet forces reached the Baltic near Riga and thereby cut Army Group North off from the Third Reich.

Then the Soviet advance came to a halt. On 1 August, insurgents in Warsaw took up arms. Western writers have accused Stalin of deliberately abandoning them. The motive was that the destruction of the Polish Home Army, all anti-Soviet, would make it easier to establish a communist Poland. Recent scholarship casts doubt on the argument that the Soviets could have successfully aided the insurgents. The Germans retook Warsaw and destroyed the city in doing so. Himmler, head of the SS units, used pro-German Russian troops. They committed the most appalling atrocities. Himmler had their commander shot afterwards.

A major offensive was launched in the south on 20 August. The Romanians surrendered and, on 23 August, the King dismissed the pro-German government and switched sides. Romanian units joined the Red Army in clearing Romania of German troops. They took over 300,000 German POWs (Murray and Millett 2001).

On 2 September 1944, Soviet troops arrived at the Bulgarian border. Bulgaria, Germany's ally, had never declared war on the Soviet Union. Now it declared neutrality. Moscow ignored this and Soviet troops flooded through Bulgaria, heading for Yugoslavia. They linked up with Tito's communist partisans and drove the Germans out. However, the behaviour of the Red Army men, looting, burning and raping their way forward, left a bitter taste. Budapest, the Hungarian capital, fell to Soviet forces in December 1944. Stalin was pursuing two goals in the Balkans: military and political. He was brilliantly successful; the only blemish was the strained relationship with Tito. Soviet troops left Yugoslavia to continue their advance. Tito made sure none returned.

The final push

In January 1945, Hitler refused to believe that the Red Army was preparing an offensive against Poland. On 12 January, the Soviets attacked across four huge fronts, from the north to Ukraine, with about 4 million men. In the south, the Soviets had a five to one superiority in men and armour and seven to one in artillery. They were also very mobile thanks to Lend-Lease. The Germans were desperately short of vehicles and fuel. Warsaw, Krakow (the Nazi overlord surrendered it to prevent its destruction) and Breslau (Wroclaw) fell. When troops reached Germany they unleashed a reign of terror, murdering thousands of civilians, looting and destroying everything in sight. They were releasing the pent up rage of three and a half years of warfare. Soviet tanks drove down columns of refugees and gunners finished off anyone who had not been squashed. Soviet soldiers were encouraged to keep revenge notebooks. In these they recorded the crimes the Germans had committed in the Soviet Union.

Stalin pitted Zhukov and Konev against one another in the race to Berlin. It began on 14 April. Hitler committed suicide on 30 April and the same day the Red Flag was flying over the Reichstag. Only on 2 May did German resistance end. Victory had come at a price. The Red Army lost over 361,000 Soviet and Polish soldiers in taking Fortress Berlin. The defeat of Germany did not bring the war to an end. War was declared on Japan and Soviet forces entered Manchuria. Fighting continued after Japan surrendered on 14 August 1945. The Japanese Guantong (Kwantung) army only surrendered on 20 August. The campaign cost 30,000 lives or 10 per cent of their forces.

Casualties

The Red Army lost at least 8.7 million soldiers, 600,000 of these during the first 20 days of the war. Another 18 million were wounded, of whom 1 million died. There were 5.3 million Red Army POWs, of whom 57 per cent died in German captivity. Only 3.5 per cent of British and American POWs in Germany died. One of the reasons for the high Soviet death rate was that they were treated as a 'superior form of cattle'. About 40 per cent of the Soviet population, or 74.5 million, lived under German occupation.

German and Axis dead and wounded on the eastern front amounted to 6 million and there were 3.1 million POWs. Of these, a third died. The younger a prisoner was, the more likely he was to die. The United States lost 405,000 troops during the war. Britain mourned the deaths of 375,000 service men and women. France lost about 600,000.

The economy

The occupied areas were the industrial heartland of the country. For instance, 60 per cent of the defence plants, 63 per cent of the coal industry, 58 per cent of crude steel and 42 per cent of electricity generation were under German control. However, much of this capacity had been moved east or destroyed. Altogether 2,593 factories were evacuated and, of these, 1,200 were already in operation by mid-1942. Up to 40 per cent of workers and technical personnel moved as well.

About 400,000 were evacuated from Leningrad and 1.4 million from Moscow during the autumn of 1941. Altogether about 16.5 million were officially transported east while up to 10 million more moved unofficially.

Pavlenko's army

One of the most extraordinary stories of the war only came to light in 1952. N. M. Pavlenko deserted from the Red Army in March 1942 and quickly found others to form a pseudo-construction unit. He recruited deserters, criminals and his own relatives and friends. By bribing the right officers, he was able to procure uniforms for 'officers and soldiers' of his 'military unit'. They looted and stole on a massive scale and even executed Red Army men. They almost got to Berlin. Military commanders in East Germany were bribed, railway wagons procured, filled with German loot and brought back to the Soviet Union during the summer of 1945. The war over, Pavlenko divided most of the booty among his men, awarded them 230 orders and medals and they were demobilised with forged documents. He moved to Kalinin (Tver) and set up an *artel*. Now calling himself

Table 14.2 Soviet economic development, 1941–45 (1940 = 100)

	1941	1942	1943	1944	1945
Gross Industrial Production	98	77	90	104	92
Arms Production	140	186	224	251	173
Light Industry	88	48	54	64	62
Global Agricultural Production	62	38	37	54	60

Source: Based on I. C. B. Dear (ed.), *The Oxford Companion to the Second World War* (1995).

colonel, he concluded contracts with various organisations to build roads, was paid 30 million rubles but, of course, never did any work. The company even had an account in the State Bank. Pavlenko acquired influence by bribing local officials. His 'army' even had a counter-intelligence unit, headed by a 'major'.

It all unravelled in November 1952. His 'army' consisted of 300 men, 50 of them armed. His empire extended to Kyiv, Odesa, Kharkiv, Moldova and Estonia. 'Colonel' Pavlenko was executed. This astonishing story reveals that, even during the repression of the post-war years, massive scams were still possible. His organisation was well equipped with transport, itself a minor miracle during the post-war years. They could forge any document. The only way he could have kept afloat until 1952 was by bribing the right comrades. Why did Pavlenko become unstuck? Possibly because some official thought that he had been short-changed by him and reported him. How many other Pavlenkos were not brought to trial? One can only guess at the extent of the shadow economy in the late Stalin period.

Vlasov and others

General Andrei Vlasov, facing encirclement by German forces south of Leningrad, asked Stalin for permission to withdraw in June 1942. Stalin refused and Vlasov and others were captured. Vlasov agreed to form what later became known as a Russian Liberation Army (ROA) out of Soviet POWs. His intention was to fight with the Wehrmacht to remove Stalin and then to turn on the Germans. However Hitler did not trust Vlasov and his troops were moved to the western front. Some units participated in atrocities. The ROA did go into action against the Red Army, on the Oder, in April 1945. It had limited success and then moved to Czechoslovakia where it supported the successful Prague uprising against the Germans. Vlasov and his men surrendered to the Americans but were handed over to the Soviets. Vlasov and his staff officers were hanged on 2 August 1946 as traitors. The Ukrainian Galicia division saw front line duty between 1943 and 1945 as part of the Waffen-SS, the most brutal of all German military formations. A Ukrainian Insurgent Army (UPA), formed in 1942, sought an independent Ukraine.

Government and Party

On 22 June 1941, half of European Russia, from Archangel to Krasnodar, was placed under martial law. Heavy and defence plants were placed under Party supervision. On 29 August 1941, the Committee for the Defence of Leningrad ordered the expulsion of 96,000 Soviet citizens who were ethnic Germans or Finns for resettlement in the east. On 31 August, all ethnic German males in Ukraine were to be organised into construction battalions and sent to the east. The same month, Germans in the Volga German autonomous republic were to be deported en masse. Red Army soldiers, in German uniforms, had parachuted into the region and asked for shelter. The locals welcomed them. A planned visit by Hitler to the region never materialised but everyone had been provided with a little Nazi flag. Now they were accused of pro-Nazi sympathies. The inmates of prisons which could not be evacuated were simply shot. Among the victims was Trotsky's sister, the widow of Lev Kamenev.

Panic spread in Moscow as the Germans advanced. On 15 August, foreign embassies, the USSR Supreme Soviet and Sovnarkom were instructed to go to Kuibyshev. Thousands were arrested for spreading rumours. Stalin was informed that, due to a lack of political education, people had begun to play cards for money in the shelters. The key day was 16 October. Law and order broke down in Moscow. Stalin prepared to leave but changed his mind. He asked Zhukov if he could hold Moscow. He replied he could if provided with fresh troops and tanks. Troops were withdrawn from the Far East theatre and the great offensive began on 5 December.

Wars cannot be won by force alone. Stalin also needed a velvet glove. A softer cultural line was adopted. Boris Pasternak (1890–1960) and Anna Akhmatova (1889–1966) again appeared in public as literature escaped for a season from its Marxist straitjacket. Now the emphasis was on the Russian nation, its culture and heroes.

Over 1,000 writers became war correspondents at the front; almost half of them lost their lives. Wartime writing was organised by Aleksandr Fadeev, a leading official of the Writers' Union. The poem 'Holy War' by V. I. Lebedev was set to music and became the battle hymn of the Soviet people. Mikhail Sholokhov wrote *A School of Hatred* in 1942; Aleksei Surkov, the poem 'I Hate'; and Konstantin Simonov, whose play *The Russian People* was performed everywhere, also penned the poem 'Kill Him'. The cruelties and the crimes of the enemy dominated all discourses.

The extraordinary times produced some great literature. Aleksandr Tvadovsky's poem 'Vasily Tvorkin', stood out. The first attempt to depict the war realistically was by Vasily Grossman. His collection of short stories, *Immortal People* (1942), won acclaim. Ilya Ehrenburg's *The Fall of Paris* won the Stalin Prize in 1942. Konstantin Simonov's *No Quarter* and *Days and Nights* (about the battle of Stalingrad), appeared in 1943 and proved enormously popular. When the cultural climate changed after the war, these writers were subjected to harsh criticism. The partisans were celebrated in Fadeev's novel, *The Young Guard*, in 1945. He was attacked in 1947 for not giving the Party a prominent enough role in the book. In the realm of music, Dmitry Shostakovich's Seventh (Leningrad) Symphony was smuggled into the besieged city and first performed in 1942. It was an instant hit. It symbolised the heroic struggle of the Soviet people and was a great success when performed in London and the US in 1942.

Why was Stalin taken by surprise by the German attack of June 1941?

- Stalin believed that he had a good understanding of how Hitler's mind worked. This, despite the fact that he had never met the Führer; nor did he speak German.

- Stalin did not believe that Hitler would repeat the mistake of Germany, in 1914–18, when it became embroiled in a two front war. Hitler was too smart for that. Britain would have to be defeated first before thoughts of attack on the Soviet Union were entertained. War with Germany was inevitable. This was clear from Hitler's *Mein Kampf* (My Struggle).

- Stalin regarded Hitler as a rational decision maker.

- 22 June was too late to attack the Soviet Union. It left too little time before winter set in.

- Stalin was flooded with intelligence reports that Germany was going to attack. Why did he ignore them? He had been receiving shoals of intelligence reports predicting an imminent German attack from June 1940 onwards. All of them had proved erroneous. Why not those predicting an invasion in June 1941? Stalin was a great falsifier of information and news. He was a master of newspeak, the new Bolshevik language. He simply did not trust intelligence reports. Much less information from dyed in the wool anti-communists, such as Winston Churchill. They were all trying to provoke a war between Germany and the Soviet Union to their mutual benefit.

- Stalin accepted the explanations given by the German ambassador in Moscow. German forces were being massed on the Polish frontier to protect them from British air attacks. They were being prepared for an invasion of Great Britain. Zhukov told him this was a lie but it made no difference. The numerous flights over Soviet territory by German planes were due to the young, inexperienced German pilots losing their bearings. Zhukov told him that they were overflying Soviet defence positions and that they were on reconnaissance missions. Stalin ignored this. One German pilot had to make an emergency landing. He was found with detailed maps of the frontier region. He was allowed to return.

- Had Stalin accepted that Germany was going to attack, he would have been forced to amend his military thinking completely. The Soviet Union would have to prepare for a defensive war. This had always been rejected in the past as defeatist.

- To Stalin, changing to a defensive posture risked provoking a German attack. It would signal weakness.

- Stalin did not put his troops on the frontier on high alert until 21 June. The order did not get through to most units since communications had been sabotaged. However it was unclear if the troops were to fight if the Germans attacked. They were not to cross into German-held territory. Stalin was afraid of giving the Germans the impression that he was preparing to attack.

- Stalin was planning an attack on Eastern Europe but detailed planning had not yet begun. This would explain why Soviet forces were so close to the Polish border. Soviet defences along the pre-1939 frontier were dismantled but the new defences about 200–250 km further west had not yet been completed. It is astonishing that Stalin, who was planning to break the German–Soviet non-aggression pact himself, did not consider the possibility that Hitler might do the same. In this case Hitler beat him to the punch.

- Stalin was master of the Soviet Union and had terrified everyone into submission. He became too self-confident about his own ability to mould foreign policy. He treated his diplomats with disdain, did not believe his own intelligence chiefs and thought he knew best. His main consultant on foreign policy was 'iron-arse' Molotov. However Molotov was unlikely to disagree with the master once he perceived that his mind was made up.

- Zhukov and Timoshenko knew that war was coming but failed to convince Stalin. Had Stalin not purged the military so thoroughly in 1937–38, when 35,000 officers met their death, a military coup would have been on the cards. Probably only the brilliant Tukhachevsky could have changed Stalin's mind. But he had been shot. Tukhachevsky had been an advocate of a pre-emptive strike against the West. This was in line with Stalin's thinking.

- The future pre-emptive strike was only conceived of as an attack on Eastern Europe. It would stop at the German frontier. The Red Army would then be built up to launch an assault against Germany and Western Europe. By 22 June, Stalin thought that it was too late for an all-out attack on the Soviet Union. Stalin believed he now had time to prepare his next move.

- Stalin began to entertain doubts on 21 June. Still he believed that if an attack came, it would be a provocation by some German officers. Stalin also was extremely suspicious of his own military and had launched a purge in 1940. He feared that they and German officers could conspire to provoke a war between Germany and the Soviet Union.

- Molotov was informed by the German ambassador, Count von der Schulenburg, that Germany had declared war on the Soviet Union. His only response was to mutter: 'What have we done to deserve this?'

■ When Stalin put out peace feelers to Hitler, on 26 June 1941, through the Bulgarian ambassador, one of the questions he put was: 'Why did you attack us?' He still could not fathom it out.

Questions

1 'Without the economic machine established by Stalin during the 1930s, victory in the Great Fatherland War would have been impossible.' Discuss.

2 Outline the nature of Stalin's foreign policy during the war.

3 Explain why and how ideology was so important to Stalin's foreign policy.

4 'Political and institutional factors owed more to Soviet victory in the Great Fatherland War than economics.' Discuss.

5 'Stalin was always bound to win the war because he had an abundance of human capital which Hitler lacked.' Discuss.

6 How did Stalin make up for the loss of high-ranking military personnel during the Great Purge when it became obvious war was inevitable?

7 'Stalin's personality cult of *vozhd* was really only consolidated during the Soviet victory in the Great Fatherland War.' Discuss.

8 'The system of rule institutionalised during the war was merely an extension of that practised by Stalin himself during the 1930s.' Discuss.

9 'Stalin was a military genius.' Discuss.

10 Without Marshal Georgy Zhukov the Soviet Union would have lost the Great Fatherland War.' Discuss.

Further reading

Catherine Andreyev, *Vlasov and the Russian Liberation Movement* (1987); John Barber and Mark Harrison, *The Soviet Home Front, 1941–1945: A Social and Economic History of the USSR in World War II* (1991); Constantine Pleshakov, *Stalin's Folly: The Secret History of the German Invasion of Russia, June 1941* (2005); Jung Chang and Jon Halliday, *Mao: The Unknown Story* (2005); Williamson Murray and Allan R. Millett, *A War to Be Won: Fighting the Second World War* (2001); Catherine Merridale, *Ivan's War: The Red Army, 1941–45* (2005); Albert L. Weeks, *Stalin's Other War: Soviet Grand Strategy, 1939–1941* (2002); Ted Gottfried, *The Great Fatherland War: The Rise and Fall of the Soviet Union* (2003); Gabriel Gorodetsky, *Grand Delusions: Stalin and the German Invasion of Russia* (1999); Richard Overy, *Russia's War* (1997).

CHAPTER 15

The onset of the Cold War

The bid by Germany and Japan for world dominance ended in bloodshed and destruction. Humankind had never experienced anything like it. Total casualties may have exceeded 70 million. Germany lost 6.5 million and Japan 2 million. Japan's war in China cost at least 15 million Chinese lives. Over 4 million Poles died as did about 2 million Yugoslavs. However Soviet losses were gargantuan. The latest research puts casualties at 27.8 million, of whom 17.8 million were military. Other sources regard 50 million as more accurate. Almost a million Soviet military personnel were sentenced (one of them was Alexander Solzhenitsyn) for various offences. Of these 157,000 were shot: the equivalent of 15 divisions. This last figure is stunning. It is the obverse of the coin of heroic sacrifice. The discipline was so savage because Stalin clearly feared losing control.

Stalin's colossal blunder in 1941 had cost the Soviet people dear. In his victory speech one senses that he was surprised to be still in power. Ironically, Stalin's misjudgement led to the Soviet Union becoming the dominant power in Europe. Only the United States was its superior. To Stalin, the world was now divided into two camps: the Soviet and the American. Stalin finished the war exhausted, frequently ill and nervous about the loyalty of his generals and the Soviet people. On the positive side, he was sure the tide of history was flowing in the direction of communism. According to Molotov, he was too cocky in 1945. This was to result in diplomatic defeats in Turkey and Iran.

The Grand Alliance

The Grand Alliance – the United States, the Soviet Union, Great Britain, France and China – was a marriage of convenience. They only agreed on one objective:

the defeat of Germany, Japan and other Axis forces. How this should be achieved and what should happen afterwards to ensure it never happened again became the subject of bitter controversy. There were two major military powers: the United States and the Soviet Union. The Americans did not want the Soviet Union to replace Germany as the dominant military power in Europe. Moscow wanted to claw back the territory ceded in 1917 and establish a buffer zone in Eastern Europe. There were three major Big Three conferences: Tehran (28 November–1 December 1943), Yalta (4–11 February 1945) and Potsdam (16 July–2 August 1945) and numerous British–Soviet meetings; the most significant being the Moscow meeting of Stalin and Churchill, 9–18 October 1944; the main outcome of this was the percentages' agreement on zones of influence in Eastern Europe after the war.

The term Big Three is a misnomer. It was always the Big Two (Stalin and Roosevelt/Truman) and a Dwarf (Churchill/Attlee). Churchill sought to cling on to the coat-tails of the Americans in order to influence policy. Roosevelt was informed by his advisers before Yalta that the war against Japan might continue until 1947 and cost a million casualties. (British military estimates were half a million killed and half a million wounded.) It was not certain that the atomic bomb would be ready either. Churchill had many policy disagreements with Roosevelt. At Tehran, Roosevelt stayed at the Soviet embassy as the US embassy was about a mile away. It was judged too dangerous to travel back and forth because of the number of German agents who were seeking to kill all three leaders. Churchill stayed in the British embassy which was adjacent to the Soviet. Roosevelt grasped the opportunity to meet Stalin on his own. He did not inform Churchill of the contents of his discussions. It was clear to everyone that Roosevelt had an enormous admiration for Stalin. The expression on his face when he talked to Stalin revealed this. During the informal sessions Roosevelt and Stalin shared jokes at Churchill's expense.

What is one to read into Churchill's decision not to attend the American President's funeral in April 1945? Whatever the reason it was a major blunder. Truman had a high regard for Churchill and the latter could have used this in discussing the post-war world. Stalin respected both Roosevelt and Churchill. The Soviet leader had good intelligence – he bugged everyone's room – and this permitted him to plan negotiations like a game of chess. Stalin charmed the western leaders. They even called him Uncle Joe. Roosevelt had an infinitely subtle mind and was as good as Tony Blair at spin. Roosevelt's death on 12 April 1945 meant that Harry Truman represented the US at Potsdam. Churchill began as Britain's representative but was replaced by Clement Attlee after Labour's great election victory.

The Big Three conferences concentrated on certain key areas.

Europe:

- Britain and the US, **at Tehran,** committed themselves to a second front in Europe in 1944 (Roosevelt had unwisely promised Stalin that it would be opened in 1942);
- **at Yalta,** the Soviets accepted that General Franco could remain in power in Spain;
- this was a victory for Churchill who feared that communists could come to power after Franco and cause problems in the Straits of Gibraltar;
- Moscow had ambitions in Tangier and Libya.

Germany:

- no agreement, **at Tehran,** on occupation zones;
- **at Yalta,** agreement on German occupation zones of 14 November 1944 confirmed (France now added);
- Germany to lose territory to Poland and the Soviet Union;
- Soviets did not reach agreement on Germany's western border or on reparations;
- **at Potsdam,** Germany to be divided into occupation zones but treated as one economic space;
- Berlin (and Vienna) to be under four-power control (including France) and divided into sectors;
- Britain and US could not agree on amount of reparations Soviet Union to receive.

Eastern Europe:

- there was no agreement, **at Tehran,** however Roosevelt and Churchill conceded Soviet domination of Poland;
- they recognised the Curzon Line as the frontier between Poland (with north-east Prussia added) and the Soviet Union;
- they did not want conflict with Stalin as they feared that the Red Army might stop advancing when it reached the German frontier;
- **at Yalta,** Britain and the US again recognised the Curzon Line as the Polish–Soviet frontier and the Soviet-backed Polish provisional government;
- provisional government was to include a few London-based Poles;
- Roosevelt was willing to sacrifice Poland to gain Stalin's support in war against Japan (made many sarcastic remarks about the Poles at Yalta);
- Churchill could not write off Poland as Britain had gone to war in 1939 to defend Poland;

- **at Potsdam,** Britain and US recognised Poland's takeover of German territory east of the Oder–Neisse rivers;

- expulsion of Germans from Czechoslovakia, Poland, Hungary and Romania agreed;

- German–Polish frontier to be agreed at a separate conference;

- Stalin felt dominant and wanted recognition of Soviet sphere of influence in eastern Europe;

- Britain and US declined to grant this.

Far East:

- **at Yalta,** agreed that Soviet Union to enter war against Japan after defeat of Germany;

- Soviets to regain territories lost to Japan in 1905 and privileges in Manchuria;

- Outer Mongolia (Mongolian People's Republic) recognised as Soviet protectorate;

- Roosevelt also granted Stalin's wishes in China without consulting his ally, Chiang Kai-shek (he regretted this a few days before his death).

United Nations:

- **at Yalta,** Soviet Union favourable to establishment of UN.

The Moscow meeting of Stalin and Churchill, 9–18 October 1944, resulted in the percentages' agreement.

At Tehran, the West had conceded Soviet domination of Poland; the Red Army was making good progress and Churchill was keen to salvage as much as possible. He proposed the percentages' deal which excluded Poland and Czechoslovakia.

	Soviet Union	West
	(%)	
Romania:	90	10
Greece:	10	90
Bulgaria:	75	25
Hungary:	50	50
Yugoslavia:	50	50

The United States was not party to this agreement and objected to it. Britain regarded the Declaration on Liberated Europe, agreed at Yalta, as superseding the percentages' agreement. Stalin did not. Since the Red Army was in control in Eastern Europe, Stalin's interpretation prevailed.

Stalin had no delusions about post-war cooperation. He told Georgi Dimitrov, the Bulgarian Party leader, on 28 January 1945:

'Capitalism is divided into two camps: fascist and democratic. We are allied with the latter but in the future we will be against these capitalists too. The Soviet model is not the only one but the best. They may be other forms: the democratic republic; the constitutional monarchy . . .'

This reveals that Stalin expected cooperation to end, but how soon?

The mood was upbeat after Yalta. A Foreign Office official remarked: 'Stalin is a great man, and shows up very impressively against the background of the other two ageing statesmen'. Churchill was ever mindful of Neville Chamberlain, the British Prime Minister, who had been duped by Hitler. 'Poor Neville Chamberlain thought he could trust Hitler. He was wrong. But I don't think I'm wrong about Stalin.' He soon changed his tune.

British attitudes changed radically after Yalta as disillusionment set in. The Russians had no interest in resolving problems on the European Advisory Commission (on post-war Germany). The British concluded that the Russians had expected to end the war on the Rhine but were surprised at the rapid advance of the Allies. They had decided to hold on to everything they had. One diplomat lamented that democracy and cooperation had different meanings in Russian. Democracy was guided democracy and cooperation meant that each power could do as it liked in its own zone. The Foreign Office did not think that the Soviets posed a military threat. They needed 25 years of peace to become a great economic power.

The USSR emerges as a future potential enemy as early as 2 October 1944. Churchill instructed the Chiefs of Staff to report on the possibility of fighting the Russians if trouble arose. Churchill was anxious about the Russian bear sprawled over Europe. 'The Russians are all powerful in Europe', he gloomily reported on 11 June 1945. He wanted the Allies to remain where they were at war's end in order to negotiate access to Berlin. However, the Americans wanted the Red Army as an ally in the war against Japan. The failure to negotiate adequate access to Berlin was to cause endless friction.

Truman did not share Churchill's fears. At their first meeting, Truman concluded: 'I can deal with Stalin. He's honest – but as smart as hell'. Truman proposed that he see Stalin alone and that Churchill could come in at the end. The British bulldog threatened not to come to Potsdam if he were confined to a walk-on role. Stalin probably thought he had three aces before Potsdam but the atomic bomb changed all that. Now he only had two. Truman probably thought he had three aces; one of them being the A bomb. Churchill knew he had no aces.

Churchill's mood completely changed after hearing about the successful testing of the A bomb. Lord Alanbrooke, the clever Chief of the Imperial General Staff, records his reaction (23 July 1945):

'It was no longer necessary for the Russians to come into the Japanese war; the new explosive was enough to settle the matter. Furthermore we now have something in our hands which would redress the balance with the Russians! The secret of this explosive, and the power to use it, would completely alter the diplomatic equilibrium which has been adrift since the defeat of Germany! Now we had a new value which redressed our position (pushing his chin out and scowling), now we can say that if they insist on doing this or that, well we can just blot out Moscow, then Stalingrad, then Kyiv, then Kuibyshev, Kharkiv, Stalingrad [sic], Sebastopol, etc. And now where are the Russians!!!'

Alanbrook knew all this was nonsense so he had to keep the bulldog in check.

The Far East

Japan began to consider ending the war and hoped the Russians might act as intermediaries. However, Moscow had no interest in facilitating a dialogue between Tokyo and Washington. It wanted to come into the war and claim an easy victory. Tokyo called on all Japanese to fight to the death. Japan would never surrender as it believed this would mean the end of the Emperor and the Japanese way of life. Truman did not agonise over using the bomb. It was a simple choice: either hundreds of thousands of US troops die taking Japan or hundreds of thousands of Japanese die in a bid to end the war quickly. On 6 August an atomic bomb was dropped on Hiroshima, killing 145,000 persons. On 8 August, the Soviet Union declared war on Japan. The following day, the Americans dropped another atomic bomb on Nagasaki, killing 70,000. Tokyo decided to surrender. The Soviets wanted to land in Hokkaido, the most northerly island. Truman said no. Moscow was not going to get an occupation zone in Japan.

On 9 August 1945, over 1.5 million Soviet and Mongolian troops invaded China along a massive front stretching over 4,600 km; wider than the European Front from the Baltic to the Adriatic. Mao's forces immediately took over the territory overrun by the juggernaut. Under the Yalta agreement, the Soviet Union was supposed to sign a treaty with China before invading. A week later, with the Russians hundreds of kilometres inside China, a treaty of friendship and alliance was signed. Outer Mongolia was formally excised from China. Moscow recognised Chiang as the legitimate head of government. Stalin toyed with the idea of detaching Inner Mongolia from China but dropped the project. The Japanese Guantong army surrendered on 15 August. Irrespective of this, the Red Army carried on into central and eastern China. Manchuria had 70 per cent of China's industries.

Mao thought that if he had Manchuria he could take China. It was a treasure trove for Mao's army. The biggest arsenal, Shenyang, alone had about 100,000 guns, thousands of artillery pieces and large quantities of ammunition, textiles and food. About 200,000 Japanese prisoners had surrendered and these were handed over by the Russians for enlistment in Mao's forces. The Russians dismantled whole factories as war booty and other installations. The equipment removed by the Russians was estimated to be worth $858 m ($2 billion in current prices). The empowerment of Mao and the booty, of course, violated the treaty with Chiang (Chang and Halliday 2005).

The Red Army did not finally leave Manchuria until May 1946. Red forces re-entered the cities. Mao's number two, Liu Shao-chi, and the commander in Manchuria, Lin Biao, who was later to become Mao's number 2, did not believe they could hold the cities. They were right. An added difficulty for the communists was that they were linked, in the civilian mind, with the hated Russians.

In December 1945, General George Marshall, Secretary of State, met Mao. The wily old fox flattered Marshall and gave the impression he preferred America to Russia. Marshall told Congress, in February 1946, that there was no concrete evidence in China that the communist army was supported from outside. This was an astonishing statement to make, given the fact that the Americans and British had been intercepting cables from Russia, including those to Mao in Yenan. The head of the US mission in Yenan was in no doubt, informing Marshall that communism was international. Marshall chose to ignore all this intelligence. He presented Chiang with an ultimatum, on 31 May, to stop attacking the communists. Mao had been on the point of abandoning Harbin and dispersing his forces, breaking them up into small bands.

Marshall's misjudgement was the turning point in the Chinese civil war. Had Chiang continued to advance the Reds might have been forced to retreat into Russia, North Korea and Mongolia. Instead Mao could secure a base, 1,000 km long and 500 km deep, along the Mongolian and Russian borders. The Russians now trained Mao's officers. They brought in 900 aircraft, 700 tanks and thousands of machine guns, among other things. Over 2,000 wagons of Japanese matériel came in from North Korea, where there were huge arsenals. Japanese prisoners of war trained Chinese pilots and showed them how to use captured equipment. Japanese medical staff introduced higher standards of treatment. About 200,000 North Koreans who had served in the Japanese forces were added to Mao's armies. North Korea also became a major base for the Reds. Russians repaired the railways and bridges in Mao-held territory and this permitted large numbers of men and matériel to be ferried rapidly to critical theatres during the decisive year of 1948 (Chang and Halliday 2005).

In November 1947, confident of winning the civil war, Mao informed Stalin that he would like to visit Moscow. Stalin decided to show him who was boss. In April 1948, with still no invitation from the master, Mao informed him he was coming in May. Stalin said yes and then said no. In July, Mao cabled Stalin telling him he planned to visit him in the near future. His suitcases were packed, leather shoes had been bought and a woollen coat made. The master then came up with a ludicrous reason why Mao could not come. Senior Party officials were off to bring in the harvest and would not be back in Moscow until November.

In September, Mao, aware that the he had annoyed the *vozhd*, sent a grovelling telegram. He now addressed Stalin as 'master'. Stalin invited him but Mao did not fancy Moscow in the winter. He asked politely for a postponement. Mao had to make do with the master's comrade for all seasons, Anastas Mikoyan, who arrived in Yenan in January 1949. Then the Nationalist government moved capital, due to Red victories, and the Russian ambassador was the only one to accompany it. Mao was in such a huff that he declined to see Mikoyan for two days. Zhou Enlai filled in. Mao never forgave the ambassador who became Soviet envoy to the People's Republic. When the ambassador threw a dinner party for the Chinese leadership, Mao never uttered a word and, according to a Russian diplomat, wore a 'mocking-indifferent expression' (Chang and Halliday 2005). The Cominform, established in September 1947, had been deliberately restricted to European parties. Mao now proposed that when he took power he set up an Asian Cominform. Mikoyan countered by saying that an East Asian Cominform (China, Korea and Japan) might be a better idea. Mao was signalling that he regarded himself as the leader of Asian communists.

The atom bomb

Stalin's spies had kept him informed about the Manhattan Project. He was aware that Germany and Japan had been trying to build one but could not produce enough enriched uranium. One of the reasons why Stalin wanted to get to Berlin first was to gain access to German nuclear research. So he informed Eisenhower that the German government had moved south and that Berlin was no longer strategically important. (This was untrue. Hitler was still in Berlin.) Eisenhower swung his armies south giving the Red Army the opportunity to take Berlin.

Moscow was informed by one of its British agents, John Cairncross, in September 1941, that Britain had established a special committee to build an atomic bomb. In September 1942, Stalin signed a secret order to begin work on uranium. Molotov was in charge. Academician Igor Kurchatov (1903–60) was appointed and became the atomic tsar. He and a few colleagues had access to mountains of intelligence information. In mid-May 1945, the NKVD took some Soviet nuclear scientists to Germany to search for pure uranium. The leading

German specialist, Professor Nikolaus Riehl, who had lived in Russia until 1919 and spoke fluent Russian, agreed to help them. He took them to the main factory producing pure uranium but discovered that the Americans had bombed it deliberately only days before. However, the team managed to collect 112 tonnes of uranium oxides. Riehl and other German engineers began work in a factory near Moscow in July 1945. The first uranium ingots were ready in January 1946. The factory was developed by ex-Soviet POWs who, on their return to the Soviet Union, had been labelled cowards for surrendering. The plant became part of the gulag. By 1950, production of pure uranium had reached 1 tonne a day. There were about 10,000 prisoners working there.

Soviet intelligence informed Stalin about the successful atomic test in New Mexico about three days before President Truman told him. Stalin's spies discovered that the Americans had enough uranium and plutonium to produce eight atomic bombs a month. On 20 August, Stalin set up a special committee, consisting of scientists and bureaucrats, to produce an atomic bomb. Beria was put in charge. The gulag was to help produce the bomb. By the end of 1945, there were about 250,000 engaged on the project, about half of them prisoners. This was double the number involved in the Manhattan Project. By 1950, Soviet numbers had risen to 700,000.

Stalin gave Beria a deadline. The Soviet Union was to possess atomic and plutonium bombs by 1948. The atomic bomb was to be an exact replica of the American bomb. When Stalin was informed the scientists wished to use Einstein's relativity theory, branded pseudoscience in the Soviet Union, he replied: 'All right, we can shoot them all afterwards, if necessary'. In June 1948, the Soviets blockaded the access routes to West Berlin in response to the introduction of the Deutsche Mark as the West German currency. One of the reasons for Stalin's inept handling of the crisis was that he did not possess a nuclear weapon. Had he done so he could have negotiated from a position of strength.

The first Soviet atomic bomb was tested successfully in northern Kazakhstan on 29 August 1949. When the Americans analysed the radioactive fallout they concluded that the Soviets had made virtually a carbon copy of the bomb they had dropped on Nagasaki. The Soviets soon had a plutonium bomb. This came as a shock to Britain and the United States. The search for spies began. Klaus Fuchs was arrested in January 1950. He had come to Britain as a refugee from Nazi Germany. Bruno Pontecorvo, an Italian working on the Manhattan Project, fled with his family to the Soviet Union in 1950. He was given a laboratory at the Institute of Nuclear Physics at Dubna, near Moscow. John Cairncross, who had informed Moscow about Britain's nuclear project in 1941, was not unmasked until the mid-1980s. Guy Burgess and Donald Maclean escaped to the Soviet Union in 1951. They lived out the rest of their lives in Moscow with the rank of a KGB colonel. The most notorious of the group was Kim Philby, who only moved to Moscow in 1963. He became a personal friend of Yury Andropov. A series of postage stamps was issued in 1990 honouring the most successful Soviet spies. Philby was among them.

The hydrogen bomb

The Americans had an arsenal of about 300 atomic bombs by mid-1949. However they thought they would need a thousand bombs to defeat the Soviet Union in a war. Washington faced a critical choice after the explosion of the Soviet atomic bomb. Negotiate an end to the arms race or build a super weapon – the hydrogen bomb? Eventually the Americans concluded that the Soviet bomb and the establishment of the People's Republic of China on 1 October 1949 were threats to their security. President Truman announced, in January 1950, that the US would continue research on nuclear weapons, including the hydrogen bomb. American scientists tried to produce a bomb several thousand times as destructive as a plutonium bomb.

Andrei Sakharov (1921–89) had all the information he needed about the US project. He concluded that the Americans would never build their bomb. He and Vitaly Ginzburg constructed their own model. Arzamas-16 was the chosen site. Again it was part of the gulag.

The Americans did manage to test a hydrogen bomb, on 1 November 1952. It was about a thousand times as powerful as the bomb dropped on Hiroshima. This made clear that it could not be used in warfare. Worldwide reaction was, on balance, negative. The Soviet hydrogen bomb, 20 times as powerful as an atomic bomb, was successfully tested on 12 August 1953. A more powerful hydrogen bomb was exploded on 22 November 1955. A new testing ground, Novaya Zemlya in the Arctic, was prepared for the next generation of these fearful weapons.

Stalin's view of the world

Stalin's view of the world was Marxist. Capitalism was doomed but this made it potentially more dangerous. A working relationship with the Americans was needed in the short term. Stalin decided there was something which was non-negotiable: he would not retreat from territory the Red Army had occupied. If he gave way in one region, the Soviet Union itself could begin unravelling.

The Soviet Union did not have the resources to develop Eastern Europe. This meant that the socialist revolution had to be postponed. In the meanwhile coalition governments were necessary. Stalin was pragmatic. The key criterion was that no government could be hostile to Soviet interests. Countries such as Romania and Bulgaria, where the bourgeoisie was weak, would pose few problems. Caution was advisable in East Germany and Czechoslovakia, where the bourgeoisie was more developed. Poland, with its deep rooted hostility towards Russia, would pose a problem. So would Yugoslavia, where Tito held sway.

Finland offered a solution to the problem. It had signed a peace treaty with the Soviet Union and Great Britain on 19 September 1944. This ended its participation in the war on Germany's side. An Allied Control Commission was set up, dominated by the Soviets. There was no military occupation but Soviet troops occupied a large base at Porkkala, 30 minutes' drive from Helsinki, the capital. Finland agreed to pay heavy war reparations. It was to remain neutral and not to enter into any organisations, military or political, which the Soviets viewed as hostile to their security.

Could the Finnish model be applied elsewhere? In Bulgaria, a communist-dominated coalition, the Fatherland Front, took power in September 1944. In March 1945, a coalition government, dominated by communists, was formed in Romania. The United States protested vigorously but Britain held back. Churchill was mindful of the percentages' agreement. He feared that if he broke his word on Romania, Stalin would do the same in Poland and Greece. Hence, before the end of the war the communists had taken power in Bulgaria and Romania.

The Smallholders' Party (Hungary was a predominantly agrarian country) won 57 per cent of the vote in the elections in Hungary in November 1945. This placed the party, a coalition of many disparate elements, in a quandary. The contemporary joke was that the party leader had won a lion in a lottery and was afraid to take it home.

Eastern Europe was agrarian, the only exception being Czechoslovakia. An obvious way of attracting support was to take over the landed estates and distribute them among the peasants. However, the farms were not to be large enough to be viable economically. This would make it easier for the communists to influence rural politics. In Hungary, 3 million hectares were distributed among 663,000 peasants, many of whom had been landless. Romania and Poland followed suit. In Poland, 5.5 million persons were moved westwards to take over German territory up to the Oder–Neisse rivers. In Czechoslovakia, the tactic adopted was to expel Germans living in Sudetenland. One of these expellees told me that the land was so fertile they had to hold back produce from the market. Otherwise prices would have collapsed.

America entertains doubts

The Soviets made it clear they would like a handsome loan, perhaps $1 billion, to help with reconstruction after the war. Truman, however, was not as accommodating as Roosevelt. He wanted to discuss Soviet policy in Eastern Europe and the Soviet Union should join the International Monetary Fund (set up at Bretton Woods, New Hampshire, in July 1944) and the World Bank (established in

December 1945). Among other things, this would have obliged Moscow to declare its gold and hard currency reserves.

The loan would be used to import machinery and advanced technology. The Americans knew that the defence sector would be given priority. American suspicions grew after perusing a speech by Stalin on 9 February 1946. The Soviet victory had demonstrated the 'victory of the Soviet *social system* . . . and the victory of our Soviet *state*'. There was nothing remarkable about Stalin's speech. But many Americans read it as hostile to everything America stood for. The State Department then asked George Kennan, chargé d'affaires in the Moscow embassy, to analyse Soviet motives and behaviour. Over a weekend, he drafted the 'Long Telegram', one of the most influential documents of the Cold War. He had a profound knowledge of Russian culture and history. He saw the Soviets as ideologically obsessed; they were 'impervious to the logic of reason'. They were implacable enemies of the United States. World communism should be viewed as a 'malignant parasite which feeds only on diseased tissue'. The pragmatic element of Stalin's policies was completely ignored.

President Truman then invited Winston Churchill, out of office and out of favour, to speak on relations with Moscow. He addressed a college audience in Fulton, Missouri, on 5 March 1946. Truman was on the platform. Churchill's 'Iron Curtain' speech was brilliant and said everything the American administration wanted to hear. From Stettin in the Baltic to 'Trieste in the Adriatic, an iron curtain has descended across the continent'. Eastern Europe was lost to communism.

The image of the Soviet Union as an expansionist power was nurtured by Stalin's behaviour in the Middle East. Molotov, in his dotage, thought the boss had been too cocksure of himself. He toyed with the idea of adding the Azeri part of northern Iran to the Soviet republic of Azerbaijan. Soviet troops were eventually obliged to leave Iran in March 1946 and the project collapsed. Then territorial demands were made on Turkey but they had to be abandoned. One of Truman's advisers talked about America having to wage atomic and biological warfare to halt Soviet expansionism.

Europe divided: the Truman Doctrine and the Marshall Plan

President Truman addressed Congress on 12 March 1947 and radically altered the direction of American policy. Britain had appealed to the United States for help in the struggle against the communists in Greece. Turkey was also facing problems. The Truman Doctrine stated that Washington would come to the aid of any state under threat. He specifically mentioned Greece and Turkey. Communism was not mentioned. The code words used were 'totalitarian regimes'. This emotive term

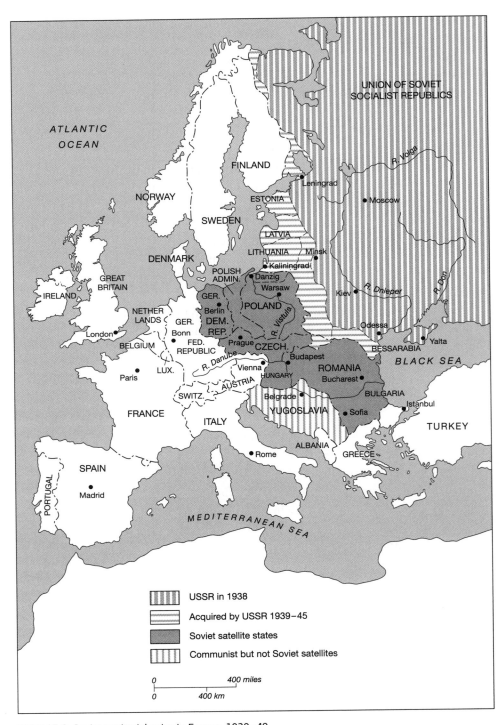

MAP 15.1 Soviet territorial gains in Europe, 1939–49

had previously described Germany, Italy and Japan. The psychological message was quite clear. The mortal threat to freedom now emanated from Moscow.

On 5 June 1947, General George Marshall declared that the United States was willing to extend loans to European states to promote integration. Poverty in Europe was the breeding ground of communism. The offer covered the Soviet Union and Eastern Europe. There was a risk that they might be smart enough to accept the proposal. Molotov wanted aid without strings but the US and its allies insisted on integration to create a single economic space in Europe. Anastas Mikoyan, the astute Trade Minister, saw a golden opportunity. Stalin thought that this would make the Soviet Union dependent on the United States. Mikoyan argued that American capital would promote the more rapid recovery of the Soviet economy and make the country more independent. Stalin did not agree and thereby missed a golden opportunity. Czechoslovakia was keen to accept aid. Stalin told the Czechs that doing so would be viewed as an unfriendly act. So Europe divided into two economic blocks. Those in the east were to develop their own trading organisation – it was called Comecon and came into being in 1949. Those in the west began the process which eventually climaxed in the formation of the European Economic Community in 1958, the forerunner of the present European Union.

In September 1947, communist leaders from the Soviet Union, Eastern Europe (but not Greece and East Germany), Italy and France met in Szklarska Poreba, Poland. Andrei Zhdanov represented Stalin. Zhdanov divided the world into two camps: the imperialist and anti-imperialist. Countries such as India and Indonesia were left outside. Zhdanov lashed the Italian and French parties for pussyfooting around. More militancy was needed. It was no defence that pussyfooting – so as not to antagonise the Americans – had been official Moscow policy. It was agreed to set up the Communist Information Bureau, the Cominform, with headquarters in Belgrade, Yugoslavia.

Conflict in Eastern Europe

Two comrades dominated the region: Georgy Dimitrov (1882–1949), had headed the Comintern until its dissolution in 1943. He later became Party boss in his native Bulgaria. The other was Josip Broz, known as Tito (1892–1980). They were as different as chalk and cheese. Dimitrov was Stalin's servile servant – the only way to survive since he was living in Moscow – but Tito was haughty and self-confident. The Red Army had presented Dimitrov with power. However, in Yugoslavia, Tito's communists had fought a guerrilla war against the occupying Germans. The Red Army had helped liberate the country but had then moved on to Hungary. Tito – a bit of a dandy – revered Stalin as the father of world communism. However he did not regard Stalin as his master.

Stalin accepted that Tito would be a dominant force in the Balkans after the war. In September 1944, Tito visited Stalin in Moscow and they worked out a new Balkan federation. On Bulgaria, Stalin advised Dimitrov, on 2 September 1946, to set up a Labour Party, not a workers' party. The reason for this was that, as Marxists were now in power, a minimalist programme was advisable. Stalin judged that the dictatorship of the proletariat was not necessary. The Bulgarians were advised not to copy the Russian communists, who had been in a totally different position. Bulgaria had laid claim to western Thrace. A war was needed to solve that problem.

Dimitrov promoted the concept of an Eastern European federation. He thought that this was inevitable and it would also include Greece. This brought down Stalin's wrath on his head. He sent him a sharp letter on 24 January 1948, ordering him to retract. Stalin thought the Americans would automatically conclude that he was behind the plan. *Pravda* weighed in on 28 January 1948, dismissing all schemes for an Eastern European federation as harmful.

On 10 February 1948, Stalin wrote to Dimitrov that if the Greek partisans (communists) could win, they should be allowed to do so. Bulgaria should take Albania away from Yugoslavia but do it in a subtle manner. There were only three federations possible in Eastern Europe: 1) Bulgaria and Yugoslavia; 2) Romania and Hungary (both non-Slav); 3) Poland and Czechoslovakia. The unification of Bulgaria, Yugoslavia and Albania should not be delayed.

In Czechoslovakia, the communists emerged as the largest party after winning 38 per cent of the votes in the republic in the elections of May 1946. Their leader Klement Gottwald (1896–1953) became Prime Minister, heading a coalition government. All Soviet troops had left the country. The communist 'takeover of power' in February 1948 was not a coup at all. Social democrat ministers and members of the non-communist opposition resigned from the government, hoping to bring it down and force new elections. This was crass stupidity. The communists cleverly turned the government crisis to their advantage with Gottwald's nomination of Party members to fill the vacant posts, which resulted in a final power confrontation with the non-communist opposition. President Edvard Beneš (1884–1948) was obliged to accept the new coalition government, now dominated by communists. The Foreign Minister, and member of the non-communist opposition, Jan Masaryk (1886–1948), died in mysterious circumstances, on 10 March. In May, a new constitution was adopted and the communists triumphed in new elections. Beneš resigned on 7 June and Gottwald succeeded him. All this had happened without a single Soviet soldier in the country. The contrast with Poland, where anti-communist feeling was highest in Eastern Europe, is remarkable.

Stalin once remarked that communism fitted Poland like a saddle on a cow. It was strategically too important to Moscow to be allowed to go its own way. Soviet troops crossed Poland to reach East Germany. Nationalists and communists killed one another in Poland by the thousand between 1945 and 1948. The communists and socialists 'won' the elections of January 1947. They merged in December 1948 to form the Polish United Workers' Party. Poland was now a people's democracy. The main opposition came from the Roman Catholic Church. It adopted a non-confrontational approach which disappointed many believers who wanted out-right opposition. However the church's attitude was that it would last for ever whereas the communist regime was only a temporary aberration.

Stalin discovered that Tito was not as malleable as other communist leaders. The boss overestimated his power. He talked about bringing Tito to heel by wav-ing his little finger. The great love affair between Tito and Stalin ended in bitter divorce. He sent the Yugoslav Communist Party a stinging letter in May 1948. Dimitrov commented that the Yugoslav leadership (he meant Tito) was 'egotist-ical, painfully ambitious and thoughtless'. Stalin had concluded that Tito could dominate the Balkan federation. Albania was not to be swallowed up by Yugoslavia. In June 1948, the Cominform condemned Yugoslavia. Tito immedi-ately expelled pro-Soviet (called Cominformists) members from his inner circle. Stalin sent military advisers to neighbouring countries to prepare an invasion of Yugoslavia. It never materalised because the United States responded to Tito's pleas for military aid. Stalin would not risk a confrontation with America. Instead he sent Ministry of State Security (MGB) agents to assassinate Tito. The latter caught, tortured and executed them. He then sent Stalin a note instructing him not to send any more agents. If he did, Tito would send one of his men to Moscow. He would not need to send a second one. Stalin backed off. To be labelled a Titoist was now the most heinous crime. Show trials in Bulgaria and Czechoslovakia resulted in death sentences. Over a million members were expelled from com-munist parties in Eastern Europe.

The German question

From Moscow's point of view, Germany was the key country in Europe from 1945 to 1991. Stalin's primary goal was security. He had to ensure that Germany never again attacked the Soviet Union. There were various options to choose from. The best was a neutral, demilitarised, unified Germany which would be capitalist. Another was two German states, East and West Germany, as a federation: one socialist the other capitalist. The worst scenario was a communist East Germany dependent on the Soviet Union and a capitalist West Germany dominated by the Americans.

Stalin expected Berlin to remain the capital of Germany. The social democrats, the SPD, were more attractive to the working class than the communists, the KPD. The communists suffered a comprehensive defeat in elections in Austria, in December 1945. The Soviet military administration decided the only option was to merge the SPD and KPD. The new party was called the Socialist Unity Party (SED). This was forced through in April 1946. The KPD was too weak in the western zones to effect a merger. The forced merger harmed the image of the communists and the Russians. Henceforth the SED was always dismissed as the Russian party in West Germany.

The Americans and British lost patience with the Soviets and set up Bizonia, in July 1946. They thereby began the process which culminated in two German states. Britain, facing austerity, could ill afford the food and consumer goods needed to supply its zone. Neither Britain nor France favoured a unified Germany. They feared they could not compete with a resurgent German economy. On 6 March 1948, the western powers announced that a separate West German government would be set up. Moscow protested and pointed out that this was a breach of the Potsdam Agreement. It was. The next step, announced on 1 June, was to introduce a new currency, the Deutsche Mark (DM) in West Germany. (It was launched on 20 June.) The Soviets introduced the East German Mark (later the DDR Mark) and included all Berlin. The DM was then declared the currency of West Berlin.

Stalin had to react. On 24 June all access routes to West Berlin were cut. The three air corridors were exempt. The Berlin Blockade had begun. Stalin's advisers told him West Berlin could not be supplied by air. President Truman was told the same. Nevertheless, the Berlin airlift began on 26 June. Berlin, previously the capital of fascist Germany, now became a symbol of heroic resistance to totalitarianism. One American officer referred to the Russians as 'rats walking like bears'. The Americans made it clear they would use the atom bomb if necessary to defend West Berlin.

Stalin was in the stronger bargaining position. However, he played his cards badly. One of the reasons for this was the ill health he suffered from time to time. When he was indisposed no decisions were taken. The blockade lasted until 5 May 1949. It cost over $224 million. From Truman's point of view it was money well spent. The blockade weakened the appeal of communism and cemented West Germany and West Berlin in the western camp. It also gave the impression that the Soviet Union was an expansionist power. Konrad Adenauer, the conservative first Chancellor of the new Federal Republic of Germany, worked tirelessly to set up a separate West German state. He feared the appeal of Marx to German workers.

In April 1949, the North Atlantic Treaty Organisation (NATO) was set up. Had it not been for the Berlin Blockade, the Americans might have hesitated about committing themselves so closely to the defence of Western Europe. West European politicians (but not the left) were delighted. American troops and nuclear bombers would now provide a security umbrella. The setting up of the Federal Republic of Germany and the German Democratic Republic (GDR) divided Germany and Europe for 40 years.

Mao comes to town

After Mao had proclaimed the founding of the People's Republic, on 1 October 1949, he waited impatiently for an invitation from Stalin to visit Moscow. None came. Zhou Enlai was dispatched to tell the Russian ambassador that Mao would like to visit Moscow to pay his regards to the master on the latter's seventieth birthday, on 21 December 1949. Stalin, who had been stringing Mao along for two years, grudgingly said yes. However it would not be a state visit. Mao would be visiting the Soviet Union as merely one of a gaggle of communist leaders. Mao did not take along any senior aide. When he saw Stalin he excluded his own ambassador. Mao expected to be humiliated and wanted to ensure that no subordinate witnessed his discomfort. He saw Stalin when he arrived and presented his shopping list.

The master needed time for reflexion. Mao was put in Stalin's bugged number two dacha, about 30 km outside Moscow. All Mao could do was to fume and look out at the snow. Then Stalin sent a succession of minions to talk to him. The objective was to draw a psychological portrait of the new Chinese Emperor. Every now and then Mao had a little treat. One of these was to marvel at the wonders of socialist agriculture. All Mao saw were some cows. He was also kept away from foreign leaders. The only one he saw was the Hungarian boss. He was keen to meet Palmiro Togliatti, the Italian communist chief. Stalin made sure he did not. Mao was seated on Stalin's right at the grand birthday festivities in the Bolshoi Theatre. The audience chanted: 'Stalin, Mao Zedong'. Mao responded: 'Long live Stalin! Glory to Stalin!' Afterwards he was packed off to his dacha. He became so frustrated that he shouted at Stalin's intermediary that he had come to do business, not to 'eat, shit and sleep'.

Stalin saw Mao on 24 December but would not discuss his pet project: an arms industry. Mao's birthday, on 26 December, went unnoticed. Mao then showed Stalin he could play him at his own game. In his dacha, he proclaimed loudly, to ensure that it was picked up, that he was ready to do business with America, Japan and Britain. Diplomatic relations were established with Britain on 6 January 1950. The British press then reported that Stalin was holding Mao under house arrest in Moscow. It worked. Stalin immediately began negotiating seriously. Zhou Enlai and other ministers were summoned from Beijing to work out the details.

A Sino-Soviet treaty was signed on 14 February 1950. Mao got his $300 million loan, over five years, all earmarked for defence. Stalin agreed to begin building 50 large industrial projects. In return, Mao conceded that Manchuria and Xinjiang were Soviet spheres of influence. The Russians were to have exclusive access to their industrial and raw material wealth. Moscow also obtained the right to acquire 'surplus' tungsten, tin and antimony for 14 years. This deprived China of the opportunity of selling these valuable products on the world market until the mid-1960s. Deng Xiaoping informed Mikhail Gorbachev, in 1989, that of all the unequal treaties China had signed with tsarist Russia and the Soviet Union this was the most onerous. China had not only to pay for Soviet engineers and technicians but had also to compensate their own enterprises for the loss of their labour. An even more important concession by Mao was that all Soviet citizens were outside Chinese jurisdiction. Stalin, at a final party, mentioned Tito again. He warned Mao that any country which went down that path would return to the fold under a different leader. At the signing ceremony, Stalin, 1.7 m tall, took a step forward in order not to appear shorter than Mao, who stood 1.8 m.

The Korean War

Mao was hungry to expand China's influence. To mollify him, while in Moscow Stalin granted him supervision of Vietnam. Then Mao switched his attention to another country he had been assigned by Stalin: North Korea.

Kim Il Sung, the communist leader of North Korea, the Korean People's Democratic Republic, went to Moscow in March 1949 to ask Stalin to help him take South Korea, the Republic of Korea. Stalin said no but when Kim asked Mao he said yes. The first half of 1950 would be preferable. Chinese soldiers could help the Koreans because both had black hair and the Americans would not be able to tell the difference. Stalin held Kim on a short leash until he had the atomic bomb.

Then, in January 1950, Kim informed the Soviet ambassador in Pyongyang that Mao was prepared to help him to attack South Korea. Stalin gave Kim the green light. War in Korea would benefit the USSR and China. North Korea and China would be dependent on Russian military aid. However, the Chinese would want their military industries developed rapidly. The Chinese had 300 million men available, were not concerned about casualties and so could fight for ever. From Moscow's point of view, if huge numbers of American troops could be sucked into Korea, it might change the balance of power in other parts of the world. Stalin started toying with the idea of taking over countries such as West Germany, Italy and Spain. Chinese troops could be used, if necessary. He even thought of attacking the US fleet on the high seas between Japan and Korea. This would mean a Third World War. 'If war is inevitable, then let it be fought now, rather than in a few years' time' (Chang and Halliday 2005).

On 25 June 1950, the North Koreans crossed the 38th parallel and penetrated South Korea. They carried all before them. The United States urgently sought a United Nations mandate. They obtained one due to the fact that the Soviet delegate in the Security Council, Yakov Malik, had been boycotting the UN. Malik wanted to return and veto the UN resolution. Stalin stopped him.

UN forces turned the tide in Korea. They crossed into North Korea and it appeared they might take the whole of Korea. Kim Il Sung pleaded for help.

Mao was for war against America but the rest of his team was against. He gambled that the United States would not invade China or use atomic weapons. He was right. Soon there were six Chinese for every North Korean soldier. The Chinese took Seoul, the South Korean capital, at the end of the year. British forces were involved in fierce fighting with the Chinese. Mao told Stalin that he wanted the war to last several years in order to 'consume' hundreds of thousands of American lives.

Many British, US and other UN prisoners were taken by the Chinese. They faced the problem of how to manage them and prevent them from escaping. They hit on the idea of identifying the leaders and guarding them closely. They discovered that only one in twenty was a leader. With these removed, the other 95 per cent became passive and easy to control. Apparently only one in twenty in any society is a leader.

In June 1951, with North Korea resembling a wasteland, Kim had had enough. He asked Mao about a ceasefire. Stalin advised it would be advantageous to negotiate. Ceasefire talks began in July 1951 but got nowhere. A desperate Kim again pleaded for a ceasefire in July 1952. Mao was not interested. He kept on demanding more and more arms factories from Moscow. Stalin was also accepting greater Chinese influence in Asia.

In February 1953, the new US President, Dwight Eisenhower, stated he might use the atomic bomb on China. This delighted Mao and he proposed a deal with Stalin. Give me the bomb and you will not be drawn into a nuclear war with America. Thereupon Stalin, on 28 February, decided to end the war. However, he immediately fell victim to a stroke and died on 5 March. Mao did not bother to go to the funeral in Moscow. Zhou Enlai stood in. He then moved on to Prague where Klement Gottwald had finally succumbed to alcoholism. Harry Pollitt, the Communist Party of Great Britain chief, asked for an audience. After a few pleasantries, Pollitt requested a $5,500 Chinese contribution towards renovating Karl Marx's grave in Highgate cemetery, in London.

The post-Stalin leadership in Moscow wanted to end the war and reduce tensions with the West. An armistice was signed on 27 July 1953. China poured 3 million men into Korea and may have lost a million of them. The Americans suffered 142,000 fatalities. The Russians lost 335 planes and 120 pilots. Among the Chinese casualties was An-ying, Mao's eldest son, killed in November 1950. He was 28. Mao showed little emotion when informed of his death.

How did the Cold War come about?

General Semen Budenny, a faithful servant of Stalin but not very bright, made an interesting remark to Stalin just after the war. He thought it a pity that Stalin had not ordered the Red Army to continue westwards after taking Berlin and Prague.

Stalin replied: 'And how could we have fed them all?' Was Stalin being serious given the fact that he knew Budenny was not very gifted upstairs?

In November 1947, Stalin told Maurice Thorez, the French communist leader, that had Churchill delayed the second front another year, the Red Army would have reached France. He paused and continued: 'We even thought of getting to Paris'. Thorez replied that the French communists had concealed arms dumps and had transmitters to contact Moscow. Stalin then told him that he would have provided more arms. 'After all, we are all communists and that is what matters', he concluded.

There are various schools of thought:

- The orthodox or classical. They blame it on Stalin's ambitions, Marxism and the presence of the Soviet army in Eastern Europe. The Russians were perceived to be expansionist. The coup in Czechoslovakia and the Berlin Blockade were seen as confirming the aggressive intentions of Moscow. Many post-communist Russian historians blame Stalin. One sees him as a 'communist imperialist'.

- The revisionist. They argue that Stalin was pragmatic and pursued limited goals – first and foremost security. The country was economically weak. He expected large loans from the United States. He thought that the United States and Britain had conceded Eastern Europe as a Soviet zone of influence – a buffer zone in case of renewed aggression by Germany. Stalin expected the West to collaborate in ensuring that Germany never became a threat again. Some historians regard the Americans and Russians as equally culpable but others, on the left, blame the United States.

- The post-revisionist. These (the leading figure is John L. Gaddis) avoid apportioning blame and examine the false conceptions the two parties entertained of one another. Both sides had misconstrued each other's intentions. This led to policies which produced a vicious circle of distrust.

- International relations specialists. They draw inspiration from the study of large organisations. Each side was a geopolitical system which followed logical rules in mobilising and projecting its power. Ideas and human beings play a minor role in this approach. The collapse of the Soviet Union dealt this school a mortal blow as some members had argued that it had predictive power. It had not foreseen the end of the Soviet Union.

The Warsaw Uprising, which began on 1 August 1944, lasted 63 days and cost the lives of 16,000 insurgents and 180,000 civilians. Norman Davies (2004) sees the dead as the first victims of the Cold War. The Red Army halted on the other side of the Vistula river. Stalin permitted the Wehrmacht and SS to slaughter the cream of the Polish bourgeoisie – implacable enemies of communism. This made the task of sovietising post-war Poland all the easier. Stalin called the insurgents a 'criminal gang'. Britain and the United States requested landing rights on Soviet-occupied territory so as to arm the insurgents. Stalin would have none of it. George Kennan, in the US embassy in Moscow, saw this decision as a direct challenge to the Big Three. For Stalin, the chance of eliminating the armed part of the Polish bourgeoisie was more important than his relationship with Roosevelt and Churchill. More seeds of distrust had been sown.

There was no hidden agenda, nor was there a grand design which was being implemented. Foreign policy was influenced by domestic politics and there were various interest groups which struggled for influence. One could argue that Stalin proceeded by trial and error within a Marxist framework. He often found it hard to make up his mind. He did not expect his behaviour in 1945–46 to lead to a long-lasting confrontation with the West. Hence he blundered into the Cold War by miscalculating western reactions to his initiatives. Once the Cold War got under way, he sought to demonstrate that the Soviet Union was a strong power. Some scholars even think he was planning the Third World War before his death. He was as paranoid in foreign as in domestic affairs.

A foreign diplomat was driving down Gorky Street in Moscow. A militia man stopped him. 'Didn't you see the arrows?', he asked. 'No. I didn't even see the Indians.'

Why was there a Cold War?

- It was almost inevitable given two conflicting, universalist ideologies: Marxism and the American dream; the Soviets expected Marxist socialism to take over the world; the Americans believed they had a 'divine mission' to bring (capitalist) peace, freedom and democracy to the world.

- Some see the conflict beginning with the October Revolution; others, the majority, in 1947.

- Marxism envisaged continuing conflict between communism and capitalism; Stalin accepted that an eventual war was inevitable; however, in 1952 Malenkov talks of the possibility of peaceful coexistence; the Soviet Union had the bomb.

- The Soviet Union and the United States had little knowledge and understanding of one another; Washington had only established diplomatic relations with Moscow in 1933.

- The Grand Alliance was a marriage of convenience; Germany and Japan had to be defeated in order for socialism and capitalism to survive; no single nation could have defeated the Axis powers.

- Roosevelt's main priority was always the war in the Pacific against Japan; Stalin and Churchill's main priority was always the war in Europe against Germany and its allies.

- Roosevelt was willing to sacrifice Poland and much else to bring the Soviet Union into the war against Japan. In early 1945, the Americans expected the Pacific war to last another 18 months, costing up to a million casualties.

- Eventually the Americans did not need the Red Army to defeat Japan. However, they had made concessions to Stalin which they could not renege on.

- Stalin believed that America and Britain had conceded Eastern Europe as a Soviet buffer zone against a future German attack, should it come. Churchill, in the percentages' agreement of October 1944, did concede Soviet hegemony in the region.

- The Warsaw Uprising, which began on 1 August 1944, soured relations between the Big Three. The Soviet refusal to allow Allied planes to land behind Soviet lines so as to help the insurgents rankled; as did Stalin's dismissal of the insurgents as a criminal gang.

- Stalin delayed the Yalta conference until the Red Army was in a dominant position in Eastern Europe. Churchill wanted Roosevelt to put more pressure on Stalin but the latter declined because of the need for Soviet help against Japan.

- Stalin did not implement the Yalta agreement on Poland.

- Stalin expected to get a $1 billion loan from the Americans. This was desperately needed for reconstruction. The Soviets stripped East Germany and Manchuria of industrial and other equipment. When the loan was not forthcoming Stalin felt let down. Stalin declined to join the IMF and World Bank; had he done so the Soviets could have applied for loans. This was a major strategic blunder on Stalin's part.

- Truman was less willing to make concessions than Roosevelt; he felt America with the atomic bomb was dominant, so the Soviets should make concessions.

- Stalin was often ill and could only concentrate on key issues; his main concern after May 1945 was to reduce the prestige of the military; otherwise they could challenge him and perhaps win; he also had to manipulate his subordinates, especially Beria, Malenkov, Molotov and Zhdanov, to ensure they did not outmanoeuvre him; hence domestic policy took precedence over foreign policy immediately after the war. Détente with the Americans would have diluted Stalin's political control. It would have involved many encounters in the political, economic, social, cultural and military spheres which would have been very difficult to monitor. There was also the danger of western ideas undermining Soviet ideology.

- Stalin perceived the delays in launching the second front in France to be a tactical decision by the Allies. Its aim was to permit the Russians and Germans to exhaust themselves fighting. Then the Allies would attack a weakened Wehrmacht. The dropping of two atomic bombs by the Americans was read as a signal that America harboured ambitions to dominate the world. Another factor was the proposal by Admiral Lord Louis Mountbatten that an atomic bomb should be dropped in the White Sea, off the coast of northern Russia, as a warning to the Russians. The message was that the bomb could be used against them.

- Stalin did not seek a confrontation with the West but his clumsy diplomacy provoked increasing tension. He did not have the energy or understanding to defuse the situation and turn things to his advantage. Molotov, had he been given more autonomy, could have done a better job but Stalin was paranoid about Molotov attempting to supplant him.

- The Soviets did not leave Iran as agreed; it appeared that they were trying to establish a Soviet Iran in the north which would link up with Azerbaijan. They were tardy in leaving Manchuria too. American pressure had to be applied. Stalin also laid claim to some Turkish territory and wanted Libya as a protectorate. All this sowed seeds of doubt in western minds.

- Mikoyan failed to convince Stalin of the benefits to the Soviet Union of the Marshall Plan. He obliged the Eastern European states to turn down the offer as well. It appeared that the USSR would not collaborate with the United States.

- On the other hand, the USSR was very defensive in China. Stalin's goal was to establish a communist Manchuria which would be a buffer against possible future Japanese aggression. He did not believe that Mao Zedong could take over the whole of China. Stalin's goal was always to avoid confrontation with the Americans in China and the rest of Asia. This was to change in 1950 after the Soviets had acquired an atomic bomb.

- The 'coup' in Czechoslovakia, in February 1948, was read in the West as Soviet-engineered. In reality it was due to the stupidity of the Czech social democrats.

- The Berlin Blockade was a diplomatic disaster for Stalin. He handled the negotiations badly and was clearly not well briefed, especially on economic matters. Berlin became a symbol of the Manichean struggle of good and evil: the Russians were the baddies and the Americans the goodies.

- France and Britain wanted a divided Germany.

- The Christian Democrats (CDU), who were to form the first West German government in 1949, wanted a divided Germany. Their leader, Konrad

Adenauer, was fearful of the appeal of communism. An American presence was essential.

■ East German politicians, when they sought refuge in West Germany, were very anti-Soviet.

■ Britain and France were too weak militarily to defend Western Europe. They wanted an American umbrella. This involved stationing US troops in Western Europe. NATO was a godsend to the West Europeans.

Questions

1 What is meant by the term 'Cold War'? Answer in relation to the worldwide balance of power after 1945. How did Stalin conceive of the 'Cold War'?

2 What were the primary goals of Soviet foreign policy in and after 1945?

3 'Perceptions rather than substance or detailed knowledge about each other's intentions determined the nature of the relationship between Stalin, Roosevelt and Churchill in 1943–45.' Discuss.

4 Summarise the main events leading to and the reasons for the establishment of a Soviet zone of influence in Eastern Europe.

5 'The Yalta conference (February 1945) was a turning point in Soviet foreign policy.' Discuss.

6 What were the key events leading up to the signing of the Sino-Soviet treaty in February 1950? What did these reveal about Stalin's attitude towards the Far East after 1945?

7 Plot the course of the Stalin–Mao Zedong relationship. Who came out on top?

8 'Communist revolution in Eastern Europe was instituted from "above" and not from "below".' Discuss with regard to individual cases of the communist seizure of power.

9 Which factor dominated the evolution of the US–Soviet relationship in the post-war years?

10 Why and when was the Cominform founded? Was it important?

Further reading

Odd Arne Westad, *Reviewing the Cold War: Approaches, Interpretations, Theory* (2000); Jung Chang and Jon Halliday, *Mao: The Unknown Story* (2005); Apor Balázs *et al.* (eds), *The Leader Cult in Communist Dictatorships: Stalin and the Eastern Bloc* (2004); Raymond Pearson, *The Rise and Fall of the Soviet Empire* (2002); Martin McCauley, *The Origins of the Cold War 1941–1949* (2003); John Lewis Gaddis, *The Cold War* (2005).

CHAPTER 16

High Stalinism

Brow-beating the military

The most dangerous challenge to Stalin's authority in May 1945 came from the military. They were the heroes and rightly so. The star was Marshal Georgy Zhukov. Stalin was very jealous of his popularity. He had to be cut down to size.

At a grand reception for Red Army commanders in the Kremlin, on 24 May 1945, Stalin made a striking confession.

> 'Our government committed many errors; there were times, in 1941–2, when we found ourselves in a desperate situation. Another people might have said to the government: you have not come up to our expectations, go!; we shall appoint another government which will conclude a peace with Germany and guarantee us a quiet life. But the Russian people did not do that.'

Then and later he commended the Russian people, not the Soviet people, for playing a decisive role in defeating Hitler. Everyone was aware that it was primarily the Russian people who had won the war in spite of Stalin's mistakes. How was Stalin to shake the growing self-confidence of the military?

Stalin never trusted the military. The NKVD began its surveillance of Zhukov in 1939. His quarters, apartment and dacha were bugged. All those in contact with him were also watched. On 26 May 1945, Zhukov invited leading military commanders and a popular singer to his dacha. They drank to Zhukov as the victor over Germany. The next day, the transcripts of the conversations were on Stalin's desk in the Kremlin. Zhukov was closely monitored as commander-in-chief of Soviet forces in Germany. In the second half of 1945, Smersh (military counter-intelligence;

literally, death to spies), headed by General V. S. Abakumov, began to collect compromising material (*kompromat*) on the marshal and his commanders.

Smersh attacked on three fronts: collect *kompromat* on Zhukov; unmask 'wreckers' in the air force and military industries; uncover links between politicians and the military. The first blow was the arrest of the commander-in-chief of the air force, Air Marshal A. A. Novikov and the commander of the Twelfth Air Army, Air Marshal S. A. Khudyakov. The latter, under torture, in February 1946, confessed that he had russified his Armenian name and had had links with British intelligence in the Caucasus. By April, he was implicating Novikov and a huge number of air marshals and politicians. Zhukov's name also came up. The Commissar of the Aviation Industry and his officials had, allegedly, supplied the air force with defective planes. On 10–11 May 1946, the military college of the USSR Supreme Court considered the evidence against those in the Aviators' Affair. Novikov and six others were sentenced to death.

Novikov confessed that Zhukov 'in a crafty and guarded form . . . tries to belittle the leading role in the war of the supreme commander in chief [Stalin], while he is not embarrassed to overemphasise his own role as army commander in the war, and he even declares that the key plans for military operations were drafted by him'. Novikov informed Zhukov that Malenkov had known all about the allegedly defective aircraft but had said nothing in Stalin's presence. Zhukov was arrogant and overbearing. He was also too greedy. Most Soviet commanders

16.1 Comrade Minister, Some Friends would Like to have a Word with You
Source: Keremput, Zagreb, 1951.

contented themselves with a wagon full of booty from Germany but Zhukov had brought back a whole train full to Moscow. Every Soviet official helped himself. A former Soviet ambassador in East Berlin and Bonn informed me that he had a splendid collection of old masters. He particularly enjoyed the Impressionists. Zhukov had overstepped the norm. On 3 June 1946, Zhukov was dismissed as commander-in-chief of land forces, head of the Soviet military mission in Germany and as USSR deputy Minister of Defence. He was made commander of the Odesa military district. Other leading military figures fell victim to Stalin's suspiciousness. Marshal Grigory Kulik and General V. N. Gordon were executed.

At a political meeting workers are apprised of the country's war plans. 'If war comes our citizens will carry atom bombs into the enemy's cities in suitcases and then they will . . .' A worker interrupts: 'I know we have more than enough bombs but where are the suitcases to come from?'

Sowing uncertainty among his subordinates

Stalin targeted the victorious military first as they posed the greatest threat to his dominance. Next in line were the politicians who had had a good war: Malenkov, Zhdanov, Molotov, Mikoyan and Beria. The tactic adopted by the boss was to promote, demote and move sideways so as to sow the maximum uncertainty among the elites.

Stalin repaired to the Black Sea for a rest in October 1945. It appears he had suffered a mild heart attack. He left Molotov nominally in charge. Stalin received transcripts and the most important documents every day. There was great speculation among the foreign press. Stalin's daughter wrote to him in December informing him of widespread rumours that he was seriously ill and that Molotov would take over. Immediately Molotov was severely criticised for his handling of foreign affairs. Another who found himself in the firing line was Anastas Mikoyan, the Commissar for Trade. He was held responsible for the food crisis. He, like Molotov, humbly asked for forgiveness from Stalin.

Georgy Malenkov was a first class administrator and was secretary for cadres in the CC apparatus from 1938 to 1946. He had proved himself Stalin's executioner in 1937. He had travelled around various republics and oblasts encouraging Party plenums to unmask enemies of the people. Over 150,000 were arrested, mainly communists in the economic apparatus. Many of them were shot. In Erevan, Armenia, he met Beria and they began to work together. Malenkov was also responsible for aviation during the war. Hence Stalin could implicate him in the Aviators' Affair when he judged it tactically opportune.

On 18 March 1946, the Orgburo was increased from 9 to 15 members. Three leaders acquired special status: membership of the Politburo, Orgburo and

Secretariat. They were Stalin, Zhdanov and Malenkov. The struggle for supremacy between Zhdanov and Malenkov got under way. The winner would succeed Stalin.

Lavrenty Beria was the most brilliant administrator around. He was elected to the Politburo on 18 March 1946 and assumed responsibility for the police and security police and Ministry of State Control. Stalin set up a commission to probe into the mistakes committed by Sergei Kruglov when Minister of Internal Affairs. The main target, however, was not Kruglov but Beria. Stalin liked to attack leaders indirectly.

Hence, by the summer of 1946 Stalin had undermined the position of his closest aides. In doing so, he deployed formidable political skill. Clearly the old man was still in overall control. The next leader of the elite to fall foul of him was Andrei Zhdanov. He was Party leader in Leningrad but Stalin brought him to Moscow in December 1945 to take overall charge of ideology. In early 1946, Zhdanov replaced Malenkov as head of the Party apparatus. Joint Party–state resolutions were signed by Stalin and Zhdanov. He was clearly Stalin's deputy.

Many soldiers had joined the Party during the war and had little grasp of ideology. Zhdanov's first task was to ensure they were given a grounding in the fundamentals of the faith at their place of work. A new propaganda weekly, *Kultura i Zhizn*, was established to help with this formidable task. A new Central Committee Higher Party School was set up to train future cadres. Stalin perceived that the Soviet intelligentsia had to be transformed into an instrument to fight the Cold War. The attack on the cultural elites, the *Zhdanovshchina* (literally the Zhdanov times), raged from the summer of 1946 to Zhdanov's death in August 1948. It should really have been called the *Stalinshchina*, as Zhdanov was merely articulating Stalin's policies. It began in August 1946 with attacks on two Leningrad journals, *Zvezda* and *Leningrad*. Then Zhdanov laid into two famous literary figures, the humorist, Mikhail Zoshchenko, and the poet, Anna Akhmatova. The humorist was a 'vulgar and minor petty bourgeois' and the poet a 'concoction of nun and harlot . . . a mad gentlewoman dashing back and forth between her boudoir and her chapel'.

Deteriorating relations with the West was a major factor in the cultural assault. G. E. Aleksandrov, a protégé of Zhdanov, published an acclaimed book on *The History of West European Philosophy*. It even won a Stalin Prize. Then Stalin changed his mind. A conference was organised, in January 1947, to tear the book to shreds. President Truman, in March 1947, called on Congress to aid Greece and Turkey in their struggle to resist totalitarian oppression. Stalin now ordered a second conference to chew and spit out Aleksandrov's book. It met for 10 days in June and over 50 speakers vied with one another in attacking the book for underestimating Russian influence on western philosophy. The proceedings were published in a new journal *Voprosy Istorii*. Zhdanov had managed to avoid chairing the first conference but Stalin obliged him to chair the second. Zhdanov

had to attack Aleksandrov and he was removed from the agitation and propaganda department. He was replaced by the up and coming Mikhail Suslov,
recently appointed a CC secretary. The latter was to prove a Stalin favourite and
Roy Medvedev thinks that Stalin had him in mind as his successor. This underlines
the importance of ideology in Stalin's world view.

After culture and philosophy came science. Two scientists had apparently
come up with a miraculous cure for cancer. They had submitted their manuscript
for publication in an American journal. In June 1947, they were arraigned before
a court of honour – a tsarist body for naming and shaming officials and officers
who had transgressed – and 800 spectators. Publishing abroad was described as
an 'anti-patriotic and anti-state act'. The object of the exercise was prophylactic:
scare scientists away from contact with foreigners. It was all very embarrassing for
Zhdanov as he had helped the scientists in their research.

Banning genetics

*Stalin dies and his guardian angel asks him where he would like to go: heaven
or hell. 'May I have an inspection tour in order to decide?' 'Of course.' The
angel takes him to heaven. Some are singing psalms; other are playing the
harp; others praying; and others whispering to one another. 'Let's see what
the other place is like.' In hell, there is wine, women and song. Everyone is
singing and dancing and having a whale of a time. 'Oh, I choose hell', says
Stalin. When he arrives the devil arrests him and drags him off to the torture
chamber. 'But, but everyone was having such a wonderful time in hell . . .'
'Oh', says the devil, 'that was only propaganda.'*

Modern genetics stems from Gregor Mendel (1822–84) who first postulated the
laws of heredity in 1866. His findings remained unknown to the wider scientific
community until 1900. Charles Darwin carried on his work. Until Mendel the
leading thinker was Jean Baptiste Lamarck (1744–1829). He pioneered the concept of the inheritance of acquired characteristics. Marx was a Lamarckian and so
was Stalin. A battle royal raged between Lamarckians and Mendelians in Soviet
biology. The leader of the former school was Trofim Lysenko and the leading
Mendelian was Nikolai Vavilov (1887–1943). The latter had been framed and
died in prison in Saratov in 1942. Lysenko called his discipline agrobiology and
Vavilov and his followers used the western term genetics.

Stalin had appointed Yury Zhdanov, Andrei's son, as head of the science
department of the CC apparatus in December 1947. He was a chemist by training
but had a great interest in the biological aspects of the discipline. His father
had counselled him against accepting as he was aware that ideology was akin to
quicksand in which many had perished. Yury was inclined to follow Mendel.

He delivered a lecture, on 10 April 1948, in which he argued that the academic debate was not between Soviet and bourgeois camps, as Lysenko claimed, but between various schools of Soviet biology. He chided Lysenko for claiming he was the main disciple of Ivan Michurin, the leading Russian Lamarckian. Lysenko immediately wrote to Stalin and complained about the lecture. The boss seized on a purely scientific argument and turned it into a political football. Stalin forced Andrei Zhdanov to draft a CC resolution condemning his own son.

A conference was held at the Timiryazev Agricultural Academy with Lysenko as the main speaker in August 1948. The boss had edited Lysenko's speech. Genetics was dismissed as a bourgeois, foreign pseudoscience and agrobiology, with Lysenko as tsar, proclaimed socialist and Soviet. Genetics was only rehabilitated in 1966. Lysenko was a charlatan but a skilled political infighter. Unfortunately for Soviet science and agriculture he caused enormous damage.

I was told at the Timiryazev Academy in 1969 that a professor of genetics had continued to train some able students in genetics in secret. He was willing to risk his life for his discipline. On visits to various plant and animal breeding institutes throughout the Soviet Union in the 1970s, I always asked about genetics. Some directors informed me that their institute had ignored the ban and had continued unofficially with genetic research. On one occasion a scientist asked: 'What is genetics?' Afterwards the director confided to me that he was the institute's Party secretary. The institute always chose the most stupid scientist as Party secretary! As a postgraduate student at the Timiryazev Academy I repeatedly asked to meet Lysenko, who lived nearby. I always received the same answer: 'Comrade Lysenko is ill and cannot receive visitors'. I wanted to shake the hand of one of the great conmen of Soviet science.

The Leningrad Affair

Stalin could not cope with his previous workload and delegated the economy to the USSR Council of Ministers. However, all key economic decisions were to be made by him. To ensure this, he created a strict hierarchy of decision making. The first to fall foul of him was Nikolai Voznesensky, chair of Gosplan from 1939 and deputy Soviet Prime Minister from 1946. A member of the Politburo, he was the leading economist in the country and had a doctorate in economics. He ran the economy and Malenkov ran the Party apparatus.

It all started with a wholesale fair in Leningrad in January 1949. The decision to hold it had been taken by the RSFSR government and the Leningrad Party. Stalin was merely informed of its progress. The boss hit the roof. Voznesensky then confessed that P. S. Popkov, the Leningrad Party leader, in 1948, had proposed that he, Voznesensky, act as Leningrad's patron. This was even worse. Voznesensky was charged with losing secret Gosplan documents and not carrying out Stalin's instructions on the economy. The RSFSR Prime Minister and the Leningrad Party and soviet leaders were accused of belonging to an anti-Party group. Beria played an important role in making the case. In March 1949, Voznesensky was dismissed as chair of Gosplan, from the Politburo and as deputy chair of the Soviet government. Voznesensky's brother, RSFSR Minister of Education, and his sister, wives and relations were also arrested. Nikolai Voznesensky and Aleksei Kuznetsov, a CC secretary but from Leningrad, were shot. These are the only two top officials executed during the post-war Stalin period. The comrades who benefited most were Malenkov and Beria. Zhdanov had died in August 1948 and could no longer protect the second capital.

Stalin and decision making

The first meeting of the Politburo after the war took place in December 1945. There were several meetings in 1945 but only two more before the death of Stalin: one in 1947 and one in 1949. The three most important policy areas after the war were foreign affairs, security and cadres. A group of six began as a foreign affairs committee but gradually embraced the whole gamut of domestic policy. Then Voznesensky was added in October 1946. Lazar Kaganovich and Nikolai Bulganin joined later. Sometimes members were selected before they became members of the Politburo. Stalin could hire and fire at will. Bulganin once remarked that one was never sure after a meeting with Stalin if one was going to return home or be sent to prison. Decisions of the ruling group became resolutions of the Politburo.

In 1944 Svetlana, Stalin's daughter, married Grigory Morozov, her first husband. Stalin did not think he was good enough for her so she moved out of the Kremlin. It had been his custom to dine with her every evening. He now repaired to his dacha at Kuntsevo, just outside Moscow. He was a lonely man and summoned the ruling circle to dine with him. Stalin usually tried to get them drunk so that they would let slip indiscretions. He would oblige them to dance Russian and Georgian folk dances. This was a bit awkward as there were no women present – apart from the maids. Then they whiled the rest of the night away watching western films. The boss particularly liked cowboy films and would comment as the translation was shouted out to him. Presumably he always played the sheriff with Trotsky as number one baddy! He would then have the pleasure of shooting him every night.

In contrast, the USSR Council of Ministers conducted business according to formal rules. There were committees embracing the various policy areas and they reported to the government. The top government ministers were also members of Stalin's ruling circle. The workload of leading officials was staggering. In June 1947, Stalin introduced a law on state secrets but left it to the government to decide what a state secret was. Inevitably, also, everything was made a secret. This immensely complicated administration and management. A government document in April 1947 commented that even young cadres were suffering from serious problems of the heart and nervous system. This had led to a rapid decline in their efficiency. Dizzy spells became almost normal among senior officials. Part of the problem was that Stalin was a night owl and wont to phone officials in the middle of the night.

Monitoring his team

Aleksei Kosygin (1904–80) was a rising star in the late 1940s. He had proved his ability during the wartime evacuation of enterprises to the east and the provisioning of besieged Leningrad. At a Politburo meeting, Stalin confided to him that he kept a dossier on the families of Molotov, Mikoyan, Kaganovich and others. All they spent on themselves, their guards and servants was listed. 'It's simply revolting', declared Stalin. (This was pure hypocrisy. Stalin had rows of dachas in the south and ordered any food or wine he wished.) The master asked Kosygin to make a list of all the privileges enjoyed by Politburo members. This made Aleksei very unpopular with his colleagues. Kosygin picked up the fact that one of the accusations against Nikolai Voznesensky was that he had had firearms in his apartment. Kosygin and his son-in-law immediately searched their dwellings and threw all weapons into a lake. They also searched for listening devices and found them. Every morning Kosygin left for work he reminded his wife what she was to do if he did not return.

The gulag becomes a liability

Stalin regarded the use of gulag labour as rational. In 1952, the Ministry of Internal Affairs (MVD), formerly the NKVD, invested 12 billion rubles (9 per cent of Gross Domestic Product) in the forced labour economy. However, output was only 2.3 per cent of the country's gross production. Nevertheless, it played a key role in certain sectors. It was the leading producer of cobalt and pewter and mined one-third of the nickel. It also mined uranium. Despite this, the MVD was always short of money. This meant that prisoners (zeks) could not be properly fed. This led to higher death rates, sometimes due to exposure to radioactivity (Lewin 2005).

Theft, embezzlement and false reporting were rife. Inmates were abused and killed. The MVD was insouciant as there was always a fresh flow of new inmates. The zeks flooded the Party and the central administrations, especially the Ministry of Justice, with complaints. Even Kruglov, Minister of Internal Affairs, admitted that the cost of a zek was greater than the value of his output. One report by a zek which the Central Committee obtained revealed that the camp administration did not pay the slightest attention to raising productivity. Zek labour was wasted on a monumental scale.

Another factor which exacerbated the crisis was that the zeks were changing. After the war, experienced military officers found themselves in the camps. They dealt very quickly with informers and linked up with criminals to challenge management. There was also a shortage of guards and this made insubordination more effective. Many now refused to work: a million days were lost in 1951 alone. It appears no one dared tell Stalin that his cherished gulag system was in a catastrophic state.

Refashioning the Party

The government administration had managed the state during the war. Politburo members had assumed responsibility for key sectors as members of the State Committee on Defence. They functioned within government structures. The Party was relegated to a cosmetic role. After the war, the huge task of reassembling the Party apparatus had to be undertaken. Then there were the liberated regions and the newly acquired territories. In Lithuania and west Ukraine there were nationalist groups which engaged in guerrilla warfare. I travelled from Moscow to Kyiv in 1957 and all tunnels and bridges were still being guarded by armed soldiers.

FIGURE 16.1 Party membership, 1942–53

Source: Based on data in Richard Overy, *The Dictators: Hitler's Germany and Stalin's Russia* (2004).

All train windows had grilles which made it impossible to leave the train unless authorised.

In 1946, Stalin chose Aleksei Kuznetsov (1905–50) as the comrade to remodel the Party apparatus. He had been an efficient second in command to Zhdanov during the siege of Leningrad and then Party boss of Leningrad and Leningrad oblast. Kuznetsov's brief did not extend to ideology. He was to produce cadres who were technically proficient and loyal to Stalin's line. He became head of the cadres directorate of the Central Committee (Lewin 2005).

Courts of honour, as explained by Kuznetsov in a speech to the whole Party apparatus in September 1947, were to be convened in the CC apparatus and all other Party and state bodies. The object of the mock trials, which could hand down punishments but not the death sentence, was to instil in officials patriotism and a love of their socialist (Stalinist) fatherland. These courts were needed because many officials engaged in anti-patriotic, anti-social and anti-state activities. Drunkenness, debauchery (too much sex) and careless handling of confidential documents by leading officials were highlighted. Such behaviour put the state at risk as the central Party apparatus – it was called the holy of holies in Kuznetsov's report – dealt with very sensitive information. Reference was made to the experience of the great purges: for example, Stalin's speech on vigilance. The intelligentsia had been warned. 'You tell your wife something; she tells a neighbour – and everyone learns state secrets', Kuznetsov said.

Just how difficult it was to keep state secrets was illustrated by the 1948 decision by the government, in the utmost secrecy, to raise prices. The news got out and there was a wild rush to buy up everything in the shops.

The courts of honour marked a surge of Russian nationalism which Stalin promoted. He amended the words of the Soviet national anthem and turned it into a glorification of Great Russia. Jews were a special target; they were denigrated as rootless cosmopolitans. The Jewish Anti-Fascist Committee (AFC) was accused of collaborating with the Americans. The great actor, Solomon Mikhoels (1890–1948), chair of the AFC, was deliberately run over by a lorry in Minsk. His death was put down to a traffic accident. Ironically one of the victims was Kuznetsov himself. He was enveloped in the Leningrad Affair and, together with Nikolai Voznesensky, was shot in 1950. The courts of honour were abandoned under Khrushchev.

During the 1930s and the war, government agencies, ministries and enterprises had been extending favours to top Party functionaries. The low living standards of the time had made such perks irresistible. These ranged from scarce consumer goods to the construction of dachas and holidays in sanatoria for the Party boss and his family. Party bosses were known to demand scarce consumer goods and other desirable products. Needless to say, the state agencies had expected favours in return. According to one report, the cosseting of the Party elite had reached 'astronomical proportions'. The risk existed that the Party elite would be swallowed up by their benefactors. The solution, adopted in 1946, was to remove the central apparatus from involvement in the economy. However, local Party bodies (all those below the Central Committee) were to continue supervising the activities of enterprises and economic agencies. The central Party apparatus was to concentrate on providing policy guidance to the government and ensuring the development of a Marxist-Leninist consciousness among the population.

There was corruption on a massive scale. Party officials were supposed to defend the public interest but, in reality, were pursuing their own private interests. Stalin was informed that many local Party bosses spent most of their time acquiring scarce goods and organising events at which huge quantities of alcohol were consumed. Naturally state agencies paid for the booze and the girls. Girls came in various guises. Lower level apparatchiks had to make do with ordinary girls; middle level comrades had more attractive girls; the bosses had sensational girls.

Kuznetsov's conclusion was that if this state of affairs persisted, it would 'mean the end of the Party'. It was imperative that Party organisations recovered their independence. But how was this to be achieved in a scarcity economy? It transpired that CC department heads formed cliques and were inaccessible to lower level officials. There was a strict hierarchy with no fraternising with those below or above. Important ministers were like feudal lords who simply ignored the Central Committee and its nomenklatura. They went directly to the Council of Ministers. The secrecy was stifling (Lewin 2005).

How was the Party apparatus to be saved? The Council of Ministers was to run the economy. The Central Committee would, among other things, help choose all top state officials and monitor the cadres department in every institution. Party apparatchiks were deeply unhappy with this reform. There was no money in ideological work. Less than two years later, Party bosses were again closely embroiled in the running of the economy.

The Party nomenklatura

The CC nomenklatura had to be reconstructed in 1946. It contained all the top state and Party positions. Listed were 42,000 key positions and incumbents. Of these, about one in four was a Party or Komsomol post and one in five an industrial position. Non-Party members occupied 1,400 of the nomenklatura positions. Two-thirds of office holders were Russians, 11 per cent were Ukrainian and 5 per cent Jewish. A major complaint was that over half of the promotions and dismissals from ministerial positions on the list were decided without consultation with the Central Committee. The relevant ministries were obliged to accept the primacy of the nomenklatura list. The directorate was also putting together another important list: reserve cadres for all leading positions.

Did the Central Committee control appointments through the nomenklatura system? Only to a certain extent. Ministers were wont to dismiss, transfer and promote officials without consulting the Central Committee. If a position became vacant, the apparatus would ask if the relevant institution had a candidate in mind. Normally the candidate was confirmed in office. The apparatus was only really needed if there was no suitable candidate available. It is worth noting that the Politburo had its own nomenklatura list. For instance, ambassadors to capitalist countries were on its list. Hence it is debatable whether the central Party apparatus actually controlled top appointments. Normally the government administration got its way. This was especially so in the defence sector.

Chaim Goldberg becomes a member of the nomenklatura. He hears that other members visit the opera. So he sends his wife, Esther, to the Bolshoi. 'Two tickets for the opera, please.' 'For Madame Butterfly?' 'No, for Mr and Mrs Goldberg.'

The economy

A woman is having a bath in a communal apartment. She sees a man peering through the window. 'What do you want? Have you never seen a naked woman before?' 'I'm not looking at you, I just want to see whose soap you are using.'

The pre-war mobilisation system which had proved so successful was restored. The armed forces were reduced from 11 million to 2.7 million in 1947 while much of military industry was switched to civilian production. Capital investment in the military economy in 1946–50 was half that of the 1938–41 period. The share of military output was 3.3 per cent in 1947 compared to 6.9 per cent in 1940. Investment in raw materials, the machine-building industries, fuel, etc. were given priority.

Soviet gross national product (GNP) grew annually by 8.9 per cent between 1946 and 1950. This was a formidable achievement given the depredations of the war and the utter chaos in many areas afterwards. Over 25 million had lost their homes; retail outlets were down by 40 per cent; a third of the capital stock had been destroyed. American Lend-Lease amounted to $9.5 billion, of which $5 billion was non-military (food, etc.). Much of the machinery provided was new technology and helped to raise labour productivity. The Russians copied it and incorporated it into their economy.

The Soviet economy was about a quarter of the American. The American atomic monopoly was countered by the build-up of conventional (non-nuclear) forces after 1947. A new biological weapons facility was built near Ekaterinburg based on designs taken from a Japanese programme (Hanson 2003). By 1950, the Soviets had 281 Tu-4s; exact copies of the American B-29 Superfortresses. This terrified the Pentagon as, with American markings, the Tu-4s could reach any target in the United States, on a one-way mission. Most remarkable and worrying for Washington was the ability of the Soviets to catch up and surpass the US in nuclear and other weaponry. For instance, the MIG-19, the first Soviet supersonic fighter, launched in 1953, was superior to its US counterpart, the F-100. This was primarily due to their pool of brilliant mathematicians, physicists and engineers. Espionage also helped greatly.

Two brilliant American engineers, Joel Barr and Alfred Sarant, dedicated communists, part of the Julius and Ethel Rosenberg atomic spy ring (the Rosenbergs were executed), moved to Prague in 1950 to avoid possible arrest and conviction in the US. They had stolen information from their American employers during the Second World War which proved crucial to building the first advanced weapons systems in the Soviet Union. They convinced Nikita Khrushchev, in 1962, to found the Soviet microelectronics industry, at Zelenograd, outside Moscow. Without them, the Soviet defence industry would not have developed so quickly (Usdin 2005).

Agriculture did not fare as well as the industrial sector. Famine in 1947 claimed many victims and was kept secret. A Ukrainian told me that his family survived on black beans which the family had been able to secret away. Millions fled the countryside and this led to the labour force in the non-kolkhoz sector exceeding the plan by almost 6 million. Living standards were still very low. It was only in 1953 that the 1940 level was achieved. Hence the last years of Stalin were hard and hungry.

The kolkhoz labour force dropped from 18.2 million in 1940 to 11.5 million in 1945. During the harvest of 1946, millions of hectares were affected by drought and another 2 million hectares of grain were not harvested. A soviet deputy in Kirov oblast reported returning from the army and finding that local kolkhozniks were eating clover and grass because there was no grain. They were obliged to leave the kolkhoz and find lumbering work for half the year in order to feed themselves and their families. The land was exhausted, it had not been manured and there were shrubs and trees growing everywhere. In the absence of horses and oxen, humans had to pull ploughs. Kolkhozniks were much worse off than workers. The latter received ration cards which guaranteed them 700 grams of bread and invalids also got rations. Those down on the farm often received next to nothing for their labour and there was no minimum wage. Widespread theft of grain was common. In 1945, over 5,700 kolkhoz chairs were sentenced and over 9,500 in 1946. In some raions, up to a half of chairs were found guilty.

Desperate times give rise to desperate measures. Nikita Khrushchev, then Party boss in Ukraine, promoted a decree, in June 1948, which permitted the exiling of those who were judged to be work-shy. It was then expanded to cover the whole country. This legislation was not to be published, ordered Stalin. Over the period 1948–53, 33,000 kolkhozniks and 13,600 members of their families were exiled to Siberia.

In December 1947, the government implemented a currency reform and abolished ration cards for food and consumer goods. The goal of the currency reform was to wipe out the profits made on the black market and control the money supply. The usual rate of exchange was 10:1. However, those with savings accounts could exchange 3,000 roubles at 1:1. Foreign citizens could exchange money at a rate of 3:1. The reforms were trumpeted as evidence of the recovery of the economy after the war. However, in reality, the government was no longer obliged to provide the urban population with a minimum level of sustenance. Workers and employees would now have to go to commercial shops and markets. State prices, expressed in the new currency, turned out to be higher.

The private plots of kolkhozniks and workers were taxed. There were two types: in money and in kind. After the war, the average plot had to deliver annually 40 kg of meat, up to 100 eggs and 320 litres of milk. The average money tax rose from 112 rubles in 1940 to 431 in 1950 and 528 rubles in 1952. There was no way a kolkhoznik could pay this tax from his wages. The only way to scrape together this sum was to take everything he grew on his private plot to the kolkhoz market. This was deliberate state policy to force food prices down. The result was that villages were reduced to penury.

The average income of a kolkhoznik, in 1950, was 1,133 rubles. Only 221 rubles, or less than a fifth, was earned from working on the kolkhoz. This reveals that it was senseless to work on the kolkhoz. Despite this, one could be exiled for not working on the kolkhoz. One earned from 211 days' work on the kolkhoz less than half of what one obtained from working the 0.25 ha of one's private plot (Pikhoya 1998).

In 1950, kolkhozes were consolidated and their number declined from 252,000 to 94,000 in 1952. The private plots of the kolkhozniks were reduced as part of this reform. Khrushchev's thinking became clear in March 1951 when a grandiose scheme to create agricultural towns (*agrogoroda*) was published in *Pravda*. The peasants were to live in multi-storeyed blocks and be provided with the accoutrements of urban life. Naturally they were to give up their private plots.

This reform appeared to have been conceived under the influence of alcohol. The reality was that, in 1950, private plots of peasants accounted for 38 per cent (and workers 13 per cent) of the global agricultural production of the country. They also contributed 46 per cent of animal products. The goal was to abolish the private sector and oblige peasants to work full time on kolkhozes. There was a minor problem. The *agrogoroda* did not exist and would therefore require substantial investment.

Fortunately, Khrushchev's grandiose plan never got beyond the pages of *Pravda*. The next day, the Party newspaper informed readers that the scheme had only been published for discussion. Malenkov had taken it to Stalin and convinced him that Khrushchev was peddling dangerous ideas. Malenkov had another go at it during the 19th Party Congress, in October 1952. At the same congress, he assured his audience that the grain problem in the Soviet Union had been finally solved. This time it was Malenkov who was living in cloud cuckoo land. Khrushchev exacted revenge after the death of Stalin when he rubbed Malenkov's nose in the dirt for making such a preposterous claim.

The doctors' plot

A surgeon sees his patient the day after his operation.
'Comrade, I have bad news and very bad news for you.'
'Well, what is the bad news?'
'You only have 24 hours to live.'
'What then is the very bad news?'
'I should have told you yesterday.'

Surveillance had revealed that some Kremlin doctors led a wild sex life, held anti-Soviet views or sympathised with landowners. It was also claimed that they had misdiagnosed the heart ailments of Politburo members Andrei Zhdanov and Aleksandr Shcherbakov (1901–45), Zhdanov's brother-in-law. The damaging evidence came from Lydia Timashuk who claimed that she had been forced to change her interpretation of Zhdanov's cardiogram. (Recent evidence appears to corroborate her initial interpretation.) Over 25 Russian and Jewish Kremlin specialists were arrested. Stalin concentrated on the Jewish connection. He informed the Presidium (formerly Politburo) on 1 December 1952 that Jewish nationalists 'believe that their nation was saved by the United States (there they can become rich, bourgeois and so on). They believe they owe a debt of gratitude to the Americans. Among the doctors there are many Jewish nationalists' (Gorlizki and Khlevniuk 2004). He claimed that Zhdanov had not died but had been murdered by the MGB chief, Abakumov. Hence Jews and the MGB were now in the firing line. On 9 January 1953, Stalin sent his inner group a bulletin stating that there was a group of terrorist doctors at work. Their aim was to shorten the lives of Soviet leaders. The 'doctors-murderers' had links to the international Jewish organisation Joint, and others to the British security service. *Pravda* published the allegations on 13 January.

Some observers think Stalin was preparing a show trial of the Jewish doctors; others see a plan to deport all Jews from the western regions to the east. It was an ugly time for Jews. They were insulted in the street and many lost their jobs.

Was Stalin murdered?

The ailing Stalin could not deliver the keynote speech at the 19th Party Congress in October 1952. He was absent for much of the time. He appeared on the last day and, with considerable difficulty, read out a seven minute address. He ensured that he was the centre of attention by advancing a new textbook on economics. It was called the *Economic Problems of Socialism* and was to pave the way to the higher stage of communism or full communism. Debate had begun among economists in 1948 and culminated at a Central Committee conference in November–December 1951. This was the sixth draft, Stalin having rejected the previous five.

Stalin then instructed his colleagues to convene a Party Congress, the first since 1939, on 28 February 1952. He was going to give an opening address. He then changed his mind. The Congress was to meet in October 1952 and he was going to content himself with a written report. Malenkov was to give the political report and Khrushchev was to perorate on Party rules. Meanwhile Stalin forwarded his notes on political economy to economists and political leaders. He declined to have them published. He wanted comments but, of course, everyone merely asked for clarification from Stalin. One daring soul, the economist Leonid Yaroshenko, actually claimed authorship of one of Stalin's ideas. He was arrested. Stalin's notes and other materials were published on the eve of the Congress to maximise their effect. The boss's economic vision of the future took centre stage at the Congress (Gorlizki and Khlevniuk 2004).

A major issue was the debate about commodity circulation and product exchange. As long as there is commodity circulation there will be money. Product exchange (industry exchanges goods for agricultural produce, for example) does not involve money. This is the moneyless economy envisioned by Marx. When product exchange takes over, the law of value is replaced by consumer demand. The latter would, according to one estimate, begin in 1970. In the last Stalin years there were several price reductions of essential goods. Eventually essentials would cost nothing. A new textbook laying out this vision was to be penned in 1953 and run to 500 pages. It was then to become the bible for all socialist countries. *The Economic Problems* was an extraordinary document. It was an example of utopian economics. For example, one cannot just abolish the law of value. Also the hope that full communism – everyone's needs are met – would be attained in 1970 was wholly unrealistic.

One of the central themes at the Congress was vigilance. There were attacks on 'enemies of the Soviet state' which presaged a purge after the Congress. Two days after the Congress, Stalin addressed the Central Committee, without notes, for an hour and a half. He centred his comments on Lenin, who was fearless when confronted with danger. The membership of the Central Committee was expanded by two-thirds and the same happened to the Politburo. It was merged with the

Orgburo and renamed the Presidium. The latter was to have 25 full and 11 candidate members. Previously it had nine full and two candidate members. The new arrivals were younger and relatively unknown. Stalin appeared to be preparing for a purge of the old leadership.

There was also an inner group, the Presidium bureau, consisting of nine comrades. Stalin then engaged in a conversation with himself about who would succeed him. It was modelled on Lenin's testament of 1922. Only Bulganin came out of the musings in a positive light. Molotov and Mikoyan were omitted from the bureau. Stalin now poured venom on them. Particular ire was directed at Molotov whom he accused of cowardice and personal betrayal. This astonished the Central Committee who had always regarded 'iron arse' as Stalin's most faithful servant. Stalin had worked himself up into an almost uncontrollable rage. Then he turned on Mikoyan using the language of the 1930s. Molotov and Mikoyan were out of Stalin's team and feared for their lives.

On 28 February, Stalin watched a film until late in the Kremlin and then invited four members of his inner team to his dacha. They left about 4 a.m. The following day, 1 March, the *vozhd* did not leave his room and made no requests. At 10.30 p.m., an aide decided to enter Stalin's room and found him lying on the floor in his own urine. Malenkov and Beria arrived about 3 a.m. on 2 March. Khrushchev got there at 7.30 a.m. A group of doctors came about an hour later and diagnosed a brain haemorrhage. The Presidium Bureau convened at noon that day. On 3 March, the doctors predicted imminent death. A radio broadcast informed the population that Stalin was ill on the morning of 4 March. He expired at 9.50 p.m. the following day.

'The mice have buried the cat', was Khrushchev's comment on the death of Stalin.

The death of Stalin could have come out of a thriller. He had dismissed Vlasik, his long term head of security at the dacha a short time previously. The guard in charge on the night of his attack, Khrustalev, was given the evening off. Why was Stalin left a whole day before someone entered his room? Why did Malenkov and Beria not immediately summon medical aid when they were told of Stalin's condition? Why did the doctors arrive almost six hours after Malenkov and Beria had seen the state Stalin was in?

The Russian historian Nikolai Dobryukha, argues that Stalin was poisoned (*Pravda.ru*, 29 December 2005). Documents relating to his health during the last 30 years of his life have come to light. They reveal that he was not afraid of doctors and had treatment for the slightest ailment. In 1947, he suffered from hypertension, chronic articular rheumatism and overfatigue. However his blood pressure – 145 over 85 – was excellent for a man of his age. Five years later, it was 140 over 80 and 70 beats of his pulse per minute. When these tests were made Stalin was suffering from influenza and fever. They are remarkably good.

Dobryukha says that Stalin was poisoned some time between the evening of Saturday 28 February and Monday 1 March 1953. The weekend was chosen because most doctors had Sundays off. The poisoner was Beria. Stalin drank some poisoned mineral water. Curiously, on 4 March newspapers controlled by him reported that Stalin had suffered a 'cerebral haemorrhage in his Moscow apartment on 2 March'. This was untrue as he had fallen ill at his dacha. Was the person who suffered the haemorrhage in Moscow a double? Was Stalin already dead at his dacha? Was his double then moved to the dacha? When the doctors examined Stalin at 7 a.m. on 2 March, at his dacha, they found him lying on his back on a sofa with his head turned to the left and eyes closed. His breathing was normal and the hyperaemia of his face was moderate. His blood pressure was 190 over 110. His right arm and leg were paralysed. The records reveal that the doctors treated Stalin for poisoning without daring to state that he had been poisoned. On 3 March, Stalin deteriorated. On the evening of 5 March the doctors had conclusive proof of poisoning. Stalin was given several doses of carbogene but his condition did not improve. Nurse Moiseeva, at 8.45 p.m., gave Stalin an injection of calcium gluconate. She then injected adrenalin. Contemporary medical opinion is that a patient in Stalin's condition should not have been given adrenalin. Was this to finish him or his double off?

Hitler stands in hell with boiling tar around his throat. Beria stands next to him but the tar only reaches up to his waist. 'Why did you get off so easily?', asks Hitler. 'I'm standing on Stalin's shoulders.'

Questions

1   Explain what is meant by the term 'High Stalinism'.

2   What structural changes occurred in the Communist Party in the period 1945–53?

3   What happened to the 'Party-state' during 'High Stalinism'? Was Stalin genuinely committed to building a Party-state after all? Answer with reference to events between 1946 and 1952.

4   How and why did Stalin consolidate his power and authority following the war?

5   Why was scientific development in the post-war period so important for the Soviet ideology of the state?

6   Why was genetics dismissed as a 'bourgeois' pseudoscience during 'High Stalinism' and how did this affect the development of Soviet science?

7   Did Stalin retain his hold over all aspects of Soviet life, both political and economic, between 1945 and 1953?

8   What became Stalin's top priority during the post-war years?

9   'Soviet political culture changed little between 1936 and 1953'. Discuss.

10   'Party corruption indicates that Stalin's hold on the Party was weakening.' Discuss.

Further reading

Yoram Gorlizki and Oleg Khlevniuk, *Cold Peace Stalin and the Soviet Ruling Circle, 1945–1953* (2004); John Keep, *Last of the Empires: A History of the Soviet Union 1945–1991* (1995).

CHAPTER 17

Bolshevik speak

'Marxism is correct because it is scientific; Soviet science is correct because it is Marxist.'

'Marxism is the religion of the [working] class, its symbol of faith.'

Stalin, 1946

One of the fascinating aspects of Stalinism was the emergence of a new language, newspeak or Bolshevik speak. It was the official language of communication adopted by the Party bureaucracy, ordinary Soviet citizens and also, later, the professional elite, including academics and scientists (scientific newspeak). It was the dominant ideological medium for public discourse from the 1930s onwards, which fused politics, science and ideology (dialectical materialism). It encapsulated modes of thought, rhetorical styles and behavioural patterns. The growing importance of the political role of language revealed a new dimension of Stalinist political culture. Initially, newspeak was an indicator of social-ideological loyalty to the regime, but gradually it developed into a political-scientific discourse underpinning the legitimacy of the regime as a modernising power during the late 1940s and early 1950s. Newspeak was a language that could not be verified or questioned; it was an indicator of accepted, undisputed and absolute truth (Marxism-Leninism). All alternative views to those stated by official state ideology were inadmissible; there were no words, concepts or linguistic categories to express counter-thoughts. Newspeak signified a complex mental transformation of ordinary citizens. The ideological streamlining of thought was justified solely on the basis of the ideological needs of the regime. Language is synonymous with identity and therefore newspeak aimed at a revolution of the mind. Its rhetorical devices in many respects built on existing ideological categories of exclusion from the 1920s.

The function of newspeak in Soviet society was multifaceted. It was not merely a 'systematisation' or 'standardisation' of daily life. Newspeak was a means of expressing loyalty to the ideology of the state as well as the social and political acceptance of the authority of the regime; it was a means of personal and professional self-identification with the regime as a whole; and it was a new ideological standard and indicator of social status and acceptability, aimed at shaping the identity and mentality of Soviet citizens. Most important, its mastery meant access to power, or at the very least the ability to survive the daily grind of the system. It was a crucial part of a new evolving social identity and social consciousness (in the form of the 'new' Soviet man and woman) that represented the utopian goals of the totalitarian regime. Newspeak reinforced the nature of the regime and its goals, which based its legitimacy on the realisation of a technocratic and, later scientific, revolution. In effect language, and the nuances of communication and expression, became central to the modernising pretensions of the Stalinist Soviet Union during the 1930s.

Newspeak reached its apogee during High Stalinism after 1945. The unprecedented cult of science and technology reflecting the potential of science to build communism (for example, the hydrogen bomb) in the late Stalinist era influenced the development of a scientific newspeak, which was a means of communication and negotiation between the scientific community and the Soviet regime. The onset of the Cold War led Stalin to draw a sharp distinction between western and Soviet science and learning. Universal science no longer existed; there was now socialist (scientific) and bourgeois science. This created problems for the Soviet scientific elite. They had the task of catching up with and surpassing bourgeois science. Were they to ignore western research and advance independently? A raft of western scientific theories had been declared un-Marxist. For example, Einstein's theory of relativity. Freud's theories on sex were also taboo. The political language of the Cold War resulted in the 'scientification' of Marxism and with it the nature of the regime itself. The new exciting discipline of cybernetics posed a potential problem for the Soviet order. Cybernetics is the 'science of systems of control and com-munication in animals and machines' (*Oxford English Dictionary*). It had taken off in the United States and was a vital component of weapons research. Grandiose claims were made about it. It could become man's best friend or even take over the world. Central to it was the computer. It applied mathematics to the analysis of human behaviour. However the Soviets found a way of turning the Cold War atmosphere to their advantage: in the mid-1950s, Soviet scientists and engineers attempted to replace the existing basis for dialogue found in scientific speak with 'cyberspeak' as a new 'mediating language' (Gerovitch 2002) between the regime and the scientific community. Cybernetics was modelled on newspeak and aimed at reforming Soviet science, both intellectually and politically through the creation of a new and more precise universal scientific language that would counter the woolly and imprecise language of Marxism-Leninism. The emerging compatibility of science and ideology during the 1940s is revealing about modes of legitimation in the Soviet regime: the application of science to politics and vice versa reinforced the legitimacy of both fields.

In the late Stalin period, Soviet intellectual life was dominated by Marxist-Leninist philosophers. They were the kings of the castle and decided which scientific theories were acceptable and which were unacceptable. They were the Party's watchdogs. Becoming a Rottweiler was the goal. Few of these sages had any scientific training. The supreme talent was manipulating the texts of Marx, Engels, Lenin and Stalin in order to win an argument. Hence a non-mathematician could outlaw a mathematical theory. Stalin saw himself as the king of the philosophers and was in many respects the main arbiter in ideological disputes about the meaning and interpretation of dialectical materialism. He was called the coryphaeus of science; a universal scientific genius. He did not automatically intervene in disputes even though scientists and philosophers appealed to him to support their point of view. He was wont to become involved in certain disciplines and not others. For example, he left his mark on biology, economics and linguistics. Indeed, in June 1950, Stalin published a lengthy article on linguistics in *Pravda* which reinstated the importance of comparative historical linguistics. Other disciplines, regarded as essential for defence, such as chemistry, physics, atomic physics and astrophysics escaped virtually unscathed.

Soviet ideological discourse was constructed to ensure that public statements could not be questioned or verified but had to be accepted as true a priori. It is very skilfully deployed in George Orwell's *1984*, which was published in 1949. He coined the expression newspeak. Winston Smith, the main protagonist, is eventually brainwashed into accepting the lies of the government. The Polish Nobel Prize-winning Czesław Miłosz published *The Captive Mind* in 1953. Both books are profoundly pessimistic and assumed that Stalinist discourse (newspeak) would dominate for the foreseeable future. Such was the impact of Bolshevik speak on the European mind in the post-war period.

Aside from providing a means of social identification with the regime and a marker of political acceptability, the fundamental reason for the emergence of newspeak was the need, by the bureaucracy, to understand intellectual debate. Since few Party ideologists had scientific training, they could not understand the arguments for and against a school of thought, say in mathematics. By creating their own language, they could manage debate. They decided what words should mean. There was never a fixed meaning for any word or term; it was always in flux. An example was dialectical materialism (diamat). There were standard definitions (ideologemes) upon which significance of words or concepts were constructed, but the meaning of the terms used in relation to ideology, for instance, realism, changed constantly. Every scientist, in order to graduate, had to pass an examination in diamat.

The Soviet Union regarded itself as the land of science but, paradoxically, under Stalin, rejected cybernetics. However, the key role in declaring it as a 'reactionary pseudoscience' was not played by scientists but by philosophers. The cultural thaw of the Khrushchev era saw it rehabilitated. In the new Party programme of 1961 it was proclaimed a 'science in the service of communism'. Cybernetics began to run out of stream in the late 1960s and by the 1990s was being blamed for holding back the development of computer technology. One reason was the obsession with the science of control. This was to be part of the scientific management of society at the beginning of the Brezhnev era. However, Brezhnev gradually realised that it could make the Party redundant. This dashed the hopes of those who wanted to apply mathematics to the management of society. Mathematical economics did surface in the chaotic Gorbachev era. Many observers find it astonishing that the Soviet Union did not grasp the great opportunities offered by science and technology to craft a modern society. The key reason may be that too many comrades were doing too well out of the existing system. The nomenklatura's prime objectives were to enrich itself and stay in power. Empowering the people put that in jeopardy.

The successes of Soviet scientists reveal that they were not brainwashed into accepting Soviet ideology. On the contrary, they very skilfully integrated the core of Marxism-Leninism, dialectical materialism, into their research during the 1950s. The various scientific schools used diamat and deployed newspeak in their internal battles and debates. A clever scientist, using newspeak, could outflank a philosopher. This was much more difficult in the humanities and social sciences. Another key to success was to enlist the support of politicians and administrators. Scientists learnt to play the political game of criticism and self-criticism. In other words, they were playing by Party rules. But these games camouflaged the fact that the conflict was, in essence, scientific and not ideological. One cannot say the discourse was ideological or scientific; according to Gerovitch (2002), it was a melange of both.

There is a parallel here between the Soviet period and early modern Christianity. Scientists had to preface every work with a biblical text and keep within the boundaries of the faith. The Pope was the final judge of whether a work was science or heresy. In the days when it was held that the sun went round the earth, it was not wise to proclaim the heliocentric view – that the earth goes round the sun. Galileo's (1564–1642) mistake was that he was overconfident that the Pope would accept his innovation. Stalin was the Pope of his day and Marxism-Leninism, the core of which was dialectical materialism, was Holy Scripture.

Box 17.1 *Definitions*

Dialectical materialism (diamat)
The science of sciences; basic principles were realism; non-reductionism; the view of the material world as an infinitely complex, interconnected and evolving whole; belief in the relative nature of human knowledge

Realism
Main goal is to reproduce accurately objective reality

Idealism
Converse of scientific; use of mathematics in research in social and life sciences

Formalism
Detached from real life

Mechanicism
Regarding human body as a self-regulating mechanism; also regarded as idealist

Metaphysical
Non-Marxist; non-materialistic

Reactionary
Non-Marxist; bourgeois

The late Soviet period divided science into Soviet and bourgeois. This had been the practice during the 1920s and 1930s but had fallen out of use during wartime collaboration. Then the concept of the unity of universal science had been adopted. When Stalin edited Lysenko's speech at the July–August 1948 session of the Lenin All-Union Academy of Agricultural Sciences, which led to the banning of genetics, he crossed out 'bourgeois' and inserted 'idealistic and reactionary'. Soviet biology became scientific biology. In other words, Lysenko's class-based analysis gave way to the concept of 'two worlds – two ideologies' in science (Gerovitch 2002). Lysenko and his followers claimed that their scientific views were Marxist and those of the geneticists were deviations from Marxism. This became the norm in the late Stalin period.

Newspeak reached its apogee during the initial phases of the Cold War. In 1946 Stalin stated that the task of Soviet scientists was to catch up with and surpass science in the world outside. Western scholarship was to be criticised and destroyed. Soviet scientific progress was measured against western science but, at the same time, western science was denigrated as a source of alien ideology. Hence there was permanent tension between the two goals of 'emulate and surpass' and 'criticise and destroy' western science. This presented thorny problems for the scientist. If he ignored advances in western science he could be accused of holding back Soviet science. Scientists got round the problem by demolishing any new western theory. They then rewrapped it under their own names and proclaimed it as yet another triumph for Soviet science. This applied also to the past. All the great scientific advances had been made by Russians.

There was another problem for scientists. The philosophers believed that western publications deliberately printed misleading scientific information. This was to send Soviet scientists off on the wrong track. It was taken for granted that valuable scientific information would not be published in the open press. This is an interesting example of mirror-imaging. Since Soviet journals did not publish the results of cutting edge research, it was assumed the same applied to the West. Soviet publications exaggerated national achievements. The same must be true of the capitalist world.

Lysenko was a skilful defender of his discipline, agrobiology, which swept genetics aside in 1948. He linked agrobiology to Marxism-Leninism and socialism and genetics to idealism and capitalism. The way to win an argument was therefore to uncover links to western theory in the work of an opponent. In newspeak discourse there were key words or categories of words, all of which indicated ideological standard and ideological legitimacy: Soviet, socialism, Bolshevism and Marxism-Leninism. These functioned as synonyms and were powerful mobilising concepts. On the other side there was idealism, reactionary, formalism, mechanicism and metaphysical (Gerovitch 2002).

In *1984*, Orwell, brilliantly illustrated newspeak in the slogans on the façade of the Ministry of Truth:

War is Peace
Freedom is Slavery
Ignorance is Strength

He is reflecting the fact that the same word has a positive and a negative connotation. A love for all nations can either be ideologically positive (internationalism) or negative (cosmopolitanism); an exclusive love for one's country can be ideologically positive (patriotism) or negative (nationalism or chauvinism). There was a Soviet slogan: we are fighting for peace. Hence war waged by a socialist state is legitimate (it defends socialism) but a war by a capitalist state is illegitimate (it defends capitalism). Those in socialist countries enjoy freedom while those in capitalist countries, who believe they live in freedom, actually live in slavery. The same concept could be translated differently. For instance, a policeman in a capitalist country was a *politseisky* whereas in a socialist state, he was a *militsioner*, a militia man. This was a variant of the good cop–bad cop routine. Cops in capitalist states were bad and those in socialist states were good.

In the early Soviet period Marxist writers contrasted Soviet internationalism with capitalist nationalism. This was to emphasise the goal of world revolution.

During the war this gave way to patriotism and afterwards the opposite of patriotism became cosmopolitanism (a euphemism for anti-Semitism). This was widely used against Jewish scientists. Ethnic Russians were patriots but Jews were cosmopolitans. There was no half-way house between these extremes: it was either one or the other. Various pairs of opposites were extensively deployed: materialism–idealism; dialectics–metaphysics; practice–formalism; objectivity–subjectivism; practicality–knowledge for its own sake. The second term labelled the target an ideological deviationist and potential enemy of Soviet society. This split the scientific community up into factions and promoted conflict. This was Stalin's objective. It permitted him to intervene and take sides whenever deemed necessary (Gerovitch 2002).

Stalin was a master of newspeak. He skilfully used the slogans of the right to defeat the left and those of the left to defeat the right. He constantly labelled his opponents deviationists from the (ever changing) Party line. He was the true Leninist, they were deviationists. The definition of a true Leninist could be manipulated by Stalin endlessly to suit his political ends. Hence the flexibility of newspeak permitted virtually any position to be ideologically undermined. If one creatively developed Marxism-Leninism one could be labelled a deviationist. If one defended the purity of the ideology one could be accused of dogmatism. Gradually newspeak spread out from the Party to embrace the whole of society.

Mathematical methods

There were rigid boundaries between scientific disciplines. This was a political device to ensure that mathematical methods were not deployed in the social and life sciences. Lysenko, for instance, refused to recognise the validity of mathematical methods in biology. His opponents had demonstrated mathematically that he was a charlatan but this availed them nothing. In the Khrushchev era cybernetics was seen by its supporters as means of introducing mathematics to the social and life sciences. Even more, it could reassemble the shattered world of science.

The goal of cybernetics was to fashion mechanisms to control the whole national economy, individual technological processes and maximise the effectiveness of government. The leading advocate of cybernetics, Admiral Aksel Berg, went off into flights of fancy. He envisaged a home computer replacing the doctor as it would tell one what to do; students would no longer need to listen to boring lectures; they would be connected to a machine and work at their own pace; those who did not believe this should commit suicide; those who opposed it would be weeded out. Berg's military background was taking over.

Cybernetics was to play an important role in establishing the material bases of communism by 1980. Optimal planning and control became goals. Cybernetic enthusiasts presumed that the inefficiency of the planned economy was due to poor data collection, information processing and control. They came up with a solution based on mathematical modelling and computer-guided decision making. They thought computers would produce a politically neutral, optimal solution. Soviet planning and management could be reformed without political upheaval. However, the sluggishness of the Soviet economy could not be solved by mathematics. It was an inherently political problem. The dream of a brave, new computerised world was bound to be shattered. There was no leading role in it for politicians. The computer would direct the country. The political class quickly realised that the way to prevent this happening was to embrace cybernetics and squeeze the life out of it. The group who could play this role would be the philosophers. The computer would have rendered philosophers redundant. Now, via newspeak, the philosopher could take over the computer and become an even more powerful philosopher. The distinctions and similarities between newspeak and cyberspeak are clearly outlined by Slava Gerovitch:

'Soviet cybernetics as a discourse modelled itself on newspeak – first as an enemy, then as a challenger, later as a substitute – and employed the same discursive techniques that made the Soviet ideological discourse flexible, adaptable and virtually universal. Like newspeak, whose dogmatic formulas allowed for a wide range of convenient interpretations, cyberspeak created room for intellectual freedom by offering a large variety of techniques of quantification, formalization, and computer modelling for any subject. Like the language of Soviet pseudo-Marxism, cyberspeak combined polysemous terminology with flexible rules of reasoning. Both newspeak and cyberspeak imposed limitations on how to speak but left much room for what could be said as long as it was said in the right way. Both Soviet political slogans and formal cybernetic models often functioned in a "poststructuralist" way: as material for play, metaphor, and ironic subversion.'

Brezhnev waffled about the scientific management of society but this concept was devoid of substance. Only the scientists wanted a mathematical model of the economy. The Party and government knew it would reveal how inefficient the economy was and how poorly managed it was. That would inevitably result in calls for reform. Then there was the problem of data collection. A central institute was to be responsible. However, local authorities fought to control data collection on their territory. That way, they could disguise what was going on and hopefully benefit from inflating the numbers they relayed to Moscow. A computer is only as good as the information which is fed into it. Computers could not save communism because the political will to reform was lacking.

The greatest achievements of Soviet science were recorded under Stalin. Many Soviet scientists were awarded Nobel prizes in physics and chemistry. The Khrushchev era is much less impressive. One is mindful of successes in space and rocket technology but the groundwork had been laid before 1953. The Brezhnev and Gorbachev periods are even less impressive. This leads to the paradoxical conclusion that scientists were most creative under the oppressive hand of Stalin. There may be a parallel with North Korea. Probably the most oppressive regime on earth had developed its own atomic bomb by the end of the twentieth century.

Document

Viktor Glushkov, a brilliant mathematician, proposed a nationwide computer network in 1964. There was no reaction from the authorities. Here he comments, in his memoirs, about the Soviet reaction to the American Arpanet (the forerunner of the Internet).

'In the late 1960s, the Central Committee and the Council of Ministers received information that Americans had designed an information network as early as 1966, that is, two years after us. Unlike us, however, they did not argue but got down to work, and in 1969 they already planned to launch the Arpanet network . . . which linked computers installed in various American cities . . . I met Andrei Kirilenko [a CC secretary] and handed him a memo that advocated a return to my original project. "Write down in detail what has to be done, and we will create a commission", he said. Then I wrote something like this: "The only thing I ask is not to create a commission. Commissions operate on the principle of subtraction of brains, not summation, and they can wreck any project". They created a commission nevertheless.'

Slava Gerovitch, *From Newspeak to Cyberspeak* (2002)

Questions

1   Define what is meant by 'newspeak' or 'Bolshevik speak'.

2   'Stalin was the first Soviet leader to acknowledge the importance of science for ideology.' Discuss.

3   'Scientific research and progress was important for Soviet leaders because science was a source of regime legitimacy.' Discuss.

4   Explore the contention that Soviet science was dominated by and subservient to the official ideology of the Soviet state between 1945 and 1953.

5 'The atmosphere of the Cold War and geopolitical status, rather than Marxist ideology, dictated the pace of Soviet scientific research.' Discuss.

6 Why do you think cybernetics was rehabilitated as an ideologically legitimate discipline under Khrushchev but was soon pushed to the sidelines?

7 'Progress in Soviet science owes more to the close empirical observation of scientific developments in the West rather than to geopolitical concerns.' Discuss.

8 How did Soviet scientists manage to work around the system and continue with their daily work? What methods did they employ to make the system work for them?

9 'Cybernetics was a language of science, whilst newspeak was a language of politics.' Discuss in relation to the emergence of the two disciplines.

10 Identify the changing nature of ideological discourse in Soviet science during the Stalin, Khrushchev and Brezhnev eras.

Further reading

Stephen Kotkin, *Magnetic Mountain: Stalinism as a Civilization* (1995); Slava Gerovitch, *From Newspeak to Cyberspeak: A History of Soviet Cybernetics* (2002); George Orwell, 'Appendix: The Principles of Newspeak', *1984* (1949).

CHAPTER 18

Stalin, Hitler and Mao

The twentieth century was shaped by three extraordinary leaders. They were convinced they were great men and inspirational leaders. They were bending history to their will. To some, they were heroes, to others villains. Were they unique? Could a clone reappear in the future? Would it be possible, like Lego™, to reassemble one again?

Background and education

Stalin	Hitler	Mao
■ Outsider; born in Georgia in humble circumstances	■ Outsider; born in Austria in humble circumstances	■ Insider; Han Chinese; born into rich, peasant family
■ Hated his father but was close to his mother	■ Hated his father but was very close to his mother	■ Fell out with his father but close to his mother
■ Good, basic education with remarkable memory	■ Good, basic education	■ Well educated including private tutors
■ Married several times, children and other liaisons	■ Slept with his girlfriend Eva Braun without having sex; fear of syphilis (almost a chapter in *Mein Kampf* devoted to it)	■ Many wives, children and liaisons
■ Sided with Bolsheviks and became a terrorist	■ In German army 1914–18 and decorated with Iron Cross	■ Little interest in peasants; cut off pigtail which was symbol of imperial Manchu dynasty
■ Sided with Lenin in 1917 and important member of his team	■ Became a terrorist in 1918; imprisoned	■ Never imprisoned for political activities
	■ Recommended political activity in Bavaria in 1925 but NSDAP (German Socialist Workers' Party) was small but was soon leader	■ 'China has to be destroyed and then rebuilt'
		■ Marxist in 1920

Pathway to power

Stalin	Hitler	Mao
▩ Began as disciple of Lenin but emerged successor after his death, displaying great psychological and tactical skill	▩ Inspirational leader and mesmeric orator whose grip on an audience had to be experienced to be believed	▩ Became the Stalin of the Communist Party of China in April 1945
▩ Came to regard himself as personification of socialist revolution	▩ Listening to the *Führer* was a quasi-orgasmic experience for some	▩ Proclaimed People's Republic of China on 1 October 1949 and became absolute ruler of 550 million Chinese; he was indispensable to the success of the revolution
▩ Poor orator; spoke Russian with Georgian accent; also spoke Armenian and Azeri	▩ Believed himself chosen by fate to lead (Freud called this the Messiah complex); natural leader	
▩ Master political infighter		▩ Poor orator; spoke in dialect and never mastered standard Mandarin; this restricted his public appearances
▩ Master of detail, especially personnel appointments	▩ Extraordinary self-confidence in public	
▩ Emerged as leader in period of instability when people desired strong leader; exceptional times produced an exceptional leader	▩ Germans were to sacrifice themselves to achieve world dominance	▩ Brilliant, ruthless political infighter
	▩ Not interested in administrative detail	▩ Chinese were to sacrifice themselves in interests of great China and world revolution
	▩ Emerged as leader in period of instability when people desired strong leader; exceptional times produced an exceptional leader	▩ Economic illiterate who demanded the impossible
		▩ Emerged as leader in period of instability when people desired strong leader; exceptional times produced an exceptional leader

Cult of the personality

Stalin	Hitler	Mao
▩ The cult began to emerge in the late 1920s because of the need for a strong leader; the internal and external threats produced a siege-like mentality in the Party	▩ He coined the expression: 'authority of the *Führer* downwards, responsibility of the *Gefolgschaft*, followers, upwards'	▩ Cult developed during Yenan terror campaign, 1942–43
		▩ Mao is 'our only wise leader'
	▩ Absolute obedience to a genius who had risen from among the people	▩ Until then no enthusiasm to study his speeches; many reluctant to chant 'Long Live Mao'
▩ Stalin emerged from this as a strong, charismatic leader; the turning point was the cult-like celebration of	▩ There was a personal bond; one thought of him as *mein Führer*, my leader	▩ Developed cult himself, especially in Party newspaper; 'Comrade Mao Zedong is the Saviour of the Chinese People', was a favourite slogan
	▩ Hitler inspired deep, even orgasmic love among many	▩ He distributed badges of his head to the elite; in 1943, portraits of Mao

Stalin	Hitler	Mao
his fiftieth birthday in December 1929	followers; there was always a love-fest when he appeared, with some swooning or collapsing	mass produced for first time and each home expected to buy one

Stalin

his fiftieth birthday in December 1929

■ Stalin was now projected as the new leader, Lenin's successor; he was the 'best pupil, heir and successor of Lenin'; however, Stalin's authority was uncertain among the rank and file Party members

■ In 1933, he boasted of the successes of the first FYP; this set off another wave of the leader cult; he was now called the inspiration behind all the successes recorded in building socialism

■ Initially the cult had been propagated by the leadership, now it was acquiring a mass base

■ Stalin became the patriarch and the hero

■ He was called the 'Lenin of today', the coryphaeus of science, indeed he was omniscient and omnipresent; he was a genius, the father of the nation

■ Stalin was the great war leader and his cult reached new heights after 1945; he became a god to many

■ Stalin's cult survived his death and the Soviet Union continued to develop

Hitler

followers; there was always a love-fest when he appeared, with some swooning or collapsing

■ Neither Stalin nor Mao attained the same level of physical devotion

■ Another talent, malevolent in the extreme, was to inspire good people to commit brutal deeds and crimes as a mark of devotion to him

■ Hitler believed leader emerged from the people because of his special gifts; considered hereditary monarchy a 'biological blunder'

■ The German philosopher Friedrich Nietzsche (1844–1900) developed the concept of the *Übermenschen*, overmen or supermen, superior leaders untrammelled by moral or societal values; this was developed into concept of prophet sent to save his nation; Max Weber (1864–1920) wrote that most desirable form of political authority emerged from 'charismatic personality'; was to act on the basis of his own will, with 'decisiveness'; this type of leader emerged in times of crises

■ Hitler's cult of personality was not grafted on to the political culture, but derived its appeal from the search for a German saviour

■ The annual Nuremberg rally, with 200,000 present in a special stadium, was the celebration of the cult

■ Hitler's cult died with him and Nazi Germany was swept away

Mao

mass produced for first time and each home expected to buy one

■ Mao's anthem 'the East is Red' became a hit; Mao Zedong Thought coined at this time; interminable Party meetings; simplistic message that mistakes were faults of others; Mao was always right; history rewritten

■ Edgar Snow's *Red Star Over China* (1937) was huge success in promoting Mao abroad; Anna Louise Strong sent on promotional tour in 1947; book *Dawn Out of China*; Mao's greatest achievement was to 'change Marxism from a European to an Asiatic form . . . in ways that neither Marx nor Lenin could have dreamt of'; all Asia will learn from China 'more than they will learn from the USSR'

■ Mao claimed that his work was influencing 'governments in parts of post-war Europe'; Stalin was not amused

■ In Moscow, in January 1950, Stalin accused Mao of being China's Tito

■ March 1958 Mao told elite: 'There has to be a personality cult . . . it is absolutely essential'

■ Hysteria broke out when he appeared in public; during great purge, 1966–67, cult reached new heights; 4.8 billion heads of Mao made; 1.2 billion portraits; Little Red Book given to everyone; Mao's works read and reread; he became the Great Helmsman; the Reddest Red Sun in our Hearts; citizens were expected every morning to put their hand on their head, then their heart and dance to show that their hearts and minds were full of boundless love for Chairman Mao

■ Mao's cult survived him and he is still revered

Authority

Stalin	Hitler	Mao
■ Expected to be removed in 1941 because of his failure to heed warnings about Germany's imminent attack	■ Undiminished by catastrophic military losses during war	■ Mao was untouchable after 1949
■ Authority grew during war as he became indispensable as leader	■ Attempt to kill Hitler in 1944 by military failed to evoke opposition to Hitler in military or society	■ His hold over the Party meant he could humiliate his closest associates
■ Even in physical decline he retained his authority; however, he always felt politically insecure	■ He felt absolutely secure as leader	■ His authority was undiminished by catastrophic economic (Great Leap Forward, launched 1958) and cultural (Cultural Revolution 1966–76) policies
■ May have been poisoned because of fear of his policies; this reveals that his authority was not absolute	■ Spell-binding authority could only be broken by his death	■ He physically withdrew to palaces in order to prevent any attempt on his life
	■ He was his own executioner	■ Despite his great authority he felt insecure
		■ His authority declined as his health deteriorated but he struck a deal with his associates that he would die as leader

The art of leadership

Stalin	Hitler	Mao
■ The ability to inspire men and women to follow; this involves articulating a desired goal which is attractive to a wide constituency; then propose a solution	■ Believed that providence had destined him to save German nation	■ Brilliant tactician in intra-Party and intra-military conflicts
■ Presented himself as the personification and implementer of the revolution; all others would derail the revolution	■ This was Hitler's central, 'pathological' characteristic; the fate of the German people was in his hands; saw himself as above law	■ Skilled at putting labels on opponents, and sidelining them
		■ Trotskyite was a potent, negative label
■ A leader needs to build up a devoted following, consisting of various circles: a small circle of close advisers; a wider group of implementers of policy; and rank and file supporters	■ Göring stated: 'Führer when you think, Germany thinks'	■ Falsely claimed vast majority of communist organisations in nationalist areas spy rings; this permitted him to purge them
■ Charisma is important as the leader will call for followers to sacrifice themselves in pursuit of a common goal	■ Retained institutions of Weimar Germany; never fashioned a new constitution	■ In Yenan province attracted many young volunteers from other regions; brainwashed to make them obedient
■ His first big idea was socialism in one country; it inspired Party members	■ Reichstag (parliament) remained responsible for passing laws but could not initiate legislation	■ Skilled at choosing subordinates who could be blackmailed because of their past
■ He defined the ideal Party member as a 'son of the working class, a son of want and struggle, the son of extreme privation'; the males loved it; they were to be 'special people'	■ On death of President Hindenburg, on 2 August	■ Created tension in Party by inventing accusation that there was a vast pro-Chiang Kai-shek (nationalist leader) spy ring in Party; scapegoats always found

Stalin	Hitler	Mao
■ Stalin was a poor speaker so he eschewed mass rallies and public speeches ■ Stalin skilled at playing one member of his team off against another; has to avoid coalitions forming against him; needs psychological insight into what motivates others; he needs tactical (short term) and strategic (long term) vision ■ His power was informal and untrammelled by law or the constitution; this reveals his great leadership skills ■ He was able to concentrate power (the right to take decisions and have them implemented) in his hands	1934, Hitler became President without an election; then the posts of President and *Reichskanzler* (Chancellor) were merged into the single office of the leader ■ *Der Führer* stopped describing himself as a dictator in the 1920s ■ *Führer* implied untrammelled power (the Messiah complex) ■ Exercised power more formally than Stalin	■ Mao never wrong ■ Great fear of Mao ■ Liked to isolate himself in his villas because of fear of assassination ■ Normal to summon colleagues to his bedside for consultations; liked to work in bed ■ Had his own special account, replenished by book royalties; these were astronomical as everyone was required to buy his books; female lovers were given money from the special account

Terror

Stalin	Hitler	Mao
■ Deployed as an instrument of legitimation ■ Unbridled violence against perceived opponents; discovered that it was effective during Civil War ■ Developed by Dzierzynski's Cheka and later refined by Stalin; torture used to extract confessions from victims ■ Hard times were blamed on hidden enemies, such as Trotskyism ■ Concept of the enemy of the people developed	■ Had more secure power base than Stalin; did not need to rely on secret police to the extent Stalin did; neither was there so much checking and verification ■ Stalin and Hitler, both former political terrorists, saw themselves engaged in a violent war against international terrorism ■ Unbridled violence to be deployed ■ Hitler saw himself as having saved Germans from Red terror; communist (Jewish-Bolshevik) threat had to be erased ■ In 1933 violence was mainly against the left,	■ Deployed terror as an instrument of legitimation ■ In Yenan used terror to discipline young cadres, 1942–43; thousands arrested and imprisoned in caves ■ Converted colleagues into jailers; former colleagues, prisoners and jailers all lived in same premises ■ Often work and living accommodation the same place; this was innovation by Mao; whereas Stalin and Hitler had secret police elites (KGB, Gestapo) and prisoners were taken away from home ■ Chinese tactic was to force prisoners to confess to being spies and to denounce others; real suspects quickly executed; mock executions ■ Mao supervised torture; forced labour for 'class enemies' ■ Mass rallies; young volunteers forced to confess to being spies; hysterical slogan-chanting; constant indoctrination meetings; no singing and dancing permitted; had to write down confessions of everything not good for Party; resistance meant person was spy; everyone informed on everyone; broke down trust between people

Stalin	Hitler	Mao
and they had to be extirpated	with concentration camps set up and torture and beatings the norm; Reichstag fire, on 27 February 1933, resulted in Hitler being granted special powers to deal with 'threat of communist revolution'; this myth was exploited in the same way as the murder of Sergei Kirov	■ After 1949, law emasculated and media tightly controlled
■ Society had to be cleansed of all segments of population which did not serve revolution		■ October 1950, nationwide campaign to eliminate counter-revolutionaries; bandits, those involved in armed resistance, of which there were millions, and spies, those who had worked for nationalists, special target
■ There was also an external enemy – the capitalist powers who were ready to attack and crush the Soviet Union	■ Violence now legally sanctioned in Germany; People's Court set up in Berlin, in 1936, to deal mercilessly with major cases of treason	■ Mao berated local cadres for being too soft; wanted more beatings, more killings; campaign lasted a year; wanted public executions for maximum effect; millions attended 30,000 rallies in Beijing; hundreds shot in head in public so that brains splattered over bystanders; trucks loaded with corpses dripping blood; children also to witness bloodletting; millions sent to labour camps (perhaps 10 million in camps in any one year under Mao)
■ Permanent tension was created to minimise opposition	■ Soviet 'enemy of the people' concept became 'alien to the people' (*Volksfremde*) in Germany	■ Order-keeping committees set up in every factory, street and village; place of residence and work recorded from July 1951
■ Stalinism was developed in a climate of fear; uncertainty and insecurity became a way of life	■ In February 1936, Gestapo freed from judicial review; they could now decide what constituted a political crime	■ In 1955, Mao said necessary to arrest 1.5 million counter-revolutionaries in next five years; 14 million state employees vetted
		■ After Hungarian revolution of 1956 Mao commented: 'We must kill and we say it's good to kill'
		■ Cultural revolution launched on 16 May 1966 when *The People's Daily* carried a coded attack on Mao's political opponents; Nie Yuanzi, Party secretary at Beijing University's philosophy department, inspired to put up a poster claiming that department under control of bourgeoisie; Mao had poster read out over national radio thereby giving his blessing to attacks on those in authority; key objective was to purge Party cadres, called capitalist-roaders; feared conspiracy against him; student Red Guards had licence to assault and kill teachers and other educated; 'smash old culture'
		■ Violence and humiliation in public; first senior official tortured to death in public was Minister of Coal in January 1967
		■ Policies resulted in about 70 million deaths

Utopia

Stalin	Hitler	Mao
■ A Marxist social utopia in which harmony would reign in society	■ Believed capitalism had fragmented German society and made it individualistic and selfish	■ Marxist social utopia closely modelled on Soviet Union but it gradually became more Chinese
■ Everyone would have their material needs satisfied; they would work together for the common good and eliminate selfishness, crime, war, cruelty	■ Wanted to create a harmonious society in which everyone worked and lived towards a common goal; classes would give way to race comrades, those of common blood – a new community	■ Mao wished to destroy old China and Chinese society
	■ A special nation in a new collective society; former egoism would be replaced by collective we	■ Favoured struggle and did not want people to become rich and lazy
■ Everyone would behave rationally and universal happiness would be attained	■ Bourgeoisie to be swept away as well as all petty bourgeois values; Hitler applauded Stalin's destruction of the bourgeoisie: 'humanly worthless'; bourgeois were culturally arrogant and 'cowardly shits' to the *Führer*	
	■ Germans or Aryans master race: everyone else was an *Untermensch*, a subhuman	■ He had world ambitions for the Chinese model and was willing to take risks to prosecute world socialist revolution
■ This is a secular version of paradise where there would be no inequality	■ World domination was goal; a biological utopia	
■ The perfectibility of human nature was a tenet of the socialist faith in the nineteenth century; it reveals a woeful lack of understanding of human nature	■ Principal enemy was Jew; German defeat in First World War due to Jews; world finance run by Jews; hence there was a world-wide conspiracy against Germany .	
	■ Citizens to live in new urban utopia; village and countryside inferior; national socialism shared communist vision of a new community but one based on service to the *Volk*, people or nation, and a shared racial identity; one that superseded class	
■ World revolution was goal as this was a universalist model	■ Class struggle in Marxism became struggle between races in national socialism; this did not mean an egalitarian society; the more able secured the best positions	
	■ The German equivalent of the Russian comrade was *Volksgenosse*, member of the *Volk*; evolution of new man and woman of primary importance; a new type of man was to emerge: fearless, brutal, intrepid, socially engineered, tall, blond, blue-eyed and gracefully proportioned; these new men would construct the new order	
	■ Those judged unfit to reproduce were to be castrated, sterilised or killed; women were entreated to have large families	
	■ First killing of undesirables – handicapped children – in 1939; in September 1940, decision taken to murder (gas) all Jewish mental patients; then all Jews	
	■ The biological utopia required the ruthless elimination of any blood which could contaminate it	
	■ World conquest would lead to the domination of the German or Aryan race	

Culture

Stalin	Hitler	Mao
■ The early Bolshevik years were very creative as various schools fought for dominance	■ As in the Soviet Union, art for art's sake was out; art was to be heroic and romantic; it was a function of the life of the people	■ Anti-western, especially anti-American from 1949
■ There was no Party line in culture	■ An artist was to draw a true picture of the inborn capacities of the people and not to distort them; art was to be simple and comprehensible; 'only art that the simple man can understand is true art'	■ Literature and art to be didactic; tightly censored, often by Mao himself
■ Stalin, who was very well read, conceived of culture as a force of production; it would help to transform the country economically		■ Cinema almost shut down; only five films made in 1952
■ Socialist realism, introduced in 1934, was to glorify achievements and paint a beautiful tomorrow; it was to inspire greater productivity	■ Hitler saw himself as an artist as well as the leader; in sculpture he wanted the physical beauty of Greek statues to be the guide; he preferred the landscapes of the nineteenth century; the architecture of the Roman and Greek world was a model; literature, which fascinated Stalin, was of little interest	■ Influence of non-communist writers and artists to be eliminated; domestic writers thrown into prison; letters intercepted; people were afraid to write down thoughts
■ Ethnic culture had to be national in form but socialist in content; this meant downgrading the achievements of the local nation and praising big brother Russia		■ 'Let a hundred flowers bloom', said Mao, February 1957; trap to discover what intellectuals thought; then could be labelled rightist
	■ Stalin's norm was socialist realism, Hitler's nationalist realism	
■ Russians were the elder brothers, other nationalities were younger brothers	■ All modern culture was 'hostile to the Volk': impressionism; futurism; cubism; Dadaism	■ In 1957, most pupils who had finished urban elementary schools and secondary education not allowed to continue education
■ Stalin read plays, novels, film scripts, listened to music and viewed art and sculpture in order to censor them; in his last years Russian culture was glorified and Soviet culture took second place	■ Classics of German literature permitted if not Jewish or un-German; blacklisted books burned, in April–May 1933; Marx topped the list	■ Cultural revolution launched 1966
		■ Mme Mao launched 'kill culture manifesto'
■ Jewish culture was unacceptable	■ Brahms and Bruckner most popular composers; whereas Stalinist political ritual was rooted in carnival – everyone was to enjoy the glorification of socialism – German displays were serious and solemn, often commemorating the dead	■ Mao had great library and love of Chinese classics but no one else permitted this luxury
	■ Soldiers could look forward to a glorious death	

The main source for Stalin and Hitler is Richard Overy, *The Dictators: Hitler's Germany, Stalin's Russia* (2004); for Mao, Jung Chang and Jon Halliday, *Mao: The Unknown Story* (2005); and Christopher Andrew and Vasili Mitrokhin, *The Mitrokhin Archive II* (2005).

Questions

1 What are the key ideological distinctions between the different types of dictatorships which evolved in the Soviet Union, Germany and China between the 1920s and 1950s?

2 Compare and contrast the methods used by Stalin, Hitler and Mao to legitimise their rule.

3 What did Stalin, Hitler and Mao understand by political authority?

4 'Each regime was characterised by a different form of utopian ideology.' Discuss.

5 Compare and contrast the leadership styles of Stalin and Mao to that of Hitler.

6 'Of the three dictatorships, Stalin's was the most socially progressive.' Discuss.

7 Did the three dictatorships conceive of social engineering in roughly the same way?

8 All three dictatorships were concerned with race and ethnicity, but did they necessarily all base their ideologies on this precept?

9 What precisely did the three dictators share in common?

10 'War and the "militarisation" of political culture were indispensable to the ideologies of the three dictatorships.' Discuss.

CHAPTER 19

The Khrushchev era

Khrushchev returns from a visit to the United States in a foul mood. He
explains to Mikoyan. 'Kennedy told me they have invented a machine that
can bring a man back from the dead. I couldn't admit we were backward so
I told him we had invented a compound than can make a man run faster than
a car.' 'No problem', says Mikoyan, 'If they bring Stalin back from the dead,
you'll run faster than any car.'

Khrushchev's rule can be broken down into several periods:

1 struggle for dominance, 1953–55;
2 the virgin lands reform, decentralisation of economic decision making,
   de-Stalinisation and the Anti-Party plot, 1955–58;
3 apogee and the Cuban Missile Crisis, 1958–62;
4 decline and fall, 1962–64.

Khrushchev was a brilliant political infighter but all at sea when he tried to
make the economy more effective. In the cultural world he promised more than he
delivered. Why was such a consummate political operator so ineffective as a policy
maker? The answer lies in his background under Stalin. The boss saw the big
picture and Khrushchev's task was to implement his orders. He was, therefore, not
involved in creative thinking about state and society. Stalin had a grasp of political
and economic reality which no successor came near to equalling. Whereas Stalin
was normally cool and methodical, Khrushchev was headstrong and impulsive.
Stalin took risks in the 1930s but afterwards avoided them. Khrushchev was a
natural risk taker. The key reason why he was not a successful policy maker was
that his perception of the problem under review was faulty. Solutions based on

imperfect intelligence rarely succeed. A major error was to regard the Party apparatus as an engine of progress. He abolished most of the central economic ministries in 1957 and passed decision making to over 100 councils of the national economy (sovnarkhozes). He quickly discovered that each sovnarkhoz attempted to enlarge its domain and become a mini-state. This was strengthened by local nationalism.

Under his leadership, Soviet citizens ate more and lived better. Endless agricultural reforms proved self-defeating. When I informed a Party official in Kazakhstan, in 1968, that I was working on Khrushchev's agricultural policy, his response was: 'You mean he had a policy!' He also told me that they ignored most agricultural reforms after 1958. Why? A new one was bound to come along which would override the previous one.

Defence and foreign affairs consumed much of his attention. He wanted to reduce the military budget so as to switch more investment to the civilian economy. The military-industrial complex did not. One way to achieve his goal was to browbeat the Americans into an arms control agreement. Sputnik, in 1957, demonstrated the superiority of the USSR in space. Mao thought that this should be used to take over the world, using nuclear weapons wherever necessary. Khrushchev had a horror of war and wanted a peaceful solution. The United States would have to accept that the Soviet Union was superior. Threaten Armageddon and the timid Yankees would submit. Instead he unleashed an arms race which only concluded with the arrival of Gorbachev.

A burning political issue was de-Stalinisation. What were its limits? Khrushchev did not think through the consequences of debunking Stalin. Most war veterans, for instance, simply rejected his charges and pointed to Stalin as a great war leader. The cultural community went along with it because it wanted to free itself from the shackles of Party censorship. The average person wanted his or her say.

By 1964, he had alienated too many interest groups. They conspired against him and ignominiously unseated him in October 1964. He became a non-person and died a sad, disillusioned man. His understanding of human nature was defective. He had thought that, under socialism, the new Soviet man and woman was evolving. In reality, the old man and woman lived on. Self-interest, manifested in growing corruption, born of a lust for material goods, characterised many in the new society. They inundated the brave souls who sought to live a selfless life in the interests of society. A fervent follower of Marx, he paradoxically shattered the communist dream for many.

Struggle for supremacy

After Lenin's death, there was a collective leadership until one comrade gained dominance. The same happened after the death of Stalin. The Soviet system favoured the emergence of a strong leader who, in turn, attempted to become a dictator. The post-Stalin collective leadership was decided even before the boss was dead. On 5 March 1953, they met for 40 minutes, from 8.00 to 8.40 p.m. The master breathed his last at 9.50 p.m. The meeting was called in the name of the Party, government and Presidium of the USSR Supreme Soviet. Nikita Khrushchev chaired the session. Georgy Malenkov stated that the Presidium (Politburo) had instructed him to present various changes in the Party and government leadership. Beria interrupted him and reported that the Presidium had decided to appoint Malenkov Prime Minister. Then Malenkov took over again. Lavrenty Beria, Vyacheslav Molotov, Nikolai Bulganin and Lazar Kaganovich were proposed as first deputy Prime Ministers. The Ministry of Internal Affairs (MVD) and the Ministry of State Security (MGB) were to be merged. The new overlord of this mighty new ministry was to be Beria. Molotov was appointed Minister of Foreign Affairs and Bulganin Minister of Defence. Kliment Voroshilov became chair of the Presidium of the USSR Supreme Soviet, nominally head of state. Stalin's Presidium, elected at the 19th Party Congress, in October 1952, was refashioned. Instead of the 25 full and 4 candidate members, there were now to be 11 full and 4 candidate members. It transpired that all these changes had been agreed the day before, 4 March, and then rubber stamped on 5 March (Pikhoya 1998).

Stalin had been head of government and overseer of the instruments of coercion at his death. These duties were split between Malenkov as Prime Minister and Beria as the top policeman. This made clear that these two comrades were now the most powerful.

Nikita Khrushchev did not obtain any government post. He was elected a CC secretary as well as being a member of the Party Presidium. The practice had grown up that the Prime Minister (Stalin) chaired Politburo (Presidium) sessions. As the Party had no executive apparatus, decisions of the Politburo were implemented by the government. Hence the Prime Minister appeared to head both the government and the Party apparatus. Malenkov also mentioned at the meeting that he, Beria and Khrushchev had been instructed to 'ensure that Stalin's papers, both actual and those in the archives, were arranged correctly'. It provided them with a mine of information on their colleagues. Khrushchev was to use this more effectively than the others.

Beria's reforms

Beria knew that he, a Georgian, was unlikely to succeed Stalin, another Georgian. He needed to make himself the power behind the throne. His principal ally was Malenkov; his chief enemy was Khrushchev. However, he was hated and feared by the whole collective leadership because of his bloody role under the master.

Intellectually he was superior to the others. Yet he was to commit the cardinal sin of clever politicians: he underestimated the opposition. For instance, he thought Khrushchev was a 'moon-faced idiot'. He turned out to be his nemesis.

Fundamental to Beria's reforms was the belief that the Party-state was ineffi- cient. Stalin, on one occasion, said he was not a Marxist. Beria was a pragmatist with a low opinion of Party officials. He said to Khrushchev: 'What is the Party Central Committee? Let the government decide everything and the Central Com- mittee busy itself with cadres and propaganda'. He was very perceptive. Had this insight been implemented the Soviet Union might still exist. But it was not a wise thing to say to Khrushchev, whose power base was the Party apparatus.

Beria immediately set up a group to look into the Doctors' Plot and several other affairs since 1945. On 2 April 1953, he informed the Presidium that Solomon Mikhoels, the Jewish actor, had been murdered. Stalin, MGB Minister Abakumov, his deputy and the Belarusian MGB chief had planned the murder. Several doctors had been implicated in the Doctors' Plot because they had known Mikhoels. The same applied to Molotov's Jewish wife. The following day, the Presidium overturned the sentences passed on the 'doctors-wreckers'. L. F. Timashuk, whose accusation of medical negligence during Zhdanov's final illness had spawned the Doctors' Plot, was stripped of her Order of Lenin. Those condemned in the Aviators' Affair, in 1946, were declared innocent.

Beria informed the Presidium that there were 2.5 million in prisons, colonies and the gulag, of which over 220,000 were classified as dangerous criminals. Most inmates had been sentenced to long terms for stealing state and private property and for economic misdemeanours (kolkhoz directors, engineers, etc.). He recom- mended that about a million be released. An amnesty followed. These men and women, angry at their unjust treatment, flooded back into society seeking justice. They had to be found jobs and integrated into society. The police were no longer to use torture or physical abuse during investigation and all the instruments of torture were to be destroyed. Many MVD projects, using gulag labour, were discontinued. Responsibility for gold and other mining of minerals passed to the Ministry of Metallurgy. Hydraulic projects were taken over by another ministry.

Beria was arrested on 26 June 1953. How Khrushchev managed to prise Beria and Malenkov apart is still a mystery. Once Malenkov had come over to the opposition, Beria's fate was sealed. Originally there had been three power bases: government, headed by Malenkov, the security services, headed by Beria, and the Party led by Khrushchev. Now there were two. The East Berlin uprising, on 17 June, was a fateful event. Beria was dispatched there immediately and only returned on 25 June. This provided the conspirators, headed by Khrushchev, with the time to plan their coup. They enlisted the help of Marshal Zhukov. He had a score to settle with Beria. The conspirators were afraid that Beria, who had many troops under his command, would activate them. Only Zhukov would have the stature to ensure the military stayed loyal. Surprisingly, no word of what was going on was relayed by Beria's contacts to him in Berlin. He suspected nothing when he returned. On entering the Kremlin, he failed to notice that the guards had changed. Instead of his own MVD troops, sailors of the Baltic Fleet were on duty. They were dressed like MVD troops but their epaulettes gave them away.

Malenkov lost his nerve when presiding at the Presidium meeting. He was supposed to tell Beria that he was under arrest. Khrushchev, according to his own account, intervened and called in Zhukov. There are two versions of what happened next. According to one account, attributed to Vladimir Soloukhin, the well known writer, Beria was taken to a shooting range in the basement of the Kremlin and shot. The other version is that he stood trial, was sentenced to death and executed in December 1953.

This was not the first occasion Baltic sailors had guarded important persons. They protected Stalin at the Tehran conference. When he met Soloukhin, Stalin asked him: 'What do you want to be in life?' Soloukhin replied: 'A writer'. This surprised Stalin but he arranged for him to go to a literary institute.

The fear of the conspirators that Beria's armed men would come to his support turned out to be justified. Immediately, the MVD Dzierzynski motorised infantry division began moving towards Moscow. A tank division was given the task of stopping them. A motorised infantry division has no chance against a tank division. There was an exchange of fire and casualties. The Dzierzynski division retreated.

Six of Beria's close associates were also shot. The reaction of the public to the Beria affair is revealing. One person wanted to know if Beria had been arrested in connection with the ending of the Doctors' Plot and the amnesty. Another wondered if Beria had terminated Stalin. Would Beria's trial be open or held in secret? Was he involved in the Berlin uprising?

Khrushchev v. Malenkov or Party v. state apparatus (1953–55)

With Beria sidelined, the way was clear for Khrushchev to challenge Malenkov for supremacy. They had fundamentally different approaches to politics and economics. Politically, Malenkov favoured a collective leadership. He, as Prime Minister, chaired Presidium sessions. Party decisions would be implemented by the government with the aid of the Party apparatus. Government ministers would dominate decision making in the Presidium and would form a majority. Malenkov, in order to revive the economy, favoured the bottom up approach. The worker or producer should be afforded more incentives. Heavy industry, especially the military-industrial complex, devoured too much investment. The time had come to concentrate more on light industry and consumer goods. This was only possible if international tension could be reduced. In August 1953, Malenkov used the word détente for the first time. In agriculture, he increased procurement prices for state deliveries, reduced taxes on private plots and thereby sought to promote kolkhoznik initiative.

Khrushchev, elected First Secretary of the Party CC in September 1953, was in the opposite corner. His power base was the Party. He set out to strengthen the Party apparatus at the expense of the state apparatus. He continued the Stalinist approach to leadership: democratic centralism. The decisions of the First Secretary were to be implemented by government. The Party apparatus was to expand and to dominate the governmental apparatus. The argument that heavy industry was consuming too many resources was nonsense. The country had to 'catch up with and surpass' the United States in armaments as well as butter. The solution to every pressing economic problem was a grand Party-government initiative. This was the top down approach.

Khrushchev launched the grandiose Virgin Lands project to solve the grain problem once and for all. Eventually 33 million hectares were put under the plough. Thousands of young Komsomol activists flocked to northern Kazakhstan but many of them were shocked by the appalling conditions and returned home post-haste.

In February 1955 Malenkov was forced to concede he had made mistakes. He was removed as Prime Minister but remained in the Presidium. Nikolai Bulganin, a suave, indecisive, goatee bearded apparatchik, took over the government. He was in Khrushchev's pocket.

Why did Khrushchev win?

- Malenkov assumed that since Stalin had been Prime Minister and had chaired the Presidium, this state of affairs would continue.

- He had always been a number two and had not developed the suspiciousness or paranoia of a number one.

- Khrushchev was hungry for power and wanted to become a strong leader.

- The Party apparatus was hungry for power and would support Khrushchev against Malenkov.

- Malenkov afforded the governmental apparatus primacy over the Party apparatus.

- Khrushchev was better at putting coalitions together than Malenkov.

- Malenkov, in power, had to devote his energies to running the government.

- Khrushchev had time to plot a coup against Malenkov.

Khrushchev's craze for maize earned him the sobriquet of comrade Kukuruznik (maize).

The Americans land on the moon. Mission Control asks: 'What do you see?'
'Well, there is a little fat, bald man planting corn [maize]!'

Maize was animal fodder and this was to increase meat production. Officially, over the years 1953–58 agricultural production rose by 50 per cent. A new slogan was launched in May 1957: 'Catch up and surpass America in per capita output of meat, milk and butter'. He was copying Stalin. For every problem find a miracle cure. 'Maize', he told his incredulous comrades, 'is a tank in the hands of the kolkhoznik and can overcome any barrier on the way to abundance.' Maize is like a male's private organ. One can imagine the obscene jokes it gave rise to. Unfortunately for Khrushchev, maize tanks cannot solve production problems and he threshed around for another miracle solution.

'What is Khrushchev's hairstyle called?' 'The 1963 harvest.' (It was very poor.)

Inevitably, the pressure to produce more and more grain, maize and meat led to massive fraud in reporting state deliveries. One tactic was to deliver cattle to the delivery point; they were paid for and then sold back to the kolkhoz at a low price; this was then repeated several times. Dead animals could also be delivered. The farms met their targets and the state paid out for imaginary meat.

In August 1958, it was decreed that cattle could no longer be maintained on plots owned by urban dwellers. This affected 12.5 million families. The cattle were immediately seized by kolkhozes and sovkhozes and slaughtered. Now these families would have to buy meat and milk from state stores. The problem was that the stores did not have the produce. Corruption and the black market expanded. At a stroke Khrushchev had destroyed a section of the population which had produced much of its own food. When his successors attempted to stimulate the private plot they failed. Animals had been looked after by the women of the household. They were no longer willing to sacrifice their time looking after Buttercup the cow. By 1961 the agricultural crisis could no longer be disguised. When the harvest failed in 1963, Khrushchev, to his credit, swallowed his pride and imported grain from the United States.

Khrushchev and the Stalinists (1955–58)

Immediately before his denunciation of Stalin at the 20th Party Congress, Khrushchev left the stage after a few minutes. Someone asked him after the speech where he had been. 'I dropped into the mausoleum for a minute to take Stalin's pulse . . . just in case.'

'Who was braver, Hitler or Khrushchev?' 'Hitler. He fought Stalin while he was alive. Khrushchev took him on when he was dead. He didn't win either.'

The big question for Khrushchev was Stalin. With a million prisoners returning home from the gulag and demanding justice, some initiative was necessary. A commission was set up, chaired by Petr Pospelov, and it collected information from the archives. The material was shocking. The Presidium split on making it public at the 20th Party Congress, in February 1956. Eventually it was agreed that Khrushchev should deliver a speech but only at a closed session. The Secret Speech, a wildly misleading title as the whole world learnt of it very quickly, was continuously amended by Khrushchev right up to the moment it was delivered. This broke the longstanding rule that all speeches had to be vetted by the Presidium before delivery.

The speech stunned the audience; at least one fainted from shock. It laid bare Stalin's crimes since 1934. Everything that went wrong was blamed on him. Some delegates immediately rejected the analysis and praised Stalin as a great leader, especially during the war. No stenographic report of the speech was permitted. An edited version was sent to all Party committees for discussion. Again there was considerable opposition to the blanket denunciation of the former leader. Immediately there were demands that Bukharin, Zinoviev and the other leaders defeated and killed by Stalin be rehabilitated. Trotsky's widow, writing from Mexico, asked for her husband to be rehabilitated. However, the Presidium decided against it and it was only in 1988 that they (except Trotsky) were rehabilitated.

Without realising it, Khrushchev had created a Party opposition. The same applied to the population at large. It consisted of two groups: those who believed that he had not gone far enough and wanted de-Stalinisation to be more radical and the others who defended Stalin and refused to accept Khrushchev's judgements. Many war veterans fell within the second group. Intellectuals, artists, academics and specialists were more likely to gravitate to the first group. The consequence was that the Party was irreparably damaged in the Soviet Union and abroad.

Why did Khrushchev deliver the Secret Speech?

- He wanted to break the spell of Stalinism and release the creative potential of the Party and people.
- He wanted to become a supreme leader and hoped that the revelations could be used against his political opponents.
- Beria had criticised Stalin; so had Malenkov; he had to seize the initiative before his rivals implicated him in Stalin's crimes.
- He had blood on his hands and needed to shift the blame on to Stalin.
- The demolition of Stalin's reputation meant that it would be easier to introduce radical reforms.

■ He hoped opposition would be weakened because it could not found its arguments on Stalinist practice.

In 1956, Khrushchev absolved from blame all those nations accused of collaborating with the German Wehrmacht during the war (1941–45). This involved many nations in the north Caucasus such as the Chechens, Ingush, Karachais, Balkars and Kalmyks. All were granted the right to return to their homeland except the Volga Germans and Crimean Tatars. When they returned the deportees found their land occupied by Russians and Ukrainians; their mosques being used as stores and their cemetery headstones used for building materials. Moscow ruefully conceded that those who returned from exile in Central Asia were the most religious group in Soviet society. The KGB noted that attacks on religion were perceived as attacks on national identity.

Khrushchev was forthright in his remarks about Jews to Polish communist leaders on 20 March 1956. They were encouraged to emulate Soviet practice by limiting the proportion of Jews in high positions to their proportion in the Soviet population.

'In the Soviet Union, 2 per cent of the population is Jewish, which means that ministries, universities – everything – contain 2 per cent Jews. I'm not an anti-Semite, indeed we have a minister who is a Jew; he's a good minister [Venyamin] Dimshits is his name, and we respect him, but you have to have limits.'

There were 23 all-Union ministries (responsible for the country as a whole) and 29 Union-republican ministries (a ministry in Moscow and in each republic) in 1957. Khrushchev was very irritated by their power. They frustrated his efforts to reform the economy. In February 1957 he hit on a bold solution. Abolish the central ministries and devolve economic decision making to 105 local bodies, called councils of the national economy (sovnarkhozes). The defence economy – the Military-Industrial Commission (VPK) which embraced nine key ministries – was excluded. The sovnarkhozes followed closely the Party krai and oblast boundaries. Hence the local Party bosses acquired more control over the economy in their bailiwick. That secured a solid base of support for Khrushchev. The governmental apparatus was thereby weakened. Government officials had to decamp to the provinces. For many of them, especially their wives, it was like being banished to the back of beyond. 'Forty kilometres outside Moscow and one is back in the Middle Ages', went a Moscow saying.

Since the main objective of the reform was political, it is not surprising that it was an economic failure. The VPK, for instance, produced many consumer goods, such as refrigerators, and it was centrally regulated. Research, development and innovation (RDI) had to be coordinated by Moscow. Since government personnel opposed the reform, they found ways of gradually moving back to the centre. Committees began to spring up in Moscow to coordinate the activity of sectors and branches of the economy.

The failed coup

The first discussions about the removal of Khrushchev took place on 20 May 1957. Lazar Kaganovich, Georgy Malenkov, Vyacheslav Molotov, Nikolai Bulganin and Mikhail Pervukhin, all members of the Presidium, were there. Then Kliment Voroshilov joined them. There was now a majority, 6 of 11 full members, against Khrushchev. The ousted leader was going to be made Minister of Agriculture. This revealed their sardonic humour. Agriculture was an Irish bog for politicians. Mikhail Suslov, the Party's ideology chief, was to become Minister of Culture and Bulganin the new KGB chief. A key comrade was Marshal Zhukov, then a candidate member. He proposed to Molotov that the post of Party First Secretary be abolished and replaced by a Secretary for General Affairs. Molotov was not quick enough to promise him the earth in order to win him over. This was to prove a fatal error. After all, Zhukov could be double-crossed afterwards.

The Presidium session began on 18 June with only eight full members present. Khrushchev was absent. Malenkov subjected Khrushchev to severe criticism. It was agreed to meet the following day when all members could be present. The slogan of catching up with and overtaking per capita American production of meat and milk was ridiculed. There was a clear majority to remove Khrushchev. Then the unexpected happened. A group of CC members, headed by high ranking military, appeared at the door. The military demanded to be allowed to attend the session. Central Committee secretaries and leading ministers demanded that a CC plenum be convened to decide Khrushchev's fate. Zhukov reminded the Presidium that tanks could break into the Kremlin and soldiers surround it. The conspirators caved in. The CC plenum turned the tables. Zhukov used military planes to get Khrushchev's supporters to the Kremlin in time. The plenum removed Malenkov, Kaganovich, Molotov and Shepilov (candidate member) from the Presidium. Bulganin, as indecisive as always, prevaricated and survived. He did not survive long. He was expelled in September 1958. Among the new full members was Leonid Brezhnev.

Party rules had been flouted in a Stalinist manner. The Anti-Party group (so called because it opposed the dominance of the Party over the government) had a majority in the Presidium. They had been overruled by a revolt of CC members, clearly orchestrated by Khrushchev. An even more disturbing development had been the threat of military force if the generals did not get their way. Khrushchev sacked Zhukov in October 1957 and removed him as a full member of the Presidium.

In March 1958, Khrushchev pushed Bulganin aside and took over the portfolio of Prime Minister himself. A Defence Council was set up and Khrushchev became commander-in-chief of Soviet forces. Five years after the death of Stalin, he had accumulated all the master's principal offices. He was on top of the world.

Khrushchev promised a thaw after the Secret Speech, hoping this would promote de-Stalinisation and thereby strengthen the Party's influence. Solzhenitsyn's *Gulag Archipelago* (published abroad) and *One Day in the Life of Ivan Denisovich* (published in Moscow) were a devastating attack on the gulag system. (It should be pointed out that Solzhenitsyn was describing a world which no longer existed.) Pasternak's *Dr Zhivago* also could not be published in the Soviet Union. Khrushchev took the award of the Nobel Prize for literature to Pasternak as a personal insult. He was culturally very conservative and could not understand modern art and music. He railed against the sculptor Neizvestny. (However he later recanted and asked Neizvestny to carve the headstone to his grave, which he did in Novodevichy cemetery, Moscow.)

Khrushchev visits a famous art exhibition at the Manege in Moscow. 'What is that stupid square with the red dots supposed to be?' 'That's a Soviet factory and its workers, Nikita Sergeevich.' 'What's that old canvas covered in green and yellow supposed to be?' 'That's a field of corn.' 'And what's that arsehole with ears?' 'That . . . that's a mirror, Nikita Sergeevich!'

On top of the world (1958–62)

Sputnik (fellow traveller) orbited the world in 1957 and demonstrated that the USSR was ahead of the United States in the space race. The detonation of the hydrogen bomb, in August 1953, had been a wakeup call to the Americans. In weapons of mass destruction, Russians were now number one. Khrushchev went to the United States, in 1959, to tell the Yanks that their glory days were over. 'We will bury you', was one of his memorable quotes. He was enormously impressed but, of course, could not say so. Self-service supermarkets were one of the innovations he brought back. The 1961 Party programme promised victory over capitalism in 10 years and the advent of communism in 20 years.

On 1 June 1962, in Novocherkassk (Rostov oblast), a group of about 10 steel workers began discussing recent food price rises. A Party official began explaining policy. An enterprise director appeared but soon fled. Workers had previously struck over poor conditions and lower pay. A crowd of 200 gathered and the military appeared. The next day, 2 June, workers carrying red flags and portraits of Lenin marched to the main square. The meeting demanded the cancellation of price rises and higher wages. The military opened fire and killed 20 demonstrators; 3 more died later from gunshot wounds; about 40 were injured and the remainder arrested. The leader of demonstration was later shot. The Novocherkassk tragedy destroyed the illusion that the food problem could be solved by socialist agriculture, led by the Party. Moscow was so shocked that state food prices were never again increased.

'Will there be queues under communism?' 'No, there will not be queues because there will be nothing to queue for.'

'How does a lizard differ from a crocodile?' 'Basically they're the same. A lizard is a crocodile which has passed from socialism to communism.'

'What do I do if I feel like working?' 'Lie down. It will soon pass.'

At the 22nd Party Congress, in October 1961, a new Party statute was adopted. In elections up to raion level, half of those elected had to be new; at oblast, krai and republican level, one-third had to be new; at CC and Presidium level, one-quarter had to be new. This made it more difficult for a Party leader to be re-elected at each level. However this threatened the stability of the Party apparatus. At the November 1962 CC plenum, a Party-state control organ was set up; previously Party and state apparatuses had their own control (supervision) bodies. Krais and oblasts were to be divided into industrial and agricultural sections; in each krai and oblast there were to be two Party organisations; one industrial and the other agricultural. This also applied to local soviets; one was to be industrial and the other agricultural. Party secretaries in agricultural raions – the largest group in the Party apparatus – were simply dismissed. Management of agriculture now passed to Territorial Production Administrations (TPAs); each embraced several raions; division into industrial and agricultural sections – called the production principle – also applied to the Komsomol, trade unions and the police. Khrushchev was dissuaded from applying it to the KGB. In exasperation, KGB boss Vladimir Semichastny asked the First Secretary: 'How am I to distinguish between urban and rural spies?' He told Khrushchev that splitting the KGB would result in a great increase of officers and generals. This won the day as Khrushchev had a great dislike of KGB military ranks and wanted to abolish them.

Decline and fall (1962–64)

The rising tide of crime and corruption shocked Khrushchev. Bribery was evident in Gosplan, ministries, the Party apparatus, indeed in every institution across the country. A Party-state control committee was set up in November 1962. It had transpired that a purely Party control body would not have the clout to deal with governmental institutions. Unfortunately it turned into a bureaucratic monster. It duplicated the activities of the CC apparatus and government in Moscow. It set up sections for all the main sectors of the economy, trade unions, the military and so on. It soon had almost 500 staff instead of the 100 originally envisaged. In 1958, the central CC apparatus consisted of 1,118 political officials and 1,085 technical personnel (secretaries, typists, etc.). The central administration of the Soviet government and ministries numbered about 75,000; it was clear from these figures that the ability of the CC apparatus to monitor the governmental apparatus was limited. The Party-state control committee proved enormously unpopular. It was dismantled by Brezhnev.

A customer asks a sales assistant: 'Wrap me up a kilo of meat.' The assistant in a sparkling white apron pulls out some spotless white paper. 'Give me your meat, comrade.'

Religion irked Khrushchev as it provided an alternative world view to Marxism. The faithful were unlikely to be enthusiastic believers in the coming communist paradise. His anti-religious policy was harsh and thousands of churches and mosques were closed down. Islam was a particular problem. In Central Asia, one scholar estimated that official Islam accounted for 1 per cent of the faithful and unofficial Islam the other 99 per cent. It later emerged that many tea houses on collective farms had, in reality, been unofficial mosques.

Russians were always hungry. Two-thirds of imported food had come from China. Mao had exported food to pay for military and civil technology. This meant the Chinese starved. This policy ended in 1962. The failure of the Soviet harvest in 1963 meant that food had to come predominantly from the capitalist world. The Americans demanded cash. Gold was sold to pay for grain shipments. This was humiliating as Khrushchev had devoted large resources and energy to improving Soviet agriculture. He lost patience with Party bosses and proposed to rotate them so that they could not become too complacent. He had alienated almost every elite group.

A July 1964 CC plenum was convened to propose Anastas Mikoyan as chair of the Presidium of USSR Supreme Soviet (President). Leonid Brezhnev was to move to the post of 'second' secretary or Khrushchev's number two. Instead Khrushchev launched into a great speech on agriculture. He proposed the setting up of specialised production associations; one for each sector. This was ill-advised, to say the least, since meat and milk production have to be planned together. Party officials were to be excluded from the management of agriculture. This was astonishing, as only two years earlier the Party was to play the leading role in agriculture. He was extremely unhappy with the contribution of the Academy of

There were two centres of power: Party and government. Which was the more influential after Stalin's death?

March 1953	Malenkov becomes head of government and also of Party apparatus. Hence one can say that Party and government are of equal significance. However, Malenkov is not permitted to hold both offices and has to cede one. He chooses to remain as leader of government. This means government is of primary importance.
September 1953	Khrushchev uses his position as Party leader to undermine Malenkov.
February 1955	Malenkov resigns as Prime Minister; succeeded by Khrushchev ally Nikolai Bulganin. This is the point at which the Party Politburo becomes more influential than the government.
June 1957	Khrushchev survives coup by Politburo members to remove him; demonstrates that Politburo is key institution in state.
March 1958	Bulganin resigns as Prime Minister; Khrushchev assumes role; now head of Party and government; he has emulated Stalin; Party post more influential.
October 1964	Successful coup by Politburo to remove Khrushchev; he automatically loses his government post; Party leader clearly more important.

FIGURE 19.1 Power in the state, 1953–64

Sciences and the Academy of Agriculture in the development of agriculture. He threatened to disband the Academy of Sciences and the Academy of Agriculture and to dispatch the agricultural institutes in Moscow and Leningrad to the countryside. The main reason for his ire was that the scientists regarded most of his initiatives as unscientific.

Alas, poor Stalin . . .

One of the most remarkable films made during the Khrushchev era was *Hamlet*. Shakespeare's play has always appealed to Russian cultural circles. It is after all the story of a lone intellectual who feigns madness to take on and defeat a corrupt, illegitimate regime. Elsinore is a suffocating, dangerous place ruled over by a murderous, paranoid dictator. Hamlet is betrayed by old friends (Rosenkrantz and Guildenstern) and, unwittingly, commits evil himself, causing the death of his innocent love Ophelia. The power of corrupt bureaucracy is revealed as Hamlet changes the name on his death certificate to survive. Those who sought to stage *Hamlet* in the 1930s were putting their lives at risk. Stalin strongly objected to the play. The allusions to himself were all too obvious. Finally, in 1964, in the dying embers of the Khrushchev era, the film version appeared. The director was Grigory

Kozintsev, screenplay was by Boris Pasternak and music by Dmitry Shostakovich. It is a visual masterpiece by artists who knew the claustrophobic, conspiratorial, murderous world of Shakespeare at first hand. It is a stunning artistic attack on Stalin's world. The cultural elite was exacting its revenge. Innokenty Smoktunovsky made his name as Hamlet and some may even prefer his performance to that of the master himself, Laurence Olivier. The film is now available on DVD, with English subtitles of course.

Crime and corruption

'Is state planning of the population possible?' 'Not as long as the means of production are in private hands.'

A Soviet diplomat takes a girl to her room in a bordello. Soon there are frantic screams: 'No, no, anything but that.' The madam hurries in and reminds the girl that the client's wishes are law. 'I know, but he wants to pay me in rubles.'

In June 1961, Nikita Khrushchev is in Vienna to see President John F. Kennedy. At a press conference afterwards he is in fine form, believing he has gained the upper hand over his young opponent.

> *'May I say, dear friends, that it is a great pleasure to be here in Vienna. However I should like to make a point about the much-vaunted western style of life. We hear a lot about how it is superior to socialism but I think the West has a glittering façade but is rotten underneath. Take, for example, corruption. I am told you can buy anyone in the West, from a girl to a seat in parliament. No, dear friends, we do not have such things in our beloved Soviet Union. The fact that everything is owned by our people precludes the corruption which I see around me. It will eventually dig the grave of the capitalist system.'*

'Excuse me, Mr Premier, but I should like to make a point about corruption', says a foreign journalist. 'I am informed that Moscow rivals West Berlin as the world capital of currency speculation. Apparently one can buy any currency on the black market there. There is nothing money cannot buy in Moscow. I wonder if you could comment on this.'

Khrushchev is struck dumb. After a pause he replies: 'I am convinced that everything you say is a capitalist lie, designed to blacken the great name of Soviet socialism. Nevertheless I shall look into the question when I return to

Moscow.' He returns to Moscow and immediately instructs Aleksandr
Shelepin, the head of the KGB, to come to see him.

> *'Comrade Shelepin, I was embarrassed in Vienna by a capitalist journal-*
> *ist's question. He spewed out some rubbish about Moscow*
> *being a hotbed of currency speculation. Surely this cannot be true.'*

Shelepin spreads out his arms and begins:

> *'Comrade First Secretary, I have to tell you that we have struck two devas-*
> *tating blows against the currency speculators. We have the problem under*
> *control. Indeed, two of the ringleaders, have been sentenced to*
> *15 years' imprisonment and had their ill-gotten gains confiscated.'*

> *'What', exploded Khrushchev, 'you mean to say that two arch-criminals*
> *who are contaminating our socialist fatherland will only go to jail for*
> *15 years. Sack the prosecutor and appoint a new one who will pass the*
> *death sentences on these two scoundrels! Do it immediately!'*

So the two currency dealers were shot.

The profit motive for private gain is fundamental to every society. However, buying and selling privately for gain in the Soviet Union was a criminal offence. A planned economy is, by definition, a shortage economy. Goods most in demand attract the highest prices when sold privately. Most officials were paid low salaries and were keen to increase their disposable income. The state erected a barrier (manned by the courts and the KGB) between the high potential of private profit and officials on low incomes. This barrier broke because of corruption. Officials could be bribed by those selling high-demand goods for private profit. This expanded until it became the shadow economy and entered the genes of society. It became a way of life.

Currency dealers appeared in earnest during the World Youth Festival in Moscow, in 1957. The official rate was 10 rubles to the US dollar but the speculators paid 20–25 rubles. Tsarist gold coins were in great demand and sold for dollars or rubles. Yan Rokotov quickly became very active. He bought tsarist gold rubles for 20 rubles and sold them on for 1,500. At this rate he could net 50,000 rubles in one evening. The Soviet population had heard rumours about a currency reform. As many of them had amassed a lot of savings, they wanted to offload as much as possible. The reform eventually entered into force on 1 January 1961, when 10 old rubles became 1 new ruble. Needless to say, one could only exchange legally a certain amount. I had my first experience with the Russian black market at the Youth Festival, in 1957.

I was invited one evening by a Russian, who spoke exquisitely good English, to meet some other Russians. They wanted to buy all the dollars I had. I explained I only had sterling. 'That's fine, we would like to buy pounds as well.' I thought that the whole episode was so far-fetched that it had to be a KGB trap. It was not. When I reported the encounter to our guide, she went white with fright. 'Don't repeat what you have told me to anyone.' I took her advice. What astonished me was that a graduate of a prestigious language institute, someone who could look forward to a successful career, was willing to risk everything to work for currency speculators. Either he had very good connections in the nomenklatura which would protect him if caught or he was just taking a risk.

Rokotov's fame spread to the gulag where he enjoyed the reputation of being a fabulously rich man. He was reputed to eat in the best restaurants in Moscow and Leningrad, always with a 'dolly bird' on each arm. In May 1961 he was arrested. Rokotov's defence was that he was an undercover militia officer and was on very good terms with the head of the currency section of the Moscow MVD. He had made it possible for him to visit expensive restaurants and spend time at health resorts. However, the KGB pressurised the MVD major and he handed over his contact. Rokotov was arrested at the Leningrad station in Moscow. He stored his assets there as well. The KGB discovered 440 gold coins; 12 kg of gold ingots and 2.5 million rubles worth of foreign currency. He and his associate, Vladislav Faibishenko, had been buying gold from Arabs and currency from small time operators (*fartsovshchiki*). These were the two Khrushchev wanted executed.

Rokotov became very rich very quickly. Hence he was satisfying a demand. As János Kornai, the eminent Hungarian economist, has demonstrated, a planned economy is, by definition, a shortage economy. The black market intervenes to satisfy repressed demand. There were many Berezka shops in which western goods and Russian furs could be bought, but only for western currency. Other currencies in circulation were diamonds and gold. Much was produced in the Soviet Union and some of it was siphoned off into the black market. Rokotov must have been buying gold as an investment. The circulation of such wealth in the black market reveals that there was widespread corruption in the Party, security, government and economic agencies. All gold and diamond mines were state owned so the valuables which appeared in the black market had to be stolen. The KGB and militia (MVD) were aware of Rokotov's activities but only decided to arrest him in May 1961. He was obviously paying bribes to many officials in Moscow in order to continue functioning. A tactic which the agencies deployed was to wait for the black marketeer to become rich and then to pounce. His assets were confiscated and became the property of the state. The law stated that they had to be sold but it

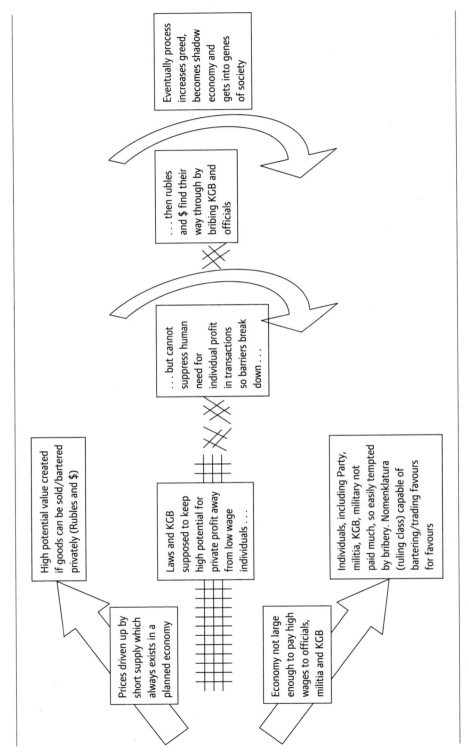

FIGURE 19.2 The roots of corruption

did not stipulate the price or to whom they should be sold. Senior officials were best placed to acquire valuable assets at knock-down prices.

The *tsekhoviki*

During the 1930s, Stalin permitted enterprises which had met their planned obligations to produce for the private sector. They were permitted to use defective spare parts to meet demand. They made these things in the factory, in a *tsekh* or shop or unit. Those who traded in these goods were known as *tsekhoviki* or shadow capitalists. They expanded quite rapidly in the 1950s and were quick to take advantage of Khrushchev's many economic reforms.

From time to time, *tsekhi* were uncovered. In 1961, Boris Roifman was arrested. It had occurred to him that there were a lot of patients in medical centres who could be put to work during their spare time. In one medical centre there were 58 knitting machines and the patients worked in shifts. Wool came from Nalchik, in the Caucasus, and sales were very well organised. The best outlets were railways stations and markets. In no time at all, the business was turning over millions. When arrested, Roifman was found to possess 100 kg of gold as well as gold coins, diamonds and other precious stones worth 2.5 million rubles. Boris's reward was a bullet in the back of the head. 'At least that means one zhid (Jew) less', screamed Khrushchev, on hearing of Roifman's execution.

Again one is struck by the fact that this scam was patently obvious to anyone who entered one of these medical centres. Patients sitting at knitting machines! The medical staff, the inspectors, indeed everyone right up to the top were presumably having their palms greased. Or perhaps they were simply given a woollen jumper to keep quiet.

The *tsekhoviki* were risk takers. Between November 1962 and July 1963 there were 80 major cases involving economic crime before the courts. No less than 163 death sentences were handed down. The rule of thumb was that these cases only involved comrades who had embezzled at least a million rubles. That adds up to a lot of theft. Others had connections which were good enough to keep them out of the courts.

Roifman was not the only one to realise that knitting machines could be good business. Maria Korshilova, director of the Moskva departmental store, had good connections. She was friendly with Ekaterina Furtseva, a CC secretary and later Soviet Minister of Culture. Through her, Korshilova managed to get permission to set up a knitting unit in the departmental store in 1961. They specialised in tennis gear and men's and women's garments. They did a roaring trade and over five years the turnover was put at 2.5 million rubles. Then the roof fell in. Her manager, Aleksandr Khaifets, was shot. She got off scot free. She claimed she had only been an observer. Shortly afterwards she moved to a high

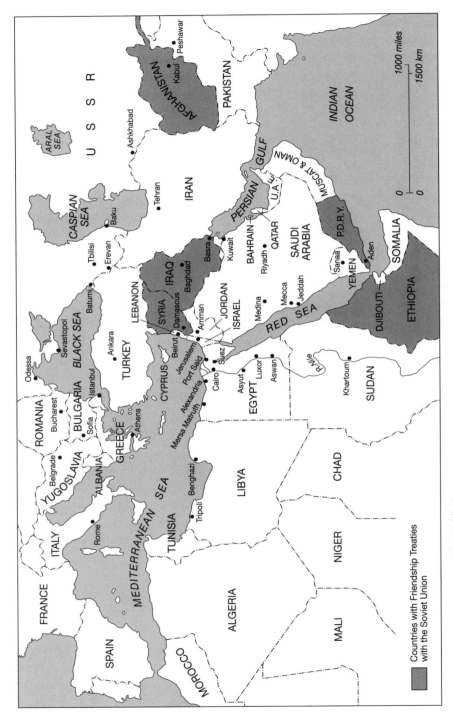

MAP 19.1 The Soviet Union and the Middle East

level position in a prominent departmental store. Evidently, it all depended on whom one knew.

Picasso forgets his invitation to an art exhibition in Paris. He has to prove he is Picasso to gain admission. With a single flourish of his pencil he draws a dove of peace and is admitted. Furtseva also forgets her ticket and is refused admission. 'But I'm the Soviet Minister of Culture.' 'You'll have to prove it. We only allowed Picasso in after he had drawn a dove.' 'Picasso. Who's Picasso?' 'Everything is in order, Madame Minister, please go straight in.'

The Moscow militia became so corrupt that criminals could actually pay them in the open. Shaya Shakerman met his MVD contacts in Mayakovsky square and handed out between 5,000 and 15,000 rubles to each of them, depending on their rank and position. Over a period of years, one officer earned a million rubles and another 600,000. This implies that they must have been sharing their wealth with a very large number of recipients. A militiaman at that time earned about 150 rubles a month.

The Socialist World

China

Mao Zedong sends Khrushchev a telegram. 'China starving. Send food'. Khrushchev replies. 'Short supplies here. Tighten your belts.' Mao wires back.' Send belts.'

Until 1949, China was always outmanoeuvred by Russia; afterwards China always came out on top. Traditionally Russians underestimated the Chinese. Modernity to twentieth century Russians meant factories belching smoke, steel production and a powerful military with nuclear weapons. This then became the dream of Mao Zedong when he proclaimed the People's Republic of China. He set about expelling foreigners and had no interest in establishing diplomatic relations with the leading world power, the United States. The only country which could help him realise his dream was the Soviet Union. How was he to inveigle the comrades in Moscow to help him? It was quite clear that China aspired to leadership of the world communist movement. So why should Moscow help Beijing supplant it as number one?

Mao's tactics were quite simple. Scare the Russians into helping China militarily. Taiwan was the primary target. Shell the offshore islands and try and provoke an American attack. Breakneck industrialisation, with the emphasis placed on the defence economy, was needed. How was China to pay for this? Collectivise the

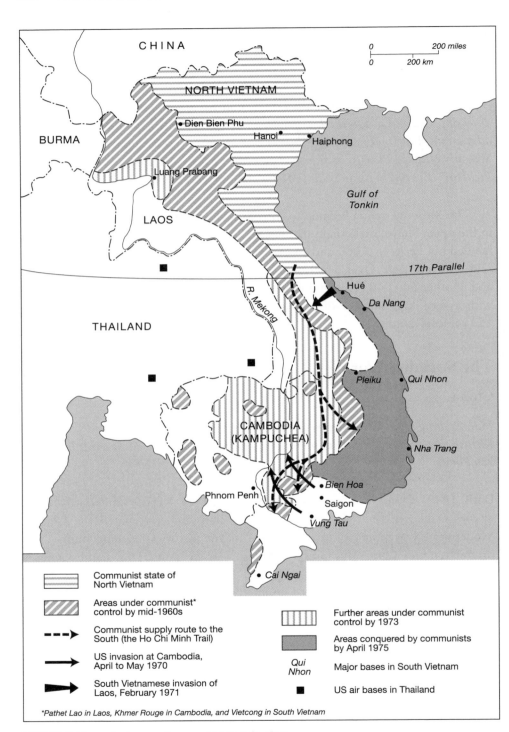

MAP 19.2 War and advance of communism in Indo-China

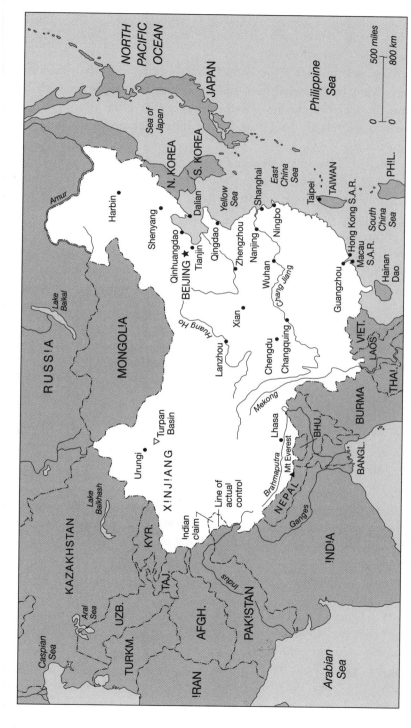

MAP 19.3 China

peasants and force them to deliver more grain and food. If they starved, so be it. China was hungry under Mao because he was hungry for a powerful industry and military. The virility symbol of a great power was an atomic bomb. China had to acquire one in the shortest possible time.

Khrushchev was no match for Mao. Infinitely better read than the autodidact Khrushchev, Mao bamboozled him with conversations peppered with illusions culled from the Chinese classics. His best interpreter often did not understand what Mao was getting at. That suited the Chinese leader fine: always keep the Russians guessing.

China shelled Taiwan's offshore islands in September 1954, hoping the Americans would threaten to use nuclear weapons to defend their island ally. Alarmed, Khrushchev scampered off to Beijing in October 1954 and promised to help the Chinese develop an atomic bomb. Mao was offended by not being consulted before the Secret Speech was delivered. He defended Stalin: 70 per cent of what he had done was good and only 30 per cent bad. Though he admitted that Khrushchev had bottle: he had 'touched Stalin'. After the suppression of the Hungarian uprising in 1956, Khrushchev needed Mao's support at the communist summit in November 1957. In return, the Soviet Union promised to provide sample atomic bombs and to help China develop its own. (China tested its first atomic bomb in October 1964.) Mao alarmed everyone by saying China was willing to sacrifice 300 million (half its population) to achieve world revolution.

Mao provoked a second Taiwan crisis in August 1958. This time he wanted the Soviet Union to provide him with a nuclear navy. The Russians gave in and agreed to build a nuclear fleet and also missiles. However, Mao was fearful that Khrushchev would engineer his removal. He slackened the tempo of industrial expansion. All the while, he was attempting to win over the Eastern Europeans to his side. He had little luck. Eventually, the only country to back China was Albania, in 1961. Well, it was a start.

In June 1960, at a communist summit in Bucharest, Romania, Khrushchev refuted Mao's assertion that world war was inevitable if socialism were to prove victorious. The Sino-Soviet split was now in the open. Zhou Enlai, when he came to the rostrum to deliver his speech, turned his back on Khrushchev and the audience, and spoke to the wall. The enraged Khrushchev, on his return to Moscow, ordered the withdrawal of over 1,000 Soviet technicians and halted work on 155 projects in China. He relented the following year and some of the projects continued. Over the years 1950–59, about 10,000 Soviet and East European specialists worked in China. About 20,000 Chinese were trained in the Soviet Union.

Khrushchev gave China the go-ahead to attack India while he was engaged in the Cuban Missile Crisis, in October 1962. He also had to ensure that Mao did not provoke another Taiwan crisis and a possible American attack. Mao excoriated Khrushchev for backing out of Cuba. The last straw was Khrushchev's signature on the Non-Proliferation Treaty, in July 1963. The Soviet leader was now denounced as a revisionist. One of the attractions of the treaty was that it prohibited the transfer of nuclear military technology to China. In October 1964, Khrushchev was criticised for the poor state of relations with China. This was rather unfair. No Soviet politician, defending national interests, could have maintained good relations with China. Mao was a nationalist and put Chinese interests first. He told Soviet ambassador Yudin: 'You can call me a nationalist. If you do, I will say your nationalism extends to the coast of China'.

Eastern Europe

'Define a secure Soviet border.' 'One with Soviet soldiers on both sides of it.'

'What's the difference between bourgeois democracy and socialist democracy?' 'The same as between a chair and an electric chair.'

'What would have happened had the first socialist country been established in the Sahara desert instead of the Soviet Union?' 'It would have run out of sand.'

Khrushchev made a pilgrimage to Yugoslavia, in May 1955, to try to woo Tito back into the socialist fold. The visit could have terminated before it began as the Soviet pilot was unfamiliar with the airport. Tito welcomed the Soviet delegation and then switched off the microphones. Ever since 1948, Tito had been called the 'fascist hangman of the Yugoslav people'. All this was blamed on Beria. The real culprit, Stalin, could not be named. At the evening reception, the debonair Yugoslavs and their consorts, resplendent in Parisian dresses, looked down their noses at the Soviets in their crumpled, ill-fitting suits. Some of them looked as if they had been pulled through a hedge backwards. Tito made sure Khrushchev imbibed too much. The British ambassador, Sir Frank Roberts, observed the scene:

> 'He had to be carried out between rows of diplomats and other guests on the arms of Tito and Rankovic, with his feet sketching out the motions of walking without ever touching the ground.'

The visit also included a trip to the island of Brioni, Tito's summer residence. The sea was choppy and the Soviets arrived seasick and with green faces. Khrushchev wanted to restore inter-Party relations but this did not interest Tito. He knew the CPSU would want to claim supremacy. Inter-state relations were acceptable. The Cominform was dissolved in April 1956, and Tito visited the Soviet Union in June. The Cominform continued to function as a department of the CC apparatus.

Another startling move in foreign policy was the withdrawal of Soviet troops from Austria. The latter was to be neutral. Porkkala naval base was returned to the Finns. The Warsaw Treaty Organisation was established in May 1955 as a reaction to NATO accepting West German rearmament. The Big Four (Russia, America, Britain and France) convened in Geneva, in July 1955. The main topic was Germany and the Soviets agreed that all-German elections were possible. On his way home, Khrushchev dropped in on Walter Ulbricht, the bespectacled, goatee bearded Stalinist leader of the GDR. He assured him that these elections would only take place with GDR consent.

Moscow needed trade with West Germany. Konrad Adenauer, the conservative West German leader, was invited to Moscow in September 1955. When the subject of the repatriation of German prisoners of war came up, Khrushchev feigned anger. He stamped his foot on the floor, indicating they were all six feet under. Diplomatic relations were established and 9,626 POWs began returning. Some preferred the GDR. This visit gave rise to one of Khrushchev's stories:

> 'Adenauer likes to speak in the name of the two Germanies and to raise the German question in Europe as though we couldn't survive without accepting his terms. But Adenauer does not speak the truth. If you strip him naked and look at him from the rear, you can see clearly that Germany is divided into two parts. However if you look at him from the front, it is equally clear that his view of the German question never did stand up, doesn't stand up and never will stand up.'

Then Khrushchev went off to India, Burma and Afghanistan. So many people wanted to see him in India that he was almost crushed to death.

'Communism fits Poland like a saddle on a cow', Stalin once remarked. It had to be forced down Polish throats. The Poles, after the Secret Speech, saw a chance to disgorge it. Wladyslaw Gomulka, recently out of prison, became the new Party leader. The key question was: is the Party in control? Moscow concluded it was and the Poles gained greater autonomy in domestic affairs but promised to support the Soviet Union in foreign affairs. Events in Hungary took a different turn and developed into a revolution. Imre Nagy was elected leader and took the country out of the Warsaw Pact. Party control was clearly in danger. The Soviet Presidium agonised about intervening militarily: it voted against and then for. Mao and Tito were strongly in favour. Blood flowed. János Kádár became the new Party leader. His brief was the 'normalisation of the country'. Budapest had to be patched up and goods sent in. This was money Moscow could ill afford. Some Hungarians had been misled into believing that the West would intervene militarily. This did not occur as Britain and France had invaded Egypt to take control of the Suez Canal. It had been nationalised by Nasser. One of the reasons for the failure of the mission was that the Americans strongly opposed it. Khrushchev weighed in by threatening to use atomic weapons if Britain and France did not back off.

Relations with America

'What is the difference between capitalism and socialism?' 'Capitalism is the exploitation of man by man.' 'And socialism?' 'Under socialism, it is the other way round.'

'Why is communism superior to capitalism?' 'Because it heroically overcomes problems that do not exist in any other system.'

'We are free', says the American. 'I can march up to the White House and shout. Down with Eisenhower.' 'Big deal', says the Russian, 'I can march up to the Kremlin and shout, Down with Eisenhower.'

The space age was launched on 4 October 1957 when Sputnik circumnavigated the globe every 96 minutes for three months. It then returned to the earth's atmosphere and burned out. Khrushchev thought this gave him the edge in the superpower contest and decided to push America to the limit. He was a risk taker but did not want war. West Berlin, surrounded by GDR territory, was the West's Achilles' heel. He called it the West's 'balls'. Every 'time I squeeze them, the West squeals'. Rustic but right. He needed to reduce arms expenditure – nuclear arms were hugely expensive – and hoped his rockets might force the Americans to talks. The Berlin crises of 1958–63 were provoked by Khrushchev. Socialism could not be built in the GDR if the frontier with West Berlin remained open. All the talent was walking away. In November 1958, the first ultimatum was delivered. Berlin should become a free city. If the Americans used force, a third world war would result.

The Americans thought that if they invited him to visit, he would become more amenable to reason. He went, in September 1959, and got on well with President Eisenhower. The Berlin ultimatum was withdrawn. His greatest regret was that he did not visit Disneyland. His security could not be guaranteed. One of the 'ducks' might shoot him. The Paris summit, in May 1960, promised much. But just beforehand Gary Powers, flying a U2 spy plane, was shot down over Sverdlovsk (Ekaterinburg). Khrushchev demanded that Eisenhower apologise publicly. That was the end of the relationship. Khrushchev went off to the United Nations and made various proposals, including moving the headquarters to Austria, Switzerland or the Soviet Union. Diplomatically he made no impact. However he was a sensation as an actor. He shouted, laughed, insulted speakers and banged his shoe on his desk.

19.1 Nikita Khrushchev and President Dwight Eisenhower
Source: A 1959 Herblock Cartoon, copyright by The Herb Block Foundation.

Yury Gagarin's first flight in space, in April 1961, was a boost. Khrushchev and the new young American President, John F. Kennedy, met in Vienna in June 1961. He thought Kennedy would buckle under pressure. On 13 August 1961, Ulbricht was permitted to build the Berlin Wall. It split Berlin in two and also surrounded the city. The Americans brought their tanks up to the wall but that was all. In 1962–63 the Soviets interfered with traffic on the air routes to Berlin and stopped a US military convoy en route to Berlin. Each time the Russians backed down. Khrushchev was an unpredictable leader. He mixed threats with offers to negotiate. He could, therefore, not be trusted. The Berlin problem was resolved in September 1971, when a quadripartite (Russia, America, Britain and France) agreement was signed.

The Cuban crisis was more dangerous. The Americans had attempted, in April 1961, to overthrow Castro's communist regime. They would try again. Khrushchev installed short range nuclear missiles in Cuba. There were 42,000

Soviet troops there. On 25 October 1962, Russian ships heading for Cuba were turned back. Plans to take out the missile sites before they became operational were almost complete. The most dangerous day was 27 October. A Soviet submarine almost fired a nuclear torpedo. On 28 October, Khrushchev announced that the nuclear missiles would be dismantled and shipped back to the Soviet Union. In a secret agreement, Washington promised to remove its Jupiter missiles from Turkey. Castro was furious. He had argued for a Soviet nuclear attack on America even though this meant the devastation of Cuba. He was not informed by the Russians of the backdown. When an official reported what he had heard on the radio, it took Castro about five minutes to take it in. He called Khrushchev a bastard, an idiot without balls and a homosexual. Khrushchev read Castro's behaviour as an attempt to drag the USSR into a war with America. The Soviet Union now had to tread very warily. Two of its allies, China and Cuba, were attempting to enmesh it in a war with the United States.

Khrushchev set about repairing fences with Castro. He was invited to make a grand tour in April 1963. Soviet military hardware debts were written off; sugar was to be imported at inflated prices and oil to be delivered at very low prices. One estimate put the benefits to Cuba at $6 billion annually.

The coup to remove Khrushchev

Who stood to gain most from the removal of Khrushchev? Leonid Brezhnev and Nikolai Podgorny (1903–83). Brezhnev, according to Semichastny, KGB boss, proposed the elimination of Khrushchev several times. A car or plane crash could be arranged. Semichastny maintains that he rejected all these suggestions. The main organiser of the coup was Aleksandr Shelepin. The Presidium met on 12 October 1964. Dmitry Polyansky delivered the main report. The main accusations are listed below. Khrushchev, holidaying in Pitsunda, on the Black Sea, was summoned to Moscow, on 13 October 1964. This time Leonid Brezhnev took the floor. He repeated the main accusations. Khrushchev responded. Then Petr Shelest (1908–96), Ukrainian Party boss, spoke. Ukraine was a traditional bastion of support for Khrushchev. But Shelest deserted him. The most carefully crafted speech was by Aleksandr Shelepin. It followed closely Polyansky's conclusions. For good measure, Shelepin added some more damning statistics: national income growth had declined from 11 per cent to 4 per cent annually during the First Secretary's stewardship. Mikoyan found some positive words, blaming Khrushchev's close colleagues. This found no support among the others. Thereby Mikoyan said goodbye to his long political career. The session ended on 14 October 1964. So too did Khrushchev's reign as Party and government leader. Stalin had handed him his baton but he dropped it. Now it would be up to Leonid Brezhnev to repair the damage. As we shall see, this task was beyond him.

When asked in retirement what he most regretted about his role under Stalin, Khrushchev answered: 'Most of all the blood. My arms are up to the elbows in blood. That is the most terrible thing that lies in my soul'.

What were the main accusations against Khrushchev?

- He had attempted to develop his own cult of personality.

- He ignored the elementary rules of leadership: he called his colleagues obscene, insulting names.

- The Party Programme, adopted in 1961, was unrealistic; not based on serious economic research, consultation with economic experts; programme far removed from reality.

- Growth between 1950 and 1956 was between 10.6 and 11.1 per cent annually; from 1959 to 1963, fell from 6.9 to 5 per cent; Khrushchev presented first period as failure and latter period as success; statistically false.

- Proclaimed priority of growth of light and consumer goods industries (group B); in reality, heavy industry (group A) grew twice as fast as group B.

- Labour productivity declined.

- Did not catch up with United States.

- Industrial reforms slowed down introduction of new technology.

- Construction of pre-fabricated five storey buildings was misguided; communications infrastructure cheaper per square metre of housing in 9–12 storey blocks.

- Twenty years after end of war, agricultural production was such that ration cards had to be introduced; 860 tonnes of gold sold to buy food from capitalist countries.

- Plans to raise living standards in the countryside failed; workday wage of kolkhoznik rose from 1 ruble 56 kopeks, in 1958, to 1 ruble 89 kopeks, in 1963; average monthly wage of kolkhoznik 37–40 rubles; compared to 1940, position worse; in 1940, each kolkhoz family received 0.8 tonnes of grain; in 1963, this was down to 0.4 tonnes.

- Economic situation after restructuring (word used was perestroika) of administration worse; sharpest criticism reserved for introduction of production principle – splitting Party, state, soviet organisations into industrial and agricultural sections; shortages of grain, vegetables, meat and milk but no shortage of administrative changes.

- In foreign policy guilty of adventurism; this had brought the country to the verge of war on several occasions.

- Suez crisis: Soviet Union within a hairsbreadth of major war.

- Berlin crisis: Khrushchev presented President Kennedy with an impossible ultimatum: either Berlin becomes a free city or there will be war; 'we are not foolish enough to think it is worth starting a war to make Berlin a free city'.

- Cuban Missile Crisis: this almost started a nuclear war; 'finding no way out of the crisis, we had to accept all American demands and conditions, including the shameful inspection of our ships'.

- China: Khrushchev called Mao Zedong an 'old boot'; he lectured the Romanian President on how to develop agriculture; he told the Algerian leader, Ben Bella, that Castro was a 'bull, charging at any red flag'.

- Economic aid to Third World a failure; Guinea received considerable Soviet investments but 'we were pushed out'; in Iraq, Soviet Union involved in over 200 projects; despite this, new leader was enemy of the Soviet Union and communists; the same happened in Syria and Indonesia; large amount of aid and arms sent to India, Ethiopia and other countries.

- Khrushchev's conduct of foreign policy caused offence; spent days, even a month abroad, at any one time, accompanied by a large entourage, including many members of his family; in 1963, spent 170 days abroad; January–October 1964, 150 days abroad; extravagant behaviour; threats to drive opponents 'three metres into the ground'; banged shoe at United Nations; he warned the West German ambassador, in Moscow: '[W]e'll wipe all you Germans off the face of the earth'; he turned his son-in-law, Aleksei Adzhubei, whom he had made editor in chief of *Izvestiya*, into his unofficial Foreign Minister.

- Khrushchev was ignorant, incompetent, caddish and an adventurer in domestic and foreign policy; an example of this was the Party Programme and the goal of attaining communism in a short time.

Source: Pikhoya, Sovetsky Soyuz: Istoriya Vlasti 1945–1991 (1998);
Lewin, The Soviet Century (2005).

'In 1952 someone said Stalin was a fool. They shot him there and then. Just the other day, someone said Khrushchev was a fool. He got eight years for revealing a state secret.'

A comrade is arrested for telling jokes and is brought to Khrushchev. 'What furniture, what carpets', enthuses the man. 'Soon everyone in our country will have such things', says Khrushchev. 'Come on, it's one or the other', says the man, 'Either you tell the jokes or I will!'

Questions

1 How did Khrushchev rise above the triumvirate of collective leadership (1953–55) and secure his position as top dog in the CPSU?

2 What impact did Khrushchev's denunciation of Stalin have on Soviet society?

3 What did Khrushchev's de-Stalinisation campaign involve?

4 'Khrushchev used "de-Stalinisation" merely as a means to legitimise his position within the CPSU. He was not fully committed to the campaign.' Discuss.

5 What were Khrushchev's major successes and failures in the spheres of agriculture, industry and foreign policy?

6 How did Khrushchev attempt to revitalise the Communist Party after its downgrading by Stalin? Did his reforms of the CPSU have the expected outcome?

7 Outline the main features of Khrushchev's policy-making style.

8 What was Khrushchev's greatest achievement in foreign policy and did ideology inform his foreign policy as much as it had Stalin's?

9 Did Khrushchev genuinely intend to democratise the Soviet Union?

10 Why and how was Khrushchev ousted in 1964? Why was he able to retain his position in 1957 but not in 1964?

Further reading

Donald Filtzer, *The Khrushchev Era: De-Stalinisation and the Limits of Reform in the USSR, 1953–1964* (1993); William Taubman, *Khrushchev: The Man and His Era* (2003); Moshe Lewin, *The Soviet Century* (2005); Melanie Ilic, Susan E. Reid and Lynne Attwood (eds), *Women in the Khrushchev Era* (2004).

CHAPTER 20

The Brezhnev era

Leonid (Lenya) was universally perceived as a dimwit. However unfair this may have been, it gave rise to a multitude of jokes at his expense. Nevertheless, everyone was expected to extol his virtues and to acknowledge him as a wise leader.

'Have you heard that Brezhnev is going to have surgery? He's having his chest widened to accommodate more medals.'

The Brezhnev era breaks down into three phases:

1   1964–68: Leonid Brezhnev emerges as the dominant Soviet leader, pushing Aleksei Kosygin aside. Attempts are made to make industry and agriculture more dynamic. Socialism with a human face in Czechoslovakia, in the spring of 1968, is the first great challenge. The Warsaw Pact invasion, in August 1968, ends an alternative, more popular brand of Marxist socialism. It also kills off reform in the Soviet Union. The deeply ingrained Russian belief in centralisation reasserts itself. The Brezhnev doctrine means that it is the comrade in the Kremlin who decides if socialism was under threat in the world-wide socialist commonwealth. Naturally the Chinese reject this. Moscow is claiming greater responsibility for the socialist world at a time of declining economic growth.

2   1969–75: The Soviet Union looks inwards and becomes culturally conservative. No real attempt is made to address the economic problems facing the country. The Party and governmental apparatuses consolidate their power. The KGB, under Andropov, becomes a force in the land as opposition from the intelligentsia and ordinary people mounts. The belief grows that the national liberation movements in the Third World are paving

20.1 Children in Kalinin (now Tver), 1965

20.2 First day at School, 1 September 1965, Novgorod

20.3 Schoolgirl in Novgorod, 1 September 1965

the way for the defeat of American imperialism. Mao provokes a war scare by killing Soviet border guards in March 1969; Russians kill many Chinese and also penetrate Xinjiang. Strategic Arms Limitation Treaty (SALT I) signed in 1972. Brezhnev signs the Helsinki Final Act, in 1975. It confirms the post-war boundaries in Europe. However, Brezhnev concedes that human rights are of a universal character.

3   1976–82: Brezhnev becomes dependent on drugs and his health gradually declines. Corruption increases and economic problems mount. Limited reform attempted but this dies with Kosygin, in 1980. Some successes in foreign policy: SALT II, signed in 1979. Sad decline into senility.

Consolidating power

A collective leadership took over from the wilful Khrushchev. However, the rules of the Soviet game meant that someone would try to become dominant. In order to ensure that no leader wielded as much destructive power as Khrushchev, it was agreed that the posts of Party leader and Prime Minister would always be held by different comrades. This meant that Brezhnev, the Party leader, and Kosygin, the head of government, were equal. This was not a natural state of affairs. Brezhnev attempted, and succeeded, in securing dominance.

October 1964	Brezhnev becomes Party leader and Kosygin Prime Minister. It is the same situation as in 1953. Kosygin acts in name of the Soviet Union internationally. No clear order of precedence. However Politburo key institution; Kosygin, of course, is a full member.
1966	Brezhnev becomes *primus inter pares* (first among equals).
August 1968	Crisis in Czechoslovakia makes Brezhnev clearly number one; Party leader is responsible for relations with all communist states; Brezhnev headed team which negotiated with Czechoslovaks; Kosygin, who opposed invasion, pushed aside.
September 1968–November 1982	Party key institution.
November 1982–February 1984	Party key institution under Andropov.
February 1984–March 1985	Party key institution under Chernenko.

FIGURE 20.1 Power in the state, 1964–82

Brezhnev promised stability. Khrushchev had tampered with the Party apparatus and this had produced instability. He had also harmed the Party's authority. Previously leaders had been distant from the people and had been regarded as wise. Khrushchev, on the other hand, was folksy, human, down to earth and full of crazy ideas. This broke the spell of Party omniscience. He had promised an earthly paradise. All he delivered were queues for basic essentials. He became the butt of myriad jokes; all representing him as a fool. Brezhnev would have to restore some gravitas to the post of Party leader.

At the November 1964 CC plenum, Khrushchev's Party reforms were annulled. The party apparatus returned to its territorial subdivisions. The Party boss assumed responsibility for everything in his raion, oblast, krai or republic. The former soviets, Komsomol and trade union organisations were reconstituted. At the September 1965 CC plenum the sovnarkhozes were abolished and replaced by branch ministries. The Party division into industrial and agricultural sections also ended.

There was a Khrushchev monster which was potentially dangerous: the Committee of Party-State Control. Its head, Shelepin, had masterminded the removal of Khrushchev. He might do the same to Brezhnev. The new First Secretary found a clever solution to this problem. The committee was renamed the Committee of People's Control. As such it did not need such a high profile official to head it. Shelepin remained its chair and also a CC secretary. However, he lost his position as deputy Prime Minister. He would later be pushed sideways to head the trade unions – a non-position for a leading politician. Brezhnev had won the first round in his battle to become dominant leader.

Agriculture

Every new Soviet leader began by lambasting the record of his predecessor. A key element was the food question. As agriculture was Khrushchev's pet sector, he was a sitting duck. Brezhnev, at the March 1965 CC plenum, launched his panacea to solve the eternal problem of producing enough food. He paraded past failures. Grain output per hectare was down to 0.7 tonnes in 1963. Grain production per head of the population in 1913 was 540 kg but in 1963 it was only 573 kg. Huge farms for the production of milk products, pork, chicken and grain were to be set up. At the May 1966 CC plenum it was decided to invest up to 10 billion rubles in irrigation projects in Central Asia and southern Russia. The flow of the northern rivers could be turned southwards. This would irrigate the dry steppes of Kazakhstan and Central Asia. This grandiose, ill-advised scheme only ran into the sand under Gorbachev. The great increase in investment benefited agriculture little. Those who gained most were the ministries and construction companies. They, however, had no material interest in the end result. One example will suffice to underline the lack of interest. Irrigation canals were built without any plastic being put under the concrete canals. At least one-third of the water trickled into the ground.

On 1 July 1966, a guaranteed minimum wage was introduced for kolkhozniks. This did not achieve much as kolkhoz pay was less than a quarter of their total income. It became clear that expanding production on the private plot would not solve the food problem.

20.4 A man's best friend, Khiva, Uzbekistan, 1973

The situation became so serious that, in 1974, a food programme was announced. This, unfortunately, signalled to everyone that there was a crisis. Why should a country with so much fertile land need a food programme? The problem was that more and more goods were going into the shadow economy. Good meat could only be obtained in the private markets. The leadership needed to cut investment so as to provide more funds for the defence budget. It decided, in 1977, to reduce the quality of vodka and tobacco. This had a negative impact on the health of the population, especially in the Russian Federation and Ukraine, which were hard drinking republics. The quality of cheese and sausages dropped, as did that of bread.

'What are the main obstacles obstructing Soviet agriculture?' 'There are four: spring, summer, autumn and winter.'

Industrial reform

There was vigorous debate in the economics journals and institutes about how to raise the effectiveness of socialist industry. A brilliant mathematical economist, V. S. Nemchinov, proposed a radical solution. Enterprises should propose their own plans and Gosplan should collate these offers and arrive at an optimal plan. Factories would, therefore, have a greater economic interest in fulfilling plans. This was called the khozraschet (economic accounting) approach.

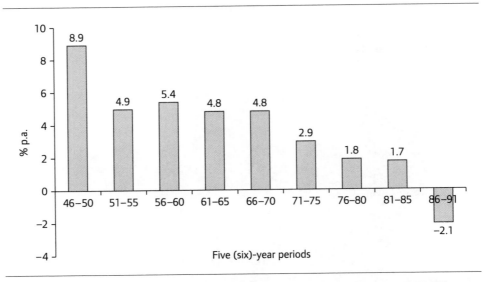

FIGURE 20.2 Soviet gross national product: average annual growth rates, 1945–91

Source: Philip Hanson, *The Rise and Fall of the Soviet Economy: An Economic History of the USSR from 1945* (2003).

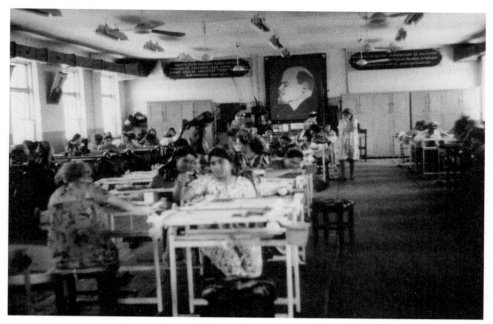

20.5 Factory workers in Bukhara, Uzbekistan, 1973

Kosygin, at the September 1965 CC plenum, declared that the abolition of the sovnarkhozes did not imply returning to the pre-1957 system. He peppered his speech with words such as market, profit and the effectiveness of capital investment. He wanted to see a great expansion of planning at the enterprise and economic association level. A basic problem was that existing prices did not reflect relative scarcity. They reflected planners' or rather politicians' preferences. Prices for coal, iron ore and sulphuric acid were low. This meant that the coal industry, for instance, was loss making. In 1964, it reported a loss of 16 per cent. In many defence industries profitability was very high. In light industry almost all production was loss making. The milk and fish industries just about broke even. The oil and gas industries were doing very well.

Prevailing wisdom states that the Kosygin reforms were a step in the right direction. However, their effectiveness was blocked by central authorities who would not give up their powers. Hanson (2003) quotes Vladimir Kontorovich to refute these arguments. According to Kontorovich, the Soviet planned economy was a coherent whole. Reforms which increased local decision making were likely to make it less effective and reduce growth rates. Kontorovich is claiming that the Stalinist economic model should be left in place. Khrushchev's sovnarkhoz reform had a negative impact and Kosygin's changes were also not, on balance, positive. The fact that they were not fully implemented by the administration prevented more economic damage.

The 23rd Party Congress

A Communist Party Congress is in progress and comrade Brezhnev is mumbling through his speech. In the gallery, some people are craning their necks to see the speaker better. One fellow asks the man in front, 'Could you move slightly to the right? Thanks. Now could you bend forward a bit? Thanks. No, that's too much?' The fellow in front asks, irritated, without turning, 'Do you want my binoculars, perhaps?' 'No thanks, I've got a telescopic sight!' End of story but there is a sequel. The fellow in the back row shoots, misses, is duly apprehended and taken to the KGB for interrogation. There follows the regular KGB routine: blinding light in the victim's face, rubber truncheons, who are your accomplices?, etc. This goes on round the clock, and in an unguarded moment in the small hours of the morning the KGB interrogator asks a question straight from the heart: 'Look, you idiot, how could you miss, with your telescopic sight?' That really hurt him. 'Try it yourself, with everybody shoving and pushing, Let me have a go, no, let me . . .'

This joke was actually based on fact. Viktor Ilyin, born in 1947, was a psychopath. He decided to kill Brezhnev so that he would be replaced by Mikhail Suslov, known to some as Misha the Insipid. He obtained two pistols and, on 22 January 1969, started firing at Brezhnev's motorcade as it drove through the Kremlin's gate. He had no idea where exactly Brezhnev was and only succeeded in killing one of the chauffeurs and wounding a cyclist. Ilyin was interrogated by none other than the future Gensek Yury Andropov, who eventually decided to send him to a mental hospital for 20 years.

The long awaited Congress met in April 1966. It was packed with Brezhnev supporters. Predictably, he launched into a litany of complaints about his predecessor. The Party apparatus had been thrown into confusion. The requirement to rotate cadres was ill judged. The delegates loved it. The Presidium became the Politburo again and the First Secretary, General Secretary or Gensek. All very Stalinist.

Culture

'What is a Soviet string quartet?' 'The Moscow Symphony Orchestra on its return from a foreign tour.'

A rabbit runs across the road in front of a school bus. 'Who is that?', asks the teacher. The children are silent. 'Well, whom do we sing so many songs about?' The children (in unison): 'It's Grandad Lenin.'

What was to replace Khrushchev's fairy-tale land of communism, shimmering on the horizon? A dose of reality? Poets such as Andrei Voznesensky and Evgeny Evtushenko and the novelist, Boris Aksenov, got positive reviews in *Kommunist*, the Party's theoretical journal. However the case of Andrei Sinyavsky and Yuli Daniel set the scene for the new era. The former was sentenced to seven years' and the latter to five years' hard labour. The main accusation against them was that over the period 1956–63 they had sent their work abroad for publication. In the KGB's view it was 'anti-Soviet'. Under the guise of literary work, they were calling for the overthrow of the socialist system. They had met Khrushchev several times. A massive propaganda campaign was launched in the media against them. The intellectual opposition came up with a new tactic. Letters, from many leading cultural figures, in defence of Sinyavsky and Daniel, were forwarded to the 23rd Congress and USSR Supreme Soviet. From the mid-1960s, this became a new way of registering political opposition. These letters were handwritten, then copied and distributed via samizdat (self-publishing). They then found their way abroad and were published there. Their contents became known to a wider audience through being broadcast by foreign radio stations, such as Voice of America and the BBC Russian service. This forced the KGB to act against the signatories.

The authorities were obliged to sharpen the legal justification for their persecution of these writers. In September 1966, an additional article was added to the Russian Federation penal code. It was now a crime to distribute 'false information harmful to Soviet state and society'. Dishonouring the Soviet state emblem or flag was also a crime.

On 5 December 1965, in Pushkin square, in Moscow, Andrei Sakharov, one of the fathers of the Soviet atomic bomb, Aleksandr Ginsburg, Vladimir Bukovsky, Andrei Amalrik, and other literary figures staged a demonstration. They demanded that the Soviet government observe its own laws. This was the forerunner of the human rights movement. Public opinion was divided into two main groups: those who sided with Stalin, such as the journal *Oktyabr*, and those who were anti-Stalinists. Brezhnev spoke of Stalin's contribution as commander-in-chief during the war. This was greeted with great applause. Twenty-five leading cultural figures fired back a riposte to national leaders. The greatest waves of all were made by Alexander Solzhenitsyn. He demanded an end to the 'subjugation' of literature to censorship. What were the authorities to do with him? Semichastny, the KGB chief, suggested he be expelled from the Union of Writers. Eighty-four writers defended Solzhenitsyn. He could not be put in prison as he had eloquently attacked the penal system in his works. Could he be persuaded to recant? The solution adopted was to revert to an old Leninist practice. Deprive the recalcitrant of his citizenship and expel him. On 15 April 1968, the Politburo decided to do this (Pikhoya 1998). The leaders admitted defeat. Internationally, they suffered an even greater defeat.

Czechoslovakia

If Solzhenitsyn was an embarrassment, there was an even greater one brewing on the borders of the Soviet Union. Brezhnev, as Party leader, was responsible for relations with other socialist states. His first great test was Czechoslovakia. He had visited Prague and accepted the removal of the Stalinist Antonín Novotný as Party leader. Alexander Dubček, a Slovak, took over. The Czechoslovak Party was convinced it had the right to develop its own brand of socialism. This became known as socialism with a human face. Dubček was not a strong leader and soon found himself being carried along by a mood which became more and more radical. This alarmed Moscow. Brezhnev went to see for himself and was assured that everything was under control. He tried to find a peaceful solution. Conservatives in Moscow began advocating military intervention. Walter Ulbricht, the GDR leader, was very keen on this as he feared contagion spreading from his southern frontier. Various meetings, sometimes with Warsaw Pact members present, sometimes with most of the Soviet Politburo, were held to try to find a solution which would satisfy everyone. The fatal mistake the Czechoslovaks made was to discount a military invasion. The Warsaw Pact intervened on 21 August 1968. Moscow had checked with Washington beforehand. The Americans, obligingly, confirmed that Czechoslovakia was within the Soviet zone of influence. The Russians wanted to set up a government of national salvation. They could not find anyone of stature to serve on it.

Military intervention in Czechoslovakia revealed that inter-party disputes about the development of socialism could not be solved without resorting to force. It demonstrated the weakness of the Soviet Party. It had authority but declining power. Khrushchev had intervened in Hungary and got away with it. The West's attention had been deflected by the Suez crisis. This time the full gaze of world opinion was directed at Prague. The legitimacy of the Soviet Party world-wide dropped. This led to the emergence of Eurocommunism in Western Europe. The Soviet Party never recovered from this self-inflicted blow.

From Prague to Helsinki

The rejection of socialism with a human face gave rise to the view that any attempt to improve socialism amounted to revisionism. It provided a bridge across which capitalist ideas could penetrate the land of socialism. The cold winds of orthodoxy became a blizzard after 1969 in the academic world. The Party apparatus had the task of imposing greater Party authority in all arts, social sciences and hard sciences. This affected history, always a volatile subject, economics (debate about introducing the market mechanism in the socialist economy was no longer acceptable), sociology, literature and other arts. More discipline was needed in the Academy of Sciences where scientists were wont to afford little weight to Party pronouncements. I was struck, as a postgraduate student in Moscow in 1969, by the lack of respect accorded Brezhnev by scientists.

Solzhenitsyn was awarded the Nobel Prize for literature in 1970. Should he be allowed to collect it and then be refused re-entry to the Soviet Union? He did not go. When the KGB discovered the first part of *The Gulag Archipelago* they acted. He was arrested, charged with treason and expelled from the Soviet Union in February 1974. He collected his Nobel Prize in 1974. Mikhail Gorbachev dropped the charge of treason and restored his Soviet citizenship. He returned to live in Russia, from the United States, in 1994.

The crisis of faith in Marxism was brought home to Vladimir Soloukhin, the writer. He visited Yaroslav Smelyakov (1913–72) just before his death. Smelyakov, a much decorated poet and a member of the USSR Supreme Soviet, had spent a lifetime exhalting Party and Soviet power. 'I have wasted my life', he told Soloukhin. This tragic admission profoundly affected Soloukhin and was one of the reasons why he never committed himself to the regime. In *Chitaya Lenina* (1989) he traced the receipts that Lenin had signed when receiving money from businessmen linked to German intelligence. Hence he contributed to the demolition of the Lenin myth.

The Politburo split on how to commemorate the twenty-fifth anniversary of the defeat of Germany. How was Stalin to be presented? The majority wanted to stress the positive aspects of Stalin's leadership. Opponents pointed out that this would result in a loss of credibility as everyone had previously condemned Stalin. Brezhnev was opposed but during the decisive meeting changed his mind. Comrade Stalin was, indeed, a great war leader.

This made life easier for the KGB. As long as Stalin was in the dog house, the opposition could pour abuse on the past and demand changes in the present. The KGB discovered opposition groups in Saratov and Sverdlovsk (Ekaterinburg). They were mainly composed of young students and workers. Gradually young radicals lost their faith in Soviet socialism. One coined the expression: minus the future plus the past equals socialism. Valery Chalidze, in 1970, set up the Committee for the Protection of Human Rights. Academician Andrei Sakharov joined. This was the new direction of protest. A Soviet branch of Amnesty International appeared in 1973. Brezhnev's signing of the Helsinki Final Act, on 1 August 1975, was a great boost for the human rights' movement. The Soviet Union now accepted that human rights were universal.

The KGB changed tactics. Those arraigned before the courts halved between 1959 and 66 and 1967 and 74. This was not because there was less opposition but because 'prophylactic' measures had been proving more effective. These ranged from a quiet word to a stern warning. Whereas 2,423 appeared in court over the years 1971 to 74, 63,108 were dealt with prophylatically. This reveals that the

KGB devoted most of its energies to combating political opposition throughout the country. Little time was devoted to catching spies. Over the same period, 114 foreigners were deported for 'ideological diversion' and 679 were denied entry visas. The KGB never troubled me on my numerous trips. Perhaps it was because I played the role of a dumb foreigner well.

Urbanisation

Urbanisation transformed the Soviet Union. It produced a new type of society. In the 1930s, millions had moved from the countryside to the towns. In many ways, they ruralised the cities. The Soviet Union became a semi-urban society in the 1960s when the majority of citizens in the Russian Federation, Ukraine and the Baltic States lived in towns and cities. Until 1958, each republic had its own definition of a town. Then it was decided that a town had a minimum of 12,000 inhabitants. Gosplan did not plan labour flows. It decided investment and left the availability of labour to spontaneity. Those who wished could move to new jobs where pay and conditions were better. Labour law permitted workers to give notice and leave. If labour was not planned then it followed that migration was also not planned. Gradually citizens gained greater control over certain aspects of their lives.

Population flows were of two kinds: out of the villages into the towns and out of the towns into the villages. In the Russian Federation, over the years 1961–66, almost 29 million arrived in towns and 24.2 million left. This adds up to a total of 53.2 million migrants. The population of the Russian Federation, according to the 1970 census, was 130.1 million. If one assumes that the population was several million less in the first half of the 1960s, this means that 45 per cent of the population moved. That is an astonishingly high figure. Various conclusions can be drawn from this. One is that almost half the population were dissatisfied with their working and living conditions in their home town or village. There was a particularly large inflow to and outflow for Siberia and the Far East. This was because of the lamentably bad housing conditions. Unfortunately for the economy, these were regions which desperately needed extra labour.

Gosplan, although it did not attempt to manage the labour supply, produced very good research studies on labour problems. One was undertaken in 1965 (Lewin 2005). Over the years 1959–63, the working population had grown by 9 million but manpower had only increased by 1.7 million. In other words, an extra 7.3 million workers had been recruited from those who worked at home and on their private plot. These were predominantly female. Not surprisingly, Central Asia had a large labour surplus. This was partly due to the increase in births, which were twice the Union average. Labour surpluses were building up in Armenia and Central Asia but in Estonia and Latvia the low birth rate meant that

20.6 Relaxing at home in Bukhara, Uzbekistan, 1973

extra labour had to come from elsewhere. Those leaving Siberia often made for the sun belt regions in the south, which already had labour surpluses.

The report stated that there had been increased investment in the east without commensurate labour incentives. On the other hand, there had been less investment in labour surplus areas. Khrushchev's cutting back on the private plot had cost 3.5 million jobs in the countryside and had exacerbated food shortages. There were seldom alternative jobs to go to. Ambitious girls moved to the towns, followed by those boys who wanted a wife. The net result was that there was not enough agricultural labour. Enterprises were obliged to assume responsibility for cultivation and harvesting and constructing and maintaining buildings on their dedicated farm. Some of the produce went to the state and the rest was theirs.

However, it meant that they had to maintain a reserve labour force for this seasonal work. Kolkhozniks soon discovered that industrial workers were paid up to three times as much as they were. Some moved to the towns and joined the factory labour force.

In 1968, a Gosplan specialist assessed the demographic situation. Over the previous 20 years, the country had experienced an extraordinary growth of its large towns and cities. The proportion of those living in small towns had declined. Between 1926 and 1960 the population of cities of over half a million had multiplied by a factor of 5.9. The number of small towns had dropped 17 per cent in the Russian Federation. Those living in towns with fewer than 10,000 inhabitants only accounted for 1 per cent of the Russian population. The pattern in the United States was the opposite. Why was Soviet experience so different? A Russian librarian once explained to me why. Prospects of promotion and the quality of life in small towns were dismal. She managed to move over time from one job to another, always moving to a larger town. Eventually she reached her goal, Moscow. She had arrived. She felt she was in a cultured, civilised environment for the first time.

In the Russian Federation there was a peculiar phenomenon: the one industry town. This applied to over 300 towns. A striking example was Ivanovo-Voznesensk, where textiles were king, or rather queen. Labour was overwhelmingly female. What did the unemployed males do? They could work on their private plot or migrate. This seriously affected social life. In some towns male unemployment reached 57 per cent. The national average was 13 per cent. Not surprisingly, labour turnover was much higher than elsewhere. Many textile factories had to attract female labour from outside. However, they did not stay long. The net result was low population growth and high levels of migration. In small towns there were 125 women for every 100 men in the Russian Federation. Gosplan did not concern itself with sexual imbalance in the labour force. It was simply left to the labour market. There was also a labour market for specialists and this enhanced the standing of the intelligentsia.

The number of *nachalniki* (bosses) and *rukovoditeli* (managers), 1.5 million in 1939, had grown to about 4 million by 1970. They were a formidable interest group. They built factories in towns where they were prohibited. Even phantom factories were added to the plan. They hoarded labour and reserves (some factories had two or three years' supplies of inputs). They built up retinues which served their every whim. Where did the money come from? It came from trading inputs and goods in the shadow economy. Slush funds were also needed to bribe inspectors and other officials. Karen Brutents, a member of the CC apparatus in Moscow, in the late 1960s, shared a room in a nomenklatura sanatorium with an enterprising comrade. He was the manager of a state enterprise employing 28 workers. However, he was very well dressed and had some expensive belongings. He had a thick wad of rubles which he ostentatiously counted in front of Brutents each evening before going to bed. Brutents discovered that the money was to pay nurses and maids for sex (Brutents 2005).

The education level of new entrants into the labour force rose appreciably. They were not satisfied with the primitive working standards of many factories and found work boring and repetitive. Since there was an increasing labour shortage, managers had to provide incentives to keep them. One way of doing this was to pay workers performing unskilled tasks the rates of a skilled worker.

The 1977 constitution

This was most notable for placing the Party in its rightful place: article 6 of the constitution stated that the Party was the 'core of the political system'. In the 1936 constitution, the Party had been relegated to article 126. A new constitution was needed as Khrushchev's Party Programme had promised the advent of communism in 1980. The country now found itself in the era of 'developed socialism'. The working class was no longer the ruling class. A 'socialist, people's state, representing the will and interests of workers, peasants, the intelligentsia and the employees of every nation and nationality of the country', had come into being. The Party statute was altered to underline the fact that the activities of institutions and enterprises were to be supervised by their Party organisations. This led to a mushrooming of Party building everywhere. No decision of importance could be taken without consulting the relevant Party body. Even more than before, becoming a Party member was necessary to make a career.

Each republic was to adopt a new constitution. In the Soviet constitution there was no reference to the official language of the state. It was assumed that all nations and nationalities would gradually merge to form a 'new Soviet people'. In the existing Azerbaijani, Armenian and Georgian constitutions there was an article about republican languages. The fear was that would be excised from the new constitution. This would mean that Azeri, Armenian and Georgian were no longer official languages. This led to large demonstrations, especially in Georgia, demanding that the local language be recognised as official. They got their way.

Oil, gas and gold

A new source of wealth appeared: hydrocarbons. West Siberia turned out to be sitting on vast reserves of oil and gas. In 1970, oil production there was 31 million tonnes. This rose to 312 million tonnes, in 1980. Exploitation of natural gas, over the same period, increased from 9.5 billion to 156 billion cubic metres. Pipelines were built to export these valuable products to the West.

The agricultural crisis forced the Soviet leadership to sell gold in order to buy food abroad.

TABLE 20.1 Gold reserves and sales (tonnes)

Year	Gold reserves	Sold abroad	Of which to purchase food
1963	1,082.3	520.3	372.2
1964	749.1	483.7	–
1965	577.1	335.6	335.3
1966	739.2	5.2	–
1967	864.4	50.2	50.2
1972	1,243.7	458.6	458.2
1973	1,032.0	382.5	382.5
1975	1,221.0	141.0	–
1976	1,001.4	362.8	362.8
1977	774.4	390.0	390.0
1978	498.0	412.0	–
1979	510.0	168.0	158.0
1980	502.0	156.0	156.0
1981	452.0	286.0	–
1982	576.0	30.0	30.0
1990	484.6	–	–
1991	514.0	269.1	–

Source: R. G. Pikhoya, *Sovetsky Soyuz: Istoriya Vlasti 1945–1991* (1998).

Dependency on foreign grain imports was growing. Whereas in 1973 imported grain amounted to 13.2 per cent of domestic production, in 1981 this had risen to 41.4 per cent. Official statistics reveal that the republics were developing at different rates. Republics were investing, per head of the population, two to four times as much as the Russian Federation. This gave rise to the strong belief in the republics that their economic problems were caused by the Russian Federation.

In 1979, the deputy Prime Minister, academician Vladimir Kirillin, delivered a trenchant speech on the state of the economy. He pointed out that a financial crisis was around the corner, industry needed radical restructuring and that the country was falling badly behind technologically. Kirillin's speech provoked such anger that he was dismissed as deputy Prime Minister and his speech was locked away for over ten years (Pikhoya 1998). What does the reaction of the leadership to Kirillin's apt analysis of the Soviet economy tell us? It was unwilling to accept a negative analysis. Kirillin, as an academician, did not have a power base in any of the three powerful networks: KGB, Party or governmental. Kosygin was careful to have Kirillin deliver the devastating verdict on the economy. Basically, it meant that Kosygin had failed as manager of the economy. If a competent technocrat such as Kosygin could not improve economic performance then no one else could.

Vladimir Kirillin came to the University of London just as Gorbachev's perestroika had got under way. Everyone expected a positive analysis. Instead he said that perestroika would not succeed and that the only hope for the Soviet Union was a market economy. I was so astonished that I was certain I had misunderstood his Russian. I asked him to repeat what he had said. He recounted the above devastating dismissal of the Marxist planned economy.

In the early 1970s, special shops were set up for KGB, MVD, government and Party officials. First class produce could be purchased only with vouchers. One could buy 200 rubles worth of vouchers and get excellent food and products to feed a family of five. The same quality goods elsewhere cost 500–600 rubles. Gorbachev determined to close down these special shops when he became Gensek. He did not and they continued to expand.

Kemerovo, in Siberia, was a centre of the mining industry. In 1979, a lecturer arrived to present the Brezhnev regime in the best possible light. The miners quickly confronted him with reality. They informed him that, in fact, they only achieved about a third of the plan. Needless to say official statistics declared that they had fulfilled the plan. The reasons for non-fulfilment were the build-up of gas; the conveyor belts broke down; there was a shortage of safety equipment and so on. The mine had a famous Stakhanovite miner. He was a member of the USSR Soviet and had many awards and medals. How had he achieved his feat? The whole mine had worked for him and he had recorded three times his official norm.

Shops in Kemerovo were full of vodka and little else. A basic test for consumer goods was to visit a store's baby food department. The only thing on the shelves was Stolichnaya vodka. It soon transpired that no one in Kemerovo bought vodka. Why not? Pure spirit was provided by the state to clean the machinery and equipment. The miners simply consumed it.

In 1980, a lecturer visited a huge meat packing plant in Zhdanov, Ukraine. Afterwards he went to lunch in the factory canteen. He ordered meat dumplings. Instead he was served potato dumplings. 'No meat', said the waitress. This meant that all the meat was being diverted into the black market. The management was clearly unconcerned if this was reported to Moscow.

The mounting food crisis provoked strikes in Sverdlovsk, Latvia, Estonia, Chelyabinsk oblast, Ukraine, Sevastopol and Krasnoyarsk krai. So worried was the CC in October 1980 that it adopted a special decree on the 'negative consequences resulting from defects in organisation and pay of workers and employees'. This was newspeak for lack of food and consumer goods.

The leading Russian poet of that period, Andrei Voznesensky, said it all in a poem about queues:

> I am 41st for Plisetskaya [famous ballet dancer],
> 33rd for the theatre at Taganka,
> 45th for the graveyard at Vagankovo,
> I am 14th for the ophthalmologist,
> 21st for Glazunov, the artist,
> 45th for an abortion
> (When my turn comes, I'll be in shape),
> I am 103rd for auto parts
> (They signed me up when I was born),
> I am 10,007th for a new car
> (They signed me up before I was born)

Fedor Kulakov, the CC Secretary of Agriculture, died from a heart attack, aged 60, in June 1978. Embarrassingly, his fatal attack had been brought on by making love to a fair maiden. On paper, the post was a death sentence for an aspiring politician. However, Soviet politics operated by different rules. There were two main candidates for the job. Fedor Morgun, first secretary of Poltava oblast. He had survived over ten years husbanding the virgin lands of northern Kazakhstan. The other candidate was Mikhail Gorbachev. He was first secretary of Stavropol krai. He had made a good impression on Yury Andropov and Mikhail Suslov when they came down from Moscow for a vacation at Mineralny Vody. Morgun was infinitely better qualified but Gorbachev got the nod. When he got to Moscow, he confided that he was unsure whether he was up to the job. 'That's all right', he was told, 'The Gensek trusts you.' Appointing him, Brezhnev said he was a 'young, energetic comrade who was well acquainted with agricultural production'. Gorbachev became a candidate member of the Politburo the following year and a full member in 1980. Since agriculture was in a worse state in 1980 than in 1978, his promotion clearly had nothing to do with agrarian expertise. To be frank, this was limited.

Consumers began to talk of acquiring goods, not buying them. They could be obtained in makeshift markets and from shop assistants. The latter kept desirable goods under the counter for special customers. They cost twice or three times as much as state goods. The price of goods depended on one's position. The ordinary customer paid high prices, the middle level official much less but the top elite paid only a nominal amount for their goods. Resentment grew towards government and Party officials who had access to special stores. Most resented of all was the most senior Party and government stratum. Their wives were ferried in chauffeur-driven black Volgas. Many cities introduced coupons for meat and butter. Letters poured into organisations responsible for the distribution of goods. Enterprises and other institutions pleaded for supplies for their war and labour veterans. If they did procure more, veterans saw few goods. They went immediately into the black market. Top officials were in the strongest position to work the black market. If goods did appear in state shops, every customer tried to buy as many as possible: some for friends and the rest for the black market. No wonder the shops always appeared empty. Muscovites were luckier than other citizens. The 1980 Olympics turned Moscow into a city brimming with food and consumer goods. They all disappeared afterwards.

Brezhnev begins his official speech opening the 1980s Olympic Games: 'O!, O!, O!' His aide whispers to him: 'The speech begins below, comrade Gensek. That is the Olympic symbol.'

The leadership was old. Brezhnev was no longer capable of grasping what was going on. Nevertheless, he was strong enough to pick up the telephone in 1980 and inform Kosygin that he was sacked. He was succeeded as Prime Minister by the aged Nikolai Tikhonov.

Who wielded influence in the late Brezhnev era? One was Andrei Aleksandrov-Agentov, his foreign policy adviser. Another was Aleksandr Blatov. They were influential when personnel appointments were being made. Some senior members of the CC apparatus met from the mid-1970s onwards to discuss how the system could be made more effective. This group also included Evgeny Primakov and high ranking KGB officers. They had experience of the outside world and understood that things had to change after Brezhnev. There was also a perception that the Russian Federation was 'feeding' the other republics. This had to stop. A loose federation was one proposal. This would ensure that each republic was responsible for its own economy.

Mikhail Suslov, *eminence grise* or the grey cardinal, died in May 1982. This was a piece of luck for Andropov. Suslov had been the Party's ideological guardian. As such he was known as the 'second' secretary (ideology). Andropov moved from being KGB chief and became the new 'second' secretary. He was now first in line to succeed the Gensek. On 7 November, the anniversary of the revolution, in bitterly cold weather, Brezhnev stood atop the Lenin mausoleum and welcomed the demonstrators as they filed past. Afterwards he went to his hunting dacha, at Zavidovo, outside Moscow. Two days later, he returned to his Moscow dacha. On the morning of 10 November, the guards found the Gensek dying. They spent half an hour trying to revive him. Andropov was the first to arrive. After hearing the guards' report he left to inform the widow. Next to arrive was Evgeny Chazov, the leadership's personal physician. He listened to what the guards had to say and then asked: 'Where is Andropov?' Party officials around the country were only informed about Brezhnev's death late that evening. One remembers being phoned at 9.30 p.m. He then tried to contact the Kremlin on the special telephone but it did not work.

A telegram was sent at 10.30 p.m. informing officials that the Gensek had died early that morning. The Central Committee gathered at 10 a.m. on 12 November in the Sverdlov hall, in the Kremlin. Andropov delivered a 15 minute eulogy. Then he asked for a minute's silence. Then he said the Party had to strengthen its unity. The 'plenum has to decide whom to elect as General Secretary'. Konstantin Chernenko, head of Brezhnev's private chancellery since 1960 and chief of the CC general department, stood up. He declared that the Politburo had instructed him to propose the 68 year old Yury Andropov as Gensek. He was a 'convinced Marxist-Leninist, broad minded, possessed great political and human qualities and had an excellent grasp of the Brezhnev style of leadership'. Chernenko stressed Andropov's commitment to 'collective, collegial leadership'. Andropov, in reply, stated that he would decide problems 'as far as possible in a collegial manner but not always to everyone's satisfaction'. He was giving notice that there would be radical changes (Pikhoya 1998).

Andropov had something special to say to Party cadres. He told them they did not understand the country or the people they governed. The greatest danger to the Soviet Union was not America or spies but the poverty and destitution of the Soviet people.

The level of corruption in the MVD and KGB was brought home to Andropov in 1980. For some reason, the head of his secretariat decided to travel home on the Moscow underground. He was waylaid, horribly beaten up and later died from his injuries. Andropov was furious and ordered an immediate investigation. It revealed that militia and KGB officers were working hand in glove with gangsters. They jointly carried out muggings, assaults and robberies. About 300 militia and KGB officers were arrested.

Andropov had the reputation of being all-seeing.

At an imaginary question and answer session, an anonymous questioner sends him a note paraphrasing an old Russian proverb that puts the blame for all rottenness on nachalstvo, *the top people. 'Isn't it true that fish start to rot at the head?' 'Of course', replies Andropov, 'but I would remind esteemed comrade Ivanov, fifth row, seat thirteen, that one starts to clean fish at the tail!'*

Under Andropov the KGB waxed in influence. It was better informed about the mood of the country than the Party or government. It was well represented in Gosplan, Gossnab and Goskomstat (state statistics). Andropov sensed that the economy was not in as good a shape as the official statistics suggested. He tried to find out the true state of affairs. Sometimes he encountered a wall of distrust. At least one economist who could have enlightened him refused to do so. He feared the Chekists would play one of their dirty tricks on him. Andropov estimated the number of potential oppositionists in the country at 8.5 million or 3.2 per cent of the population. He was aware that their numbers would grow if the social and economic problems facing the country were not addressed successfully.

It quickly became evident that Andropov's number two was Konstantin Chernenko. He chaired sessions of the Politburo when the Gensek was absent. On paper, he had enormous powers. However, the Gensek knew that he suffered from emphysema and could not sustain a heavy workload. With Chernenko as his preferred successor, there was no danger of a palace coup. Andropov immediately set up a CC economic department to oversee the economy. He recruited Nikolai Ryzhkov from Gosplan, made him a CC secretary, and put him in charge. An engineer by training, Ryzhkov had made his name in Uralmash, a huge defence plant, in Sverdlovsk (Ekaterinburg).

As a Chekist, Andropov understood the role of information. Politburo sessions took place on Thursdays. On Friday morning, radio and TV reported on the 'Politburo in session'. This was revolutionary. Hitherto Politburo discussions were regarded as top secret. He also sanctioned the publication of bad economic news. Corruption in Moscow's Gastronom was laid bare in November 1982. Many citizens saw this as confirmation that the Party and governmental apparatuses were hopelessly corrupt. Restore order and discipline were his slogans.

The KGB raided shops, hotels, restaurants, cinemas and even apprehended passers-by. Nothing was sacred. They even penetrated that most beloved of Russian institutions: the bath house. Whom were they looking for? Citizens who should have been at work. They sought out those on *komandirovki*, business trips. This had become a perk for many and was often a paid holiday. Now they had to pay for their hotel and travel. In fact, this was not terribly onerous as both were very cheap. Stories circulated that Chekists in Moscow were willing to overlook absence from work for a small consideration. It turned out that they were crooks making a fast buck.

When Andropov visited a factory, workers were on their best behaviour. At the obligatory meeting afterwards, one after the other demanded greater production discipline. They told the Gensek what he wanted to hear. He, in turn, warned the bosses, starting from the minister, that they were also included in the new drive for labour discipline. About 150 Chekists were seconded to the MVD to deal with the corrupt Moscow retail trade. An insider later wrote that, apart from a few big names, only the little people were sent to prison. The fat cats, first and foremost in the Party apparatus, continued to enjoy their embezzled wealth. He made the point that corruption always originated in the Party apparatus and then spread outwards. The KGB gave permission for newspapers to publish investigations into corruption. An avalanche of articles, film scripts and thrillers appeared throughout the country. The mafia was now accepted as part of the political system. Anyone could pen a story about good Chekists battling bad mafiosi. Any amount of factual material could be smuggled into the piece. Readers loved it. All mention of Stalin's crimes now disappeared from the press. Self-censorship became the new watchword for Party functionaries. A long biography of Marshal Tukhachevsky ended with the laconic phrase: his life ended tragically.

New blood flowed into the CC apparatus in Moscow. Egor Ligachev had had considerable Party experience in Siberia. He was known as fanatically keen on a healthy lifestyle. He demanded that everyone engage in sport and skiing. He reduced the amount of vodka sold and became a great patron of the local theatre. Grigory Romanov moved from being first secretary of Leningrad oblast to become CC Secretary for Defence. Aleksandr Yakovlev, ambassador in Canada, was brought back to become director of the Institute of the World Economy and International Relations. He had impressed Gorbachev during his visit to Canada in May 1983. Yakovlev arranged for Gorbachev to visit Canadian grain farms. On one, after being told how much land was cultivated, he asked the owner: 'Where are all the workers?' 'My son and I and a hired help run the whole show', he told the incredulous Gorbachev.

Andropov still had a clear mind. He instructed Nikolai Tikhonov, the Prime Minister, to pay close attention to the food problem. As regards Gorbachev, he advised him to spend less time talking about the drought and bad weather and more time about bringing in the harvest. This was a slap in the face for Misha. He was CC Secretary for Agriculture yet Andropov had placed the greater responsibility on the Prime Minister. The subject of the dacha then came up. The regulations were that a dacha could not occupy more than 25 square metres; the veranda around it was not to be more than 10 square metres and no higher than 2.5 metres. Some dacha owners got round these restrictions in ingenious ways. One excavated a two metre deep cellar to increase space! 'It has come to my notice', said Andropov, 'that a certain comrade has built a 120 square metre dacha. He then sold it for 32,000 rubles. His son and daughter also acquired land on which they are, with the help of papa, building their own dachas. Comrades, this is not right and, from my point of view, constitutes an abuse of one's official position.' One day after Mikhail Suslov, Brezhnev's all-powerful ideological secretary, died his family was thrown out of the dacha they had lived in for over a decade. This was to underline that a dacha was a perk and also that those who lose power lose everything.

Korean Airlines KAL 007

On the morning of 1 September 1983, information reached Moscow that an American R-135 spy plane had been shot down over Sakhalin. It turned out to be a Boeing 747 Korean airliner en route from Anchorage, Alaska, to Seoul, South Korea, with 269 passengers on board. How could a Russian pilot, in a Su-15, confuse a huge Boeing 747 with a small spy plane? There had been a spy plane over Soviet territory but it had already left Soviet airspace by the time the unfortunate Boeing appeared. Why was it so far off course? Why was it not ordered to land in Sakhalin? These and other questions poured into Moscow. On 5 September, the commander of air defences conceded that at night, in cloud, it was not possible to distinguish between a spy plane and an airliner. On 8 September, US Secretary of State George Shultz and Soviet Foreign Minister Andrei Gromyko, in Madrid, exchanged insults and blamed one another for the tragedy. Then the Russians took an unprecedented step. They organised a press conference in Moscow, addressed by Marshal Nikolai Ogarkov, Chief of the General Staff. He defended strongly the Soviet position. He also sent a chill down western spines by saying that if another plane appeared in Soviet airspace it would also be shot down. The international atmosphere was as cold as a penguin's foot.

In 1996, the pilot who had shot down the plane admitted that he knew it was a civilian airliner. 'But for me, this meant nothing. It is easy to turn a civil plane into a plane for military use.' He insisted that he had flashed his lights and fired warning shots. However he had not attempted to radio the plane or describe the Boeing 747 to ground control.

Chernenko steps up

A burglar breaks into President Chernenko's apartment in Moscow and steals all his books. The President is very disappointed. He had not finished colouring them in.

President Chernenko phones up the Guinness Book of Records. 'I want to claim a record. I have finished my jigsaw puzzle of the Kremlin in only three months.'

Guinness: 'So what! That is not a record.'

Chernenko: 'But, but it says on the box: 4–6 years.'

Andropov spent 6 of his 15 months in power in hospital. He died on 9 February 1984. The following day, the Politburo met. Tikhonov proposed Chernenko as Gensek. Others supported him, including Gorbachev. It was agreed unanimously and a special CC plenum would formally elect him. Who would be number two? The Politburo was split in two factions: the oldies and the youngsters. The oldies feared that if Gorbachev took over they would be pensioned off. However, it was agreed that every Thursday Gorbachev should wait for a phone call from the half-dead or perhaps half-alive Chernenko. If he gave the go-ahead, Gorbachev could then chair the Politburo meeting. Chernenko ended Andropov's persecution of officialdom. However several implicated in the Moscow trade scandal were shot (Pikhoya 1998).

The most important project was drafting a new Party Programme. What type of socialism existed in the Soviet Union? Was it developed socialism or developing socialism? This archaic theme was deemed important. I once asked a member of the Academy of Sciences what the difference was between developed and developing socialism. His reply was brusque. 'There is no difference and it is all nonsense anyway.'

Chernenko's death, on 10 March 1985, brought the Brezhnev era to an end. The post-Brezhnev era had experienced the communist fundamentalism of Andropov. He had had great faith in the anti-imperialism struggle in the Third World. He had tried to re-ignite fear in the hearts of officials and workers. His dialysis machine gave rise to some terrible jokes: 'Comrade Andropov is the most switched on comrade in Moscow. He can light up any party'. These revealed that he was no longer to be feared.

Crime and corruption

The great Uzbek cotton scam

In Tashkent, the Uzbek Minister of the Cotton Industry calls together the main officials dealing with the industry. It is 1959.

'We have a problem', he says, 'there is no way we can fulfil the plan this year. Comrades, can anyone come up with a solution?'

'Comrade Minister, we cannot resolve this question without the participation of our beloved Party leader, Sharaf Rashidov.'

'Comrades', says the Party leader, 'every problem has a solution. You say you do not have enough cotton to meet the plan. We need to engage in some creative accounting so as to ensure that we meet the plan. We cannot fail as the consequences could be disastrous for all of us.'

'What do you suggest, comrade Rashidov?'

'First decide what the shortfall is. Then work out how many wagons that means. Then fill up the wagons with leftovers and other rubbish.'

'*But the cotton processing plants in our republic, Kazakhstan, Ukraine and the Russian Federation will not accept rubbish as cotton.*'

'*Oh, yes, they will, if you make it worth their while. I mean you will have to pay bribes to everyone. And I mean everyone. There is no way we can palm off leftovers as cotton without the USSR Minister of the Cotton Industry finding out. So everyone in the ministry has to be kept sweet. Then there are the militia and the KGB. Leave them to me. Where will the money to pay bribes come from? Moscow will pay us for imaginary cotton and we shall have a slush fund. The more we inflate the cotton figures the more money will flow from Moscow.*'

And so began the great Uzbek cotton scandal. The scam was so simple, it was absolutely brilliant. A thought flashed through Rashidov's mind. If this scam works, it will work for every other product. Think of the possibilities this will open up.

On 26 January 1984, the Moscow KGB arrested two Uzbek nationals. They were the director and his assistant of an Uzbek cotton factory. They immediately offered a bribe of 40,000 rubles. One of them had 400,000 rubles on his person and the other 700,000 rubles. The Uzbeks were accused of forging documents to show that the Uzbek enterprise had delivered 150 tonnes of cotton to the Moscow factory. Over the period January–March 1984, many Uzbek enterprise directors and others were arrested. Money and valuables worth 2.3 million rubles were confiscated. Ministers in Kazakhstan, Turkmenistan and Azerbaijan were also arrested. The prosecutors estimated that the Soviet state had paid for 5 million tonnes of imaginary cotton. Moscow had paid at least 3 billion rubles too much. This only covered the previous five years. Then there were all the scams involving other products.

The cotton and a multitude of other scams were no secret to the Party, government and KGB in Moscow. No action was taken because the Brezhnev clan was strong enough to prevent legal action. Since the godfather, *Il Padrone*, of the whole operation was the Uzbek Party leader, the Party itself would suffer humiliation if Rashidov were brought to trial. There was also the point that there was an informal contract between Moscow and the republics which permitted scams. In this way they remained loyal to Brezhnev. However, there was one comrade who was determined to bring the crooks to justice: Yury Andropov. As head of the KGB from 1967, he had built up thick dossiers on the misdemeanours of the national elite. A puritan himself, he found it difficult to understand the lure of money, valuables and sex. He was outraged to discover that a director of a state farm in Uzbekistan had set up his own harem there. In 1977, Andropov had evidence that Rashidov had bribed a deputy chair of Gosplan with mink coats and other presents to site an airport near his home. On another occasion, Rashidov had sacked the Uzbek KGB chief for arresting corrupt Party officials without first getting permission from the local Party committee. Rashidov kept Leonid Brezhnev happy. He bought the Soviet leader at least half a dozen luxury European sports cars to add to his collection. He also built several expensive hunting lodges for the Gensek to cater for his passion for hunting. However, in 1982, with Brezhnev's health in terminal decline, Andropov decided to pounce. This aversion to corruption had a political side. If he could implicate the Brezhnev clan in nefarious dealings, he stood a good chance of succeeding Brezhnev as Party and national leader.

He moved against Galina Brezhneva, Brezhnev's daughter. Another target was Yury Churbanov, deputy head of the USSR MVD and Brezhnev's son-in-law. Then there was Semon Tsvigun, deputy head of the KGB and Brezhnev's brother-in-law. Eventually Andropov did succeed Brezhnev and then began sweeping the Augean stables clean. Andropov died on 9 February 1984. His widow was convinced that he was murdered since he was threatening the comfortable existence of too many corrupt leaders. Hence the Uzbeks were unlucky. Had their arrest been delayed a couple of weeks the great Uzbek cotton scandal might never have hit the headlines.

The trial took place in Moscow in September 1988 and was a sensation. The main accused were Yury Churbanov, the Uzbek Minister of Internal Affairs and a whole phalanx of other Uzbek MVD officers. Telman Gdlyan and Nikolai Ivanov were the main investigators. They related that the head of the MVD in Bukhara oblast had been caught red-handed in April 1983 accepting a bribe of 1,000 rubles. In many oblasts of Uzbekistan, extortion was being practised on a massive scale. The resolution of problems of planning, supply and the selection of new cadres depended on paying bribes. Promotion depended on paying the appropriate bribe. The greater the rent (bribe) which could be extracted from the post, the higher the bribe needed to procure it. These bribes ensured the support of one's superiors at the republican, oblast or raion level, while providing protection for oneself. All subordinates had to pay bribes as a matter of course. If someone resisted, he was threatened with loss of office and arrest.

Rents (bribes) were applied as a tax. They were calculated carefully and had to be paid on a regular basis. The command-administrative system produced the cult of personality, ostentatious and obsequiousness behaviour by the clan around the Party leader, problems were passed over in silence and cadres were chosen and promoted according to corrupt criteria. The going rate to become a soviet deputy was 2,000–3,000 rubles a month. Orders, decorations and Party membership could be acquired at an appropriate price.

This system led to senior officials accepting bribes and stealing vast sums from the state. For instance, A. K. Karimov (not to be confused with Uzbek President Islam Karimov), Party boss of Bukhara oblast, had amassed over 6 million rubles; and the director of the Bukhara trade organisation had salted away 4.5 million rubles. The director of Tashkent airport had done very well for himself. The deputy head of a trade organisation near Tashkent promised to return 10 million rubles on the understanding that all charges against him would be dropped. Raion Party leaders also became rich. One was discovered to have 18 million rubles and 200 kg of gold (rings, bracelets, etc.) squirreled away. It is fair to say that the sums uncovered by the investigators may have been only the tip of the iceberg of the personal fortunes of the elite.

Two of those accused did not appear in court. A former Uzbek Minister of Internal Affairs and a former first deputy minister committed suicide beforehand. Another comrade who killed himself, in April 1985, was the Party leader in Kashkardarinsky oblast. For over 20 years he was the self-styled Lenin of the oblast. His subordinates fawned over him and he amassed a huge fortune. One estimate put it at tens of millions of rubles, mainly in gold. One of his raion Party secretaries returned 600,000 rubles and gold bonds worth 500,000 rubles to the state. One of his daughters was unfortunate. She was caught red-handed trying to hide a sack which contained 300,000 rubles.

Gdlyan and Ivanov were very busy in Uzbekistan. They began their investigations in 1980 and eventually over 4,500 officials were sentenced by the courts. The Uzbek Minister of Internal Affairs turned state's evidence and provided a wealth of detail. Eventually four secretaries of the Uzbek Party Central Committee; the Prime Minister; the deputy chair of the Supreme Soviet (parliament); seven oblast and raion first Party secretaries; first deputy USSR Minister of Internal Affairs; the Uzbek Minister of Internal Affairs; three deputy ministers; eight heads of oblast MVD organisations; and numerous trade, supply and administrative officials found themselves in court. Among the crimes uncovered were court cases in which the evidence was fabricated to convict innocent individuals; and sane persons were dispatched to psychiatric hospitals.

The investigators identified about 20 criminal clans in Tashkent in 1985. They had divided up Tashkent, Tashkent oblast and the raions of the republic among themselves. There were clashes from time to time because of disagreements over territory. In order to gain prestige the heads of each clan maintained close relations with *vory v zakone* (thieves in law). The clan chiefs built up a fund to support those who ended up in jail. This included those dealing in drugs and those caught bribing officials unsuccessfully. The chiefs resolved all conflicts which arose, including those involving losses at card games. The gangsters were wont to gamble up to 300,000 rubles on a card game. What was the reaction of the Soviet MVD to these revelations? An MVD general laconically remarked: 'Don't mention organised crime to me'.

Andropov, now Gensek, worked with Rashidov's competitors in an effort to unseat him. Uzbekistan was divided into three great political clans: the Samarkand, Bukhara and Tashkent clans. Rashidov was tsar of the Samarkand clan. Andropov did not succeed in removing Rashidov. The latter died on 31 October 1983 by his own hand. Inamzhon Usmankhodzhaev, from the Bukhara clan, succeeded him. The cotton scandal finally brought him down in January 1988. The Party agonised about putting a republican Party boss on trial but eventually did. He was sentenced to 12 years in December 1989. His trial confirmed the view of many Soviet citizens that the Party had degenerated into a mafia organisation.

All oblast Party secretaries and Central Committee secretaries, the Prime Minister and speaker of parliament admitted paying Rashidov bribes. The money was not put in envelopes but in suitcases because the sums were astronomical. One paid 1.5 million rubles; another 1 million rubles; another 800,000 rubles. Rashidov's personal fortune was put at over 100 million rubles; it is quite clear that this is merely a guess. Rashidov and his wife used to travel around Uzbekistan in a special train. It stopped at the oblast centres to permit the local Party and other bosses to offer gifts to Rashidov's wife. She put them in the train. She was particularly partial to money, gold jewellery and precious stones.

Telman Gdlyan wanted to bring home to everyone the extent of corruption in Uzbekistan. In April 1988, he arranged for a special flight from Tashkent to Moscow. On board were eight suitcases of valuables. There was a lot of money; piles of 3 per cent government bonds; valuable jewellery; pendants with 70 diamonds; bracelets; tsarist gold coins and so on. There was 4.7 million rubles in cash; the gold jewellery and artefacts weighed 43.2 kg and were worth at least 4 million rubles. Uzbekistan appeared to be a land of fabulous wealth.

As regards corruption, was Uzbekistan an exception or was it the norm? In neighbouring Kazakhstan something occurred which provides a clue. In 1969, in Karaganda oblast, there was a large group of *tsekhi* specialising in the lucrative fur trade. The organisation was headed by highly qualified lawyers. One Dunaev had been head of a legal consultancy; and Epelbeim was head of the criminal law section of the MVD High School. It all began when Snopkov, a businessman, set up a *tsekh* in a state enterprise specialising in the fur trade. It was soon receiving huge amounts of untreated fur. The group managed to obtain two Party Politburo and Soviet government decrees which transferred untreated fur from light industry enterprises to their group. Various *tsekhi* were set up in enterprises in the oblast with about 50 per cent of output going directly into the black market. The business was doing so well Dunaev invested all his savings, 18,000 rubles, in it. After making a few million rubles, they decided to open an office in Moscow. Not in an ordinary office block but in the Metropol hotel, near Red Square. Soon branches were being opened everywhere. Snopkov almost became a deputy of the USSR Supreme Soviet. Dunaev then commissioned a leading lawyer, a doctor of law, to evolve a theory of embezzlement. He was to advise on the most effective way of enriching oneself illegally. This was the Soviet version of the perfect crime. Dunaev paid a militia major in Moscow 8,000 rubles a month to keep him apprised of present and imminent dangers.

Investigators tried to discover who had lobbied the Party Politburo to provide such advantageous decrees to the group. They were not permitted to pursue the matter. The Politburo was taboo. However Dinmukhamed Kunaev, Party boss of Kazakhstan, was a candidate member of the Politburo in 1969. Is it possible that Kunaev lobbied the Politburo to issue the decrees? As Party leader he would have known about the fur scam. If Kunaev did so the implications are stunning. It would mean that a republican Party leader and a member of the all-powerful Politburo knowingly engaged in a scam. Of course, he would have gained materially from the scam. This would put Kazakhstan on a par with Uzbekistan. Is it fair to assume that the other Central Asian republics, Kyrgyzstan, Tajikistan and Turkmenistan, were administered along the same lines?

In a lecture on 10 September 1985, the USSR Procurator General stated that in the previous five years, 2 million citizens had been arrested and accused of large scale embezzlement of state property. This led to 1.3 million court cases. The investigators calculated that 386 million rubles had been stolen in 1976 and the amounts rose thereafter. The largest number of court cases was in Uzbekistan, followed by Krasnodar krai, Rostov oblast and Arkhangelsk oblast.

Comrade Shchelokov is coming

On 13 December 1984, Nikolai Shchelokov put on his general's uniform with his hammer and sickle medal, 11 Soviet orders, 10 other medals, 16 foreign awards and his USSR Supreme Soviet deputy badge. He then took his Gastin-Rannet revolver and shot himself in the head. He was found face down in a pool of blood in the vestibule of his Moscow apartment. His wife, Svetlana, had committed suicide at their dacha at Serebryanny Bor, near Moscow, on 19 February 1983. So ended the life of an extraordinary couple. Galina Vishnevskaya, the wife of Mstislav Rostropovich, regarded the Shchelokovs as friends. Shchelokov had befriended the cellist after he had been ostracised by the Soviet establishment for placing his dacha at the disposal of Alexander Solzhenitsyn. It had been an extraordinary gesture. At the time, Shchelokov was the Soviet Minister of Internal Affairs. The reason for the démarche was his intense hatred of Yury Andropov, the head of the KGB and the prime mover against Solzhenitsyn. Andropov, in turn, loathed Shchelokov whom he regarded as a common criminal.

Shchelokov had become Soviet Minister of Internal Affairs in 1968. Andropov took over the KGB in 1967. Hence Shchelokov was the Soviet Union's top cop and Andropov the top spymaster. Andropov was powerless to do anything until 1981 when he began taking action against members of Brezhnev's family. Shchelokov tried to protect them but to no avail. When Andropov became Gensek, he immediately sacked the Soviet MVD chief. He was succeeded by Vitaly Fedorchuk, formerly Andropov's head of the Ukrainian KGB. Fedorchuk sacked about 100,000 officers and placed the MVD under the supervision of the third department of the KGB.

When Brezhnev chose Andropov to head the KGB in 1967 he was careful to appoint as his deputy Semon Tsvigun, who was his brother-in-law. Shchelokov's deputy as MVD chief was Yury Churbanov, Brezhnev's son-in-law.

In 1968, Shchelokov made a grand tour of Central Asia. He arrived in Tashkent, en route from Kazakhstan. His host was the Uzbek Minister of Internal Affairs, Khaidar Yakhyaev. The minister was amiable and remarked that Uzbek fresh fruit and vegetables were first class. Could the minister send some to Moscow? Yakhyaev began sending him fresh fruit and vegetables two or three times a year. Lower level officials actually paid for the goods. In 1970, Yakhyaev was in Moscow to meet Shchelokov. The Soviet minister was wearing a dark suit. He said that his suit had been made for him in Moldova by a Jewish tailor. He wondered if there was a tailor in Tashkent who could make him a similar suit. If so, he would like to order one. The Uzbek said that he would make inquiries when he got back to Tashkent. Then the minister said it might be possible to buy a suit off the peg in Moscow. The Uzbek cottoned on to the fact that Shchelokov was asking for a bribe. He had 2,200 rubles in his pocket. He took the money and gave it to the minister. The latter took it, thanked him and then put the money in a drawer.

Shchelokov was a connoisseur of jewellery and an avid collector. In 1973, the Soviet MVD was carrying out a routine inspection of the Uzbek MVD. Shchelokov suddenly arrived from Moscow. He was shown around various militia centres but he was really interested in visiting a jewellery factory. He made it clear to Yakhyaev that he was expecting jewellery and money. He explained that he needed to take home some special jewellery for his wife. No mention was made of actually paying for the jewellery. On his departure, the Uzbek handed Shchelokov an envelope containing 5,000 rubles; a woman's gold bracelet, worth 350 rubles; gold rings and diamond ear-rings worth 1,500 rubles. Shchelokov was also given eight rolls of cloth worth 800 rubles, in addition to boxes of fruit and vegetables and various other presents.

Yakhyaev was again in Moscow in the summer of 1976. He gave Shchelokov a package containing 10,000 rubles; two Japanese cups worth 350 rubles; a gold watch worth 800 rubles; and a Philips electric shaver costing 230 rubles. The

Uzbek had previously received the Japanese cups and the electric shaver as a bribe from another official. Then Shchelokov instructed him to acquire a diamond ring for his wife. In 1977 he handed over 10,000 rubles to the Soviet minister; beads worth 200 rubles; a golden tie pin worth 1,000 rubles; 20 Karakul skins worth 400 rubles. The Uzbek minister had acquired the skins as a bribe. The skins were delivered to Shchelokov's office in a suitcase and the suitcase was returned empty except for a calendar. Shchelokov was not the only top official the Uzbek minister was providing with presents. Vodka, fruit and vegetables were the most popular presents.

One estimate of the jewellery and other valuables squirreled away by the Soviet minister for his wife is 250,000 rubles. After exhibitions, Shchelokov did not return all the valuables. He retained some in his office, his dacha and his apartment in Moscow. Another tactic was to 'send' valuables to Eastern European leaders. On one occasion Gustav Husak, the Czechoslovak Party boss, was the supposed recipient. Needless to say, he never received the valuables. They were added to the Shchelokov collection.

In 1980, Shchelokov hit on the idea of making a two part film about his time as minister. A budget of 50,000 rubles was earmarked for the project. A certain Erontev was put on the payroll as a laboratory assistant. He was also given a Zhiguli to travel around in. In reality, he was the Shchelokov family masseur. A lady was paid 8,000 rubles from state funds for some repair work over the period 1978–82. She was Shchelokov's daughter's private maid. Another person lived at state expense in a government dacha from 1980 to 1983. Actually he worked in a research institute where he was writing a candidate (PhD) dissertation for a relative of the minister. In October 1982, he was added to the staff of the Soviet MVD. He was also promoted to militia colonel.

The 1980 Olympics opened up new vistas. Three Mercedes were acquired to ferry important guests around. The Olympics over, Shchelokov decided that the cars were too good to return to the state. He acquired one, as did his son (who occupied an important position in the Komsomol) and his wife. Shchelokov was an entrepreneur in his own right. The MVD identified persons who had valuables and then charged them with theft and other crimes. It was normal to confiscate the property of the guilty person. The minister had first choice and removed the most valuable items. These items were then sold in special shops. He traded in a wide range of goods, from jewellery to cars. One interesting case involved stamps. The MVD raided apartments in Tallinn, Leningrad, Moscow, Odessa and other cities. They confiscated large stamp collections. These were returned to their rightful owners. However, the most valuable stamps were missing. The ministry had retained them. Gradually these stamps appeared at auctions in the West and sold for fabulous sums.

Intourist

I was in Krasnodar in May 1979. The director of the hotel I was staying in, Intourist, said: 'Today, 9 May, is Victory Day. Your driver has been given the day off so why not spend the day with me here in the hotel?' I agreed but said I would come after attending the Victory Day parade. We spent the afternoon and evening in conversation. She was one of the most cultured, intelligent Russian women I ever encountered. I was looking forward to debating Marxism-Leninism with her. Ideology was a subject most students found very difficult to grasp. Hopefully I would gain some new insights into it to help in my teaching.

'Tell me about the new English writers. What are they writing about?' she asked. She could neither read nor speak English but devoured everything she could obtain in translation.

'You will be interested to know that one of them, John Berger, an English Marxist, has just published a new novel.'

Her response surprised me. 'I don't want to hear of English Marxist writers, we have enough Marxists here. Let's talk about other writers', she said. So we did.

Then I approached the subject of Marxism-Leninism, explaining that students found the subject difficult. She gave me a withering look and scornfully replied: 'No educated person discusses Marxism-Leninism!' She, a leading member of society in Krasnodar, was telling me that the official Soviet ideology was not worth wasting one's breath on!

We eventually got on to the subject of her management of the hotel. I remarked that the hotel only appeared to be about 20 per cent full. So how did she fulfil the plan, which would have been about 80 per cent? She smiled and replied:

'I go to Sochi several times a year and we come to an arrangement. The plan is always fulfilled.' I was not cheeky enough to ask how much money was involved. It occurred to me that if the hotel was 20 per cent full and the plan was 80 per cent, the hotel would receive food, beverages and other things based on 80 per cent capacity. What happened to the 60 per cent? Of course, the food and other deliveries were never made. They were sold directly on the black market. She received a modest salary as director but had a large supplementary income. This scam could not have been kept a secret. There were too many people involved. The Party boss of Krasnodar krai must have known of it and been collecting a rent from it.

In the evening, her assistant arrived.

'May I present my assistant to you? As you can see she is a very beautiful woman.'

She was. Very slim, she was dressed in a tight blue costume. She belonged to a very select group. She was a stunning Russian redhead. Sex dripped from her. The director looked at her. 'You are not permitted to go up to his room', she said like a matron.

Then turning to me she said sternly: 'If she comes to your room, you are not to let her in. Understood?' 'Understood.'

Here was one of the paradoxes of the Soviet Union. Sex in the hotel was out but fiddling the hotel books was in.

The great caviar scandal

In 1977, Andropov decided to proceed against the notoriously corrupt Soviet Ministry of the Fish Industry. It was to be a warning to other corrupt officials. The deputy minister, Rykov, was arrested, as was another top official. (This was as high as Andropov could go. The minister, the mastermind of the black market dealings, was untouchable. He was eventually pensioned off in late 1978.) The investigators identified various criminal clans specialising in bribery and embezzlement in Georgia and Krasnodar krai. Their key members were trade and food officials. In 1978, in Sochi, the director of the Okean store, the director of the meat and fish trade organisation, the director of the Sochi freezer plant and many other food officials were taken into custody. Some higher level officials were arrested; the most senior being Andrei Tarada, a secretary of the krai Party apparatus. He supervised the krai's trade and local industry. Under his guidance, the *tsekhoviki* flourished and underground factories mushroomed. He collected huge rents from the black marketeers.

Once, when Gensek Brezhnev was coming, Sergei Medunov, the krai Party boss, phoned Tarada. He demanded that he collect enough money from the underground millionaires to buy an appropriate present for the Soviet leader. When Tarada was arrested investigators found 200,000 rubles and a fortune in gold in his possession. He also had hundreds of savings books. Presumably there was one for each businessman who was paying bribes. The KGB put pressure on Tarada and he promised to cooperate. One night he absconded from prison and the case was dropped.

Krasnodar krai became a battleground between Andropov's KGB and Shchelokov's MVD. The latter seized the initiative and called a conference in Sochi to discuss how to speed up the investigation into the Okean scandal. Yury Churbanov arrived from Moscow to oversee discussions. Viktor Naidenov, deputy Soviet Procurator General, was also there. The latter was invited for a chat at one of the Party's dachas. He sensed danger and immediately returned to Moscow. Then a huge propaganda operation was set in motion. Specially selected persons wrote to Moscow complaining that they had been subjected to illegal methods of investigation. They had been forced to make false confessions. These letters were sent to the Party Central Committee in Moscow. Eventually, in August 1981, the USSR Supreme Court sentenced the deputy Soviet Minister of the Fish Industry, Rykov, to death.

The Okean scandal also embraced Rostov oblast, a major centre of the black economy under Brezhnev. The Party boss had struck up a relationship with Rykov. Everything caught by the Far East fishing fleet in Vladivostok – fish, caviar and the like – was sent to Rostov-on-Don for processing. These valuable products went straight to underground factories. The most valuable product was caviar and it was exported. The caviar was put in tins and labelled fish. The whole operation fell apart one day when a KGB officer opened his tin of fish and found it contained caviar. Many trade officials in Rostov oblast were arrested and shot. The state prosecutor could not calculate how much money had been involved in the scam.

Andropov had to wait until June 1983 before Sergei Medunov could be removed. He was dropped from the Party Central Committee, along with Yury Shchelokov. Krasnodar krai was famously corrupt under Brezhnev. Between 1976 and 1981, the population of the krai increased 4 per cent but the number of crimes rose by 32.4 per cent. The number of crimes per 10,000 of the population was the highest in the Russian Federation.

The phantom factory

One of the most successful factories in Moscow oblast during the 1970s was the Great Oktyabr plant. It fulfilled its plan year after year. Normally enterprises complained to their ministry that the necessary inputs had not arrived or were inadequate to fulfil the plan. The Oktyabr plant was different. It was a model of its kind. Eventually, officials in the Party apparatus thought that the director should be rewarded for his exemplary work. It was decided to award the plant the Red Banner of Labour. Inspectors were dispatched to bring the good news to the director and to write up the citation. When they got to the address of the plant, they found an open field. They checked but could not find the enterprise. No other local factory could help them. They suddenly realised that the Oktyabr plant did not exist; it was an imaginary factory. The 'phantom' director was shot.

How many other Oktyabr plants were there in the Soviet Union? There was one in Baku which made shoes or rather maintained it made shoes. There was another near Lake Ladoga. How was it possible to run a 'factory' for years without the authorities finding out? A lot of bribe money must have been distributed. An imaginary factory had to be registered, be given a state plan, obtain the inputs to fulfil the plan and then distribute the output to other enterprises and organisations. What, in fact, happened? The inputs were obtained but diverted to various underground factories where goods were produced. These were then sold on the black market. Presumably part of the output was delivered as state deliveries to some plants. This would give the impression that there really was an Oktyabr plant.

Afghanistan

The Soviet Union imported goods from India, Japan and other Asian countries through Afghanistan. The goods were very valuable and included the finest silks. They crossed into Central Asia by boat along the Syr Darya river. Once on the Soviet side, some of the goods were stolen before they were sent on to other parts of the Soviet Union. The corrupt officials and ship personnel dug pits in which they stored the stolen goods. This flourishing business lasted many years. It was cut short by the Soviet invasion of Afghanistan in December 1979. Then a different type of business developed. Afghans used Tajikistan as their entry point to Central Asia and the rest of the Soviet Union. They traded mainly in drugs. The Soviet border guards had to be bribed in order to allow the Afghans through. One Ukrainian was given 50,000 rubles. He packed 40,000 rubles into a chest and dispatched it to his family in a Ukrainian village. He was shot.

During the war in Afghanistan, two members of the Soviet embassy in Kabul, one a former Tajik Minister of Justice and the other a secretary at the embassy, could not resist the temptation of going into business with the locals. This meant they were doing business with the mujahidin. They traded in gold, acquired in various countries, and this was to procure weapons abroad. Unfortunately for them, one consignment was checked at Sheremetevo airport, in Moscow. It was found to contain 23 kg of gold, worth over 1 million rubles. The two diplomats were executed.

Another more daring case involved members of the Soviet military mission in Kabul. The mujahidin urgently needed weapons to counter the overwhelming superiority of the Soviet army. One member of the mission, Guseinov, found a simple solution. He and his colleagues simply sold weapons and equipment destined for the Soviet army to the mujahidin. Hence they were providing the weapons which were used to kill Soviet soldiers. They were paid mainly in gold. It was laundered world-wide by Armenians because they were the most skilled and had the necessary network. However, the fraud was eventually discovered. A military court in Moscow sentenced Guseinov and seven other members of the mission to death.

What happened to honest MVD officers who tried to bring corrupt officials to book? Penza, in 1974, was a salutary warning to them. Georgy Didichenko, deputy head of the Penza MVD decided to take action against criminal organisations involved in vodka, liquor and confectionery enterprises, meat factories, restaurants and other businesses in the city and Penza oblast. It was clear to him that an organised criminal group, composed of top officials, was active. They had their own sources of information and armed guards. The oblast was under their control. They were so sure of themselves that they ignored the investigation in its early stages. Didichenko discovered that the deputy head of the Party agitprop department was involved. Then the Party hit back. The Procurator who had authorised the investigation was summarily sacked. Didichenko received a phone call at home. He was informed that if he continued with the investigation he would lose his only daughter. The investigation ended. Four years later Didichenko was sacked and warned to keep his mouth shut if he wished to enjoy his pension.

Diamonds are a comrade's best friend

The Moscow glitterati were enamoured of diamonds. Women especially are fascinated by them and this gives them value. If a hood wanted to ingratiate himself with a Party boss, he gave the latter's wife a diamond ring or bracelet.

Andropov had a huge number of files (known as *kompromat*) on the misdemeanours of the Brezhnev family and clan. A special target was Galina Brezhneva, the Gensek's wild daughter, and her husband, Yury Churbanov. She took as a lover a handsome 32 year old opera singer, Boris Buryatsky, nicknamed Boris the Gypsy. She put him in an apartment on Chekhov street. He gathered around him many members of the creative intelligentsia and the criminal world. Through him they all had access to Galina and through her to the Gensek. One of Galina's passions was collecting diamonds. She discovered that the Politburo was going to increase the retail price of diamonds. Naturally she bought as many as she could. She kept some and sold others to shops at handsome profits. This was one of the ways the Moscow elite made money. Viktor Kantor, the director of the Sokolniki departmental store, bought 322,886 rubles worth of diamonds from his store and then sold them on. His profit margin was as high as 150 per cent.

On 30 December 1981, the apartment of Irina Burgrimova, a well known lion tamer, was broken into and a whole collection of diamonds stolen. The thieves were real professionals. In order to gain access to the building, they had brought a New Year's tree and claimed that it was for one of the residents. In early January 1982, at Sheremetevo airport, a person was detained and found to have some of Burgrimova's stolen diamonds on him. The investigation led back to Boris the Gypsy. His apartment was searched. Semon Tsvigun, Andropov's deputy and Brezhnev's brother-in-law, protested against the targeting of the Brezhnev family. On 19 January 1982, Mikhail Suslov, the Party's chief ideologist, called him in. The meeting was very heated. Tsvigun went back to his dacha, pulled out a revolver and shot himself. All these events were too much for the ascetic Suslov. On 25 January 1982, he suffered a heart attack and died. The same day Andropov ordered the arrest of Galina and many of her circle. Suslov's death was a stroke of luck for Andropov. There was a vacancy now for a Party Central Committee secretary. He manoeuvred himself into the position in May 1982. The way was open to succeed the ailing Brezhnev.

The great Moscow food scandal

The Soviet Procurator General confirmed to the Party Central Committee what Andropov knew already. Many MVD officers regarded their jobs as a quick way of enriching themselves. They engaged in blackmail, extortion, embezzlement, the fabrication of evidence and so on. Many of them were heads of criminal gangs. One of the top protectors of corrupt Party officials, Andrei Kirilenko, was quietly given his pension in September 1982. Then, in October 1982, the KGB set up a sixth department to combat economic crime. The first major arrest was that of Yury Sokolov, the director of Eliseev, the leading food store. On 30 October 1982, the KGB caught him red-handed accepting a 300 ruble bribe from the deputy head of a fish store. Yury's deputy and four others were arrested.

Sokolov was famous in Moscow and a comrade to know. Eliseev's was the best food store in town and never seemed to have difficulty in procuring produce. Anyone who was anyone in the capital shopped there. He had had a good war and afterwards worked as a chauffeur. His penchant for defrauding customers led to his downfall. He was sentenced to a year's corrective labour but this was quashed. He managed to enrol in the prestigious Plekhanov Institute of Economics and then went into trade. Yury employed a direct approach. In 1963, he identified the comrade who decided who would become deputy director of departmental store number one. 'If you give me the job, I'll pay you a bribe of 300 rubles a month.' He got the post. In February 1972, he became director of Eliseev's.

The secret of his success was his ability to get to know the right people. One special target was Galina and her circle. His contacts reached right to the top: to Viktor Grishin, the Moscow Party boss. He was wont to come to work and inform his deputy that he had been talking to Grishin the evening before. Another variant was that Brezhnev's son had come to see him. He had the direct number of the Soviet Minister of Trade and his deputies. As a result, he had no problems getting all he needed for his store. Shchelokov provided protection, a 'roof', for him. He intervened as early as 1969 to save him from trouble. Sokolov also got himself elected to Mossovet, Moscow city council. All the leading lights in the trade world were Mossovet deputies.

Why was Sokolov in court? He was accused of cheating customers. One tactic was to adjust the scales. In this way customers paid for more than they received. Another was to change the classification of the goods. Class 3 became Class 1 and so on. Another ruse was to write off 0.3 per cent of incoming goods as damaged. If the turnover was 3 million rubles a week, he pocketed 10,000 rubles. However, the most lucrative part of the business was collecting rents or bribes. Everyone below him had to pay a bribe in order to stay in the chain. Correspondingly, he had to pay a bribe to everyone above him. The court accused him, during his ten years as director, of receiving 297,675 rubles in bribes. The state confiscated 112,325 rubles from him. What had happened to the other 185,350 rubles? He had paid most of it out as bribes to higher level officials. Needless to say, the higher ups also expected free food and the latest delicacies.

The KGB had promised Sokolov a light sentence or even an amnesty if he turned state's evidence. He believed them and revealed the extent of corruption in Moscow's ruling circles. The other defendants were given prison sentences but he was sentenced to death. Afterwards officers came into his cell and demanded millions of rubles to secure his release. He did not have the money and they knew it. 'I knew they were going to shoot me. They kept asking me for money I did not have', he confessed. Yury was executed on 14 December 1984. More senior officials than Yury had received prison sentences. His death sentence made no sense in the eyes of many observers.

Georgia and Azerbaijan

These republics had a reputation for shady dealings. In Tbilisi, in 1979, a Georgian official confided to me: 'We Georgians regard it as our national duty to cheat Russians'. They also practised on one another. He provided me with some examples of how they outwitted the Russians. One example concerned lemons which were always in great demand. They were secreted in tea chests and dispatched to Moscow and Leningrad. Vasily Mzhavanadze had taken over as Party boss in 1953. Andropov finally managed to engineer his removal in 1972. Eduard Shevardnadze, who had been Minister of Internal Affairs, 1965–72, took over. Shevardnadze's boss had been Shchelokov. In 1971, at a meeting in Moscow, the latter chided Shevardnadze that 50 per cent of highway police in Georgia demanded bribes. On his return to Tbilisi, Shevardnadze took an ordinary car and drove around the city. He discovered that Shchelokov was wrong; 100 per cent of highway police wanted a bribe. He sacked the lot. Soon the new men were demanding bribes. Several attempts to remove Mzhavanadze failed because of his close links with Brezhnev.

At an official reception, Shevardnadze noticed that Mzhavanadze's wife was wearing a diamond ring which had disappeared from a museum and had long been on Interpol's wanted list. He discovered that Ogari Lazishvili, a big underground hood, had presented it to the first lady of the republic. This was reported to Moscow and Andropov pounced. Shevardnadze wanted a big sensation to shock the Georgian public into realising Mzhavanadze had to go. In the summer of 1972 a secret factory for making weapons was discovered in Sukhumi. Guns were sold to Georgian and other criminals. Georgia became a source of weapons for Chechens. Mzhavanadze moved to Moscow with his family. He was provided with an apartment, dacha and a handsome pension. The climate did not suit him. He moved to Ukraine where he had very good contacts. His wife was the sister of Volodymyr Shcherbytsky's wife.

Shevardnadze was very active. Within 20 months he had removed 20 ministers and members of the Georgian Party Central Committee; about 100 oblast and raion Party secretaries went; about 10 mayors and their deputies lost their jobs; something like 40,000 Party and state officials were purged; over 30,000 were arrested. A special target was Ogari Lazishvili. He had very good contacts in Moscow and it took Shevardnadze some time to prise him out of the republic. The new Party boss became very unpopular in some circles. There were two attempts to assassinate him. On 12 April 1976 a bomb exploded outside the government building in Tbilisi. On 9 May 1976 the Opera House in Tbilisi was burnt down shortly before Shevardnadze was due to attend the 9 May victory celebrations.

In 1969, Geidar Aliev, KGB boss in Azerbaijan, launched a campaign against corruption, centred on the Party leader of the republic. Aliev was so skilful that he became the Party boss. Under the guise of rooting out corruption and combating Islam, Aliev propelled his own clan into leading positions. According to one author, the 'Caspian Sea caviar mafia, the Sumgait oil mafia, the fruit and vegetable mafia, the cotton mafia, the customs and transport mafias all reported to him, enriched him and worshipped him' (Remnick 1994). Aliev knew that Brezhnev was susceptible to flattery and expensive gifts. In 1982, he presented the Gensek with a ring set in a huge jewel, portraying him as the Sun King, surrounded by 15 smaller precious stones representing the Union republics. 'These are like planets orbiting the sun', he explained. Overcome with emotion, Brezhnev burst into tears in front of the TV cameras (Andrew and Mitrokhin 2005).

The mafia

There was no all-Union mafia; it always controlled a specific territory. The southern parts of the country were more attractive because they were economically more developed. Funerals were used to demonstrate the power of mafia. The hoods appeared in Mercedes, wore dark suits and sunglasses and copied the dress and style of the Chicago gangsters of the Al Capone era.

The mafia first appeared in the Russian Federation during the Khrushchev era when reforms introduced the economic mechanism. This permitted black marketeers to establish contacts with officials and the police. In 1958–59, the annual loss to the Soviet economy through black market dealings was put at 1.5–2 billion rubles. By the early 1970s, the mafiosi were a social phenomenon. They travelled around in Mercedes, wore diamond rings, lived in detached houses and flaunted their wealth. The underground economy took off as more and more raw materials were stolen from the state. Gangsters targeted the underground businesses. They burnt their vehicles, homes and dachas and kidnapped their children. It was the first time this phenomenon had appeared in the Soviet Union. The businesses needed protection, guards and information. Eventually the underground businesses and gangster groups merged. Various meetings were arranged in the north Caucasus to reach agreement. The *tsekhoviki*, besides paying the mafia for protection, had also to pay rents (bribes) to officials. They had to pay the administrative organs for protection against the militia and the militia in turn to leave them alone. Gradually a system emerged where the Party boss, the dominant official in a region, often collected rents from the underground businesses and from the mafiosi. The larger the black economy in his region, the richer he became. The MVD under Yury Shchelokov was closely involved. The party bosses needed a 'roof' in the Party Central Committee in Moscow. Those who performed this function naturally expected to be handsomely rewarded.

As the black market expanded throughout the Soviet Union in the 1970s, more money became available to bribe officials. One estimate of the black economy, in 1989, put it at 70–90 billion rubles annually. This is a western estimate, and, given what one now knows about the black economy and corruption, is certainly far too low. By the late 1970s, white collar criminals were consorting openly with the leaders of Soviet industry. In 1980, the director of Rosmash, a huge engineering enterprise and part of the military economy in Rostov-on-Don, was observed talking at a reception to a leading hood. Most enterprises in the military economy produced consumer goods as well. Some of these, and those produced in the enterprises' *tsekhi*, were sold in the military Voentorg shops throughout the country.

The first article about organised crime appeared in *Literaturnaya Gazeta* on 20 July 1988. It identified Moscow, Leningrad, Tambov, Penza, Yaroslavl, Perm and some small towns in Moscow oblast such as Pushkino as major centres in the Russian Federation. Kyiv, Lviv, Odessa, Donetsk, Dnipropetrovsk headed the list in Ukraine. Moldova was also high on the list. Many mafia groups were headed by sportsmen or ex-sportsmen; professional recidivists and small, unnoticed economic actors such as someone serving in a pizzeria. This article must have come as a shock to many readers but it only touched on the problem. It omits many of the major centres of organised crime in the country. However, it was a daring piece of journalism for its time and almost cost the journalists their jobs.

This was the world which Yury Andropov had been determined to take on. In the Party apparatus his two main targets were Volodymyr Shcherbytsky, the Ukrainian Party boss, and Viktor Grishin, of Jewish extraction and the top Party comrade in Moscow. Belarus was another target. During his short period in

20.7 A bathing party, Odesa, Ukraine, 1973

office (November 1982–February 1984) about one-third of the top Party Central Committee apparatus and government officials were sacked. The Party bosses in 47 of the country's 150 oblasts were removed; in Ukraine 9 out of 25 were dismissed. Odesa was a special target.

In 1980–81, the amount of socialist property stolen was put at 100 million rubles. In 1981, over 5,000 officials, accused of stealing 3.4 million rubles, were sentenced. In the same year, 1,111 communists appeared in court on criminal charges. A militia officer in Krasnodar krai became famous for taking on Bella Borodkina, known as Iron Bella, the head of the trade mafia. By March 1983, she had embezzled at least 1.5 million rubles. The lady was sentenced to death. In Moscow, in 1984, 15,066 were arrested of whom 2,121 were in senior positions. In the MVD, about 100,000 were sacked, including over 5,000 Party members. Andropov's arrests broke some of the decades long links between organised crime and top officials. Immediately after Andropov's death top state officials met with the leaders of Moscow's criminal fraternity about how to re-establish links with Party, government and the Moscow city authorities.

The KGB identified about 300 officials who were mafia bosses and at least 100 of these were militia officers. In 1983, there were 606 death sentences and 512 in 1984. This declined to 140 in 1987 under Gorbachev, when some of the shadow economy activities had been legalised. An amnesty freed half of those sentenced

20.8 Waitresses, Odesa, Ukraine, 1973

to prison. Did the Andropov purge change anything? The problem for Andropov was that those promoted to fill the boots of the dismissed came from the same apparatus. Many of them had been collecting rents for their Party bosses and for themselves. The feeble Chernenko did not have the energy to bother about corruption in high places. However, the KGB continued arresting trade officials in Moscow, despite Grishin's efforts to prevent them.

Grishin desperately wanted to succeed the ailing Chernenko as Gensek. Chernenko died on 10 March 1985 but Grishin lost out. On 1 April, 400 MVD and KGB officers arrested Vladimir Kantor, director of the Sokolniki store. When they went to his apartment they were confronted with a door resembling that in a Swiss bank. Secreted away, he had a superb collection of Czech and other glass; a fine collection of cigarette lighters; black wood carvings; a collection of diamond rings; rings with rubies and many other precious stones. Kantor had hidden away his wealth not from the militia but from thieves. There were 749 pieces of jewellery and coins made of precious metals weighing about 10 kg: gold, silver and much else. The horde was valued at 613,589 rubles. He was sentenced to eight years in prison and had his property confiscated.

The Chechens, specialists in black market dealings and violence, made their presence felt for the first time in Moscow in 1983. They became involved in buying second-hand cars from private individuals who wanted more than the state would offer. Usually three Chechens worked this scam. The first would show interest and pass the owner on to a second Chechen. The deal was to be completed by a third Chechen. Usually the owner ended up with no car and no money. They main rivals were Azeris, who dominated the private fruit and vegetable market as well as flowers.

Russians loved gold teeth. It was a mark of a person's wealth. As a consequence, private dentists multiplied and became rich. Where did they get the gold from? Gold was a state monopoly and could not be bought? They obtained it from the flourishing black market in gold.

If the son of a member of the nomenklatura committed a murder, he faced years in prison. How was he to escape this fate? His father would go to the Serbsky Institute and ask if it would admit his son. For a consideration, the son was examined and declared insane. He stayed in the clinic, made a remarkably fast recovery and was released after a few months.

The socialist world

China

In March 1966, the Communist Party of China broke off relations with the CPSU. It accused the Soviets of betraying socialism. Soviet diplomats in Beijing were under virtual siege. As they evacuated their embassy in 1967 they were taunted and spat at. This provoked a wave of anti-Chinese emotion in the Soviet Union. China denounced the invasion of Czechoslovakia in 1968, saying it was similar to that by Hitler in 1938. Soviet foreign policy was 'social imperialist and social-fascist'.

This led to new thinking about China in Moscow. President Leonid Brezhnev (he assumed the presidency after the 1977 constitution was adopted) and Marshal Andrei Grechko, Minister of Defence, did not fear America most. They feared China. This was because they perceived the United States leadership to be rational decision makers but the Chinese were capable of anything. Hence defence planning had to contend with two main adversaries. Most conventional forces were located in the east, just in case China attacked. Mao had attacked in March 1969, when 32 Soviet border guards had been killed near Zhenbao (Domansky island). The Russians counter-attacked and killed 800 Chinese. Soviet tank forces penetrated Xinjiang, from Kazakhstan, and wiped out Chinese forces, in August. The Brezhnev doctrine made Mao nervous and he thought it could lead to the Soviet Union attacking China.

Mao needed a powerful ally and invited President Richard Nixon to China. Although astute in foreign policy, the American President none the less failed to grasp that China needed America more than the reverse. In July 1973,

US Secretary of State Henry Kissinger promised to help China modernise its military aircraft industry. Moscow's worst nightmare was becoming reality: a Sino-American alliance aimed at it. The Americans shared intelligence with the Chinese. They told them that Brezhnev had considered taking out China's nuclear capability. How would Washington react? Would America consider a joint mission? In 1977–78, China talked about an alliance of the Third World against the Soviet Union. This was abandoned in 1979 when Deng Xiaoping began his reforms. He sought a rapprochement with Moscow. China wished to develop its domestic economy as quickly as possible. This required a stable international environment.

Eastern Europe

The invasion of Czechoslovakia, in August 1968, established the Brezhnev doctrine. Moscow was to decide if socialism was under threat in its satellites. However, it never used military force again. After 'normalisation', four divisions were left in Czechoslovakia. Charter 77 emerged but the regime did not become unstable. One of the reasons for this was that there was no economic crisis in the country.

Poland was different. Large increases in food prices were announced as a Christmas 1970 present by Wladyslaw Gomulka, the Party chief. These led to riots and the replacement of Gomulka by Edward Gierek. Moscow knew that if it invaded there would be a lot of bloodshed. As if to prove that he had learnt nothing from the 1970 events, Gierek announced substantial increases in food prices in 1976. This time unrest led to the increases being rescinded. Poland was clearly a powder keg.

The election of the Bishop of Krakow, Karol Wojtyla, as Pope in 1978 provided a great moral boost to the anti-communist mood in Poland. The Roman Catholic Church had no intention of leading the opposition to the regime. John Paul II's message to Poles when he visited his homeland in 1979 was: 'Do not be afraid'. Acute food shortages during the summer of 1980 led to the formation of the Solidarity trade union movement, led by Lech Walesa. On 13 December 1981, the regime demonstrated that it had not lost its nerve. General Wojciech Jaruzelski imposed martial law (but he carefully avoided using this term), banned Solidarity, arrested its leaders and set out to 'normalise' the country. Moscow had decided not to intervene but had to give the impression that it would intervene. Jaruzelski fell for the ruse. As most of the male leaders of Solidarity had been arrested, women stepped into the breach. They sidestepped the political police, forged papers, ran underground seminars and produced a clandestine mass-circulation newspaper. In vain, the authorities tried to suppress it. The Polish establishment was male so they thought that their main enemies were male. In house searches, things which were deemed female, such as nappies, were routinely ignored. Important material could be hidden under a pile of dirty nappies. Thus women played an important part in the eventual dissolution of communism. Afterwards they melted away as their political goals had been attained.

The banning of Solidarity caused some tension in the Soviet Union. Lecturers were quizzed by angry workers who wanted to know what had changed. Previously there had been calls for solidarity with Polish workers. Now their organisation had been banned. Why were Polish workers being treated in this way? The Hungarians went their own way but were careful not to challenge Party rule. Negotiations between the two German states led to the Basic Treaty, effective from June 1973. The two states exchanged permanent representatives, not ambassadors.

Ministry of Foreign Affairs

Key Responsibilities	Key Objectives	Successes	Failures
■ Relations with US, Japan, Western Europe and developed capitalist states ■ Indirectly relations with China, North (Democratic Republic) Vietnam and North (People's Democratic Republic) Korea	■ Reducing influence of United States (main adversary) ■ Separating Western Europe and US ■ Undermining NATO ■ Undermining European Union	■ 1957 Sputnik great breakthrough ■ Gagarin's flight, in 1961, even greater boost ■ US nonplussed at Soviet technological advances ■ US withdrawal from Vietnam, in 1975, another high point ■ Jimmy Carter condemned the national disgraces of 'Watergate, Vietnam and the CIA', 1976 ■ US self-doubt at highest level; high point of Soviet influence world-wide	■ Failure to force West out of Berlin ■ Unable to conclude arms agreements to reduce Soviet defence spending ■ Fear of US nuclear first strike in late Brezhnev era and under Andropov ■ Peace offensive fails to prevent deployment of EuroMissiles (Pershing, etc. in response to deployment of SS-20s across Soviet Union) ■ Soviet Union loses world-wide influence after Afghan invasion, 1979

KGB and CC International Department

Key Responsibilities	Key Objectives	Successes	Failures
■ Relations with communist, workers' and other progressive parties in	■ Promoting national liberation movements world-wide	■ Brilliantly successful in science and technology espionage ■ Played large role in keeping Soviet military equal of West	■ Many KGB defectors meant that US and West had much information on active measures ■ Weakness of Third World M-L states was that they concentrated on

Key Responsibilities	Key Objectives	Successes	Failures
Eastern Europe, China, North Vietnam, North Korea and pro-Soviet countries of Third World (Party Gensek dominant influence in relations with ruling M-L parties)	■ Opposing Zionism everywhere ■ Protecting Marxist-Leninist states from internal enemies ■ Espionage, especially involving science and technology ■ Disinformation campaigns to undermine US and western world (called active measures) ■ Promoting peace and anti-nuclear movements	■ Outmanoeuvred CIA overall ■ CIA officer Aldrich Ames, in 1985, best agent KGB ever had in US ■ Other Americans spied for money ■ Very successful in identifying potential US traitors ■ Active measures (disinformation, etc.) very successful in Third World, especially India ■ Cuba becoming M-L state great coup ■ Castro, on balance, great asset ■ Nicaragua, Guatemala, Grenada (Salvador Allende first Marxist President of Chile) ■ Angola, Democratic Republic of Congo, Burundi, Mali, Guinea, Dahomey, Mozambique, Somalia, Ethiopia, Algeria, Laos, Cambodia, all came into Soviet camp at one time or another ■ Egypt and Syria at times pro-Soviet	security and eliminating opposition and ignored economic development ■ Main policy in Africa in 1970s was to increase arms supplies to client states but proved disastrous for these states ■ M-L influence in Nicaragua and Guatemala declined ■ Castro often difficult to restrain as he wished to promote world revolution more rapidly than Soviet Union ■ Afghan invasion (December 1979) led by KGB but military and political failure ■ This revealed intelligence weak ■ Andropov obsessed with Zionist influence world-wide ■ Also very nervous about expansion of Chinese influence in Third World ■ Overestimated appeal of M-L worldwide ■ Wasted resources on massive scale ■ Lost polemical war with China ■ Little influence over North Vietnam (basic error by Washington to assume that Moscow decided policy in Hanoi) and North Korea ■ Invasion of Czechoslovakia, in 1968, gave birth to Eurocommunism ■ End of Marxist philosophical dominance in France, etc. ■ Increasing KGB and Party corruption undermined ideological appeal

FIGURE 20.3 Foreign policy, 1957–85

Andrei Gromyko was Foreign Minister from 1957 to 1985. He was conservative, concerned not to provoke US and had little interest in Third World and national liberation movements. He was also not concerned about the dissident movement in the Soviet Union. He loathed Boris Ponomarev (1905–95). He did not share

Yury Andropov's concern about Zionism and the potential of the national liberation movements.

Yury Andropov was head of the KGB from 1967 to 1982. He devoted great energy to combating internal dissent in the Soviet Union and confronting Zionism everywhere. He was excited about the prospects of national liberation movements undermining US power world-wide. As late as 1982 he believed the Soviet Union was winning the ideological battle with the US.

Boris Ponomarev worked in the CC International Department from the 1950s and retired in 1986. He distributed largesse to West European communist and workers' parties and was active in promoting Third World anti-imperialist movements, channelling large resources to them.

The outside world

United States

After the American astronauts land on the moon, Brezhnev summons the leaders of the Soviet space programme. 'The Party and government instruct you to land cosmonauts on the sun as soon as possible.' 'But the temperature of the sun is so high; we'll not be able to get near it.' 'Do you think I'm a fool? We'll send them during the night.'

In April 1967, Brezhnev wanted an arms agreement with Washington. However, Cuba had troops in Angola, Ethiopia and elsewhere. The US made it clear that it would not enter into arms control negotiations while Castro was pursuing his revolutionary ambitions in Africa and Latin America. This led Brezhnev to write to Castro. If he did not rein in Che Guevara and his revolutionaries everywhere, the Soviet Union would not prevent an American invasion of Cuba. Castro was in an even weaker position in 1970 after the sugar harvest failed to reach its goal of 10 million tonnes. About 10,000 Soviet and East European advisers were dispatched to advise the Cuban government how to run the country. Strict rules of conduct were laid down. If an adviser spent a night with a Cuban senorita, he was on a plane home the next day.

Castro did not keep his revolutionaries on a short leash in Latin America. He directed the campaign which brought the Sandinistas to power in Nicaragua in 1978. The Cubans had broken the codes used by President Samoza's troops and so were in a position to deal them devastating blows.

The United States and North Vietnam began peace talks in May 1968. The new President, Richard Nixon, promised to end the war. A peace settlement was agreed in late 1972. The United States left South Vietnam in February 1973, leaving their local allies in the lurch. The communists took Saigon in April 1975, and renamed it Ho Chi Minh City. It was a traumatic defeat for the Americans.

After the Arab–Israeli war, in June 1967, President Lyndon Johnson invited Aleksei Kosygin to visit Glassboro'. As the Russians could not find it on any of their maps (it is halfway between New York and Washington), they assumed that the invitation was a hoax. After this demonstration of ignorance about their major competitor, the Institute for the Study of the United States and Canada was set up in the Academy of Sciences. The two leaders discussed the Middle East and Vietnam but made no progress. President Johnson accepted an invitation to Moscow. Czechoslovakia intervened.

Richard Nixon's arrival in the White House, in 1969, changed matters. He had a superb grasp of foreign relations. America wanted out of Vietnam and it needed Soviet help to extricate itself. Nixon and Henry Kissinger came up with the idea of linkage. Washington would accept that there was nuclear parity between the superpowers, would not interfere in the Soviet empire and would grant access to western investment and technology. The concept of the rollback of communism was consigned to the dustbin of history. The key goal was stability of relations. Arms negotiations were on the agenda. Détente had broken out.

Zhou Enlai proposed talks with the incoming President Nixon, in November 1968. Nothing came of this initiative. However, Nixon did make it to Beijing in February 1972. The Americans could now contemplate playing China off against Russia. The Soviets were keen to slow the arms race and SALT I was signed by Nixon and Brezhnev, in Moscow, in May 1972. Brezhnev's first trip to America, in June 1973, resulted in a summit with Nixon at Camp David and San Clemente, California. The outlines of SALT II were agreed. The superpowers agreed to contact one another if nuclear war threatened. Superpower summits were becoming part of the international agenda. Presidents Ford and Brezhnev met in Vladivostok in November 1974. Progress was made on SALT II. But Brezhnev's planned visit to America in 1975 never materialised. After seven years of endeavour, SALT II was signed by President Jimmy Carter and Leonid Brezhnev in Vienna in June 1979. However, President Carter's relations with Moscow collapsed over Cuba. There was a Soviet brigade there which the Americans demanded be removed. Brezhnev refused. The next arms negotiations, in Geneva in June 1982, were the strategic arms reduction talks (START). The superpowers were now discussing cutting back their arsenals. This was a great step forward.

Kissinger decided, in 1976, that America had got so little out of détente he would no longer use the term. The new term which gained currency was Cold War II. Moscow intervened in Afghanistan, in December 1979, because it suspected that President Hafizullah Amin might be turning traitor. It was a KGB-led invasion and one of its tasks was the assassination of Amin. Andropov, then KGB chief, hoped that a breakthrough in Afghanistan would reveal to the world that communism was the ascendant political system. Afghanistan increased tension to fever pitch. Was this the beginning of a Soviet push to the Indian Ocean? US athletes boycotted the Moscow Olympics in 1980, and the Soviets and their allies (but not Romania) reciprocated in Los Angeles in 1984. The Carter doctrine proclaimed that the Persian Gulf was of prime strategic importance to the United States. The Afghan adventure estranged the Soviet Union and the Muslim world and turned into its Vietnam. Russians took to calling the country 'Af-gavni-stan' or 'Af-shit-stan'.

President Ronald Reagan sensed that the Soviets were weak. He wanted to eliminate all nuclear weapons. He decided to increase defence expenditure as a stick to bring Moscow to the negotiating table. American strategists began talking of a six month nuclear war to finish off Russia. Reagan maliciously referred to the Soviet Union as the 'evil empire'. He received no response during his first term (1980–84) because Soviet leaders were incapable of replying coherently.

Were the Soviets weak? Perhaps politically but certainly not militarily. Over the years 1974–82, the Pentagon estimated that the Soviets had produced, for example, 5.9 times as many intercontinental ballistic missiles (ICBMs) as the United States (2,035 compared to 346); 2.7 times as many tanks; twice as many tactical aircraft; and 38.1 times as many field artillery pieces and multiple rocket launchers. Actually they underestimated Soviet output during this period. Washington calculated that the Soviets had produced 30,000 nuclear warheads and 500–600 tonnes of enriched uranium. The real figures were 45,000 warheads and 1,200 tonnes of weapons grade uranium. As regards tanks, 64,000 had been produced rather than 50,000. This enormous arsenal had been built up to counter the perceived American advantage in mobilising for war. Providing fuel in case of war led to many oil refineries being built around the country. Their production far exceeded demand in a peacetime economy. Huge strategic reserves of raw materials (aluminium, etc.), grain and other products, needed in wartime, were built up around the country.

Ivan goes to see the doctor. 'Doc, I'm having a problem with my health.' The doctor says: 'The problem is you're too fat.' 'No, I want a second opinion.' 'OK, you're ugly as well.'

Questions

1 What was 'developed socialism' and how did it change the nature of Soviet society?

2 Was the period 1964–82 necessarily an 'age of stagnation'?

3 What reforms were carried out in the spheres of the economy, foreign policy, and culture between 1964 and 1985?

4 'Brezhnev had no political style. He was nothing more than a neo-Stalinist.' Discuss.

5 Did Brezhnev manage to unify state and society; and if so, how?

6 How much of a role did ideology play in the determination and expression of Brezhnev's foreign policy?

7 What were the key problems facing the Soviet leadership in the 1970s and early 1980s?

8 Did corruption drastically increase under Brezhnev or was this merely a continuation of previous trends?

9 Why was the shadow economy so pervasive in the USSR?

10 Why was Andropov chosen as Brezhnev's successor, and what reforms did he introduce in the fields of domestic and foreign policy?

Further reading

William J. Tompson, *The Soviet Union under Brezhnev* (2003); Edwin Bacon and Mark Sandle (eds), *Brezhnev Reconsidered* (2002); Matthew J. Quimet, *The Rise and Fall of the Brezhnev Doctrine in Soviet Foreign Policy* (2003).

CHAPTER 21

The Gorbachev era

'Who supports Gorbachev in the Politburo?' 'No one. He can walk by himself.'

> 'We cannot go on like this any longer, we have to change life radically, break away from past malpractices.'
>
> Gorbachev, 1985

> 'The stuffiness in the country had reached a maximum; after that only death . . . We stole from one another, took and gave bribes, lied in reports, in newspapers, from high podiums, wallowed in our lies, awarded medals to one another. And all of this from top to bottom and from bottom to top . . . We cannot live like this any longer. Everything must be done in a new way.'
>
> Ryzhkov (1992), reflecting on 1985

The period can be divided into four parts:

1 perestroika, glasnost, acceleration: 1985–87;
2 radical political and economic reform: 1988–89;
3 attempts at market reform, reaction and indecision: 1990–91;
4 from the attempted coup to the dissolution of the Union: August 1991–December 1991.

The election of Gorbachev was not a foregone conclusion. There were two groups in the Politburo. Whom would the oldies prefer? A key role was played by Gromyko, the leader of the oldies. He had discussions with Gorbachev, the leading youngster. The other possible candidate was Viktor Grishin. Who would make a more credible leader, in the eyes of the Party and the people? Not all members of the Politburo were in Moscow when Chernenko died. Volodymyr Shcherbytsky was in Canada. According to formal Politburo rules, Shcherbytsky should have been present and voted. He would have voted for Grishin. Another who was not present was Dinmukhamed Kunaev, Party boss in Kazakhstan. He arrived too late. He might also have voted for Grishin. Gromyko made up his mind that Gorbachev was the preferred candidate. This was an important decision; he had now moved camps. The decisive voice was that of Grishin. He unexpectedly proposed Gorbachev as chair of the committee arranging Chernenko's funeral. This was the seal of approval. Gorbachev could now be proposed as Gensek.

At the Politburo meeting on 11 March, Gromyko spoke first. He listed Gorbachev's qualities: his unquenchable energy; his desire to do and achieve more; his attitude to people; he always put the interests of the Party, the interests of society and the interests of the people before his own; he had a great amount of Party experience; he had chaired meetings of the Secretariat and Politburo with skill and in a Party spirit. Grishin echoed Gromyko's views. Eduard Shevardnadze praised Gorbachev as he had once praised Brezhnev. Gorbachev thanked everyone for their support. We 'are living through a very difficult period of transition. Our economy needs rejuvenation as does our democracy and foreign policy . . . we must move ahead, identify defects and remove them'.

Acceleration (*uskorenie*): 1985–86

Gorbachev regarded economic reform as necessary but not urgent. The concept of acceleration had emerged in 1983, He was an impatient leader. He operated according to the placebo principle: willpower could solve any problem. He was ill qualified to regenerate the Soviet economy. He believed that the planned economy was infinitely malleable. One could pick and choose reforms and thereby improve the whole.

Only a few insiders knew that the Soviet economy was lagging behind the West. Acceleration revealed to the general public the real state of affairs. It was perceived as the fastest way of increasing living standards. Instead of warning the population of the difficulties ahead, Gorbachev chose to promise everyone higher living standards in two or two and a half years. This would come about due to the rapid expansion of the machine-building sector. More machines would mean that more consumer goods could be produced.

The leadership assumed that national income was growing at about 3 per cent annually. In reality, the growth rate was only 1 per cent. Analyses pointing out weaknesses were ignored. Gorbachev and some other Politburo members favoured economic reform and organised a conference in July 1984 on prices and subsidies.

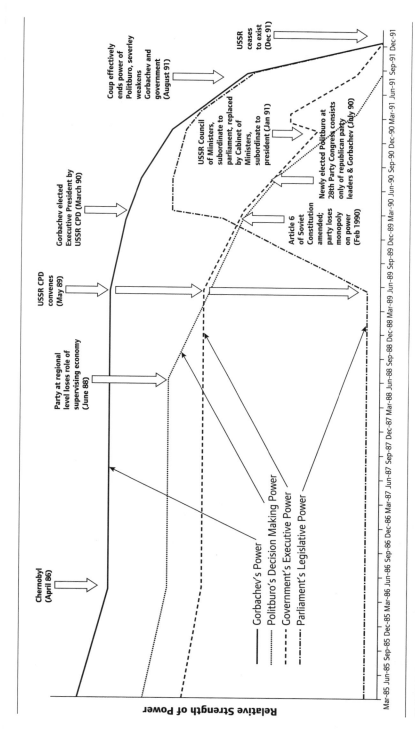

FIGURE 21.1 Power in the USSR, 1985–91

Gorbachev's contribution was characterised by 'persistent ambiguity and vacillation'. This was due to his inability to articulate a coherent price policy because he could not grasp the essentials of the problem. The Chernenko period is usually regarded as one of paralysis. However, some of the most radical economic reforms of the period 1986–88, such as permitting private cooperatives, individual economic activity and relaxing the foreign trade monopoly, were approved under Chernenko. In sum, the Gorbachev leadership knew what it wanted but did not know how to achieve its goals. It expected specialists to come up with a miraculous formula to solve all economic ills. Gorbachev complained to President George Bush, at the Malta summit in December 1989, that he was plagued with poor economic advice.

Alcoholism

A Party boss is making love to his secretary. 'No, no, leave the door open to show everyone we're not drinking.'

Gorbachev became known as Minsek or mineral water Gensek. Vodka was a staple of Soviet life and Misha wanted to take it away. A start had begun under Brezhnev and then given greater impetus under Andropov.

My own experiences under Brezhnev made me very sceptical of the success of any official anti-alcohol campaign. I was in southern Ukraine, in 1974, visiting a rice farm. That day, Pravda had announced a campaign against drinking. As someone who did not have a taste for vodka, I was delighted. At lunch, the table was covered in food, a few bottles of vodka and soft drinks. I chose some delicious looking pear juice. The director knocked the glass out of my hand, saying: 'A man does not drink pear juice; it is only for women'. Chastised, I had to drink a few obligatory toasts in vodka. As the vodka quickly ran out, I prepared to return to pear juice. However the director reached between his legs and brought forth a bottle of vodka. I weakly commented that Pravda had announced an anti-alcohol campaign. He waved this aside and we carried on drinking. He retrieved several more bottles from the floor. When everything was finished he called one of the waitresses over. He set the fair maiden on his knee, fondled her, and said: 'Darling, bring us some strong, black coffee'. After imbibing it, we all sobered up. It was then possible to inspect the farm. One could now tell a rice paddy from a hole in the ground.

In 1985, the state's income from the alcohol monopoly was almost 14 per cent of budget revenues. During the years 1985–88, the loss of revenue as a result of the anti-alcohol campaign cost the USSR 67 billion rubles or 9 per cent of 1985 GNP; 17 per cent of that year's revenue or nearly four times the health budget (Aron 2006). Overall, the budget deficit was 45.5 billion rubles in 1985. This climbed to 93 billion rubles in 1988.

At a Politburo session in April 1985 devoted to combating alcoholism, Gorbachev waxed eloquent about the evils of booze and its impact on future generations. Production had to be sharply curtailed. A commission was set up, headed by Egor Ligachev and Mikhail Solomentsev, the only teetotallers in the Politburo. As a Moscow wit observed, this was tantamount to sending a virgin to close down a brothel. Later, when Nikolai Ryzhkov, the Prime Minister, protested about the excesses of the campaign Gorbachev and others rebuked him. To them, Ryzhkov was putting economics ahead of morality. Hence, Gorbachev saw the campaign as a moral crusade. He was incapable of grasping the damage the loss of revenue would do to the budget.

In May, a decree was adopted which aimed at turning the country into a 'dry zone'. Even though it proposed the expansion of wine and beer production, this was ignored. Distilleries were closed down wholesale; as were those making glass tumblers. Vines in Armenia, producing the best cognac in the country, were ripped up. The same thing happened in Crimea, home to the famous Marsala wine. It had taken a century to develop them. So distraught was Professor Golodriga, a famous viticulturist, at the vandalism in Krasnodar krai that he committed suicide. Vineyards were cut back 30 per cent over the years 1985–88.

Home made hooch, *samogon*, rushed in to fill the void. Sugar began disappearing from shops; so did sweets and tomato paste. Everything was being turned into alcohol. One of the consequences of the campaign was to drive drinkers to switch to the hard stuff. One recalls: 'I only survived because I was poisoned by some chemical cleaning agent quite early on and I couldn't drink it any more. After that I stuck to eau de cologne.'

Repression

Corruption was part of the political and economic culture of socialism. Almost every official used his position for personal gain. A legal case could be put together against practically anyone. Hence the reason behind the anti-corruption campaign was political, not legal. Once the official had been removed, the vacancy could be filled by a Gorbachev nominee. One of the ministries targeted was the Ministry of Foreign Affairs. Diplomats in Tokyo had been buying Japanese consumer goods, especially for the youth market, and shipping them back to Moscow in containers. They were then sold on the black market for high prices. Diplomats in other countries did the same. Eventually they made so much money they started taking it out of the country and selling it for dollars. The CIA began buying large quantities of rubles to fund their 'friends' in the Soviet Union. Inevitably, the KGB picked this up. Many diplomats were dismissed, arrested and jailed.

Another target was foreign trade. V. Sushkov, deputy Minister of Foreign Trade, was targeted. He had been responsible for purchasing machinery and equipment in western countries. He was put in Lefortovo prison and accused of accepting bribes from western suppliers. The KGB demanded incriminating information about Nikolai Patolichev, the Minister of Foreign Trade. The latter had been close to Brezhnev and the KGB was trying to put a case together accusing him of links to Japanese intelligence. Sushkov's wife was also arrested. Sushkov was given 13 years and his wife 11 years. Gorbachev had personally sanctioned Sushkov's arrest (Pikhoya 1998).

Another high profile arrest was that of G. D. Brovin, Brezhnev's reception secretary. A massive press campaign followed in which lurid details of his alleged corruption were provided. He had actually been arrested in the CC building and the first interrogation began there. He was put in prison and the KGB threatened to shoot him without trial if he did not confess (Pikhoya 1998). He was sentenced to a long term in prison.

Then there was the Uzbek cotton scandal which extended into Azerbaijan and Kazakhstan, also cotton growing areas. Again the main purpose was political. MVD chief Fedorchuk devoted himself to collecting material on Stavropol krai, Gorbachev's former base. The *kompromat* was so embarrassing that Gorbachev engineered the sacking of Fedorchuk in January 1986. At the 19th Party Conference, the editor of *Ogonek*, a popular journal, accused several leading Party officials of corruption. This was the final straw. Gdlyan and Ivanov were reined in.

The investigations into corruption, begun under Andropov, broke an informal agreement. The centre had been aware that the republican elites had been embezzling large sums. Moscow had paid in order to cement their loyalty and subordination. Now these elites were being arrested, humiliated and sent to prison. The republics began to exact revenge. By late 1986, it was clear that Moscow was facing rising nationalism. Gorbachev was to pay a heavy price for his anti-corruption campaign.

In February 1986, in *Pravda*, Tamara Samolis, a well known journalist, published an article in which she reflected the views of innumerable letters to the editor. The drift of the letters was that the 'Party-administrative stratum', the middle level officials, was holding up the transformation of the country. A similar perception began to gain ground in the Party leadership. The leading light was Aleksandr Yakovlev, head of the CC department of propaganda. He forwarded Gorbachev, at the end of 1985, a wide ranging document. He proposed a two party system, based on the CPSU; the election of a Soviet executive President; the democratic transformation of the country; and pro-market economic reform. Gorbachev only found a few of them acceptable. He regarded the evolution of an opposition as inevitable. He was not afraid of it and was confident of his own powers. One can say that he consciously began to dismantle the totalitarian system from 1986.

Gorbachev's team

Egor Ligachev was elected to the Politburo and became number two in the Party. Nikolai Ryzhkov, head of the CC economic department, and Viktor Chebrikov, head of the KGB, also became full members. The oldies were now outnumbered. Anatoly Lukyanov became head of the CC general department. Other important members of the team were Valery Boldin, head of the Gensek's personal secretariat; Vadim Medvedev, member of the Presidential Council; Georgy Shakhnazarov, the political scientist; and Anatoly Chernyaev, a specialist in international relations. The most important unofficial member was Raisa Maksimovna, Gorbachev's wife. When I became the editor of the English edition of Gorbachev's memoirs, his aide laid down the ground rules. 'Number one', he said, 'is that you do not contradict Raisa Maksimovna.' Enough said.

In April 1985, Boris Yeltsin, first secretary of Sverdlovsk oblast, received a phone call from CC secretary and candidate member of the Politburo, Vladimir Dolgikh. He was invited to become CC Secretary for Construction. Yeltsin regarded this as a demotion and refused. The following day, Egor Ligachev phoned him and demanded that he submit to Party discipline. Yeltsin moved to Moscow.

In June 1985, Gorbachev proposed that Andrei Gromyko move into the vacant position of President. This was a neat solution. The Gensek could now appoint his own Minister of Foreign Affairs. Eduard Shevardnadze, Georgian Party boss, was chosen. Besides being Georgian, he had an imperfect command of Russian and had no diplomatic experience. He was made a full member of the Politburo. It was clear that Gorbachev was going to play a major role in foreign affairs himself.

Grigory Romanov retired and thereby left the Politburo. Tikhonov was packed off with his pension in September 1985. Nikolai Ryzhkov became Prime Minister. In December 1985, Viktor Grishin was put out to grass. The Gensek now had a clear majority in the Politburo. Boris Yeltsin was chosen as the new Party first secretary of Moscow.

The 27th Party Congress

It opened on 25 February 1986, the same day as the 20th Congress which had shaken the world in 1956. Gorbachev lamented the fact that there was so much inertia; perestroika was clearly needed. Then he dropped a bombshell. 'It is impossible to win the arms race', he said. The United States had won and the

Soviet Union had lost. He then turned to glasnost. Without it, there could not be democratisation. The political creativity of the masses could not find expression if it did not take root.

After the Congress, Gorbachev divided up duties among his team. He demonstrated a huge appetite for work, taking on much more than Andropov. Ligachev, in turn, had fewer responsibilities than his predecessor. The Gensek wanted to avoid having a powerful number two during a period of transition. However, there was a price to pay. It made decision making less efficient. This was compounded by the fact that some of the duties of one official overlapped with those of another. The Gensek, in his personnel policy, always set out to create competing agencies. This system of competing and overlapping functional elites demanded a strong leader who could manage them from the centre. If poorly managed, the result could be policy paralysis.

Chernobyl

All this paled into insignificance at 1.26 a.m. on the morning of Saturday 26 April when reactor number four of the Chernobyl atomic power station exploded. Gorbachev was told at 5 a.m. A special commission of top scientists, headed by academician Legasov, was immediately sent there. However, they were quite incapable of comprehending the seriousness of the situation. They sent no information back to Moscow for two days. All 43,000 inhabitants were evacuated from Pripyat, 3 km from the plant, on the afternoon of 27 April. By then they had been exposed to almost 64 hours of radiation. The Soviet media remained silent about what was happening. The Politburo met on 28 April to discuss the disaster. The area contaminated by radiation was estimated at 600 square km. The next day the situation was worse. However, the May Day parades in Kyiv and many other cities, within the zone of contamination, went ahead. Ryzhkov and Ligachev visited Chernobyl on 2–3 May. Ryzhkov decided to evacuate people from a 30 km zone around the reactor. On 2 May, everyone was evacuated from the village of Chernobyl, 7 km from the plant.

There was the risk of a second explosion in reactor number four. Radioactive magma was seeping through the cracked concrete floor. Were it to come into contact with the water table underneath, an explosion at least ten times as powerful as Hiroshima would result. This would devastate Europe. On 13 May, thousands of miners were ordered to dig a tunnel in the sand under the rector in order to pour in concrete to prevent seepage. On 14 May, Gorbachev finally decided to appear on television and report to the people. Thousands of troops were brought in the 'liquidate' the Chernobyl problem. In September, radioactive graphite had to be removed by hand from the roof of the reactor. A man could only work 45 seconds because of the level of radiation. By November the reactor had been sealed in a concrete and steel sarcophagus. Chernobyl had cost 18 billion rubles but also thousands of lives. The heroes were the fire-fighters and soldiers who gave their lives to save their country and Europe from a nuclear catastrophe.

Chernobyl ended any belief in the socio-economic acceleration of the country. The Soviet budget deficit in 1985 was 17 billion rubles and in 1986 it was three times as much. One-quarter of enterprises failed to fulfil their plan and 13 per cent were loss making. What was to be done?

More radical measures

In August 1986, Gorbachev went off on a grand tour of the Soviet Far East. He became increasingly disillusioned with what he encountered. 'Officials', he averred, 'are either instinctively or deliberately ignoring perestroika.' For the first time, he identified middle level government and Party bureaucrats as the culprits. He claimed that the people wanted to participate in perestroika but the dead hand of bureaucracy frustrated them.

In October 1986, at a Politburo meeting, Gorbachev provided information on people's problems as expressed in letters to the CC. There was widespread resentment at the lack of food in the shops. Even more annoying was the spread of commercial shops which sold goods, many of them manufactured in state enterprises, at high prices. Gorbachev was also criticised for developing his own cult of personality. Higher prices for alcohol and meat caused great offence. One Leningrad writer stated that he did not like the way the Gensek was conducting domestic policy. 'Far too many words and no action!' The 'law on unearned income is now targeting those who grow fruit and vegetables. The real culprits are being left unmolested'. A Muscovite writer was very direct. 'Your utopian projects to save the Soviet Union are leading to total disillusionment with the policies of the Party . . . Corruption and speculation surround us everywhere.' Gromyko revealed that he opposed the 'new thinking' (Pikhoya 1998).

On 11 December, Ryzhkov reported on the draft law on the socialist enterprise. This law permitted the election of managers and the setting up of workers' collectives. If managers were to be elected what did this mean for ministries? Full self-financing and self-accounting were envisaged. This did not make much sense, given that prices were low and material inputs were decided by government. The critics were proved right. This law led to endless wrangling over who should be manager. Workers, of course, favoured a comrade who would make life easy for them. There were many confrontations between management and workers' collectives. It all contributed to a further decline in industrial production. Without being unkind, one can say that this law was one of the most ill-advised economic reforms. Instead of solving problems it made them worse. It revealed that Nikolai Ryzhkov, the Prime Minister, lacked a basic grasp of economics and finance. In his

21.1 Martin McCauley with Mikhail and Raisa Gorbachev

defence, one can say that, as an engineer, he had had no training in these policy areas. One of his problems was that he was unaware of this.

On 25 December 1986, the Politburo agreed to legislation on joint enterprises with foreign companies. As someone who acted as adviser to western companies engaged in joint ventures, my conclusion is that they did not work. Or, put differently, they worked for the Soviet partner but not for the foreign one. The approach to business on the Soviet side was totally different. They always worked on the short term. A contract was valid until the ink was dry on the document. They then began renegotiating it. There was also the problem of language. How did one convey the concept of profit? After all, it was a taboo word under socialism. After having come up with a translation of various terms, one had then to attempt to teach the Soviet side their meaning. In my experience, most Russians were natural capitalists, that is, bandit capitalists. Investment went straight into their private pockets. A joint venture was a sure way of losing money – fast.

As things had not gone as well as expected, Gorbachev drew the usual Bolshevik conclusion: it was the fault of the cadres. They had to be renovated from bottom to top. There were to be competitive elections. Now glasnost came into play. Ordinary members could have their say and influence who was considered worthy of the job. In other words, the hallowed nomenklatura system was being undermined.

Yeltsin on the offensive

A very thorny question had to be addressed. What had given rise to the present crisis and who was responsible? A Politburo meeting in January 1987 brought matters to a head. Yeltsin was very provocative. The present members of the Politburo were responsible. He proposed to give each of them marks out of ten. In his opinion, little had happened in many parts of the country since the April 1985 CC plenum. Shevardnadze came up with a clever formulation to save face. Under Brezhnev, decisions had been taken by a small clique and the Politburo had been ignored. Gorbachev took exception to the proposal that the performance of Politburo members should be reassessed. He claimed that mistakes in cadre policy and the administrative structure were responsible for the slow development of perestroika. One can see here the beginning of the split between Gorbachev and Yeltsin. Yeltsin was too radical. He had offended the Gensek. The latter informed Vorotnikov that little had changed for the better in Moscow under Yeltsin. Boris's days at the top were coming to an end.

Glasnost

The driving force behind glasnost was Aleksandr Yakovlev. He wanted to cut through the lies which pervaded public life. Without glasnost, he believed perestroika was doomed. In the summer of 1986 he became responsible for the mass media. He made Vitaly Korotich editor of *Ogonek* and told him to tell the awful truth about the past. He appointed Egor Yakovlev, no relation, editor of the newspaper *Moskovskie Novosti* (Moscow News). It became the standard bearer of glasnost. Yakovlev released many films which had been blocked by the censors, beginning with *Repentance*. He returned over 400,000 churches, mosques, synagogues and prayer houses to believers (Aron 2006). He told the Politburo time and again that glasnost could only strengthen socialism while doing his best to end one party rule.

Nikolai Gumilov, the poet, was rehabilitated. Great writers and poets who had been banned for decades, such as Mikhail Bulgakov, Boris Pilnyak, Evgeny Zamyatin and Anna Akhmatova reappeared in print. Yakovlev abandoned Marxism but was to part company with Gorbachev, who held to his socialist principles. There was a desperate search for something positive in the past. Lenin was held up as the great revolutionary whose legacy had been betrayed. Vladimir Soloukhin, the novelist, threw some cold water on this and presented Lenin as cruel and the father of the gulag. He had also taken money from the Germans before 1917.

In September 1987, the Politburo set up a commission on the rehabilitation of the victims of repression. It had two functions: one was to uncover the dark truths about the past and the other was to accord justice to those who had been wrongly treated. In his speech on the occasion of the seventieth anniversary of the October revolution, in November 1987, Gorbachev faced two ways. He could not bring himself to break with the past. This underlined one of the Gensek's traits: intellectual indecisiveness.

The conservative camp struck back on 13 March 1988 when Nina Andreeva, a Leningrad chemistry teacher, published an article in *Sovetskaya Rossiya*. Indirectly, she represented those who thought that Stalin should be rehabilitated. There was also a streak of anti-Semitism in the article. Research revealed that some sentences had been lifted from Zhdanov's anti-cosmopolitism. Ligachev initiated it and the final draft emerged from the CC organisation department. A rebuttal of her views was only published in *Pravda* 23 days later. It was drafted by Aleksandr Yakovlev and Vadim Medvedev. The irreconcilable differences between the Politburo's Ligachev and Yakovlev were now in the open.

Elections to local soviets were held during the summer of 1987. In some cases electors had a choice of candidates. The opportunity was seized by some citizens to express their opinions by adding comments to the official posters. These ranged from asking for more food and shoes to 'Russians go home', in Estonia.

A snapshot of the state of affairs was provided in May 1987, when a young German pilot, Matthias Rust, flew his Cessna plane from Leningrad to Moscow, following the railway line. He landed in Red Square. Air defences had followed him all the way and had him in their sights many times. They never fired. No one would give the order to shoot. Why not? The commander-in-chief was Gorbachev and he was in Berlin. KGB chief Chebrikov wanted to deport Rust to West Germany for trial but Gorbachev insisted he be tried in the Soviet Union. The Gensek grasped the opportunity to sack the Defence Minister (he was replaced by General Dmitry Yazov) and bring 150 generals and officers before military courts or relieve them of their duties. The minister, Marshal Sokolov, and the commander of air defences, General Koldunov, had taken a hard line in negotiations on arms control with the Americans. More malleable successors could be appointed. Yazov was chosen because he was regarded as a very ordinary general. Unfortunately for the Gensek, very ordinary generals can be easily misled.

Economic woes

Ryzhkov reported on the state of the economy to the Politburo in April 1987. Economic growth had declined; there was a hole in the budget; investment in housing should be cut; price rises should be considered; the trade deficit with the West was now $4 billion due to the fall in the price of oil and the dollar. Valentin Pavlov, head of the State Committee on Prices, pointed out that prices for resources and labour had dropped; the oil, gas and coal sectors were now loss making. Under these conditions, it was not possible for these sectors to move to self-accounting. However, unofficially, some enterprises were prospering. The Tula agro-industrial complex had amassed four years' reserves of metal inputs. This means it had acquired, via the shadow economy, huge quantities of metal which was in great demand.

Despite the above gloomy analysis, Gorbachev informed the Bulgarian Prime Minister, in April 1987, that every machine-building ministry would be able to draft and implement plans which would mean that 100 per cent of output by 1990 would be world standard (Brutents 2005). Gorbachev did not understand how enterprises would react to reform. He ruefully admitted, in 1988, that he had not anticipated the 'social egoism' of managers who, on increasing profits, immediately distributed them to the workforce as bonuses. Nikolai Ryzhkov, the Prime Minister, also admitted a fundamental error. He failed to link rises in wages to increased labour productivity. These examples testify to the economic naivety of the Soviet leadership. Gorbachev was consistently asked to define exactly what perestroika entailed. He was quite incapable of articulating a coherent response.

Dependency on grain imports increased during perestroika. The usual caveat about Soviet grain statistics as shown in Table 21.1 applies. The figures for grain production are almost certainly too high. The financial situation was even worse. The country was increasingly becoming dependent on foreign loans. This had its effect on domestic policy. The slogan of acceleration was abandoned in 1988 and replaced by a new one: a strong social policy. The consumer goods sector was now given priority.

Yury Sokolov, Leningrad Party boss, reported a worrying tendency: the appearance of informal associations. Many were related to defending historical monuments, which were disappearing fast. A mass movement defended the

TABLE 21.1 Production and import of grain, 1983–88 (million tonnes)

Year	Soviet Grain Production	Imports	Imports as Percentage of Soviet Grain Production (%)
1983	122.9	29.6	23.4
1984	123.5	52.8	42.1
1985	124.9	36.4	29.1
1986	123.6	29.1	23.5
1987	123.8	33.8	27.3
1988	104.4	28.0	26.8

Source: R. G. Pikhoya, *Sovetsky Soyuz: Istoriya Vlasti 1945–1991* (1998).

TABLE 21.2 Hard currency debt (billion $)

Year	Debt
1981	24.7
1985	27.2
1986	39.4
1987	38.8
1988	40.8
1989	46.3
1990	57.6
1991	52.2

Source: R. G. Pikhoya, *Sovetsky Soyuz: Istoriya Vlasti 1945–1991* (1998).

Astoria hotel against demolition. The poet Sergei Esenin had ended his life there. Similar movements sprang up in Moscow. They brought together disparate groups of people. Some were defenders of old buildings, some pro-perestroika, some opponents of perestroika, some nationalists and so on. They gradually became more and more politicised. Delegates to the upcoming 19th Party conference were to be selected in multi-candidate elections.

On 6 May 1987, in Manezh square, in Moscow, about 500 took part in an unofficial demonstration. This was an unheard of event. They carried slogans ranging from 'Down with those who are sabotaging perestroika' to 'We demand a meeting with Gorbachev and Yeltsin'. Yeltsin, as Party boss of the city, had to decide how to react. He invited the leaders of the demonstrators to meet him and express their demands. The meeting lasted over two hours. Among the complaints was the destruction of old Moscow and the Americanisation of Russian life. Yeltsin was taking a risk by agreeing to meet and discuss with the protest leaders. He was setting a dangerous precedent. Some of the leaders were clearly members of the opposition. The main group protecting Moscow monuments was *Pamyat* (Memory). It was nationalist and anti-Semitic. The number of requests by groups to hold meetings in Moscow immediately mushroomed.

An important confrontation took place at a Politburo meeting on 10 September. Ligachev was in the chair as Gorbachev was on holiday. Ligachev rounded on Yeltsin for permitting Moscow city council (Mossovet) to regulate the holding of meetings and demonstrations in the capital. The Moscow rules were expected to be copied by the whole country. This was a dangerous development for the Party. It meant that city soviets would decide this important question without any official Party input.

On 12 September, Yeltsin, still fuming, sent a letter of resignation to Gorbachev. It contained a virulent attack on Ligachev. Boris could no longer work with him. He offered to resign as Moocow Party boss and as a candidate member of the Politburo. Disillusionment seeps from every line of the letter. It put the Gensek in a very difficult position. He was in Crimea putting the finishing touches to his book *Perestroika. New Thinking for Our Country and the World.* Yeltsin phoned him but he avoided a direct answer.

Things came to a head at the October CC plenum. Yeltsin had not prepared a speech but the Gensek insisted he speak. It was not entirely coherent. His speech took up two pages of the published minutes. Analysis of his contribution occupied 48 pages. It was expressed in language reminiscent of the 1930s. Each member of the Politburo took it in turn to pour vitriol over Boris. The Gensek spoke last and bared his teeth.

News reached Gorbachev, on the morning of 9 November, that Yeltsin had tried to commit suicide. He had stabbed himself in the chest with a pair of scissors. Yeltsin was psychologically at a low ebb. Despite this, on 11 November he was brought before the Moscow Party bureau, given another verbal lashing and dismissed as First Secretary. The following day he was sacked from the Politburo. Gorbachev had punished him severely for his rebellion. However, it was a Pyrrhic victory. Gradually Yeltsin became the unofficial leader of the opposition. He had been cast out by the Party haves and became the champion of the have nots. He gave interviews to the foreign press and never missed an opportunity to trumpet the failure of reform and provide his prescription for success.

Nationalities

An old Russian Jew, with a long white beard, is sitting on a park bench studying a Hebrew grammar. A KGB officer peers over his shoulder and engages the old man in conversation.

KGB officer: 'What is that book with the strange writing you are reading?'
Old Man: 'A Hebr ew grammar.'
KGB officer: 'But you are not likely to go to Israel at your time of life.'
Old Man: 'Alas, you are right. I know that my dream of seeing the Promised Land will remain a dream. However they speak Hebrew in Paradise too.'
KGB officer: 'How do you know you are going to Paradise? What happens if you go to Hell?'
Old Man: 'Oh, I already speak Russian.'

Officially the nationality problem had been solved. In common with many other Party statements, this did not coincide with reality. Russians were the elder brothers and the natives younger brothers. An unofficial contract had developed under Brezhnev. It permitted state embezzlement in the republics. Andropov had broken this unofficial agreement. The situation was made worse by the failure of perestroika to improve living standards. The superiority of Russians was now put in question. Estonians, to quote only one example, were convinced they could run their republic more efficiently than Moscow.

KGB chief Chebrikov, in December 1986, advised Gorbachev to include the nationality question in discussions on renewing cadres. The non-Russian intelligentsia had become more confrontational. He had plenty of evidence of emerging nationalism. In the spring, in Yakutia, Russian and Yakut university students had fought one another for three days. Then about 600 young Yakuts demonstrated in front of the local Party building. Their slogans were very provocative: 'Yakutia for the Yakuts' and 'Russians get out!'

On 11 December 1986, Gorbachev informed the Politburo that Dinmukhamed Kunaev, first secretary of the Party in Kazakhstan, had resigned. Nursultan Nazarbaev, Prime Minister of Kazakhstan, had asked him if he could appoint Kunaev Soviet ambassador to a Third World country far away. He also advised Gorbachev to appoint a Kazakh to succeed the Kazakh Kunaev. The Gensek ignored this advice and appointed Gennady Kolbin, formerly first Party secretary of Ulyanovsk oblast. He was formally elected by a Kazakh Party CC plenum, on 16 December. The following day, in Almaty, Kazakh students rebelled and called for a Kazakh Party leader. The crowd grew to several thousand, mostly young people. The KGB and militia tried to disperse the crowd. They were pelted with stones, pieces of wood and anything else that came to hand. Eventually two militiamen and one demonstrator died and over 1,200 were injured, almost 800 of these militiamen. Many KGB and MVD vehicles were destroyed.

Kazakhs had a lot to complain about. Nuclear tests were contaminating the north-east of the republic. The cosmodrome, Baikonur, was also there. Russians accounted for almost 40 per cent of the population of Kazakhstan. The south was poor and Kazakh. The ethnic Kazakh elite was divided into several *zhus* or clans. The poor state of the economy led to about 400,000 Russians leaving the republic between 1979 and 1988.

During the summer of 1987, Crimean Tatars renewed their campaign to return to their homeland from exile in Central Asia. Khrushchev had transferred Crimea from the Russian Federation to Ukraine in 1954. The Tatars, one of the 50-odd nationalities deported by Stalin in 1944, had been rehabilitated under Khrushchev. The Volga Germans and the Crimean Tatars were the only two nationalities not permitted to return to their homelands after rehabilitation. This was because Russians and Ukrainians had taken over their property.

The bloodiest inter-ethnic conflict, however, took place in Nagorno-Karabakh, a predominantly Armenian enclave in Azerbaijan. Demonstrations had begun, in 1986, for its transfer to Armenia. Violence broke out in February 1988. The local soviet passed a motion requesting the Soviet government to transfer the territory to Armenia. This provoked a sharp reaction from Azerbaijan. The territory was, and always would be, Azerbaijani. The conflict was significant for two things: republican elites were in open conflict with Moscow and it was the first inter-ethnic conflict covered live by the national media.

On 27 February, in Sumgait, near Baku, Azeris began attacking Armenians and destroying property. Officially 32 persons died and over 100 were injured. The local militia did not intervene. Barbarities occurred. Marshal Dmitry Yazov, the Minister of Defence, reported that two women had had their breasts cut off, one woman had her head severed and another was skinned alive. Some members of the Politburo wanted martial law but Gorbachev, as ever, sought a compromise. He reminded his colleagues that force had not worked in Afghanistan. A territorial rearrangement in Armenia and Azerbaijan would lead to an avalanche of claims by other nationalities.

The Baltic republics began edging towards independence. In June 1988, the pro-independence movement Sajudis was established in Lithuania. National fronts appeared in all republics. Their supreme soviets declared the national language the state language, replacing Russian. This discriminated against the 'occupying' Russians. In Belarus, members of the cultural intelligentsia complained about limitations placed on the use of the Belarusian language (Pikhoya 1998).

Non-Russian elites were laying claim to power in their regions. In essence, they were saying this was the price of loyalty to Moscow. They did not wish to secede – except in the Baltic – since they benefited financially from their relationship with Moscow. There was another factor at play in Central Asia, Tatarstan, Bashkortostan and the north Caucasus: Islam. The deportees, on their return to the north Caucasus after 1956, continued to be the most religious Muslims in the Soviet Union. Attempts to promote 'scientific atheism' were sharply rebuffed as locals equated attacks on religion as attacks on their national identity. The KGB gloomily concluded that Islam was dominant and that Soviet law was ignored. Andropov conceded that Russian cultural institutions were empty and that locals did not wish to mix with Russians. There had always been tension between official and unofficial Islam. By the Gorbachev era official Islam had been discredited throughout the Soviet Union. As a consequence, unofficial Islam was rapidly expanding its influence. The Iranian revolution, in 1979, acted as a stimulus to religious activity in Azerbaijan and elsewhere.

The 19th Party Conference: June 1988

The conservative Politburo members opposed the further blackening of the Soviet past and wanted greater ideological discipline. The more radical members,

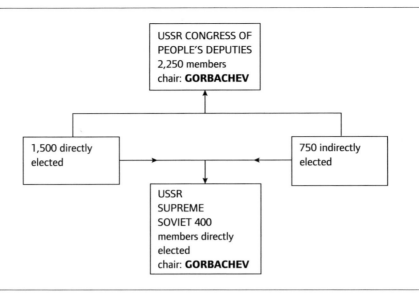

FIGURE 21.2 USSR Congress of People's Deputies

Yakovlev, Shevardnadze, Ryzhkov and Medvedev were clearly in the minority. Gorbachev, as usual, chose not to lead any faction. He always sought the middle ground and tried to cobble together coalitions for his policies. Yakovlev, speaking for Gorbachev, went on the offensive. He presented a stark choice: do we continue with perestroika or go into reverse? He won the argument. Ligachev's star began to fade and he gradually lost the right to chair Secretariat sessions.

The Gensek recommended that the local Party boss become the chair of the local soviet. In this way, the Party and the soviets would grow together or even fuse. The USSR Congress of People's Deputies, extinct since Lenin's day, was resurrected. Fifteen hundred members were to be directly elected in multi-candidate contests and 750 nominated by social organisations, such as the Party and Komsomol. The Congress would elect from its members a Supreme Soviet of 400 members. They would be full time law makers. Over time, it was envisaged that all 2,250 members would serve in the Supreme Soviet. This reform transformed the role of the chair of the Supreme Soviet. Hitherto, the chair of the Presidium of the Supreme Soviet, was a decorative function. It was held by Andrei Gromyko. As Gorbachev wanted the position for himself, he pushed Gromyko into retirement.

The conference revealed that the Party had split into two wings. There were the reformers, headed by Gorbachev and Yakovlev, and the opponents of the present course of perestroika. One of these was the writer Yury Bondarev. He likened perestroika to a plane which after its take-off had no idea where it was going to land. Perestroika had no clear goals or direction. It destroyed without putting anything new in place.

Yeltsin made quite an impact. He touched on a sensitive nerve. He attacked the Party nomenklatura's privileges: special polyclinics, special shops and the like. There 'can be no special communists in the Party', he thundered. The little people in the country loved it. His call for multi-candidate elections to all Party posts struck a chord. Then he became cheeky. Would the delegates rehabilitate him by removing the charges made against him at the October 1986 plenum? It was normal for a comrade to be rehabilitated after his death. He would prefer it while he was still alive. Predictably, a torrent of abuse descended on his head.

Gorbachev had no doubts that the Party apparatus was the main reason for the problems of the country. He had received a letter from a village soviet deputy who informed him that everything in the village had collapsed. The shop had been shut and the main road was in disrepair. The Politburo had stated that villages needed to be connected to a gas supply. What was a local official's response? 'Let the Politburo put in gas!' Officials toadied up to those above and were deaf to the pleas of the people below (Pikhoya 1998).

In September, the Politburo considered the reorganisation and slimming down of the Party apparatus. It had lost its role as the supervisor of the economy at the June conference. Over 1,000 departments and sectors in the CC and republican apparatuses were dissolved. The only departments left were those concerned with agriculture and the defence sector. The net result was a sharp decline in Party authority throughout the country. The Secretariat had historically ensured that all the documents necessary to reach decisions on the Politburo agenda were available. This had now ended. Ligachev reported that these changes involved dismissing up to 800,000 comrades. This had produced confusion and a decline in discipline. Gradually, Party cadres began to regard the Gensek as the source of all their problems. Many feared dismissal would result in a sharp fall in their living standards.

Another group which came in for sharp criticism was the intelligentsia. A campaign began in the second half of 1987 and continued until early 1989. This was a period when workers and peasants were being favoured over the intelligentsia. The main critic was Ligachev but Gorbachev echoed his sentiments. It was claimed that it was disgraceful if a professor's son became a professor; likewise if a diplomat's son became a diplomat. This was nepotism and had to be stopped. Many diplomats were recalled from foreign postings. In 1988, Gorbachev said that if a steelworker's son became a professor it was cause for celebration. 'We have to prevent a university professor's son becoming a professor', he claimed. This also extended to journalists. Some had their careers ruined at this time.

Gorbachev's behaviour was amazing. He had mounted the nomenklatura ladder, rung by rung, to the top. Once there he was bent on destroying it. He was losing support in the nomenklatura at the time when ordinary people had begun to express openly their disappointment at the results of his policies. His visit to Krasnoyarsk oblast, in September 1988, was a chastening experience. Anger at rising prices, shortages and ecological problems were compounded by the unpopularity of Raisa Maksimovna. Where the Gensek went, she was sure to go. She was an easy scapegoat. She was bright, dressed well, wore jewellery and visited shops when abroad. She was even rumoured to have a credit card.

In December 1988, Gorbachev visited America and addressed the United Nations. An official recommended that Raisa Maksimovna refrain from shopping and wear only clothes made in the Soviet Union. Back in Moscow, still glowing from his welcome in New York, Gorbachev summed up three years of perestroika. Great progress had been made. It had caused 'concern, even fear among the political elites of the United States, and even Thatcher'.

Radicalism and conservatism: 1989–90

The upcoming 1st Congress of People's Deputies (CPD) involved multi-candidate elections. A huge number of staff from the CC apparatus began moving to the new USSR Supreme Soviet apparatus. The centre of power was shifting. Elections to the CPD permitted the formation of movements, national fronts, single issue groups and an array of social democratic and religious formations. One could be elected with the backing of the Party apparatus or even against it. High profile journalists, scientists and artists could stand as independents. The politics of choice had returned. The dispossessed nationalities now raised their voices. Soviet Germans wanted their autonomous oblast reinstated and Ingushi wanted territory lost to north Ossetia restored. *Pamyat*, Russian nationalist and anti-Semitic, got involved. Inter-ethnic conflicts within republics, suppressed for decades, flared up again. Events in Tbilisi, Georgia, on 8 April 1989, took a tragic turn. Gorbachev was abroad and Ligachev was in charge in Moscow. It was decided to disperse demonstrators using gas and spades. Nineteen died and hundreds were injured.

The elections provided a national platform for Boris Yeltsin. He was nominated in over 200 constituencies but chose Moscow. He won in a landside: over 89 per cent of the vote. Other well known names who became deputies were academicians Andrei Sakharov and Dmitry Likhachev and the poet Evgeny Evtushenko. Radical economists, such as Gavriil Popov (a future mayor of Moscow), and lawyers such as Anatoly Sobchak (a future mayor of Leningrad) were also there. The best way to be elected was to oppose the Party apparatus. This was the case in Moscow, Leningrad and Sverdlovsk. There were rumours of a conspiracy to remove Gorbachev.

Gorbachev had to engineer his election as chair of the USSR Supreme Soviet. This would be an extremely important post. As Gensek and chair he would dominate Soviet politics. The Congress opened on 25 May 1989 and the whole country stopped to watch television. Later, proceedings were shown in the evening and late into the night. People arrived for work the next day half asleep. Every republican and national grievance was aired. The Soviet Union was an empire. However, it was a strange one. Normally the metropolis lived off the periphery but in this case the opposite was true.

Gavriil Popov announced that an Inter-regional Deputies' Group was to be formed. This signalled an official opposition in the CPD. Among its co-chairs were Boris Yeltsin, Andrei Sakharov and Yury Afanasev. The main points of their programme were: recognition of private property and greater sovereignty and economic autonomy for the republics.

Economic problems

The law on cooperatives was adopted in May 1988. They developed rapidly and in 1990 about 1 million persons were involved. At the beginning of perestroika there were three banks: Gosbank, Stroibank and Vneshtorgbank. By the middle of 1991, there were over 1,500 banks in operation.

In January 1991 the Russian Supreme Soviet legalised private property. It applied to land, capital and the means of production. Private enterprises could now be set up. They could hire as many employees as they liked. This law overturned the existing planned economy. The Russian Federation began acquiring

21.2 Kolkhoz market, Nizhny Novgorod, 1989

all-Union enterprises and property on its territory. Oil, gas and mining were gradually taken over. The motivation was also political. The life blood of the Soviet Union was being sucked away. Attempts began to take over Party property.

The economy gradually disintegrated. Food producing regions would not fulfil state orders. They wanted to barter their produce for something else. There were queues everywhere, especially for tobacco and vodka. Gorbachev told a joke in America about a man who got tired of queueing for vodka. 'I'm going to shoot Gorbachev', he said. After a while he returned. 'Well, did you shoot him?' 'No.' 'Why not?' 'The queue was longer than the vodka queue!' It's a good joke but Gorbachev did not tell the second part of it. One of those in the queue commented sternly, 'We'll never build communism if we keep running from queue to queue. You should have stayed there and done the job'.

The public attitude to authority became more and more hostile. During the spring and summer of 1989, there were 51 mass demonstrations, involving over 350,000 people, in Moscow and other cities, in support of Gdlyan and Ivanov. They had accused many members of the Politburo of taking bribes.

Gorbachev becomes Soviet President

With rising opposition in Russia, Gorbachev decided to set up a CC Bureau for Russia. He followed this with a Russian Communist Party. Elections to the 1st CPD led to the formation of Democratic Russia, an umbrella political movement. It quickly established itself in all major Russian cities. One of Yeltsin's proposals was to establish the post of President of Russia. He or she was to be elected by the people. Gorbachev reacted by having himself elected President of the USSR, not by the people, but by parliament. Article 6 of the Soviet constitution was amended. Nursultan Nazarbaev, Party leader in Kazakhstan, surprised Gorbachev. He asked for the post of President to be introduced in the republics.

Russia declares itself sovereign

Elections to the 1st CPD had revealed that Democratic Russia dominated Moscow and Leningrad. Formally, 86 per cent of deputies were communists but this did not mean much as the Party had split into various factions. Most deputies were heads of enterprises and agencies. Workers and peasants only accounted for 6 per cent of the deputies. The security services, including the KGB, were well represented. Democratic Russia had come up with policies which undermined the CPSU: reduce waiting time for housing from ten to three years; and a private plot for every Muscovite. In the Ukrainian elections, the Party leader estimated that anti-communists made up about a quarter of deputies. There was a joke about a Bolshevik in Odesa who had just celebrated 70 years of membership in the CPSU.

When asked why he had chosen the Party, he said that he had joined 48 parties in 1920 in the hope that one of them would win. Vladimir Kryuchkov, the KGB chief, thought that the country was near to breaking point (Pikhoya 1998).

Gorbachev was being caught in a vice. On one side, the Russian Supreme Soviet wanted to acquire more and more power. On the other side, the Russian Communist Party was dominated by conservatives. There was danger closer to home. Anatoly Lukyanov, who had taken over as chair of the USSR Supreme Soviet when Gorbachev became President, was visibly joining the opposition. As the second most important person in the state, he was in a position to harm the President. Gorbachev either failed to sense the danger or discounted it. The Gensek was trying to expand the middle ground but found that it was becoming narrower and narrower.

The publication in the official press, on 5 May 1990, of a letter by military officers to the President of the Soviet Union, set a new precedent. The officers sharply criticised the President for his handling of the Nagorno-Karabakh crisis. Under any previous leader, this would have been regarded as treason. The May Day demonstrations revealed the depths of anger and resentment. Thousands of people marched behind banners such as: 'The Politburo should retire'; 'Down with the CPSU'; 'Down with Marxism-Leninism'; 'Pension off Gorbachev'. Even more significant was the appearance of the Russian tricolour which had been banned since 1917.

Gorbachev did all in his power to prevent the election of Yeltsin as chair of the 1st Russian Congress of People's Deputies, in May 1990. His preferred candidate was Aleksandr Vlasov, formerly Soviet MVD chief. However he was a poor speaker and no match for Yeltsin. Boris thundered about the many years of central imperialist rule by the Party apparatus.

The new Russian government was much more reform-minded. The Prime Minister was Ivan Silaev, an industrial manager. Grigory Yavlinsky, chair of the Soviet State Committee on Economic Reform and one of the authors of the 500 day programme, became deputy Prime Minister. Boris Fedorov, who had experience of international financial institutions, became Minister of Finance.

On 12 June, the 1st Congress adopted the declaration of the sovereignty of the Russian Federation. This stated that Russian laws now took precedence over Soviet laws. This was a bitter blow for the Gensek. Russia would only now accept those policies which were deemed beneficial. Constitutionally the break-up of the Soviet Union began that day.

The constituent Congress of the Russian Communist Party (RCP) took place in June 1990. Most delegates at the RCP Congress attacked the CPSU Politburo, especially Gorbachev and Yakovlev. Ivan Polozkov was elected First Secretary. All Russian members of the CPSU automatically became members of the RCP as well. However the election of Polozkov as leader led to a mass exodus from the CPSU.

Pro-reform members simply refused to join the RCP. A high profile member who left the CPSU was Boris Yeltsin. He made his dramatic exit at the 28th Congress.

The 500 day programme

The Shatalin–Yavlinsky 500 day programme was published in September 1990 and the Russian Supreme Soviet soon passed it. Nikolai Ryzhkov and academician Leonid Abalkin drafted a proposal for a socialist market economy. Gorbachev was faced with two opposing reform models. As usual, he tried to find a middle way. A joint Russian and Soviet committee was set up to draft a compromise programme. However, the USSR Supreme Soviet was becoming more resistant to reform. A Soyuz group of deputies had formed, opposed to Gorbachev's leadership. Their protector was Anatoly Lukyanov.

The domestic political situation was becoming more tense. Georgia, Lithuania and Estonia declared sovereignty in March; Latvia in May; Russia, Uzbekistan and Moldova in June; and Ukraine and Belarus in July. Republic governments now claimed precedence over Moscow.

Gorbachev's solution was to propose a Union of Sovereign States. In August, the Politburo received information that a Democratic Union had come into being and was proposing the removal of Gorbachev and the dissolution of the CPSU.

21.3 Martin McCauley outside the magnificent pre-1914 Palace of Commerce, Nizhny Novgorod, 1989

Reports expressing fears that the Soviet Union would disintegrate were received from western Ukraine and Lithuania.

The RCP judged the 500 day programme 'anti-Soviet and a capitulation to capitalism'. On the morning of 21 September, a car in which Boris Yeltsin was travelling was involved in a traffic accident. Another car suddenly collided with Yeltsin's vehicle. He suffered light concussion. The incident happened the day after Yeltsin had asked an American delegation to arrange a meeting between him and President George Bush. Was it an assassination attempt? One of the results of the incident was that the Yeltsin–Gorbachev relationship, which had been developing during the summer, began to cool.

The constituent congress of Democratic Russia took place in Moscow in October 1990. It had nothing good to say about Gorbachev. There was more bad news for the Gensek. Party organisations had begun to dissolve. On 1 January 1990, there were 19.2 million communists but on 1 January 1991 there were only 16.5 million.

Changing institutions

In November 1990, Gorbachev, in order to streamline government, decided that a cabinet would replace the Council of Ministers. It would be subordinate to him and not parliament. Nikolai Ryzhkov, the Prime Minister, under enormous strain, had become quite desperate. No one obeyed him. A Presidential Council had been in existence for a short time but it was to go. It became a Security Council. At the 6th CPD in December 1990 a deputy from the Chechen-Ingush autonomous oblast accused Gorbachev of breaking up the Soviet Union. She called for a vote of no confidence. About 400 voted to remove the President but the majority voted against, including Yeltsin. The most sensational event was an emotional speech by Eduard Shevardnadze, the Minister of Foreign Affairs. He announced his resignation and warned the country of the threat of dictatorship. Gorbachev insisted that Gennady Yanaev be elected Vice-President of the Soviet Union. To be polite, he was a political lightweight. Gorbachev thought that he would implement his policies. He could not have been more wrong.

The Baltics

According to Vladimir Kryuchkov, Gorbachev had agreed to use force against the 'extremists in Latvia and Lithuania'. Another source states that a document had been drafted to introduce presidential rule. Gorbachev never signed it. The Lithuanian Party was clamouring for it so as to 'restore order'. On 10 January 1991, Gorbachev forwarded an ultimatum to the Lithuanian Supreme Soviet to implement fully the Soviet constitution there. The same day, he instructed the

Minister of Defence, the head of the KGB and the Minister of Internal Affairs to use force in Vilnius. The Alpha special unit was sent to Vilnius. On 11 January, Alpha and the other security forces, together with local worker volunteers of the committee of national salvation, occupied the House of the Press. During the night of 12–13 January, army and KGB units moved to seize the television centre in Vilnius. In the resulting conflict, 14 persons died. Citizens began building barricades around the Supreme Soviet (Pikhoya 1998).

These events provoked a furious response across the Soviet Union. Donetsk miners demanded the resignation of Gorbachev and a truly democratic and economic transformation of the country. Gorbachev claimed that he had not given any order to send the military or use force in Lithuania. Yeltsin then called on Russian troops not to obey orders to suppress dissent in the republics.

The Vilnius tragedy revealed that the Soviet government was willing to use force to keep the Union together, irrespective of public opinion. Force might now be used to resolve the political crisis in Russia. The most important lesson drawn by Yeltsin and his supporters was the need to establish a Russian army to defend Russia. Returning from Tallinn, Estonia, on 14 January, Yeltsin stated that the leaders of Russia, Ukraine, Belarus and Kazakhstan wished to sign a quadripartite treaty. These four republics would not wait for the signing of the Union Treaty.

Immediately after Vilnius, Gorbachev began planning a referendum on the continued existence of the Soviet Union. It was to take place on 17 March 1991. Voters were asked if they 'deemed it necessary to retain the USSR as a renewed federation of equal sovereign republics?' The referendum was an attempt to forge a third way between the old USSR and independence for the republics. The leaders of the parliaments of Estonia, Latvia, Lithuania and Georgia declared that they did not wish to sign a new Union Treaty. Yeltsin and his supporters seized the opportunity to add a question to the Union referendum in the Russian Federation. Voters would be asked if they were in favour of a President elected by popular vote.

In February 1991, KGB chief Kryuchkov forwarded his assessment of the political situation to Gorbachev. Shadow capitalists irritated him. They added nothing to production and there had to be a more just way of distributing goods. Privatisation was leading to the enrichment of some people. This, in turn, was having a political impact. If this continued a new bourgeoisie would emerge with all the consequences that entailed. Democratic Russia and the Russian Supreme Soviet were his bugbears. He favoured clipping the wings of the shadow capitalists and the press. If the crisis demanded it, the Soviet Supreme Soviet could propose provisional institutions to the President. A great propaganda campaign would be needed to unite the people to save the Soviet Union. Here was Kryuchkov, six months before the attempted coup of August 1991, informing Gorbachev of what was going to happen.

Yeltsin under siege

On 15 February 1991, 270 Russian communist deputies demanded the convocation of the 4th Congress. It was hoped to achieve this before 17 March and dismiss Yeltsin as chair of the Russian Supreme Soviet. Yeltsin replied by making a 40 minute speech on television. On 21 February, in the Supreme Soviet, several deputies demanded his dismissal. They also wanted the cancellation of the Russian referendum about electing a Russian President. Parallel with this, the CC apparatus engaged in intensive discussions with leaders of the autonomous republics in Russia. Their goal was to convince them to abstain from the Russian referendum. On 1 March, miners in the Kuzbass, in Siberia, went on strike. Among their demands were the dissolution of the CPSU and the dismissal of Gorbachev.

As expected, a large majority, 76 per cent, voted in the referendum for the retention of the Soviet Union. However the majority of voters in Georgia, Moldova, Latvia, Lithuania and Estonia did not participate. In Russia, 71 per cent favoured keeping the Union. However, voters in Sverdlovsk oblast rejected the Union, as did half of voters in Moscow and Leningrad. About 71 per cent of Russian voters favoured the election of a Russian President.

On 25 March, the Soviet Cabinet of Ministers passed a decree banning demonstrations and meetings in Moscow. Some Russian deputies asked Prime Minister Valentin Pavlov (he had succeeded Ryzhkov, who had suffered a heart attack) for protection against Democratic Russia. The communist tactic was to demand that Yeltsin give an account of his policies to the Russian Congress, convening on 27 March, and then dismiss him. On 26 March, Gorbachev transferred control of the militia in Moscow and Moscow oblast from the Russian government to the Soviet MVD. When the Congress opened there was a huge military presence, with hundreds of vehicles, around the Kremlin. Many deputies demanded that Gorbachev withdraw the military. Ruslan Khasbulatov, deputy chair of the Supreme Soviet, was dispatched to talk to the President but he refused to remove the military. The Congress then adjourned. The same evening, there was a huge demonstration in support of the Congress. Despite the fact that this was illegal, the security forces did not intervene. Clearly Action Plan 28, the carefully elaborated tactic by the communist faction in the Congress to overthrow Yeltsin, had failed. It had been elaborated by the CC apparatus behind the backs of their Russian comrades. Another objective had been to introduce a state of emergency in Moscow. The military were withdrawn (Pikhoya 1998). Gorbachev was the loser.

The speech of Colonel Aleksandr Rutskoi, an Afghan veteran, and member of the CC, RCP, caused a sensation. He informed the RCP that its goals were no longer those of the people. He was leaving the Communists of Russia faction and setting up his own parliamentary group: Communists for Democracy. Ninety-five deputies had agreed to join, including part of the Communists of Russia faction.

This meant that the RCP had split. This move may have saved Yeltsin from defeat. Yeltsin not only retained his position as chair of the Supreme Soviet but was also granted additional powers to introduce reform.

The failure to remove Yeltsin added urgency to the need for a new Union Treaty. The President met, on 23 April, the leaders of Russia, Ukraine, Belarus, Uzbekistan, Kazakhstan, Azerbaijan, Kyrgyzstan, Tajikistan and Turkmenistan at the dacha, 35 km outside Moscow. These were dubbed the 9+1 talks. They agreed that a new Union, a new constitution and new elections were necessary.

At a CC plenum meeting on 24–25 April 1991, Gorbachev was showered with criticism by Party functionaries. He snapped and stated he would resign as Gensek. A hastily convened Politburo meeting asked him to withdraw his resignation but he refused. It then went back to the CC plenum. However, members lost their nerve. Presented with a clear opportunity to dismiss Gorbachev, they opted out. Only 13 voted for his dismissal and 14 abstained. The culture of obedience had prevailed.

Election of a Russian President

The election was set for 12 June 1991. Yeltsin was supported by Democratic Russia and a host of parties and movements which had sprung up since 1990. Communists chose former Soviet Prime Minister, Nikolai Ryzhkov, as their candidate. Vladimir Zhirinovsky, leader of the Liberal Democratic Party, added his name at the last moment (his party owed its origins to the KGB). A key question was who was Yeltsin going to choose as his running mate? Eventually he hit on Colonel Aleksandr Rutskoi, believing he would bring in the military vote and some communists. The winner had to obtain a majority of registered voters, not a majority of those who voted. Yeltsin obtained 57.3 per cent, Ryzhkov 16.9 per cent and Zhirinovsky 7.8 per cent. Yeltsin was sworn in, in the Palace of Congresses in the Kremlin, on 10 July. A new national anthem (but without words) was based on music by Glinka. For the first time since 1917, the Patriarch of all Russia blessed the incoming ruler, President Boris Yeltsin. Russia had been resurrected.

Another anti-Gorbachev move

The Novo-Ogarevo negotiations concluded on 17 June and the draft Union treaty was forwarded to the republics. The same day there was a closed session of the Supreme Soviet. Gorbachev was subjected to searing criticisms. Marshal Yazov reported on the withdrawal of forces from Germany, Hungary and Poland. Gorbachev had cut the armed forces by 500,000, including 100,000 officers; many of them had no pension; the military call-up had been disrupted, partly because republics opposed it. If this state of affairs continued, there would soon be no armed forces. Boris Pugo, the Minister of Internal Affairs, stated that criminality and inter-ethnic conflicts had mushroomed. Since August 1990, the MVD had confiscated about 50,000 firearms and tonnes of explosives. Kryuchkov asked why Gorbachev's policies were so popular in the West. Valentin Pavlov asked for and was granted additional powers which placed him on a par with the President. Alarmed, Gorbachev turned up at the next day's session. He denounced Pavlov's speech and called for a vote in his favour. He got it. However, it was now clear that Gorbachev had lost control of the Supreme Soviet.

On 23 July, republican and Soviet leaders gathered at Novo-Ogarevo. 'I sense a dangerous tendency', declared Gorbachev. It was necessary to sign the Union Treaty as soon as possible. The chosen date was 20 August. Significantly, neither the CPD nor the Supreme Soviet was to be a signatory to the new agreement. Russia, Ukraine, Belarus, Kazakhstan, Azerbaijan, Uzbekistan, Tajikistan and Turkmenistan would sign. Those opposed to the treaty went on the offensive. On the same day, *Sovetskaya Rossiya* published an appeal: 'Word to the people'. Signatories included almost all those who would form part of the Emergency Committee in August. It was a virulent attack on those who wished to break up the Soviet Union.

The last CC plenum took place on 25–26 July 1991. A new Party programme and preparations for the next Party Congress were on the agenda. Delegates insulted the Gensek and the level of noise precluded rational debate. The draft programme was a remarkable document. It was a social democratic programme not a communist one. It was to be debated at the Congress which was to take place in November–December 1991.

Gorbachev, Yeltsin and Nazarbaev met, in Novo-Ogarevo, on 29 July. Vice-President Yanaev, KGB chief Kryuchkov, Minister of the Interior Pugo, Minister of Defence Yazov and the head of the State Radio and Television Committee were to be sacked. The new Prime Minister was to be Nazarbaev and the new President Gorbachev. Since the KGB had bugged Novo-Ogarevo, Kryuchkov and the others soon learned that they were to be fired. What were they to do? The CPD and Supreme Soviet could not dismiss Gorbachev as President as he had been elected for five years. That is, unless he was judged to be physically or mentally incapable of fulfilling his duties. Action Plan 28, the attempt to introduce a state of emergency, in March 1991, had failed. In April, the Security Council began working on a document which would introduce a state of emergency. Gorbachev, on several occasions, mentioned the need for 'emergency measures'. On 3 August, the day before he left for his Foros residence, he said, in the Cabinet of Ministers, that the situation in the country was 'exceptional'. It was necessary to take 'emergency measures'. Then Gorbachev added: 'The people will understand this'.

On the eve of the April CC plenum, at which Gorbachev offered his resignation, a group began drafting state of emergency legislation and the establishment of a provisional Soviet state committee of administration. Aleksandr Tizyakov, a member of the extraordinary committee on 18 August, and representatives of the military-industrial complex, among others, worked on the draft law. Members of the State Committee of Administration were to include Oleg Shenin, 'second' secretary (ideology) to Gorbachev with the authority to chair Secretariat meetings; Oleg Baklanov, deputy head of the Security Council; Valery Boldin, head of Gorbachev's personal secretariat; Yazov; Pugo; Kryuchkov; Yury Prokofev, Moscow first Party secretary; and Vasily Starodubtsev, chair of the Soviet Peasants' Union.

The plotters had to gain the support of the KGB, military and militia. They obtained this. During the summer of 1991 the Cabinet of Ministers increased food deliveries to military, MVD, KGB and railway forces officers. This was a significant move at a time when there was little to buy in the shops. On 20 July, the KGB leadership convened a meeting with KGB republican chiefs. The meeting was, ostensibly, to discuss the rise in criminality. Measures to cope with a possible 'paralysis of executive organs', in collaboration with the MVD, were discussed. Another factor which emboldened the plotters was the avalanche of letters which flooded in from ordinary Party members. They attacked Gorbachev and demanded that order be restored. This created the illusion that grass-roots support for a coup was strong.

Gorbachev was warned about the coup. Gavriil Popov informed the US ambassador, Jack Matlock, of the names of the coup leaders. This information was to be relayed to Yeltsin, who was in the United States. Secretary of State James Baker informed Minister of Foreign Affairs Aleksandr Bessmertnykh. Matlock informed Gorbachev that American intelligence had picked up that there was going to be a coup. Gorbachev was unruffled. He said he had everything in hand.

On 6 August, Kryuchkov instructed two of his senior officers, V. Zhizhin and A. Egorov, to undertake a feasibility study on the introduction of a state of emergency. General Pavel Grachev, commander of airborne troops was added. Their conclusion was not very encouraging. Kryuchkov refused to accept this. On 14 August, Kryuchkov informed Egorov that Gorbachev was mentally confused and could not work. The necessary documents to introduce a state of emergency were to be prepared. They were ready the following day. Kryuchkov then met Zhizhin, Egorov and Grachev. Oleg Baklanov joined them. They agreed on measures necessary to ensure stability. The vertical and horizontal lines of Party and government command were to be re-established. All parties and social organisations were to be closed down. These proposals were to be presented to Gorbachev, in the interests of saving the motherland (Kryuchkov 1996, vol. 1).

The KGB forwarded increasingly negative information to Gorbachev. This was to convince him that the country was becoming ungovernable. He was told that Yeltsin had flown to Almaty to meet Nazarbaev and other republican leaders. This was a bitter blow. On 17 August, a declaration, 'From words to action', was published. It was reminiscent of the 'Word to the people'. It was signed by a group for the convening of a constituent congress of a national patriotic movement. Vladimir Zhirinovsky's Liberal Democratic Party signed as well.

There were various groups of leading Party and government officials who were keen to reverse Gorbachev's policies.

- CC secretary for defence industries Oleg Baklanov; Aleksandr Tizyakov, head of a group of defence-related enterprises; Valery Starodubtsev, chair the Peasants' Union (opposed to private farming); and Minister of Defence Dmitry Yazov.

- Those who had gravitated to the top of the Party under Gorbachev. These included Oleg Shenin, now 'second' secretary (ideology); Vladimir Ivashko, deputy Gensek; and Valery Boldin, Gorbachev's right-hand comrade.

- The *siloviki*, the heads of the power ministries; Defence, Internal Affairs and the KGB. Kryuchkov was the brains and the organiser. Yazov's military would do the 'dirty' work of restoring order. Kryuchkov did not invite Boris Pugo, the MVD chief, to participate in the drafting of the necessary documents. He was also not at the crucial meeting on 17 August. It would appear that he was included in the conspiracy only because he was MVD chief. The KGB and military were to play the decisive roles.

- Those state officials who would lose their positions after the signing of the treaty: deputy President Gennady Yanaev; chair of the Supreme Soviet Anatoly Lukyanov; and Prime Minister Valentin Pavlov.

Crime and corruption

It is 1990 and any Jew can emigrate to Israel. Moshe Rabinovich appears at Moscow's Sheremetevo airport with two suitcases and a tall, thin box. 'What is that?', asks the Russian customs official. 'Not what but who', replies Moshe, as he retrieves a huge portrait of Stalin in a beautiful frame. 'But why do you want to take a portrait of Stalin to Israel?', asks the astonished official. 'I have great respect for comrade Stalin. He beat Hitler and made the Soviet Union a world power.' 'OK, proceed.' Moshe lands in Tel Aviv. The Israeli customs official points at the tall box and asks, 'What is that?' 'Not what but who', replies Moshe as he withdraws the huge portrait from the box. The official becomes very angry. 'Why are you bringing a portrait of that criminal to Israel?' 'I'll tell you. When I feel homesick, I'll just glance at this portrait and my homesickness will disappear.' 'OK Proceed.' Sasha, Moshe's nephew who emigrated to Palestine in the 1930s, meets him and takes him to his home

at Beersheba. Moshe withdraws the painting from the box. 'Who is that?',
asks Sasha. 'Not who but what is that, you should ask. Just look at the
frame. It is made of 20 kg of gold.'

Mikhail Gorbachev inherited a corrupt empire. A new Gensek, a new broom, was the rule. Cotton is part of the agricultural economy. As Party secretary for agriculture, from 1978, he would have been aware of the Uzbek scam. He had been Party leader in Stavropol krai, next door to the notoriously corrupt Krasnodar krai. Rostov oblast, just as corrupt, was not far away. The MVD had identified over 3,000 criminal gangs across the country.

Who would become head of the MVD? The comrade who was chosen to maintain law and order was Aleksandr Vlasov. In 1984 he became the Party leader of Rostov oblast. In January 1986, Gorbachev chose him as the new MVD chief. He was familiar with the problems of organised crime. His first comment to the MVD leadership surprised some: 'You have been devoting too much time to combating white collar crime'. As the new minister, he immediately arrested some of his predecessor's men.

Prostitution was also a growing problem in the capital and elsewhere. In 1985, the most successful madam in Moscow was Nina. She recruited village girls who were in financial difficulties. Nina charged 100 rubles as a minimum and 150 rubles for a night. Her business flourished and embraced taxi drivers who delivered clients to the door. A phone line was put in to permit a client to choose which girl he wanted. She was closed down but prostitution, the flesh business, quickly expanded. It was taken over by pimps working for criminal groups.

Gorbachev introduced two reforms which turned out to be godsends for the mafia. The first was the anti-alcohol decree of May 1985. This criminalised the activities of drinkers and had the same effect as the 16 January 1920 law on prohibition in the United States. Bootlegging became a major industry and huge fortunes were made. The American mafia had taken off. Exactly the same happened in the Soviet Union. The Russian mafia took off. Russians and their vodka cannot be parted.

The anti-alcohol campaign meant that everyone with access to vodka became a bootlegger. There was a woman who was in modest circumstances. She began speculating in vodka. Soon she had a nice dress and shoes, then an apartment and then a car. Taxi drivers began to make a good living guiding customers to a side street where a car was parked. The vodka was sold at twice or three times the normal price. Those who benefited most were the mafiosi. They made fortunes. Moscow restaurants were full of customers who appeared to be always drinking tea or coffee. In fact, the teapots were full of vodka and it was drunk from tea and coffee cups.

When Boris Yeltsin became the Moscow Party boss, the MVD forwarded him a memorandum stating that organised crime was becoming a growing threat.

'What organised crime? Who is organising it? This is for someone else', was his dismissive comment.

The Azeris were important in the black economy in Moscow. They controlled imported goods and part of the Berezka foreign currency shops. The Kursk bureau de change was under their wing and they ran three markets. Azeris had links to Turkey, Iran and Pakistan. They controlled the fruit and vegetable markets and almost all of the floral business. They had to beat off strong competition from the Baltic States and Ukraine. The floral business was one of the most lucrative but also most dangerous. An investment of 1 million rubles could be turned into 3 million rubles in a week. They supplied their markets with fresh produce from Azerbaijan. Lorries would have papers stating that they were going to deliver to state stores. Once inside Moscow they switched to new papers which revealed the goods were for the markets.

The 1987 law on cooperatives was like manna from heaven for the mafiosi. Some paid 50,000 rubles a month for a licence. They invented a list of goods they produced and staff they employed. The mafiosi used dirty money to pay the rent and used new money to buy property and accumulate capital. Private banks appeared to cope with the cash of the more successful cooperatives. Curiously, Aleksandr Vlasov, the MVD chief, did not permit the militia to inspect the papers or enter the premises of the cooperatives. The law on the cooperatives turned the whole of the country into a bazaar. In 1988, national income increased by 60 billion rubles. The cooperatives contributed one-quarter of this (Brutents 2005).

A momentous reform was the withdrawal of the Party from involvement in the economy in June 1988. Party bosses had been the glue which had kept the command-administrative system functioning. Party leaders were now to concentrate on ideology. However there is not much money in ideology. Did this mean the end of the glory days of the Party bosses? Of course not. Most of them had the skills to go into business on their own behalf. They had all the contacts and the know-how. The CC apparatus in Moscow began to move money abroad.

In October 1988, Vadim Bakatin, the mild-mannered Party boss of Kemerovo oblast, a mining region in Siberia, replaced Aleksandr Vlasov as MVD chief. The latter became Prime Minister of the Russian Federation. The KGB leadership changed as well. Vladimir Kryuchkov replaced Viktor Chebrikov. In January 1988, Rafik Nishanov had replaced Inamzhon Usmankhodzhaev as Party boss in Uzbekistan. The latter was arrested in October 1988. This was a momentous decision to take. It was the first time a republican Party boss had been arrested for corruption. Over the years 1984–88 about 58,000 officials in Uzbekistan were sacked. This included roughly three-quarters of central Party cadres and 3,000 militia officers.

In January 1989, Bakatin conceded that criminality was rising quickly throughout the country. The number of crimes was up 40 per cent in one year. In 1990, about 2,000 criminal groups were identified in Ukraine alone.

In April 1989, a new Soviet law permitted citizens planning to move to Poland, Czechoslovakia or Hungary to take all their resources with them. This allowed crime bosses and others to transfer their assets abroad. They found Hungary most congenial. They quickly bought up companies, hotels, restaurants and villas. Here was a simple way of laundering money and moving it on to the West. Cyprus quickly became an attractive destination. The courts were busy during the years 1985–89. Six hundred and twenty-nine millionaires were arrested and accused of theft, fraud and embezzlement. The main route to riches was stealing from the state. How many other millionaires escaped the net?

In late 1989, I travelled to Moscow to meet a KGB colonel to negotiate a contract with Intourist. Westerners were to join a boat which was to sail down the Volga, visiting towns en route. Then they would cross the Black Sea into the Mediterranean, visiting Greece, Turkey, Israel and finally Italy. I was taken to a fine, wooden dacha in Arkhangelskoe, just outside Moscow. The area had been traditionally off-bounds to foreigners. The colonel pointed out the homes of his neighbours: 'that one belongs to the Patriarch; that one to a member of the Politburo' and so on. We spent three days there negotiating the contract. The splendid dacha had ample sleeping accommodation. The next morning I discovered that there were other dacha guests: mice. They had gnawed their way through a canvas bag to get at bars of chocolate. This was a formidable achievement. I concluded that Russian mice had the sharpest teeth in the world! In order to prevent further damage, I left the chocolate out for them the following night.

The contract was to be in English and Russian. I drafted the English version and then proposed a Russian translation as the colonel did not speak English. Passages such as 'so and so shall be responsible for' were translated into Russian using the future tense. The colonel interrupted me: 'If we put this in the future tense nothing will happen. In order to get a Russian to act you we have to put it in the present tense'. This was a very interesting comment. It then occurred to me that all Soviet Five Year and annual plans were expressed in the future tense. He was telling me that they had little impact.

Negotiations over, the colonel said: 'With your contacts in London, I was wondering if you could arrange for a bank to extend me a $2 million loan?' I humoured him by saying I would approach a bank when I returned to London. His behaviour was instructive. He negotiated on behalf of Intourist thereby confirming it was an agency of the KGB. He wanted a huge loan, presumably to further other KGB business deals. There was a positive side to doing a deal with the KGB. If a deal was struck they had the power to implement it.

One request I made did not find favour. I mentioned that a personal meeting with Gorbachev would make the tour a roaring success. His reaction revealed that his influence did not extend to the inner circle around the Gensek.

I also acted as adviser in negotiations with the Soviet Ministry of Communications in 1989–91. The plan was to lay a fibre-optic cable from Berlin to Japan. At that time, NATO opposed such deals as it thought that the transfer of civilian technology would benefit the military. The main contractor was a large American corporation. Negotiating in the Soviet Union proceeded in stages. One never met a high ranking official at the first stage. One only moved to a higher level if there was a chance of success. The higher up one got the more likely the deal became. Fibre-optic cable was the cutting edge of technology and the KGB had a great interest in it. The Ministry of Communications, of course, was part of the military-industrial complex. The American side had brought along their chief research engineer. He regaled the Soviet side with their latest achievements. The following day a high ranking official suddenly appeared. Presumably he was a KGB general. The Soviets, of course, were fascinated by the technical detail. They, in turn, tried to give the impression it was old hat to them. Afterwards I asked the engineer if they really had developed the product which had aroused the greatest interest. 'Of course not', he said, 'but you have to bait the hook so as to catch their attention.'

We also held discussions with the Russian Federation Ministry of Communications. Their engineers were ill informed about high level technology. As regards theory, they were first class and grasped quickly the essence of the technology. This underlined the fact that Soviet ministries did not share important information. This wall of secrecy held back the technological development of the country.

In December 1989, the official rate of exchange of the dollar was changed to $1 = 5 rubles. This was an attempt to undercut the speculators who had been trading at 15 rubles to the dollar. The reform made little impact as there were already over 100,000 hard currency speculators operating in Moscow alone. Valentin Pavlov, the Soviet Minister of Finance, was proud of the fact that he played the black market in currency and made a handsome profit.

The best news of all for the black marketeers was the proposed 500 day programme, in 1990. One of its goals was to encourage entrepreneurial behaviour. The plan stated that the 'logic of the transition to the market involves the use of shadow (black) capital in the interests of everyone in the country'. A pro-market reformer, Galina Starovoitova, went even further. 'The black economy has the most dynamic, entrepreneurial businessmen. They have established structures and links with abroad which only need to be legalised.' Readers of *Pravda* could hardly believe their eyes. Here was a proposal to transform the black economy into the official economy.

Bakatin was pushed aside in December 1990 when Boris Pugo, Party leader in Latvia, took over. Pugo had previously been the Latvian KGB chief. Boris

Gromov, the Afghan veteran, was made his first deputy. A major reform by Bakatin had been the decision to permit locals to take over their republican MVD. An unexpected side effect of this occurred in Estonia. All officers with Russian sounding names were soon dismissed.

Was the Soviet Union uniquely corrupt? No, all communist states follow the same pattern. Marxist economics attempts to suppress the market economy and also the profit motive which results in personal gain. Both are fundamental to human society. Buying and selling privately at a profit was a crime in the Soviet Union. Since the planned economy was, by definition, a shortage economy, pent up demand eventually generated sources of supply. The less efficient the planned economy became, the more rapidly the shadow economy developed.

The shadow market also thrives in non-Marxist market economies. One estimate of the shadow market in Italy, in 2003, was that it amounted to 27 per cent of GDP. In Greece it was even larger. What about the former communist states of Eastern Europe? A conservative estimate would be that the shadow economy is about equal to the official economy. This leaves open the possibility that in some states it is the dominant sector. In Russia, in 2003, it was at last one-third of the economy. Bribery is also widespread in leading economies.

The socialist world

In a speech to the United Nations in New York in December 1988, Gorbachev spelled out his understanding of universal human values. Among these was the right of all peoples to choose their form of government. East Europeans wanted to know if this applied to them. He had stated, in March 1985, that the Brezhnev doctrine (the right of the Soviet Union to intervene in the domestic affairs of socialist states) was dead. Gorbachev was fêted everywhere he went in Eastern Europe. One can forgive him for believing that socialism there was secure. He told everyone to engage in perestroika. He believed that this would strengthen socialism. It had the same effect as in the Soviet Union. It fatally undermined it.

In Poland, communists lost elections in June 1989 and joined a coalition government under an anti-communist Prime Minister. In August, the Hungarian authorities permitted tens of thousands of East Germans to pass into Austria. The Czechoslovaks allowed trains packed with East Germans to travel to West Germany. In East Berlin, in October 1989, Gorbachev told locals that history punishes those who are left behind. The dinosaur Erich Honecker was replaced as Party leader but nothing could save the GDR. Soon after, the opening of the Berlin Wall (based on a misunderstanding) opened the floodgates and led to the unification of Germany the following year. Even in Romania, the seemingly impregnable President Nicolae Ceausescu and his wife were shot in December 1989. Soviet-style socialism had expired.

Gorbachev did his best to repair relations with China. However his visit, in May 1989, although a resounding personal success, greatly embarrassed the Chinese leadership. Young Chinese wanted perestroika and glasnost but the leadership was terrified of losing control of the country. Gorbachev's presence gave the democratic movement a great fillip. This sealed its fate. Deng Xiaoping sanctioned the Tiananmen Square massacre in June 1989. The leadership had drawn the conclusion that the Soviet experiment of simultaneous political and economic reform was inadvisable. Political reform was put off for several decades while economic reform could proceed.

America and the West

The first Gorbachev–Reagan summit took place in Geneva, in November 1985. It helped that Grim-Grom Gromyko had given way to the smiling Georgian, Eduard Shevardnadze. The two day summit broke the ice. Gorbachev, who started out regarding Reagan as a political dinosaur, gradually saw him as a man he could do business with. Reagan underlined the fact that no one could win a nuclear war. They had to combine to prevent one. Neither Gorbachev nor Reagan was good at detail but the American President had a finer grasp of political reality than Gorbachev. Reagan's instinct informed him that the Soviet Union was a declining power and keen on a deal. Reagan wanted to eliminate nuclear weapons and, by so doing, the arms race and the Cold War.

New thinking in foreign affairs made its appearance in May 1986. The class approach was dropped and the Soviet Union wanted to be a partner in solving the world's problems. One of the Gensek's proposals was that nuclear weapons be phased out by 2000. Afghanistan was a 'running sore' and he wanted out.

A deal was almost reached at the Reykjavik summit, in October 1986. Reagan accepted Gorbachev's suggestion that nuclear weapons be phased out. However, he would not concede that testing of the Strategic Defence Initiative (Star Wars) be restricted to the laboratory. Overall, the Americans thought the summit had failed. Gorbachev surprised everyone by saying it had been a success. This was then echoed officially by Washington. In reality, Gorbachev had negotiated poorly and had made many concessions on arms. Back in Moscow there was panic. Skilled journalists were given the task of putting a positive gloss on Gorbachev's performance.

Gorbachev coined the expression 'common European home' in Paris, during his first official visit to Western Europe in February 1986. France was chosen because it had a nuclear deterrent. His vision of a nuclear-free world caught the public imagination. Gorbymania had been set in motion. When Mrs Margaret Thatcher, the British Prime Minister, visited Moscow, in March 1987, she poured cold water on the idea of a nuclear-free world. However, she and Gorbachev got

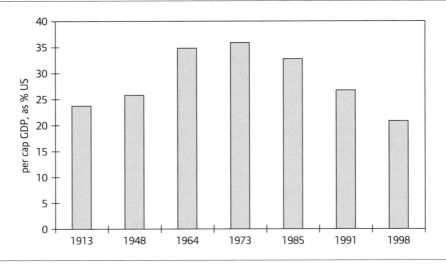

FIGURE 21.3 Russia-USSR per capita GDP as a percentage of US, various years, 1913–98

Source: Philip Hanson, *The Rise and Fall of the Soviet Economy* (2003), Figure 9.3, p. 244.

on famously and she told the Gensek she was a great fan of perestroika. She was to become an important link between Moscow and Washington.

In Washington, in December 1987, Gorbachev and Reagan signed an agreement which eliminated a whole category of weapons. Gorbymania took off. The first Gorbachev–Bush summit took place in Malta, in December 1989. The American President offered an economic partnership but was struck by Gorbachev's lack of understanding of a market economy. The 'Cold War', declared Shevardnadze 'has been buried at the bottom of the Mediterranean'. The bipolar world had become the unipolar world. America now saw itself as the hegemon of the earth.

Saddam Hussein's invasion of Kuwait, on 1 August 1990, was a severe test for the developing Soviet–American relationship. Gorbachev was in a quandary. Iraq was an ally and there were thousands of Soviet soldiers stationed there. He bit the bullet and said he would cooperate with the United States to put a stop to Iraqi aggression. He desperately needed western credits to prop up the Soviet economy. He could not jeopardise these by siding with Hussein. The Americans offered him $1.5 billion to buy grain. In London, in July, Gorbachev made another plaintive plea for lots of money. He reminded President Bush that the West had found $100 billion to fight the Iraq war. Why could it not come up with the same amount to save perestroika? He came away empty handed. The main reason was that giving Gorbachev the money was tantamount to throwing it away. The President had no clear vision of how to reform his economy. The two leaders met

21.4 Boris Nemtsov (governor) and Mrs Margaret Thatcher, in the Palace of Commerce, Nizhny Novgorod, 1989

for the last time in Moscow in July 1991. The Strategic Arms Reduction Treaty was ready for signature. Bush then repaired to Kyiv and told the Ukrainians that independence was not the same as democracy and freedom. An independent state could be oppressive. This was dubbed Bush's 'Kiev chicken' speech. His hosts did not enjoy it. It was clear that America wanted the Soviet Union to hang together rather than to splinter.

> 'The collapse of the Soviet Union was the greatest geo-political disaster of the twentieth century.'
>
> Vladimir Putin

Questions

1 What is meant by the terms perestroika, glasnost and *demokratizatsiya*?

2 What were Gorbachev's precise plans for the USSR? Did he really want to 'democratise' the system?

3 Examine Gorbachev's policies towards the Communist Party, the USSR Congress of People's Deputies and the executive presidency.

4 Outline the nature of Gorbachev's leadership style.

5 How did Gorbachev legitimise his political position within the CPSU?

6 Was it inevitable that Gorbachev's reforms would fail?

7 Was the dissolution of the Communist Party of the Soviet Union a result of Gorbachev's policies?

8 'Yeltsin was more than a political opponent; he was a thorn in Gorbachev's side.' Discuss.

9 Which phase of Gorbachev's reform package (1985–91) proved decisive in the eventual collapse of the USSR? Was Gorbachev directly responsible or was he essentially a bystander?

10 Why did Gorbachev become an executive President?

Further reading

Archie Brown, *The Gorbachev Factor* (1996); Martin McCauley, *Gorbachev* (1998); George W. Breslauer, *Gorbachev and Yeltsin as Leaders* (2002); John Lewis Gaddis, *The Cold War* (2005).

CHAPTER 22

Strengths and weaknesses of the Soviet system

Communist federations appear to have a limited shelf life. The Soviet Union was a federation; Czechoslovakia was a federation. Yugoslavia was a federation. They are no more. The other communist state in Europe which disappeared was the German Democratic Republic. It was one of many communist unitary states. However it was swallowed up by a federation, the Federal Republic of Germany (West Germany). In Europe, communist federations failed while capitalist federations flourished. Why was this?

Before attempting to analyse the most important factors in the demise of the Soviet Union, it is necessary to arrive at an understanding of how the country was run. This study adopts the view that the Soviet Union was a mono-hierarchical or mono-organisational system. In other words, there was one centre of power. After Stalin, the centre of power was the Party leadership. In a normal state, state organs would have dominated. This rejects the approach, prevalent in Western scholarship during the 1970s and 1980s, that the Soviet Union was gradually moving towards a pluralist society. The interplay of various interest groups, allegedly, was fashioning a new society. The ministries and other institutions of the Party-state were splintered into factions and lobbies. The communist and capitalist systems were gradually converging. Despite the mountains of scholarship devoted to this approach, the much criticised totalitarian model provides more insights into the functioning of the Soviet system. This model did not fail. It was demolished by the Gensek who believed he could put a more 'civilised' and 'moral' model in its place.

A striking factor in support of the mono-organisational model is the power of even the most decrepit Gensek. Brezhnev, in 1980, in his dotage, was able to pick up the telephone and dismiss Aleksei Kosygin, Prime Minister since 1964. Chernenko, physically weak, was able to block any new initiatives. Party bosses strongly opposed the election of enterprise managers under Gorbachev but were powerless to derail the policy. Some military enterprises were to be switched to civil production despite the strong opposition of the leaders of the military-industrial complex. Ministries and other institutions did lobby the centre. However, they never acquired the power to force the centre to cede to their demands. They pleaded and begged and eventually accepted the centre's decision (Ellman and Kontorovich 1998).

The concentration of decision making at the centre led to a neglect of feedback from below. Gorbachev was a radical leader who rode roughshod over the interests of subordinates. He ignored negative feedback and ploughed on. Astonishingly, it took over six years of root and branch reform before an attempt was made to remove him. He provoked an acute political and economic crisis but his right to take decisions was not challenged. The fact that his decisions were often only partially (or not) carried out is beside the point. The Gensek had the right to decide. The culture of obedience to the leader was instilled in Party members. At the 28th Party Congress they voted for policies they detested. At the Congress, the conservative Egor Ligachev, the darling of the delegates, only received one-quarter of the votes for Gensek. The new programme, vehemently criticised during the Congress, received 90 per cent of the votes.

Obedience to the leader's line prevailed. Members were obliged to observe Party unity. During Party plenums and Congresses the Gensek and his supporters were submitted to ferocious criticism. That became acceptable. What was not accepted was voting against policies proposed by him. I followed the 28th Congress on television, in Estonia. It was amazing to watch delegates tear into the Gensek and then vote meekly for the policies which they had previously condemned. A classic example was the new Party programme. It was social democratic and not Marxist. Yet it was passed easily. Hence this study of the Soviet Union concentrates on the rulers and their policies.

■ The failed coup sentenced the Soviet Union to death. It permitted Yeltsin to dominate Gorbachev and gradually to achieve Russia's ambition of destroying the Soviet Union and establishing a weak Commonwealth of Independent States.

■ The big idea of the Soviet Union was communism. Russian political culture favoured the emergence of a strong leader and ideology. Russians were by nature collectivist. They favoured a strong leader and a strong state. Marxism was a utopian ideology, meaning it could never be implemented. It assumed that a person could only achieve happiness within a collective, never as an individual. The profit motive or private gain, the generator of economic advance from time immemorial was declared a vice not a virtue. Hence the basic human instinct of man and woman, to make money, was denied.

German society was communal so Marx's concept of a mass society with the individual achieving fulfilment and happiness within the commune was broadly German. Marxism spread like wildfire among certain sections of the intelligentsia in Russia from the 1890s onwards. It offered a sophisticated, European philosophical understanding of the human condition. It also claimed certainty. It was moral – condemning the exploitation of man by man and woman by woman – and envisaged everyone working for the common good. It promised social justice and the arrival of an earthly paradise. Gradually all conflicts would be eliminated as human beings acted rationally for the good of society.

No wonder it was attractive in a backward European country which was just beginning the process of industrialisation and modernisation. The engine of progress for Marx was the working class, meaning an industrial working class. When capitalism, the private ownership of the means of production, distribution and exchange, had reached its zenith, the dictatorship of the pro-letariat – those who sold their labour for a wage – would usher in the era of socialism. The higher stage of socialism – communism – would follow. In the former workers would be rewarded according to their labour but in the latter according to their needs. The problem that Russian Marxists faced was that Russia only had a small but growing working class. Orthodox Marxists con-cluded that Russia would have to industrialise before it could move forward to socialism. Vladimir Ulyanov (1870–1924), better known as Lenin, disagreed. A revolutionary party, known as Bolsheviks, could seize power and industri-alise rapidly. Russia could be the first country to achieve a Marxist revolution but could not sustain that revolution without other, more developed states becoming socialist. To Lenin, during the First World War (1914–18), Russia was the weakest link in the capitalist chain of countries. Remove one link and the chain would break. Lenin and the Bolsheviks took power in Russia on 25 October 1917. They waited with bated breath for news from Berlin, Vienna, Paris, London or Milan that revolution had broken out. It never came. Russia was on its own. Soon after taking power, the Bolsheviks were plunged into a bitter Civil War (1918–20). The Party was militarised and had to use coercion to stay in power.

The victory of socialism was declared in the 1936 constitution with the Soviet Union having built the 'fundamentals'. This meant it was now in the lower stage of communism. In 1952, Stalin expected the country to reach the higher stage, full communism, in 1970. Khrushchev was a fervent Marxist-Leninist but with an unsure grasp of theory and history. He proclaimed the imminent arrival of the Soviet Union at the foothills of communism: this time it was 1980. The spell of Marxism-Leninism was broken under Khrushchev.

He did more than any other leader to undermine the faith. Hence one can say that there was a crisis of faith from the Khrushchev era onwards.

The concept of developed socialism made its appearance under Leonid Brezhnev (1964–82). The communist future had been discredited so Brezhnev reversed to developed socialism. A slow economic decline set in after 1975 and little was done until the arrival of Mikhail Gorbachev in 1985. Brezhnev, in his declining years, and his successors Yury Andropov and Konstantin Chernenko often gave the impression of being more dead than alive. Gorbachev had to remove the discredited concept of developed socialism and came up with developing socialism. This was puzzling. Was the Soviet Union going backwards?

Soviet leaders after Stalin were treated with scant respect. Brezhnev was dim-witted and the butt of many jokes.

Brezhnev instructs his clever assistant to write him a ten minute speech. 'Remember, just ten minutes,' he admonishes. After returning, Brezhnev is furious and berates the assistant mercilessly. 'You fool, I told me to write me a ten minute speech but it took twenty minutes to deliver.' The assistant quietly replies. 'But comrade general secretary I gave you two copies!'

I asked a member of the Academy of Sciences what the difference was between developed and developing socialism. He replied: 'There is no difference. It is all nonsense'. Clearly Marxism-Leninism was no longer a motivating faith. Gorbachev began moving towards social democracy.

However, there were still many true believers – those who kept the faith despite the evidence of their own eyes. I asked the Russian Minister of Finance, in 1990, what percentage of Party members were Marxists. His reply surprised me. 'Twenty per cent', he said. Another analyst suggested that one-third of Party members were committed to Marxism, another third were in the Party for career advancement and another third were thinking of leaving.

■ Industry: In 1914, Russia was the eighth most developed country in the world. Stalin's rapid industrialisation achieved formidable success. One of the reasons for this was that the country was almost autarkic – it did not need to import to industrialise. One of the few exceptions was rubber. Stalin followed a Marxist mode of industrialisation – start industry everywhere. The aim was to industrialise evenly across the country. This meant transporting raw materials and finished products hundreds, often thousands, of kilometres. Large industrial towns were set up in isolated areas. If free labour was unwilling to move there, Stalin used coercion. Most of the labour in the north, for example, was convict labour. Stalin never accepted the liberal market concept that free labour is more productive than unfree. The planners favoured large enterprises, employing thousands. They also dispensed welfare and became communities in their own right.

The Soviet economy grew substantially but it was extensive growth, based on setting up new enterprises. Several attempts at making the system more efficient were attempted under Brezhnev (1964–82) but the huge rise in oil prices in the early 1970s rendered reform less urgent. The Soviet Union became a leading oil and natural gas exporter. Growth rates began to slow in the late 1970s as raw materials became more expensive to exploit. In reality, by 1970, there were two economies which existed side by side: the official or planned and the shadow economy. The latter was growing faster than the official economy as shortages began to bite. Gorbachev had an imperfect understanding of how the Soviet economy worked – economics was one of his blind spots. He introduced many economic reforms which, in reality, made matters worse.

■ The Military-Industrial Complex (VPK):

VPK (Voenno-promishlennaya komissiya) Military-Industrial Commission; established in 1957 by Dmitry Ustinov; he remained in charge until he became Minister of Defence in 1976; consisted of nine key ministries which were responsible for military research and development (R & D) and defence procurement; many ministers remained in post for a quarter of a century; it employed most of the country's best scientists and engineers.

The Bolsheviks saved Russia from disintegration in 1917–22. The military economy took precedence. Stalin was so successful that Nazi Germany was defeated in 1945. All key enterprises were in the defence sector. The Academy of Sciences undertook much of the fundamental research. There were amazing achievements. The atomic bomb in 1949; the hydrogen bomb in 1952; the first space vehicle, Sputnik, in 1957; the first man, the first woman, the first dog in space and so on. So alarmed were the Americas that they set up the National Aeronautics and Space Administration (NASA) to get to the moon first.

Part of the Soviet success was due to espionage. Mountains of intelligence flowed into the VPK. To take one example: radar. The Soviets moved from zero in 1940 to be world leaders by 1956. They could not have achieved this without good spies but that is only part of the story. They had the scientists capable of understanding and developing the ideas from America and elsewhere. If this was so why did the Soviets fall behind in the arms race? One of the key reasons was the gulf between scientists and engineers. In the Soviet Union scientists enjoyed enormous prestige. Engineers were second class citizens. This explains why so many brilliant ideas never got beyond the drawing board. A Soviet scientist never got his hands dirty by helping in an engineering laboratory. In other words, research was brilliant but development was weak. The military-industrial complex in the Soviet Union accounted for at least 40 per cent of national income. No one knew the exact figure, not even the leader.

■ Agriculture: The rural sector was always the Achilles' heel of the Soviet system. The country could never market enough food to feed the population adequately. It could produce the food but it lost about one-third between the field and the consumer. Khrushchev began importing US grain 1963 and Brezhnev enthusiastically followed.

The above analysis of industry, the military-industrial complex and agriculture only embraces the official economy. There was another economy which can be called the grey (legal private trade in goods) and black (illegal private trade in goods) economy. A collective name would be the shadow economy. Here everything which was traded outside the official, state economy is referred to as the shadow economy. János Kornai, a leading Hungarian economist, has called the official or state planned economy a quintessentially shortage economy. Where there are shortages there will always be those who are willing to meet repressed demand. Since all private trade (except the kolkhoz markets) was illegal, private trading was a high risk activity. Since it was illegal, its practitioners had to pay bribes to stay out of labour camps or, in some cases, stay alive.

The planned economy, or the command administrative system, could not supply all the required goods. Stalin permitted enterprises, after fulfilling the plan, to market privately up to 5 per cent of the plan output. These goods were sold in special shops. Defective parts and goods which could not be included in state deliveries were recycled and sold privately. In a shortage economy, this opened the door to widespread speculation. One enterprise, producing sewing machines, managed to make 600 extra machines for the shadow economy out of defective spare parts. In fact, it was in the interests of the factory to produce defective machines. They could be repaired quickly and sold privately.

Stalin always exhorted enterprises to overfulfil the plan. One does not have to be an economist to realise that if one factory overfulfils its plan, another underfulfils its plan. In an economy in which there were never enough inputs to meet plan targets, the acquisition of extra inputs to meet one's state deliveries became a matter of life and death. Under Stalin, the price of failure could be the gulag. One might even be accused of wrecking and sabotage. An army of fixers (tolkachi) came into being. Their job was to acquire inputs by legal or illegal means. They traded what their enterprise produced 'on the side' for the desired inputs. In other words, the market made a comeback.

The networks which had been built up flourished under Khrushchev. Those involved became known as *tsekhoviki* or shadow capitalists. The word derived from workshops (*tsekh*), the part of the enterprise devoted to private production and sale. One state furniture factory devoted 10 per cent of its time working for the state and 90 per cent for itself (Brutents 2005). Many military enterprises were dual purpose. They produced for the military and civilian markets. They were very well placed to take advantage of the shadow economy. In some enterprises the number of transistor radios rejected as unfit for military use could be as high as 99 per cent. The military had their own retail outlets, the Voentorg. Under Brezhnev, the shadow capitalists came into their own.

■ The Arms Race: Many commentators aver that the arms race brought down the Soviet Union. This is not so. According to published statistics, defence expenditure under Gorbachev did not rise. However, it is true that the Soviet leadership realised that the country could not compete with the US. Arms expenditure was crippling the Soviet Union. The arms race is only one of many variables which, when combined, provoked the demise of the country.

President Ronald Reagan wanted to abolish nuclear weapons. He increased defence expenditure to force the Soviets to the negotiating table. He then changed tack. Why? In November 1983, there was a NATO war exercise code-named Able Archer, which the Soviet military misinterpreted as a preparation for a nuclear strike against them. This scare also caused Reagan to soften his anti-communist rhetoric. He was mindful of one of the many quips of President Richard Nixon (1968–74): 'I can go into my office and pick up the telephone and in 25 minutes, 70 million people will be dead'. Ronald Reagan did not want to go down in history as a mass murderer. The arrival of Gorbachev changed everything. The arms race went into reverse.

■ Nationalities: The Russian Empire extended across many time zones and stretched to the Pacific, the borders of Afghanistan, Persia and the Ottoman Empire. The Soviet Union inherited this territory and hence was also an empire. Over 100 nationalities inhabited the Soviet space. They ranged from Europeans such as Germans, Poles and Hungarians to Muslims to Buddhists to tree worshippers. Ethnic Russians always made up a majority of the Soviet population. The last census, in 1989, counted over 145 million Russians out of a Soviet population of just over 285 million. Had the Soviet Union survived, Russians would have been in a minority before the end of the century. However, if one adds 44 million Ukrainians and 10 million Belarusians, the Slavs accounted for over two-thirds of the Soviet population. Muslims were the next largest group, at over 41 million.

The major nationalities had their own republics. The Soviet constitution of 1936 even included the right of a republic to secede from the Soviet Union. This was only on paper since Stalin was the final arbiter and his attitude was that new republics (Estonia, Latvia and Lithuania in 1940, for example) should join the Soviet state not leave it. Stalin's nationality policy left his successors with almost intractable problems. The Volga Germans had been deported in 1941 to Siberia and Central Asia and many other nationalities, the majority Muslim, were also deported to Central Asia from 1944 onwards. They had all been accused of collaborating with the German Wehrmacht. All these charges were revoked under Khrushchev but not everyone could return home. Volga German territory had been occupied by Russians and Ukrainians and the Crimean Tatar land also occupied by the Slavs.

Each republic had its own Communist Party (except Russia until 1990), its own Academy of Sciences (except Russia until 1990) and so on. This produced national elites who developed a strong sense of national identity. It was only natural that many of them believed they could run their own territories better than the Russians or Ukrainians. This applied most strongly to the Baltic republics, Estonia, Latvia and Lithuania, which had been forced into the Soviet Union against their will. Gorbachev blithely believed that the nationality problem had been solved. However, one of his predecessors, Yury Andropov (1982–84), had warned officials about the perils of Russian arrogance. Glasnost reopened old wounds and long festering grievances. Gorbachev's solution was to propose a Union of Sovereign States and transform the sham federation which he admitted the Soviet Union was into a genuine federation.

■ The Burden of Empire: By 1991 every socialist state was a net recipient of Soviet largesse. One of the worst offenders was the German Democratic Republic; until the 1980s the showpiece of socialist planning in the region. It was resource poor, especially in fuel. Moscow increasingly had to subsidise it. Hans Modrow, the last GDR Prime Minister, plaintively appealed to Gorbachev: 'The GDR is the Soviet Union's child. Please care for us'. It is impossible to put a figure on what the East European empire was costing Moscow during the Gorbachev era. East European states aimed to run a trade deficit with the Soviet Union because that meant that they were getting credit from Moscow. It was rational economic behaviour from their point of view.

Afghanistan was an 'open wound', to quote Gorbachev. That disastrous adventure ended in February 1989. Elsewhere in the Third World, it appeared that the Soviet version of Marxism was on the march. Countries such as Ethiopia, Angola, Mali, the Democratic Republic of the Congo and Mozambique all declared themselves part of the socialist crusade against western imperialism. The problem was that they were all poor and often involved in civil wars. The East Europeans also chipped in. The East German speciality was to train the secret police in the new socialist states. An unkind critic once referred to these graduates as Himmler's henchmen. Other communist states, such as Laos and Vietnam, expected Soviet largesse. In the latter, despite enormous aid, Moscow had only limited influence.

The favoured son in the western hemisphere was Cuba. The Soviet Union took Cuba's sugar and paid well over the world market price for it. Cuba was useful for the Soviet military as a listening post next door to the US. Western communist parties expected subventions. Relations with the Italian Communist Party (PCI) were good. A high level Soviet Party functionary would travel to Italy to meet the PCI secretary. The Party comrade did not want the interpreter to know how much money was being passed over. So he turned his back on him and traced numbers in the air with his finger. Only the Italian comrade could see them. It was always the same Party comrade and the same interpreter. On one occasion the interpreter committed a faux pas. Entering the conference room, he observed that there were four chairs arranged side by side. Since he knew there were only three bottoms he removed one and placed it against the wall. When the Party comrade entered the room he immediately retrieved the chair and placed it alongside his own. He suffered from haemorrhoids and needed to sit between two chairs! When the interpreter saw this he burst out laughing.

■ The mortal blow which buried Soviet communism was arguably moral, intellectual and cultural. These factors are just as important as the economic and technological ones. The Soviet Union until the 1920s was in the avant-garde of world literature, painting, sculpture, music and many other arts. Stalin and his circle reverted to a more conservative cultural approach: one that would serve the building of socialism. Many observers were bemused by the Soviet refusal to engage with world culture and the persecution of artists and writers who wanted to experiment. Had the Soviet Union engaged with the world, it would have gained enormous prestige. Arguably it would have conferred greater legitimacy on the communist system than any series of economic statistics. Its cultural policy was utterly self-defeating. By 1985, Mikhail Gorbachev and, especially, Aleksandr Yakovlev, had come to the conclusion that a moral regeneration of the country was necessary. The lies had to be swept away and the truth told about the country and its past. Glasnost unleashed this revolution. Large numbers of educated came to regard the regime as illegitimate. Workers wanted a state that would deliver the goods.

■ Youth: Jazz was all the rage in the Soviet Union in the 1920s. Then the country went serious as Stalin attempted to shape the new Soviet man and woman.

Jazz just did not fit in. Folk music was favoured. The transistor radio changed all that. For the first time Soviet young people could hear western jazz and pop. They loved it. The Americans realised this and made sure there was plenty on offer. There was an insatiable appetite for things western. In the early 1970s I was asked by a girl if I could give her a western fashion magazine. On another occasion I was asked what the word 'groovy' meant. Soviet youth developed an encyclopaedic knowledge of western pop music. I was often asked whom some pop star had recently married. Was it true that so and so were breaking up?

Young people delighted in singing western pop songs. I asked one of them what the words meant. She did not know, but it was the in thing to do. Two cultures gradually emerged: the official and the unofficial. The official was conservative with classical and light classical music – but not atonal music – and folk music favoured. The ballet was above criticism. Jazz and rock were out. Youth reversed these priorities. Rebellious youth delighted in provoking the stuffy ruling class. Under Gorbachev, western pop culture flooded in and Russian groups imitated their western idols. The cultural war had been lost.

■ Leadership: What is leadership? The ability to lead a team, identify a problem, arrive at a solution and ensure that it is implemented. The leader needs to possess the skill to outmanoeuvre opponents and to think long term. Gorbachev was brilliant at tactical manipulation to maximise his advantage. He could outwit his adversaries. He was gifted but these gifts did not extend to strategic, long term, thinking. He lacked the imagination to perceive the consequences of his policies. Gorbachev was often too nice for his own good. A leader needs to be constantly suspicious of the motives of others and to have sharp claws when necessary.

Foreigners will be always be grateful to Gorbachev for ending the Cold War and managing the demise of the Soviet Union without a civil war. If the chief goal of leadership in the Soviet Union was the strengthening of the Party and the country, then he was a failure. He inherited a superpower so some of his predecessors must have been brilliant leaders. The two outstanding leaders of the communist era were Vladimir Lenin and Iosif Stalin. Lenin had a charisma which only Stalin eclipsed. One of the reasons for Lenin's elevated status was that many worshipped him as the saviour of Russia and the world. Stalin then claimed the role of chief disciple. He laid down the Leninist canon. Those who disagreed with him were anti-Leninists and hence counter-revolutionaries, hence heretics. This was brilliant Marxist theology. His successors were just ordinary comrades. Khrushchev played the buffoon; Brezhnev was inept and senile during his last years; Andropov and Chernenko were dying when they assumed the highest office. After this parade of incompetents, Gorbachev had to look good.

■ The New Elites: A bloody revolution ushered in the communist era in 1917. There was no bloody revolution when it disappeared in 1991. Why was this? The reason is that the ruling class until 1991 became the major part of the ruling class after 1991. In other words, in 1991, there was no social revolution; no transfer of power from one class, to use Marx's term, to another. The Red ruling class became the blue and white ruling class in Russia. Only in Kyrgyzstan (temporarily) and the Baltic States did the communist elite lose power. The economic empowering of the Red ruling class began under Khrushchev and accelerated under Gorbachev. The latter's economic reforms provided the right environment for enrichment.

The law on cooperatives permitted new cooperatives to be set up, mainly in the service sector. They immediately became a magnet for money laundering. Organised crime was developing fast and needed an outlet for all the cash generated. Cooperatives were a perfect haven for such cash. Cooperatives required various licences to be legal so bureaucrats were bribed to provide the requisite paperwork. This could not be hidden from the KGB so they had to be given their cut as well. An unholy trinity of Party, state officials and the KGB made money hand over fist. Some enterprises were permitted to export and import on their own account. They lacked the know-how but the KGB possessed it. Another money making racket was spawned. As the Soviet economy collapsed, the ruling class became more and more daring. The Soviet army, before leaving the German Democratic Republic, sold off anything that a German would buy – even tanks. A lucrative racket was to buy huge quantities of cigarettes, get them through customs by paying bribes and then sell them for a handsome profit in the Soviet Union. Mafia groups controlled the Soviet cigarette market under Gorbachev.

One of the most skilful institutions at maximising wealth was the Komsomol, the young communist league. Prior to Gorbachev everyone had assumed that if a comrade wanted to make a career in the youth organisation he must be pretty dim. This was the impression that Komsomol officials made on me. However, they turned out to be very clever. Their dullness was only a mask. The Komsomol was supposed to turn out smart communists but instead was producing smart capitalists.

Some of the oligarchs, such as Mikhail Khodorkovsky who became the richest man in Russia before his fall in October 2003, began their money-making careers in the Komsomol. Most of the Russian oligarchs were already dollar millionaires under Gorbachev. Mikhail Fridman, for example, transferred some of his wealth to Prague. After all, one could never be sure that the good times would continue. He had begun his financial career by cornering the market in Bolshoi theatre tickets. Teams of impecunious students took it in turn to queue for tickets when they went on sale. Anyone else was elbowed out of the way. Mikhail then flogged the tickets on the black market. Then he espied another niche: he went into the window cleaning business, again using hard-up students to do the labour. Today he is head of Alpha Bank and one of the richest men in Russia. The Soviet Union disposed of its property in Eastern Europe after the collapse of communism there in 1989–90. One of those empowered to do this in East Germany was Vladimir Putin.

In the late Gorbachev era, a beautiful, well-dressed research student arrived at the University of London. However, her research topic was incoherent and poorly focused. Since she was intelligent, it was clear that this was not her real research subject. The task was to discover what she really wanted to study. One day, her supervisor arrived late and offered profuse apologies. 'I'm terrible sorry for being late. I needed my hair done and I had to wait until Marcel could fit me in.' 'Oh', said the Russian, 'in Moscow I tell my hairdresser when I want my hair done.' Very revealing. It transpired that she had been sent to study a very important subject: How does the capitalist ruling class in England manage to stay in power? How do capitalists keep workers in their place? How does one stop revolution? Researchers had been sent out to all developed capitalist countries to study the phenomenon of the capitalist ruling class. It is not too fanciful to assume that when she returned to Moscow, she said the following: 'Comrades, we communists are the ruling class in Russia. What do we have to do to stay in power today? The answer is quite simple. We transform ourselves into the capitalist ruling class of Russia.'

Explanations for the collapse of the Soviet Union

- The Soviet system never really worked; hence its demise is akin to the disappearance of a mirage.

- Economic failure; the Soviet Union revealed early economic vitality but its strength was sapped during its last three decades by the exhaustion of natural resources, negative demographic developments, the advent of computers or some other unavoidable occurrence.

- Political failure; the ruling class destroyed the system in order to take possession of the publicly owned economy.

- The collapse was the result of policies which were intended to achieve something else; this is the theory of unintended consequences.

- A mixture of political and economic factors; the decline of economic growth over a long period; the role of the West; the role of the intelligentsia; the loss of faith in Marxism which destabilised the country; the ill-considered policies adopted by Gorbachev; there was also the moral dimension; large sections of society regarded the regime as illegitimate.

- Nationalism: the national problem was always dormant; it flared up under Gorbachev's glasnost; the anti-corruption campaign by Andropov and Gorbachev broke the informal agreement between the non-Russian republics and Moscow that the centre would turn a blind eye to some of the scams the republics were operating; the humiliation of national elites stoked the fires of nationalism.

- Corruption: this accelerated under Brezhnev and Gorbachev; it penetrated the regional Party apparatus; it linked up with enterprises and the black market for mutual enrichment; this promoted the view of most citizens that the Party was corrupt; corruption weakened central control.

- Religion: it made a comeback under Gorbachev to fill the vacuum left by the collapse of faith in Marxism; the concept of repentance for past crimes emerged.

- Gorbachev was quite aware that his policies in Eastern Europe would lead to the collapse of communism there; this was the price he was willing to pay to end the Cold War; however, he presumed that Eastern Europe would remain socialist.

- The collapse was the result of unintended consequences of government policies; the economy played a key role here; in an attempt to stimulate a slowing economy, the leadership adopted policies which fatally weakened the political and ideological pillars which sustained the system; this brought down the whole edifice; hence the economic crisis did not cause the collapse of the Soviet Union; the economic situation after 1992 was worse but this did not lead to the demise of post-communist Russia; ill-advised political decision making was the key variable.

- The demonstration effect of the West; glasnost revealed how backward the Soviet system was; citizens wanted rapidly rising living standards which the command administrative system would not deliver.

- The military burden was unsustainable; arms agreements ended the fear that the West would attack; why should citizens make sacrifices (lower living standards) if there was no real threat?

- The command administrative system was not innovative enough to keep up with world trends. The technology was increasingly obsolete; sooner or later wholesale modernisation would be needed; the system could not cope with this (Ellman and Kontorovich 1998).

The conclusion of this study is that poor leadership provoked political and economic collapse. A major weakness was the Party-state system. The Party never possessed the technical expertise to run the country. That should have been the role of the government. Instead the Party was always setting goals and interfering in the economy. The country needed a reforming Prime Minister who had the support of the Party leader. However, the Party leader realised that a stronger government meant a weaker Party elite. This was because the government could have run the economy without the Party. Kosygin, who was dismissed in 1980, was the last Prime Minister who favoured radical economic reform. After his death, the economy went into rapid decline. This meant a drop in living standards for most people. Andropov was in office for too short a time to make a difference. He knew that radical reforms were necessary. However, he turned his face against market-oriented reforms. Gorbachev's attempts at economic reform provoked a collapse. One of the reasons for this was that economic reform needs time to produce positive results. Gorbachev was impatient and introduced more radical reforms to accelerate growth. He eventually wrecked the system. He was quite unqualified for the role he had to play. He had little understanding of economics. This meant he was swayed by economists who promised him success. When it did not materialise, he listened to more radical economists. None of these economists had ever worked in a market economy, let alone industry. They were all theoreticians. They assumed that the planned economy was infinitely malleable. Reformers could pick and choose policies and the economy would improve as a result. Hence they had no understanding of the consequences of any of their reforms.

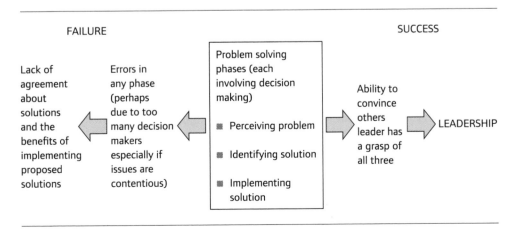

FIGURE 22.1 Achieving successful leadership

A man buys some Lenin stamps. He returns the next day and complains they don't stick. 'You're spitting on the wrong side, comrade.'

Questions

1 What were the main characteristics of the 'one-party state' or 'mono-organisational system'? Did these alter at all during the existence of the Soviet Union; if so, during which eras and why?

2 Which institutions (political and economic) made up the mono-organisational system? Answer in relation to the eras associated with Stalin, Khrushchev and Gorbachev. Which leader in your estimation mastered the running of the system?

3 'The weakness of the Soviet system at times constituted its greatest strengths.' Discuss in relation to informal practices and networks.

4 What do you consider to have been the main obstacles to successful economic/political reform in the Soviet Union?

5 'The Soviet political experiment 1917–91 was characterised by a cyclical pattern of reaction and reform.' Discuss.

6 'Ideology dominated some periods of Soviet history but not others.' Discuss.

7 'Bolshevik political culture was determined by a mixture of tsarist traditions, terror and the political pragmatism of Soviet leaders.' Discuss.

8 'The Bolshevik mindset never fundamentally changed between 1917 and 1989, just re-fashioned from time to time to suit needs and circumstances.' Discuss.

9 'All Soviet leaders experimented with Marxism except Brezhnev.' Discuss.

10 Using the leadership chart in Figure 22.1, draw up a list of policies during the Soviet period. Break them down into perception of problems; proposed solutions; and implementing solutions. The most innovative leaders were Lenin, Stalin, Khrushchev and Gorbachev. Repeat this exercise for all these leaders. Who was the most successful leader according to these criteria?

Further reading

Michael Ellman and Vladimir Kontorovich (eds), *The Destruction of the Soviet Economic System* (1998); T. H. Rigby, *The Changing Soviet System: Mono-organisational Socialism from its Origins to Gorbachev's Restructuring* (1990).

On the totalitarian analysis of the Soviet system, see traditional studies including Merle Fainsod, *How Russia is Ruled* (1970); Leonard Schapiro, *The Communist Party of the Soviet Union* (1966); *The Origin of the Communist Autocracy* (1977); Zbiegniew K. Brzezinski, *The Permanent Purge: Politics in Soviet Totalitarianism* (1956); Carl J. Friedrich and Zbiegniew K. Brzezinski,

Totalitarian Dictatorship and Autocracy (1965); Robert Conquest, *Power and Policy in the USSR* (1967); as well as the 'new totalitarian' and marginally revised approaches on the 'revolution from above', Robert C. Tucker, *Stalinism: Essays in Historical Interpretation* (1999); *Stalin in Power: The Revolution from Above, 1928–1941* (1991); Robert Conquest, *The Great Terror: A Reassessment* (1990).

CHAPTER 23

Russia reborn

'What has Yeltsin done in three years that the communists couldn't do in seventy?' 'Make communism look good.'

Aleksandr Tsipko, an anti-Marxist, inveigled his way into the CC apparatus and became a Gorbachev adviser. He concluded that many apparatchiks had already abandoned Marxism by 1985. They were Russian nationalists and avid readers of 'village prose'. This literature portrayed the lost rural Russian world and its values. It was clearly anti-Marxist but patrons in high places protected it. During the Gorbachev era, the apparatus was divided into conservatives, ready to defend Marxism, and pragmatists. Nikolai Portugalov, a leading German specialist, congratulated Tsipko: 'Sasha, you are a genius. It took you four articles to say what can be said in one sentence. Marxism is bullshit and the Bolsheviks, led by Lenin, are a bunch of criminals!'

The passion to destroy the Bolshevik past was overpowering. Russia could now return to its pre-1914 roots. This, of course, was an illusion. The apparatchiks effortlessly put on new clothes and paraded as democrats and patriots. This meant there would be no social revolution as in October 1917. The economy collapsed and self-proclaimed saviours emerged. Yeltsin was tsar. He had two main objectives: ensure that communists never returned to power and rebuild Russia. This meant primarily revitalising the Russian economy. The spectre of hunger hung over Moscow during the winter of 1991–92. There was no time to lose.

The saviour who presented himself was Egor Gaidar, a brilliant mathematical economist. Scion of a famous family, he had belonged to the privileged elite. He possessed the finest command of Russian among his peers. A member of the Party, he was no believer in Marx. His gods were headed by Adam Smith, the founder of modern market economics. The solution to Russia's ills was simple. Introduce a market economy as quickly as possible. Cut loose from the other post-Soviet states. It was a Russia-first option. It would be troublesome but, after all, there is no gain without pain. Yeltsin had another option. Grigory Yavlinsky proposed a common economic space which enveloped those states which wished to collaborate with Russia. Yeltsin chose the Russia-first option.

Egor Gaidar immediately set about assembling his team to destroy the old economy and build the new. He phoned his friend, Anatoly Chubais, in St Petersburg. 'Tolya, come to Moscow and let's build the new Russia together.' The offer was irresistible. Chubais, a talented economist, did have some experience of a market economy. He had a stall selling flowers and soft toys at St Petersburg railway station.

Boris Yeltsin was nicknamed Boris the Boozer because of his penchant for vodka. He was a sensitive soul and easily slighted. A product of the Party, he decided he did not need a political party. He wished to stand above factional politics. There were three centres of power: the government which concerned itself with the economy; the Congress of People's Deputies, the outer parliament, and the Supreme Soviet, the inner parliament; and the presidential administration. The last was the only new institution. In reality, it was an updated version of the CC apparatus. It served the President. In a democracy, the leader's political party performs this function. Russia was not yet a democracy.

Gaidar launched shock therapy in January 1992. The goal was to open Russian industry up to the winds of international competition. Sort the wheat out from the chaff. Some prices were controlled. However, the centre had little chance of imposing its will as the country was in chaos. In order to function, the government required money but it could collect little tax. That left international loans. Washington adored Gaidar and Chubais. They accepted American recipes for the regeneration of the Russian economy. The money was channelled through the International Monetary Fund (IMF).

A cynic described shock therapy as all shock and no therapy. The promised results never materialised. Inflation roared ahead and deprived people of their savings. These were huge and had to be eliminated in order to bring supply and demand into balance. There were, in reality, two economic policies being pursued. One was radical and one was conservative. The government pressed on with the radical approach because this was essential in order to secure western loans. The conservative was centred in the presidential administration. It sought to protect as much of Russian industry as possible. Its head, Yury Petrov, had emerged from the military economy. Hence there was no single economic approach.

'Democracy is a fight without rules.'

18 year old Russian

The political scene was also fragmented. Yeltsin was advised to draft a new constitution and hold new parliamentary elections. He declined. He also chose not to transform Democratic Russia into his political party. The CPD had many representatives of the economy, especially the defence sector. They wished to protect whatever they could from Gaidar's shock therapy. Confrontation between the CPD and Yeltsin burst forth as early as April 1992. Yeltsin acted liked a communist apparatchik: he cut deals with everyone. He was like Gorbachev desperately waiting for the economic dawn which never came. The CPD voted to subordinate the government to parliament. It had the necessary two-thirds majority to amend the constitution. Yeltsin met it head on. He called a referendum on 11 April 1993. The people could choose between him and parliament. In the meanwhile, Yeltsin agreed the CPD could vote in the next Prime Minister. Out went the despised Gaidar and in came Viktor Chernomyrdin. He managed the gas industry so the CPD thought he was one of them. The gas man quickly disappointed them by espousing market economics. In order to please the West, Boris Fedorov, a keen advocate of market reform, was installed as Minister of Finance and deputy Prime Minister. Yeltsin was playing the game of checks and balances again.

The Chechen Ruslan Khasbulatov, speaker of parliament, changed sides. He became an implacable critic of the President. This was evidence that Khasbulatov believed that Yeltsin's days were numbered. The way was open to impeach Yeltsin. The vote fell 72 votes short of the required 689. Had he lost the vote, the President would have dissolved parliament, using force if necessary. He also survived the referendum on 25 April.

The new Russian constitution

'Russian politics is Russian roulette.'

Boris Berezovsky, oligarch

Yeltsin ruefully admitted the error of his ways and a new draft constitution was published on 30 April. The Supreme Soviet also published its draft constitution. They were incompatible. Yeltsin's constitution envisaged a presidential republic and that by parliament, a parliamentary republic. Controversy raged during the summer. The President disappeared from time to time. President Clinton could not locate him for four days. President Bill was told that President Boris was in a place without a telephone.

On 21 September 1993, by presidential decree, Yeltsin dissolved the CPD and the Supreme Soviet and announced new elections to a Federal Assembly (a Duma with 450 members and a Federation Council with two representatives from each Russian republic and region). The Duma was to consist of 250 deputies elected in a first past the post ballot and 250 on the basis of party lists. To qualify, a party needed to secure at least 5 per cent of the national vote. Democratic Russia was delighted. It praised the President for breaking the 'vicious circle of the power struggle'. Nationalists called Yeltsin an 'outlaw' and democrats *dermokraty*, from the Russian word for shit.

It was a coup. Constitutional procedures were ignored. Boris had the full backing of Washington and London. Opponents convened an extraordinary Congress in the White House and a new President who was Yeltsin's deputy President, Aleksandr Rutskoi; and new ministers of defence, security and internal affairs were sworn in. Now there was dual power in Russia. Arms were handed out. It was shaping up to be a replay of August 1991. On 28 September, the White House was blockaded. Those who wished to leave could but no one was permitted to enter. Electricity, water and telephones were cut off.

The first violent confrontations took place on 2 October between demonstrators and the militia in the square opposite the Ministry of Foreign Affairs. On 3 October demonstrators broke through cordons to the White House. Some of the

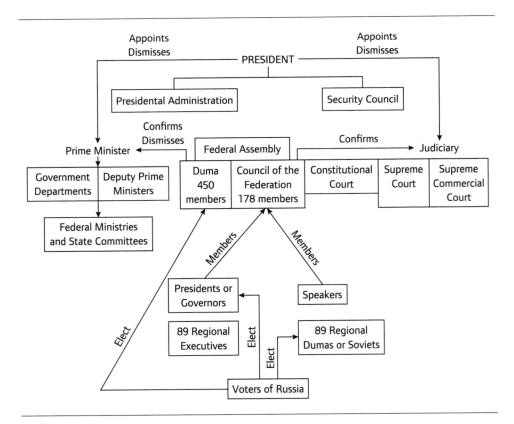

FIGURE 23.1 Key institutions of the Russian Federation (1993 constitution)
Source: *Bandits, Gangsters and the Mafia*, Pearson Education (McCauley, M. 2001).

banners read: 'Hang Yeltsin'; 'Judas Yeltsin'. Rutskoi was jubilant. 'We've won', he shouted, 'it's time to finish off the fascist dictator Yeltsin.' The Moscow mayor's office was sacked. Another target was Ostankino, the television centre. If they took it, the demonstrators could proclaim their victory and demand obedience from the population. On the morning of 4 October, Yeltsin ordered troops to fire on the White House. Quickly the top four floors were gutted. The defenders surrendered just before 6 p.m. The number of dead was between 20 and 170.

There is another version of these events. The opposition fell into a carefully prepared trap. The defence of the White House was amateurish, as was that of the mayor's office and Ostankino. The militia was withdrawn from the streets of Moscow and troops left the White House. Television reported that Ostankino had been seized by demonstrators. This was completely untrue. Once the demonstrators had used force, Yeltsin was able to claim that he was acting in self-defence. The President revealed that he was willing to spill blood to overcome the opposition. The conflict in the White House had been, in the main, between far left communists and the President. Gennady Zyuganov, leader of the Communist Party of the Russian Federation, ensured that he was on holiday when the fighting started. He only returned when calm had been restored. Ivan Rybkin, head of the Agrarian Party, the communists' sister party in the countryside, had been in the White House. When he realised the danger he made himself scarce. He was to collaborate closely with Yeltsin as speaker of the first Duma. Communists were not interested in taking power. They were more concerned about personal wealth than wealth redistribution.

The draft constitution was not a presidential constitution but a super-presidential constitution. The President was akin to a tsar. He was head of state, elected for four years and appointed the Prime Minister. He, in turn, selected the members of the government. Only the Prime Minister had to be confirmed by the Duma. It was virtually impossible to remove the President.

Duma elections

The election campaign was enlivened by the clown prince of Russian politics, Vladimir Zhirinovsky. Called Mad Vlad by some, he was an unashamed populist. Critics called his party, the Liberal Democratic Party of Russia (LDPR), neither liberal, nor democratic nor a party. It was his personal vehicle. He promised every woman a man and everyone free vodka. He was nationalist, anti-Semitic and hammered the new business elite. The Yeltsin camp expected a third of the votes on 12 December 1993. The trouble was that Yeltsin had decided he did not wish to form a broad coalition to campaign for votes. This was a mistake. His ministers set up their own parties. Egor Gaidar's was called Russia's Choice. It was not Russia's choice. It only polled 15.5 per cent of the votes. About 30 per cent of the electorate voted for radical economic reform. The surprise packet was the LDPR. It obtained

22.8 per cent of the votes. Hence the President did not have a working majority in parliament. He would have to cut deals as before. The constitution was passed but only electoral fraud ensured this. Had the constitution been rejected, the Duma elections would have been invalid. This set a precedent. Electoral fraud became part of the Russian political process.

Yeltsin and his lifestyle

After the December elections the President again played the magician: he disappeared. He repaired to his dacha-sanatorium outside Moscow and tried the patience of everyone. He was almost always in a foul mood. He stayed away from the Kremlin for weeks. His two years in power had changed him. Previously he had been a workhorse, staying in the Kremlin until late evening. He even worked on Sundays. Now he was a shadow of his former self. Depression and insomnia were constant companions. Vodka was not far from his elbow. Economic failure appeared to be affecting him profoundly. Was the bloodletting of October 1993 preying on his mind?

The decision-making process became even more haphazard. Ad hoc decisions became the norm. Boris loved the trappings of power and the opulence of the Kremlin. He hired and fired with gay abandon. Given his inability to concentrate for long, those close to the ailing tsar wielded great influence. He was comfortable with the former kings of Soviet industry. He also surrounded himself with young go-getters whom Gaidar called nincompoops. They were intellectually undemanding. Like a latter-day Roman emperor, he hosted huge dinners with generous libations. The bathhouse or sauna was part of this lifestyle. His waistline expanded.

There was an inner circle consisting of officials, mostly concerned with defence and security. Then there was his tennis coach, at least as long as he played tennis. It is striking that no liberal or democrat was a member of his charmed group. They all helped themselves to economic favours. Those in the outer circle found direct access to the President barred. They had to negotiate with his gate keepers, of whom Aleksandr Korzhakov, a former KGB officer, became the most influential. Yeltsin's back pain flared up from time to time. Blockage of the coronary arteries became a problem. He often took pain killers, washed down by alcohol. Heart attacks became inevitable. He suffered one in July 1995, and another in September, at Shannon airport, when he was unable to leave the plane to greet the Irish Prime Minister. Eventually he underwent a quintuple heart by-pass operation.

The Duma and the presidency

Political parties came and went; only the Communist Party stayed. It was normal for an aspiring politician to form his own party as the best way of getting into the

Duma. There was always an anti-Yeltsin majority in parliament, headed by the communists. Electioneering for the Duma elections of December 1995 received a stimulus from Zhirinovsky. He referred to the Lenin era as rape, the Stalin period as homosexuality, the Khrushchev years as masturbation, the Brezhnev years as group sex, and the present time as impotence. He declared the era of impotence over and that orgasm had begun. Hedonism would rule in Vlad's Russia. There was a beer lovers' party which handed out free beer. The communists, as expected, won the election with 34.9 per cent of the vote. Our Home is Russia, the main pro-Yeltsin party, came second and the LDPR third. Again the President lacked a parliamentary majority. According to one analyst, pro-reformers polled 43 per cent of the vote in 1993 but only 38.2 per cent in 1995. How did the President handle the Duma? He cut deals which involved paying large bribes. If the money was right, any piece of legislation could be approved.

The favourite to win the presidential election in June 1996 was the communist Gennady Zyuganov. The President appeared out of it. What could he do? Things came to a head at the World Economic Forum at Davos, Switzerland, on February 1996. Western bankers fawned over Gennady as if he were certain of inheriting the Kremlin. Even the legendary George Soros, the financier and philanthropist, thought that he would make it. Anatoly Chubais was shocked by the gullibility of the foreigners. 'There are two Zyuganovs: one for foreign and one for domestic consumption', he bellowed. There would be civil war if the communists won as they said they would renationalise all property which had been privatised. The barons of industry, the oligarchs, became alarmed. Gradually seven came together to engineer Yeltsin's re-election. They became known as the seven wise men and other sobriquets which are unprintable. Chubais was to be their front man. This plan had to be sold to the tsar. His campaign team, headed by Korzhakov, told him everything was fine. Eventually Boris arrived at one of his typical solutions: Chubais was to become his campaign manager but the Korzhakov team would remain. The two could slug it out for influence. As a politician said, they were like two bears but Russia was only big enough for one of them. There was talk of bribing every electoral official to falsify the results. This might cost $600 million. Some of the oligarchs were for arranging a pretext to postpone the election.

Boris's campaign style was to ask people what they wanted and then say: 'You've got it'. Eventually these added up to about a fifth of 1996 budget. The government did not have the money. After the election all the promises were rescinded. Some electors were not taken in by promises. So a show was put on everywhere he went. He even talked of becoming a matchmaker for the beautiful girls he saw. Zyuganov's main line was that privatisation had to be reversed. Chubais spread the rumour that the communists would prevent a person from having two jobs. 'Vote communist and bring back the KGB', was another line. Zyuganov was circumspect. He avoided words such as socialism and communism.

He tapped into the latent Russian fear of the outside world. There was a world-wide conspiracy to suborn Russia and all other countries. Yeltsin was a past master of invective. 'Zyug Heil!', a play on the Nazi 'Sieg Heil' or hail the victory, was one offering. General Aleksandr Lebed became a candidate late in the campaign. Chubais reasoned he would take votes from the communists. Yeltsin became so jittery that he planned another coup, in March 1996. He was going to dissolve the Duma and declare a state of emergency. He was talked out of it, mainly by Chubais. In the first round, Boris scored 35.3 per cent and Lebed 14.5 per cent. There was a deal that the latter would advise his supporters to vote for Yeltsin in the second round (necessary because no candidate had obtained 50 per cent in the first round). Boris got 53.8 per cent in the second round. This was one of the most unlikely presidential results of all time. Common sense would suggest that the numbers were massaged. The oligarchs were exultant. One of their number, Vladimir Potanin, became deputy Prime Minister. They had now crossed the threshold of political power. What was Chubais's reward? He became head of the presidential administration. He was now number two in Russia.

The figures in Tables 23.1 and 23.2 reveal the shocking decline of the Russian economy after 1991. It performed more poorly than eastern Europe and was way behind China. In 2002, Russian GDP was still below the level of 1973. Why was Russia's performance so poor during the 1990s?

- After 60 years, the planned economy was so deeply embedded that only its destruction could herald the new dawn of a market economy; Russia had no diaspora to turn to for capital and know-how.

- The situation was not so severe in Eastern Europe which had experienced about 35 years of central planning; hence it was easier for these economies to return to the market.

- China had only had just over 20 years of central planning before experiments with the market began; it could draw on its diaspora for capital and know-how.

- The Russian state was weak after 1991; collapse was deeper than in Eastern Europe.

- The defence sector dominated the Russian economy in 1991; it proved extremely difficult to move from military to civil production; in many cases it was almost impossible.

- Many of the military enterprises were in closed cities, isolated from the rest of the country.

- The sheer size of the country made it extremely difficult to integrate enterprises into a market economy; Eastern Europe was small and compact in comparison.

TABLE 23.1 Annual per capita GDP growth (%)

	1928–40	1950–59	1959–76	1976–91	1991–98
USSR	3.8	2.9	3.2	0	−7.5
Eastern Europe	–	3.2	3.5	−0.8	1.8
China	–	5.2	1.2	5.6	7.0

Source: S. Rosefielde, 'Russia: An Abnormal Country', *The Economic Journal of Comparative Economics* (2005).

TABLE 23.2 Russian GDP (billion $)

1973	872.5
1991	1,094.1
1998	655.4
2001	790.6
2002	825.3

Source: S. Rosefielde, 'Russia: An Abnormal Country', *The Economic Journal of Comparative Economics* (2005).

- The severity of the climate imposed high costs on development; this applied especially to the Far North (the exception is Norilsk Nickel).

- Transport costs were high because of the size of the country; local markets were weak because of low purchasing power.

- The Russian economy was dominated by hydrocarbons (oil and natural gas) and mineral extraction; other sectors were neglected.

- Russian industry (except for optics, laser technology) was not internationally competitive and did not begin to catch up.

- Agriculture before 1991 could not feed the Russian population; labour productivity was low because of low motivation; there was little capital investment in this sector.

- Russian bureaucracy hindered the development of a market economy; there were more bureaucrats in post-communist Russia than under the communists; this was because officials could collect rents (bribes) from those engaging in economic activity.

- Privatisation was carried out to prevent the communists coming back to power; hence the prime motive was political and not economic; privatisation in Russia went far beyond that in Eastern Europe.

■ Privatisation permitted the emergence of oligarchs (barons of industry); the leading oligarchs became enormously wealthy and also influential in politics (the Minister and deputy Ministers of the Oil Industry served the interests of the oil oligarchs and not the state).

■ Privatisation was theft on a massive scale, unparalleled in economic history; the state lost vast revenues.

■ Tax and import exemptions granted by the President cost the state large sums.

■ Secure property relations and the rule of law were slow to develop; without these a market economy only develops slowly; it takes less than a day to set up a company in England but months in Russia.

■ Russia received poor economic advice from foreign institutions (IMF, World Bank, etc.); foreign advisers attempted to impose a US-type model which was inappropriate to Russia.

■ Russian economic policy making was poor; as bad as under Gorbachev; this was because no one had experience of a market economy, let alone how to move to the market; another problem was that Russian policy makers were not aware of the depth of their ignorance.

■ Russia was poor at tax collection so could not service its infrastructure, health, social sector.

■ Low tax collection meant that borrowing from oligarchs and international institutions was needlessly high.

■ Corruption reduced economic growth (3 per cent annually is a 2005 estimate); the estimated total amount of money paid in bribes in Russia grew from $36 billion in 2001 to $319 billion in 2005; the average private bribe rose from $62 to $97 over the same period; corruption in education (colleges and universities) went up from $450 million to $580 million; however, corruption in the health services declined from $600 million to $400 million; officials pocketed $3 billion in 2005; of this the executive branch of government accounted for 87 per cent, parliamentary deputies 7 per cent, and judges 6 per cent; Russia, in 2005, was rated 95th of 145 world countries for corruption; it is now on a par with Iraq, Iran and Sudan.

■ Many Russians do not take easily to capitalism, in marked contrast to the Chinese.

■ Organised crime and monopolies slow down the emergence of small and medium scale companies.

■ The Russian government does not favour foreign control of strategic industries, such as oil, gas and minerals; this has led to little foreign investment and transfer of know-how in these sectors.

- Many foreign investors have had their fingers burnt; George Soros, as smart as they come, lost over a billion dollars and has abandoned Russia.

- There are success stories, notably Ikea, but they are predominantly in the consumer goods sector.

Bandit capitalism

During the 1990s, Russia pursued two economic policies. One was inspired by western neo-liberal economic theory, shock therapy and its successors, and the other by Russian experience. Neo-liberal fundamentals were:

- Privatisation was to be pushed through as quickly as possible. Poorly executed privatisation was deemed better than no privatisation. Black market wheelers and dealers were to be welcomed. If they possessed the skills to succeed in the planned economy, they would flourish in a legal economy.

- Inflation would be high in the beginning and would cause hardship. It was over 2,600 per cent in 1993. It would be brought down by balancing the budget. In other words, the social security burden would be cut drastically. Citizens would have to pay gradually for health and education. Unemployment would be considerable in order to transfer labour to more productive jobs.

- Structural reform was important. This meant, in effect, inefficient companies going to the wall.

- The central economic ministries should be phased out and the management of the economy left to the market. Russia would be able to export oil, gas, minerals and timber successfully.

Side by side with this philosophy, alien to most Russians, was the old economic philosophy. The essentials were:

- The state provides subsidies to industry and regions. These had to be off-budget to satisfy the IMF. The presidential administration would look after the off-budget funding. This money came from the Russian banks. They received loans from the Russian Central Bank at advantageous rates of interest. In return, the commercial banks, owned by the oligarchs, received government accounts. They paid no interest on the money which flowed in. They made substantial profits from exporting oil, gas, etc. but some of the profits had to be channelled to loss-making enterprises. Banks were not interested in people's savings or extending loans to small businessmen and women. The banks' bad debts were written off by the government from time to time. The government, desperately short of cash, issued short term bonds. These collapsed in August 1998 when foreigners lost their investments.

■ Privatisation was rigged to favour outsiders; these were the clans around Yeltsin with Anatoly Chubais the main actor. The government deliberately bankrupted enterprises so that outsiders could take them over. In the short term, the outsiders concentrated on gaining control of the energy sector. In 1995, 60 per cent of the business elites were from the former communist nomenklatura, as were 75 per cent of Yeltsin's government and entourage and 75 per cent of regional elites. This ensured their collaboration. Ordinary Russians and the middle classes (doctors, scientists, etc.) opposed privatisation because it enriched existing and new elites. Deals were struck with mafia entrepreneurs. Over the period 1992–99 over 133,000 companies were sold for a grand total of $9.25 billion or $69,000 per asset or less than the cost of a new Mercedes. Revenues from 22,400 industrial enterprises amounted to $347 million or $15,500 a time. Construction companies went for an average of $7,000 each. Russia's privatisation was the biggest giveaway ever. Compare this to Brazil's $67 billion between 1990 and 1998.

Banking was a bonanza. Private banks could be established from 1988. Often the new bankers were former Central Bank officials with the right contacts to secure loans. The surest way to wealth was to borrow huge amounts from the Central Bank, change the money into dollars, transfer it abroad, then declare bankruptcy and vanish. However, the loot had to be shared with the Central Bank officials who had agreed to the scam.

Russia was looted by all and sundry. An estimated $220 billion in raw materials, icons, gold, diamonds, and so on left the country during the 1990s. It was placed in offshore accounts (the Russian term for an offshore account is *offshorny schet*) and invested in property in London, Paris, Berlin, Rome, the Canary Islands and other lucrative milieux.

The loans for shares scam

The biggest money spinner for the oligarchs was the loans for shares scheme. Yeltsin needed money to fight the 1996 election campaign. The scheme was very simple. The bankers would lend money and, in return, would manage the state's shares in large companies. The seven wise men or the seven leading bankers agreed among themselves which state companies they wanted to take over. Vladimir Potanin was to get Norilsk Nickel, which produced nickel, cobalt and controlled the world palladium market. Yukos was to pass to Mikhail Khodorkovsky. There were supposed to be two bidders for each contract. The winners extended the government credit for three years but gain control and management of them for five years. Eventually they could buy a controlling block of shares as the government could not repay its loans. There were 12 auctions but the winners had been decided beforehand. Just to ensure there were no unwelcome bidders, local airports were mysteriously closed. Khodorkovsky's Mentep acquired 45 per cent of Yukos for $159 million. There was another bid for $355 million but it was disqualified. Menatep, Khodorkovsky's bank, was the registering agent! It gained another 33 per cent by promising to invest $150 million. Yukos's real value was at least $10 billion. Yukos was a 'nice little earner', as the immortal Arthur Daley, star of the ITV programme *Minder*, would have commented. Boris Berezovsky and his partner Roman Abramovich acquired 51 per cent of Sibneft for $100.1 million. The company was really worth $5 billion (in 2005, Abramovich sold his share to Gazprom for an estimated $9 billion).

The second presidency

The doctors worked a miracle and Yeltsin managed to get through his inauguration on 7 August 1996. However he walked stiffly, took the oath of office haltingly and gave the impression that he was only half alive. Clearly he was President but did not rule. According to the Constitution, the Prime Minister acts in his place. However, it soon transpired that Anatoly Chubais was intent on playing this key role. He linked up with Boris's daughter, Tatyana Dyachenko. They controlled access to the President and were his main conduit of information.

Aleksandr Lebed was a problem. He performed a miracle in the Caucasus when he negotiated an end to the first Chechen war (1994–96). In essence, this meant recognition of Chechen independence in the future. His opponents accused him of betraying Russia. Lebed talked about military unrest and the country being ready to explode. If Boris expired, Lebed was in pole position to take over. In October, the Minister of the Interior accused Lebed of planning a creeping coup. Framed, Lebed was sacked. Boris dragged himself back to the Kremlin just before the New Year and spoke to the nation on the radio. He was not presentable enough for television. He had a sorry tale to tell. The country was in a mess but 1997 would be better.

Boris Nemtsov, handsome, partly Jewish and the darling of the media because he provided good copy, became deputy Prime Minister. His brief was to sort out the public utilities. This included breaking up the natural monopolies. He was aware of the magnitude of his task. There were two market economy models in Russia. There was the 'government-monopolistic, mafia-corrupt model'. The other was 'democratic capitalism'. The former was being 'implemented on a grand scale in Russia'. The President agreed and was determined to steer the country from 'bandit capitalism' to 'people's capitalism'. One of Nemtsov's initiatives was to oblige officials to travel in Russian rather than foreign cars. Most of them ignored him. He was red faced once when his Volga broke down in central Moscow. He had no client network – he came from Nizhny Novgorod – and this doomed him. He did have a sense of humour and enjoyed telling a joke about Ivan, who went to Paris on a business trip. 'Buy me a sexy French bra', his wife said. 'Buy you one, my darling, but you have no breasts', he replied. 'Well, I buy you briefs', she retorted.

The Prime Minister departs

Boris's attention was now concentrated on the presidential elections in June 2000. He needed a candidate who could win. In March 1998, he sacked Viktor Chernomyrdin, the Prime Minister, Anatoly Chubais and the Minister of the Interior. It is still unclear why he did this. He referred to Viktor as an exceptionally decent, conscientious and devoted man. However, he had to go. Chernomyrdin had struck up a close relationship with Al Gore, the US Vice-President. Their talks, in the United States in March 1988, were dubbed the meeting of the future Presidents. Then Chernomyrdin went off to Odessa to talk to the Presidents of Ukraine and Moldova without informing Boris. Perhaps Boris was simply protecting his back. Was there a Prime Minister in waiting? No. Yeltsin said he would act as Prime Minister. Then someone pointed out that it was unconstitutional. This reveals that the sacking of Chernomyrdin was a sudden decision.

Andrei Kirienko, a partly Jewish banker and businessman from Nizhny Novgorod, was proposed as Prime Minister. The average response was: 'Kiri-who?' He was that unknown. He was an excellent choice from Boris's point of view. As an outsider who had no client base in Moscow he would be dependent on the President. Boris restricted his room for manoeuvre further by making Boris Berezovsky acting secretary of the Commonwealth of Independent States. This permitted oligarch Boris to expand his business interests further. It also revealed that he was the Yeltsin family's business manager. Then, in May, Chubais became chair of the United Energy System of Russia, responsible for the generation and distribution of electricity throughout the land (he still holds this position). All the oligarchs would have to deal with him. Battles between Anatoly and the oligarchs would continue to the mutual benefit of Yeltsin.

Financial meltdown

The financial crisis deepened as Kirienko floundered. Interest rates soared but devaluation was regarded as a poor option. That left international loans. Chubais was dispatched to Washington to tell the Americans that if Russia did not receive money a big, bad dictator would take over and threaten America with nuclear weapons. The IMF agreed to a $10 billion loan over three years. When the first tranche, $4.8 billion arrived, the government acted. The ruble was to float and servicing of international debt would be suspended for 90 days. Insiders cashed in their government bonds, changed the rubles into dollars and then moved the money offshore. When the dollars ran out, it was time to devalue and default. Chubais was quite frank. Russia had conned the IMF out of about $20 billion. He claimed Russia had no other option. The winners were the smart oligarchs and government insiders. The losers were foreign banks, financial institutions and the average Russian. The last saw their savings wiped out again; the first time having been 1992. Even those with dollar accounts lost as the banks did not have sufficient dollars to meet demand. The burgeoning middle class was decimated. Many went back to the provinces. Why should they have any faith in the market economy?

Many expected Boris to resign as President. Instead he appeared on television and said he would soldier on to the end of his term. Evgeny Primakov came in as Prime Minister. He was no lover of the market economy or the United States. He sought social peace through stabilisation. Collect more tax and cut government expenditure. Primakov lasted until May 1999. He was sacked a few days before the Duma was to vote on impeaching the President. Deputies thought better of attempting to remove the President in such a tense political atmosphere. Boris's gamble had paid off. The next Prime Minister lasted until August. Some Chechens had invaded Dagestan and attempted to establish an Islamic republic. A hard man was now needed to deal with the Islamic threat. He turned out to be Vladimir Putin. There were bombs in Moscow in August and September; the latter killing 94 and injuring over 200. Another multi-storey block was blown up. In Buinaksk, Dagestan, a bomb exploded and killed 64. More were killed in Volgodonsk. Who was responsible? The FSB (successor to the KGB) was caught red-handed placing bombs outside an apartment block in Ryazan, south-east of Moscow. They said it was a training exercise. Were the Chechens the guilty party? They denied involvement. It is still unclear who bears responsibility.

The Dagestani incursion set off the second Chechen war, which is still raging. Vladimir Putin came in as Prime Minister to deal with the crisis. Boris told his friends that he regarded Volodya (Vladimir) as his heir apparent.

A new Duma

The communists won the Duma elections in December 1999. They polled 26 per cent of the vote, followed by Edinstvo (Unity), which supported Putin. Independent observers put the communists at 33 per cent and Edinstvo at 15 per cent. Electoral fraud had become the norm. The average Russian voter was apathetic. Putin moved quickly to secure a Duma majority. He struck a tactical alliance with the communists. Sixty-six of the independents came over to Edinstvo. It now had a two-thirds majority to push through legislation if opposed by the Federation Council.

The tsar departs

A car and trailer break down on a road outside Moscow. The driver signals for help and a car stops. 'I wonder if you can help me', he says. 'Well as I am the acting President of Russia, I shall do my best to help a citizen of our great country. What is the problem?' 'Well, I have two bears in the trailer and they have to be taken to Moscow zoo by 4 p.m. or I will lose my job.' 'Oh, I think I can do that.' 'Here is a thousand rubles for your trouble.' Later that evening the man is in Red Square, in Moscow, and sees Putin arm in arm with the two bears. He is furious and goes up to him and says: 'Mr President, you promised me you would take these bears to Moscow zoo by 4 p.m. and it is now 7 p.m. I will lose my job.' 'Oh, no', says Putin, 'I did take them to Moscow zoo but we had such a great time and as I have 400 rubles over, I'm taking them to the movies!'

On 31 December 1999, Boris stunned viewers with his New Year's message. Everyone had expected a Santa Claus act but he announced he was stepping down and nominated Vladimir Putin as his successor. He asked the people to forgive him for failing to realise the dream of a new, dynamic, rich Russia. To Putin he simply said: 'Take care of Russia'. The acting tsar was brutally frank about the tasks awaiting him. Russia's GDP had almost halved during the 1990s and was only a tenth of that of the United States and a fifth of that of China. Labour productivity in electricity generation and raw materials was about world average but elsewhere it was about a quarter of the American. Russia now had 1 per cent of the global market whereas the US had 36 per cent and Japan 30 per cent. Forty per cent of the Russian population lived in poverty. The American road had failed. Russia now had to find its own way and rediscover patriotism, national pride and dignity. Russians favoured a strong state and a strong leader.

The Commonwealth of Independent States (CIS)

It consists of 12 countries. In other words, the old Soviet Union without Estonia, Latvia and Lithuania. The Baltic States are now members of NATO and the European Union. There are three main development models in the CIS: Belarus, where there has been no privatisation and which retains a Soviet-type economy; Kazakhstan, where companies, especially in oil and metals, are sold to foreigners but must employ young Kazakhs who will eventually take over; and Uzbekistan, which has joint ventures with foreign companies; no company is owned by foreigners; Japan and South Korea have invested in Uzbekistan and there is a car plant, managed by Koreans, in Tashkent.

Only Belarus, Kazakhstan and Uzbekistan have living standards comparable with those of 1991. Georgia has few natural resources and hence little foreign

investment. There are ongoing problems in Abkhazia and South Ossetia. Ukraine
has privatised but there is little foreign interest. The shadow economy accounts for
an estimated 70 per cent of economic activity. The post-Soviet rulers in Georgia,
Ukraine and Kyrgyzstan were removed in revolutionary upheavals in 2004–05.
Georgia and Ukraine are forging a closer relationship with the United States.

The CIS is a loose confederation dominated by Russia. It exported oil and gas
at discounted prices until 2005. The political will for closer integration is missing.
The orange revolution in Ukraine has increased tension within the organisation.
Russia's Gazprom substantially increased the price of gas to Ukraine in 2006 and
followed suit in Moldova and Georgia. Moscow's present policy is to capitalise on
its energy monopoly. The greatest problem facing Russia is security. The threat of
militant Islam is ever present and this is leading to closer military cooperation in
Central Asia. The other long term problem is China.

How to strike a deal

The son of a high ranking Russian official killed his partner in a fit of rage in Paris.
He was immediately arrested and put in jail. The Russian Foreign Minister arrived
in Strasbourg for a Council of Europe meeting. However, his main concern was
to secure the release of the official's son. 'What do you want in exchange for his
release?', he asked. 'There can be no deal. We cannot overrule the French judi-
ciary', he was told. Shortly afterwards a FSB general arrived in Paris. 'What do
you want to release him?', he asked. Eventually a deal was struck. The general
gave the French authorities the names of two of their agents at the centre of the
French government. The son returned to Moscow.

Relations with America

The Bill and Boris show kept everyone entertained during the 1990s. Yeltsin
struck up a good relationship with Clinton and the latter put up with Boris's
drunken antics. Russia was a weak power in need of loans during the decade and it
was Yeltsin's job to smooth the way for Anatoly Chubais to do the negotiating.
Washington prodded the IMF into providing the money. The house of cards
collapsed in 1998. Moscow defaulted, many foreign banks and investors lost
mountains of money and it looked as if Russia would go into free fall. A miracle
occurred. When Yeltsin handed over to Vladimir Putin things were looking up.
The mounting oil price transformed Russian finances. By 2005, its foreign debt
was down to $85 billion and it was paying back loans before time. Foreign
currency reserves were approaching $150 billion. Under Putin, the Russian
government and companies borrow money in the international money markets.
They no longer need any foreign largesse. America and Russia are allies in the war

against terrorism but competitors in almost every other sphere. America now needs Russian oil more than Russia needs America.

The *nouveaux riches* are known as New Russians. All jokes about them present them as thick and uncultured.

A New Russian buys a top of the range Mercedes. A week later he is back and buys another one. Another week passes and he is back again to buy another one. The assistant is puzzled. 'Why do you need to buy a new Mercedes every week?' 'Quite simple. The ashtrays were full.'

A New Russian buys a Rolls Royce. The next day he is back and complains to the assistant that it only goes up to 200. 'What is wrong with that?', asks the assistant. 'I live at No. 220.'

Questions

1 Was there a democratic revolution after 1991? If not, why not?

2 Why did western-style political parties not form after 1991?

3 How important was bandit capitalism for the development of the Russian state after 1991?

4 How was it possible for the oligarchs to accumulate such vast wealth in the decade after 1991?

5 Explain the key differences between neo-liberal (western) and Soviet approaches to economics.

6 Compare Yeltsin and Gorbachev as leaders.

7 Why did the Russian state not disintegrate after 1991?

8 'The Russian political scene, after 1991, was dominated by conflicts between populist, pragmatist and conservative figures.' Discuss.

9 What foreign policy goals did Russia pursue after 1991?

10 Why did the Commonwealth of Independent States remain weak after 1991?

Further reading

Martin McCauley, *Bandits, Gangsters and the Mafia Russia, the Baltic States and the CIS after 1992* (2001); Archie Brown (ed.), *The Demise of Marxism-Leninism in Russia* (2002); Alexander J. Motyl, Blair A. Ruble and Lilia Shevtsova (eds), *Russia's Enlargement with the West: Transformation in the Twenty-First Century* (2004); Archie Brown and Lilia Shevtsova (eds), *Gorbachev, Yeltsin and Putin: Political Leadership in Russia's Transition* (2001).

Biographies

Akhromeev, Marshal Sergei Fedorovich (1923–91), first deputy Chief of the General Staff, 1979–84, Chief of the General Staff of the Soviet Armed Forces and first deputy Minister of Defence, 1984–88; military adviser to Gorbachev, 1989–91; committed suicide.

Aliev, Geidar (Haydar) Ali Rza Ogly (born 1923), first secretary, Communist Party of Azerbaijan, 1969–82, first deputy chair, USSR Council of Ministers, 1982–87, member of Politburo, 1982–87; too conservative for Gorbachev; President of Azerbaijan, 1993–2003.

Andropov, Yury Vladimirovich (1914–84), chair of the KGB, 1967–82, General Secretary of the CPSU, 1982–84; chair of the Presidium of the USSR Supreme Soviet (head of state), 1983–84; member of the Politburo, 1973–84.

Baklanov, Oleg Dmitrievich (born 1932), USSR Minister of General Machine Building, 1983–88; secretary of CC (military–industrial complex, chemical industry), 1988–91; one of the conspirators, August 1991.

Beria, Lavrenty Pavlovich (1899–1953), a political gangster and brilliant administrator who was kind to his family; a Georgian, he was Stalin's butcher in the Caucasus and succeeded Ezhov in 1939; he headed the Soviet atomic programme; he was outmanoeuvred by Khrushchev after the death of Stalin and executed.

Bessmertnykh, Aleksandr Aleksandrovich (born 1933), head of the American department, USSR Ministry of Foreign Affairs, 1983–86; USSR deputy Foreign Minister, 1986–88; first deputy USSR Foreign Minister, 1988–90; USSR Minister of Foreign Affairs, 1990–91; dismissed for not siding with Gorbachev in August 1991.

Boldin, Valery Ivanovich (born 1935), adviser to Gorbachev on agriculture, 1985–87; head of the general department, Party CC, 1987–90, Gorbachev's Chief of Staff, 1990–91; member of the Presidential Council, March 1990; one of the conspirators, August 1991.

Brazauskas, Algirdas Mikolas (born 1932), secretary, CC of Communist Party of Lithuania, 1977–88; first secretary, Communist Party of Lithuania, 1988–90; chair, Lithuanian Supreme Soviet (head of state), chair of the Lithuanian Democratic Labour Party, 1990; President of Lithuania, 1992. He and the majority of Party members broke with Moscow in 1990 and supported the independence of Lithuania.

Brezhnev, Leonid Ilich (1906–82), First Secretary, then General Secretary of the Communist Party, 1964–84; chair of the Presidium, USSR Supreme Soviet (head of state), 1960–64 and 1977–82; member of Politburo, 1957–82.

Chebrikov, Viktor Mikhailovich (born 1923), chair of the KGB, 1982–88; secretary, Party CC, 1988–89; member of the Politburo, 1985–89.

Chernenko, Konstantin Ustinovich (1911–85), General Secretary of the Party, 1984–85; chair of the Presidium, USSR Supreme Soviet (head of state), 1984–85; member of the Politburo, 1978–85.

Deng Xiaoping (1904–97), lost posts during Cultural Revolution (1966–76), rehabilitated, 1973; resigned as deputy Prime Minister, 1980; proponent of market reforms; responsible for Tiananmen square massacre; paramount leader of China.

Ezhov, Nikolai Ivanovich (1895–1940), a 'bloody dwarf' and 'iron people's commissar'; Ezhov gave his name to the bloodiest period of the purges, the *Ezhovshchina*; he succeeded Yagoda in September 1936 and, in turn, gave way to Beria in April 1939; in his desk, Ezhov kept the bullets, wrapped in paper, with the victim's name on each, which had terminated the lives of Bukharin, Zinoviev and other top leaders.

Fedorchuk, Vitaly Vasilevich (born 1918), chair of the Ukrainian KGB, 1970–82; chair of the USSR KGB, 1982, Minister of Internal Affairs, 1982–86.

Frunze, Mikhail Vasilevich (1885–1925), a leading Red commander during Civil War; he sided with Stalin against Trotsky in military affairs; he was author of the 'unitary military doctrine' which envisaged that the military should be used for offensive action.

Gorky, Maxim (1868–1936), regarded by many as the father of Soviet literature, he became the most famous communist writer in the world living, of all places, in fascist Italy; he returned to Moscow in 1931 and his death may not have been altogether natural.

Grachev, General Pavel Sergeevich (born 1948), Afghan war hero who sided with Yeltsin during the attempted coup, August 1991; he promised to order the military not to use weapons; then appointed by Gorbachev chair of the Russian Committee on Defence and Security; also made deputy USSR Minister of Defence; Russian Minister of Defence, May 1992–June 1996.

Gromyko, Andrei Andreevich (1909–89), 'Grim-Grom' was USSR Minister of Foreign Affairs, 1957–85; chair, Presidium of USSR Supreme Soviet (head of state), 1985–88, when Gorbachev took over; member of Politburo, 1973–88.

Honecker, Erich (1912–94), succeeded Walter Ulbricht as first secretary of the SED, the East German Party, 1971; chair of the GDR Council of State (head of state), 1976–89; Gorbachev undermined his position in east Berlin in October 1989; Egon Krenz then took over.

Jaruzelski, Wojciech (born 1923), first secretary, Polish United Workers' [Communist] Party, 1981–89; head of state, 1985–89; President of Poland, 1989–90.

Kaganovich, Lazar Moiseevich (1893–1991), true to Stalin to the end; he even denied being a Jew; was Party leader in Moscow in 1930 and helped Khrushchev's career; Jews complained about Kaganovich's anti-Semitism; Stalin told him to shave off his beard as he did not want a rabbi near him; once said there were six Stalins; so mercurial was the dictator.

Khasbulatov, Ruslan Imranovich (born 1942), first Deputy chair (speaker), Russian Supreme Soviet, 1990–91; speaker, Russian Supreme Soviet, 1991–93.

Khrushchev, Nikita Sergeevich (1894–1971), First Secretary, Party Central Committee, 1953–64; chair, USSR Council of Ministers, 1958–64; member of Politburo, 1939–64.

Konev, Marshal Ivan Stepanovich (1897–1973), one of the most successful Red Army commanders during the 1941–45 war. Promoted Marshal of the Soviet Union in 1944; his front advanced to Berlin and to Torgau where they linked up with US forces; his forces then moved south and took Prague in May 1945; was first deputy Minister of Defence and commander in chief of ground forces, 1946–50.

Kosygin, Aleksei Nikolaevich (1904–80), deputy chair, USSR Council of Ministers, 1946–53, 1964–80; member of Politburo, 1960–80.

Krupskaya, Nadezhda Konstantinovna (1869–1939), Lenin's wife but not his great love (that was Inessa Armand); she was a faithful wife but her memoirs are disappointingly shallow; Stalin browbeat her and she died disillusioned.

Kryuchkov, Vladimir Aleksandrovich (born 1924), head of foreign intelligence, USSR KGB, 1974–88; chair of KGB, 1988–91; member of Politburo, 1989–90; leader of conspirators, August 1991.

Kulakov, Fedor Davydovich (1918–78), first secretary, Stavropol Party kraikom, 1960–64; secretary (agriculture), Party CC, 1965–78; member of Politburo, 1971–78.

Kunaev, Dinmukhamed Akhmedovich (1912–93), first secretary, Communist Party of Kazakhstan, 1960–62, 1964–86; member of Politburo, 1971–87.

Ligachev, Egor Kuzmich (born 1920), first secretary, Tomsk Party gorkom, 1965–83; secretary (personnel, ideology, agriculture), Party CC, 1983–90; second secretary to Gorbachev, 1985–88; member of Politburo, 1985–90.

Lukyanov, Anatoly Ivanovich (born 1930), head of general department, Party CC, 1985–87; secretary, Party CC, 1987–88; first deputy chair, USSR Supreme Soviet, 1988–90; chair, USSR Supreme Soviet, 1990–91; one of the conspirators, August 1991.

Medvedev, Vadim Andreevich (born 1929), rector, Party Academy of Social Sciences, 1978–83; head, department of science and education, 1983–86, head, department for liaison with communist and workers' parties of socialist countries, Party CC, 1986–88; secretary, Party CC, 1986–88; member of Politburo, 1988–90; he lost all his positions at 28th Party Congress, July 1990; member of Presidential Council, July 1990; adviser to Gorbachev and moved to Gorbachev Foundation.

Moiseev, General Mikhail Alekseevich (born 1939), Chief of Staff, Soviet Armed Forces, first deputy USSR Minister of Defence, 1988–91; acting USSR Minister of Defence, August 1991.

Molotov, Vyacheslav Mikhailovich (1890–1986), Soviet Minister of Foreign Affairs, 1939–49, 1953–56; first deputy chair, USSR Council of Ministers, 1953–57; member of Politburo, 1926–57; member of anti-Party group defeated by Khrushchev in June 1957; readmitted to the Party under Gorbachev.

Nazarbaev, Nursultan Abishevich (born 1938), chair, Council of Ministers of Kazakhstan, 1984–89; first secretary, Communist Party of Kazakhstan, 1990–91; member of CPSU Politburo, 1990–91; President of Kazakhstan, 1990–.

Ordzhonikidze, Grigory Konstantinovich (1886–1937), prominent Georgian revolutionary who was influential during the industrial drive of the 1930s; became Commissar for Heavy Industry in 1932 but could not cope with Stalin's ruthlessness; committed suicide.

Pavlov, Valentin Sergeevich (1937–2003), chair, USSR State Committee on Prices, 1986–89; Soviet Minister of Finance, 1989–91; Soviet Prime Minister, 1991; one of the conspirators, August 1991.

Podgorny, Nikolai Viktorovich (1903–83), first secretary, Communist Party of Ukraine, 1957–63; chair (head of state), Presidium, USSR Supreme Soviet, 1965–77; member of Politburo, 1960–77.

Popov, Gavriil Kharitonovich (born 1936), professor of economics, Moscow State University, 1977–88; editor-in-chief, *Voprosy ekonomiki*, 1988–90; mayor of Moscow, 1990–92; leading member of Russian Greek community.

Primakov, Evgeny Maksimovich (born 1929), director (Arabist), Oriental Institute, USSR Academy of Sciences, 1977–85; director, Institute of World Economy and International Relations, 1985–89; chair, Soviet of the Union, USSR Supreme Soviet, 1989–90; director, Russian foreign intelligence service, 1991; personal Gorbachev envoy to Saddam Hussein during the Gulf War; Russian Foreign Minister, 1996; Prime Minister 1998–99.

Pugo, Boris Karlovich (1937–91), chair, Latvian KGB, 1980–84; chair, CPSU Central Control Commission, 1990–91; Soviet Minister of Internal Affairs, 1990–91; one of the conspirators, August 1991; committed suicide.

Romanov, Grigory Vasilevich (born 1923), first secretary, Leningrad Party obkom, 1970–83; secretary (defence industry), Party CC, 1983–85; member of Politburo, 1976–85.

Rykov, Aleksei Ivanovich (1881–1938), Stalin's ally in the battle against Trotsky after Lenin's death; later became a member of the right opposition, with Bukharin, against Stalin's polices, especially forced collectivisation; executed after show trial.

Ryzhkov, Nikolai Ivanovich (born 1929), secretary and head of industry department, Party CC, 1982–85; chair, USSR Council of Ministers, 1985–91; member of Politburo, 1985–90.

Shaposhnikov, Marshal Evgeny Ivanovich (born 1942), commander-in-chief, Soviet air force and deputy USSR Minister of Defence, 1990–91; Soviet Minister of Defence, 1991; commander-in-chief, strategic first strike forces, 1991–93.

Shatalin, Stanislav Sergeevich (1934–97), academician; drafted, with Yavlinsky and others, the 500 day programme; member of Presidential Council, 1990; resigned from Party after Vilnius killings; supported Yeltsin during Russian presidential campaign, June 1991; joined Democratic Party of Russia, June 1991; co-chair, Movement for Democratic Reforms (international), July 1991.

Shcherbakov, Vladimir Ivanovich (born 1949), member, Soviet commission for perfecting administration, planning and the economic mechanism, 1988; chair, USSR state committee on labour and social questions, 1989–91; deputy, March–May 1991, first deputy Soviet Prime Minister, May–November 1991; Minister of Economics and Forecasting, May–November 1991.

Shcherbytsky, Volodymyr Vasylevych (1918–90), chair, Ukrainian Council of Ministers, 1961–63, 1965–72; first secretary, Communist Party of Ukraine, 1972–89; member of CPSU Politburo, 1971–89.

Shevardnadze, Eduard Ambrosievich (born 1928), first secretary, Communist Party of Georgia, 1972–85; Soviet Foreign Minister, 1985–90; Soviet Minister of External Affairs, 1991; member of Presidential Council, 1990–91; member of Politburo, 1985–90; chair (head of state), State Council of Georgia, March 1992; President of Georgia, 1995–2003.

Silaev, Ivan Stepanovich (born 1930), Soviet Minister of Civil Aviation, 1981–85; deputy chair, USSR Council of Ministers, 1985–90; chair, Russian Council of Ministers, 1990–91.

Sobchak, Anatoly Aleksandrovich (1937–2000), USSR people's deputy, 1989–91; mayor of Leningrad-St Petersburg, 1990–96.

Starodubtsev, Vasily Aleksandrovich (born 1931), chair, All-Russian Kolkhoz Council, 1986–91; USSR Farmers' Union, 1990–91; one of the conspirators, August 1991.

Tikhonov, Nikolai Aleksandrovich (1905–97), chair, USSR Council of Ministers, 1980–85; member of Politburo, 1979–85.

Trotsky, Lev Davidovich (1879–1940), worked closely with Lenin during October Revolution; USSR Commissar for War, 1918–25; lost all posts, 1925; deported to Turkey, later went to Mexico where he was murdered, almost certainly on Stalin's orders.

Tukhachevsky, Marshal Nikolai Mikhailovich (1893–1937), a major military thinker, his career was cut short because of suspicions that he was not loyal to Stalin; autocratic by nature, he was of noble Polish origin; was promoted Marshal of the Soviet Union in 1935; in 1936 he was first deputy Commissar for Defence; tortured and executed; he was rehabilitated posthumously under Gorbachev.

Varennikov, General Valentin Ivanovich (born 1923), commander-in-chief, Soviet border troops, deputy USSR Minister of Defence, 1989–91; one of the conspirators, August 1991.

Vlasov, Aleksandr Vladimirovich (born 1932), first secretary, Rostov Party obkom, 1984–86; USSR Minister of Internal Affairs, 1986–88; chair, Russian Council of Ministers, 1988–90.

Yagoda, Genrikh Grigorevich (1891–1938), one of Stalin's bloodiest police chiefs, he himself fell victim to the executioner's bullet; some referred to him as the Mephistopheles from the (Jewish) Pale; head of the NKVD, 1934–July 1936.

Yakovlev, Aleksandr Nikolaevich (1923–2005), father of glasnost; Soviet ambassador to Canada, 1979–83; director, Institute of World Economy and International Relations, USSR Academy of Sciences, 1983–85; secretary (propaganda, culture, foreign policy), Party CC, 1986–90; member of Politburo, 1987–90; adviser to Gorbachev, 1990–91.

Yanaev, Gennady Ivanovich (born 1937), secretary, 1986–89, deputy chair, 1989–90, chair, All-Union Central Council of Trades Unions, 1989–90; secretary, Party CC, member of Politburo, 1990–91; USSR Vice President, 1990–91; one of the conspirators, August 1991.

Yavlinsky, Grigory Aleksandrovich (born 1952), pro-reform economist; co-author with Shatalin of the 500 day programme; deputy chair, Russian Council of Ministers, 1990; co-leader of Yabloko Party.

Yazov, Marshal Dmitry Timofeevich (born 1923), commander-in-chief, Central Asian military district, 1980–84; Far East military district, 1984–86; USSR Minister of Defence, 1987–91; one of the conspirators, August 1991.

Yeltsin, Boris Nikolaevich (1931–2007), first secretary, Sverdlovsk Party obkom, 1976–85; head of construction department, Party CC, secretary, Party CC, 1985; first secretary, Moscow Party gorkom, 1985–87; first deputy chair, USSR State Committee for Construction (Gosstroi), 1987–89; chair (speaker, head of state), Russian Supreme Soviet, 1990; President of Russia, 1991–99.

Zhdanov, Andrei Aleksandrovich (1896–1948), the guardian of Soviet cultural orthodoxy, from socialist realism to the xenophobia of the late 1940s; led the defence of Leningrad, 1941–44; died suddenly.

Zhukov, Marshal Georgy Konstantinovich (1896–1974), most prominent and successful Red Army commander during the 1941–45 war; fought Japanese at Khalkin-Gol, in Mongolia, 1939; Chief of General Staff and deputy Commissar for Defence, January–July 1941; became commander of entire western front; responsible for defence of Stalingrad; participated in battle of Kursk; his troops reached Berlin in April 1945; struck up a good relationship with Eisenhower; then became commander of Soviet occupation forces in Germany; demoted to commander of Odesa military district in April 1946; became deputy Minister of Defence after the death of Stalin; Minister of Defence under Khrushchev but dismissed; brilliant, rude man who was undoubtedly the leading military man of his generation.

Glossary

ABM Treaty Anti-ballistic missile treaty, signed by the US and the Soviet Union in 1972; part of the Strategic Arms Limitation Treaty (SALT I).

Agitprop Department of Agitation and Propaganda, CC apparatus; originally written and oral propaganda, the task of the official was to mobilise the population to achieve the economic goals set by the state by raising Party awareness; it was thought the more dedicated a communist was, the better he or she worked.

All-Union Ministries could be either All-Union, i.e. responsible for the whole of the country, or republican, responsible for their own republic, but subordinate to Moscow; hence there was a USSR Ministry of Agriculture and 16 republican Ministries of Agriculture.

Almaty Meeting See CIS.

Anti-Party Group Those in the Presidium (Politburo) in 1957, almost all representing government ministries, who opposed the transfer of responsibility for the implementation of economic plans from the government to the Party; Khrushchev was almost defeated but after victory he removed all his opponents from the Presidium. None of his defeated opponents ever made a political comeback; the Party dominated economic decision making until 1988 when Gorbachev, at the 19th Party Conference, removed the Party from economic management.

Apparatchik Paid Party, but also state, official.

ASSR Autonomous Soviet Socialist Republic. A territory, within a Soviet republic, inhabited by non-Russians, indeed non-Slavs (Russians, Belorussians and Ukrainians) (e.g. Komi ASSR), which had its own government; the Communist Party organisation in an ASSR was equivalent to an obkom; in reality an ASSR was totally subordinate to the capital of the republic in which it was situated; hence autonomous did not mean independent; most ASSRs were in the Russian Federation.

August Coup The attempted coup of 19–21 August 1991.

Belovezh Agreement See Minsk Agreement and the CIS.

Black Earth Zone or Chernozem One of the most fertile soils in the world, it runs as a triangle with its tip in west Siberia and then crosses southern Russian and northern Ukraine.

Bolsheviks When the Russian Social Democratic Labour Party (RSDRP) split in 1903, those in the majority were known as Bolsheviks; in October 1917 the Bolsheviks or Communist Party took power.

Brezhnev Doctrine The right of the Soviet Union to intervene unilaterally if it deemed socialism to be in danger; in March 1985, Gorbachev informed Eastern European leaders that the doctrine was dead; he repeated this at a meeting of the Warsaw Pact, in April 1985; it was renounced officially by Gorbachev, during a speech in Yugoslavia, in March 1988; spheres of influence were abandoned, officially, in July 1989; James Baker, during the Romanian events of December 1989, stated that the US had no objection to the Soviets intervening; he had not grasped that Moscow could no longer intervene militarily in Eastern Europe; such an eventuality, Shevardnadze believed, would have ended perestroika.

Cadres Personnel; Party cadres were Party officials; Stalin coined the expression: 'Cadres decide everything!'

Candidate Member a) Before a person could become a full member of the Communist Party he (she) had to serve a probationary period during which he (she) was referred to as a candidate member; b) candidate members of the Party Central Committee and Politburo could attend, speak but not vote.

CEC (TsIK) All-Russian Central Executive Committee of the soviets; acted in the name of the Congress of Soviets when it was not in session; main state institution until mid-1918 when Sovnarkom overtook it; it was multi-party but in the inner group, the Presidium, there were only Bolsheviks; head of CEC technically head of state; became USSR CEC in 1922 and, in 1936 constitution, USSR Supreme Soviet.

Central Committee (CC) Central Committee of the Communist Party; this body acted in the name of the Party Congress when the latter was not in session; contained all the most important Party officials, government ministers, leading army and navy personnel, top ambassadors, academics, etc.; elected at each Party Congress; the first meeting after election was known as a plenum or full meeting of candidate and full members; according to the Party statutes there were to be at least two plenums per year; the first meeting was the 1st plenum, the next, the 2nd plenum, until the next Party Congress, then the first meeting after that became again the 1st plenum, and so on.

CC Apparatus (*Apparat*) Consisted of departments, such as cadres department, and others which paralleled state institutions (e.g. transport, agriculture); responsible for implementing Politburo, Orgburo and Secretariat decisions; drafted policy documents to assist Politburo elaboration of policy; was responsible for selecting leading cadres in Party and state and monitoring their activities; played key role in ideological education of society; supervised all local Party and state organisations; in 1946 its economic departments, such as agriculture and transport, were abolished and removed from central supervision of economy; reason for this was, apparently, large scale corruption of Party officials by economic ministries and enterprises; central economic role restored in 1948; in 1946–48 new departments formed, including agitprop (agitation and propaganda); Party–Komsomol–trade unions, international relations, heavy industry, consumer goods industry and machine building, administrative department to supervise security services, planning, trade and finance, apparatus responsible for supervising 115 ministries and all republican and local Party bodies; in 1958, the CC apparatus in Moscow counted 1,118 officials and 1,085 technicians (typists, etc.); in contrast, there were about 75,000 officials and technicians in the central governmental apparatus; all these had to be monitored by the CC apparatus; in 1940, in the country as a whole (excluding the central Party apparatus) there were 116,931 Party officials and 37,806 technical staff; in 1947, there were 131,809 officials and 27,352 technical staff; in 1953, there were 125,005 officials and 28,710 technical staff; but in 1963, there were 96,909 officials and 20,595 technical staff (administering 24,290 local Party organisations).

CC Secretariat Set up by the 8th Party Congress, 1919; until March 1920 there was only one secretary – Yakov Sverdlov until his death in March 1919; and then N. N. Krestinsky; then E. A. Preobrazhensky and L. P. Serebryakov added in March 1920; each secretary responsible for a group of CC departments; secretaries could decide issues which were not important enough to go to Orgburo; hence Secretariat was a board; in 1921, decisions of Secretariat, in absence of objection by members of Orgburo to be treated as decisions of Orgburo; two and Stalin was elected the first General Secretary (Gensek), in 1922, but at that time the post was not regarded as conferring much power on the incumbent (the title of Gensek was dropped at the 17th Party Congress, in 1934, and Stalin's official Party position was secretary of the CC until 1953); in 1946, the CC Secretariat met several times a day, as and when required; it prepared the agenda and relevant materials for Orgburo meetings and checked that the decisions taken by it and the Politburo were fully implemented; also supervised the appointment of leading cadres in Party and state institutions; there were four secretaries in August 1946; between 1953 and 1966 the top man was called the CC First Secretary; after 1957 the CC apparatus assumed responsibility for the economy and a CC secretary was senior to a USSR Minister; in 1987, there were 11 CC secretaries, including Gorbachev; when Gorbachev became Gensek in 1985, Ligachev was elected to chair the secretaries' meetings and he became known unofficially as second secretary (his main responsibility was ideology).

Cheka The All-Russian Extraordinary Commission for Combating Counter-Revolution and Sabotage; founded in 1917 it was the first Bolshevik secret police force whose task was to ensure the Bolsheviks stayed in power; it changed its name several times and from 1954 was known as the KGB.

CIS Commonwealth of Independent States; established on 8 December 1991 by Russia, Ukraine and Belarus in Belovezh Forest, near Brest, Belarus; they reasoned they had the right to dissolve the Soviet Union because they had been the original signatories setting up the USSR in 1922; at a meeting in Almaty, Kazakhstan, on 21 December, other states were admitted: Armenia, Azerbaijan, Kazakhstan, Kyrgyzstan, Moldova, Tajikistan, Turkmenistan, and Uzbekistan; eventually Georgia also joined and this left Estonia, Latvia and Lithuania outside; Gorbachev fought hard to keep the former Soviet Union together and felt betrayed by Yeltsin, whose goal was to destroy the Union.

Classes There were two classes in the Soviet Union: the working class and the collective farm peasantry (kolkhozniks), and a stratum, the intelligentsia.

CMEA See Comecon.

Collectivisation Common ownership of the land had begun in 1917 but had made little progress by 1929 when peasants (there were about 25 million peasant households) were not given a choice about joining a kolkhoz or collective farm; on land not previously farmed, sovkhozes or state farms were set up; collectivisation was completed in 1937; in practice, several villages were lumped together and declared a kolkhoz; peasant opposition was dealt with brutally, by using military force, deportation or expulsion; initially almost everything was collectivised but in March 1930 the private plot around a peasant's cottage was legalised; as of May 1932, he could legally sell any surplus (after paying taxes) in an urban kolkhoz market where demand and supply determined prices; the more efficient farmers, kulaks, were not permitted to join the kolkhozes as they were viewed as class enemies; hence Stalin deliberately eliminated the most successful farmers from agriculture; the Soviet state never developed socialist agriculture to the point that the demand of the population for food was met; by the 1980s about one-third of marketed produce came from the private plots, occupying less than 5 per cent of arable land.

Comecon Council for Mutual Economic Assistance; set up in 1949 by Stalin it came alive after his death to assume the function of a socialist Common Market; its membership eventually included Cuba, Mongolia and Vietnam but by the mid-1980s it was becoming a liability for the Soviet Union; Yugoslavia became an associate member in 1964; it was dissolved in June 1991.

Communist A member of the Communist Party.

Communist Party of Russia, also Communist Party of the Russian Federation Russia was not permitted before 1990 to have its own Communist Party as Lenin believed this would allow Russians to dominate the young Soviet state too easily; there was a Russian Bureau under Khrushchev but it was dissolved in 1965; the RCP was founded in 1990 and elected Ivan Polozkov its First Secretary, much to the disappointment of Gorbachev, who regarded the Russian party as a bastion of conservatism.

Conference Differed from a Party Congress in that not all Party organisations were represented (an exception was the 19th Party Conference, 1988); in the early years of the revolution logistics made it difficult to convene a Congress rapidly to deal with urgent business; a conference did not have the right to elect members to the Central Committee and the Politburo.

Congress Most important meeting of the Party, soviet, trade union or other organisation; at a Congress, which had to meet once during a five year period, the Communist Party reviewed its record over the period since the previous Congress and laid down goals for the future; a new Central Committee was elected and it, in turn, elected a new Politburo and Secretariat; the last Party Congress before it was banned by Yeltsin was the 28th in July 1990.

Conventional Forces Non-nuclear forces.

CPSU Communist Party of the Soviet Union; the party was founded in 1898 as the Russian Social Democratic Labour Party (RSDRP) (until 1917 all social democratic parties were

Marxist) but split, at its 2nd Congress, 1903, into Bolshevik (majoritarians) and Menshevik (minoritarians) factions; it assumed the name of Russian Communist Party (Bolsheviks), 1918, and adopted the name CPSU in 1952; throughout this book this party is referred to as the Communist Party; in 1987 there were about 19 million Party members, but on 1 July 1991 this had dropped to 15 million; each republic had a Communist Party (except the Russian Federation until 1990) and collectively they made up the CPSU; each republican Party had its own CC, Secretariat, etc.; leader of Party in each republic was called First Secretary.

CPSU Programme The agenda of the Communist Party; the 1961 Party Programme, envisaging the foothills of communism being reached in 1980, was still valid when Gorbachev became General Secretary; it was urgently in need of revision but this became a battleground between radicals and conservatives.

CSCE Conference on Security and Co-operation in Europe; the inaugural meeting was in Helsinki on 3 July 1975; the foreign ministers of the 33 European states (Albania was absent), as well as the United States and Canada, participated in the follow up conferences; the CSCE developed into a forum for East–West debate on political, economic, social, cultural and security issues; on 1 January 1995 it became the Organisation for Security and Co-operation in Europe (OSCE).

Democratic Platform A radical group within the Communist Party whose programme was published in *Pravda* in March 1990 which demanded, among other things, the renunciation of a single state ideology and that the Party should reject communism as its goal; its leading members were expelled and others resigned and some founded other parties, such as the Republican Party of the Russian Federation.

DemRossiya The Democratic Russia movement came into being in 1990 in order to support democratically minded candidates during the elections to the RSFSR Congress of People's Deputies, especially those associated with Yeltsin; it was an umbrella organisation which contained a wide range of parties and movements and failed to develop into a viable political party; one of the issues on which it could not agree in 1991 was whether Russia would be better off if the Soviet Union were destroyed or not; their views were close to those of the Inter-Regional Group and Memorial; they became the largest opposition group to the communists in 1990, having, before their splits, over 4,000 members; among leading members were Boris Yeltsin, Yury Afasanev, Anatoly Sobchak, Gavriil Popov, Nikolai Travkin and Sergei Stankevich; Yeltsin's victory in the presidential election of June 1991 owed much to the support of this movement; by 1996, it has shrunk to a small group.

District See raion.

Five Year Plan The first Five Year Plan spanned the period October 1928–December 1932, the second, 1933–37, and so on; plans were drafted by Gosplan and had the force of law; non-fulfilment of the plan was, therefore, a criminal offence; extremely detailed norms were laid down and this reached ludicrous proportions, e.g. the amount of fat in milk in Estonia was laid down by Moscow!

G7 Group of advanced industrial states, consisting of the United States, Japan, Great Britain, France, Italy, Germany and Canada; the Soviet Union wished to join and transform it into G8; Gorbachev attended the G7 meeting in London during the summer of 1991.

GDR German Democratic Republic; in 1945 the eastern part of Germany was occupied by the Red Army and was called the Soviet Occupied Zone of Germany; in 1949 this territory was renamed the GDR in response to the establishment of the Federal Republic of Germany; it was also known as East Germany and its capital was East Berlin; the ruling Communist Party was called the Socialist Unity Party of Germany (SED) and there were other parties, such as the Christian Democratic Union of Germany, which were subordinate to the SED; the GDR merged with the Federal Republic in October 1990.

Glasnost A key element of Gorbachev's reforms which involved openness in economic and political decision making and the open discussion of all questions and freedom of information; this latter aspect led to vigorous debate about the Soviet past, including the crimes of the Stalin era. Glasnost was a key theme at the 19th Party Conference and was confirmed in the conference resolutions.

Gorkom City Party committee, headed by a first secretary.

Gosplan State Planning Commission of the USSR Council of Ministers responsible for drafting economic plans and checking on their implementation; founded in 1921, it continued to 1990; it produced Five Year Plans, annual plans, quarterly plans, etc.; each Soviet republic had its own Gosplan whose task was to provide inputs for USSR Gosplan in order to draft the next plan and check on plan implementation; after 1985 Gosplan lost influence as the Soviet economy gradually fragmented; in 1990, when Gorbachev replaced the USSR Council of Ministers with a Cabinet of Ministers, Gosplan became the Ministry for Economics and Forecasting.

Gosstroi State Committee for Construction.

Gosteleradio State television and radio: the Soviet equivalent of the BBC before it lost its broadcasting monopoly.

Ideologists Those Party officials and academics who were concerned with propagating and developing Marxism-Leninism; every university student was required to pass an examination in Marxism-Leninism before graduating; Gorbachev complained with justification that the great majority of these communists merely justified the present and did not attempt to develop creatively the ideology; however, under Brezhnev the concept of developed, mature or ripe socialism was coined and Gorbachev began with developing socialism; the negative western term for these officials is ideologue.

IMF The International Monetary Fund, based in Washington, which is concerned with macro-economic issues; it was founded in 1945 as a result of the Bretton Woods agreement.

INF Intermediate range nuclear forces.

INF Agreement Signed on 8 December 1987 by the United States ad the Soviet Union to eliminate a whole category of nuclear weapons, land based nuclear intermediate range weapons with a reach between 500 and 5,500 km.

Inter-Regional Group Deputies in the USSR Congress of People's Deputies and the USSR Supreme Soviet who formed the group in the summer of 1989 and who defended human rights, the introduction of private property, a multi-party system and a democratic rule of law state; its members included Boris Yeltsin, Andrei Sakharov, Yury Afanasev and Gavriil Popov.

KGB Committee of State Security; established as the Cheka in 1917 by Lenin to ensure that the Bolsheviks stayed in power; under Stalin its task became to keep him in power; there was a USSR KGB and each Soviet republic had its own KGB, subordinate to the KGB whose headquarters were in the Lubyanka, Moscow; the KGB was responsible for domestic and foreign intelligence; in the military, the GRU was responsible for intelligence gathering but the KGB checked on the political loyalty of the armed forces.

Kolkhoz Literally, collective economy; members farmed the land as a cooperative but, in reality, had little say in what was produced as this was laid down in the annual state plan; before 1966 there was no guaranteed wage, if the farm made a profit wages were paid, if not, no wages were paid; most peasants preferred to concentrate on their private plots.

Kolkhoznik A member of a kolkhoz.

Komsomol Lenin Young Communist League; for those between 14 and 28 years, except for the organisation's leadership; most young people belonged to it and almost everyone who joined the Communist Party had previously belonged to the Komsomol; there was a USSR Komsomol and one in each Soviet republic; like the Communist Party its leadership were full time officials; in the early 1980s the Komsomol had over 40 million members.

Kosygin Reforms Launched by Aleksei Kosygin, chair of the USSR Council of Ministers, 1964–80, to give enterprise more control over what they produced and marketed; one problem which arose was what to do with surplus labour in an enterprise as it was not possible just to sack them; Kosygin was a technocrat and his reforms promised well but were interrupted by the invasion of Czechoslovakia in August 1968; afterwards reform was a term which fell out of use as centralisation was reimposed; Kosygin lacked the willpower to fight for power and from being seen as the Soviet leader in 1964–68 was gradually pushed aside by Brezhnev who was clearly *primus inter pares* by the early 1970s.

Krai Administrative sub-division of a Soviet republic containing within it a territory inhabited by another (non-Slav) nationality, called an autonomous oblast; can also be translated as territory.

Kraikom Krai Party committee, headed by a first secretary.

Kulak Peasants were divided into poor, middle and rich by Lenin and the Bolsheviks; a poor peasant did not have enough land to live off, the middle peasant did and the rich produced a surplus for the market; in West European terms the kulak would have been a moderately well off farmer.

Left Communist Bukharin was leader of this group in Party Central Committee, October 1917–18; favoured the immediate introduction of socialism and a revolutionary war against Germany; Lenin wanted peace and achieved this at Brest-Litovsk.

Lend Lease US military and food aid to Allies during the Second World War; authorised by Congress in March 1941 to aid Great Britain, it was extended to China, in April, and the Soviet Union in November 1941; about 22 per cent of aid or $10 billion went to Soviet Union.

Lysenkoism Trofim Denisovich Lysenko was an agro-biologist who made a glittering career under Stalin undermining the existing scientific thinking in agricultural science and genetics; very skilfully propagated the 'theory' of the inheritance of acquired characteristics which promised higher yields; was a vigorous opponent of genetics, arguing that it was bourgeois pseudoscience; reached the pinnacle of his influence in 1948; Khrushchev would not listen to those scientists who condemned him as a charlatan and it was only in 1966, under Brezhnev, that genetics was rehabilitated fully and Lysenko dispatched to the rubbish bin of science; his pseudoscience cost Soviet agriculture dearly.

Memorial Society Formed to remember the victims of Stalin's oppression; politically it became active in early 1989 and concentrated on making public the Russian and Soviet past and laying bare the crimes of the Stalin period; later became part of DemRossiya.

Minsk Agreement This agreement between Russia (Boris Yeltsin), Belarus (Stanislau Shushkevich) and Ukraine (Leonid Kravchuk) was the death blow to the further existence of the Soviet Union under Gorbachev; the agreement states that the Soviet Union as a subject in international law has ceased to exist.

Muzhik Russian peasant.

MVD Ministry of Internal Affairs responsible for law and order; there was a USSR MVD and each Soviet republic had its own MVD, subordinate to Moscow.

NATO North Atlantic Treaty Organisation, founded in 1949.

NEP New Economic Policy; introduced in 1921 by Lenin as a compromise after war communism (1918–21) had failed and the country was facing economic ruin and the fear that the peasants would not deliver food to the cities; was not well received by communists who saw it as a defeat and a retreat from socialism; under NEP the commanding heights of the economy (energy, communications, heavy industry, etc.) stayed in state hands while light industry and agriculture reverted to private ownership; trade was again legal. Soviet Russia recovered and by the mid-1920s the country was again achieving the gross domestic product of 1913; for the peasant it was the golden era of Soviet rule; NEP was brought to an end by the victory of Stalin in the struggle to succeed Lenin when he launched the first Five Year Plan (October 1928–32); during NEP there was a developed system of producers' and consumers' cooperatives, and a vibrant tradition of cottage industries, but all this was destroyed deliberately by Stalin who forced peasants to join collective (kolkhoz) and state (sovkhoz) farms, mainly to ensure that the state could feed workers during the industrialisation drive; detailed plans for farms were laid down by Gosplan and it was the responsibility of the Party secretary to ensure implementation.

19th Party Conference A rare event, the previous conference had taken place in 1941, and convened by Gorbachev between Party Congresses, and more significant than a CC plenum, to push through radical policies; the Party was withdrawn from economic management and it also lost its right to nominate candidates for state and soviet posts; glasnost was also promoted through conference resolutions.

Nomenklatura Nomenclatura or nomenclature: consisted of a) list of positions which the Party regarded as important and required Party assent to be filled b) list of persons capable of filling these positions; there was the Party nomenklatura and the state nomenklatura; each Party body, from the obkom upwards, had a list of nomenklatura appointments it could fill; the longer a first Party secretary remained in an oblast, for example, the greater the number of posts he could influence; in this way nepotism and corruption crept into the Party apparatus; for example, important Soviet ambassadors – to Washington, Bonn, etc. – were on the nomenklatura list of the Politburo; in August 1946, the CC secretaries drew up a list of 42,894 leadership positions in Party and state organsiations; about 12 per cent of these belonged to the top stratum (ministries and Party); often a minister was asked to suggest the best candidate for a top position in his ministry when it fell vacant.

Non-Black Earth Zone or Non-Chernozem Zone Not very fertile but the Russian heartland, it extends from Moscow to southern Russian where the black earth zone begins and eastwards to Siberia; under Brezhnev considerable attention and investment was devoted to this region since if depopulation continued there was a risk that vast tracts of the Russian heartland would return to the wilderness.

Novo-Ogarevo Gorbachev's dacha near Moscow at which republican leaders (including Yeltsin) debated the formation of a genuinely federal state to succeed the Soviet Union with President Gorbachev during the spring and summer of 1991; the outcome was the draft Union of Sovereign States; these talks were also referred to as the 9 + 1, nine republican leaders and Gorbachev; the Baltic republics never participated in these deliberations, having demanded their independence.

Obkom Oblast Party committee, headed by a first secretary.

Oblast Administrative subdivision of a Soviet republic; oblasts were subdivided into raions, as were cities; can also be translated as territory, province.

Organ Agency.

Orgburo Organisational bureau; established in March 1919; lower in status than Politburo; Lenin said: 'The Orgburo allocates resources and the Politburo decides policy'; Politburo held 19 joint meetings with Orgburo and Orgburo met 110 times on its own between April and November 1919; responsible for organisation and selection and development of Party cadres; contact with local and regional Party bodies; collecting reports on Party activity and information; in 1946 (had almost ceased to function during war) reform Orgburo was to assume responsible for local (below level of CC) Party organs: it summoned them, heard their reports and proposed improvements; meetings were regular and fixed in advance.

Orgotdel Organisational department, CC apparatus; its tasks included Party organisation, cadres, etc.

Orgpartotdel Department of Party organs, CC apparatus; responsible for cadres, among other things.

Perestroika Restructuring, renaissance, reformation, the word goes back to the eighteenth century and was also frequently used by Stalin in the sense of changing Party structures; under Gorbachev the work came to mean an all-embracing modernisation of the Party and state; it was to touch and transform all aspects of life, from the cradle to the grave.

Politburo Political Bureau of the CC; was the key decision-making body of the Communist Party; set up formally at the 8th Party Congress, 1919; called the Presidium between 1952 and 1966.

Presidium Inner council or cabinet, hence supreme body; the Politburo of the Communist Party was known as the Presidium, 1952–66; the USSR Supreme Soviet Presidium contained all the worthies in the state and Party; the chair of the Presidium of the USSR Supreme Soviet was the head of state, hence he was sometimes referred to as President; the term President officially entered the Soviet constitution in 1989 when Gorbachev was elected Soviet President; the USSR Council of Ministers (Soviet government) also had a Presidium, consisting of key ministers – hence it was similar to a cabinet; at CC plenums and other meetings, important persons would sit on a podium facing the delegates; this was also known as a Presidium.

Procurator General The top law official in the Soviet Union, he headed the USSR Procuracy; each Soviet republic had its own procuracy, as did each raion, oblast and krai.

Prosecutor General See Procurator General.

Raikom Raion Party committee, head by a first secretary.

Raion Administrative subdivision of an oblast, krai and city; can be translated as district.

RCP Russian Communist Party, founded 1990, dissolved 1991; between 1918 and 1925 the Communist Party was known as the Russian Communist Party (Bolsheviks), becoming the CPSU in 1952; the Russian Federation was the only Soviet republic which did not have its own Communist Party (until 1990): in Ukraine there was the Communist Party of Ukraine, in Estonia, the Communist Party of Estonia, etc.; all these parties were subordinate to the CPSU in Moscow; despite the form of organisation it was a strictly centralised party; one of Gorbachev's proposals, in the late 1980s, was that the republican communist parties should become autonomous parties, running their own affairs but still under the umbrella of the CPSU; hence he was proposing a federal Communist Party; the RCP was a disappointment to Gorbachev since it was dominated by conservatives, reluctant to implement perestroika.

Referendum On 17 March 1991, Gorbachev launched a referendum in order to gauge support for a successor state to the Soviet Union, the Union of Sovereign States; there was a majority in favour of keeping the Union but other republics added questions to the Union referendum, e.g. Yeltsin asked Russian voters if they were in favour of a directly elected Russian President, which they were; he was elected President of Russia in June 1991; this was one of the unforeseen consequences of the referendum.

RSDRP The Russian Social Democratic Labour or Workers' Party was founded in Minsk in 1898 but it split in 1903 into Bolsheviks and Mensheviks; it was modelled on the German SPD and until 1917 all social democratic parties were Marxist.

RSFSR Russian Soviet Federated Socialist Republic or the Russian Federation or, simply, Russia; it was the largest of the 15 Soviet republics and its capital was also Moscow.

RSFSR Congress of People's Deputies First convened in March 1990 with Yeltsin as speaker; it was a super-parliament and it elected from among its members a RSFSR Supreme Soviet with a rotating membership which exchanged some members at each new Congress; Russia was the only Soviet republic with a Congress as all the others declined to elect one and proceeded directly to the election of a Supreme Soviet which then enjoyed popular legitimacy; it was dissolved by a presidential decree in September 1991.

Rootless Cosmopolitanism A term which became synonymous with anti-Semitism in the late 1940s in connection with the turn towards Russian nationalism and xenophobia.

SALT Strategic Arms Limitation Talks; discussions on the limitation of nuclear weapons which got under way in 1969 between the USA and the USSR; in 1972 the SALT I treaty was signed and in 1979 the SALT II treaty emerged; due to the Soviet invasion of Afghanistan the Americans did not ratify SALT II.

Science The Russian word *nauka* is the same as the German *Wissenschaft* and is much wider than the English term science (which was only coined in the 1830s); all intellectual activity can be called *nauka* in Russian and the person involved a scientist; hence scholars in the humanities were also known as 'scientists'.

SDI Strategic Defence Initiative, also known as Star Wars; conceived in 1983 by President Reagan as a space system to prevent incoming nuclear missiles penetrating the United States; it was more psychological than military but it was a useful bargaining chip for the Americans since the Soviets could never write it off, even though their top scientists did not give it much credence.

Secret Police See KGB.

Secretariat See CC Secretariat.

SED Socialist Unity Party of Germany; the ruling Communist Party in the GDR, it was founded in April 1946 and dissolved in 1990; under Gorbachev, its General Secretary was Erich Honecker, until 1989, then Egon Krenz.

Shock Worker Called *udarniki* during the first FYP and superseded by the stakhanovites; a worker who leads by example and sets the norms for his fellow workers.

Short Course The official Stalinist version of Bolshevik history, published in 1938 as *The History of the Communist Party (Bolsheviks) Short Course*; it continued to appear in new editions until 1983.

Soviet a) Council b) citizen of the USSR c) name of the country; soviets first emerged during the 1905 revolution and then blossomed after the February 1917 revolution; it was all the rage, there were soviets of workers' deputies, soviets of peasants' deputies, soviets of soldiers' deputies, soviets of long distance train travellers, etc.; the most influential was the Petrograd Soviet of Workers' and Soldiers' Deputies which spawned the October revolution; the October revolution was called a Soviet revolution, the government was called the

Soviet of People's Commissars, etc.; the term became synonymous with worker power; Lenin changed his mind about the future role of the soviets and in his April (1917) Theses he stated that Russia would be a republic of soviets; Lenin and the Bolsheviks handed power to the 2nd Congress of Soviets in October 1917, but power soon slipped way from them as they opposed Lenin's prescriptions for revolution; they had ceded primacy to the government by mid-1918 and it in turn to the Politburo of the Party by 1921; soviets ran the countryside and towns and performed the function of local government but never had the power to tax independently of the centre or keep local state taxation; their finances were determined in Moscow; they had to implement Gosplan directives; Gorbachev attempted to reinvigorate them in 1988 but by then the Party boss ruled the localities; he hoped they would take over from the Party at local level and implement perestroika but they lacked the skill and personnel to do this.

Soviet–German Non-Aggression Pact or Stalin–Hitler Pact Signed by Molotov and Ribbentrop on 23 August 1939 (Stalin and Hitler never met); it envisaged that the Soviet Union and Germany would not attack one another and that if war did ensue elsewhere both states would remain neutral; the key part of the agreement was the secret protocol which the Soviets denied existed until the late 1980s; it divides Eastern Europe up into zones of influence with the Soviet Union taking eastern Poland, Latvia, Estonia, Finland, Lithuania (as the result of an amendment) and Bessarabia; Germany bagged the rest of Europe; the original agreement turned up in the private papers of von der Schulenburg, the German ambassador to Moscow at the time, after his death.

Soviet Republic There were 15, of which the Russian Federation was the largest and Estonia, Latvia and Lithuania were the last to join, in 1940; each republic had its own government, many ministries and its own Communist Party which was, of course, part of the CPSU; the local Communist Party had its own Central Committee and a Bureau (playing the same role as the central Politburo) (Ukraine was the exception and had a Politburo); the communist parties split in many republics into pro-nationalist communist parties and pro-Moscow communist parties; this occurred in all three Baltic republics; the pro-nationalist communist parties then supported the bid for independence; under glasnost, many informal associations (so called because they were not officially registered) sprang up and these included popular fronts, especially in the Baltic republics.

Sovkhoz Literally state economy; set up on land not previously cultivated, it was run like a factory with a guaranteed minimum wage, higher than those of the average kolkhoznik; operatives were classified as workers and enjoyed their social benefits.

Sovnarkhoz Council of the National Economy; adopted by Khrushchev in 1957 and initially there were 105 which covered the whole country and were responsible for all economic activity on their territory (except military, security and other vital tasks which remained centralised); Khrushchev thought that by devolving decision making to the local level, economic efficiency would result; in fact the sovnarkhozes attempted to become mini-states in their own right; they were abolished in 1965, after Khrushchev's removal as Soviet leader.

Sovnarkom The Council of People's Commissars, the government of the country, 1917–46, when it was renamed the USSR Council of Ministers; Commissars then became Ministers;

there was a All-Union Sovnarkom, each Soviet republic and autonomous republic also had its Sovnarkom; the government resigned formally at the end of each legislative period; in reality the Union government ruled; the Soviet Union, according to the 1977 constitution, was a federal state but Gorbachev admitted that it was, in reality, a unitary state; federalism was a sham.

Soyuz Union; People's Deputies at all levels were members; established December 1990 to defend the integrity of the Soviet Union and it argued that a state of emergency was the only way to restore order and ensure the survival of the Soviet Union; its leading members were Yury Blokhin, Viktor Alksnis, Evgeny Kogan and Sergei Baburin; among the membership were representatives of the military-industrial complex, the KGB, the MVD and the Party apparatus; in the USSR Congress of People's Deputies and the USSR Supreme Soviet Soyuz was the largest anti-reform faction but did not command a majority.

Staraya Ploshchad Old Square, the headquarters of the Party CC until August 1991; it is close to Red Square.

START Strategic Arms Reduction Talks; negotiations on the reduction of strategic weapon systems, between the United States and the Soviet Union, then Russia, which resulted in the START I agreement in 1991 and the START II agreement, 1993.

State Procurements Output bought by the state and laid down by the plan in advance; in industry this applied to most of an enterprise's output but in agriculture it could vary; kolkhozes and sovkhozes had to meet state procurement plans first before they disposed of any of their produce; naturally they attempted to keep back as much for themselves as possible, sometimes stating that they did not have enough to meet the plan; the person responsible for ensuring that farms met their state obligations was the first Party secretary.

Strategic Nuclear Weapons Those nuclear weapons which can be fired from one continent to another.

Stavka General Staff of the Red Army and Navy during the Great Patriotic War (1941–45).

Supreme Soviet Set up by the 1936 Soviet Constitution, the USSR Supreme Soviet was bicameral: Soviet of the Union and Soviet of Nationalities, the number of deputies in the former was based on population, while the number of the latter was fixed; the houses were of equal status and often met in joint session; a parliament only in name (until 1989), key decisions being taken by the Communist Party and the government; the chair of the Presidium of the USSR Supreme Soviet was Soviet head of state; each Soviet republic and autonomous republic had its own Supreme Soviet but they were unicameral; each house had its own commissions and committees were joint bodies; all important state legislation was passed by the USSR Supreme Soviet which normally only met twice a year, for a few days at a time; in 1989 the USSR Congress of People's Deputies elected a USSR Supreme Soviet with a rotating membership, some members being dropped and others elected at each new Congress; the RSFSR Congress of People's Deputies, convened in 1990, also elected an inner RSFSR Supreme Soviet, again with a rotating membership.

Tactical Nuclear Weapons Short and medium range nuclear weapons for the theatre of war.

Territory See krai.

20th Party Congress Convened in February 1956, it is famous for the secret speech (it was held behind closed doors) of Khrushchev laying bare Stalin's crimes since 1934; he did not use the expression Stalinism to describe what he was analysing but referred to it as the cult of the personality; the speech ended the claims to infallibility of the Communist Party; it became a focal point of interest under glasnost.

Union of Sovereign States Gorbachev intended it to be the successor state to the USSR but the attempted August coup was timed to prevent its signature; afterwards it was too late and the dissolution of the USSR and the establishment of the CIS consigned it to the dustbin of history.

USSR Union of Soviet Socialist Republics; also known as the Soviet Union.

USSR Congress of People's Deputies Convened during the early years of the revolution, it was resurrected in March 1989 as the supreme agency of state power; its 2,250 deputies were elected for five years and there was to be a Congress every year; of the 2,250 deputies, two-thirds were directly elected, there were to be multi-candidate elections, with open campaigning beforehand; the other 750 deputies were elected indirectly, according to lists proposed by political and social organisations; for instance, the Communist Party received 100 seats; Gorbachev chaired it; it was a super-parliament and from its membership it elected a USSR Supreme Soviet, or standing parliament, with a rotating membership which exchanged some members at the next Congress; according to the amendments of the Soviet constitution, the Congress could amend the constitution, if a two-thirds majority approved; the Congress elected Gorbachev President of the Soviet Union; the Congress, on 5 September 1991, voluntarily dissolved itself and conceded power to the RSFSR Congress of People's Deputies but there were deputies who were members of both.

USSR Council of Ministers The Soviet government, headed by a chair or Prime Minister; dissolved in 1990 and replaced by a Cabinet of Ministers, headed by a Prime Minister.

USSR Council of the President or Presidential Council It was established in March 1990 and functioned until December 1990 with all members being nominated by Gorbachev; was dominated by the power ministries (Security, Internal Affairs, Defence) but its precise functions were unclear; was replaced in early 1991 by the newly constituted USSR Security Council which lasted until the attempted coup.

USSR Soviet (Council) of the Federation Established under Gorbachev as a supra-government for the Soviet Union, consisting of the President, Vice-President and senior representatives from each of the 15 Soviet republics; ceased to exist in August 1991 and should not be confused with the Council of the Federation, the upper house of the Russian parliament, established in December 1993.

USSR State Council The successor to the USSR Soviet of the Federation but again was only consultative.

USSR Supreme Soviet Founded in 1936, it was the supreme agency of state power in the Soviet Union, according to the constitution; was bicameral, the Soviet of the Union and the

Soviet of Nationalities and in 1985 had 1,500 members; elected for four years and had to meet twice a year, amounting to about a week altogether; elected a Presidium (39 members since 1977) from among its members and the chair was the head of the Soviet state; until Podgorny became chair of the Presidium in 1964, the position had never been politically significant; Brezhnev made himself head of state in May 1977 and Podgorny was sent packing; Andropov and Chernenko also made themselves head of state but Gorbachev, in July 1985, suggested Gromyko for the post and he remained there until 1988 when Gorbachev himself took over; the USSR Supreme Soviet was superseded by the USSR Congress of People's Deputies in March 1989; confusingly the Congress then proceeded to elect its own USSR Supreme Soviet but the latter was subordinate to the former.

VLKSM All-Union Leninist Communist League of Youth or Komsomol.

VSNKh (Vesenkha) Supreme Council of the National Economy; founded in December 1917 and responsible for the whole economy and state finances; as of June 1918 it became in effect the Commissariat for Nationalised Industry; there were local VSNKh to run industry; under NEP enterprises were grouped together in trusts but still managed by VSNKh; in 1924 a VSNKh was set up in each republic responsible for industry there; in 1932 it was divided into Commissariats of Heavy Industry, Light Industry and Timber Industry.

VTsIK All-Union Central Executive Committee of the soviets; became the USSR Supreme Soviet in 1936.

VTsSPS All-Union Central Council of Trade Unions, the central trade union body.

Warsaw Pact Organisation The Pact was founded in 1955 as a response to the Paris Treaties of October 1954 which had admitted the Federal Republic of Germany to NATO; the original members were the Soviet Union, Poland, Czechoslovakia, Hungary, the GDR, Bulgaria, Romania and Albania; Albania left in 1961; the Pact had also a Political Consultative Committee which was attended by foreign ministers; the Pact never permitted the East German Volksarmee to set up its own General Staff, for instance; all advanced military technology was manufactured in the Soviet Union and the Soviet army was the best equipped; the Pact was dissolved on 1 July 1991.

Bibliography

Acton, Edward (1990), *Rethinking the Bolshevik Revolution*, Edward Arnold, London.

Andreyev, Catherine (1987), *Vlasov and the Russian Liberation Movement*, Cambridge University Press, Cambridge.

Andrew, Christopher and Oleg Gordievsky (1990), *KGB: The Inside Story of its Foreign Operations from Lenin to Gorbachev*, Penguin, London.

Andrew, Christopher and Vasili Mitrokhin (1999), *The Mitrokhin Archive: The KGB in Europe and the West*, Penguin, London.

Andrew, Christopher and Vasili Mitrokhin (2005), *The Mitrokhin Archive II: The KGB and the World*, Penguin, London.

Applebaum, Anne (2003), *Gulag: A History of the Soviet Camps*, Allen Lane, New York and London.

Arendt, Hannah (1986), *The Origins of Totalitarianism*, Harcourt, New York.

Aron, Leon (2006), *Journal of Democracy*, Vol. 17, No. 2.

Axell, Albert (2003), *Marshal Zhukov: The Man who Beat Hitler*, Pearson Education, Harlow.

Baberowski, Jörg (2003), *Der rote Terror: Die Geschichte des Stalinismus*, DVA, Stuttgart.

Bacon, Edwin and Mark Sandle (2002), *Brezhnev Reconsidered*, Palgrave, Basingstoke.

Baehr, Peter and Melvin Richter (eds) (2004), *Dictatorship in History and Theory: Bonapartism, Caesarism and Totalitarianism*, Cambridge University Press, Cambridge.

Balazs, Apor, Jan C. Berends, Polly Jones and E. A. Rees (eds) (2004), *The Leader Cult in Communist Dictatorships: Stalin and the Eastern Block*, Palgrave Macmillan, Basingstoke.

Banac, Ivo (ed.) (2003), *The Diary of Georgi Dimitrov, 1933–1949*, Yale University Press, New Haven, CT.

Barber, John and Mark Harrison (eds) (1991), *The Soviet Home Front, 1941–5: A Social and Economic History of the USSR in World War II*, Longman, London.

Barber, J. and M. Harrison (eds) (2000), *The Soviet Defence Industry Complex from Stalin to Khrushchev*, Macmillan, Basingstoke.

Barros, James and Richard Gregor (1995), *Double Deception: Stalin, Hitler and the Invasion of Russia*, Northern Illinois University Press.

Breslauer, George (2002), *Gorbachev and Yeltsin as Leaders*, Cambridge University Press, Cambridge.

Brown, Archie (1996), *The Gorbachev Factor*, Oxford University Press, Oxford.

Brown, Archie (ed.) (2002), *The Demise of Marxism-Leninism in Russia*, Palgrave Macmillan, Basingstoke.

Brown, Archie and Lily Shevtsova (eds) (2001), *Gorbachev, Yeltsin and Putin: Political Leadership in Russia's Transition*, Carnegie Endowment for International Peace, Washington DC.

Brutents, Karen (2005), *Nesbyvsheesya: neravnodushnye zametki o perestroike*, Mezhdunarodnye Otnoshenii, Moscow.

Brzezinski, Zbiegniew K. (1956), *The Permanent Purge: Politics in Soviet Totalitarianism*, Harvard University Press, Cambridge, MA.

Chang, Jung and Jon Halliday (2005), *Mao: The Unknown Story*, Jonathan Cape, London.

Cherkashin, Victor with Gregory Feifer (2005), *Spy Handler: Memoir of a KGB Officer*, Basic Books, London.

Clements, Barbara Evans (1994), *Daughters of Revolution: A History of Women in the USSR*, Harlan Davidson, Arlington Heights.

Clements, Barbara Evans (1997), *Bolshevik Women*, Cambridge University Press, Cambridge.

Conquest, Robert (1967), *Power and Policy in the USSR*, Harper and Row, New York.

Conquest, Robert (1990), *The Great Terror: A Reassessment*, Hutchinson, London.

Dallin, Alexander and F. I. Firsov (eds) (2000), *Dimitrov and Stalin, 1934–43: Letters from the Soviet Archive*, Yale University Press, New Haven.

Davies, Norman (2004), *Rising '44*, Viking, London.

Davies, R. W., M. Harrison and S. G. Wheatcroft (eds) (1994), *The Economic Transformation of the Soviet Union, 1913–1945*, Cambridge University Press, Cambridge.

Davies, R. W. and Stephen G. Wheatcroft (eds) (2003), *The Years of Hunger: Soviet Agriculture 1931–1933*, Palgrave Macmillan, Basingstoke.

Davies, Sarah (1997), *Popular Opinion in Stalin's Russia: Terror, Propaganda and Dissent, 1934–1941*, Cambridge University Press, Cambridge.

Dear, I. C. B. (1995), *The Oxford Companion to the Second World War*, Oxford University Press, Oxford.

Easter, Gerald M. (2000), *Reconstructing the State: Personal Networks and Elite identity in Soviet Russia*, Cambridge University Pres, Cambridge.

Edmondson, Linda (ed.) (2001), *Gender in Russian History and Culture*, Palgrave Macmillan, Basingstoke.

Ellman, Michael and Vladimir Kontorovich (eds) (1998), *The Destruction of the Soviet Economic System: An Insiders' History*, M. E. Sharpe, Armonk, NY.

English, Robert (2000), *Russia and the Idea of the West: Gorbachev, Intellectuals and the End of the Cold War*, Columbia University Press, New York.

Evangelista, Matthew (1999), *Unarmed Forces: the Transnational Movement to End the Cold War*, Cornell University Press, Ithaca, NY.

Fainsod, Merle (1970), *How Russia is Ruled*, Harvard University Press, Cambridge, MA.

Filtzer, Donald (1993), *The Khrushchev Era: De-Stalinisation and the Limits of Reform in the USSR, 1953–1964*, Macmillan, Basingstoke.

Fitzpatrick, Sheila (1992), *The Cultural Front: Power and Culture in Revolutionary Russia*, Cornell University Press, Ithaca, NY.

Fitzpatrick, Sheila (1994), *Stalin's Peasants: Resistance and Survival in the Russian Village after Collectivization*, Oxford University Press, Oxford.

Fitzpatrick, Sheila (1994), *The Russian Revolution*, 2nd ed., Indiana University Press, Bloomington.

Fitzpatrick, Sheila (1999), *Everyday Stalinism: Ordinary Life in Extraordinary Times: Soviet Russia in the 1930s*, Oxford University Press, New York and London.

Fitzpatrick, Sheila (2000) (ed.), *Stalinism: New Directions*, Routledge, London and New York.

Fitzpatrick, Sheila and Yuri Slezkine (eds) (2000), *In the Shadow of Revolution: Life Stories of Russian Women from 1917 to the Second World War*, Princeton University Press, Princeton, NJ.

Fitzpatrick, Sheila, Alexander Rabinovich and Richard Stites (eds) (1991), *Russia in the Era of NEP: Explorations in Soviet Society and Culture*, Indiana University Press, Bloomington, Indiana.

French, Marilyn (2003), *From Eve to Dawn: A History of Women*, Vol. III *Infernos and Paradises*, McArthur, Toronto.

Friedrich, Carl J. and Zbiegniew K. Brzezinski (1965), *Totalitarian Dictatorship and Autocracy*, 2nd ed., Praeger, New York.

Gaddis, John Lewis (2005), *The Cold War*, Allen Lane, Penguin, London.

Gerovitch, Slava (2002), *From Newspeak to Cyberspeak: A History of Soviet Cybernetics*, MIT Press, Cambridge.

Getty, J. Arch (1985), *Origins of the Great Purges: The Soviet Communist Party Reconsidered, 1933–1939*, Cambridge University Press, Cambridge.

Getty, J. Arch and Oleg V. Naumov (1999), *The Road to Terror: Stalin and the Self-Destruction of the Bolsheviks*, Yale University Press, New Haven, CT.

Gill, G. and R. Pitty (1997), *Power in the Party: The Organization of Power and Central-Republican Relations in the USSR*, Macmillan, Basingstoke.

Glantz, David (1998), *Stumbling Collosus: The Red Army on the Eve of War*, University of Kansas Press, Lawrence.

Gorbachev, Mikhail (1991), *The August Coup: The Truth and Lessons*, HarperCollins, London.

Gorbachev, Mikhail (1996), *Memoirs*, Doubleday, London.

Gorlizki, Yoram and Oleg Khlevniuk (2004), *Cold Peace: Stalin and the Soviet Ruling Circle, 1945–1953*, Oxford University Press, New York.

Gorodetsky, Gabriel (ed.) (1994), *Soviet Foreign Policy, 1917–1991*, Frank Cass, London.

Gorodetsky, Gabriel (1999), *Grand Delusions: Stalin and the German Invasion of Russia*, Yale University Press, New Haven, CT.

Gottfried, Ted (2003), *The Great Fatherland War: The Rise and Fall of the Soviet Union*.

Gregory, Paul (2001), *Behind the Façade of Stalin's Command Economy*, Hoover Institution Press, Stanford, CA.

Gregory, Paul (2004), *The Political Economy of Stalinism: Evidence from the Soviet Secret Archives*, Cambridge University Press, Cambridge.

Hahn, Gordon M. (2002), *Russia's Revolution from Above, 1985–2000: Reform, Transition, and Revolution in the Fall of the Soviet Communist Regime*, Transaction Publishers, New Brunswick, NJ.

Hanson, Philip (2003), *The Rise and Fall of the Soviet Economy: An Economic History of the USSR from 1945*, Longman, Harlow.

Harris, J. R. (1999), *The Great Urals: Regionalism and Evolution of the Soviet System*, Cornell University Press, Ithaca, NY.

Harris, Jonathan (2004), *Subverting the System: Gorbachev's Reform of the Party Apparatus, 1986–1991*, Rowman & Littlefield, Lanham, MD.

Haslam, Jonathan (1983), *Soviet Foreign Policy, 1930–33: The Impact of the Depression*, Macmillan, Basingstoke.

Haslam, Jonathan (1984), *The Soviet Union and the Search for Collective Security, 1933–1939*, Macmillan, Basingstoke.

Haslam, Jonathan (1992), *The Soviet Union and the Threat from the East, 1933–1941: Moscow, Tokyo and the Prelude to the Pacific War*, Macmillan, Basingstoke.

Heinzig, Dieter (2004), *The Soviet Union and Communist China 1945–1950: The Arduous Road to the Alliance*, M. E. Sharpe, Armonk, NY.

Hildermeier, Manfred (2001), *Die Sowjetunion 1917–1991*, R. Oldenburg, Munich.

Hildermeier, M. and E. Müller-Luckner (eds) (1998), *Stalinismus vor dem II. Weltkrieg. Neue Wege der Forschung*, Oldenbourg, Munich.

Hochwald, Abraham (1997), *Und wenn der Rabbi lacht*, Brockhaus, Wuppertal.

Hoffmann, David L. (2003), *Stalinism: The Essential Readings*, Blackwell, Malden, MA.

Hoffmann, David L. (2003), *Stalinist Values: The Cultural Norms of Soviet Modernity, 1917–1941*, Cornell University Press, Ithaca, NY and London.

Hoffmann, Joachim (1999), *Stalins Vernichtungskrieg 1941–1945*, Herbig, Munich.

Hosking, Geoffrey (2006), *Rulers and Victims: The Russians and the Soviet Union*, Harvard University Press, Cambridge, MA.

Ilic, Melanie, Susan E. Reid and Lynne Attwood (eds) (2004), *Women in the Khrushchev Era*, Palgrave Macmillan, Basingstoke.

Keep, John (1995), *Last of the Empires: A History of the Soviet Union 1945–1991*, Oxford University Press, Oxford.

Kelly, Catriona and David Shepherd (eds) (1998), *Constructing Russian Culture in the Age of Revolution: 1881–1940*, Oxford University Press, Oxford.

Kennedy-Pipe, Caroline (1998), *Russia and the World, 1917–1991*, Arnold, London.

Khlevniuk, Oleg V. (1996), *Politburo: Mekhanizmy Politicheskoi Vlasti v 1930-e gody*, Moscow, Rosspen.

Khlevniuk, Oleg V. (2004), *The History of the Gulag: From Collectivization to the Great Terror*, Yale University Press, New Haven, CT and London.

Kotkin, Stephen (1995), *Magnetic Mountain: Stalinism as a Civilization*, University of California Press Berkeley.

Kotz, David M. (1997), *Revolution from Above: The Demise of the Soviet System*, Routledge, London.

Krivitsky, W. G. (2004), *In Stalin's Secret Service*, Enigma Books, London.

Kryuchkov, Vladimir V. (1996), *Lichnoe Delo*, 2 vols., Olimp, Moscow.

Kuromiya, Hiroaki (2005), *Stalin*, Longman, Harlow.

Lewin, Moshe (1968), *Russian Peasants and Soviet Power: A Study of Collectivisation*, Allen & Unwin, London.

Lewin, Moshe (1985), *The Making of the Soviet System*, Methuen, London.

Lewin, Moshe (2005), *The Soviet Century*, Verso, London.

Lieven, Dominic (2000), *Empire: The Russian Empire and Its Rivals*, John Murray, London.

Litvin, Alter and John Keep (2005), *Stalinism, Russian and Western Views at the Turn of the Millennium*, Routledge, London.

Lugovskaya, Nina (2003), *The Diary of a Soviet Schoolgirl, 1932–1937*, Glas, Moscow.

McCauley, Martin (1998), *Gorbachev*, Longman, Harlow.

McCauley, Martin (2001), *Bandits, Gangsters and the Mafia: Russia, the CIS and the Baltic States since 1992*, Longman, Harlow.

McCauley, Martin (2002), *Afghanistan and Central Asia: A Modern History*, Longman, Harlow.

McCauley, Martin (2003), *The Origins of the Cold War 1941–1949*, 3rd ed., Longman, Harlow.

McCauley, Martin (2003), *Stalin and Stalinism*, 3rd ed., Longman, Harlow.

McCauley, Martin (2004), *Russia, America and the Cold War, 1949–1991*, 2nd ed., Longman, Harlow.

Maddison, Angus (1995), *Monitoring the World Economy, 1820–1992*, OECD, Paris.

Maddison, Angus (2003), *The World Economy: Historical Statistics*, OECD, Paris.

Martel, Gordon (ed.) (1999), *The Origins of the Second World War Reconsidered: A. J. P. Taylor and the Historians*, Allen & Unwin, London.

Martin, Terry (2001), *Affirmative Action Empire: Nations and Nationalism in the Soviet Union, 1923–1939*, Cornell University Press, Ithaca, NY and London.

Mawdsley, Evan (2000), *The Russian Civil War*, Birlinn, Edinburgh.

Mawdsley, Evan and Stephen White (2000), *The Soviet Elite from Lenin to Gorbachev: The Central Committee and its Members*, Oxford University Press, Oxford.

Mawdsley, Evan (2003), *The Stalin Years: The Soviet Union 1929–1953*, Manchester University Press, Manchester.

Medvedev, Vladimir T. (1994), *Chelovek za spinoi*, Russlit, Moscow.

Medvedev, Zhores A. and Roy A. Medvedev (2003), *The Unknown Stalin*, trans. Ellen Dahrendorf, I. B. Tauris, London.

Merridale, Catherine (2000), *Night of Stone: Death and Memory in Russia*, Granta, London.

Merridale, Catherine (2005), *Ivan's War: The Red Army, 1941–45*, Faber and Faber, London.

Motyl, Alexander and Amanda Schnetzer (eds) (2004), *Nations in Transit: Democratization in East Central Europe and Eurasia*, Rowan and Littlefield, New York.

Murphy, David E. (2005), *What Stalin Knew: The Enigma of Barbarossa*, Yale University Press, New Haven, CT.

Murray, Williamson and Allan R. Millett (2001), *A War to be Won: Fighting the Second World War*, Harvard University Press, Cambridge, MA.

Naimark, Norman M. (2001), *Fires of Hatred: Ethnic Cleansing in Twentieth-Century Europe*, Harvard University Press, Cambridge, MA.

Nove, Alec (1992), *An Economic History of the USSR, 1917–1991*, Penguin, Harmondsworth.

Orwell, George (1949), *1984*, Gollanz, London.

Overy, Richard (1997), *Russia's War*, Penguin, Allen Lane, London.

Overy, Richard (2004), *The Dictators: Hitler's Germany, Stalin's Russia*, Penguin, Allen Lane, London.

Payne, M. J. (2001), *Stalin's Railroad: Turksib and the Building of Socialism*, University of Pittsburgh Press, Pittsburgh, PA.

Pearson, Raymond (2002), *The Rise and Fall of the Soviet Empire*, Longman, Harlow.

Pikhoya, R. G. (1998), *Sovetsky Soyuz: Istoriya Vlasti 1945–1991*, Izdatelstvo RAGS, Moscow.

Pleshakov, Constantine (2005), *Stalin's Folly: The Secret History of the German Invasion of Russia, June 1941*, Weidenfeld and Nicolson, London.

Pons, Silvio (2002), *Stalin and the Inevitable War, 1936–1941*, London and Portland, OR, Frank Cass.

Raack, Richard (1995), *Stalin's Drive to the West, 1938–1945: The Origins of the Cold War*, Stanford University Press, Stanford, CA.

Rayfield, Donald (2004), *Stalin and His Hangmen: An Authoritative Portrait of a Tyrant and Those Who Served Him*, Viking, London.

Razzakov, Fedor (2004), *Bandity vremen sotsializma (Khronika rossiiskoi prestupnosti 1917–1991)* (www.chelny.ru).

Rees, E. A. (ed.) (1997), *Decision-making in the Stalinist Command Economy, 1932–1937*, Macmillan, Basingstoke.

Rees, E. A. (ed.) (2004), *The Nature of Stalin's Dictatorship: The Politburo, 1924–1953*, Palgrave Macmillan, Basingstoke.

Rees, E. A. (2004), *Political Thought from Machiavelli to Stalin: Revolutionary Machiavellism*, Palgrave Macmillan, Basingstoke.

Reese, R. R. (1996), *Stalin's Reluctant Soldiers: A Social History of the Red Army, 1925–1941*, University of Kansas Press, Lawrence, KS.

Reese, R. R. (2000), *The Soviet Military Experience: A History of the Soviet Army 1917–1991*, Routledge, London.

Remnick, David (1994), *Lenin's Tomb: The Last Days of the Soviet Empire*, Random House, New York.

Rieber, Alfred J. (ed.) (2000), *Forced Migration in Central and Eastern Europe*, Frank Cass, London.

Rigby, T. H. (1979), *Lenin's Government: Sovnarkom 1917–1922*, Cambridge University Press, Cambridge.

Rigby, T. H. (1990), *The Changing Soviet System: Mono-organisational Socialism from its Origins to Gorbachev's Restructuring*, Elgar, Aldershot.

Roberts, Geoffrey (1995), *The Soviet Union and the Origins of the Second World War: Russo-German Relations and the Road to War, 1933–1941*, Macmillan, Basingstoke.

Rohwer, J. and M. S. Monakov (2001), *Stalin's Ocean-Going Fleet: Soviet Naval Strategy and Shipbuilding Programmes, 1935–1953*, Frank Cass, London.

Rosenberg, G. and Siegelbaum, Lewis H. (eds) (1993), *Social Dimensions of Soviet Industrialization*, Indiana University Press, Bloomington.

Rosenfeldt, N. E. (1990), *The Origins of the Stalinist Political System*, Cambridge University Press, Cambridge.

Rosenfeldt, N. E. *et al.* (eds) (2000), *Mechanisms of Power in the Soviet Union*, Macmillan, Basingstoke.

Rosefielde, S. (2005), 'Russia: An Abnormal Country', *The Economic Journal of Comparative Economics*, Vol. 2, No. 1.

Rousso, H. (ed.) (1999), *Stalinisme et nazisme: Histoire et mémoire comparées*, Eds Complexe, Brussels.

Ryzhkov, Vladimir (1992), *Perestroika: Istoriya Predatelstv*, Novosti, Moscow.

Samuelson, Lennart (2000), *Plans for Stalin's War Machine: Tukhachevsky and Military-Economic Planning: 1925–1941*, Macmillan, Basingstoke.

Schapiro, Leonard (1966), *The Communist Party of the Soviet Union*, Methuen, London.

Schapiro, Leonard (1977), *The Origin of the Communist Autocracy*, 2nd ed., Macmillan, Basingstoke.

Schattenberg, Susanne (2002), *Stalins Ingenieure Lebenswelten zwischen Technik und Terror in den 1930er Jahren*, Oldenbourg, Munich.

Service, Robert (1999), *The Russian Revolution, 1900–1927*, Macmillan, Basingstoke.

Service, Robert (2003), *A History of Modern Russia from Nicholas II to Putin*, Penguin, London.

Service, Robert (2004), *Stalin: A Biography*, Macmillan, Basingstoke.

Shlykov, Vitaly (2006), 'Back into the Future, Or Cold War Lessons for Russia', *Russia in Global Affairs* (http://eng.globalaffairs.ru), April–June.

Shukman, Harold (1977), *Lenin and the Russian Revolution*, Batsford, London.

Shukman, Harold (ed.) (2003), *Redefining Stalinism*, Frank Cass, London.

Siegelbaum, Lewis H. (1992), *Soviet State and Society between Revolutions, 1918–1929*, Cambridge University Press, Cambridge.

Siegelbaum, Lewis H. and Andrei Sokolov (eds) (2000), *Stalinism as a Way of Life: A Narrative in Documents*, Yale University Press, New Haven, CT.

Smith, Jeremy (1999), *The Bolsheviks and the National Question, 1917–1923*, Macmillan, London.

Soloukhin, Vladimir (1989), *Chitaya Lenina*, Posev, Frankfurt-am-Main.

Starr, S. Frederick (1994), *Red and Hot: The Fate of Jazz in the Soviet Union, 1917–1991*, Limelight Editions, New York.

Stites, Richard (1991), *The Women's Liberation Movement in Russia: Feminism, Nihilism and Bolshevism, 1860–1930*, Princeton University Press, Princeton, NJ.

Stites, Richard (1992), *Revolutionary Dreams: Utopian Vision and Experimental Life in the Russian Revolution*, Cambridge University Press, Cambridge.

Stone, D. R. (2000), *Hammer and Rifle: The Militarization of the Soviet Union, 1926–1933*, University of Kansas Press, Lawrence, KS.

Suny, Ronald Grigor (1998), *The Soviet Experiment: Russia, the USSR, and the Successor States*, Oxford University Press, Oxford.

Suny, R. G. and T. Martin (2001), *A State of Nations: Empire and Nation-making in the Age of Stalin*, Oxford University Press, New York.

Suvorov, Viktor (1990), *Icebreaker: Who Started the Second World War?*, Penguin, New York.

Taubman, William (2003), *Khruschev: The Man and His Era*, WW Norton & Company, New York and London.

Todd, Allan (2002), *The European Dictatorships: Hitler, Stalin, Mussolini*, Cambridge University Press, Cambridge.

Tompson, William J. (2003), *The Soviet Union under Brezhnev*, Longman, Harlow.

Tucker, Robert C. (ed.) (1991), *Stalin in Power: The Revolution from Above, 1928–1941*, W. W. Norton, New York.

Tucker, Robert C. (1999), *Stalinism: Essays in Historical Interpretation*, Transaction, New Brunswick, NJ.

Usdin, Steven T. (2005), *Engineering Communism: How Two Americans Spied for Stalin and Founded the Soviet Silicon Valley*, Yale University Press, New Haven, CT.

Watson, Derek (1996), *Molotov and Soviet Government: Sovnarkom, 1930–1941*, Macmillan, Basingstoke.

Wade, Rex (ed.) (2004), *Revolutionary Russia: New Approaches*, Routledge, London.

Weeks, Albert (2002), *Stalin's Other War: Soviet Grand Strategy, 1939–1941*, Rowman & Littlefield, Oxford and Lanham, MD.

Werth, Nicolas (2002), *Ein Staat gegen sein Volk*, trans. Bertold Galli, Piper, Munich.

Westad, Odd Arne (2000), *Reviewing the Cold War: Approaches, Interpretations, Theory*, Frank Cass, London.

Wheatcroft, S. G. (ed.) (2002), *Challenging Traditional Views of Russian History*, Palgrave Macmillan, Basingstoke.

White, G. Edward (2004), *Alger Hiss's Looking Glass Wars: The Covert Life of a Soviet Spy*, Oxford University Press, New York.

Zaleski, E. (1980), *Stalinist Planning for Economic Growth, 1933–1952*, Macmillan, London.

Index